Praise for Tim Cook

"Tim Cook can really write. We've had trouble putting down Cook's gripping yet scholarship-driven *At the Sharp End*. This is the one book of many war titles coming out this season most likely to fully satisfy readers' hunger for our military history." —*Toronto Star*

"An authoritative and brightly written narrative."—*The Gazette* (Montreal)

"Cook has produced an impeccably researched and immensely readable account of the Great War. The mark of a good historian is finding new ways to tell a tale we thought we knew, and Cook has that quality in spades." —*The Globe and Mail*

"Exhaustively researched and written with great narrative momentum, *At the Sharp End* creates an unforgettable canvas of Canada's men at war." —*Hill Times* (Ottawa)

"Cook's First World War history arrives with a difference … it is the common foot soldier that drives the narrative … [A] magnificent and accessible history of the Great War." —*Sun-Times* (Owen Sound)

"Provides an intimate look at the Canadian men who fought in World War One … An engrossing, moving experience." —*London Free Press*

"*At the Sharp End* is a landmark work of military scholarship and gripping narrative … Featuring never-before-published photographs, letters, diaries, and maps, the book recounts … the Great War through soldiers' moving eyewitness accounts." —*Scene* magazine (London, Ontario)

"Despite a multitude of books on the First World War, in my opinion, this stands alone. Whether you are interested in the strategy and personalities of the top brass, the real experiences of the sharp end soldier, or both, this is definitely a must for the discerning reader." —*Esprit de Corps* military magazine

Praise for *Shock Troops:*
Canadians Fighting the Great War, 1917–1918, Volume Two

Winner of the Charles Taylor Prize for Literary Non-Fiction
Shortlisted for the J.W. Dafoe Book Prize
Finalist for the Ottawa Book Award

"Tremendous detail and almost unstoppable narrative momentum ... Through these stories of horror and heroism, what shines through most brilliantly is the complex humanity of the characters." —Jury, Charles Taylor Prize 2009

"Cook has written what will surely be the definitive history of the Canadian Army in the First World War." —*Edmonton Journal*

"If you want to know more about the Canadian experience in the Great War, these books are a fine resource—exhaustively researched and yet vividly accessible." —*The Star Phoenix* (Saskatoon)

"Compelling narrative ... [Cook's] easy-going style, interesting personal stories and attention to detail engage the reader." —*Ottawa Sun*

"Tim Cook knows more about WWI than you ever will." —*National Post*

"Military scholar John Keegan described how military history ought to be written—'rigorously but vigorously, with emotional passion but intellectual dispassion' ... [and] *Shock Troops* and its predecessor, *At the Sharp End*, reach this lofty standard. They will remain essential reading for historians and anyone interested in the Canadian Expeditionary Force for years to come." —*Guelph Mercury*

"The one title ... we've most been looking forward to this fall comes from Ottawa's Tim Cook ... *Shock Troops* is every bit as readable as its bestselling predecessor. Bravo." —*Toronto Star*

"Gripping history." —*The Gazette* (Montreal)

"Splendid ... Welcome representatives of the new military history. There is much on fighting and weapons and much on generals, but also much more on the ordinary soldier ... These are superb books, brilliantly researched." —*The Beaver*

PENGUIN CANADA

AT THE SHARP END

TIM COOK is the curator of the South African and First World War galleries at the Canadian War Museum, as well as an adjunct research professor at Carleton University. He is the author of *No Place to Run* and *Clio's Warriors*, as well as *Shock Troops: Canadians Fighting the Great War, 1917–1918, Volume Two*, which won the 2009 Charles Taylor Prize and was nominated for the J.W. Dafoe Prize. He lives in Ottawa with his family.

Also by Tim Cook

No Place to Run

Clio's Warriors

*Shock Troops: Canadians Fighting the Great War,
1917–1918, Volume Two*

TIM COOK

AT THE
SHARP
END

CANADIANS FIGHTING THE
GREAT WAR, 1914–1916

VOLUME ONE

PENGUIN
CANADA

PENGUIN CANADA

Published by the Penguin Group

Penguin Group (Canada), 90 Eglinton Avenue East, Suite 700, Toronto, Ontario, Canada M4P 2Y3 (a division of Pearson Canada Inc.)

Penguin Group (USA) Inc., 375 Hudson Street, New York, New York 10014, U.S.A.
Penguin Books Ltd, 80 Strand, London WC2R 0RL, England
Penguin Ireland, 25 St Stephen's Green, Dublin 2, Ireland (a division of Penguin Books Ltd)
Penguin Group (Australia), 250 Camberwell Road, Camberwell, Victoria 3124, Australia (a division of Pearson Australia Group Pty Ltd)
Penguin Books India Pvt Ltd, 11 Community Centre, Panchsheel Park, New Delhi – 110 017, India
Penguin Group (NZ), 67 Apollo Drive, Rosedale, North Shore 0745, Auckland, New Zealand (a division of Pearson New Zealand Ltd)
Penguin Books (South Africa) (Pty) Ltd, 24 Sturdee Avenue, Rosebank, Johannesburg 2196, South Africa

Penguin Books Ltd, Registered Offices: 80 Strand, London WC2R 0RL, England

First published in Viking Canada hardcover by Penguin Group (Canada), a division of Pearson Canada Inc., 2007
Published in this edition, 2009

1 2 3 4 5 6 7 8 9 10   (CR)

Copyright © Tim Cook, 2007

Maps copyright © Crowle Art Group, 2007

The credits on page 598 constitute an extension of this copyright page.

Manufactured in the U.S.A.

LIBRARY AND ARCHIVES CANADA CATALOGUING IN PUBLICATION

Cook, Tim, 1971-
At the sharp end : Canadians fighting the Great
War, 1914-1916 / Tim Cook.

Continued by: Shock troops : Canadians fighting the
Great War, 1917-1918.
"Volume One".
Includes bibliographical references and index.
ISBN 978-0-14-305592-1

1. Canada. Canadian Army—History—World War, 1914-1918.
2. Canada. Canadian Army. Canadian Corps—History.   3. World
War, 1914-1918—Campaigns—Western Front.   4. World
War, 1914-1918—Canada.   I. Title.

D547.C2C555 2009   940.4'1271   C2009-902754-2

Visit the Penguin Group (Canada) website at **www.penguin.ca**

Special and corporate bulk purchase rates available; please see
www.penguin.ca/corporatesales or call 1-800-810-3104, ext. 477 or 474

For Sarah, Chloe, and Emma

CONTENTS

AT THE SHARP END

Hurtling through the air, artillery shells crash down on the enemy lines in a series of explosions that sends sandbags, clods of earth, and body parts in a geyser of solid eruptions. In the Entente lines several hundred metres away, the ground quivers and buckles in a continuous series of ripples. A newly arrived Canadian infantryman, nervous and sweating, stands ready in the front lines, minutes away from going "over the top" for the first, and possibly last, time. With steel helmet perched awkwardly on his head, his breath coming in quick, shallow gasps, he grips the wooden stock of his Lee-Enfield, Mark III rifle like an anchor. The bayonet, seventeen inches of cold metal, rises up past his face, pointing to the sky above the muddy trench parapet wall of rotting sandbags, now frayed and oozing wet mud after too much rain.

The minutes tick down, and thousands of soldiers, spread out along the battered front-line trenches, shift in anticipation or throw themselves against the forward trench wall as the roar of incoming shellfire is picked up by ears attuned to decipher the wail of war. The Canadian infantryman turns to his more experienced sergeant standing next to him, blurting: "I suppose in a few moments, Sarge, we shall be making history." The sergeant, staring up at the fire-streaked sky with a stony face, says nothing for a few seconds before turning and eying the new man. "History be blowed," the sergeant growls. "What you have got to make is geography."[1]

In this war of muddy metres, geography is indeed the trench soldiers' primary concern. As the front-line troops pull themselves up ladders to climb over the sand-bagged trench walls, the difference between life and death, between a successful operation or one that leaves a soldiers' formation hanging on the barbed wire in bloody swaths, is their speed in crossing the several hundred metres known as No Man's Land that separate the two opposing trenches. As the experienced sergeant rightly knows, these metres of *geography* are the only thing that matters to the infantry in these desperate moments as they advance through enemy fire and tangled barbed wire; but it is the *history* of these men that continues to fascinate us to this day.

CANADA'S GREAT WAR ran from August 4, 1914, to November 11, 1918, some 1,561 days. Though the last shells and bullets fell silent at 11 A.M. on that Monday in November, the fury of the fighting has reverberated throughout the twentieth century, and into this millennium. The meaning of the war, however, has changed. Competing strands of memory from participants, propagandists, and historians, among others, have shaped how the war has been viewed by succeeding generations, and what it continues to mean today.

The war's ten million battlefield dead was surely a horror, but the influenza pandemic of 1918–1919 killed at least twice—some estimate up to five times—that number worldwide. There were also, by one count, more than twenty million lives lost in car crashes between 1898 and 1998.[2] So why is a Remembrance Day not observed for casualties of influenza or the vehicularly mangled, as it is for the fallen of the Great War on November 11 of each year?

Clearly the Great War has come to be considered something more than a war. Indeed, even during the enormous conflict, the term "Great War" was being used to describe the new type of industrial warfare and a new scale of slaughter. The war was both the end of an era and a harbinger of the future. Like the trenches that divided Europe, the Great War marked the birth of the modern, dividing everything before it from the bloody century that would follow in its wake.[3] It was also a tragedy, a manmade disaster—and one, many believed in the years that followed, that could have been avoided. It was not a case of invisible microbes or lead-footed motorists claiming innocents, but of leaders gambling with lives, sacrificing millions of their citizens. It is a story of catastrophe and cataclysm: the wealthiest, seemingly most advanced nations of the world locked in a death match of nearly unfathomable fury, which, by the third year of the war, left combatants clawing for little more than survival. But they refused to lay down arms as they were driven on by the grief and anger of a blood sacrifice that overwhelmed all hopes of a peaceful resolution.

The war and its aftermath reshaped people and nations. It raised powerful national aspirations or, in some cases, frustrations that were later channelled or twisted into ideologies like Fascism and Communism. Festering wounds buried beneath the criss-crossing scars remade Europe's political face and the fractious former imperial colonies. The conflicts in Northern Ireland, Rwanda, Yugoslavia, Palestine, and Iraq, among others, all had their origins in the Treaty of Versailles settlements, which formally ended the war. Some scholars note that the industrial and institutionalized slaughter of the Holocaust had its emotional and intellectual genesis in the systematic and callous slaughter of the trenches.[4]

IN CANADA, a nation of not yet 8 million in 1914, 430,000 men and women served overseas, and more than 61,000 were killed. Another 138,000 were wounded in battle, many crippled for life. With Canada's twenty-first–century population pegged at a little more than 32 million, the proportional Great War losses today would be approximately 250,000 dead and more than 550,000 wounded. In 1918, almost every community mourned a generation lost to the killing fields of Flanders and the Somme, marking their sacrifices with monuments, statues, and cenotaphs across the Dominion. The enormous exertion of the Canadian forces in Europe brought a new-found respect for Canada and led to greater autonomy for the nation on the world stage. The war made heroes and martyrs.

While dozens of scholarly and popular general works have been devoted to Canada and the Great War, and hundreds, perhaps thousands, of additional monographs or articles have explored events during the period of 1914–1918, only a few studies have chronicled the full experience of combat in the Canadian Corps, and what it meant to those men who were forced to partake in the vicious, relentless, and mind-numbing arena of kill or be killed. This book offers a detailed history of the Canadians at the sharp end of battle, and their painful process of learning how first to survive on the battlefield, and then how to effectively wage war on the Western Front.

During the Great War, the Canadian Corps—the nation's 100,000-strong fighting formation—came to be regarded as elite troops within the British Expeditionary Force, under whose operational umbrella it fought. From their brilliant victory at Vimy Ridge, in April 1917, to the end of the war, the Canadians never lost a battle. But they had not yet earned that elite reputation in 1914. The Canadian forces, like all formations, went through a tactical evolution, and even the best divisions and units suffered high casualty rates. The Canadians could not, and did not, avoid this difficult learning curve. Winston Churchill, as a participant in and historian of the war, called the grinding, butchering battles of 1916 on the Somme a "blood test."[5] Certainly this was the case for the four Canadian divisions when they fought there, and during their previous two years on the Western Front. But the Canadians learned to fight within this strange, brutal battlefield, and they emerged from this "blood test" as one of the most respected and feared of all formations involved in the war.

THIS BOOK IS A HISTORY that addresses both success and failure among the Canadian forces. To whitewash defeat is not only to skew history but also to denigrate the memory of the men who struggled against horrendous conditions and an obstinate and highly skilled enemy. But defeat must be understood in the context of the times. Hindsight is useful for dissecting problems of the past, but we must remember that the decisions of soldiers and commanders were often made under terrible duress, without full military intelligence about the confusing and changing situation at the front.

Even a two-volume history must have its limits, and this one takes as its focus the combat effectiveness of the Canadian Corps, in which the vast majority of all enlisted personnel served, and how that effectiveness was shaped by technology, tactics, command, discipline, and morale. The reputation of the Canadians and their commanders is front and centre, but since this is a history of the Canadian Corps, little is included about the Canadian Cavalry Brigade, which was rarely attached to the corps, or about the 13,000 Canadian aircrew personnel who served within the British flying services and outside the corps' influence.

The focus here is on the infantry at the sharp end: those who faced the enemy and bore the heaviest brunt of the fighting. Nothing could have been accomplished on the battlefield without the infantry who, through their tenacity and skill, ground out victory on one of the worst battlefields in human history. The "poor bloody infantry," in the words of Canadian infantryman John Harold Becker, "did all the fighting, most of the dying and in addition had to dig ditches, build emplacements, carry tons of material and then go on short rations and live in crummy residences."[6] The infantry were those called on to advance into the dirtiest holes and claw their way forward. And with the infantry suffering a little more than four out of five of all battlefield casualties on the Western Front, they deserve to be the centre of this history of combat.[7]

One of Canada's most famous Great War veterans was a man who never picked up a gun. Canon Frederick Scott was a padre with the 1st Division and a poet of high standing. His poems and fearlessness in ministering to soldiers under shellfire made him a hero in the Canadian Corps. Scott noted that he never expected to survive the war, but when he found himself alive at the end, he published his memoir, *The Great War as I Saw It*. In its pages, Scott captured much of the beauty and brutality of the war, the camaraderie he saw among the men, and their desperate struggle to survive. While his memoirs offer insight into the plight of the soldiers to whom he ministered, the book's title provides a useful jumping-off point for an exploration of the multiple narratives among Canadians at war. Scott's war— as he saw it—was not like anyone else's war: he was an old padre among young warriors; he was in a privileged position as an officer and as a "star" poet in the age before television and radio; and he suffered the agony of burying his son on the Somme in 1916. The war Scott saw was unique to him, although it intersected with the experiences of tens of thousands of other Canadians at the front.

Indeed, the Canadian Great War on the Western Front consisted of several hundred thousand individually experienced wars, from those lasting only a few days—revealing the unfortunate tendency of new men to be killed or wounded during their first tour at the front—to those of rare soldiers who served, and survived, from August 1914 to November 1918. Every soldier's story was different. Two men who enlisted on the same day and who served together in the same unit might have different experiences in the trenches, suffer different wounds, even participate in different battles.

"Often a simple foot soldier in the first-line trenches sees things of which staff officers have but an inkling," wrote Lieutenant Colonel Joseph Chaballe of the 22nd Battalion.[8] Through their letters, diaries, and memoirs, the soldiers left us first-hand testimonials to the trials of the trenches. Many were compelled to write the war out of their system, reconstructing or regurgitating their experiences to avoid being consumed by them. These testimonials reach across the decades, and their words, whether passionate and detailed observations or quickly jotted notes, provide moving glimpses into the war experience that cannot be garnered solely from the official records.

To gain a full understanding of the battlefield dramas, a historian must place these eyewitness accounts within the context of the Canadian Corps' experiences on the Western Front. Nearly a decade of research into the official and unofficial records held at Library and Archives Canada, the Canadian War Museum, and other archival repositories has unearthed official reports, casualty returns, lessons-learned documents, and countless other forms of documentation. References from war diaries, after-battle reports, and orders were compared against map references and reports to higher formations. Only by reading the records of individual formations at all levels of the military hierarchy can one begin to reconstruct the history from the ground up and understand the complex interplay among divisions and brigades, as well as sections and even individuals. Such reconstruction provides an understanding of how the Canadians fought, and how at times the tide of battle was turned by the action of a handful of men. These documents, augmented by Canada's civilian-soldiers' eyewitness accounts, form the core of this study.

It was the infantrymen who most often faced the blizzard of steel, chemicals, and high explosives, and it was the infantrymen whom the generals ultimately relied upon to deliver victory. "They're loaded like pack animals, their shoulders are rounded, they're wearied to death, but they go on and go on," wrote Lieutenant Coningsby Dawson, a thirty-two-year-old British-born novelist who was twice wounded while serving with the Canadian Field Artillery. "There's no 'To Glory' about what we're doing out here; there's no flash of swords or splendor of uniforms. There are only very tired men determined to carry on. The war will be won by tired men who could never again pass an insurance test, a mob of broken counter-jumpers, ragged ex-plumbers and quite unheroic persons."[9] It was the infantry who fought and died for the shattered and cratered geography of No Man's Land. And through the blood test of battle, it was these soldiers at the sharp end of war—these ordinary Canadians called upon to perform the extraordinary—who ultimately defeated the German armies, forever changing world history.

THE WESTERN FRONT

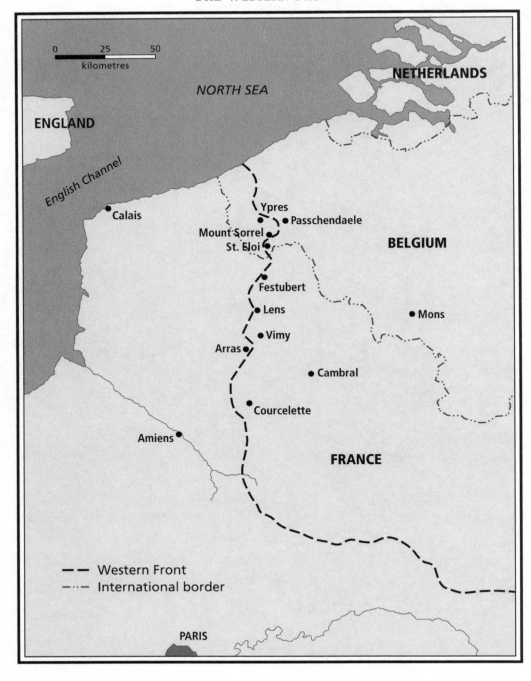

ENGLAND

NORTH SEA

NETHERLANDS

English Channel

BELGIUM

Calais

Ypres

Passchendaele

Mount Sorrel

St. Eloi

Festubert

Lens

Mons

Vimy

Arras

Cambrai

Courcelette

FRANCE

Amiens

0 25 50
kilometres

– – Western Front
–·–·– International border

PARIS

CHAPTER 1

EUROPE MARCHES

"The lamps are going out all over Europe; we shall not see them lit again in our lifetime," spoke a sorrowful British Foreign Secretary Sir Edward Grey as Britain slipped into war.[1] Despite this moving statement implying the inevitability of the forthcoming tragedy, the nations of Europe did not go to war in 1914 accidentally. While none of the great powers can escape blame, examinations of prewar German foreign policy conducted after the war revealed—once historians sorted through the propaganda and official publications that suggested all nations had been acting in self-defence—that Germany was willing to risk a war in order to forestall an expected future attack by Russia and France. In attempting to shift the centre of power in Europe towards itself, Germany first planned to break the delicate balance that had kept the European powers from each other's throats for decades. But the causes of the Great War are complex. The great powers embraced war in August 1914 through calculated plans and ultimatums that proved impossible to rescind. The kings and foreign ministries had deep grievances or goals that propelled them to conflict. All were bound by a complicated system of alliances, and when an unpopular Austrian archduke was assassinated in late June 1914, this proved to be the spark that set the world ablaze. The inferno would rage for five years and consume ten million soldiers and countless millions of civilians, shatter empires, and usher in the bloodiest century in human history.

IN THE SUMMER of 1914, Europe was a tinderbox. No war involving all the great powers of Europe had occurred since the defeat of Napoleon in 1815.

Nineteenth-century wars in Europe remained limited, largely through the desire of all nations to ensure a balance of power. But that did not stop the Europeans from using force to leverage power and prestige, and most sent their armies to carve out new colonies, with Britain and France leading the scramble. Between 1800 and 1914 the proportion of the earth's surface occupied by European countries, colonies, or former colonies rose from thirty-five to eighty-four percent. Under Queen Victoria's six-decade reign, Britain's control expanded to cover one-fourth of the world's surface. The sun may have never set on the British Empire, but the glory of the radiant queen had brought Britain into increasing friction with Germany, which also, under Kaiser Wilhelm II, wanted a lofty place in the sun.[2]

In the quest for power, both Britain and Germany, followed by other great powers of Europe—France, Russia, Austria-Hungary, and Italy—embarked upon an arms race. New battleships, new armies, new civilian technology such as railways and telegraphs, were all employed to expand and project power. Mutual suspicion spread in the capitals. Chiefs of staff and army planners devised plans to win quick wars of movement: although few were comfortable in predicting success, a long, drawn-out war would be catastrophic, and so most military planners found ways to forecast decisive victories for their political masters.

The diplomats were hardly more sanguine. Fear drove old enemies to become allies of convenience. France and Russia joined together in 1892—a clear indication that each was desperate for security and willing to overlook the incongruence of an autocracy supporting a republic, and vice versa. Britain, aware that it risked being left out in the cold, and certainly out of Europe, sided with its historic enemy, France, in 1904. Together they formed the Entente Cordiale, and three years later Britain signed a treaty with Russia. The Triple Entente was fragile at best, with its three principal members distrusting each other and, for the most part, competing with one another over key strategic areas in Europe and around the globe. But the Entente had a surprising resilience, and survived several German diplomatic manoeuvres intended to drive a wedge between these old rivals. The Triple Entente provided evidence that even antagonists can put aside their differences for the sake of survival.

This Triple Entente left Germany encircled and shackled to a corpse: the ancient and decaying Austro-Hungarian Empire, which encompassed dozens of ethnic groups and at least eleven different nationalities. On the verge of disintegration as a result of the various challenges of emerging nationalism, Austria-Hungary suffered the impending loss, alternating between acquiescence and anger. But the Central Powers of Germany and Austria-Hungary knew full well the dangers of being almost entirely encircled, so they also later formed an uneasy and informal alliance with Turkey. Nonetheless, by 1914 the Central Powers were outnumbered by the total population of the Triple Entente countries: 259 to 156 million. The final great power, Italy, coyly eyed the other strategic blocs, waiting to see where it could find the most advantageous position. Its stance was probably the worst kept secret in Europe, however, since its leaders were hungry for parts of the Austro-Hungarian Empire, and most diplomats and soldiers assumed that after some courting it would join the Triple Entente. All countries brokered treaties for mutual protection, even as they feared that the balance of power was shifting. These treaties of mutual security created mutual concern, and they also bound countries to one another, dragging them together down the sinkhole of war.

THE ARMS RACE was at full throttle when the Russo-Japanese War of 1904–1905 proved that the white Western nations could be defeated by the then-called Orientals. The Russian forces were soundly beaten, its navy annihilated at the Battle of Tsushima, and its land forces driven from the battlefield or forced into capitulation. Almost all the European armies sent observers to study the preparation, training, and engagements, and they were graciously hosted by the senior Russian and Japanese commands.

These soldier-observers were particularly keen to determine how the Japanese forces had defeated the Russians. Unlike the open battles of the South African War (1899–1902), the decisive engagements in the Russo-Japanese land conflict had been siege affairs. Trenches had dominated the battlefield; yet the Russian machine guns had been unable to stop the aggressive Japanese infantry from overrunning their dug-in positions and bayoneting them to death in a fury of hand-to-hand fighting. Many of the official military observers concluded that the superior iron-willed discipline of the Japanese soldiers had allowed them to overcome the inherent advantages of the defensive-minded Russian troops hunkered down in their trenches.[3]

A cult of the bayonet found its high priests, and the word "steel" became gospel in most armies. The French were especially quick to recognize the effectiveness of offensively minded troops led by aggressive officers who would overcome the formidable power of defenders, even those in trenches. Few dissented, as the new priests preached to the converted. The French had a burning desire to recapture the lost provinces of Alsace and Lorraine, ceded to Germany after the disastrous Franco-Prussian War (1870–1871), and this could only be accomplished through rapid offensive operations. While the French incorporated the lessons of the Japanese victory into their attack doctrine, it was less frequently stated that this victory was paid for with thousands of Japanese corpses.[4]

The South African War, in which the British had finally run the Boer insurgency to ground through the use of mounted patrols and concentration camps, had proved that battles could be won by aggressive commanders striking hard and fast. The next major European war might be won in a number of weeks, so European military leaders predicted, if their generals and troops were aggressive enough to seize victory. Some naysayers spoke out, of course, such as Ivan Bloch, a widely read Russian banker who warned in his polemic *The Future of War* that conflict between major powers would lead only to mutual suicide and a breakdown in society that would eventually result in socialism's destruction of the capitalist system. But few soldiers paid much attention then—or now—to bankers predicting that war was no longer possible without the decimation of national economies.

The price of modern war in blood was undeniable, even among the most horse- and lance-enamoured general. The new weapons technology ensured that future wars would be, if anything, conflicts of enormous firepower. By the late nineteenth century, chemical propellants and high explosives increased the range and lethality of rifles to beyond 1,000 metres, and artillery fire to several thousand more. Breech-loading guns equipped with rifled barrels, which more effectively propelled ammunition, further increased the distance and accuracy of small arms and larger field guns. An infantryman at the Battle of Waterloo in 1815 could fire his musket to a maximum effective range of 100 metres and at a rate of two rounds per minute; an infantryman at the beginning of the twentieth century, using breech-loading rifles with clips containing five or ten rounds of ammunition for rapid fire, could tear apart advancing enemy troops at four or five times that distance, and at five to seven times the rate of fire. Smokeless powder, in use since the 1880s, and the ability of the infantry to fire while lying down with rifles fed by clips, made it harder to spot the enemy on the battlefield. When an infantryman and his comrades revealed themselves, it was often through a hail of bullets.

New weapons, such as the Maxim heavy machine gun of the 1880s, allowed for a blizzard of fire—up to 500 rounds per minute. A single weapon now contained the firepower of several dozen riflemen. Within this storm of steel, quick-firing artillery field guns, with hydraulics—which placed the barrel on a slide to absorb the recoil with buffers, and therefore prevented the dislodging of the weapon's gun carriage—allowed for nearly continuous firing of up to 20 rounds per minute for short durations. High explosive shells that detonated like dynamite bursts and shrapnel shells that sent hundreds of metal balls spraying the battlefield added to the killing power of the artillery.

But battles could not be won by sitting in ditches. The necessity of sending the infantry forward into the face of dug-in riflemen who were protected by sweeping machine-gun fire and supported by artillery left more than a few generals and staff officers awake at night wondering how to overcome the power of the defensive. The lessons of past wars seemed to indicate that motivated soldiers could advance to victory on the battlefield, moving incrementally and spread out to create more diffuse targets. They would be supported by their own artillery, but this alone would not be enough to overcome dug-in defenders. Firing as they closed in on the enemy, the advancing infantry would hide in the folds of the land. After collecting themselves some 100 metres from the objective, a final push by soldiers wielding bayonets would drive through the enemy's forces. Casualties would be high, but few defenders—even those dug in—could withstand a charge of cold steel. Resolve was valued over firepower; élan was cultivated instead of passive defence. As the European armies engaged in large-scale mock battles and hammered out mobilization plans to bolster their regular forces with civilians, it was not machine guns, massed rifle fire, or high explosives that ushered in war, but two assassins' bullets in the Balkans.

TERRORIST GAVRILO PRINCIP, a nineteen-year-old Bosnian Serb, animated by dreams of greater power for Serbia in the Balkans, assassinated the heir to the Austrian throne, Archduke Franz Ferdinand, and his wife on their wedding anniversary on June 28, 1914, in Sarajevo. Princip's revolutionary organization, the Black Hand, a small, poorly funded group that was supported by Serbian military intelligence, was part of a loose assembly of agitators that had been targeting Austrian officials in the hopes of establishing an influential Serbia to control united Slav territories, many of which remained within the Austro-Hungarian Empire.

The victim, Franz Ferdinand, was an unattractive leader, disliked by most of his subjects and largely considered ineffectual. Yet he became a far more important martyr in death. The Hapsburg monarchy's response to the killing of one of its own was uncharacteristically swift. Serbia had long been seen as a conspiratorial enemy, and the infelicitous positive response to Ferdinand's death in Serbian newspapers did little to temper Austrian desire for revenge. The Serbian government's failure to adequately denounce the killing for fear of rival, ultra-nationalistic political parties gaining ground left it seemingly implicated or complicit in the assassination.

After an outpouring of grief turned to anger in Austria, the Hapsburgs saw a chance for a final reckoning with their enemy. Calls for war among senior political and military leaders were now less opposed as, ironically, the strongest proponent of peace among the small ruling circle had been the archduke before his murder. Now, his death was cited as a motivation for war. After nearly a month of escalation and planning, Austria issued an ultimatum. It ordered Serbian officials to renounce terrorism and allow Austrian police forces—largely viewed as the army—to ensure internal security in that country or face a war. Serbian officials did not want war with the Austro-Hungarian Empire, which dwarfed it in size, but giving up Serbia's sovereignty was viewed as worse. The Serbs drew the line at accepting a foreign police force to exert internal security, even as they agreed to most demands. This compromise went a long way in swaying international public opinion towards the Serbs; however, Austria took this pretext to rid itself of an annoying neighbour. The Austro-Hungarian Empire declared war on July 28, a month after the archduke's assassination. In the minds of many Hapsburgs, and especially the military leaders, this was a war for survival: if Serbia was not taught a harsh lesson, the rest of the tenuous Empire might soon fragment. Surprisingly, Chief of the General Staff Franz Conrad von Hotzendorff, who desperately wanted war against Serbia, wrote to his lover, "It will be a hopeless fight ... [but] it must be waged, since an old monarchy and a glorious army must not perish without glory."[5] Perhaps these are simply the kind of words old generals write to their younger mistresses, but they suggest that Conrad may not have been the most inspiring of leaders.

The assassination might have led only to a minor war, not unlike the conflicts that had ravaged the Balkans in the previous few years. In fact, most of the monarchical great powers believed Austria's response to be justified, if perhaps heavy-handed. But the arms race had excited nationalistic passions, and now Germany's Kaiser Wilhelm, who had ascended to the throne in 1888 before his thirtieth birthday, and who had, over the years, displayed an irrational mix of bombast and inconsistency, made the fateful choice of supporting Austria's war.

The Austrians had cleared their war against Serbia with Germany first, realizing that they needed the protection of its armies against Russia, which might attack to support Serbia. The outraged Kaiser, who did not like to see royalty gunned down, gave unconditional support to the Austrians chomping at the bit for their limited war. This "blank cheque," as it came to be known in later years, convinced Austria to act aggressively when it might have been more cautious, especially given that the Russian czar had publicly declared his support for fellow Slavs and had assisted Serbia and other Balkan armies in their wars against Turkey in 1912.

Only in the days leading up to Austria's declaration of war on July 28 did the vacillating Kaiser realize that his support might result in a war spreading out from the Balkans to infect all the great powers. After British Foreign Secretary Sir Edward Grey rushed to Berlin to head off war, but also to warn Germany that Britain could not stand aside in a general European conflict, the Kaiser panicked. But a German call to pull back the Austrians from war fell on deaf ears in Vienna, which was intent on avenging the newly beloved archduke.

CZAR NICHOLAS II of Russia—with his massive army made up of peasants and workers from across the vast country—set in motion the mobilization of Germany, and ultimately provoked the Europe-wide war. As multinational as Austria, Russia was also just as unstable, but equally resilient. The humiliating loss to Japan in 1904–1905 had been followed by an insurrection that required Nicholas to accept reforms and to experiment in establishing a political cabinet. Few thought the czar would risk another defeat in war. The Russian link to Serbs in language and history notwithstanding, advisors to the czar noted that Serbia's humiliation by Austria-Hungary might change the balance of power in the region and would allow the Austrians to amass most of their military forces opposite the Russian front, as opposed to its currently divided armies. This realization, added to old-fashioned rivalry and xenophobia—and a belief that moribund Austria-Hungary would not be acting without Germany's tacit support—led the Russians to order full mobilization on July 30, the day after Austria began bombarding Belgrade, the capital of Serbia. As was true for the other great powers, mobilization in Russia would raise the standing army by a factor of three or four—from about 1.4 million men to around 5 million.[6] Russian troops would soon be marching, and Austria-Hungary found itself in a two-front war, exactly the conflict that its generals had argued for years that it should not fight, for it likely could not win.

This show of force by the Russians reverberated through the capitals of all the European powers, particularly Berlin. But the July Crisis had inflamed passions in many countries, with a slew of intellectuals, politicians, and soldiers embracing war as a means to cleanse the septic inertia that had supposedly infected many nations and workers. While social Darwinism—the idea that war would weed out the weak and allow the strong to carry on—had germinated roots in many countries, it was the mobilization of forces that pushed the great powers to war.

MOBILIZATION MEANT the calling-up of reserve forces; it was escalation but not war. Even before mobilization, some 3.6 million professional soldiers were under arms in the Entente and Central Powers; but the call-up of reservists initially tripled or quadrupled the forces available, and then later increased them again by drawing on other segments of society.[7] Mobilization also meant putting complicated war plans into effect: calling out reserve forces, establishing strategic trains and arms depots, and transporting and concentrating forces at the borders to prepare for invasion or defend against it. It was a significant step towards war.

While Russia was considered a lumbering giant by the rest of Europe, its army had gone through a modernization period in the years prior to 1914. The forces were so large that basic weapons like rifles or uniforms were still in short supply, but its behemoth size still terrified the German high command. Eastern Germany could not hold out for long against the Russian forces. Luckily for the Germans, the Russian military was plagued by commanders who possessed consummate skill in snatching defeat from the jaws of victory.

The Germans had predicated all of their complicated war plans on speed. Positioned as a central land power, and equipped with the most efficient railway system in Europe, Germany could mobilize its forces more quickly than Russia or France, and then move them along interior lines to meet developing threats. But when Russia went active, the Germans would have to follow almost immediately to maintain their advantage. A quick victory required decisive and swift military action. The time for diplomatic negotiations would be over. The Russian actions also allowed the Germans to portray the war as a defensive one, which helped to galvanize support, at least within the country.

Outside German territory, most of the great powers believed that Germany's support of Austria in its war on Serbia had raised the stakes from a limited Balkan war to one that risked a continental conflict. While Germany had been aggressive in the last two decades in pursuing its desire for greatness through *Weltpolitik,* or world policy, it was not a militaristic regime, notwithstanding what wartime Allied propaganda would suggest in belittling and condemning German *Kultur.* In fact, some of the aggressive German foreign policy was an attempt to rally the disparate states of the federated Empire: Prussia, the most powerful state and most closely linked to the Kaiser, but also Bavaria, Saxony, Baden, and Württemberg, some of which had their own kings and tax systems. Germany was playing a dangerous game of brinksmanship, and now it, and most of Europe, was teetering on a razor's edge.

But none of this mattered when the German general staff began full mobilization: its plans called for a quick victory against France, followed by the defeat of Russia. The German troops would not turn back once they began to march towards the western frontiers. Only a quick war could offer any hope of victory, and sitting on the defensive while encircled by enemies would only lead to inglorious defeat.

Germany did not want to go down in history as having lost its place of prominence in Europe because of timidity.

THE FRENCH detested the Germans for having inflicted a humiliating defeat on them during the Franco-Prussian War four decades earlier—long enough for the wounds to fester and for the old men to forget why they had lost. The German annexation of the two eastern French provinces of Alsace and Lorraine had ensured that those wounds would never heal. While Germany remained the stronger power militarily and economically, the French had bided their time effectively, slowly isolating their Teutonic enemy. Like all the great powers in the first decade of the new century, France had rearmed. The lessons of the Russo-Japanese War and the humiliation of the Franco-Prussian War, in which large French forces had been bottled up and forced to surrender, impelled the French to embrace the cult of the offensive. Under Chief of the General Staff Joseph Joffre—a round little man of an even temperament that allowed him to accept heavy casualties without ever spoiling his appetite—the French army embraced the spirit of élan and the power of the bayonet. This offensive spirit was exhibited at both tactical and strategic levels. France's attack operation was called Plan XVII. As the name indicated, it was neither particularly inspiring nor innovative; in fact, it called for little more than a full charge eastwards to recapture Alsace and Lorraine, and the Germans could well guess exactly where the French were going and when. They would be prepared. But France was anxious to redress old defeats, and it was not about to abandon its strong alliance with Russia; nor would it allow a quick war to end without seeing its forces occupy their old provinces, which would then be brought back into France's bosom.

The British Parliament was far less certain about committing the country to war, even when German troops began to march. Britain had always aimed to keep a balance of power in Europe, and its traditional strength came from its navy, not its small regular army.[8] Britain's cabinet was initially split over the war, but the efficient, if brutal, German invasion of Belgium in early August allowed powerful orators like Prime Minister Herbert Asquith, Winston Churchill, and David Lloyd George to convince and cajole the recalcitrant cabinet members to accept that this was a war against a brutal oppressor, a violator of international law, and a bully of the weak. The British bulldog would defend "Brave Little Belgium," as the country had pledged to do since 1839.

WITHIN THE SPAN of a few days in late July and early August 1914, what appeared initially to be the Third Balkan War had spiralled into the First World War. As Europe marched, most eager soldiers felt that they would be home before Christmas. Such dreams disappeared in a haze of firepower and millions of dead and maimed. This world war, soon to be known as the Great War, would consume men at shocking rates for more than four years.

CHAPTER 2

"THE COUNTRY WENT MAD!"

Canada at War

"Thus came the war," wrote Stephen Leacock, the Canadian humorist and professor at McGill University. "For Canada it came out of a clear sky—the clear sky of vacation time, of the glory of the Canadian summer, of summer cottages and bush camps; and for the city population the soft evening sky, the canopy of stars over the merry-go-round resorts in the cool of the summer evening."[1] In fact, the war was not quite so surprising, as the lead-up events had been well covered in most papers across the country. Nor was Canada quite so idyllic, especially for those toiling in factories and mines. But few would anticipate that the great powers would indeed embrace war so readily.

WHEN WAR WAS ANNOUNCED in Canada on August 4, tens of thousands of Canadians took to the streets in an orgy of military pageantry. A sea of Union Jacks draped the country. "When the war broke out—you could not believe it unless you were there," remembered Bert Remington, an eighteen-year-old who, in his words, was "five foot nothing and 85 pounds soaking wet. The country went mad! People were singing on the streets and roads."[2] Remington was turned down because of his size and age, but later joined the forces as a bugler and made his way to France before being wounded in 1916.

Prime Minister Sir Robert Borden and his cabinet had greeted the war with decidedly less enthusiasm. The dour Nova Scotia–born prime minister, with his greying hair parted down the middle, imposing chin, and bright eyes, had been the country's leader since 1911, when he had taken the Conservatives into power, surprising almost everyone by defeating the silver-tongued Sir Wilfrid Laurier, who had been prime minister for more than fifteen years. Yet Borden and his colleagues quickly realized, like many parliamentary winners before and since, that it was harder to govern than to stand as official opposition. Scandals and mismanagement plagued the government, a deep depression stagnated the economy, and most political pundits assumed the Liberals would soon be returned as the ruling party.

But the war threatened to upset everything. No one was sure of Britain's response, but few doubted that Canada would stand by its side. As a dominion within the British Empire, Canada had no control over its own foreign policy. When Britain was at war, Canada was at war. But as a self-governing dominion, the Canadian people would choose the extent of their commitment. The government could have responded to Britain's call with a battalion of volunteers, as it had fifteen years earlier during the South African War. But Canada was a far different country in 1914: expansions in population and prosperity had made the nation surer of itself, and many influential groups and individuals were demanding that such growth required new responsibilities.

By the decade before the war, Canada was the third largest national land mass on earth, behind only Russia and China.[3] The country spanned some seventy-seven million hectares, with only the future province of Newfoundland keeping the Canadian "wolf" at bay and choosing to remain a British colony.[4] The 1911 Census had counted 7.2 million inhabitants, although the number had risen by at least half a million in the three years since then. Despite waves of immigration creating a more culturally diverse society, Canada was firmly white Anglo-Saxon in spirit and in its political institutions—except for Quebec, which always remained distinct. It was also predominantly rural, with sixty-five percent of Canadians living outside the major cities.[5] Canada was a country of potatoes and wheat, of wood and coal. It is not surprising that the British sometimes pictured the rugged Canadians as little more than frontiersmen and cowboys living rough on the frontier of the Empire.

By 1914, however, many Canadians felt that the Dominion had come into its own, some brave Canadian imperialists going so far as to proclaim that the country might some day become the new centre of the British Empire. Canada was a country of vast spaces, but the geography of empire tied it together, with British culture, the All Red Line of linked telegraphs, the Union Jack, and the monarchy and everything it represented standing as symbols of liberal progress. Most Canadians saw themselves as proud members of the Empire. But not everyone shared this sense of allegiance. Some, particularly those carving out a new life for themselves, took notice of the war but assumed it had little to do with them. These Canadians went on with their lives and were less prone to the jingoism of fiercely imperialist-minded Canadians who would soon demand that Canada support the Empire. While most Canadians were emotionally, politically, and mentally intertwined with the small island that controlled a quarter of the world, the declaration of war was still a shock. Sir William Thomas White, Canadian minister of finance, worriedly remarked that war between the great powers would signal "the suicide of civilization."[6] The question on everyone's lips was whether Canadians would embrace the war beyond waving flags and singing songs or allow the European great powers to embrace their suicidal solution alone.

IN MONTREAL, English and French citizens showed their martial enthusiasm by singing "Rule Britannia" and "La Marseillaise." "Canada, an Anglo-French nation, tied to England and France by a thousand ethnic, social, intellectual and economic threads, has a vital interest in the maintenance of the prestige, power and world action of France and England," observed Henri Bourassa, an influential member of Parliament for Quebec, founder and editor of the prestigious *Le Devoir,* and later a vociferous critic of Canada's war effort.[7] English and French in Canada were united behind the war at first, the true gulf being between rural and urban centres. Most farmers continued to stoically work the land, assuming—and rightly at first—that this was a big-city war.

In the cities, it was hard to sleep, because of both the raucous celebrations and the excitement that drove neighbours and family members to talk and speculate till all hours. Canadians realized that they were living through momentous times.

In a war portrayed as one of good against evil, liberty against despotic militarism, British justice against German *Kultur* (which became shorthand for German aggression, unthinking obedience, and military autocracy), little moderation was exercised. Everyone was an expert, and few questioned the assumption that the war would be over by Christmas. Many were already working out German reparations and settlements. Those who questioned how war would end quickly with the proliferation of machine guns and artillery bit their tongues. But so few of those weapons were available to Canadian soldiers that the public could be excused for its ignorance.

If modern weapons of war were scarce in the Dominion, there remained a lot of manpower. Many militia units had already anticipated the conflict and had accepted men to fill the ranks before war was declared. After August 4, however, the units were officially open for business. No one was quite sure what the Borden government wanted, but no militia colonel was willing to sit back and wait. The armoury doors were unlocked on August 5 to long lines of men in their best suits and hats, eager for a chance to serve king and country. Some had waited all night with nervous, shuffling feet, and they crashed through when the doors opened in the morning. In Toronto, at the University Avenue Armouries, it was necessary to post guards with fixed bayonets to keep the frenzied, patriotic, would-be soldiers at bay.

But it was a buyer's market. After shoving and jostling to the front, thousands across the country were bitterly disappointed to find they did not meet the military's high medical and physical standards. Recruiting sergeants selected men with military experience first, and many of these were recent British immigrants who had served in the South African War. The unwanted left the armouries discouraged and disappointed, some blinking away tears; many had the double disappointment of first being received in the ranks and then finding they failed the stringent medical exams that demanded good teeth, high arches, and healthy lungs; that they fall between the ages of eighteen and forty-five; and, initially, that they measure over five foot three for the infantry, and even taller for the artillery, in which gunners were required to lug heavy shells and guns. "The Medical Officer has weeded out misfits as ruthlessly as a gardener weeds a plot of ground," wrote one man who passed.[8] Those who did not meet the requirements were most often denied service. Harold Peat, a gawky, unlikely soldier from Edmonton, was initially turned down after his medical examination revealed his small chest. When he implored the doctor to

In major urban centres, armouries, such as this one in Ottawa,
became the focal point for thousands of men who tried to enlist.

reconsider, he was told roughly, "We have too many men now to be taking a little midget like you."[9]

But Peat refused to be cowed and returned the following day, pretending to be Belgian and demanding retribution for his people. He was soon in the ranks. Bribes and threats worked for other men, as did appeals to close friends who were now in positions of authority. G.T. Boyd was turned down during the medical examination because of his poor eyesight, but he knew the orderly sergeant and offered him a bottle of alcohol to "lose" the doctor's assessment.[10] Boyd was soon wearing the khaki uniform. Men pleaded that it was not fair to keep them out of this "war for civilization" because of flat feet or a persistent cough. The likely apocryphal story of the angry potential recruit barking through a mouth of missing teeth that he wanted to shoot Germans, not bite them, captured the frustration of men who had been blocked by medical inspections. South African War veterans talked their way into the ranks at the age of forty-five or older, rubbing shoe polish into their hair, and, on second attempts, remembering to also dye chest hairs. Many succeeded, and those who failed found that within months the authorities raised second and third contingents, increasingly relaxing some of the more stringent medical regulations until, by 1916, the malformed, maladjusted, and minuscule were routinely embraced by a man-hungry military.

No single reason for Canadians' decision to enlist stands out; what appealed to one man might have no effect on another, but all had a range of allegiances that often intersected and overlapped. Many were caught up in the excitement of war and felt the need to serve. And the desire of young men for adventure cannot be discounted. "I wanted to see the world and I thought this would be a good opportunity," remembered Robert Christopherson, a five-foot-seven retail worker. "I didn't see how else I was going to ever get out of Yorkton, Saskatchewan."[11]

Many men believed in the justness of Canada's war effort. "All idea of war and soldiering had long gone out of my mind," wrote one Canadian destined to serve in a Highland battalion, "but it came to me like a flash that if ever there was a war that appealed to the chivalry and patriotism of all right-minded men, this one was."[12] Some men enlisted on a lark, or after a few drinks with the boys. Alfred Andrews, a lawyer from Qu'appelle, Saskatchewan, was railroaded in late August after office mates "pointed out [that since] I was Canadian born and had no ties, it was my duty to enlist." He didn't, but two more weeks of pressure left him in an unbearable position. "We had a rather heart-breaking farewell at home but Mother and Father bore up well. We all felt that I wouldn't come back and I gave away a lot of my things."[13] Others had deep consultations with family members, realizing that a wife and children would suffer hardship without the principal wage earner in the home. The pull of Empire overcame many worries of family, however, and these concerns were soon assuaged by support groups such as the Canadian Patriotic Fund, which would raise and administer millions of dollars for soldiers' dependants.[14]

Militia men suffered particularly fierce pressure to enlist. Some 59,000 active militia men filled 35 cavalry regiments, 39 field artillery batteries, 106 infantry regiments, and an assortment of engineering units, service corps, and medical units. They, along with the 54,318 trained militia and Permanent Force soldiers who had already left the service, created a deep pool of military men that dwarfed the mere 3,110 professionals then in the Permanent Force.[15] Of the roughly 1.95 million men of military age in Canada, it was these experienced military men who would form the backbone of the overseas Canadian forces.[16] Many militia units enlisted en masse, or with only a few embarrassed members begging off for family or economic reasons. J.M. MacDonnell recounted that his entire artillery battery stepped forward on the first day of the war: "It seemed not only the natural thing to do but the inevitable thing to do."[17] They had been practising at war for years, even if it had been in short summer camps that were more rowdy, laddish getaways than anything else, and it took incredible willpower to resist the urge to serve in the real thing. However, wives had permission to veto a husband's enlistment, and men who had sneaked off and abandoned their families were still being plucked from the ranks well into 1915, at which point this matrimonial right of interdiction was quietly dropped.

Similarly, soldiers under the age of eighteen needed parental consent. The young had been weaned on stories of military bravery, and most had practised at war in the mandatory school cadet classes in all provinces but Saskatchewan.[18] Wanting to escape an unhappy home life, or seeking a break from manual labour in the factories or mines, youth eagerly enlisted, moving from short pants to military trousers and embracing their emerging masculinity.

However, more than a few men must have felt as conflicted as George Broome, who enlisted at the age of eighteen. He sent two letters to his mother within the span of a week in late June/early July 1915. The first asked her to sign a consent form to allow him to serve; the second, after some sober thought and discussion with family, was more hesitant. In it, he bluntly suggested to his mother, "I should not go for many reasons which are hard to express. I thought only of honour & country but other things count and when I see all the able bodied men laying around the city doing nothing I feel that I am not needed. Possibly you had better not send your consent and let me out. Two or three lines saying you do not wish me to fight will free me but it is as you wish."[19] It is unclear whether his mother followed through with his request, but Broome did not officially need a consent form at the age of eighteen and so went overseas. He turned nineteen in the training camps and then went to France, where he saw action from early 1916 until he was shot in the spine at Vimy Ridge. He died a paraplegic from secondary infection on November 7, 1917, at the age of twenty.

"Hungerscription" forced some men to enlist in search of employment after two economically depressed years, but most of the first recruits gave up good jobs.[20] Privates received one dollar a day, plus ten cents more for overseas service, with higher ranks receiving better wages. The private's wage was about the equivalent of the poorest paid labourer, but food and board were also supplied—although most would soon query if what the army served qualified as food. Private Robert Christopherson had enlisted out of patriotism, remarking, "It never occurred to us that we were going to be paid."[21] It surely must have occurred to the majority of others. But this was not an army of hobos, and most recruits had left jobs to enlist. Initially, many patriotic employers promised to hold soldiers' jobs for them until their return. For much of the war, civil servants continued to draw their civilian salary in addition to their military pay.[22] But despite the generosity of some employers, many family men purchased insurance to care for dependants in case of their own deaths.

Thousands of the initial enlistees were recent British immigrants. They had come to seek a new life in Canada, but found that carving it out of the dense forests or endless plains, while living in a sod hut, was far more difficult than the cheery "Last Best West" that recruiting posters had promised. "They say war is hell," read the notice nailed by one man to the door of his shack. "But what about homesteading?"[23] Other new Canadians were anxious to return home on a government-paid trip. At Toronto's University Avenue Armouries in early August, Medical Officer G.S. Strathy wrote in his diary that in the recruitment drive for the 10th Royal Grenadiers, "the men enlisting were nearly all British born and of various types, some 'out of works' and 'no goods,' with a great many ex-service men, and a large sprinkling of patriotic men without any military experience, who felt duty bound to defend their country."[24]

A postwar survey of the 30,617 men who formed the First Contingent of the Canadian Expeditionary Force (CEF) revealed some striking information about their place of birth. The vast majority of men—18,495—were born in Britain.

Canadian-born men made up 9,159 of the ranks, while 652 men were born in other British colonies. The number of American-born soldiers was high, at 756; 523 more were born in other "foreign countries"; and the remaining 1,032 men did not provide a country of birth.[25] Of the privates and non-commissioned officers (NCOs), thirty percent were Canadian-born. However, among the more prestigious officer positions, of which the First Contingent had some 1,500, almost seventy percent were born in Canada. By the end of the war, the total number of Canadian enlistees had risen to just over fifty percent.[26]

But too much should not be made of the high initial content of British-born in the ranks. Canada was a land of immigrants, and men who were born in Britain but had come to Canada and settled here for fifteen or twenty years—who thought of themselves as Canadian—would have been classified as British-born. As well, many of the British men were single and had military experience. These "ribbon men" were exactly the type of veteran that the recruiting sergeants and officers selected first to fill the ranks.[27] One wonders how many men pulled stunts like that of Harold Baldwin, a bronzed twenty-four-year-old farmhand. He was initially turned down because of his height of five foot four, but he reapplied the next day, this time lying about four years of service with the Imperial regular army.[28] No way to confirm or disprove his status was available, so the unit eagerly took him, even though he had never served a day in his life. Whatever the case, however, it is clear that British-born men enlisted far out of proportion to their numbers in Canada.

CANADA WAS A PROUD British dominion supporting the mother country, but many Canadians were also moved by the ongoing plight of Belgians, whose country had been almost entirely overrun in the first weeks of the war. Atrocity stories were heard about burnt libraries, outrages against women, babies skewered on bayonets, and summary executions: some were propaganda, but many were true. Patriotic relief organizations raised money for Belgian refugees, and men like Georges Vanier, a French Canadian equally comfortable in either language, and destined for greatness as a governor general, wrote, "I could not read the accounts of Belgian sufferings without a deep compassion and an active desire to right, as far as it was in my power, the heinous wrong done."[29]

If this war was a chance for many to right wrongs done to outsiders, it also might be a chance to right historic inequities within Canada. While this was a white man's war, many Natives felt the pull of their warrior traditions, while others hoped that their loyal service would win greater rights for their neglected and cheated people. Native warriors were prized scouts and snipers, although those living in urban areas might have secretly grinned or groaned over such broad, stereotyped characterizations. Natives were therefore eagerly enlisted, even though some commanding officers worried that the enemy might not extend the full rights of war to the "savages," and would execute them upon capture. Few warriors were deterred by such worries, however, and no records exist indicating that such atrocities took place on the battlefield. By war's end, some 4,000 Natives had enlisted.

Francis Pegahmagabow of the Parry Island Band was one of the first. Peggy, as he was known to his friends, served throughout the war and was awarded three Military Medals, becoming one of only thirty-nine men in the entire CEF to receive such a distinction. He would achieve legendary status as a sniper and scout, as would many other Native warriors. The majority of Natives, however, simply did their duty and were soon respected as equals, holding positions of responsibility and even receiving commissions. But despite their wartime sacrifice and service, equal rights would be a long time coming to these ill-used members of Canadian society.

While Natives were often accepted in the ranks, other visible minorities remained excluded from the First Contingent. Blacks and Japanese occasionally found their way into subsequent contingents, but it was not until the summer of 1916, when recruiting sources had largely dried up, that army officials overlooked many of the racist beliefs prevalent in the forces—beliefs reflecting those of the larger society—and allowed minorities to serve.[30] But even then, as in the case of blacks, they often found positions only in non-fighting labour battalions, although some Japanese Canadians served as infantrymen in the 10th and 50th Battalions. However some combat soldiers of colour did serve, and one of them, Curly Christian, had the sad distinction of being Canada's only quadruple amputee to survive the horrors of the battlefield.

THE WEST COAST experienced a genuine war scare as rumours circulated of German cruisers making for Victoria and Vancouver to bombard the cities. One virulent rumour suggested that a great naval battle had been fought in the Atlantic and that the Royal Navy had been sunk. A supposed conspiracy of silence had covered up the defeat, but now the British Empire was vulnerable. The premier of British Columbia, Sir Richard McBride, was so worried that he sent agents to the United States to purchase two submarines then being built in Seattle.[31] This move helped to calm the agitated public, and in one fell swoop McBride's subs doubled the size of the Canadian navy. The German cruisers never arrived, although they did raid in the Southern Hemisphere before they were sunk by a British squadron. While the Royal Navy was not destroyed, it was pulled back to home waters. Britain's ally, Japan, provided warships to guard the west coast, which was hard for some Canadians to take, especially since racist feelings towards Asians ran high. The war shattered many things, including, at times, pride.

These real threats, when combined with the fear in central Canada that German-Americans would band together in cross-border raids to capture Canada, drove many men to enlist. Canadians felt threatened. This was not just a war overseas. It was a war of defence, both to keep the Hun at bay and to defend the liberal, democratic ideals that underpinned the sovereignty of the nation and the British Empire.

While the militia units were recruiting to capacity in the big cities, much confusion remained as to what the government wanted. Minister of Militia Sam Hughes cleared things up by embracing utter chaos. Hughes was Canada's war leader for the first two and a half years of the war. With his close-cropped grey hair, iron jaw, and furious stare, the sixty-one-year-old Hughes was loud and boisterous. He craved to be the centre of attention. And now he was. Hughes gladly accepted the role, revelling in the publicity engendered by headline-grabbing diatribes and hyper-patriotic speeches. Despite his proven instability and volatility, Hughes was a powerful orator who had strong ties with the militia and the powerful Orange lodges of Ontario. Having been labelled a "martial madman" by the Liberals before the war, he now accepted the mantle of Canada's war leader.[32]

Hughes's office in Ottawa was soon the centre of power, and his military secretary, Charles Winter, was consistently forced to deal with long lines of contract-beggars waiting to receive a piece of the procurement pie from Hughes. Notoriously unreliable at delegating authority, Hughes nonetheless soon established a number of cronies—usually with honorary military ranks—to assist him in spreading around lucrative war contracts. Many such contracts would later lead to scandal. Hughes did not mind, and continued to blunder forward, broken china strewn in his wake.

For the moment, the money seemed limitless and little if any oversight of spending was carried out. Hughes liked to offer lucrative contracts as he saw fit, but this warlord-like behaviour was not appreciated by the cautious Minister of Finance White, who blanched as funds were spent with abandon. Canada was not a rich country, and White scrambled to secure loans, first from Britain, then the United States, and finally the Canadian people in the form of war bonds. None of this mattered to Hughes. He was a man of action; he let others figure out how to pay for things. Sitting with his feet up on the desk, Hughes barked out orders and dispensed largesse. The minister was the driving force behind the initial Canadian war effort and as cocksure in the righteousness of the cause as he was in his own abilities.

While civilians rushed to fill the ranks, it was not until August 6 that the Borden government authorized the raising of units to serve voluntarily overseas with the British forces. Britain asked for one division, and Borden's cabinet allowed for 25,000 men to be raised, enough to fill the infantry, artillery, and support units in an 18,000-man division, and to allow for about 7,000 reinforcements. With these orders, the professional soldiers began to implement Canada's mobilization plan, which called for military districts across the country to draw together militia units, select the best men, and send them off to Petawawa, Canada's then biggest military camp.

Hughes took one look at the plan and threw it away. This was his war, and he was never happy with a plan that he had had no hand in crafting.[33] Instead of a controlled mobilization implemented through existing military districts and based on the regions' proportional populations, Hughes offered a free-for-all, taking all who wanted to join the crusade. Colonel Willoughby Gwatkin, the British soldier whose misfortune it was to serve as chief of staff, looked on in disbelief.

The fiery Hughes had no faith in "barroom loafers," as he referred to the professional soldiers. Since his election to Parliament in 1892, he had dedicated himself to fighting the "regulahs" tooth and nail. No, the professionals were not needed.

Hughes turned to his "boys" to fill the ranks. Canadian civilian-soldiers, he believed, had the innate skills of war bred into them. They could ride like cowboys and shoot like hunters; Canada's war effort would be carried forth on their broad, suntanned backs. How the myopic clerk or malnourished factory worker fit this vision was left for the officers to figure out. Minister Hughes did not worry himself about such inconsistencies.

On the night of August 6, Hughes sent out 226 telegrams to militia commanders across the country, deliberately bypassing the regular channels of communication through the Permanent Force–operated military districts. It was, in his words, "a call to arms, like the fiery cross passing through the highlands of Scotland or the mountains of Ireland in former days."[34] The controlled, planned mobilization schedule would be ignored; the country's militia colonels would raise Canada's new army. It was chaotic, but surprisingly effective. Hughes's actions—much criticized by historians—caught the flavour of the time and the scramble to serve. The minister also scrapped the training grounds at Petawawa, a town that was nowhere near a port, and moved the site to Valcartier, 25 kilometres northwest of Quebec City.

The latter seemed like an especially odd move since nothing but sandy fields made up the landscape at Valcartier, which was located on the east bank of the Jacques Cartier River and surrounded by the Laurentian Mountains. Liberal critics smelled a scandal and condemned Hughes for issuing patronage contracts to former Tory member of Parliament William Price, who came from a long line of legendary lumber pioneers. Hughes and Price shrugged off the Liberal questions, invoking the need for expediency while at the same time ensuring that Tory financial backers and party friends were well rewarded. But the Valcartier camp was soon a marvel. Latrines, water works (which had to be moved the first time since they were set up next to raw sewage), huts, parade grounds, electric lights, railway tracks, and a telephone exchange were built in less than two weeks. And, as Hughes crowed, Valcartier had the most extravagant rifle range in the world—at more than 1.5 kilometres long and equipped with over 1,700 targets. Valcartier was a success story, but one that Hughes's critics snickered was probably his last in the war. It was a good thing that the camp was built in record time, too, since eager soldiers from across the country were soon converging on the spot.

CHAPTER 3

CONTROLLED CHAOS

Valcartier

Valcartier became one of Canada's largest cities almost overnight. The first troops began to arrive via Canadian Northern Railway on August 18, and the trickle soon turned into a flood. Officers devised everything on the fly. Minister Sam Hughes—acting true to form—had not helped matters by sending Canada's only Permanent Force battalion, the Royal Canadian Regiment, to Bermuda as a garrison unit. The professional soldiers of this regiment, many of them South African War veterans, would have provided less-experienced soldiers with much-needed instruction in drill and tactics, as well as the intangibles of combat. This new Canadian army also desperately needed leaders and experienced soldiers to arrange for the feeding, clothing, and training of the motley force of volunteers.

With sawdust filling the sky from the legion of carpenters and labourers who worked day and night to meet the demands of Hughes's new army, soldiers arrived by the hundreds on trains coming in from across the country. They had all left behind loved ones and cheering crowds. "I have given it no end of thought and I feel it would be a great education for me and that I would not be selfishly restraining myself from doing my bit in this empire struggle for humanity," wrote Ralph Adams to his worried mother. "I can't always be near you and home, you know mother, but I always remember it dearly just the same."[1] Nearly every recruit who came to Valcartier shared this sentiment in one way or another, despite the men's sense of adventure and their patriotic belief in the cause. Some entire militia regiments arrived intact, such as the 48th Highlanders from Toronto, but most militia units had been asked to reduce their recruits down to a single company (known as a "double company" then) of 250 men. Taking matters into their own hands, some of the more enterprising men left behind simply jumped on bikes or trains and showed up at Valcartier looking for a uniform and a rifle. Many men wore bowler hats or South African pith helmets. Multicoloured militia uniforms sprinkled the ranks, designed more to impress women than to assist men in hiding from the enemy in the field. "We were a funny-looking bunch," remembered Wally Bennett, a nineteen-year-old clerk from Calgary, who arrived in a fancy blue suit and wore it for weeks before he received his uniform.[2]

WITH ABOUT 10,000 EXTRA MEN filtering into the camps over August and September, it was almost impossible to achieve any real soldierly training. Much of the time was spent in filling out forms and undergoing inoculations that left everyone sick for several days. Before being injected, soldiers swore an oath and agreed to abide by the King's Rules and Regulations.

The military fetish for filling out forms and documents coincided with the studying of legal and constitutional documents in Ottawa. As Canada's army was training for battle, it was uncertain whether the provisions of the Militia Act allowed militia units to serve outside the country. After much hand-wringing, the government authorized battalions to be included as part of the Canadian Expeditionary Force (CEF), which would be considered an Imperial contingent, although paid for by the Dominion government. Officers received commissions in the militia, as well as temporary Imperial commissions in His Majesty's Land Forces.[3] Not until the end of 1916 would the Canadian government reclaim the CEF—and the hundreds of thousands of men and women who formed it—as part of the Canadian volunteer militia on active service, defending their country abroad. Who ultimately controlled the Canadian forces had worried few in the heady days of 1914, but it became a more pressing matter as the Canadian war contribution grew and hundreds of thousands were fighting in various theatres of battle.

Meanwhile, at Valcartier, sleeping accommodations and food needed to be organized. Uniforms and weapons would be issued as they arrived, and training would follow shortly thereafter. The job of organizing this ad-hoc force fell to a small group of professional soldiers, led by Brigadier Victor Williams—the adjutant general who was desperately needed in that role, but who Sam Hughes instead made camp commandant until a British officer was later appointed. Williams was "temperamentally unfit" to deal with the chaos and, much to the merriment of the men, was not a strong public speaker. "'You are a fine lot of men; I don't think,' pause for breath, 'I ever saw a finer lot,'" recounted one wicked soldier.[4] J.S. "Buster" Brown, who would rise to fill a senior staff officer position during the war, felt that Sam Hughes had sent Williams to Valcartier "to fail."[5] He did not do so, but Williams and his small staff of twenty-five officers felt a terrible strain as thousands of troops poured into the camp.[6] Someone was always barging into the staff's tents demanding something: mediation in a conflict or an order to carry out some work. At one point, the 2nd Battalion had five commanding officers in the course of one day, all of whom had laid claim to the coveted office and who pleaded their case before Williams.[7]

With the Canadian government authorized to raise a division, the question of who would command it was of immediate concern. Sam Hughes had visions of himself leading his boys into battle, but he was not willing to drop the reins of political power. Staying true to form, Hughes decided to keep both jobs. However, Prime Minister Borden, who usually allowed Hughes a lot of rope—even if it tended to find its way around the mercurial minister's neck—reined him in, demanding that he choose between the roles of minister and general. The British War Office

The minister of militia and defence, Sam Hughes, was the single most important figure in Canada's war effort in the first two years of the war, although most senior officers found his meddling ways tiresome and damaging.

well remembered the difficulties with Sam Hughes when he had served in South Africa—where he had proven his worth as a soldier but had eventually been sent home in disgrace for gross insubordination. The British recoiled from the very thought of having the unstable politician in the field. After British Secretary of State for War Lord Kitchener suggested forcefully that Hughes could do greater good in Ottawa, the minister came to his senses, although he would continue to meddle in most aspects of the overseas force.

The British offered one of their senior generals to the Canadians to fill the position of division commander. Lieutenant General Edwin Alderson was a thirty-six-year veteran of the British army, who had fought with distinction in South Africa. In that war, Canadian mounted troops had served under his command, and it was felt that he had an understanding of these "rough colonials." The Canadians had emerged from the South African War with a reputation as good fighters, but also as unconventional soldiers who bristled at regular army discipline.[8] Like the Australians, the Canadian rough riders had often fought the British when discipline had been imposed on them. Many therefore viewed them as brawlers, not soldiers.

The experienced Alderson was ordered to transform the Canadians into a fighting force. At his age of fifty-five, this position was likely not Alderson's first choice of command, but the British only had two corps at this point, commanded by Douglas Haig and Horace Smith-Dorrien. While command of a division usually went to a major general, perhaps the British hoped that Alderson's higher rank would show their faith in the Canadians, and certainly it might allow him greater leverage against civilian interference. True to his nature, Hughes would later have himself appointed first major general, and then lieutenant general. Cheeky indeed, but perhaps not out of character for a man who, during the South African War, had demanded not one but two Victoria Crosses—the coveted medal that represented the Empire's highest award for bravery. Sam Hughes would remain an ever-present irritant to Alderson's command.

AT THIS POINT, Alderson was in England, waiting to assume his position as commander when the Canadians crossed the Atlantic. Before this could happen, however, the force had to be brought together at Valcartier, and in the absence of an on-site division commander, much of the burden fell to the three infantry brigadiers who would lead the bulk of the Canadian division's strength. All three were appointed by Sam Hughes. Many feared that he would elevate political cronies to these positions of power. To his credit, he looked for the best men—although it did not hurt if they were Conservatives.

The commander of the 1st Brigade, fifty-five-year-old Malcolm Mercer, was a Toronto lawyer, a prominent member of society in that city, and former commanding officer of the 2nd Queen's Own Rifles of Canada. At six feet tall with a ramrod-straight bearing, and sporting a soldierly moustache that nearly covered his mouth, Mercer looked every bit the soldier. Before the war, he and Sam Hughes had travelled throughout Europe together, observing military manoeuvres and furiously taking notes on how to upgrade Canadian military capabilities; in the process, both had concluded that war with Germany was unavoidable.[9] While Mercer had never led troops in battle, he had devoted much of his life to soldiering. Mercer was a leader of men, and enjoyed their company, but he also had an interest in art, and dabbled in painting. He never married, although he cared for his three unmarried sisters and an elderly bachelor brother.

When war broke out, Hughes asked him to recruit a militia regiment, and, in early September, to take command of the 1st Brigade. While the Canadian brigades at Valcartier went through a dizzying array of changes, the final structure of Mercer's brigade—about 4,000 men strong—consisted of four battalions. The 1st Battalion was commanded by F.W. Hill, a former mayor of Niagara Falls, and the unit drew its strength from London, Stratford, and Windsor. The 2nd Battalion was composed of men from at least nine militia regiments from Ottawa, Toronto, and Peterborough. Its commander, David Watson, was a newspaper editor from Quebec City and a friend of Sam Hughes who would eventually rise to command a division. The 3rd Battalion drew largely from Toronto militia regiments, and was commanded by Robert Rennie, a fifty-two-year-old businessman and militia colonel. "The Dirty Third" became the nickname for the battalion after Rennie heard that the men were crawling with lice (as were most troops at Valcartier) and admonished them to clean themselves or they would be left behind.[10] Rennie would soon learn one of the truisms of war: almost every campaigning infanteer in history has been plagued by body lice. The 4th Battalion was under the leadership of Arthur Birchall, a British officer on loan to Canada who had penned a widely read book on infantry tactics. His recruits came primarily from Barrie, Hamilton, and Brantford.

The new expeditionary force battalions were composite groups of militia regiments, with stray individuals attached to them to meet the necessary quotas. At Valcartier, Hughes continued to impose his stamp on this fledgling army, by stripping the militia regiments of their historical names and instigating new, numbered battalions. For example, the 90th Winnipeg Rifles and the Queen's Own Rifles of Canada, militia regiments that had defended the country against Fenians and helped to pacify the west, were blandly renamed the 8th and 3rd Battalions. This was not simply another megalomaniacal decision by Hughes, although many soldiers saw it that way, but an attempt by the minister to create a new esprit de corps. The introduction of the numbering system was intended to prevent divisive arguments about what traditions would be observed within battalions that were formed from several proud militia units. Few soldiers liked the change, however, some being vocal in their opposition. In an example of the men's resistance to the new system, many numbered battalions refused to mask their former militia names and kept their unofficial designation throughout the war. But such allegiances were soon largely artificial, and battalions such as the 48th Highlanders of Canada (who formed the core of the 15th Battalion) or the Victoria Rifles of Canada (from Montreal, and forming the 24th Battalion of the Second Contingent) soon lost their initial composition as a result of the ceaseless wastage of the trenches. Men from across the country would later blur the geographical distinction and homogeneity of units.

By early September, sixteen battalions had been created, numbered sequentially from 1st to 16th, and a seventeenth battalion was later added to accommodate stragglers. Each battalion was commanded by a lieutenant colonel, and had a strength of about 1,000 men. The battalion subsumed four infantry companies of about 225 men each. Companies were the primary combat units for the battalion, and each was commanded by a major—although in battle, as a result of casualties, a captain or even a lieutenant would be forced to take command. Within each of the four companies were four platoons, each of about fifty men, most of whom were riflemen in 1914. These fighting sub-units were led by lieutenants, but they relied heavily on senior NCOs—sergeants and corporals—to ensure that orders were carried out. NCOs have been the backbone of every army in history, and the new Canadian army proved no exception. Almost all of the NCOs had military experience, and they used it to assist officers judiciously in exerting control, to enforce discipline, to ensure proper training, and to aid in the transition of civilians into soldiers. They also led the privates into battle: within each platoon were four sections of about ten to twelve men, each headed by a sergeant. Although men formed close allegiances within their sections and platoons, the larger battalion was the soldiers' family and home. Every man could probably recognize a comrade from his battalion by sight, and most would jump at the drop of a hat to save a battalion-mate in a fight.

Men from across the country were represented in the fighting battalions, artillery batteries, and auxiliary units. However, Ontario and the West provided the most soldiers, while the Maritimes and Quebec produced far fewer troops, and neither of the latter two regions had its own distinct infantry battalion in the First Contingent. Ontarians and Westerners often had more immediate links to the Empire, with more recent British immigrants settling in those regions, while Maritimers and French Canadians tended to see themselves as more established Canadians. Moreover, in the case of French Canadians, they did not speak the army's sole official language and had fewer identifiable ties to the Empire. Although 1,245 French Canadians were recorded at Valcartier, they were spread throughout a number of units—with concentrations in the 12th and 14th Battalions—and many were English-speaking men from Montreal.[11] The noticeable absence of a French-Canadian unit from the order of battle was a justifiable concern among Quebec nationalists. But Sam Hughes, a fiercely devoted senior member of the Orangemen Protestant fraternal organization, had little time for French Canadians, and less for worrying about equality in cross-national representation.[12] However, members of Parliament, and even authorities at the Department of Militia and Defence, came to their senses and organized a French-Canadian battalion in the Second Contingent.

IN ADDITION to the absence of a French-Canadian unit, senior command appointments for French-Canadian officers were lacking. Many believed that

Brigadier General F.L. Lessard—who had served with distinction in South Africa, and subsequently in senior command positions in the Permanent Force—should have commanded a brigade, and might have easily been groomed for command of the Canadian division. But Hughes's prejudice towards professional soldiers—and French-Canadian ones at that—surfaced again, and Lessard was relegated to an administrative role.[13] Instead, one of the brigade commands went to Richard Turner, a wholesale merchant from Quebec City.

But Turner was more than a merchant: he was one of Canada's few identifiable military heroes at the start of the war. The sharp-faced forty-three-year-old colonel was fluently bilingual and had served as president of the Canadian Cavalry Association. Far more important was the purple ribbon he wore on his chest to signify the Victoria Cross he had earned during the South African War's Battle of Leliefontein on November 7, 1900. As part of a small rearguard force, a young Turner had held off a large Boer commando unit, sacrificing himself and his men to allow Canadian guns and a British baggage train to retreat. Even though he had been shot through the throat, the bespectacled, slightly bookish-looking Turner had kept fighting. He was impeccably brave and most of his men were in awe of him.

All of these attributes made Turner a good choice as a brigadier, although his friendship with Sam Hughes had not hurt his cause. Turner took command of the 3rd Brigade, with the 13th, 14th, 15th, and 16th Battalions under his command. He wrote in his diary a few weeks later: "I am studying hard [,] as there is a lot to learn."[14] Indeed there was, and neither he, nor the other brigadiers—none of whom had ever commanded any unit larger than a battalion—were ready for battle in their new roles.

In Turner's brigade, Lieutenant Colonel Frederick Loomis commanded the 13th Battalion, a Highland unit constituted almost entirely of Montreal's 5th Royal Highlanders of Canada. The 14th Battalion, the Royal Montreal Regiment, also drew most of its strength from Montreal, which was not surprising since this city was Canada's largest and had a rich military history. By war's end, Montreal contributed an astonishing 56,000 men to the CEF.[15] At one point, three militia colonels vied for command of the 14th Battalion, but the coveted position was eventually given to Lieutenant Colonel F.S. Meighen. One of its four companies was designated as French Canadian.

The 15th Battalion was a Toronto battalion consisting again of almost a single militia regiment, the 48th Highlanders of Canada. Its commander was Lieutenant Colonel John Currie, a member of Parliament and long-time militia officer. Finally, the 16th Battalion, known throughout the war as the Canadian Scottish, drew from four regiments: the 72nd Seaforth Highlanders from Vancouver, the 79th Cameron Highlanders of Canada from Winnipeg, the 91st Canadian Highlanders from Hamilton, and the 50th Gordon Highlanders from Victoria. The 16th was commanded by Lieutenant Colonel R.G. Edwards Leckie, and each of these four militia regiments formed an independent company that had its own tartan and celebrated its distinctive traditions. But within those four companies were men drawn from every province in Canada; forty-seven of the counties in England; all but two of the counties of Scotland; twelve of the counties in Ireland; four of the counties in Wales; all of the dominions; nine American states; and Mexico, Italy, France, Holland, Denmark, and Sweden. Of the 1,200 men in the oversized 16th Battalion, 850 of them had previous military experience.[16]

ONE OF THE FOUR MILITIA UNITS that formed the 16th Battalion, the 50th Gordon Highlanders, had been commanded before the outbreak of war by Arthur Currie. Born in Ontario, just outside of Strathroy in 1875, Currie was the third of seven children. He was trained as a teacher, but like so many young men of his generation, Currie went west to find his fortune. He soon became a land speculator in Victoria's boom economy and, as befitting a respected member of the community, Currie became a militia officer, rising to command an artillery battery and then the Highland regiment. Sam Hughes and Arthur Currie knew each other and had served together on the executive of the Dominion Rifle Association. Both men were strong-willed, and Currie and Hughes had had minor run-ins before the war, but their relationship was one of mutual respect. The minister took notice of the six-foot-four lieutenant colonel, who had developed an impressive reputation and had furthered his knowledge by reading the latest tracts on command and tactics and taking militia courses offered by the professional forces. However, as a land speculator Currie had been less successful, and his finances had been severely strained in the recession of 1913–14. When boom prices crashed, he was stuck with overpriced land and little hope of selling it to recoup his costs.

In August 1914, the thirty-eight-year-old Currie was facing bankruptcy. He was stuck in the losing game of shifting money among several accounts to cover his debts when the war broke out. Currie had long been identified as an important military figure, and Sam Hughes offered him command of Military District 11, covering west coast recruitment and training, which would allow him to stay at home and perhaps save his business. But Currie's men, fearing that his talents would be wasted in an administrative role, urged him to turn down the offer and take a fighting command. Further, Currie's second-in-command in the 50th Highlanders happened to be Major Garnet Hughes, the minister's son, who insisted to his father that Currie was far too competent to languish in Canada. Minister Hughes reconsidered and offered Currie command of the 2nd Brigade. Currie demurred, but after a long talk with Garnet, during which the two of them walked around and around the horse track at Willows Race Track, Currie agreed to take the brigade.[17] Temporarily avoiding thoughts of his financial woes, Currie then turned his full attention to military preparation. But in his desperation, Currie absconded to Valcartier without repaying more than 10,000 dollars that he had taken from his regiment to cover his debts.[18] This pilfering would later haunt the colonel as he rose through the ranks.

Currie's 2nd Brigade consisted mainly of Western troops. Many were ranchers and farmers, but even city folk took pride in being portrayed as frontiersmen. The 5th Battalion was known as the Fifth Western Cavalry, and soldiers wore this name on their shoulder straps throughout the war. The men of this battalion came from a number of mounted troops, and were teased mercilessly by the rest of the ground-pounders for their now less glamorous role among the infantry. "The Disappointed Fifth," "The Wooden Horse Marines," and the "The Fifth Mounted Foot" were just some of the mocking nicknames thrown in their direction.[19] But the "Old Man" of the battalion, the forty-four-year-old Lieutenant Colonel George Tuxford, had a commanding presence, and soon his "cavalry" were embracing the foot soldier role.

The 6th Battalion was formed around the Fort Garry Horse from Winnipeg, while the 7th Battalion, under command of the charismatic William Hart-McHarg—a South African War veteran and a crack sniper who had represented Canada in several international shooting competitions—drew men from British Columbia. The final unit, the "Little Black Devils," composed mainly of the 90th Winnipeg Rifles, was renamed as the 8th Battalion, but the Black Devils fought hard to retain their militia identity. The commander of the 8th was the demanding British regular officer, Louis Lipsett, who would acquire a reputation for reckless bravery and absolute professionalism. When Currie's brigade arrived in England, the 6th Battalion was replaced by the 10th Battalion, which had been recruited from Calgary.

THE ARTILLERY was the second largest arm of the newly raised force. Militia Director of Artillery Edward W.B. Morrison, a South African War veteran and editor of the *Ottawa Citizen* newspaper, had been appointed commander of the artillery. Having won a gallantry award in South Africa, "Dinky" Morrison—at five feet, six inches tall—was much admired by all who knew him. He also had a keen eye for finding talent in soldiers. However, when he was appointed to command, the first person he cast an eye over was himself, and he was found wanting. Morrison was a skilled gunner, but he knew he was not ready to command three brigades of artillery. He therefore stepped aside to take over the artillery's 1st Brigade, the other two artillery brigade commanders being John J. Creelman, a long-time Liberal militia man from Toronto, and J.H. Mitchell, a forty-nine-year-old former commanding officer of the 2nd (Toronto) Brigade. In response to Morrison's move, a surprised Hughes bit his tongue and gave the position of artillery commander to Lieutenant Colonel Harry Burstall, who had twenty-five years of experience, had graduated from the staff college at Camberley, and was current Commandant of the Royal School of Artillery at Quebec. Burstall was a strong candidate, but was sadly—at least in Hughes's eyes—a member of the small professional Canadian army, which the minister generally detested. But Hughes could find no one more qualified for the position from the militia, and so the quiet Burstall took command.

Burstall's force had 18-pounder artillery guns (named after the weight of the shell they fired), of which six (later four) were grouped into a battery, with three (later four) batteries making up a 750-man brigade. Unlike the infantry battalions that were composed largely of individual men and components of militia regiments, the artillery militia batteries generally enlisted as complete units. They were therefore initially a more cohesive force, and most had trained extensively with their 18-pounder field guns, the workhorse of the army. Capable of a range of some 6,000 yards at this point in the war, the gun fired shrapnel and high explosive shells—although the latter were not introduced until several months into the war, when it was evident that explosives would be needed to damage the deeply fortified trench systems.

The blast from high explosive shells could kill from dozens of yards away, often collapsing internal organs or ripping limbs from the torso. The shrapnel shell was primarily an anti-personnel weapon, containing 375 metal ball bearings that were projected downward in a shotgun-like blast. These shrapnel balls, also accompanied by shell splinters from the shattered casing, shredded flesh, bone, and even steel barbed wire. However, both types of shells were in short supply for the Entente forces during the first two years of the war, with the troops suffering under the weight of enemy bombardments with often little ability to respond with equivalent fire. But the shells would be manufactured en masse from mid-1915 onward, and an estimated 100 million 18-pounder shells were fired by the British and Dominion forces during the war—the equivalent of 44 shells per second, every second of the day, for the duration of the 1,561 days of war.[20]

The second component of the artillery—the 4.5-inch howitzers—was missing at Valcartier, and the Canadian gunners would have to wait to receive these guns until they arrived in England. The howitzer, unlike the 18-pounder field gun, had a barrel that could be angled up to 45 degrees, therefore firing a high, heavy round that could pound enemy fortifications. As the war progressed, the gunners would receive more guns, bigger guns, and more shells. At Valcartier, however, most of the gunners drilled in getting their field guns to the front: drivers urged the six horses per gun forward into mock battle situations that allowed the gunners to unlimber the guns, situate them, and then fire off imaginary rounds.

THE CANADIANS might have thought of themselves as natural-born warriors, but soldiers are not made in a few days. Neither are armies. None of the infantry brigadiers had ever commanded any unit larger than a battalion, and had never commanded in battle. As the brigadiers and their hastily constituted staff tried to round up commanding officers for units under their command, establish training, and generally corral the men—all with no divisional staff to assist—the true leader of the camp was Sam Hughes. In an age before television and radio, most of the new Canadian soldiers had never seen Hughes, but all had heard rumours of his many antics. They soon gained personal knowledge of this larger-than-life-figure as he strode through the camp like a whirlwind.

"It wouldn't have surprised any of us if somebody had assassinated" Sam Hughes at Valcartier, remarked infantryman D.H.C. Mason, so loathed was the minister by certain parts of the forces.[21] Others, however, found him a grizzled, fatherly, and necessary figurehead to lead Canada's nascent army. Hughes stayed close to the action in the camp, even keeping a house on the edge of the grounds to oversee the training. Here, he only caused problems. Exerting his considerable power, Hughes appointed men at the drop of a hat and belittled officers who quaked before him. When he was not happy with the intensity of bayonet fighting, he grabbed a rifle from a surprised private and showed the men how to jab and disembowel an imaginary enemy. Reducing officers to trembling invalids played well with the crowd of guffawing privates, but it did little for discipline and the tenuous hierarchy of command. Hughes's instability ensured that the command within infantry battalions was constantly changing, as he appointed and demoted officers on a whim. Officers did not know if it was wiser to hide when Hughes came by, and fear having someone appointed over them, or to try to prove their mettle in the hope of gaining recognition, at the same time risking that some offhand remark by the minister might result in their being appointed commander of a latrine-digging platoon. As Hughes moved from one part of the camp to another, and the blizzard of activity with him, responsible officers tried to undo the damage. "It seemed that his personality and his despotic rule hung like a dark shadow over the camp," wrote Canon Frederick Scott.[22]

Despite these disruptions in the division's routine, the men's focus was on learning to soldier effectively. Officers crowded around old textbooks and manuals to remember the intricacies of drill movements. Lower down the chain of command, the rank and file tried to carry out their orders, many of which seemed to be barked at them in a new language, half of which consisted of profanities. Nothing was easy. Tents were put up by struggling civilians as the more experienced soldiers laughed at their discomfort. All winced when the tent cities were moved from spot to spot to satisfy some plan hatched at headquarters, which seemed to change every two or three days. The veterans shook their heads in resignation and said that this was just the army way, while new soldiers had a chance to practise their recently learned swear words, with the ubiquitous "bloody" and "fuck" rolling off the tongues of men who might previously never have uttered anything harsher than a "darn."

How much it hurt morale to purposelessly erect and tear down tents is difficult to gauge, but such activities did lead to the men learning some of the most important soldiering skills, such as grousing and gossiping. Amidst these pointless exercises, the new soldiers also embarked upon drill and basic military training, which began to bring this disparate army together. The men marched together, ate together, and slept together. The patriotic talked with the adventurous about getting into the war before it ended by Christmas; the upper-middle class tried to decipher the language of the working man; the spiritual bunked next to common criminals. New recruits learned not to go to their officers with relatively trivial problems such as too tight-fitting uniforms, instead turning to mates who were swimming in their clothes. In this masculine world of soldiering, all had to learn how to wield needle and thread.

SEVERAL THOUSAND at the camp would not make it overseas with the First Contingent, finding themselves to be deemed unfit for various reasons. Officers immediately began to weed out these unfortunates. Some men were held back from overseas service because of their failure to observe the rules at Valcartier. Teetotaller Sam Hughes had demanded a dry camp with no alcohol, which earned him the sobriquet "the foe of booze." Bibulous officers and rankers grumbled, and more enterprising men found ways to smuggle booze into the camps from Quebec City or through family and friends who sent it along clandestinely, by methods such as placing bottles in baked bread. Soldiers loved to cheat the system, but the use of alcohol caused problems. Private Roy Macfie wrote to his sister, "It is a good thing they can't get whisky here or there would be a war."[23] The red-haired and freckled Roy, who resembled actor Spencer Tracy, would serve the entire war with his two brothers, one of whom would be killed in 1917 at the age of nineteen, the other wounded. Roy would survive, having earned two Military Medals for bravery, and return to Canada to raise a family on a farm near Parry Sound, where the backbreaking work beginning at four in the morning was not dissimilar to the trench fatigues that he endured during the war.

The closeness of Quebec City meant that venturesome men on leave from Valcartier could imbibe a lot of beer and get into a lot of trouble in a short time. "The worst threat you could make to a man was that he'd be sent home," remembered Company Sergeant Major Charles Price of the 14th Battalion, but an undercurrent of illegal activity nonetheless continued in the camps.[24] Regimental officers culled the misfits, the insubordinate, the alcoholic, and the moronic. In all, more than 5,000 men were sent home. However, not all of these men were dismissed at the hands of a stern officer. Some of the married and underaged who had disappeared from homes or jobs had the unpleasant fate of being caught up to by enraged wives and parents, who demanded that they be sent home.[25] These men were indeed dismissed from service, as enough men remained to fill the ranks, and the army did not want angry wives and parents accusing it of stealing deadbeat husbands or pimple-faced teenaged sons.

Others simply could not stomach the discipline and drill, the incessant saluting and polishing, which drove many men to the brink of madness. This type of discipline, later known as "chicken shit," plagued most civilian-soldiers. The Canadians would acquire a reputation not only for developing a hearty disdain towards this rote drill but for exhibiting outright insubordination. Their behaviour was rarely as bad as the rumours suggested, but the Canadians liked to think of themselves as rowdy scrappers, especially in relation to the British. The men of the First Contingent were without doubt extremely lax about observing army discipline that demanded strict hierarchies. Two chums who enlisted at different ranks were no longer allowed to talk to one another as pals, or so the regulations insisted. Officers and NCOs were known to settle scores with unruly privates with their fists, as opposed to going through regular military channels. Some embarrassed officers had to plead with their men not to call them by their first names when around more senior officers. Captain P.G. Bell of No. 3 Field Ambulance recounted the irreverence of a new soldier from Calgary, who was operating as a driver for a group of senior officers when the vehicle hit a big hole and lurched. According to Bell, "He turned pleasantly to the officers, [and said] 'You guys had better call the roll to see if you are all present.'"[26] The rules of soldiering took a lot of getting used to for most civilians.

The camp was plagued by laddish behaviour. Although the average age of the Canadian soldier was a relatively mature twenty-six, practical jokes were played ad nauseam.[27] A favourite was to pull up the pegs of other soldiers' tents or divert water by secretly digging rivulets that caused runoff, either from rain or latrines, into a neighbour's sleeping area. Rivalries quickly sprang up between units, with soldiers taking pride in standing together with those in their unit. Fist fights were not uncommon, especially between overzealous camp guards and men returning home late from leave.[28]

When the first payday was finally arranged, the new Canadian officers were so unschooled that they simply asked men to line up and receive their money. No record books were used to track received funds, so some enterprising soldiers went from line to line, battalion to battalion, and made a financial killing. "The soldiers do wild things here sometimes," wrote Roy Macfie to his sister. "If the prices at some of the little stores don't suit them or they don't serve them quick enough, they just make a raid on it and clean it out. There was a company came in and put up a big tent[,] it would be as big as our barn, and put in a moving picture outfit, and a piano and a kind of a band, and charged .10 admission. It went alright the first night but the next night they showed the same pictures again and they started to yell, and one man climbed up on the platform and yelled, 'down with the tent boys,' and down it came and they set fire to it."[29] The cashbox was never found. Civilian contractors learned that it was in their interest to price their wares reasonably.

THE INFANTRY BATTALIONS continued to march and drill, and occasionally shoot. The Canadian infantryman's primary weapon was the Canadian-built Ross rifle, Mark III. The history of the Ross was long and convoluted, but the Canadian army's adoption of the weapon emerged from the government's desire to purchase 15,000 Lee-Enfield rifles during the South African War. When the Canadians were denied Lee-Enfields due to British priority of access to the weapons, the then-Liberal minister of militia, Frederick Borden, saw clearly that Canada's army needed its own rifle. Tests began in 1901, and Sir Charles Ross's rifle was accepted. Despite repeated design problems—including, most seriously, jamming during rapid fire—the government adopted the rifle with the official opposition's support. Dozens of modifications to the gun resulted only in increasing its barrel's length from 28 ½ to 30 ½ inches and its weight from 7 ½ to 9 ½ pounds, making it more unwieldy. When Hughes was given the portfolio of minister of militia in 1911, he continued to champion the Ross, having invested much politically and emotionally in what he called "the most perfect military rifle in the World today."[30]

At Valcartier, few were worried about all the fuss over the Ross. Yes, it had a history of blowing the bolt back into the firer's face, but few such accidents had

Toughening up the men through long marches. Note that the infantrymen are carrying pieces of wood rather than rifles, attesting to the unprepared state of the First Contingent at Valcartier.

occurred. Of course, the infantry were shooting under optimum conditions as they practised, with no one trying to kill them as they pinked away at paper targets. Even in this relatively safe environment, though, the quirky Ross revealed its flawed nature as many of the rifles failed during the rapid fire of five or ten rounds. The gun's bayonet also had a disconcerting tendency to rattle off and land unceremoniously at the shooter's feet during firing. Amidst the jostling and friendly catcalls traded between the best and worst shots in the battalion, some of the men must have pondered how the rifle would handle in a real battle. Despite its faults, the Ross rifle would be the weapon the Canadians carried overseas to "pink the enemy every time," or so Hughes wasted no opportunity to tell journalists.[31]

While training was episodic, the mobilization of the Canadian troops to Valcartier was a success. "There is quite a lot of fun watching some of the visiting women coming thru camp in automobiles when some hundreds of naked men are standing under the showers," wrote Private Harry Coombs from Simcoe County, who had been conducting surveying in Peace River Country in northern Alberta when the war broke out. "The poor 'loidies' do not see much of the camp but should remember the bottom of the machines well as that is all they care to look at, except a few who have nerve enough to look around and they get cheered roundly."[32] In addition to opening up the camp to civilian spectators, a beaming Hughes called three reviews in September to show off his army to politicians and other dignitaries. The soldiers took it in stride, but standing for hours in the pouring rain only made the rankers and officers view Hughes as a buffoon. The minister took no notice—the limelight was too blinding.

BY THE END of September, Prime Minister Borden had decided that all fit men of the First Contingent could go overseas. Sam Hughes burst into tears. At the camp, cheering could be heard throughout the day and night as word passed through the anxious ranks. There was even an impromptu dance in the dark, with men serving as each other's partners in joyous rapture. Roy Macfie wrote that he was so excited about leaving that he could barely get the words down on paper to his sister; but he worried about the quality of the troops—likely himself included. "We have a pretty poor bunch of officers in our company, if they take us to the front, I think there will

Soldiers left behind loved ones, family, and friends.
How many of these men returned to them?

be some bad mixups. The captain is a nice old chap in fact they are all too nice, the[y] just play around like a lot of kids and they can't keep order."[33]

A little more than 31,000 men marched to the harbour at Quebec City, singing both new and old marching songs, as well as "O Canada," often to the skirl of bagpipes and drumbeats. Passing by the historic Citadel, they arrived to see Canada's most prestigious ocean liners. Massive ships that embodied the strength of the British Empire had been pulled from the major shipping companies to serve as transport ships during the war. They were an awe-inspiring sight, and several thousand men could be crammed onto the largest of these vessels. The Canadian heroes would be travelling in a style befitting them—or so many believed until they were led into third-class steerage.

The loading of men was easy in comparison with the military supplies, artillery pieces, and some 7,000 horses, which left the officers and civilians in charge utterly perplexed. The solution ultimately arrived at involved loading everything that could fit into the hull of one ship and then moving on to the next one. Allotted cargoes ended up in the wrong vessels, and troops were marched onto ships and then off again. The latter resulted in the loss of a few men to desertion but also the gain of a few stowaways and much appreciated alcohol from well-wishers and loved ones who crowded the docks to see their sons, husbands, and fathers off to war. In the end, some 30,617 men went overseas with the First Contingent.

Despite the confusion a sense of excitement prevailed. Bands played the boys off with patriotic songs in a pageantry of celebration and militarism. Well-wishers waved as the First Contingent soldiers stood on the decks, or anywhere they could find a spot. On October 3, the thirty great ships, hastily painted in wartime grey, slipped their moorings. It was the largest single movement of Canadians in the history of the country. Thousands of tearing eyes had last looks at loved ones. Thousands of those soldiers of the Crown would never see Canada again.

CHAPTER 4

CARNAGE

Opening Moves

As the First Contingent sailed for England, few Canadians thought that the fighting would endure past December. The combined forces of Britain, France, and Russia would assuredly send the Kaiser's minions, shackled to a corpse, reeling back into their Hunnish lair.

Certainly Austria's inept opening offensive against Serbia seemed to prove the weakness of the Central Powers. Entente newspapers noted with glee how the Austrian forces had launched themselves at tiny Serbia, only to be strongly rebuffed. Although the Austrians vastly outnumbered the Serbs, they were weak in firepower, having too few artillery guns, most of which were obsolete. While the Serbs were even more poorly equipped, with soldiers often lacking boots and modern rifles, many of them had recent combat experience from the Balkan Wars. They were also fighting for their very survival. While this was no one-sided victory—the Serbs suffered some 17,000 casualties, the Austrians 24,000—it was nonetheless a humiliating defeat for the Austrians.[1] This bloody rebuke also revealed to all armies that launching an offensive against prepared defenders—even poorly equipped ones—would be costly.[2]

The Hapsburgs suffered a striking defeat on the Serbian front, but in their campaign against the Russians nearly lost the war before it had started. The Austro-Hungarian high command, led by Chief of the General Staff Franz Conrad von Hotzendorff, found itself in a two-front war. To meet two enemies on a dual front,

Conrad divided his forces, but a number of confusing orders and counter-orders delayed the mobilization, and then transfer, of the Austrian force to the Russian front, and left much-needed soldiers either on trains or waiting for them when they could have been defending against the Russian onslaught.

The Austrians were relying on their stronger German allies to knock France out of the war in six weeks and then turn eastward to defeat Russia in a series of joint attacks. Conrad's forces on the Galician front numbered 31 divisions of some 500,000 men, with a handful of additional divisions to arrive in early September.[3] Against this enormous force, the Russians fielded an even larger army of about 750,000 men in 50 divisions. The Russians had their own problems of inadequately armed soldiers, incompetent generals, and unwieldiness in their armies, but they lumbered forward and defeated the Austrians in a series of bloody engagements in the last ten days of August and into September. The attacks, which involved battering ram frontal assaults, showed little innovation. The Austrians called on the Germans to attack the Russians in the east and draw off some of the pressure, but their Teutonic allies were fighting for their lives as well—their main effort being on the Western Front—until they scored a decisive victory at the Battle of Tannenburg in late August, when two Russian armies were shattered. Tannenburg bought the Germans time to regroup in the east, but they could not relieve the pressure on the Austrians, whose smaller armies were wasting away.

It would be an understatement to suggest that the opening phase of the war had not gone well for the Austrians. The far smaller, if tougher, Serbian force had bloodied them and sent them reeling, although the Austrians would later return and punish the Serbs, raping and pillaging their way through the small country, and inflicting the highest ratio of losses of killed to mobilized troops suffered by any nation in Europe. Like the armies of Austria's ally Turkey, the invading Austrian armies often took the opportunity to rid themselves of long-standing enemies, be they civilian or military. In Turkey, the Armenian minority was subjected to a genocidal ethnic cleansing that resulted in an estimated 1.5 million dead. This systematic massacre went unpunished and largely unremembered for several decades.

In early September, the primary concern of the Austrians was the Galician front, where the Austrian armies had been driven back, leaving behind 100,000 dead, at least that many prisoners of war, and much of their heavy weaponry, including 216 guns and 1,000 locomotives.[4] The Austrians retreated before the Russians, eventually digging in around their great fortress at Przemysl, which anchored the new Austrian line in the northeastern part of the Empire, until it fell in March 1915.[5] Austria had started the war to achieve limited gains and was now fighting an unlimited war of survival.

ON THE WESTERN FRONT, the Germans were pitted against the Belgians and French, as well as a small British professional force that had arrived in Belgium to fulfill treaty obligations. The Germans had the most powerful and hard-hitting army in the world, with its forces raised to around four million men. But their war plans demanded a decisive, quick action, as any delay would allow their enemies to surround them. This opening military move was a race against the clock, as well as the enemy.

The German forces were under the command of Helmuth von Moltke the Younger, the nephew of the respected chief of the German general staff Moltke the Elder, who had orchestrated the victories over France in 1870–1871. The nephew was now looking for an equally decisive victory. His armies would march through the weaker Belgian frontier, sweep down into France, encircling Paris, and then hammer the French defenders against the anvil of another German force along the eastern border. This had been the gist of the famed Schlieffen Plan since 1905, although it had been modified by each new group of staff officers tinkering for success.

The Schlieffen Plan had been tested and retested, revised and reconceptualized, from 1890 to 1905 under the man who gave it his name. Like Moltke the Younger, Chief of the General Staff Alfred von Schlieffen had also worried about how to win a two-front war. He modified his own plan incessantly, first having his forces fight on the defensive in the west while the bulk of his armies defeated the Russians in the east, and later, in the final version, defending in the east against the Russians, while achieving a quick victory against the French in the west, before turning back to the east. War games and operational studies suggested that the reverse was not possible, as it was assumed that the Russians would simply retreat back into the open expanse of Russia, as they had against Napoleon in 1812.

In the west, Schlieffen's master plan called for an encircling operation as the bulk of the massive German armies swept through Belgium, where the "last grenadier on the right wing should brush the Channel with his sleeve," before sweeping down through France.[6] It was a bold plan, except that he based it on more troops than the Germans had available and, far worse, it was reliant on a rigid timetable that allowed for few delays. A tenacious Belgian or French defence or a logistical breakdown might allow the French to recover. No time was built in for prior negotiations or de-escalation. When the military writ dropped, the troops began their relentless march.

Schlieffen's successor, Moltke the Younger, embraced the same plan, although he had less confidence in a knock-out punch against the French, who had rearmed heavily during his tenure as chief of the general staff. He eventually reduced the right wing by half to strengthen the centre, although the sweeping armies still remained a powerful force. Moltke was a pessimist by nature, but perhaps he had been shaken when the great Schlieffen wrote in 1909 that future war would be made up of several battles and that a decisive battle would not likely bring victory.[7]

Moltke reinforced his centre to hold off the French armies, whose plan of attack was obvious in its simplicity: to charge to the east and retake Alsace and Lorraine. Moltke's relatively small force on this front—ten divisions, each of some 15,000 to 20,000 men—would inflict catastrophic losses on the French in the opening phase of the war. However, after the war, Moltke was scapegoated by many German officers and historians for having supposedly ruined the master plan that could have brought victory. In reality, the Schlieffen Plan was an irresponsible operation that brought Britain into war in response to Germany's invasion of Belgium and then somehow expected German troops to fight and march some 500 kilometres over forty-two days. The highly trained Imperial German Army almost made it, too.

THE INVASION OF BELGIUM was necessary to avoid a string of powerful French forts and defensive systems located along this country's eastern frontier, and because any movement to the south was blocked by Switzerland's mountains. Capturing

Belgian forts and railways was essential to any success of the wheel-like, counter-clockwise arc of advance, but Moltke the Elder had also offered an important warning that many of his successors seemed to have forgotten: "No plan survives contact with the enemy." The Germans put all their stock in their single knockout blow, and had precious few fallback plans in case the Belgians and French were not overwhelmed.

The Belgians based the defence of their small country on their fortresses at Liège and Namur, considered one of the strongest defensive systems in Europe. King Albert realized that the Germans would likely invade, but he also feared that the French would meet them in an encounter battle on his territory, thereby leaving his country as the battlefield. Wherever the great powers fought, however, few of them seemed interested in living up to the 1839 treaty that guaranteed Belgian sovereignty. The Kaiser dismissed the agreement as a mere scrap of paper. The Belgians found out quickly, on August 2, that Germany certainly did not respect their sovereignty when it demanded passage through Belgian territory with no more than twelve hours' notice. This was tantamount to declaring war. King Albert ordered mobilization, but few within the country or outside felt that "Brave Little Belgium"—its pathetic moniker in Entente newspapers—had a chance of surviving for long against the German behemoth. And indeed, it did not.

Three German armies of sixteen corps—some 600,000 men in a spearhead role—stormed across the territory, sweeping and smashing the small Belgian army before them. The military was crushed, but Belgian civilians fought tenaciously to defend their land. Small groups of irregulars—considered terrorists by the Germans and freedom fighters by the Belgians—stalked the occupying forces, killing them in hit-and-run attacks. These pinpricks by the *francs tireurs*—or "free shooters"—became more serious as they targeted the lines of communication through acts ranging from ripping up train tracks to ambushing vulnerable lorries. Supplies were essential to keep the invading German forces fed and armed if they were to meet their rigid timeline. Desperate to stem the losses, the Germans declared these ambushes to be terrorist attacks, and therefore illegal under the Hague Conventions, the loosely interpreted laws of war. That the free shooters often wore civilian uniforms seemed further evidence of a revolt by a conquered people.

The Germans responded with an iron fist. When their troops were fired upon, they rounded up terrified civilians and executed them as an example to others. A brutal policy of oppression was enacted, similar to what had worked successfully in Germany's African colonies. Stories of atrocities filtered back to Entente and neutral countries through eyewitness accounts to be reported in the press, and were then used as fodder in countless public and private demands for an unlimited war effort against German militarism and brutality. The rape of women, the public executions, and the burning of ancient manuscripts at the University of Louvain were held up as the fruits of German *Kultur*. An official British inquiry into these atrocities confirmed the accuracy of many of the rumours.[8] Its official report, when combined with sensational newspaper stories and eyewitness accounts, reassured many that the war was a crusade to save Belgium from the horrors of these brutish oppressors. While some of these atrocity stories were overplayed, many were based on real events, and this brutal occupation resulted in the deaths of more than 5,500 civilians.[9]

AS THE GERMANS SUPPRESSED the obstinate Belgian defence, the French were anxious for battle. They had suffered badly during the Franco-Prussian War when their troops had mobilized slowly and ineptly, often being stuck in transit on trains when they should have been on the battlefield. In this rematch, the French general staff had worked out a rapid mobilization, and as soon as Germany declared war, offensive operations were implemented. The unimaginatively titled Plan XVII unimaginatively called for ten corps of troops to invade the eastern frontier and recapture the provinces of Alsace and Lorraine. It was exactly what the Germans expected, and one wonders if the first sixteen versions of the plan were any more innovative. About half the number of troops were posted to the French–Belgian border, as it was expected the Germans would violate Belgium's sovereign space, but few French military planners thought their primary enemy had the troops to make much progress, or simply did not want to believe that the Germans were capable of the audacious action of marching their armies hundreds of kilometres through another country to invade France.[10]

In northeast France, the French and German armies ran into each other in Lorraine in what became known as the Battles of the Frontiers, a series of engagements starting in the middle of August. In fierce battles of attack and counter-attack, the Germans drew the eager French into devastating killing grounds where German firepower shredded the French attackers. The prewar offensive spirit, combined with Chief of the General Staff Joseph Joffre's ordering of his forces forward in an *offensive à outrance,* meant that often the most pressing tactical or strategic issue was the speed with which the French forces could close with the enemy. Firepower, on the other hand, was the Germans' primary tactical approach to battle, as their goal was to strategically fix and hold the French forces on this front to allow the Schlieffen Plan to be unleashed.

Attacking across open ground, even the French quick-firing 75mm field gun could not suppress enemy fire, and too often the infantry were smashed by dug-in German defenders firing from the relative safety of their positions. Communication among battalions, brigades, divisions, and corps was episodic at best, and often the battles were fought in a piecemeal style and without proper support. Initially successful French attacks broke down in confusion, leaving troops abandoned and destroyed by the Germans' superior weight of fire. While communication remained a problem for the Germans too, it was easier for dug-in defenders because they knew whence the enemy was coming. The French dead lay rotting in shocking numbers, their bright blue and red uniforms having often made them easier to spot from a distance. But even had they been wearing khaki or camouflage, they would have been cut down in the open by the wide scythe of small-arms fire and shrapnel. After some gains, the French offensive crumpled along the front.

By the end of August, the French had suffered a shocking quarter of a million casualties. The result appeared to be a repeat of the Franco-Prussian War, but worse and more humiliating. Soldiers and refugees retreated from the east, with panic and despair racing through the ranks. Dozens of generals were fired. "Papa Joffre," as he was sometimes known, responded in his customarily imperturbable manner, refusing to acknowledge the terrible setback but also ordering summary executions of deserters to restore order. The rout was brought under control, but the army's morale had been severely damaged. Even worse, however, Joffre realized that the German right hook was stronger than he had estimated, and it was now sweeping counter-clockwise through Belgium and northern France.

Luckily for the French, however, the Belgian forts had held up the German advance for ten precious days—five times longer than the Schlieffen Plan had allowed for in this phase. By mid-August, the lead forces of the German armies were on the march, but they were behind schedule. The sweat-grimed faces of the German infantry stared down on their targets, and Entente forces were swept before them. The British professional army of 100,000 men in one cavalry and five infantry divisions were part of that general retreat.

The British had gone to war to protect their interests in Europe, but it was also a war in support of international law and the rights of small nations. The Germans worried about fighting in a two-front war against Russia and France, whose combined national populations and armies vastly outnumbered them. To add Britain to that mix would severely strain any hope of victory in a long war, but Germany was not particularly worried about the British army. Britain's power had always been its world-class navy, and German staff officers well versed in military history knew that Britain's approach to war over several centuries was to control the oceans, isolate countries through embargo, and then slowly strangle them of food and war supplies. Britain was not a land power, and its professional army of about 100,000 men was tiny in comparison with the other great powers' forces. The Kaiser wrote off the British force as a "contemptible little army," a phrase that was almost too perfect for propagandists. Later historians, too, resisted no opportunity to note the irony that those "contemptibles" would play a key role in stopping the Germans in 1914, and, over the next four years, would eventually expand from this meagre base to an army of more than five million.

BRITAIN'S INITIAL DEPLOYMENT of the British Expeditionary Force (BEF) arrived on the French left flank around the Belgian city of Mons on August 23, just in time to be overrun by overwhelming German forces. But the phlegmatic British infantrymen fought resolutely, their professional marksmanship taking a heavy toll on the Germans. With the British regulars firing up to fifteen shots per minute with their Short Magazine Lee-Enfield (SMLE) rifles, the Germans thought they had encountered a force equipped entirely with machine guns. The SMLE's .303-round cartridge, encapsulated in a full metal jacket, moved faster than the speed of sound and could penetrate nine inches of brick. It left gaping, bloody holes in the advancing German troops, who were often shot down at ranges of 200 or 300 metres, close enough for the marksmen to pick out the details of their victims. But despite this advantage, the weight of numbers and the individual sacrifice of German troops slowly overwhelmed the British. The "old regulahs" began a desperate and punishing march to the south, stopping and deploying sacrificial rearguard forces day after day, before retreating again, and staying only a few steps ahead of the disciplined force on its heels.

This open warfare revealed the difficulty of the command and control system, in which British generals were out of touch with their troops. British commander-in-chief Field Marshal Sir John French was also at odds with the nation's French allies, who he felt had abandoned the British. Allies they were, but the long history of mistrust and rivalry made coalition warfare exceedingly difficult. At one point, General French was so exasperated that he ordered a return of the British soldiers to England, willing to abandon his ungrateful Gallic allies to their fate. Secretary of State for War Lord Kitchener stepped in with a cool head and convinced his general to rethink the catastrophic order, but coalition fighting, especially when one's side was losing, was never without friction.

Exhaustion and lassitude struck the British "Tommy" (a moniker the soldiers adopted from Kipling's poem of the same name) in the retreat that often required eighteen hours of marching per day for more than two weeks straight—some 375 kilometres in total. Discipline took over, and men were so tired that they marched in their sleep. It is no wonder that some of them believed that angels had come down from heaven to intercede on their behalf. Other stories, rumours, and hallucinations focused on magical bowmen, dressed in medieval armour, who beat back the Hun, skewering them with arrows.[11] These rumours circulated throughout the army, and then among civilians at home, who were further convinced that Britain was indeed on the side of the angels in this war for civilization. But it was the Tommies' SMLEs rather than angelic arrows that kept the Germans at bay. Constant rearguard actions that held off the advancing German vanguard bought time for the ragged BEF to keep marching south to safety. The exhausted British got the better of the Germans, but both sides paid in blood.

THE ENORMOUS RIGHT WING of the invading German force was on the verge of sweeping south to victory and enveloping Paris before crashing into the French rear areas, lines of communication, and retreating forces from the Battles of the Frontiers. While some of the French formations would have been able to reverse themselves to meet this onslaught, the destruction of their vulnerable logistical lines, which delivered all the food and ammunition, would have been catastrophic. The French army would have surely collapsed. But as they neared their goal, the marching German columns began to separate, forming gaps in their lines. Advancing over hundreds of kilometres and having suffered tens of thousands of casualties, exhausted German troops began to lose contact with units on the flanks, and gaps were therefore opening up between their forces. The greatest problem was on the far right wing, which had lost its coherency through its need to guard vast tracts of captured French territory and mask isolated strongpoints of French defenders with armed formations to ensure that these trapped defenders did not break out and attack the German vulnerable rear areas and lines of communication. The German First Army commander, Alexander von Kluck, made the fateful decision to avoid enveloping Paris, and instead pass in front of it to shorten the distance involved in hammering the French Fifth Army to the east of the city.

The French, who had already evacuated key cabinet ministers from Paris, were alerted to the opening by aerial observers. The Entente retreat ended on September 6 in one of the key turning points of the war. The military governor of Paris rallied together a motley force. They hit the Germans hard, caving in their flank in what became known as the First Battle of the Marne. The BEF, at the end of its long retreat, also responded with a vigorous thrust into the gaps forming between the German lines, whose commanders were bedevilled by poor communications and, at first, quite unsure about how to respond in a unified manner. After four days of battle, the Germans pulled back on September 9, closing the vulnerable gaps, but also surrendering any chance of crushing the French forces in the field. The Germans had come within a hair's breadth of knocking France and Britain from the war. The Miracle of the Marne would result in four more years of attritional warfare.

THE EXHAUSTED ARMIES faced each other down. Frontal attacks were beaten back in a hurricane of fire as the forces dug in to the ground, first taking refuge in ditches and then expanding them into trenches. Both sides launched probing assaults along the line, moving north, back up France, in the hope of finding a seam in the enemy's defences. This would later be called the Race to the Sea, but somewhat ironically, as neither side wanted the sea, and it was not much of a race as both sides were limping like men with two broken legs. The initial war of manoeuvre had degenerated into a bloodstained crawl.

In the race to find an open flank, both sides found only more waiting troops, dug in and protected by heavy fire. But still they went north. Behind these flanking battles, the French and German forces left a trail of trenches, like slime from a slug. The trail solidified into coherent trench systems, and soon the defenders were putting up barbed wire and establishing permanent machine gun posts to sweep the ground.

The image of the deadly machine gun firing in fixed arcs as it mowed down troops remains paramount in the popular memory of the Great War. But it was the artillery that was the true killer. Doctors estimated that more than half of all wounds received during the war were caused by the artillery's guns.[12] The crash of high explosive shells, whirling shrapnel, and shell splinters proved early in the fighting that artillery would decide the fate of empires. For those caught in the open, shrapnel and high explosives wreaked havoc.

Yet the gunners were also vulnerable. During the manoeuvre battles of 1914, in which gunners fired over open sights against targets they could see, they had suffered crippling casualties from small-arms fire. The guns were therefore withdrawn behind the thickening trench lines, and gunners began to fire indirectly on their targets, usually a few kilometres away, sight unseen. The fire was fairly inaccurate, but could still be deadly against troops in the open.

Several engagement battles after the Marne proved that the war would not be over by Christmas. Perhaps the most important was the British Expeditionary Force's desperate stand at Ypres, from October 20 to November 24. The British tore apart an onslaught of clumsy German attacks, with their experienced riflemen pouring rapid-fire into enemy ranks behind the steadying effects of protective trenches. The "old contemptibles" turned back the final German campaign of 1914 on the Western Front, leaving thousands of inexperienced troops slaughtered in its wake, but the First Battle of Ypres also destroyed much of what remained of Britain's professional force.

AS WINTER GRIPPED the Western Front, both the Central and Entente armies were exhausted. The losses had been horrendous: the French had lost 800,000 men, some 300,000 of them killed and the rest wounded or taken prisoner; the British professional force had suffered a total loss of 95,000, forcing Kitchener to turn to civilians to fill the ranks; and the Germans had lost 750,000 men in "conquering themselves to death."[13] Politicians, soldiers, and generals could barely imagine how they, their allies, or foes had withstood such high casualty rates. Why had the armies not collapsed? In fact, most professional soldiers had predicted short wars because they believed that the armies, forced to rely on civilians or part-time soldiers, could not endure the horrendous casualties of war. The resilient civilian-soldiers proved they could, although the Austrians and the French nearly buckled under the effort in the first month of fighting. This initially limited war soon became a war for civilization. Diplomacy and a search for peace were overshadowed by the terrible number of casualties that could only be answered by victory. Fear and anger drove the war effort, with pundits claiming that a loss could mean the end of a country, a culture, or an empire. No alliance was yet willing to seek, let alone sue, for peace, despite severe military setbacks.

THE GERMANS had proven that they were not invincible. They had failed to score the decisive victory they needed in the west in order to escape the two-front war dilemma. But they had overrun most of Belgium and some twenty million hectares of France. Much of the industrial heartland of northeastern France, including essential coal-producing areas, was now in German hands. In a war of materiel, which the full economy of nations would soon be devoted to winning, this occupied industrial land would prove essential to supporting the hundreds of thousands that would soon be joining the ranks, first through voluntary means and then, in most countries, compulsorily.

Along the Western Front, the Germans also had the luxuries of standing on the defensive and fighting outside of Germany's borders, thereby ensuring that the Fatherland was not ravaged by war. The French, Belgians, and British, the latter two acting as France's junior partners in the opening stage of the war, had to attack to recover occupied territory. The Germans were able to choose the best ground, usually high points, which offered the clearest firing lanes and permitted the digging of trenches on the reverse sides of hills or slopes to protect against artillery fire. The Entente forces in the West would be at a continuous disadvantage throughout the war as they forever struggled to overcome superior enemy fortified positions. With no flanks left to turn, the only possible way to throw the German occupiers back was a frontal assault into their lines, which were protected by awe-inspiring firepower from small arms, machine guns, and artillery. And even if the front line of the trenches could be pierced, secondary lines contained the break-in forces that were severely weakened from their initial assault, allowing counterattacking forces to drive them out. In the coming four years, some of the fiercest battles in the history of warfare would be waged over this broken ground in ruthless engagements of attrition.

The costly manoeuvre warfare phase at an end, the front stagnated over the winter of 1914–1915. But the defenders used the time to protect themselves. Trenches were dug deeper; millions of sandbags were stacked above them to provide better protection against snipers' fire and shrapnel shell bursts; and communication trenches were connected to secondary lines of defence, and ultimately to the rear. A vast underground city sprang up along what would become known as the Western Front. In between the two armies was the blasted landscape of No Man's Land, which weaved some 700 kilometres from Switzerland to the North Sea, and which would rarely shift east or west during the next four years of war.

Despite the million-man armies that would soon be echeloned in strength along the Western Front, by the end of 1914 all of the great powers were too weak to win but too strong to lose. A long war of attrition would grind away millions of lives before these enormous armies showed signs of cracking. Victory was nowhere in sight. Perhaps the British war hero and minister of war, Lord Kitchener, summed the situation up best when, baffled and disillusioned, he declared: "I don't know what is to be done. This isn't war."[14]

CHAPTER 5

"DRINKING AND GETTING INTO ALL THE TROUBLE THEY CAN"

The Canadians in England, 1914–1915

As titanic battles raged in Europe, the Canadians lay anchored in Plymouth Harbour in mid-October after their ten-day voyage across the Atlantic. At the last moment, the convoy had been diverted from Southampton due to German submarine threats in that region. For the almost 31,000 men on board the ships, this did not feel much like war. The trip had been long and claustrophobic. Although periodic scares about German submarine attacks had rattled some nerves, most of the men took solace in the Royal Navy escort of warships. Officers tried to conduct some training on board, but that was never easy with many of the men feeding the fish with their vomited meals. The rank and file groused and complained about the food and the officers' access to alcohol, but the voyage was largely uneventful, except for the occasional man who fell overboard, was murdered, or died of natural causes.

While in harbour waiting to unload, the Canadians stood on the rails, tired but excited and rambunctious. Wild rumours circulated, and then jumped from vessel to vessel, that the war might end before the Canadians even set foot on English soil. Every day spent on the water was one less day to fight the Hun, who was—according to the supposedly well-informed rumour mongers—in full retreat and soon to

Canadians arrive at Plymouth, October 1914.

surrender. The strain of waiting wore on all, and Private Alfred Andrews, who turned twenty-six on board ship, observed men getting "into fights over little things. Everyone's nerves were on edge."[1] These anxieties were assuaged a little by the citizens of Plymouth who lined the docks to greet the Canadians. Calls went back and forth: "Are we downhearted?" "No!" followed by more cheering.[2]

But the enormous armada took time to disembark, especially with equipment strewn haphazardly in the ships' holds. Private Harry Coombs of the 9th Battalion noted in his diary, "there was a mutiny over the supper tonight, the fellows not taking kindly to macaroni and water."[3] The drinking water became more brackish and foul. After Canadian soldiers held up signs asking for food, Plymouth residents responded with cartloads. At least one infantryman remarked that he felt like a monkey in a cage, as small vessels packed with home-baked goods and fruit were rowed out to the isolated Canadians, but most soldiers munched away cheerfully as staff officers sweated out how to unload the ships.

NEWSPAPERS COVERED the Canadian arrival, gloating that the Dominion forces from Canada and Newfoundland had come to assist in the fight against German militarism. The Kaiser was said to have heard of the First Contingent's arrival in thirty ships and predicted vengefully, "They will go back in thirty rowboats!"[4] It was probably an apocryphal story, but the Canadians took great delight in retelling it throughout the war.

Although it took several days to fully unload the armada, the Canadians were soon arriving into the waiting arms of cheering civilians. Those left behind and waiting for the orders to set them free looked on glumly as the first groups of "Canadian cousins" were greeted with hugs, kisses, and hearty handshakes. Private Alfred Baggs, an English-born member of the 2nd Battalion, described it as a "triumphal procession."[5] However, according to R.F. Haig of the Fort Garry Horse, a few civilians were disappointed to find that the Canadians were not entirely brown-skinned, decorated in feathers, and dressed in pelts.[6]

While there were few "red Indians" and voyageurs, most Dominion soldiers took pride in their unruliness, fulfilling the expectations of some curious onlookers. It is perhaps not surprising that British officer J.F.C. Fuller, who would become one of the leading tank theorists during and after the war, commented that the Canadians had all the raw material to make a strong force, but only after six months of training and "if the officers could all be shot."[7] His blood may have been up a bit when he made this comment since he was nominally in charge of a group of Canadian troops who were to unpack the ships on which they had arrived. When he ordered the Canadians back onto the vessels to unload the supplies, they told him to stuff himself, as they hadn't crossed the Atlantic to be baggage handlers. A shocked Fuller decided not to press the matter and ordered some British troops to carry out the work.

Fuller's comment on the officers was harsh, but it was echoed by other Canadians too, if perhaps in less stark terms. Captain P.G. Bell wrote privately in his diary after spending time with other commissioned men, "I think one of our weak points is our officers. It is useless to disguise the fact that many of them have not the usual qualifications expected in an officer, that is to say they are crude and do not place the proper amount of respect on their uniforms."[8] But many officers rose to the occasion. Lieutenant Colonel Russell Boyle, commander of the 10th Battalion, stood over six feet tall and cut a handsome figure. A veteran of the South African War, he had been wounded in that war but returned to Alberta to take up ranching. He gained a reputation as a tough militia officer before the war and brought his men under control, proving that there were many ways to enforce discipline. At the first parade, he tore off his coat and threw it down. Staring down the men, he barked defiantly: "I'm just an ordinary private, as far as you're concerned, as far as I'm concerned. There were four men on that boat [who] said they'd like to punch the hell out of me. Now I invite you four men, if you have the guts enough to come up, and we'll have it out right here."[9] No one moved, and the four men found interesting things to stare at on the ground. Boyle won over his men.

As the First Contingent was made up of many old soldiers and eager civilians, their outlook on discipline was quite unlike that of the near robot-like professional Imperials. Many in the First Contingent did not respond well to insults and derision, but they gave their leaders respect if they earned it. Often those leaders did not stand on higher rank. The diminutive Private Harold Peat observed that the Imperial military authorities "could not understand how it was that a major or a captain and a private could go on leave together, eat together and in general chum around together.... As far as discipline was concerned, we were a joke."[10]

WHILE THE CANADIANS shrugged off saluting and acts of deference to their betters, they had heart and many were anxious to fight. Edward Seaman of the 3rd Battalion, who had come to Canada from Britain in 1907 and had bought some rocky farmland near Muskoka, stepped off the ship, fell to his knees, and kissed the English soil.[11] It was good to be back in England, although he also noted that he

A church service for the 8th Battalion at Stonehenge.

was a Canadian. These were men who believed in their ideals and were keenly disappointed when they heard that they were to undergo additional training before being let loose on the Germans. The First Contingent moved to Salisbury Camp, the old army training ground 145 kilometres southwest of London. It was also home to the Druid ruins of Stonehenge, and surrounded by small villages and hamlets with plenty of stone churches and taverns.

After arriving by train, the order went out for the cramped Canadians to have a week of leave, since few preparations had been made for them at Salisbury. They went off in groups large and small, proudly wearing the maple leaf badge. Many did not get further than the local pubs that surrounded the training areas; some adventurous ones found their way to London. While many embarked upon sightseeing tours, an identifiable minority got into trouble. The Canadians were feted with free drinks at local pubs. Strong English beer led to drink-fuelled bar fights and vandalism; shocked civilians seemingly encountered colonials peeing in every alley they turned down. "They think of nothing but drinking and getting into all the trouble they can," wrote a disgusted and worried Private Roy Macfie of his companions.[12] The overworked and exhausted Colonel Arthur Currie had been labouring from dawn to midnight almost every single day since he had arrived to command the brigade in late August, but he caught wind of the ruckus and sent officers to London to investigate. They came back with news of the rowdy exploits. Currie and the others realized that while this might be construed as simple colonial brashness, it had to be brought under control or the Canadians would be considered by the British as little more than an armed unruly mob. Although Currie withheld leave passes for some of his troops, the damage had been done. The First Contingent was portrayed in the press as wild men from a northern wasteland—as better brawlers than soldiers. That suited many of these "old originals," who cultivated this wild reputation—even when it was no longer true later in the war, when most British generals viewed the Canadians as among the most disciplined soldiers in the Empire.

AFTER THE BLOWOUT PARTY, the drunks and sightseers were gathered on Salisbury Plain, the Canadians' home until February 1915. The gentle, rolling fields of Salisbury had for years been the British army's training ground for summer manoeuvres. But the location was never intended for use as a camp over the winter, and certainly not to accommodate troops under canvas. The rain started falling on October 23—"solid sheets of driving rain"—and barely stopped for four months.[13] The thin soil over chalk in the region meant that water pooled rather than sinking into the ground. The torrential downpours created small lakes, and more than 60,000 boots trekking through them soon churned the ground into a sea of mud. Violent windstorms blew down the tents, and the men were constantly sodden and clammy. Colds were soon rife throughout the camp, and later a small epidemic of spinal meningitis broke out, killing twenty-eight men, although the rumours often pegged those numbers at ten times that figure.

While many Canadians were anxious to go straight into battle, the high command realized the importance of training soldiers to withstand the strain of combat on the Western Front. "All expect two or three weeks in England," wrote one NCO from the Royal Montreal Regiment, "some time on the lines of communication, and a winter of sieges of some fortress on the German frontier. Of course it may be quite different, but that is the general guess."[14]

It would indeed be quite different, and the British felt the need to invest more than a few weeks in training their new soldiers for the coming siege war. They could do so since their French allies were holding down most of the front-line trenches along the Western Front. But getting these new troops ready for battle was considered an urgent priority, as 1915 was expected to be the year when the enemy would be driven back in a series of offensives.

Lieutenant General Edwin Alderson was the general officer commanding of the Canadian Division—the name that had by this time officially replaced the term First Contingent, although not in the hearts of many men. His thirty-six years in the Imperial army had left him with enormous experience, and he set about meeting with his officers to gauge the quality of his troops. W.A. Griesbach, who would rise to command an infantry brigade during the war, remarked that Alderson "was no genius," and that "his perception was not remarkable, and he had no very great sense of humour."[15] But he took to his task of training and leading the Canadians with drive and patience. While Alderson was a "horsey" general who had authored three books on soldiering and horses and been a Master of Foxhounds—even acquiring a reputation for eccentricity in the South African War for carrying his hunting horn with him during the campaign—his long experience in the army had given him a good understanding of the infantry.[16] He must have been pleased to observe the number of officers and men with military experience, but he realized that the Canadians had a long way to go before they were battle ready. Close-order drill, marching, trench digging, and bayonet practice were all necessary, if unglamorous, skills that the infantry had to master before they could move on to higher-level and combined-arms formation training. It was back-breaking, muscle-aching work, and all the more miserable when it was done in wet, rotting clothes.

FOLLOWING THE ORDERS of Sam Hughes, the Canadian training camp was "dry," even if the ground was not.[17] After marching and training in driving rain and the ankle-deep mud, soldiers wanting a drink would have to be content with coffee and tea. That arbitrary decision was unacceptable to many of the men who promptly made their way to nearby villages, converging on the taverns. With locals standing the boys drinks and Canadian soldiers being paid significantly better than their British counterparts, an explosive situation was in the making. Soldiers became drunk and disorderly, fighting among themselves and terrorizing the local civilians. Private James Gilbert noted that some of his companions were

Lieutenant General Edwin Alderson commanded the Canadians from their arrival in England until May 1916. Although he was an experienced British officer, the highly politicized and partisan machinations of Canadian politicians and soldiers led to his downfall.

"guilty of the grossest excesses, and the English began to call us a bad lot. Children would run when they saw us coming, and ladies would not associate with us."[18] Frank Fox, a deeply religious medical orderly who prayed and sang hymns at night, echoed Gilbert's observation, confessing to his diary, "So badly did they [Canadians] act that ... people became rather frightened of them."[19] Little news of this aberrant behaviour made its way back to Canada as a result of censorship in both countries, but General Alderson heard about it from his army superiors, who demanded that he rein in his unruly colonials.

Responding to the pressure, Alderson sent a dispatch from his command head-quarters at an old inn, Ye Olde Bustard, to the War Office in the last week of October 1914: "I ... find that it is absolutely necessary that there should be canteens for sale of beer in camp."[20] Most of the soldiers were pleased with their comman-der's decision to revoke the "dry" policy, and "prolonged cheers" greeted the announcement.[21] As Lieutenant Victor Tupper, grandson of former prime minister Sir Charles Tupper, noted in a letter home, "Our commander-in-chief, Major-General Alderson, seems to be a fine fellow; he has won the hearts of all ranks by fighting Sam Hughes and establishing wet canteens. He said, in short, that we had been treated as schoolboys long enough, and that in the future we would be handled like men."[22] Within a week, beer was being served to the men, although at first the wet canteens did not consist of much. Currie reported that never did he observe "a dirtier looking or more foul smelling bar room."[23] Private Harry Coombs saw it differently, writing that night after night he could see "a howling drunken mob shivering and having one H[ell] of a time."[24] As more Canadians arrived in the camps in England, however, the wet canteens improved. Soon, they contained more than just beer—they provided a dry spot to get out of the rain, tables for writing letters, and even pianos in the more upscale establishments. William Curtis, a member of the 2nd Battalion who would later be killed in action, was one of the few dissenters. "The wet canteens spoil it [the camp] to a certain extent," he wrote home in a letter to his mother.[25] Few of his comrades agreed, and sales in November and December topped over a hundred thousand dollars.[26]

While Alderson's wet canteen policy was popular with most men, notwithstand-ing the horrified teetotallers, it put him on a collision course with Sam Hughes, who had already made his way to England. Hughes had been so excited about his success in pulling together the First Contingent that he could not leave them alone. As the great convoy had sailed from Quebec, he had raced to New York and taken a fast ship to England to arrive ahead of them.

Hughes strutted throughout London in uniform. He talked up the Canadian war effort, promising men and supplies in off-the-cuff speeches. "How many men will Canada commit?" asked journalists. "How many do you need?" roared Hughes. His figures of available men were always rising: 100,000, 300,000, and even half a million men if needed. Prime Minister Borden was angry and shocked when he heard of such unauthorized pledges, although he too would later be guilty of committing men without consulting his cabinet or military authorities. The cabinet urged Borden to bring Hughes back to Canada, and at least one party member wrote worriedly to Borden that Hughes's bluster "compels me to take the charitable view that I believe the man is insane."[27]

AS HUGHES RETURNED HOME to run his ever-expanding ministry of militia and defence, the Canadians began to step up training on Salisbury Plain. Around the camp, grimacing soldiers trekked through ankle-deep mud, one hand clutching the greatcoat at the neck, the other holding the nearly obligatory cigarette. Conditions were so bad that the Australians diverted their troops to Egypt instead of allowing them to wallow in the muck of southern England. The Canadians grumbled, but intense training kept them busy. Though graveyard coughs and dripping noses plagued most men, route marches of 10 kilometres in full kit were not uncommon. As they passed other British troops or civilians, many must have felt that Canada had sent along a contingent consisting solely of consumptives.

The marching was made all the worse by the poor quality of the Canadian-made equipment. The army-issued boots had soles with a thin leather cover over a cardboard-like substance. Boots were reduced to a sodden mess within a few days. The soldiers soon called them "Sham-shoes," a play on Sam Hughes, and marvelled at the heavy hobnailed boots they received from the British after the shoes disintegrated. R.H. Whittaker of the 3rd Battalion noted in a letter home that each boot felt like it weighed five pounds, and that because of the boots' sturdiness, with their reinforced iron horseshoe heels, his feet were "all blistered."[28] More marching would soon break them in.

The infantrymen's Oliver equipment was equally poorly designed. The webbing—a tangle of leather straps and pouches—allowed for the carrying of ammunition, and for equipment to hang off while in full battle order. But the leather ammunition pouches were ill-placed over the stomach, making it hard to crawl. The pouches also did not hold enough ammunition in comparison with British equipment, and the leather straps cut the men under their arms. On top of these problems, many sets of the leather had been improperly cured and constricted on the wearer after they got wet, creating a straitjacket of sorts. The Oliver equipment was, in the words of Lieutenant Colonel John A. Currie of the 15th Battalion, "a joke."[29] Again the Imperials came to the rescue, offering British-made Webb 1908 equipment.

However, some deficiencies the British could not help the Canadians overcome. The MacAdams shovel, patented by Sam Hughes's secretary, Edith MacAdams, was a combination of metal shovel and sniper's tool that could be fired through while supposedly offering protection. It was not a terrible concept in theory (the idea being to provide the infantryman with some armour), but it was useless as a shovel and lethal to use as a shield since its thin metal could not stop a high-velocity round. The soldiers voted with their hands, tossing away the tools and keeping the army-issued entrenching shovels that came apart for easy carrying. Although Edith MacAdams—and her shovel—have long been the butt of many jokes, few at home could imagine the firepower unleashed at the front. Most of the 25,000 shovels were sold as scrap metal before they got anyone killed.

The Canadian high command slowly sorted out their kit problems, and the Canadian soldier's appearance became similar to his British companions, except in minor details. Men wore a peaked cap, which they quickly modified by pulling out the wire to create a more foppish, jaunty look. Canadians were willing to stomach the minor punishments they received when they were caught ruining their uniform for the sake of a small degree of unique identity and personal style. Steel helmets would not be issued for another year and a half, but another form of headdress was the British trench cap, known as the "Gor-Blimey." It was popular from 1915 to

1917, although it looked a little goofy since its earflaps, when not in use, were tied up over the cap, creating an odd, baggy pile on the head.

The uniform for the rank and file was a tight-fitting khaki serge tunic, with a stiff collar and seven brass buttons, which the men considered superior to the British five-button version. Members of the First Contingent also wore special coloured epaulettes on their shoulders, which, as their numbers thinned out in the months and years to come, distinguished them as the oldest combat veterans in the Canadian forces. Underneath the tunic, a collarless grey flannel shirt soaked up sweat. The lower torso was covered by khaki-coloured trousers, worn high to the belly button, and held in place by suspenders.

Woollen-socked feet went into the hobnailed British boots. Puttees were worn around the ankles and lower leg, imitating the old British soldiers who had served in inhospitable places where rocks and insects had to be kept out of footwear. In preparation for the demands of the Western Front, and to match the distinctive appearance of the British soldier, the Canadian infantryman learned that the khaki-coloured cloth was wound up from ankle boot to knees, while artillerymen and cavalrymen did it in reverse to be distinct. Sergeants harassed the men to ensure that the puttee did not reach within four inches below the knee.

Natty-looking greatcoats offered some warmth and often doubled as a blanket or pillow. The two rough army blankets almost always had to be supplemented by additional clothing in the winter months. Razors and shaving brushes were issued to keep the soldiers clean-looking, but were not to be applied to the upper lip, where it was illegal to shave for the first half of the war. Some officers, like Lieutenant Colonel E.S. Wigle of the 18th Battalion, ordered the enforcement of this rather bizarre rule, citing the quasi-scientific principle that a moustache allowed the infantry to better aim their rifles.[30] But most officers turned a blind eye to such nonsense. Big, bushy moustaches that mimicked the much-loved "Old Bill" character of the British cartoonist Bruce Bairnsfather were popular among the men, while others used their razors to shape the "Charlie Chaplin," which was named after the popular actor. NCOs and old soldiers embraced the handlebar, while officers were encouraged to stick to a clean, thin "toothbrush" moustache. With moustaches as a sign of masculinity, many a pink-faced youth who had slipped into the ranks cultivated what few hairs he could find above his lip. Tooth, hair, and boot brushes allowed for the upkeep of appearances; a mess tin and water bottle were essential for men who would live the next several years like homeless people; and other tools, like a rifle oil bottle and pull-through—a weighted cord that was pulled through the rifle barrel to clean it—as well as a bayonet and scabbard, were all part of the soldiers' kit.

Most of the infantry battalions looked the same, except for the kilted units, which included the 13th, 15th, and 16th Battalions of the First Contingent, and later the 42nd, 43rd, 72nd, 73rd, and 85th Battalions, as well as several additional units broken up as reinforcements. The kilted battalions fought hard to keep their distinctive uniforms, even though they were warned of facing the cold with bare knees. Pride in unit and traditions barely deemed a response to such pathetic cautions to be necessary. Far more contested were the battles within Highland units to determine the unit's tartan colours.

Following the success of the maple leaf cap-badge in the South African War, where the badge had become a rallying symbol for the Dominion troops, the Department of Militia issued another maple leaf badge, on which "CANADA" was superimposed. Most units accepted it and then promptly designed their own cap badges.[31] These distinctive badges, as well as shoulder titles and collar numerals, usually contained the numbered battalion and the word "OVERSEAS." All were worn with pride.

Officers dressed differently from their men. As men of higher social or educational class, and sometimes with political connections, the officers were the leaders in this hierarchical force. Their uniforms were tailored and nattier in appearance, including a collared shirt and tie. A coveted leather Sam Browne belt was worn across the waist and chest. Officers were expected to purchase their own uniform and kit, and most were armed with the Colt .45 automatic pistol, or the Webley or Smith & Wesson revolver. These were good side arms, and could make a mess of a human body at close range. Advertisements and salesmen hocked their wares to naive officers and men: insect powder, "waterproof" pyjamas, and special periscopes were among the "necessities" purchased. Most of the material was embarrassedly dropped after officers reached the trenches. Later in the war, as officers were killed and wounded, or were moved into higher echelon posts, promotion from the ranks brought experienced and hardened rank and file into the gentleman's class, and blurred the distinctions of class, bearing, and education between leaders and led. Such action also ensured, however, that the officers better understood the enormous pressure on their charges, thereby strengthening the bonds that tied fighting units together.

SINCE THE MAJORITY of the First Contingent had some family roots in Britain, many joyous reunions with loved ones occurred during the troops' time in England. Thousands of Canadian families also crossed the Atlantic to be near their menfolk. While this privilege was usually reserved for those with sufficient resources, or those who had family with whom they could stay, it helped to ease the burden for some soldier-civilians. Men were even allowed to leave the camp to stay with their families at night. But this development was not universally popular. Some commanders, such as the sourpuss Lieutenant Colonel John J. Creelman, complained in his diary, "the wives here are interfering considerably with their husbands' work....These women should never have been allowed to leave Canada and in time they will become an annoyance."[32] The women did not leave, but within a few months orders were passed making it illegal for soldiers to stay overnight outside of the camps, after it was found that the privilege was being abused by men who were not married and had taken up with local women.

With the introduction of the wet canteens, the number of alcohol-related incidents sharply dropped. Unfortunately, the anxiety among officials did not. Although serving beer was not a major concern, the British and Canadian military authorities were worried about soldiers being victimized by "immoral" women while under the influence of drink. The two vices were thought to go hand in hand—and they usually did. Lectures, threats, and appeals to engage in moral activity were absorbed by some. More often, these young men on the biggest adventure of their lives cast caution to the wind, as evidenced by the alarming number of cases of venereal disease (VD) in the overseas expeditionary force. During the four months at Salisbury Plain, some 1,249 men were recorded in the medical logs as having contracted some sort of VD.[33] By the end of the war, some 15.8 percent of overseas enlisted men had contracted a form of VD, almost six times the rate of British troops.[34] According to the predictions of some of the more agitated reformers, idle women with lax morals, when supplied with "heedlessly liberal" separation allowances and access to alcohol, would result in a whole crop of bastard "war babies" and diseased soldiers.[35] The shifting of blame and responsibility for the soldiers' high rate of disease onto women was similar to the argument employed in justifying the closing of bars and taverns when soldiers were caught dead-drunk within. The Canadians, of course, were not alone in drinking or engaging in sexual dalliances. Worry spread throughout Britain that soldiers—both Dominion and Imperial—would wreak havoc as they embarked on drunken rampages, spreading disease and making themselves unfit for campaigning on the Western Front.

DESPITE THE ATTRACTION of adventure, it was tough for these young men to be away from their loved ones and the stabilizing force of their families. One lieutenant, Ian Sinclair, wrote a sad letter to his parents over Christmas, lamenting, "This was the first time that I have ever been away from home" over the festive season.[36] And Robert Hale, a twenty-two-year-old from Montreal, captured the sentiments of many men when he wrote: "Please always remember me in your prayers and think of me sometimes. Dear Alice, don't bury yourself now but go on and enjoy yourself. If I am spared through this war I am coming back to you. I did not know how much I loved you until [I left] and then my heart broke."[37] Hale would return to his beloved Alice with three war wounds, and even though they broke up during the war, they married in 1920. But not all of the men who left for almost half a decade and passed through hell were so lucky.

CHAPTER 6

"AN IRON DIVISION FOR SERVICE IN AN IRON WAR"

January–February, 1915

"We didn't come here to salute," complained twenty-five-year-old Fred Bagnall, a prewar student from Prince Edward Island. "We came here to fight."[1] By early 1915, bodies and attitudes were hardening amidst the rain, mud, and misery of Salisbury Plain. Lieutenant General Alderson's senior staff devised training based on British regulations, and began the process of equipping and readying the division for battle. The Canadians were learning how to fight.

Musketry training was essential for the infantry battalions. Infantrymen were first instructed to hold, march with, and clean their Ross rifle, and usually with an experienced Imperial sergeant howling abuse at them. "Gentlemen," one British NCO instructor shouted at a group of men as Sergeant Alexander McClintock watched with a smile, "when I see you handle your rifles, I feel like falling on my knees and thanking God that we've got a navy."[2] The rapid fire of the BEF regulars became the goal to emulate, and Canadian infantrymen practised charger loading—driving down the single five-round stripper clip with one's thumb into the rifle's magazine, and ramming the action closed—and then firing. They were expected to hit their targets from a distance of up to 500 metres, but the range of the Ross was good up to 2,500 metres. No one ever killed anyone at that range, but effective marksmen equipped with periscopes could hit targets at 1,000 metres. But that was still an enormous distance, from which an enemy target as seen by the naked eye would appear as little more than a pinprick.

The Ross bayonet was also employed in "Hun-sticking" exercises. Straw bags were the victims, and soldiers got their blood up in mock battles. Lunges to the head were to be avoided, as the bayonet might glance off the skull. Infantrymen were also warned that a bayonet through the shoulder blade would likely get stuck, and they would have to pull hard to extricate it from the bone. Private Harold Baldwin, who was desperate to avenge the death of his brother in the First Battle of the Marne, recounted the advice from one grizzled Scottish veteran: "If you push it in too far, you canna get it oot again, because this groove on the side o' it makes the 'ole airtight; as soon as it is jabbed into a man the suction pulls the flesh all over it and you canna chuck it oot…. If a twist won't do it, stick your foot on the beggar and wrench it oot; if that won't do it, just pull the trigger a couple of times and there you are—she will blow oot."[3] Baldwin and his mates were urged to aim for the abdomen, which would ensure there would be no more "little Fritzes." Few expected

Canadians on Salisbury Plain.

the bayonet to beat the rifle while running across an open field, but it was terrifying to be on the receiving end of a cold steel charge.

To advance on the battlefield, the infantry were instructed to move in short bounds of 20 metres, and then go to ground. Once there, and behind some sort of cover, a section of a dozen men would build up a weight of fire to allow another section to advance. The four sections of the platoon worked together, and much of the training at Salisbury focused on these platoon and, later, company-level advances. The battalion's four Colt machine guns, manned by teams of five specialists, were also incorporated into this attack doctrine—although the machine gun was viewed largely as a defensive weapon at this point in the war. It is perhaps surprising that the Germans more eagerly embraced the value of the machine gun than did the British, who still clung to their riflemen, especially since the British had conquered and kept much of their colonial empire at the barrel of the Maxim machine gun. In a further example of short-sightedness, the ordinary Canadian riflemen had no training on the machine gun, which was considered a specialist weapon.

But infantry tactics involved more than simply shooting and stabbing. The infantry had to learn how to fight together. The machine guns of 1914 had torn terrible holes in attacking troop formations, but they could be overcome if enough troops advanced, firing and moving as they went. The close-order drill used by Lord Wellington's armies during the Napoleonic Wars was impossible to carry out on the modern battlefield: soldiers moving forward in tightly packed groups would soon be reduced to tightly packed corpses. Diffusion was necessary to present fewer targets to the enemy. But this in turn made it harder for officers to exert control over the troops, who would be out of earshot, and perhaps even sight, if they were using the contours of the land for cover. Furthermore, massing troops helped to build up the necessary firepower to overcome the defender; if troops were spread more thinly to avoid presenting grouped targets, then more weapons would be needed to achieve the necessary firepower ratios. No easy solutions were to be found. These were hard lessons that would have to be learned on the battlefield and paid for in blood.

WHILE MUCH OF THE TRAINING in England was rudimentary by later standards, it must be evaluated within the context of the time. Although the constant cold rain and resulting sickness of the soldiers disrupted training, a core of every unit kept at it day after day. Much of the drill was intended to boost the men's confidence in their ability to find ways to survive on the battlefield. Infantry instruction manuals such as *Rapid Training of a Company for War*, penned before the war by Lieutenant Colonel Arthur Birchall, who was now commanding the 4th Battalion, were remarkably far-sighted documents. As a result of the failures during the South African War, the British had understood that it was necessary that the "soldier is now taught to use his brains and to take advantage of the ground and cover.... In other words, our men are regarded as human beings," not as replaceable machines.[4] The infantry would be commanded by their senior officers, but it was incumbent on those at the sharp end to exploit situations should the chance arise, or should their superiors be wounded or killed.

As the infantry learned to fight together—to understand voice commands over the roar of the battlefield or to know when to shoot and when to advance—the other arms of the division were also undergoing intense training. Both the infantry and the artillery practised fighting rearguard actions, firing and retreating to more secure positions while in close contact with the enemy.[5] The majority of Canadian batteries were equipped with the quick-firing 18-pounder, the most common field gun in the British and Canadian artillery arsenal. Though the barrel clanged back and forth after firing each shell, the gun's hydrostatic recoil buffers and recuperators absorbed much of the shock. This meant that the gun and carriage stayed pointed at the target and did not require recalibration with each shot, thus increasing speed and accuracy. The 18-pounder shell weighed as much as its name indicated and could be fired to a distance of 6,000 metres, although this later increased to 9,000 when more efficient propellants were introduced. Each battery of four guns required not only gunners but also ammunition drivers, wagons, and about 170 horses, most of which were used to pull the guns or ensure a steady flow of ammunition from rear dumps to forward gun positions. The Canadian Division in total had some fifty-four 18-pounders, eighteen 4.5-inch howitzers, and four 60-pounders as part of a heavy battery.

Despite the challenge of trench warfare, the artillery continued to focus on mobile warfare tactics: riding the guns to the front, unlimbering them, setting them up, firing, and then moving on again. While the fighting to date had proven that mobility was subsumed to the near-static application of firepower, this type of rapid advance and retreat would prove essential in the first significant Canadian battle. Unfortunately, the gunners were reduced to these actions since they were continually stymied in their efforts to employ live ammunition due to shortages in available shells. Most gun teams fired fewer than fifty shells during their four months in England.[6] It was hard to master one's job as a soldier without ammunition or shells, but forward-thinking officers tried to find solutions to this dilemma and use the troops' time to best effect. One such officer was Andrew McNaughton, a prewar militia officer and professor of engineering at McGill University who lectured gunners on the importance of factoring in the effects of weather, temperature, and wear on the guns, as all of these affected the flight of a shell over several thousand metres. The charismatic McNaughton was partially successful in getting his message across, and in the years to come he would rise to become one of the most innovative and important gunners in the entire British army.

THROUGHOUT THE WINTER of 1914–1915, the British continued to assist the Canadians, providing expert trainers and all-important lessons-learned documents garnered from the experiences at the front. Though none of this could replace the role of combat in testing the Canadian Division's mettle, this training, when combined with the prewar militia or South African War military experience of many men, meant that Alderson's civilian-soldiers were not starting at the bottom of the learning curve.

As the Canadian Division went through final training in January and early February, it conformed to the size and balance of a British division. One of the units left behind was the Motor Machine Gun Brigade, composed of the oddball armoured cars. The armoured car unit had been raised by Raymond Brutinel, an expatriate French officer who had made millions in Canada through verve and an adventurous spirit. At the outbreak of war, he offered to raise an independent force of motorized machine-gun cars for Sam Hughes. Supported by powerful politicians, Brutinel purchased the cars in the United States and equipped them with two Colt machine guns. Although the cars' armour was moderately thick (between one and two inches), they lacked a covered top, making their crew susceptible to shrapnel air-bursts and small-arms fire. Brutinel was a forceful champion of his cars, but the British thought they unbalanced the firepower of the division, and Alderson was convinced to leave them behind.[7] This strange justification revealed a force that had not yet understood the importance of firepower, and was more interested in questions of command, control, and proportionality. Brutinel's armoured cars would cross over to Europe by the end of the year, but his machine-gunners would fight on their feet for much of the war. On the Western Front, the cars were welcomed by the infantry, who greeted the added firepower with open arms, although they were less convinced about the pioneering role performed by Brutinel's men in forging a doctrine of indirect heavy machine-gun barrage fire, which passed over the front-line troops' heads to harass enemy targets.

The Canadian Cavalry Brigade would also go overseas, although it remained separate from the Canadian forces for much of the war. Horse-drawn artillery and a mixture of British and Canadian cavalry units formed the brigade. While the cavalry continued to see itself as an elite arm—as it had been considered for centuries—its war on the Western Front was ultimately marked by disappointment and prolonged waiting for a rare chance to exploit an infantry break-in. The era of the warhorse was seeing its last.

The fledgling Canadian air force was even less lucky, and was strangled in its infancy. Sam Hughes had been initially unimpressed by the value of aircraft, deriding them as "an invention of the devil."[8] Canada, he rightly noted, would have a hard enough time raising an army, let alone an air force. But he allowed two intrepid aviators to accompany the First Contingent overseas, although their obsolete aircraft, a Burgess-Dunne biplane, was never even assembled after disembarkation. Although some 13,000 Canadians would serve in the British flying services, Canada's lack of interest in establishing its own force meant that this aeronautical effort was dispersed. In the absence of an ardent champion like Raymond Brutinel, a Canadian air force never got off the ground until the final months of the war—but by that point it was too little, too late.

A far more successful unit was Princess Patricia's Canadian Light Infantry (PPCLI). Raised privately by charismatic millionaire Hamilton Gault, who spent more than

$100,000 of his own money, the PPCLI initially allowed only experienced British soldiers and university men into the ranks. Others sneaked in of course, but the unit drew from a high calibre of soldier: of the original 1,049 men, 771 wore decorations or medals.[9] The PPCLI, to which the governor general's daughter lent her name, went overseas with the First Contingent, but because of its experience it was attached to a British division. It was soon fighting in France while the Canadians continued to train in England. The PPCLI served with the 27th Division to much acclaim, fighting in several battles including at Frezenberg in May 1915, where the unit was nearly annihilated in a desperate stand in the southern part of the Ypres salient. It recovered as a result of a large influx of graduates drawn from McGill and Queen's universities, and would join the Canadian Corps in late 1915.

INFANTRY BATTALION, 1916

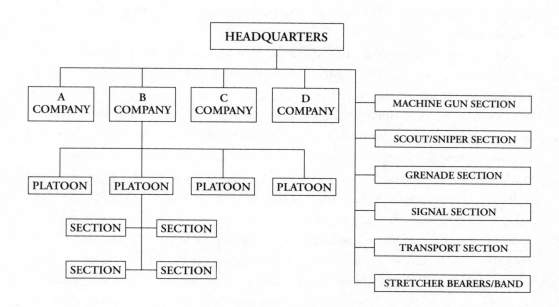

Despite the success of these unique units, the main hitting power of a Canadian division came from its infantry battalions. Commanded by a lieutenant colonel and officially a thousand strong, a battalion consisted of four companies, each composed of four platoons. Runners, signallers, scouts, and a machine-gun section of two pairs of Colts rounded out the battalion in early 1915. The soldiers identified with their platoon mates most closely, although a strong affinity was also felt for the battalion. Each battalion was numbered, and by the end of the war forty-eight infantry battalions were at the front, designated between the 1st and 116th, with the intervening units broken up for reinforcements, as well as another 140 or so battalions (the 117th to the 258th) also disbanded and fed to the original 48 battalions. Ignoring their bland numbers, battalions quickly acquired informal names like the "Dirty Third," "Mad Fourth," "Bell's Bulldogs," or "Van Doos"—these belonging to the 3rd, 4th, 31st, and 22nd Battalions respectively. These titles strengthened ties through a more colloquial identification. The terrible casualties at the front required the cannibalization of newer units, thereby leaving front-line battalions with an increasingly less homogenized regional link. Soon, men from across Canada might be in what was once a Montreal or Nova Scotia battalion, especially with 4,500 to 6,000 men passing through each of the forty-eight infantry battalions during the war.

A brigadier commanded a brigade of four battalions; and three brigades formed a division of about 12,000 infantrymen.[10] Another 6,000 men formed the artillery, engineering, medical, and service units. At 18,000 strong, the division of 1915 was the smallest self-contained fighting formation in the war. It was at the divisional level that the grouping of units made a real difference, the sum of battalions and artillery batteries being greater than the parts. Artillery, engineers, field ambulances, and logistical units were at the disposal of a major general, and could be deployed against a small portion of the front to assist the infantry, one infantry brigade being supported by almost the full weight of the division. Several divisions formed a corps (four in the case of the Canadians, but usually between three and five for the British), and three to four corps were usually grouped together to form an army, although this constantly changed according to geographical area and operational circumstances. At the army or corps level, an attack along a large front could use the artillery from a number of divisions, in addition to the heavy guns controlled by the corps, to concentrate and maximize firepower.

By the time the Canadians arrived in 1915, the British Expeditionary Force was commanded by Field Marshal Sir John French and consisted of two armies of some sixteen divisions and an Indian corps. The BEF continued to expand, and by 1918 the British had five armies of eighteen corps and some sixty divisions on the Western Front under command of Field Marshal Sir Douglas Haig. For the soldiers fighting at the front, however, the vast majority would never meet Haig, and few had any idea in which army they were serving. The corps level was also thoroughly unimportant to most soldiers (except for the Canadians or Australians) and most servicemen identified with their division as the largest formation that mattered to them.

THE CANADIAN CORPS was still more than six months away from its birth when, on February 4, 1915, the men of the division lined up in the pouring rain on Salisbury Plain to be reviewed by the King. George V's appearance brightened the day, and the Canadians—water dripping from noses and down backs—stood proudly at attention. Then, thousands of Canadians marched past him, in their final ceremony before they left for France. Five of the original infantry battalions were left behind—the 6th, 9th, 11th, 12th, and 17th Battalions, much to their bitter disappointment—to augment a new division already being raised in Canada, or to be fed piecemeal into the twelve line battalions at the front should these formations be cut up in battle.

Within the Canadian Division, the infantry and artillery had trained hard and were deemed ready for battle. They were ably supported by engineers, medical units, signallers, and those units that would feed and keep them armed. When soldiers looked back at their four months on Salisbury Plain, they often derided it as a waste of time. "If ever a bunch of greenhorns landed in France," wrote Private Harold Peat, "we of the First Contingent were that same bunch."[11] It was hard for many soldiers to see beyond the mud that slathered everything, including memories. But it was an important period for the Canadians, who were lucky to miss the hard battles of 1914 and who were given the necessary time to learn the basic principles

CANADIAN CORPS, 1916

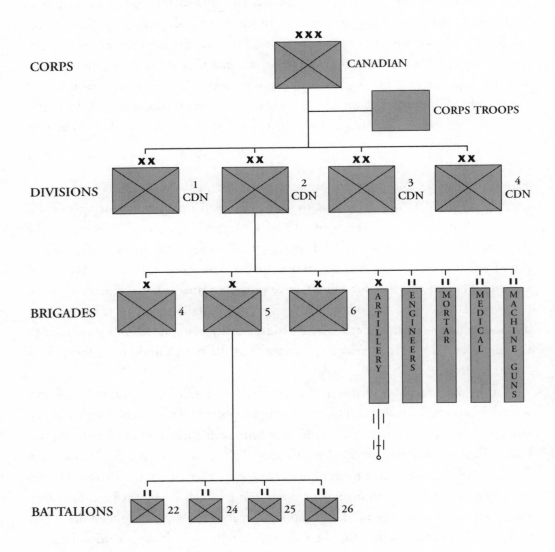

of warfare. The men had also toughened up, both physically and mentally. "On Salisbury Plain, chastened by suffering, saddened by yearnings for home, wounded to the quick by misunderstandings with our English instructors, tortured by the vilest winter climate on earth, often prostrated by sickness of the body, or by deeper sickness of the spirit, out of all this man-breaking and heart-breaking we were being hammered and wrought into an army unit," wrote twenty-five-year-old Lieutenant Arthur Chute, a former war correspondent: "Out of hell fire, came an Iron Division for service in an Iron War."[12]

CHAPTER 7

WELCOME TO THE WESTERN FRONT

February–April, 1915

Private George Bell of the 1st Battalion wanted to get into the fight at the front badly, but not enough to miss a night of partying. Aware that the Canadian Division was about to ship across to France, Bell—an American printer from Detroit who had crossed the border into Windsor to enlist—and his good mate, John Smith, stole two passes from the orderly room and decided to have one last blowout in a local town. Bell and Smith were already serving three days of punishment, confined to barracks, for doing the same thing a week earlier, when they had gone to London. Before they had been caught, however, Smith had met a woman and married her in the course of a wild day of drinking and carousing.

Bell and Smith evaded the guards that patrolled the areas between Salisbury Plain and the local towns, and celebrated their good fortune in going to France. Waking up the worse for wear, they stumbled back to camp only to find that their battalion had left and they were charged with the serious crime of desertion. But the two troublemakers inveigled their way into going across the channel with another unit and arrived in St. Nazaire in the Bay of Biscay, where the Canadian Division was forming up in mid-February. They sheepishly met up with their battalion, and suffered the two-week field punishment of extra pack labour for their offence. As Bell noted, "Marching the two hours under a sixty-pound pack was something else and it gave us plenty of time for reflection…. While we may have been a bit deficient in discipline and some of the fine points of military etiquette, our eagerness to get into the big show was not lacking."[1] With these words, Bell could have been speaking for the entire Canadian Division. The Canadians—18,517 of them, along with 4,764 horses—had trained on Salisbury Plain for four months, and they were desperate to get to the front.[2]

AS IN MANY THINGS military, the Canadians faced another case of "hurry up and wait." A delay of several days occurred while the entire division was issued cold-weather kits. Fingerless woollen mittens and leather jerkins were much appreciated, especially since they showed off the two-inch strip on the men's shoulders that read "CANADA." Foul-smelling jackets of goatskin that had been improperly treated were viewed with disgust after the soldiers took on the appearance and smell of a large herd of goats. A close look at the coats had turned many a man's stomach. The "bloody (literally) coats were dotted in many places with the actual flesh of the deceased animals still sticking to them," wrote Private Harold Baldwin.[3] Officers had not been impressed by the impromptu bleating chorus of "ba-a-a, ba-a-a, ba-a-a" from cheeky soldiers, but few of the rank and file were ordered to pick up their smelly jackets after most were unceremoniously dropped by the side of the road. They became the property of the small army of French civilians who shadowed the Dominion troops, selling to them and stealing from them when they had a chance.

The Canadian Division's first casualty occurred within hours of the troops' setting foot on French soil, when Corporal John McMaster, a thirty-three-year-old weaver from Hespeler, Ontario, fell under a train, where his arm and leg were severed.[4] Another 7,795 Canadians would die from accidents and diseases while serving overseas. That was a lot, but far fewer than in previous wars, in which disease and pestilence laid waste to armies.[5] Accidental deaths remained a constant problem in the war, exhausted and nervous men rarely being the best candidates to be carrying loaded rifles.

The French greeted the Canadians with open arms, many of which contained souvenirs and fresh fruit. Excited troops purchased them before climbing into cramped rail cars. The rail cars labelled *40 hommes ou 8 chevaux* made such an impression on the soldiers that almost all of them mentioned the experience in their letters and memoirs. In the absence of seats or lavatories, this forty-six-hour trip to the front was transportation unfit for heroes.

Rumours spread among the bored and anxious troops about their destination. Was it the Swiss frontier, India, or the persistently hoped for exotic destination of Egypt? Anywhere but the Western Front, or so predicted the rumour mongers. But in fact that was exactly where they were needed, and headed. They would be a welcome addition to the British order of battle. With the core of the BEF destroyed in the titanic battles of 1914, the French and Russians, who had continental armies of millions now, sneered that the British were not pulling their weight in the military alliance. Lord Kitchener had put out his famous plea for men in Britain, and they had answered by the hundreds of thousands, but all were still undergoing training.

THE CANADIANS were the first division to join Sir John French's seventeen-division BEF that was not a regular formation from the British army.[6] The British had learned the hard way that inexperienced troops suffered high casualties, and so the Canadians were apprenticed to British ones in late February and early March in the Armentières region, near the Franco-Belgian border. The Canadians appreciated the guidance and were a little awed by the experienced Tommies, who were matched up one to one with the Dominion troops. They were far less impressed, however, with their new underground homes.

The Western Front was an underground city that ran some 700 kilometres from the North Sea coast, slowly sweeping to the east, and ending in the Swiss mountains. Belgian forces were stationed at the north of the line, in the last part of Belgium still under Entente control. The British were dug in to the south around Ypres, where they had made their famous stand. The French—the land power to Britain's indomitable navy—held most of the line further to the south. As the war progressed, the British, with their dominion and colonial forces, would take over more of the line, but in the first two years of the war, the French bore the brunt of the fighting.

By early 1915, aerial observers who flew over the front would have seen the muddy, chewed-up, blasted landscape stretching a few kilometres in either direction—but then the green, pastoral countryside continuing on either side. A pilot who landed in these fields in the summer would have encountered wildflowers in bloom, freshly tilled land, livestock, and little evidence of the monumental struggle raging not far off. In the war zone, however, the forces were confronted with position warfare, where the spade was as necessary as the rifle. Artillery tried to blast its way through

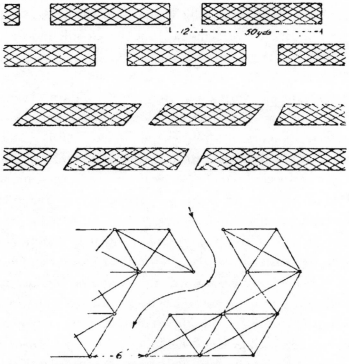

GAPS IN ENTANGLEMENTS.

Not to Scale.

There should be " knife rests " or other obstacles handy for blocking gaps.

Note the staggered gaps in between the wire that forced attackers to mill about spending precious time trying to find them. As well, machine-gunners and riflemen often trained their weapons on the gaps as they were ready-made kill grounds.

the trench bulwarks to allow the infantry, as in days of old, to breach the defences. Instead of punching through stone castle walls, however, the infantry would now first have to crash over sandbags, and then deep trenches, before reaching the rarely seen green fields beyond. But the front-line trench system was only the first barrier. Both armies faced off against each other over No Man's Land, the ravaged area between the armies that neither side could capture, and which ranged in width from 50 to 1,000 metres, depending on the position of the front. Barbed wire slowed attacks, but this early in the war it usually consisted of only a few strands. Still, the nineteenth-century American invention designed to keep cattle from straying beyond grazing fields would prove to be a devastating feature in corralling soldiers within the blasted region of the Western Front.

INTO THE TRENCHES went the Canadians. But "trenches" was perhaps too glamorous a word. The front-line trenches were little more than ditches. Battered and soggy, they offered little protection against whirling shrapnel. Luckily, though, at this point in the war, most of the gunners on either side had neither the skill nor the sensitive fuses to time shells to explode over the heads of troops in narrow trenches when firing from several kilometres away. Sandbags were used to build up the front and back of the trenches to offer further safety from machine-gun and sniper fire, from not only the enemy but also one's own troops in secondary positions. But despite such efforts, the trenches were a far cry from the perfectly symmetrical practice fortifications the soldiers had built in England. A battalion's four- to six-day tour in the forward trenches usually accounted for the graves of at least a few men.

The first experience of fire for new men was terrifying and exhilarating. Finally, after months of training, they were at the front and doing their bit. But the other-worldliness of the trenches was immediate. Dirty ditches were now home. The clatter of death-dealing machine guns played along the front. The night lit up with wondrous flares and explosions, as soldiers were treated to lethal fireworks. In this world where all activity above ground was done at night, those flares and explosions piercing the darkness removed the cloak of safety.

The Canadians were amateurs, and they knew it. Partnered with British units, the Dominion troops studied the fine art of surviving trench warfare: how to fortify trenches with scraps of wood when wooden A-frames and corrugated iron were in short supply or left in the rear area; how to make jam-pot grenades from old cans, gunpowder, and nails; how to heat tea in the morning with only a match and a pinch of fuel. Victor Lewis of the 10th Battalion remembered cringing in the trenches when a shell screamed past overhead; a gruff battle-tested British Tommy told him gently, "Come on now, straighten up.... nothing to be afraid of."[7] Lewis straightened up, taking another step in the long march towards becoming a soldier. But the British troops were not foolish, and they also taught the Canadians to "flop" at the sound of an arriving "whiz-bang," and when to move with speed. Ottawa officers in the 2nd Battalion were surprised to meet a hometown lad, Lieutenant H.S. Maunsell, who had studied at the Royal Military College in Kingston before enlisting with the Royal Warwickshire Regiment. As one of thousands of Canadians who served in the Imperial forces, he instructed his fellow countrymen on the tricks of survival.

The Dominion troops even began to sing the Imperial songs, adopting them as their own but later updating them with references drawn from Canadian battlefield experiences.

We beat 'em on the Marne;
We beat 'em on the Aisne;
We knocked 'em out of Armenteers,
An' here we are again.[8]

This song was perhaps more appropriate—and certainly more soldierly—than many of those sung by inexperienced, if cheeky, troops in the camps of England, including:

We are Sam Hughes's army
No bloody good are we
We cannot march, we cannot shoot
No bloody good are we.

The first weeks of March were a time of coming face to face with the static nature of the front. The enemy was never seen, and the infantry were warned not to put their heads above the trench to look for him. The first night the Canadians were in the line, German troops called out in singsong, taunting voices: "Come out, you Canadians! Come out and fight!"[9] The Canadian response was, according to one war journalist, unprintable.

The experience at the front began to dispel some of the chauvinistic ideas that had been drilled into the soldiers' heads through loose talk and propaganda. Private Ian MacTavish, who would later take a commission in the British army, noted in a letter home that his unit had already lost a few men to stray fire. He warned friends: "When the general advance comes, I expect we shall pay dearly for it as I can tell you the German soldier is by no means to be despised. Their shooting is accurate and their wire entanglements are thoroughly constructed."[10] Soldiers could be killed in many ways in the trenches, and careless men did not last long—even the experienced ones were taken by indiscriminate bullets or shells. "If you make a mistake," warned the British Corps commander to whom the Canadians were attached, "you will not get a chance to make a second one."[11]

THROUGH FEBRUARY AND MARCH, the Canadians lost a trickle of men to stray shelling, sniper fire, and sickness; 278 casualties were recorded during March alone.[12] On the Western Front, the ratio of deaths to woundings was about 1 to 4, so of the 278 casualties, roughly 70 of those would have been killed, with many others maimed for life. The first few deaths in a company or platoon profoundly shook the survivors. Collections were sometimes taken up to be sent home to widows or orphans. However, the loss of life quickly overwhelmed the meagre earnings of the soldiers, and they had to convey their grief through agonizingly penned letters containing heartfelt words and soft-pedalled platitudes. It was hard to find the glory in a man's death when he was shot through the head while digging a latrine. Somehow the survivors tried.

Private Alfred Baggs, a thirty-year-old clerk, described his first night in the line: "We had no sooner entered the trench than we sank almost up to our knees in thick clay, mud and water." After the men settled in, a sentry standing waist-high above the sandbag parapet was killed "when a sniper put a bullet right through his head: he simply dropped, exclaiming, 'I'm hit,' blood running from the wound, his nose and mouth."[13] The same bullet ricocheted out of his head and lodged itself in another man's wrist. According to Baggs, that first tour yielded a number of casualties, largely due to the inadequate trenches that offered little protection from shrapnel or bullets. So heavy was the artillery fire along the front that Lieutenant Colonel John J. Creelman confided to his diary, "I expect that a lot of men will lose their minds out here and others their hearing because the noise made by a shell bursting alongside is terrific."[14]

With the two sides deadlocked, firepower ruled the battlefield. Both sides could direct devastating fire on opposing troops, but the defenders had the advantage of being in protective trenches. Attacking infantry had to go overland, exposing themselves to enemy bullets. From positions of greater protection, defending machine-gunners, riflemen, and gunners could lay down curtains of fire, often indiscriminately, and still cause terrible casualties. As one U.S. Civil War general had noted some fifty years earlier, "one rifle in the trench was worth five in front of it."[15] What was the use of several machine guns on both sides discharging 500 bullets per minute in interlocking fields of fire? With barbed wire slowing and channelling

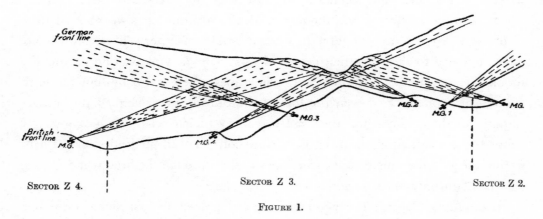

FIGURE 1.

EXAMPLE of chart given to Machine Gun Officer on taking over a sector of trenches (Z 3), showing lines of fire which his four guns must cover from their battle (*i.e.*, defence) emplacements.

Note the interlocking of fields of fire from two or more machine guns to create a nearly impassable arc of fire.

attackers into kill grounds where the machine guns swept back and forth, and several lines of defenders dug in, the front had been reduced to a stalemate. But it was the Germans who were occupying France and Belgium, and therefore it was the Entente forces that had to attack. They paid the price.

THE CANADIAN DIVISION typically held a 5,000- to 7,000-metre section of the front during a static warfare phase. Of the three infantry brigades, two were forward, and one in reserve. Each of the two forward brigades would have two battalions forward and two in reserve. Further echeloning the force, those battalions would have two of their companies "up" and two in reserve—each commanded by a major. A second-in-command oversaw some of the company's administrative work, and he was supported by a small headquarters consisting of a company sergeant major, a company quartermaster sergeant, and a few batmen and drivers. The companies would have their four platoons of four sections each in various parts of the front-line trenches. Each of the platoons was commanded by a lieutenant, and the company also counted 8 sergeants, 10 corporals, and 188 privates at full strength. But few infantry companies were ever up to full strength, as their numbers were dragged down by losses not yet replaced with reinforcements, as well as by those sick, on course, or on leave. Most infantry companies tended to function at between seventy and eighty-five percent of their full strength. There might be a section of ten or eleven men, commanded by a corporal, for every 20 or 30 metres of the front, but this would change depending on the availability of the trenches and required density to hold the front. Too many men crowding the trenches made better targets for the artillery; too few left trench lines vulnerable to enemy raids. This layering of defences—the echelon of units from platoons all the way up to divisions—allowed for a buffer zone several kilometres thick to blunt any attack and provide time for reinforcements to be rushed forward to hold the front or to counterattack. Front-line troops and defences could be lost in shocking numbers without ever losing a trench system. In 1915, no attacking force was able to pierce such defences and keep the momentum of the attack moving forward to break out through the other side.

Both the British and German defensive doctrines called for immediate counter-attacks to drive attackers from the trenches. The sanctity of ground, dictating that not an inch was to be given up, was linked to the supposed morale and endurance of the infantry. While the holding of all ground was costly, it was thought to contribute to the fighting mentality of the men. To give any ground—even muddy, devastated farmers' fields—was deemed a loss; and too many losses, when combined with the horror of the trenches and the unending casualties, might lead to a slow rot of morale and eventual mutiny in the ranks. A fine line separated victory and defeat on the Western Front, but with no way to break through the enemy lines, victory would be predicated on a strategy of attrition. Each side had to grind down the enemy, by killing men and depressing morale to the point where an attack might finally cave in the defences. Therefore, Alderson had warned his Canadians "to hold the front trenches at all costs and in the event of any trench being lost, to counter-attack at once."[16]

In these attritional battles, death on the Western Front was rarely glorious. Heroic charges and last stands were quickly eradicated by snipers who shot men in the head as they crouched at the firestep (a wooden bench that allowed men to see over the trench walls) or by stray shells that obliterated the unlucky as they made their way back and forth in the trenches. However, though the front was terrible, much of the terror was a show of sound and fury. The millions of bullets and tens of thousands of shells that were fired were often to little effect, as the trenches offered good protection. "I have just returned from my first tour in the front line trenches," wrote Lieutenant J.E. Ryerson. "At first I was inclined to duck every time a bullet sang by or a shell whizzed overhead, but in a day or two I got used to it, so long as they didn't 'bang' right over my head."[17] Ryerson learned to stay in his trench, but he was killed a year later on the Somme.

Soldiers soon developed a sixth sense of survival. High explosives, nicknamed "Jack Johnsons" (after the American heavyweight boxer who delivered a powerful punch), and shrapnel shells, nicknamed "whiz-bangs" (as they tended to be smaller, faster shells), could be identified by their very sound in flight. Experienced men soon learned when to duck and when to throw themselves up against a trench wall or down dugout steps. The trenches most often protected against these shells, except for direct hits, but an increasing number of infantrymen were being lost to head wounds received from shrapnel exploding over the trenches. Soft military caps were no match for whirling metal balls and jagged steel splinters from disintegrating shell cases.

AS THE FIGHTING to date had made clear to both sides, the prewar tactics of advancing over open ground, hoping to engage with the enemy at bayonet point, had proved disastrous in the first months of the war. The use of rapid-firing rifles, machine guns, and indirect artillery bombardments had reduced most ground assaults to bloody routs. Attackers responded by adding a few machine guns to augment their firepower and hoped that their pitiful expenditures of artillery would destroy enemy fortifications. They did not. Although the artillery on both sides had few shells to fire and rarely hit anything as narrow as a trench, the shells could make quick work of a body of men in the open. Offensive operations continued, but success was uncommon. Aware of their precarious positions in the front lines, the defenders on both sides dug in deeper, setting up interlocking fields of fire. The front solidified and stagnated as armies went underground into the trenches to escape the open killing fields. Infantrymen who, out of frustration, tried to fire their rifles above the trenches often fell victim to more skilled snipers who preyed on such emotions. It was best to sit and wait to be relieved. A new type of bravery was needed: the ability to simply hold one's nerves together and find a way to endure.

Garrisoning the front lines consisted of long periods of boredom intermixed with short periods of absolute terror. Sentries were posted day and night to watch for the enemy; working parties shored up trenches through back-breaking labour; rifles and feet were inspected; soldiers were dragged out at "stand-to," fully equipped and ready for battle at dusk and half an hour before dawn, as these were the times when it was expected that an enemy would attack. The stand-to was a part of the discipline and drudgery of the trenches: it kept men busy and allowed officers and NCOs to see the rank and file. If rations came forward to the front, it was also a good time to provide a small shot of rum to the men to warm them and reward them for surviving another night in the trenches. Those men on criminal charges—for everything from "dumb insolence" (which could be a mean glance or muttering under one's breath against an inane order) to more serious offences like being found asleep at one's post—received no rum while they served out their sentences in the trenches and rear areas. Punishment could include pay stoppages and extra fatigues, such as cleaning latrines or carrying rations. Men who committed more serious offences, such as desertion or showing cowardice in the face of battle, faced general courts martial. Several crimes could, and did, result in the death penalty. Military justice was indeed an oxymoron much of the time, and justice, military-style, was often ruthlessly and sometimes cruelly applied to enforce discipline.[18]

THE CANADIANS were involved in their first battle on March 10, 1915, in support of a large British and Indian offensive at Neuve Chapelle, with the well-defended Aubers Ridge 5 kilometres behind it as a secondary objective. It is not surprising that, as untried troops, the Canadians were put on the flank, where they would get a taste of battle but nothing too costly—unless the British forces in the centre made a breakthrough, in which case the Canadians would be thrown into the gap as an exploitation force. In the first phase, however, the role of Alderson's men was to mount a diversionary attack and keep the Germans busy with small-arms and artillery fire. The Canadians were not to leave their trenches, but to simply keep up a heavy rate of fire in order to stop the enemy from shifting its reserves over to the real battle front. With the trenches only 70 metres apart, it was an exhilarating time for most infantrymen. "For three hours we fired as rapidly as we could force clips of ammunition into the magazine and for days my shoulder was sore from the recoil of the rifle," wrote Private George Bell. "We took no particular aim, had no particular target, and it is doubtful if we killed any Germans, but it kept the enemy from making a counterattack and from sending reinforcements to the section of the line being attacked by the British."[19] More effective were artillery field pieces that engaged enemy strongpoints and identified sniper's nests.

The real fighting was happening on the right flank, where four British and Indian divisions made initial advances in the British army's first offensive operations of the year. But after first capturing the village of Neuve Chapelle, the attack stalled as communication was cut between front and rear, with chaos overtaking the battle. Rigid control at headquarters ensured that the initial successful attack was not repeated, and subordinates at the front were left stranded and unwilling to move forward without directions from headquarters. Within the rigidly hierarchical army, some front-line officers were so terrified of acting on their own initiative that they refused to press the enemy without direction from above, even though the Germans were in full disarray. The British still had a lot to learn about this new warfare, and the campaign broke down after three days and 13,000 casualties. Neuve Chapelle was a harsh lesson in how not to fight on the Western Front.

In support of the operation, the Canadians lost a hundred men, which seemed like a lot for a mere diversion, but few complained. However, more than a couple of battalion commanders barked that the Canadian Ross rifles had jammed during the rapid-firing exercise. Although reports were written drawing attention to the rifle's deficiencies, these problems were overlooked or not acted upon in the euphoria of the division's part in supporting the British in battle. Canada had begun to do its part at the front, but few suspected they would soon be called on to save the British army from catastrophic defeat.

CHAPTER 8

TRIAL BY FIRE

Second Battle of Ypres, April 22, 1915

"The Ypres salient is about the worst place one could imagine. We get shot at from three sides, and the support trenches come in for a hotter fire than the front lines," complained Lieutenant A.G. Mordy, who would serve throughout the war, except during his eighteen visits to the hospital resulting from two extended bouts of gas poisoning, and gunshot wounds to the right knee and left shoulder.[1] Since mid-April, the Canadian Division had been garrisoning the northern part of the Ypres salient, which, in its entirety, extended some 27 kilometres, but only roughly 13 kilometres at the base. The salient, known to the soldiers as "Wipers," jutted into the enemy lines, and had been the scene of some of the bloodiest fighting of the war. British regular and territorial soldiers had withstood a series of desperate onslaughts by German forces at the end of November 1914 against their entrenched positions around Ypres. More than 180,000 casualties had been suffered by British, Indian, and German troops, and while many had been cleared from the battlefield, thousands lay rotting where they fell. The Ypres salient was an enormous open graveyard.

Having paid for Ypres in blood, the Entente was unwilling to retreat from the salient even though it was surrounded and subject to accurate artillery fire by German guns directed by enemy observers on Passchendaele Ridge a few kilometres to the east. The shattered city of Ypres, with its once magnificent 500-year-old Cloth Hall, stood behind the lines. Now it was in ruins, even though the city was still inhabited by civilians unwilling to be forced from their homes. For the Belgians, and for many Canadians who had enlisted to free Belgium, the city had strong emotional value since it was the last major Belgian centre that was not yet occupied. Ypres was also a gateway to the all-important Channel Ports, which were an essential logistical portal for military supplies. In this sense, the salient was worth protecting as it acted as a buffer zone that would keep many of the main roads leading to Ypres on the outer range of enemy shellfire. But the infantry holding the front were under no illusions about the danger of their position.

TO THE NORTH AND EAST of Ypres, within and outside the salient, were green farmers' fields. Small woods cut parts of the battlefield, but the terrain was relatively flat. Still, soldiers would find many areas of "dead ground" in the undulations of the land, which allowed troops to move about the battlefield protected from observation—although snipers situated themselves so that they could kill unsuspecting men as they emerged from predictable spots.

Many a farmer from Ontario, Quebec, the West, or the Maritimes would have identified with the look of these fertile fields, and perhaps pined for their own land at home. But few of those farmers would have recognized the smell that emanated from the ground. Human and animal feces had been used for years to enrich the soil: the cropland had literally been soaked in shit. As well, a foul-smelling mist hung over the area, charged with the reek of churned-up earth from high explosives and the pungent sharpness of rotting men with abdominal gases escaping from their distended and bloated bodies. Rusting barbed wire, old tins of bully beef and other garbage, and tonnes of metal from all manner of armament littered the front.

The Canadians were also surprised to find houses, churches, and farms on or near the battlefield, though most structures had been reduced to rubble. Incredibly, some civilians still remained within the salient, clinging to their homes in small villages like St. Julien or Langemarck. Hares could be bagged for dinner, and potatoes and onions dug out of abandoned gardens by enterprising soldiers under the cover of darkness. Although a few stubborn houses and barns survived, most soldiers stayed away since enemy gunners were ranging the distance of their shells by them.

If the structures above ground were mostly destroyed, those below ground were little better. Dismayed Canadians soon learned that taking over trenches from the

French was an unfortunate fate, for their allies had developed a bad reputation for leaving their lines in a filthy condition, either due to slothful behaviour or, to be more charitable, because they could not bring themselves to dig in comfortably while much of their country was occupied. Whatever the reason, the scene that awaited the Canadian troops was nothing less than shocking. The trenches stank of urine and feces, as the French were haphazard about the establishment of proper latrine systems, preferring, it seemed, to urinate and defecate anywhere they could find a corner. Far worse was the smell of decaying men. Maggoty corpses greeted the Canadians. Most had their eyes and tongues eaten out by rats, and the corpses varied in states of decay, with patches of rotting, leather-like skin or even bare white bone protruding from the walls, floors, and from over the parapet. "We were walking on oozing bodies in the bottom of the trench. There'd be a hand or a foot sticking out of the trench in front of your face. It was horrible," recounted Ian Sinclair, a University of Toronto graduate who would rise from lieutenant to lieutenant colonel over the course of the war.[2]

The defensive parapet of sandbags along the top of the trench was thin, and enemy snipers soon learned they could fire right through them. Because of the high water table in the Ypres region, the trenches were shallow, and despite the sandbags, most soldiers still had to walk doubled over as they sloshed through the mud and water. Communication trenches linking the rear to the front seemed to have been laid out by drunken sailors, and many had been collapsed by shellfire. By mid-April, then, the front-line Canadian units were working furiously: during the day they stayed below ground, at night they moved about in the open, digging or shoring up trenches.[3] All the while, they did so amidst a graveyard of unburied bodies. Disinfectant was rushed to the front, but new bodies were added every day and night as German snipers and artillery increased in activity. Unlike some of the previous defenders of the region, the Canadians almost always carried out their dead. Despite this work, parts of the line were untenable due to the prevalence of dead, rotting corpses, and weak sandbag defences. Still, commanders urged the men onward as they worried that increased activity in the enemy lines was a sign of a potential future attack.

THE GERMANS had their own plans for *Disinfection*, the code name for the first lethal chlorine gas attack in the history of warfare. Germany was now involved in a two-front war, against Britain and France in the west and Russia in the east, exactly the situation they had tried to avoid with their ambitious 1914 Schlieffen Plan. The failure of that plan had resulted in the firing of Moltke the Younger, and his subsequent replacement by Minister of War Erich von Falkenhayn. The new minister realized his forces needed to break the deadlock, especially with Germany having already suffered several hundred thousand casualties. But shellfire and attacking troops had failed to punch through the enemy's trench systems.

Poison gas presented a potential solution to the deadlock. Germany had the most powerful chemical dye industry in the world, and it turned to these factories in this industrial war. The high command hoped that chlorine gas, even though it had been effectively outlawed in the Hague Conventions, could deliver a devastating blow. The Conventions stipulated only that gas could not be used in gas shells, noted a few officers engaged in legal sophistry, but most senior commanders realized that such details would not allow the German army to escape condemnation. Nonetheless, these were desperate times. If gas could be transported to the front and then released, a stiff wind would blow the chlorine over the enemy lines, where it would sink into the very crevices and trenches that blocked any sort of break-through. Despite these expectations, most German generals argued against unleashing such a monstrous weapon. "Poisoning the enemy as one would rats affected me as it would any straightforward soldier," wrote one senior German general. "I was disgusted."[4] Others wisely noted that aside from the issue of introducing a new and unpredictable form of warfare, weather would be an important factor. Except for a spell in spring, the prevailing winds blew towards the German lines over a greater part of the front, ultimately giving the Entente an inherent advantage.

While no one liked the idea of gassing men like cockroaches, an increasingly desperate German high command knew it had to do something. The Duke of Württemberg, commanding the Fourth Army as it faced Ypres, finally agreed to employ chemical weapons.

But the Germans were quite unsure about what the effects of gas might be, and early tests using tear gas had proven useless. They hoped that this chlorine attack might do more than make the enemy's eyes water; but if it did fail, the high command at least thought it might be a diversion to cover the movement of eight divisions to prop up the Austrians on the Eastern Front. Austria remained in a precarious situation against Russia, and it soon appeared that it would be facing another front against the Italians. Italy had been waiting for the Entente and Central powers to exhaust one another. Like most of the other great powers, the Italians wanted more territory, and they went to war in May 1915 on the side of the Entente in hopes of hastening the demise of the "sick man of Europe" that was the Austro-Hungarian Empire. But the Italian forces proved utterly inept, bordering on suicidal, and were perhaps more of a burden than a benefit to the Entente, as they siphoned off men and supplies that were continually needed to bolster their failing war effort.

While the Austrians soon found themselves engaged heavily with the Italians in the terrible attritional battles of Izonso, the Russians, too, were now massing for a new offensive. As well, an Anglo-French amphibious offensive against Turkey was soon to be launched, and Falkenhayn was not sure his allies could hold out, although Bulgaria was soon enticed to the Central Powers' cause, and Serbia would be overrun by the end of the year. Under these strategic hammer blows, Falkenhayn planned that throughout 1915 his forces on the Western Front would largely hold on the defensive, although the gas attack might set the Entente back on its heels. Few in Falkenhayn's command thought that a breakthrough was possible, and few plans for exploitation were put in place should the operation succeed.

BY THE MIDDLE OF THE MONTH, both the British and French in the Ypres salient had warnings from spies and deserters that the Germans planned to use poison gas against their front. The French, characteristically, did not share the information with lower commands, hoarding the intelligence at headquarters. Although the British did not understand how the gas would be used, they at least sent cautionary notes down to lower-level formations, including the Canadians. The effects of poison gas were hard to imagine, as most soldiers' only frame of reference for such a substance was city gaslights. Most officers were more worried about the increased activity in the German lines rather than some vaporous agent.

The Canadians accepted the warning and tried to find out more about this gas. Major Andrew McNaughton, commander of the 7th Battery, Canadian Field Artillery, was allowed to fire off ninety rounds to "search" the German lines. He later admitted that this was one of his best days of the war, since his battery had previously been so constrained in firing shells. The 7th Battery had no success, but McNaughton had the right idea. The Germans had brought up more than 5,730 steel canisters filled with 160 tonnes of lethal chlorine gas. These had been installed in the front lines under the German parapet of sandbags, and gas pioneers were waiting anxiously for the proper wind to turn on the taps. It would soon come.

The Canadian Division was situated between the 28th British Division on the right and the 45th Algerian Division on the left. This latter formation consisted of two brigades of African-born Zouaves and Tirailleurs, plus two additional African battalions. General Alderson had a 3,800-metre sector at the apex of the line that ran along the northeastern part of the rounded salient. Richard Turner's 3rd Brigade was situated on the left, Arthur Currie's 2nd Brigade on the right, around the apex of the salient's curve to the south, and Malcolm Mercer's 1st Brigade would be held in reserve. From left to right, the 13th, 15th, 8th, and 5th Battalions held the front lines. Reserve and command units were some 1,000 metres behind them at positions like Locality C and St. Julien, both of which held commanding views of the battlefield. All would become fierce sites of action in the grim days to come.

THE AFTERNOON OF APRIL 22, 1915, was warm and sunny. Canadians in the front lines were enjoying a respite from the incessant German shelling that had been falling around their positions during the preceding week. The most pressing order of the day appeared to be a communiqué to 3rd Brigade headquarters that the Division had 100 mouth organs waiting to be picked up. Many men were sunning themselves in the trenches and waiting for their rotation to the rear of the front lines. The false quiet ended abruptly at 4 P.M., when the Germans unleashed a heavy bombardment on the salient, and the city of Ypres behind it. Enormous shells from large-calibre siege guns pounded Ypres, collapsing buildings. Canadians called them the "Wipers Express," as they reminded men of London subway trains. Soon, fire and smoke billowed up from the city's ruins. Streams of panicking refugees fled with their possessions and loved ones.

But worse threats than artillery fire were to come. An hour after the bombardment, an ominous green-grey cloud, 6 kilometres wide and more than half a kilometre deep, seeped out from the enemy lines. The Germans had released 160 tonnes of chlorine liquid from steel canisters, via rubber hoses. The liquid chlorine cooled to a cold cloud with an ominous hissing sound. Pushed by a strong breeze, the densest parts of the cloud blew south, passing through the 45th Algerian and 87th French Territorial divisions to the left of the Canadian sector.

One by one, the French guns fell silent. As the enormous cloud enveloped and obscured position after position, insidiously seeping into the very crevices that sheltered soldiers from conventional fire, the French defenders were smothered.

This large-scale gas attack reveals the extent of the gas clouds that could be released from canisters brought into the front lines. Cloud attacks were an unpredictable method to deliver gas, and could turn on the attacker if the wind changed.

Most fled in terror. Flight sealed their fate, ensuring that they travelled within the cloud for a longer period of time and breathed more deeply because of their exertion.

Screaming and choking Algerians, without rifles and equipment, ran within and from the death cloud, many passing through the Canadian lines, struggling for breath and grunting, "asphyxiate, asphyxiate."[5] Colonel E.W.B. Morrison recounted seeing the red-panted Zouaves and French soldiers stumbling from the front, "faces flecked with blood and froth. Frequently these men would fall down under the feet of the mob, and roll about like mad dogs in their death agonies."[6] Yet isolated groups held their ground or took up positions in the rear, harassing the German attackers who cautiously followed the chemical cloud. The Canadians had only minutes to react before the outer edge of the cloud reached them. Most survived the effects of the dissipated gas, but a 6-kilometre gap opened on their left where the Algerian and French divisions were effectively shattered. For the moment, nothing was stopping the Germans from driving south to cut off the entire salient, capturing more than 50,000 troops, including the Canadian Division.

The untried Canadians reacted quickly. Lieutenant Colonel Frederick Loomis, a forty-five-year-old construction contractor from Montreal, ordered the "Kilties" of the 13th Battalion, eyes streaming tears and lungs wracked with hacking coughs, to shift their defensive axis and extend the line several hundred metres to the south to create a new line to cover the yawning gap.[7] Major D. Rykert McCuaig moved A Company over and bent it back to meet the German threat. Within minutes, *picklehaubes,* the German spiked helmets, could be seen moving along the flanks. The infantry fired at the enemy, finding many targets on the previously empty battlefield. McCuaig remained a force, travelling everywhere in the next three days, inspiring the men and pushing them to the point of collapse, and then past it. He would be wounded and captured during a fighting retreat on April 24. But here, on April 22, the Highlanders held on even as their ranks were thinned out by enemy fire and probing attacks. On the flanks of the gap, small groups of Canadians and Algerians fought together but were vastly outnumbered. Outposts were overrun, but slowed the enemy attack.

Men sacrificed all so that others could live. One of them, Lieutenant Guy Drummond, a twenty-seven-year-old millionaire from Montreal—dashing, fluently bilingual, and groomed for a political career—was shot in the throat and killed as the Canadians fought to close the gap. He would become one of Canada's Lost Generation: a man of enormous potential whose life was snuffed out before he reached his prime. The 13th held fast, refusing to give ground. Their stalwart defence helped to contain the German assault over the next three days.

About 2 kilometres behind the 13th Battalion's now extended and vulnerable front, understandable confusion had arisen at the 3rd Brigade headquarters at Mousetrap Farm. Under small-arms and artillery fire, Brigadier Richard Turner and his brigade major, Garnet Hughes, received faulty intelligence suggesting that the enemy was pushing through the lines and that the Canadian left flank was overrun. In fact, the Germans were driving forward, but their advance had been temporarily checked by the 13th Battalion, isolated groups of French and Algerian defenders, and the Germans' own caution in following the death cloud.

THE SLENDER AND BESPECTACLED Brigadier Turner was one of Canada's few prewar heroes. His physical courage, and later his moral fortitude in standing up to superiors, were beyond doubt, but in his first battle he showed little understanding of how to control his forces and how to react to the "fog of war"—the confusion and chaos that clouded the battlefield as thousands of men fought hundreds of individual battles over several square kilometres of broken ground. Faced with a bewildering array of conflicting reports, Turner proved here, and later, that he was incapable of deciphering the true situation at the front. Such disentangling was no easy task, but it was one of the essential requirements of command. Unfortunately,

A Canadian hero from the South African War, Richard Turner fared less well as a senior battlefield commander.

his troops suffered for his failure. Furthermore, his superiors were often led astray, as too often the reports and orders coming from his brigade headquarters were panicky and unclear, thus giving the wrong impression.

Turner's staff sent out several pleas for assistance between 6:30 P.M. and 7:10 P.M., reporting that their front was alternately "retiring" and being "driven in" by enemy assaults; one egregious report noted that they had "no troops left. Need ammunition badly. We are forced back on G.H.Q. Line."[8] Turner's forces were far from the G.H.Q. Line, which ran northeast to southwest, starting about 600 metres south of St. Julien, and while one can have some sympathy for the 3rd Brigade staff among the swirling confusion, not knowing where its battalions were located was indeed a terrible error, especially since the 13th Battalion was still holding its ground tenaciously. But Turner was right in communicating to his senior officers that the French retreat had left a yawning gap on his flank that had to be closed. As he wrote in his aide-memoir a few days after the battle, "At 6:30 P.M. on the 22nd April, I really thought all was lost."[9]

Alderson's divisional headquarters, several kilometres from the front and across the canal, responded to the 3rd Brigade's seemingly desperate situation by ordering Brigadier Arthur Currie—then organizing the defence to the east, a line that had not yet been attacked—to send one of his reserve battalions to support Turner. Hours later, though, Turner realized that his flank was intact, although the Germans had driven as deep as Kitcheners Wood, where they captured a number of British guns. Although this type of confusion occurs in battle, it did not reflect well on the 3rd Brigade. The event went largely unnoticed, however, as the Entente command was reeling. It seemed possible that the salient would be lost, and the next few hours would be critical. The Germans had to be stopped—or at least forced back on their heels.

WHILE THE INFANTRY on the left flank were trying to contain the German advance, Major William King's 10th Battery of the Canadian Field Artillery, consisting of four 18-pounders, held an important part of the front, just north of St. Julien. King's gunners had the unenviable task of covering several hundred metres of open flank with no infantry in front of them—except for the enemy's, which was slowly infiltrating its way forward. The guns had to hold. Firing an average of six shells per minute—but up to twenty in short, mad bursts—the gunners exploded a rain of steel over the advancing German troops from the 233rd Regiment. With 375 metal shrapnel balls in each shell exploding downwards in a blast of whirling metal, the German infantry were shredded, forced to retreat, leaving behind shrapnel-riddled corpses.

This gunfire supported the 13th Battalion's weak flank, which was vulnerable to the northeast. But the Germans continued to push into the Canadian lines, with the coming darkness masking their movements. King, a thirty-seven-year-old veteran from the South African War, whose military career stretched back twenty-three years, realized he was soon to be overrun. Although his gunners were firing shrapnel shells over open sights in a direct-fire role, the enemy was working around his troops' flank, and had moved to within 500 metres. Just when it appeared that the guns would be lost, a small detachment of sixty riflemen and a lone Colt machine-gun team from St. Julien came to the gunners' rescue.

THE COLT MACHINE GUN was used by British and Canadian soldiers in the South African War. The gun and tripod weighed about seventy-five pounds, and a small team of four to five could fire several hundred belt-fed .303-calibre rounds per minute. The number-one man fired the gun while the number-two man fed him bullets. The other team members ran ammunition up in heavy boxes or frantically placed the bullets into the cloth firing band that would feed into the gun. However, the Colt was not reliable in sustained combat. The gun was exceedingly difficult to keep clean, and its hundreds of intricate pieces made it vulnerable to jamming. Some gunners cursed it while others, like Armine Norris, who noted that the Colt was his "first love," learned to make it purr.[10] Despite its propensity to break down, and its operational quirkiness, the four Colts to a battalion provided essential firepower to hold the front.

Working forward from the strongpoint of St. Julien, nineteen-year-old Lance Corporal Fred Fisher of the 13th Battalion was one of the gunners who had fired his Colt almost continuously since the gas attack, engaging the Germans and buying important time for the Canadians to consolidate their lines. With Major King's

YPRES—THE GAS ATTACK: APRIL 22, 1915

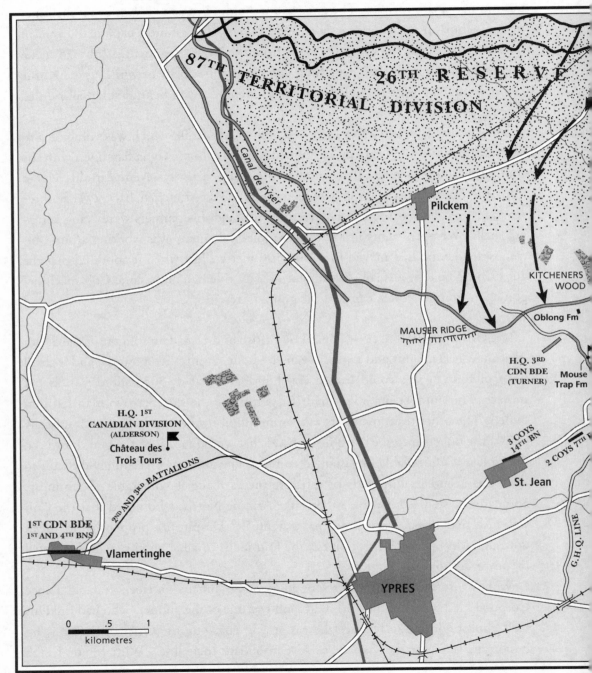

87TH TERRITORIAL DIVISION

26TH RESERVE DIVISION

Canal de l'Yser

Pilckem

KITCHENERS WOOD

Oblong Fm

MAUSER RIDGE

H.Q. 3RD CDN BDE (TURNER)

Mouse Trap Fm

H.Q. 1ST CANADIAN DIVISION (ALDERSON)

Château des Trois Tours

2ND AND 3RD BATTALIONS

3 COYS 14TH BN

2 COYS 7TH B

St. Jean

G.H.Q. LINE

1ST CDN BDE
1ST AND 4TH BNS

Vlamertinghe

YPRES

0   .5   1
kilometres

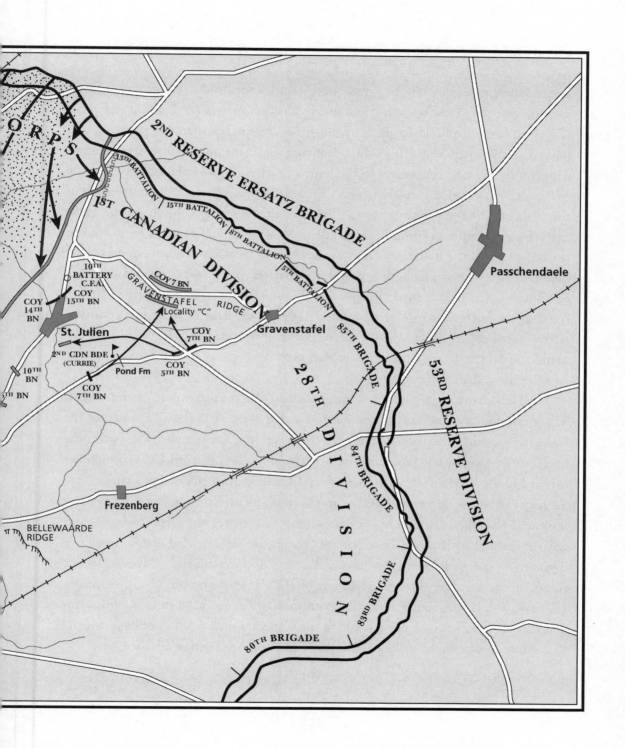

ORPS

2ND RESERVE ERSATZ BRIGADE

1ST CANADIAN DIVISION

13TH BATTALION

15TH BATTALION

8TH BATTALION

5TH BATTALION

Passchendaele

10TH BATTERY C.F.A.

COY 7 BN

GRAVENSTAFEL RIDGE

COY 14TH BN

COY 15TH BN

Locality "C"

COY 7TH BN

St. Julien

Gravenstafel

85TH BRIGADE

2ND CDN BDE (CURRIE)

Pond Fm

COY 5TH BN

28TH DIVISION

53RD RESERVE DIVISION

10TH BN

COY 7TH BN

5TH BN

84TH BRIGADE

Frezenberg

BELLEWAARDE RIDGE

83RD BRIGADE

80TH BRIGADE

batteries in danger, the young Fisher moved his team forward to engage the enemy. As a member of the "Suicide Club," the informal name given to specialist units such as machine-gunners or bombers who were called upon to do the most dangerous jobs, his five-man crew was cut down one by one, ultimately leaving him to fight it out alone. Fisher refused to retreat from his increasingly untenable position, and poured round after round into the advancing Germans. Each time the Germans dangerously exposed themselves in the hope of garnering glory through the capture of King's overextended guns, Fisher and King drove them back. The intervention of the Colt machine-gun team allowed King to halter his horses, hitch up the guns, and retreat to a safer position near St. Julien. Fisher, too, escaped, but he was killed the next day when a bullet took him in the chest as he again held swarming enemy infantry units at bay. His body was never recovered, but he was awarded Canada's first Victoria Cross of the war. Three other Canadians in the Second Battle of Ypres received the Victoria Cross, the Empire's highest award for bravery, but countless acts of sacrifice and extraordinary service went unrecorded as soldiers all over the battlefield fought to the bitter end, sometimes killed to a man and leaving no one to write the gallantry award citation.

The Canadians were barely holding on along the northern part of the salient. Many at divisional and corps headquarters to the west of Ypres were not sure the Canadians could stem the tide as the nature of the catastrophe was becoming evident. Alderson ordered military engineers from the 2nd and 3rd Field Companies forward to the Ypres Canal in preparation to demolish the bridges that spanned it.[11] Such an extreme action would likely contain the German advance, but this plan also indicated that the high command was willing to sacrifice three full divisions and what remained of the two French ones. Losing the salient and elements of five divisions would have been a monumental defeat. To blow up the bridges was a last resort, no doubt, but also an indication of the desperate nature of the situation. However, the British and French high commands did not have to make this grim decision just yet. Their hope rested with the Canadians: all would not be lost if the Dominion troops could strike hard and fast to slow the German advance.

CHAPTER 9

DESPERATE COUNTERATTACK

Midnight to 8 A.M., April 23, 1915

With the northern part of the salient collapsing under the weight of the German advance, and the French and Algerian divisions in full retreat, the Entente commanders were desperate to restore the situation. What the British high command needed most was time to react to the unfolding disaster—time that had to be bought at any price. Canadian Divisional Commander Edwin Alderson ordered Brigadier Richard Turner to launch a counterattack against Kitcheners Wood, a 2.5-hectare stand of oak some 1,500 metres west of St. Julien and 4.5 kilometres northeast of Ypres. It was the most southern point of the enemy advance through the now empty French and Algerian lines. While Alderson was largely out of touch with the battle, he was attempting to exert some control. But most soldiers—whether at divisional headquarters or in the front lines—understood that the Germans had to be stopped at Kitcheners Wood if any hope of re-establishing a strong line of defence was to be gained. This would be the first major Canadian operation of the war.

Turner pulled together his reserve forces, which included the 16th Battalion, a Scottish kilted unit, and the 10th Battalion, largely composed of men from Calgary. Neither Turner nor his staff had a firm idea as to where the Germans were, or of the strength of their numbers in Kitcheners Wood. But only six hours had passed since

This artistic rendition depicts the Canadian attack on Kitcheners Wood on April 22–23, 1915, the first Canadian offensive operation of the war. Note the Highlanders from the 16th Battalion and the author's inclusion of the recaptured British field guns that were lost earlier to the Germans.

the gas discharge, and all hoped that a swift attack might send the enemy reeling. At the tactical level, Kitcheners Wood (which many soldiers must have assumed was named after the famous minister of war, but was really a spot where previous French formations kept their cooks to prepare meals for front-line units) looked down into St. Julien and the Canadian lines centred around Mousetrap Farm. If the enemy still held the high ground when the sun came up the next day, the Canadians would pay dearly for it, as massed fire would be directed into their compromised positions.

Lieutenant Colonel R.G. Edwards Leckie of the 16th Battalion, a former Vancouver mining engineer with South African War experience, had been told only that the Germans "occupied this wood, and we were to drive them out." Highlander J.E. Lockerby, a nineteen-year-old bank clerk from Prince Edward Island who had enlisted on the third day of the war, remembered, "Our officer remarked very casually that we were going to attack the wood and drive the Germans back at the point of the bayonet. Everybody seemed pleased with the idea of it."[1] The Canadians displayed a naive jauntiness. With no time to reconnoitre the ground, it would be at best a blind charge against a dug-in enemy position. A surprise attack in the dark, supported by only a light artillery bombardment, would shock the enemy—or so everyone hoped.

A LITTLE BEFORE MIDNIGHT, the Canadians made last-minute adjustments to their kit, and then formed up in eight waves, shoulder to shoulder, to the hurried whispers of NCOs. Bayonets were fixed, as the objective was only some 500 metres away. Little was said among the men, but all knew that this would be a night for cold steel. Some chums shook hands and offered awkward platitudes about seeing friends on the other side; others kept feelings to themselves, staring stoically ahead.

Advancing in dense columns was the easiest way to travel in the darkness up the gentle ridge of the skyline, but experienced men winced at the thought of even one enemy machine gun catching them in this massed formation. It would be a slaughter. Lieutenant Colonel Russell Boyle of the 10th Battalion had a chance to confirm the existence of a probable machine-gun position on the flank at Oblong Farm, but decided against it because it fell out of his attack scheme and was considered "not our job."[2] Leaving this threat unmasked and uncaptured was a terrible error by the Western rancher, and a sign of Canadian tactical inexperience. Boyle would not live to learn from his oversight, however, as he would be shot during the battle, dying in agony three days later at a makeshift hospital.

The two battalions, totalling some 1,600 men, advanced towards the darkened wood. Under a low, cloudy moon, progress was good, with the mass of troops passing abandoned farms and skirting small groves of trees. Then the silhouetted soldiers ran into an unmarked fence some 200 metres from their objective. While hundreds of sweating, nervous men scrambled over the obstacle, the Germans became aware of the activity in the dark. They responded with flares that lit the battlefield as bright as day, casting a ghastly green tint on the upturned faces of men. The Canadians had only a few seconds before muzzle flashes flickered from the woods.

Masses of Canadians were caught in the open. Tracer bullets arced through the air. The columns of advancing troops, now in a series of ragged lines, temporarily faltered as men were snapped backwards by Mauser bullets travelling two times faster than the speed of sound. But within a minute, officers ordered a bayonet charge. It must have felt like an hour for the men under fire. Major Dan Ormond of the 10th Battalion, who would soon take over the battalion after his commanding officer and second-in-command were killed, remembered the chaos of that charge over broken ground. His most vivid memory was of seeing a man on fire like a human torch, likely lit up when one of the flares he was carrying was hit and ignited. "All officers of the company making the attack were killed or wounded before reaching within 75 yards of the German trench."[3] Caught in the hurricane of bullets, some soldiers advanced, as one Highlander recounted, with their hands before their faces.[4] The firestorm was unlike anything the Canadians had ever faced.

MOST OF THE CANADIANS "did not get far," remembered J.E. Lockerby. "The bullets were coming so thick that at first I expected to get hit every minute, then after a while, I thought when so many had missed me, I must be one of the lucky ones." But his luck ran out. "It seemed to take the whole side of my chest off, but when I recovered from shock I realized that it was only in the shoulder and the arm. I dropped in my tracks and could not move."[5] Hundreds of writhing and still bodies covered the battlefield.

But not all the men were cut down. Survivors from both battalions reached the German positions in the woods, panting and looking to even the score. John Matheson of the 10th Battalion, who had served four years with the 9th Royal Scots before coming to Canada, recounted how his mates fought "with a vengeance ... a few 'Huns' were taken prisoners, but damned few. We had enough to do to take care of ourselves and our own wounded to bother about prisoners."[6] While the Canadians were in no mood to take prisoners, some of the confusion also arose from small pockets of Germans attempting to surrender on one front while other groups continued fighting, sometimes only 20 or 30 metres away. The politics of surrender was always fraught with danger, but in this case—in the first chaotic night battle of the war, the Canadians having crossed a terrible killing ground—prisoners would

*This rare photograph depicts Canadian infantry dug in at the Second Battle of Ypres.
Note the rough trenches and lack of sandbags.*

only be taken after victory was ensured. The official war diary of the 16th Battalion noted laconically, after a number of German prisoners were found executed: "Men were cautioned against dealing harshly with prisoners."[7]

Having broken the German positions, the remnants of the two battalions found themselves lost, overextended, and vulnerable. Control was all but impossible in the dark, with most officers down and the rank and file dispersed. No telephones, lights, or message-carrying pigeons were available, and even voice control was drowned under the din of explosions and rifle fire. Isolated pockets of soldiers were on their own. Natural leaders in the ranks rallied their comrades. Sergeants and corporals organized a desperate defence, aware that when the Germans recovered they would likely counterattack quickly to push back the Canadians, who now controlled the important high ground. During the early hours of April 23, the surviving members of the 10th excavated shallow gun pits for themselves and the wounded inside the southern edge of the woods. The men of the 16th were bolder, with Leckie eventually rallying enough soldiers to push through the trees and establish a patchwork defence on the other side. In all, the Canadians recaptured four lost British artillery pieces and established a new set of trenches 900 metres into enemy-held territory. "We gave them an unholy scare and checked their advance," wrote Leckie, and this was true, but the counterattack had cost more than two-thirds of the 1,600 men involved.[8] By the morning of April 23, the 10th had been reduced to 5 officers and 188 enlisted men; the 16th Battalion had only a few more, with 5 officers and 260 other ranks.[9]

NOTWITHSTANDING THEIR SETBACK at Kitcheners Wood, the Germans continued to inch forward to the west, close to the Yser Canal. Some units even crossed over it, but they were driven back by French and Belgian troops on the western side. Unable to secure a foothold over the canal, the Germans looked to complete the surprising success by cutting off the salient with a drive southwards. It would be launched from atop Mauser Ridge, a slight rise running east–west along the northern part of the now collapsed salient, overlooking the entire battlefield and behind most of the Entente lines. To purchase much-needed time for the British to bring reinforcements up from the rear, Alderson and his superior, General Herbert Plumer, commander of the 5th British Corps, ordered Brigadier Malcolm Mercer to launch the 1st and 4th Battalions in a counterattack against the Germans atop Mauser Ridge.

These two Canadian battalions were supposed to be supported by a flanking two-battalion French attack, but this support failed to materialize, as the French were in no shape to launch any offensive operations, no matter what their senior officers told the British. Without the French, the primary Canadian assault would be a narrow frontal attack over open ground. The commanding officers, Lieutenant Colonels F.W. Hill and A.P Birchall of the 1st and 4th, respectively—both experienced British officers, the former a prewar mayor of Niagara Falls and the latter a professional British soldier on loan to the Canadians—were in a terrible predicament. The horizon had begun to lighten. With no time to reconnoitre the front, the Canadians did not know what was out there, but they suspected the enemy was dug in to shallow rifle pits, with good fields of fire, and alert to an expected attack. But the high command believed that the Germans could be dislodged, or at least that the initiative had to be taken back from the enemy to ensure they did not keep pushing south and cut off the salient.

With increasing evidence that no French support was forthcoming, the Canadians were forced to attack alone, sometime around 6 A.M. Although the 1st Battalion's war diary noted that the "attack was launched under artillery, machine-gun, and rifle fire and without [supporting Canadian] artillery preparation," the operation started well, with sections leapfrogging one another, alternately advancing, firing, or digging in with their personal entrenching tools.[10] With many of the men having trained in this type of small-unit attack in Canada as part of the militia summer camps, and then having honed these tactics in the months of training in England, the Canadians made a strong advance. But they had a long way to go— about 1,500 metres from the start line. And the attack was mounted in daylight. The Canadians were easy targets, and the Germans began to concentrate an escalating crescendo of fire that was barely hindered by the trickle of artillery fire coming from sixteen supporting Canadian field guns and howitzers.

"AHEAD OF ME I see men running. Suddenly their legs double up and they sink to the ground. Here's a body with the head shot off. I jump over it. Here's a poor devil with both legs gone, but still alive," recounted Private George Bell of the 1st Battalion.[11] There were few places for the Canadians to take cover on a battlefield that—in the words of Private Frank Betts, a twenty-one-year-old farmer— was "as level as a billiard table."[12] While it must have looked that way to a man under massed bullet fire, the land was in fact marked by slight undulations that provided some cover, but certainly not enough for two battalions' worth of men. Firing from behind barbed-wire-protected trenches, the Germans called down artillery fire when the Canadians hit the halfway mark to the objective—about thirty minutes into the battle.

It was a "hideous chaos," remarked one survivor.[13] Despite the terrible conditions, the two battalions fought for most of the day, with Canadian Colt machine-gunners and snipers finding their targets, and the rest of the infantry keeping their cohesion and discipline under a murderous rain of fire. Their bravery and endurance attested to the Canadian élan, even if the operation was from very early on clearly little more than a suicide mission. After the initial assault went to ground, the Canadians launched a second push in mid-afternoon.

These troops got closer to the enemy front—within about 300 metres—but they too were shot to pieces.

The intensity of the German fire was evident in the 1st and 4th Battalions' casualty figures: the former lost 406 men, and the latter counted 503 killed, wounded, or missing, including Birchall and the second-in-command.[14] No two Imperial battalions could have done better than the 1st and 4th, but these battalions should not have been ordered to throw themselves into the maw of battle, creating a buffer zone with their own bodies to keep the Germans from pushing south.

After the war, Canadian official historian Colonel A.F. Duguid wrote privately that the 1st and 4th Battalions' attack "unquestionably checked a German advance directly on Ypres," and was comparable in importance to the "attack in the dark by the 10th and 16th Battalions."[15] The Kitcheners Wood assault was described by none other than French general Ferdinand Foch as "the finest act in the war."[16] It was not, and the attack on Mauser Ridge was the more difficult operation to carry out. But they were both impressive, if desperate, feats of martial courage and élan.

Desperate attacks occur in war and, as grim as it sounds, the duty of a soldier is to sacrifice himself, if ordered, for the greater good. But did the frontal assault against Mauser Ridge over 1,500 metres of nearly flat ground achieve anything? Pressure was reduced on the Canadian garrison at St. Julien, but the cost of nearly 1,000 men was surely too high for this temporary relief. The counterattack, and the all-day battle that followed, also stopped the cautious Germans from advancing. But would it have been wiser to dig in instead, set up fields of fire with nearly 2,000 Ross rifles, 8 Colt machine guns, more than a dozen artillery pieces, and then smash the German forces as they attacked in the daylight across the open ground? The Germans had to go through the Canadian front if they wanted to drive south and cut off the salient, and they would have paid a terrible price.

Part of the problem also lay in coordinating with the French, who simply abandoned the Canadians. Nor were the Dominion troops helped by the tactical adherence to a clumsy doctrine that called for fierce counterattacks to recover lost ground without any reconnaissance—or any thought of how the two shattered battalions might have actually been able to hold the ground against determined enemy attacks that would surely have followed should the 1st and 4th have captured their objectives on Mauser Ridge. Nevertheless, the Canadian counterattacks succeeded in pushing the Germans back, buying time for the British and Canadians to organize a defence.

BUT PERHAPS A BAYONET charge was in fact the Canadian soldier's best hope since his Ross rifle was consistently failing him in battle. As prewar trials indicated, the Canadian-made Ross jammed repeatedly during rapid-fire operations. The straight pullback bolt did not provide enough leverage to remove spent casings. During the desperate Second Battle of Ypres, soldiers could not loosen the bolt, finding it necessary to use the boot heel or the handle of an entrenching tool. Sweating, dirty hands were cut open in frustration. Not all the rifles failed, and some units had few problems, but on the battlefield hundreds of Canadian infantrymen decided for themselves, disgustedly throwing away their Ross rifles and picking up British Lee-Enfields or even German Mausers from the dead. Private T.W. Law shared his anger with a sweetheart at home: "I have seen darling when we were in action the boys kicking the bolts back and then having another shot and for the whole five rounds they had to do this. There is talk of us getting Enfields and the sooner the better and give us a chance to fight for our lives for after the first ten rounds with the Ross it is only good to us as a club."[17]

After the battle a bitter debate ensued over the merits of the rifle: supporters pointed to poor British mass-produced ammunition as the culprit; detractors called it a useless rifle better suited for hunting than warfare. Undoubtedly, the finely crafted Ross jammed partly due to the use of mass-produced and uneven ammunition, but it was also not as robust as the Lee-Enfield, which mostly functioned despite uneven batches of ammunition, and dirt and mud getting into its works. The commanding officers were almost evenly split over the Ross's suitability, with those men who had been appointed by Hughes or were loyal to him often speaking in the rifle's favour. But clearly the soldiers had begun to lose faith in it as a weapon. The Ross rifle was eventually phased out by the end of 1916, although specialist snipers continued to use it. In the meantime, however, Canadians using this weapon scrambled to defend themselves against the German onslaught.

SCATTERED CANADIAN FORMATIONS were hanging on by their fingertips twelve hours after the first gas attack. During that time the Canadian Division had lost over 2,100 men. These casualties were brutal even by Western Front standards, since the brunt of the fighting had largely fallen on five battalions. But the Dominion troops had earned the grudging admiration of the Germans, who realized that their easy advance up to this point would now shift to a struggle to overcome first-class soldiers. One German prisoner blurted to his Canadian captors: "You fellows fight like hell."[18]

THE OPEN FLANK: APRIL 23, 1915, 12:00 A.M. TO 8:00 A.M.

Legend:
— Positions at 12:01 A.M.
— Positions subsequently occupied

0   .5   1
kilometres

Map labels:
15TH BN
13TH BN
13TH BATTALION
Keerselaere
(15)
Langemark
Steenbeek
Pilckem
MAUSER RIDGE
Canal de l'Yser
YPRES
COY 7 BN
3 COYS 7 BN
2ND CDN BDE
COY 15 BN
COY 14 BN
St. Julien
COY 3
HQ 2ND CDN BDE
Pond Farm
GUN AREA
2ND C.F.A.
Frezenberg
51ST RESERVE DIV
26TH GERMAN RESERVE CORPS
2 COYS 3 BN
2 COY 2 BN
6 BN
10 BN
12:01 A.M.
10 BN
16 BN
HQ 3RD CDN BDE
3RD FD COY C.E.
G.H.Q. LINE
52ND RESERVE DIVISION
KITCHENERS WOOD
Oblong Fm
2 COYS 2 BN
3 COYS 2/E. KENT
COY 14 BN
Hampshire Fm
Turco Fm
2 COYS 5/K.O.R.
3/MX.
2 & 3 BNS
1:30 A.M.
2
COYS
14 BN
GEDDES' DETACHMENT
GUN AREA 3RD C.F.A.
St. Jean
3 COYS 2/E. KENT
2 COYS 3/MX.
6:00 A.M.
1 AND 4 BNS
2 COYS 3/MX.
3/MX.
1ST BN 4TH BN
1ST CDN BDE
2ND FD COY C.E.
N0.
4 CDN
1 AND 4 CDN BATTALIONS

CHAPTER 10

ATTACK AND HOLD

April 23, 1915

Most of the Canadian infantrymen had now gone a full day without sleep. They had suffered under the strain of constant shell and small-arms fire, bursts of adrenaline and terror, and a lack of food and water. On the left flank, only twelve Canadian and four Zouave companies covered some 12,000 metres of front.[1] The 13th Battalion still held the key left shoulder of the Canadian line and had spent the night repelling attacks from the front, the side, and even the rear. British and French artillery support came from the other side of the canal, but all along the front the Canadians were vastly outnumbered and outgunned.

ALL OF THE REMAINING Canadian reserve battalions were ordered into the line, as well as several British battalions formed into an ad-hoc force known as Geddes' Detachment, which filled the 3-kilometre gap between Kitcheners Wood and Mauser Ridge. This formation fought heroically throughout the day, beating back several German attacks and ensuring that the Canadians further to the right, around St. Julien, were not enveloped.

The 2nd and 3rd Battalions had moved forward across the canal at midnight on April 22. Behind them, throngs of refugees streamed from the burning city of Ypres. Charred bodies lay strewn in the streets and along the side of the road. The air was black with smoke but lit eerily by the flames, shellfire, and flares. As the Canadian reserve units from the 1st Brigade pushed into this maelstrom, the Germans shelled them, pounding bridges and roads in the hope of slowing this support force. Private R.J. Clarke of the 3rd Battalion saw at least "twenty men of the battalion killed on the main road by shrapnel," and he, too, would be wounded only hours later.[2] While the entire front was under fire, Hellfire Corner, an infamous intersection on Menin Road, which led out of Ypres, became renowned for its danger. No one lingered there, and even the corpses were soon blasted out of existence by the never-ending shellfire.

Brigadier Turner had been apprised of the successful but costly attack against Kitcheners Wood by an officer who delivered a hastily scribbled message in the middle of the night. The officer staggered into the dugout, handing over the blood-splattered note, but could say very little as a bullet had ripped out his throat and shattered his chin. The situation had stabilized but was still precarious. No one was sure what the morning would bring. Under these conditions, Turner sent an urgent plea to Currie to send whatever reinforcements he had left to fill the gap north of his command post at St. Julien. This was not an unreasonable request since Currie's forces had not yet been attacked, even though the brigadier thought it was only a matter of time until they were. Aware that the battle's centre of gravity was on the left flank, around Kitcheners Wood, Currie ordered the last of his reserves—three companies of the 7th Battalion—to strengthen Turner's line.

While the Canadian-held front at Ypres appears small on most maps, Currie's men had to run and dodge across 1,000 metres of broken ground with full kit. The British Columbians from the 7th Battalion made their way crouched over, harassed in the gloom by German shell and shot. Platoons and sections got mixed up, but Currie's force arrived to strengthen Turner's front. A senior officer in the 7th Battalion, Major Victor Odlum, a wealthy Victoria newspaperman and experienced militia officer who had also served in the South African War as a private, played a key role in establishing the forward defence at the essential post of St. Julien that day. Years after the war, he recounted seeing his younger brother running towards the front later in the day, carrying desperately needed ammunition. By chance their eyes met, they waved to each other, and, seconds later, he saw his brother Joseph atomized by a direct hit from a shell. Odlum bit back his tears and continued to oversee the desperate defence.[3] Later in the same battle, Odlum's cousin would be killed, as would his friend and commanding officer, Lieutenant Colonel William Hart-McHarg, who was shot through the stomach as he and Odlum reconnoitred the front.

Odlum and his men were fortified around Keerselaere (south of the 13th Battalion and north of St. Julien) at around 3 A.M. on April 23. The 7th Battalion's infantrymen were ready to repel further advances expected the next day, and they later helped to support the 13th as its surviving officers pulled back from exposed lines to a more secure position closer to St. Julien.

WITH HIS FRONT STABILIZED by the early hours of April 23, Turner ordered Lieutenant Colonel David Watson's 2nd Battalion to support the 10th and 16th, to allow their vulnerable and overextended survivors to get back to the Canadian trenches from their position in the southern edge of Kitcheners Wood, where they had moved to better defend against enemy shellfire. These battalions' ever-dwindling numbers were depressing and shocking. Private Sydney Cox of the 10th remembered sergeants ordering the men to sound off in numbers, as they were spread throughout the wood in many shell craters and so not visible to each other. "Every time you numbered, you were a lower number than you were the time before. You didn't feel so good about that."[4]

"When dawn at last broke ... we found the German trench almost enfilading us," wrote Lieutenant Hugh Urquhart of the 16th Battalion, who would later rise to command a battalion before being maimed by a terrible wound through the spine. "I looked at my wristwatch thinking it must be noon, the minutes seemed long, but it was only 6:30 A.M. Looking backwards ... we could see our dead lying over the field, and the terribleness of last night's work came home to us." Many of the Canadians had been killed almost immediately or succumbed to their wounds; others were badly wounded and in agonizing pain. When stretcher-bearers tried to help them in the open ground, German snipers fired at them.

As the remains of the counterattacking force dug in to the hard earth, attempting to expand their trenches, the German artillery opened up: "One shell blew some men out of the trench, one shell burst overhead. The shock seemed to kill the men, for there was no scratch on them," wrote Urquhart. In other cases, soldiers were literally blown to pieces, the bodies shredded by the force of the explosion, flesh reduced to pulp, the remains shovelled into a sandbag or left smeared in the mud. The shattered remnants of the two battalions clung to Kitcheners Wood after hastily fortifying their shell-crater defences and shallow trenches. "At a certain stage of the game," noted Urquhart, "one officer in a trench on our right seemed to go literally crazy, shouted most ridiculous fire orders and kept passing information which we know to be wrong. We endeavoured to stop his shouting, but without avail. Much to our relief, he got wounded."[5] The strain of battle was terrible, but help was coming.

IN THE EARLY MORNING of April 23, the 2nd Battalion was rushed to the front to dig in along the southeast edge of Kitcheners Wood and relieve what was left of the 10th and 16th Battalions. Officers and patrols who were sent out to reconnoitre the battlefield disappeared after the sounds of heavy gunfire—an ominous sign. Nonetheless, a company from the 2nd Battalion was ordered forward in another clumsy attack. They advanced under the cover of a heavy mist and before dawn's first light. About halfway to the wood, the mist suddenly evaporated, leaving the company of 200 men vulnerable on the open ground. Surprised Germans quickly opened fire. Private Alfred Baggs of the 2nd Battalion gives a vivid account of his private battle during two days of fighting.

> The rifle and machine gun fire was so severe that it was quite impossible for the men who were not hit to make any further headway without getting wiped out; consequently they were ordered to retire ... we dug in with almost no cover: you may believe me that we dug that trench as fast as it was possible.

Baggs goes on to note that a few rescue parties tried to pull in the wounded, but the Germans "killed many by keeping up a very heavy fire on us."[6]

As the sun rose on April 23, Baggs's platoon was ordered to reinforce the ravaged front trench held by the reduced forces of the 10th and 16th Battalions, again going forward across a killing zone. To get there they had to travel 100 metres in the open with only knee-high mustard grass as cover, all the while advancing towards the enemy lines. Not knowing where they were headed and unable to look around without drawing fire, many of the Canadians crawled in circles. Baggs kept coming upon dead and wounded Canadians, the latter of whom were trying to crawl back to the rear but were hopelessly lost. He finally got his bearings by tracking the sun and following blood trails through the crushed mustard. When Baggs came to the edge of the grass, he was horrified to find a gap of some 15 metres of open ground between his platoon's position and the Canadian front line. And so the Canadians rested at the edge, caught their breath and, as Baggs noted in his diary, "made a dash for it," passing the bodies of their companions in their desperate sprint. Baggs dove headfirst into the shallow ditch in Kitcheners Wood, the bullets kicking up dirt around him. Looking around at exhausted and bloody survivors, he realized that the new Canadian trenches he had just risked his life to fortify were overextended and enfiladed. After two hours of trading fire with the enemy, massing German troops forced the Canadians to pull back—and that meant braving the gap again. This time, the Germans had a machine gun and sniped at the Canadians who ran back one at a time. They queued up in a line of death, men quietly saying goodbye to one another, aware that their chances were slim but that those behind them had it worse, as they would only get their turn to run after the enemy had been alerted to the action.

Several of Baggs's exhausted mates, men he had trained with for months, were killed around him. When Baggs's turn came to run, he was so demoralized and dispirited after the rush and fall of adrenaline that he could not find the energy to run the whole way, even as light artillery shells were added to the small-arms and machine-gun fire directed against him. Panting and sweating, he walked the final few metres into the mustard grass, his back and shoulder hunched in tension as he expected a bullet through the spine every step he took. He somehow survived—a testament to the chanciness of war. No doubt he looked at the shamrock tattoo on his left wrist a few times during the day and wondered how long his luck could last.[7] His luck would in fact last for the entire war, although he was later shell-shocked on the Somme.

Despite the near annihilation of Baggs's company, two other 2nd Battalion companies had captured key positions that strengthened the Canadian line south of Kitcheners Wood and to the east. Here, the machine-gunners and riflemen of five platoons, situated in two strongpoints known as Hooper's House and Doxsee's House, held the Germans at bay. With wide and unobstructed fields of fire, the Canadian infantrymen cut the enemy to ribbons. Sergeant H.C. Ablard, one of the 2nd Battalion's best marksmen, climbed into the second storey of the ruined Doxsee's House and shot down at least eighteen enemy troops before he, too, was felled by a bullet. The garrison here held on until April 24, when they were finally overwhelmed by fire and enemy troops after St. Julien fell on their right flank.

However, by noon on April 23, the Canadians had dug a string of defensive trenches, linked in part by manned shell holes, creating a nearly continuous line to protect against German probing attacks coming from the vicinity of Kitcheners Wood. While most of the surviving Canadian troops—numbering some 14,000—were now committed to battle, the defence was very much an engagement of small groups of enlisted men separated from their officers. The four Colt machine guns per battalion provided essential firepower, but the Canadians found themselves in a desperate battle to the finish, with both their rifles and machine guns jamming. Despite their fending off of German assaults, the enemy weight of return fire was increasing, with deadly accurate artillery shells raining down on the front and rear positions. "When the German guns open fire on you," wrote one Canadian, "all you can do is sit tight and hope to God a shell does not drop in the trench."[8]

LOSSES BEGAN TO MOUNT, but the hard-as-nails Canadians would not be easily dislodged. It was a gut-wrenching time for all, however, as the remaining Canadian reserves were thrown into the line. Losses were heavy. Lieutenant Colonel David Watson of the 2nd Battalion, the forty-six-year-old manager of the *Quebec City Chronicle,* had time to reflect on his unit's first two days in battle, confessing to his diary, "My God!! What an awful night we had."[9] But still the Canadians fought on, defending key positions like St. Julien and defeating a new series of German attacks.

Infiltrating German parties, heavy artillery fire that cut communication lines, and the normal friction of battle had left Currie out of touch with Turner's 3rd Brigade command headquarters. But the fact that the 3rd Brigade's artillery batteries were pulling back along the front was a grim signal that the brigade was in trouble.

Currie's forces still held the apex of the original line, but the brigadier was preparing a second strongpoint at Locality C, a shallow trench running along the skyline at the eastern end of Gravenstafel Ridge, roughly 900 metres behind the front line held by his 8th and 5th Battalions. It offered good fields of fire and could be a strong forming-up position, either for a counterattack or as a secondary line of defence.

By the end of April 23, the Canadian-held front had stabilized. But General Alderson's divisional headquarters, situated behind the Yser Canal, had lost control of the battle. The British had begun to feed battalions and brigades piecemeal into the salient, but these troops often received orders from Alderson or other British divisional headquarters to carry out desperate attacks over open ground in broad daylight without proper reconnaissance. Several British battalions were shattered in their doomed attempt to follow such incompetent orders.

With almost no centralized command, individual Canadian battalions, companies, and platoons held out as best they could. The fighting on April 22 had been controlled by the brigadiers, but they had soon lost touch with most of their units once their reserves were committed to holding the line. The fighting on April 23 was therefore a battalion commander's battle, with most units fighting in isolation, cut off by sweeping fire and severed communications. The training they had undergone in England, including months of discipline and drill, helped exhausted warriors deal with the stress and confusion on the battlefield, but breaks and fissures erupted throughout units as men cracked under the strain of stress. In some of the fiercest fighting, Lieutenant Colonel George Tuxford of the 5th Battalion—a forty-five-year-old Welsh-born farmer and cowboy from south Saskatchewan, who was a legend among Westerners for leading the longest cattle drive in history from his farm in Saskatchewan across the Rockies—issued orders that any man attempting to retreat was to be shot.[10] While his soldiers had received no food during the last two days, most of the men did not need the motivation of such threats and fought to the bitter end. By darkness on April 23, most had not slept for forty-eight hours. During the lulls in the battle, wasted men crumpled forward, sometimes sleeping on their feet or face-first in the dirt. They were difficult to distinguish from the dead.

Officers sacrificed their own much-needed rest to crawl around No Man's Land, searching for signs of impending attack and gathering ammunition and water bottles from the fallen. "I began to get jumpy from the constant strain on my nerves and want of sleep but everybody was the same," wrote Lieutenant William Johnson to his wife.[11] The sleep-deprived Dominion troops tried to snatch a few hours of rest, but weary sentries called the men to stand-to almost every hour to protect against real and imaginary German attacks.

EVEN WITH THE FRONT STABILIZED, hundreds of wounded lay bleeding in the lines. Those who could drag themselves out of their craters stumbled to the rear or were assisted by other walking wounded. Through the clouds of cordite that hung over the battlefield, the instinct to survive drove men to pull themselves back along the shell-cratered ground with broken legs or to stumble to the rear while cradling bloody stumps where once hands had been. "I, myself, once saw a man run down a road on the exposed ends of his tibia and fibula, flinging aside with each step the torn remnants of his foot, attached to his leg by a few tendons," recounted one horrified medical officer.[12]

Dressing stations were inundated with hundreds of men at a time. The conventional wounds were terrible, the internal gas wounds even worse. The chlorine irritated and destroyed the alveoli, causing fluid discharge within the lungs and impairing the exchange of oxygen. Even worse, the chlorine mixed with water to form hydrochloric acid that burned tissue. In the end, men drowned in their own searing fluids. It was an ugly death. Victims writhed on the ground, making gagging, choking sounds, pulling at their clothes, vomiting "greenish slime," propping themselves up to gasp for help, and then falling back exhausted from their struggles.[13] As one Canadian described the ghastly fate of a gassed companion, "The wheezing and frothing from his mouth like that of a horribly bloated bull-frog, the dilated eyeballs, the pondscum-green discolouration of face and neck, and the gurgling sound issuing from his throat, ironically simulating the hissing of escaping gas cylinders."[14] The worst cases of gassing were untreatable. Overwhelmed medical units did their best to administer morphine or alcohol to the terrified men who were slowly suffocating. Tragically, the victims often remained conscious up to the last minutes of their lives.

As bad as the gas wounds were, far more men were killed by conventional weapons. Hundreds and then thousands passed through the advance dressing stations, where surgeons, stretcher-bearers, and medical officers did their best to comfort and care for the wounded. A cigarette, a sip of water, and a comforting word could soothe a man as he waited in line to have his blood-soaked bandages changed. "We have had all varieties of wounds—some bad fractures, etc. with shrapnel—relatively few heads, chests or abdomens—I suppose they haven't survived," wrote Captain P.G. Bell of No. 3 Field Ambulance. "Many wounds to the face: noses shot away, bullets in ears, but only 3 or 4 men with eyes destroyed."[15]

Among the dead and dying at a dressing station, who were often laid out under the fall of shells as they waited for treatment, shell-shocked men cried, trembled, or simply stared with vacant, haunted eyes. The unending and nearly inhuman stress of battle had broken the minds of men, just as the shells and bullets had shattered bodies. Captain Francis Scrimger, a slight, thirty-four-year-old bespectacled surgeon with the 14th Battalion, who would be awarded the Victoria Cross for his bravery in caring for the wounded in the front lines, described in his diary a man who "was deaf and dumb and quite insane and babbling, as a result of the shell fire. He was not wounded. Two officers went temporarily insane from loss of sleep, anxiety and the nervous strain of constant big shells. A third was on the verge of similar conditions." Scrimger, who would work on repairing the shredded flesh of his fellow Canadians—"legs and arms crushed and heads torn open"—also felt himself losing control by the end of the second day, and suffering almost unbearable anxiety as the shells exploded around him and his patients.[16] But he did not break, and continued to tend to the injured men. Few would have suspected before the war that ordinary men like Scrimger, men seemingly far from filling the mould of the ideal hero, would rise to the occasion under such terrible strain. But most of the Canadians did, and their quiet heroics staved off defeat at Ypres.

CHAPTER 11

TO THE LAST MAN

April 24, 1915

Private Harold Peat of the Dirty Third watched the blur of shells skimming over his shallow trench all day on April 23 and 24. Some of the shells travelled so low that several times his cap was pulled from his head, and the enormous atmospheric pressure from one high-calibre shell nearly pulled him entirely out of the trench when it roared over him.[1] While many of these shells obliterated his comrades-in-arms, Peat survived the battle, though the shrapnel he took in the back and shoulder knocked him out of the war. But that was not a bad result for Peat, as he met his future wife while recovering in England, and then returned to Canada to write his memoirs, which became the subject of a Hollywood film in which he starred as himself.[2]

In the early morning hours of April 24, the 5th, 8th, 13th, and 15th Battalions still held much of the original front lines, but they were at the far end of a now narrow divisional front that had been caved in from the German pressure coming from the north of the salient. These four battalions had spent the last two days strengthening their position with barbed wire and sandbags. Overlapping fields of fire were established by digging new slit trenches, expanding shell craters, and positioning Colt machine guns to rake the battlefield. The Canadian garrisons also defeated probing German attacks, especially on the far left, still held grimly by the 13th Battalion, now supported by the 7th and 14th Battalions, with the 2nd, 3rd, 10th, and 16th in a jumble to the south of Kitcheners Wood. Farther to the west, the 1st and 4th Battalions were dug in and better supported by British troops. Having suffered severe losses, the Canadians now had twelve weakened battalions facing some twenty-four German battalions.[3] All knew a massed enemy assault was not long in coming.

At 4 A.M. on April 24, the Canadians fell victim to the second chlorine gas attack in the history of warfare, accompanied by an intense ten-minute artillery bombardment that shattered many of the Canadian trenches. The survivors pulled themselves out of the smoking ruins only to find tendrils of gas creeping over the front, soon to smother their positions. The 8th and the 15th Battalions took the full brunt of the gas, but soldiers on the flank, in Tuxford's 5th Battalion, as well as those echeloned in rear positions at Locality C, also found themselves gagging through constricted lungs.

Although less widespread than the first chlorine attack, this 1,000-metre-long wall of lethal chemicals was also denser, with some wispy fumes rising up to 15 metres. "It is impossible for me to give a real idea of the terror and horror spread among us by this filthy loathsome pestilence," recounted Major Harold Mathews of the 8th

This artist's rendition of the battle illustrates the Canadian defence against gas. Cloths wetted with urine or water were held against nose and mouth, as troops strained through tearing eyes to see the advancing Germans.

Battalion.[4] The soldiers had suspected that they might encounter gas again after its devastating first use, and word had already been passed down the line that the gas used two days earlier had been chlorine, identified by men with backgrounds in chemistry or soldiers who almost daily encountered the strong smell of chlorinated water in making their tea. When the second cloud was unleashed, soldiers were frantically ordered to wet a cloth bandage with water or urine and hold it against mouth and nose as an ad-hoc respirator.

These improvised devices kept many of the men from suffocating, but the insidious gas killed the skittish, the uninformed, and the weak, who could not muster the will to perform such unpleasant acts of self-preservation. As the heavier-than-air gas rolled over the Canadian lines, it seeped into and filled every crater and shell hole. "The chlorine was heavy," T.S. Morrissey observed, "and it lay in the trench and the boys were smothered to death."[5] Those Canadians already wounded by shrapnel or bullets had been bandaged and placed at the bottom of the trenches or dugouts, awaiting stretcher services to transport them to clearing stations in the rear. With the poison pooling in low-lying areas, these men suffered heavily. John N. Beaton, then stationed at Locality C with the last remaining company of the 7th Battalion still under Brigadier Currie's command, wrote in a letter to his father following the battle, "It was the poisonous gases that killed a lot of our poor fellows. They did not have a chance to fight."[6]

Those who were standing and firing, with their rags and pads over their mouths, were generally able to keep above the suffocating vapours of gas once the cloud had moved past them, but the chlorine clung in some deep trenches for two hours, dispatching all those who could not get out. However, even those who had stood above the trenches, avoiding gas at the peril of being hit by small-arms fire, were affected—and a wetted cloth was a poor shield against lung-searing gas. Infantrymen with streaming eyes fought the urge to rip away their paltry protections as they felt themselves suffocating. An official account from the 15th Battalion reported that men complained of "the effect of having cotton batting in one's lungs ... some died and the remainder were practically useless."[7] Another postbattle report noted that at least thirty-three 15th Battalion men had been killed by gas, and many more who suffered such deaths likely went uncounted.[8] These gas fatalities contributed to the battalion's staggering 675 casualties, most of which occurred on April 24. This was the worst one-day loss suffered by a Canadian battalion in the entire war.

Yet most of the Canadians survived the gas, even if many were knocked unconscious or rendered insensible, or were to suffer from damaged lungs for the rest of their chemically shortened lives. Ashen-faced from oxygen deprivation, choking and puking soldiers fired at the shadowy figures following the death cloud. The spike-helmeted infantrymen of the 2nd Reserve Ersatz Brigade advanced tentatively behind their own gas cloud, staying far back from its terrifying outer edges. They marched slowly and cautiously, betraying their faith in the gas by advancing in four columns of tightly packed men. Few seemed worried about being exposed in the open since they expected to encounter nothing except corpses. Instead, they moved face-first into heavy small-arms fire. The Canadians' Ross rifles fired 174-grain .303-calibre bullets that travelled roughly 730 metres per second. The force of the round bowled over advancing troops and tore apart flesh and bone. Added to the Canadian troops' massed rifle fire, Lieutenant Colonel Louis Lipsett of the 8th Battalion had arranged for an SOS artillery barrage from the 2nd Field Artillery Brigade to land in front of his lines in case of attack. Within minutes, the bodies of the German dead lay in piles; the wounded writhed in agony, but the defenders, still reeling from the gas, took little pity.

Despite this tenacious defence, the weight of German artillery fire and forces was too heavy for the gassed troops. On the 15th Battalion's front, the 3rd Brigade's artillery batteries were in the western part of the salient, situated around the G.H.Q. Line and helping to defend against the German onslaught there. That left the gassed Highlanders with little artillery support, and within an hour the left side of the 15th Battalion gave way under the strain.[9] Even their commander, Lieutenant Colonel John A. Currie, lost his grip. Gassed, exhausted, and having seen his men shot to bits, he snapped, and deserted from the front. He was found in a rear dugout, insensible, perhaps drunk, and definitely shell-shocked. But not all of the Red Watch (15th Battalion) men were broken. C Company held its ground, with pockets of infantrymen fighting it out as German troops overran their position on both sides, and until most of their ammunition was used. The company was annihilated or captured almost to a man.

By around 6:30 A.M., the enemy had surged through the 15th Battalion's front and was streaming towards Locality C and St. Julien, a little further to the west. The 13th Battalion remained on the left, still stalwartly holding its lines after being reinforced by three companies of the 14th Battalion, who were in a dangerously exposed position with Germans now on three sides. The 14th Battalion seem not to have enjoyed the confidence of General Alderson, because of some disciplinary problems they had suffered in England and perhaps, some thought, because the battalion had a French-Canadian company; but they performed like combat veterans at this point and throughout the battle.[10] These seven companies of the 13th and 14th Battalions had been shelled all night and day, and had suffered hundreds of casualties due to the weak sandbag breastwork built up from the trenches, which could not impede a high-velocity bullet round. Despite their poor positions, however, the two battalions beat back a series of attacks, and even conducted a fighting retreat once they were in danger of being cut off by German troops who poured through the 15th Battalion's now-broken flank. But many of the 13th and 14th Battalion men were cut down as they retreated, and others were captured after sacrificing themselves to save their mates.

One of the 14th Battalion's men to be killed at this point in the battle was Private C.D.B. Whitby, a journalist for the *Montreal Star,* who had started a regimental newspaper on the voyage across the Atlantic. His journalistic offering had enjoyed so much success that he had been made the unofficial historian of the battalion.[11] He was lost in the smoke and confusion of the vicious firefight, as was his draft history, which he had been compiling since arriving in England. The battle thus killed not only men but their history, too.

The Germans advanced through the narrow gap between the 13th and 14th on the left and what was left of the 15th on the right, their target Locality C atop Gravenstafel Ridge. This position was garrisoned by only one company of the 7th Battalion, but its commander, John Warden—a forty-four-year-old veteran of the Spanish–American and South African Wars—was a legendary fighter who would go on to command a battalion. The Germans were streaming through the lines, but Warden's men, bolstered by small groups of the gasping, choking Highlanders who had rallied at Locality C, punished the Germans and forced them to ground. At several points in the day, the Germans attempted to advance on the Canadians, and in desperation even tried the tactic of donning the uniforms of captured British soldiers. They nearly made it to the Canadian lines before Warden spotted the strange sight of British troops, some covered in blood, emerging from the direction of the enemy lines. He ordered his troops to open fire; a fellow officer countermanded the order, horrified at shooting British troops. Warden bellowed the order again. Trusting their commander, the rank and file opened fire, and the Germans in British uniforms were shot to pieces.[12] The enemy spent the rest of the day bombarding Locality C. "Hell all day," jotted Corporal A.L. Mackay quickly in his diary. He didn't have time to write more, and not much more was left to say.[13]

By noon on April 24, most of the Canadian battalions had been shattered into company and platoon-level units, which were now largely unconnected to their battalion headquarters. Locality C and St. Julien remained strongpoints along the now collapsed salient, with a number of companies—both British and Canadian—spread out between them to help link the battle groups. Command and control had broken down. However, the 13th and 14th Battalions still held their overextended front on the left and the 8th and 5th still clung on tenaciously on the right, even though both had been forced to turn their flanks to meet German troops infiltrating past them. In fact, some platoons and sections were dug in to create all-around defences, as units were being attacked from all sides.

The Canadian Division's headquarters were still several kilometres in the rear and slow to receive information from the front. When information arrived at all, it was often already inaccurate and sometimes contradicted by ever-changing events. The responsibility therefore fell to the two brigadiers, Turner and Currie (the third brigadier, Mercer, was largely left out of the battle since he was in reserve when it started and his units were sent into the line piecemeal without him at the command), their battalion commanders, and even company commanders to issue orders and react to the constantly shifting and dangerous circumstances. Communication between the battalion and brigade levels was spotty at best. The Germans having pushed into the Canadian lines in several places, no continuous trench system linking the positions remained, and most telephone lines had been cut under the artillery bombardments. The use of flags and lamps to convey messages attracted sniper fire, and quickly proved useless over the wide battlefield that was often covered in smoke and dust.[14] Runners were called on to brave sniper fire so that officers could keep in contact, but too often they never returned from their desperate missions. As no other way to determine the fluid situation was available, a battalion commander would often grab a trusted subordinate to accompany him and run, bent over, across the open fields in an attempt to coordinate the defence. With the Germans pushing on several fronts and reserves used up, the situation was desperate. Pockets of defenders surrendered, but often only after they were wounded, ammunition was spent, or their Ross rifles had jammed. Others were, in Turner's words, "blown out of position after position."[15]

On the left flank of Turner's front, the situation went from bad to worse on April 24. Turner's headquarters at Shell Trap Farm were bombarded throughout the day. Bleeding, moaning soldiers were lying on the floor of Turner's headquarters, and bullets would periodically pass through the weak sandbag defences that had been piled up against the walls. At one point, a dud shell crashed through the roof, landing on the floor and leaving the house "rock[ing] like a boat."[16] Amidst this chaos, Turner was dealing with both frantic messages emanating from the front-line units and demands for information coming from the rear. Turner's own communications were often cut, and the runners he sent out disappeared in a hail of shrapnel and rifle fire.

At the front, the 2nd and 3rd Battalions were engaged in continuous and fierce firefights, and extricating them from their ongoing battles was proving difficult. The enemy was also finding the seams in the Canadian defence by pushing into the rear areas, cutting off forward units, and leaving those in the rear without a clear appreciation of the unfolding battle. A senior divisional staff officer, Lieutenant Colonel G.C. Gordon-Hall, noted that Turner's brigade headquarters "lost control of its battalions during the critical hours of the fight."[17] The situation would get worse.

WITH ONLY INTERMITTENT COMMUNICATION, the exhausted, slightly gassed, and increasingly shell-shocked Turner misunderstood orders from divisional headquarters at 1 P.M. to strengthen his present line and "hold on."[18] Instead, forty minutes later, he ordered the retirement of all his troops to the G.H.Q. Line. In the confusion of the fighting, with orders late or never arriving, Turner must have thought that his front was untenable. But he was not panicking. One runner noted that while he was at Turner's headquarters he saw the exhausted general writing a message, when a shell burst a few feet away. "Pretty close," remarked Turner, without looking up. The runner jotted down in his diary, "Nerve of that sort helped me a great deal."[19] However, despite his personal bravery and inspiring stoicism under fire, Turner's grave tactical error in ordering his battalions to fall back to the G.H.Q. Line—resulting from either a misinterpretation of the divisional order or his desire to take matters into his own hands—could have resulted in the annihilation of the entire Canadian Division.

Only an exhausted and gassed man could have put faith in the G.H.Q. Line, which was far too glamorous a name for what was little more than a shallow ditch, partly facing the wrong way and easily enfiladed by enemy fire. Unfortunately, the move only crammed troops into a nearly defenceless trench and made them easier victims for shellfire. The existing trench system consisted mostly of shallow trenches and pits, which offered protection to individuals but not to large units. The G.H.Q. Line was a far easier target to observe and hit than the positions the Canadians had spent the last two days and nights fortifying. Even worse, the G.H.Q. Line ran northeast to southwest, the wrong direction from which to defend against units from the north of the salient. The line was likely the worst spot to hold with massed troops in the northern part of the Ypres salient, though Canadian divisional engineers worked feverishly to strengthen it with sandbags and deeper trenches. The fortifiers succeeded under heavy shellfire, and their actions likely saved hundreds of lives.

Many front-line officers must have shaken their head in disbelief when Turner's order reached them at around mid-afternoon on April 24. A few officers asked for a confirmation order as they thought it was some sort of German ruse.[20] Sadly, it was not. But to follow the order would be nearly impossible since all along the front the infantry was engaged with the enemy, some as little as only 25 metres from opposing forces. How were these men to stop firing, jump out of their trenches, and run several hundred metres to the rear? It would be a turkey shoot. Those defenders still alive with the 13th Battalion after some sixty hours of fighting, for instance, would have more than a kilometre and a half to travel, over open ground and in broad daylight.

But they had to follow orders, and at this point no single battalion commander, or anyone below him in rank for that matter, had any idea as to what was happening along the front. Perhaps the whole salient was about to be cut off? Perhaps Currie's brigade had fallen during the second gas attack? Whatever the case, Turner's men would follow their orders. As those in the front lines prepared for their fighting retreat, grieving comrades were forced to leave many of the wounded behind. Others picked up buddies and tried to carry them, making them slow-moving targets. The enemy snipers and machine-gunners swept the open ground with fire as the Canadians pitched across it in broad daylight. Pockets of resisters, sections and half sections, sacrificed themselves to hold off the enemy with all remaining ammunition so that their retreating friends might have a chance to survive.

LIEUTENANT EDWARD BELLEW, a third-generation soldier before retiring from the 18th Royal Irish Regiment to work as a harbour construction engineer in New Westminster, British Columbia, had been appointed machine-gun officer for the 7th Battalion. With the Germans closing in, he almost single-handedly allowed for dozens of his companions to retreat, as the 7th Battalion still held critical ground at Keerselaere on Turner's front. He and his loader kept up a deadly arc of fire from their Colt machine gun, and even though he was cut off (by enemy troops working behind him), and then wounded, he kept firing. With his comrade killed beside him, Bellew finally used up all of his ammunition, but he still had the presence of mind, despite his injuries and with the Germans closing in on him, to destroy his gun. And instead of surrendering, he picked up a rifle and bayonet and charged the enemy. Somehow he survived, but he remained a prisoner of war until 1919. The British government kept the award of his Victoria Cross a secret until his release, fearing he would be treated harshly in the prisoner-of-war camp or that the Germans would crow about his incarceration.

Many of the Canadian units on this front reacted badly to Turner's seemingly suicidal order. An angry Lieutenant Colonel Watson of the 2nd Battalion at first ignored the order, informing Turner's headquarters that he could hold on and had already destroyed several enemy attacks. But Turner's headquarters brooked no opposition and again ordered a retreat. Watson tried to organize a fighting force composed of companies retreating in staggered, measured bounds—which involved retreating a short distance, going to ground, firing at the enemy to allow other units to retreat, and then retreating again. Discipline and training allowed the 2nd Battalion (and other Canadian units caught in the same dilemma) to retreat in the face of such pressure, but later, in an official report, Watson informed Turner and the brigadier's superiors at divisional headquarters that "it was during this retirement that we sustained our heaviest losses" in the entire battle.[21] With the remnants of several battalions now holding the new G.H.Q. position, their location attracted artillery fire, which caused further casualties as the dishevelled infantry tried to dig into the earth to escape its fury.

As damaging as this action was to the units under Turner's command, it had equally serious implications for Currie's forces on the far right. This pullback from the rubble of what had been St. Julien and the surrounding area created a wide gap of 3,000 metres between the two forward brigades, leaving Currie's flank dangerously exposed. Upon realizing that the forces on his left had disappeared—and would soon be replaced by German troops—Currie sent several urgent requests to Turner and his good friend Garnet Hughes to return their forces to the original line. His first communiqués went unanswered, and subsequent ones elicited only terse statements that the 3rd Brigade had no men to spare. A postwar assessment by Canadian official historian A.F. Duguid privately condemned Turner's actions and noted that if the Germans had exploited the gap, they might have "cut off all the troops in the eastern and southern fronts of the Salient."[22]

With no units available to Currie to cover Turner's grievous tactical error, the 2nd Brigade was in a desperate situation. He had no reserves left to plug the gap. At the front, the 5th and 8th Battalions, as well as the motley force at Locality C, were still beating back German attacks, suffering under overwhelmingly heavy shellfire and the aftermath of the gas attack. Currie could take no men from there without weakening this critical anchor. Aware that his forward force would soon be decapitated, Currie prepared to pull back the remaining Canadian battalions, or what was left of them, especially companies of the 5th and 8th Battalions, to Locality C on Gravenstafel Ridge.

In the firing line, the fighting was nearly non-stop. Sergeant William Alexander Alldritt of the 8th Battalion, a thirty-three-year-old former physical director for the YMCA, had been firing his Colt machine gun for nearly three days straight, stopping only when the ammunition ran out or the barrel glowed red hot. He penned his final diary entry on April 24, during one of the short lulls in the pressure: "Germans massing. Frith, dead. Eccles, dead. Robertson and Roberts and Burns of my gun team killed and Hamilton, Flower wounded. Relief did not arrive but reinforcements did. Nearly all of the 3rd Brigade wiped out and both the other brigades lost heavily."[23] Alldritt's position was overrun in wave attacks, and he was captured on the battlefield. In a twist of fate, his mud-stained diary was found by German soldier Richard Hilbert of Dittersdorf, who later forwarded it to Alldritt's family in Winnipeg. It was a tangible legacy of their son's service, even as he languished in a German prison; Alldritt did not return home until the summer of 1919, almost a full five years after he left Canada, and he died at the young age of fifty-two, his constitution weakened permanently from his harsh incarceration.

Pressure was felt all along the front. The Canadians had suffered staggering casualties, the first and second lethal gas attacks in the history of warfare, and rifles that did not work, all the while being vastly outnumbered by conventional enemy forces. Yet key strongpoints of defenders were holding out, drawing upon hidden reserves of willpower and endurance, making the Germans pay for every advance. At the feet of blood-stained infantrymen still firing lay the bodies of the wounded and slain. Most of the survivors had bullet holes through tunics and caps, their water bottles and pieces of kit having been blown away by shrapnel. Almost everyone left alive and still fighting had missed death or maiming by mere inches. Yet they fought on. If only a few reinforcements could be brought forward to stem the tide, the Canadian front might still hold. What was most maddening to Currie was that at least two British battalions were languishing at the G.H.Q. Line preparing for a counterattack to stabilize Turner's front. The attack was cancelled by early afternoon, but still the British refused to move to support Currie and his overextended men.

Having appraised the desperate situation, Currie made the controversial decision to leave his troops and go to the rear to seek out a senior British officer and gain control of these yet uncommitted units. If he did not get reinforcements, he would be forced to pull back, exposing British units on his right flank. He had warned the British of this, but still the high command had not reacted. Again, the delay in transmitting and receiving information hampered the fighting men. While Currie knew that a brigadier's place was not to go running around the battlefield, his battalion commanders had better control of the ever-changing situation than he or his staff. He instructed them to fight it out or retreat to stronger lines depending on the circumstances. G.S. Tuxford of the 5th and L.J. Lipsett of the 8th worked together to ensure that in the case of a fighting retreat the Germans did not wedge them apart. "Our losses were exceptionally heavy," recounted Tuxford. "We were short of S.A.A [small arms ammunition]. We were gassed. We were without rations, and but little water. We had been promised help, which they either would not or could not give us, and for which we felt justly aggrieved."[24] Seemingly abandoned by the troops behind them, it fell to the battalions and companies of the 2nd Brigade to fight it out on their own. They beat back at least five frontal attacks during the day.[25]

CURRIE REALIZED that only a personal appeal from himself would convince the British to commit further troops, and he resolved to make the trip and impress on them the difficult conditions at the front. Advancing back through artillery fire at around 3 P.M., the grim-faced Currie, whose hair was always dapperly parted in the middle but was now a sweaty mess from his alternately running through artillery bombardments and diving into shell craters, reached the headquarters of Major General Thomas Snow of the 27th Division. Snow had a well-deserved reputation as the rudest man in the British army. He seems to have particularly disliked the Canadians, and he had no sympathy for their plight. In fact, he thought them incompetent. Forget the gas or the overwhelming attacks; forget the desperate yet successful counterattacks; forget the fact that Currie's front was now entirely unhinged because of Turner's retreat. Snow refused to consider how to help the Canadians taking the brunt of the fighting.

A dishevelled Currie, eyes bloodshot from the gas, no doubt confirmed every prejudice already carried by Snow. Without any time to collect his thoughts, Currie tersely and professionally reported his situation and asked for reserve units. But the British general would have none of it, belittling Currie's unorthodox action of coming to the rear in person, questioning whether the "colonial" had lost his nerve and abandoned his troops. While Currie must have seemed dispirited as a result of the prolonged fighting and almost three days without sleep, he in fact had a firm understanding of the desperate situation. After he again calmly reiterated the situation, Snow boorishly cut him off, screaming, "Have you come to teach me my profession and dictate to me how I shall handle my Division?"[26] Currie bit his tongue, especially since Snow's only encouragement was to return to the front and "give them hell, give them hell." Currie later noted, rightly, that Snow's admonition was the most "stupid remark" he had ever heard.[27]

Unsoldierly in appearance, Arthur Currie had a sharp mind for war and understood the necessity of careful planning. He would rise to command the Canadian Corps by the summer of 1917.

Currie kept his cool and soon left the dugout, realizing that he was on his own. Major C.H. Mitchell from Canadian Division headquarters ran into Currie after the fiery meeting and remarked on the brigadier's steely resolve to fight it out to the end.[28] Indeed, it appears that Snow, having thoroughly misinterpreted the situation at the front, was the one in desperate need of a rest. Further attesting to Snow's unhinged state, he did in fact release five British battalions to fill the gap between Currie and Turner, but maliciously did not bother to tell Currie. A discouraged Currie left assuming he had failed to convince Snow to release his reserves. However, on his way back to the front, Currie picked up some stragglers in the rear—about 200 men, many suffering from gas poisoning—and led them in a well-disciplined march back into the mouth of hell. Along the way, Currie must have wondered if the British had decided to sacrifice his force in the hope of saving the salient.

Currie's unconventional action had done little to stabilize the front, but it had been the correct path. On this occasion, the former land developer revealed tactical flexibility and open-mindedness that would shine forth further as the war progressed. Yet even Currie had lost control of his forces at times in the battle and had been engaged in a shocking shouting match with one of his junior officers, betraying the pressure under which he, and all officers, laboured.[29]

In contrast to Currie, Turner had reacted poorly to the friction and confusion of battle, and his effective abandonment of St. Julien and Currie's brigade on the far right should have resulted in his being fired. Later on April 24, Turner also went to divisional headquarters to find more troops, as his men were nearly played out. Instead of offering sympathy for the 3rd Brigade's three days of continuous warfare, Alderson was dismayed to learn that Turner's men were on the G.H.Q. Line, and ordered him back to the front to protect Currie's flank. Turner refused, calling it suicide. And at this stage it was. Neither man understood the other's position, and bad feelings developed between the exhausted and frazzled generals. Alderson considered relieving Turner of his duties, but he had no one with whom to replace him. He also realized that the Canadian government might condemn him—or even demand his resignation—if he sacked a Victoria Cross–winning hero who had held out through three days of brutal warfare. A steaming Turner returned to the G.H.Q. Line and bravely rallied his men for one last defence.

On the right flank, with British counterattacks abandoned in the early part of the day, the Germans launched another major operation during the mid-afternoon. Under a withering artillery barrage, Currie's forces at Locality C again held off the German infantry. It was another desperate stand against overwhelming odds, and although the Canadians were outnumbered and outgunned, they refused to break. Dozens, however, were cut down.

"I should not call this war—it is slaughter," wrote a desperate Private Samuel Archer. "I crawled half a mile to get my wounds dressed.... The shells were bursting all around me, and bullets coming in all directions over my head, while the dead were lying everywhere. No matter where you went you could see nothing but dead bodies."[30] Escaping the charnel house was a relief for Archer, but the ever-thinning ranks of the Canadians could not hold on much longer, although they were ably supported by Canadian field guns that had moved forward into range and saturated the enemy front with high explosives and shrapnel.

But the entire Canadian Division—or what was left of it—was in great danger of being split in two by the German advance, which now held St. Julien. With German and Canadian forces jutting into each other's lines, utter confusion reigned over the battlefield as soldiers were shot at from all directions. But the situation did not last long. Late in the day, a British counterattack by Snow's five battalions drove the Germans back along the front, especially those in the gap between the 2nd and 3rd Brigades, allowing time for Currie to extricate his forces from the now overextended and dangerously vulnerable position. Even though the Germans continued to outnumber the British and Canadian troops, they had been fought to a standstill. But it had cost another day of blood and sacrifice, and postwar forensic historians would determine that a shocking 3,058 Canadians were wounded, captured, and killed on April 24.[31] "Imagine Hell in its worst form," wrote Sergeant William Miller. "You may have a slight idea what it was like."[32]

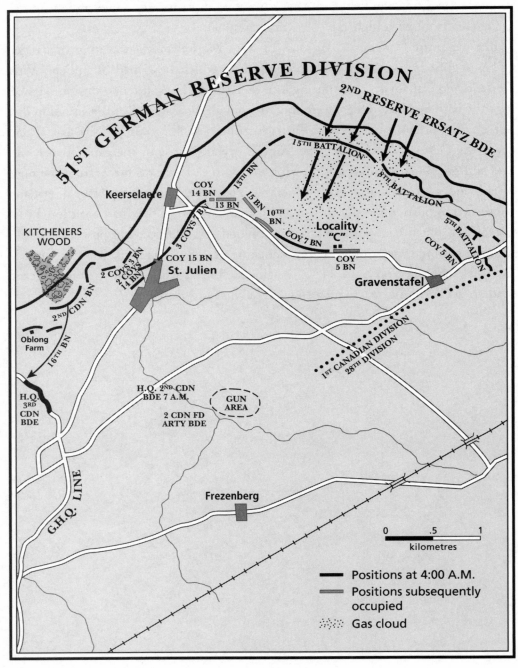

A FIGHTING RETREAT: APRIL 24, 1915, 4:00 A.M. TO 10:00 A.M.

51ST GERMAN RESERVE DIVISION

2ND RESERVE ERSATZ BDE

15TH BATTALION

8TH BATTALION

5TH BATTALION

Keerselaere

COY 14 BN

13TH BN

13 BN

15 BN

10TH BN

Locality "C"

COY 7 BN

COY 5 BN

KITCHENERS WOOD

3 COYS 7 BN

COY 15 BN

St. Julien

2 COYS 3 BN

2 COYS 14 BN

Gravenstafel

2ND CDN BN

Oblong Farm

16TH BN

1ST CANADIAN DIVISION

28TH DIVISION

H.Q. 3RD CDN BDE

H.Q. 2ND CDN BDE 7 A.M.

GUN AREA

2 CDN FD ARTY BDE

G.H.Q. LINE

Frezenberg

| | 0 | .5 | 1 |
kilometres

━━━ Positions at 4:00 A.M.

━━━ Positions subsequently occupied

∴∴∴ Gas cloud

CHAPTER 12

A REPUTATION FORGED

"We must hang on," declared Brigadier Arthur Currie to his troops.[1] The tenacity of most Canadian infantrymen was never in doubt, even though they had suffered crippling casualties. And throughout April 25, exhausted and battered beyond recognition, they continued to endure shellfire and repel attacks. German officer Rudolf Binding, who fought in one of the forward assault battalions, described the condition of the stubborn Canadian defenders who sacrificed their lives to hold the line: "A sleeping army lies in front of one of our brigades, they rest in good order, man by man, and will never wake again—Canadian divisions. The enemy's losses are enormous."[2]

With British and French reinforcements finally arriving in larger numbers on the fourth day of the battle, the remains of the Canadian battalions were systematically relieved throughout April 25. Before this relief arrived, however, several Canadian units—especially what was left of the 5th, 7th, 8th, and 10th Battalions—were driven out of their trenches, and finally out of the strongpoint at Locality C. These battalions had retired in the face of enormous pressure, but they did so in disciplined retreats, the remains of platoons and sections supporting one another with concentrated fire. Equally common was the banding together of fragments of former units into informal battle groups after battalions and companies were effectively destroyed by massive casualties to the officer corps and the rank and file. Within this chaos, the Canadians continued to remain an effective fighting force. Perhaps the independent spirit that had got many of the Canadians into trouble in England was revealing itself again on the battlefield, and these now fire-hardened veterans realized that they did not require officers to corral them to fight for their very lives. This tactical improvisation would remain a staple among the Canadian fighting forces for the next three and a half years of war.

In several engagements on April 25, the pursuing Germans thought the Canadians were routed, but each time they tried to close the gap they were met with heavy rifle fire. These were the final enemy pushes against the Canadians, most of whom were relieved by the end of the day. Survivors dragged themselves to the rear, exhausted after going some eighty-five hours without sleep and almost as long without adequate water and food. Many of the men suffered terribly, hacking through gassed lungs, while others stared blankly, faces covered with days of stubble, black from sweat and dirt, bloodshot eyes revealing unspoken horrors. "Our losses were terrible, and the sights I saw I shall never forget," wrote twenty-nine-year-old Private Percy Kingsley of Humboldt, Saskatchewan.[3]

Some of the survivors never recovered from their ordeal and were sent home, either with shattered minds or corrupted lungs. The 1,410 captured as prisoners would begin a new punishing war of survival behind barbed wire; almost half of the prisoners had been wounded, and eighty-seven would die of their wounds in captivity.[4] Frederick Fraser of the 8th Battalion recounted how, while he lay wounded in a makeshift hospital, the position was captured and the enemy infantry bayoneted all the Canadian prisoners who could not walk to the rear.[5] But not all captured men were brutalized. Lieutenant Clyde Scott had been shot and left for dead, his near-lifeless body thrown on a pile of corpses. Back home, his parents were informed of his death and held a memorial service in Perth, Ontario, his mother receiving a Silver Cross medal to mark her son's sacrifice. But a curious dog found him in the heap of bodies, and a sympathetic German soldier carried him to a doctor, where he was subsequently operated on and saved. Although crippled for life, he would return home, marry, and have a daughter, Barbara Ann, a future Olympic gold medal skater.[6]

Engaged in fighting retreats across the front, many Canadians felt guilty about leaving behind the wounded, and more than a few believed that they had abandoned men to execution.[7] Others volunteered or were ordered to act as a hopeless rearguard force to enable their companions to survive. Private G.D. Scott of the 7th Battalion had been part of one such small reserve force that went into combat on April 24. "It was like throwing a cup of water on a burning house, for our two sections amounted to twenty-eight men in all." During the fighting, Scott was wounded in the side, and many of his friends were killed around him. Their surviving officer used a bloody bandage as a white flag. Only ten men were left alive at the time of their surrender. For this little group of "dazed and stupefied" survivors, the fighting was over, but captivity would last another forty-four months.[8] While some captured Canadians were undoubtedly killed on the battlefield, most were taken prisoner and survived their harrowing trip to the enemy's rear.

The most influential atrocity story at the time was the supposed crucifixion of a Canadian soldier to a barn door, bayonets through hands and feet. The story became a powerful legend, and while many Canadians claimed to have seen the crucified Canadian, all told different versions of what had happened. Investigators were later unable to find corroborating stories, and many witnesses recanted under interrogation, admitting that they had not actually seen the crucified soldier but had been told about him by trusted sources.[9] Where this supposed crucifixion would have taken place—especially since the Canadian lines constricted during the battle (thus leaving all witnesses presumably behind German lines)—bothered few survivors in retelling the story with much venom. The Christ-like image of the executed Canadian reinforced the importance of crusading against such an inhumane enemy. The story struck a chord, being widely believed in the Canadian forces and passed on to reinforcements. It was also employed as a justification by some to show no mercy to the Hun in future battles. The only way to deal with a German foe that used poison gas to exterminate men and that crucified prisoners, opined Barlow Whiteside, a graduate of McGill University, was to "exterminate" them.[10]

THE SAVAGERY OF BATTLE was a terrible shock for the infantrymen who took the brunt of the fighting. "I have often wanted to see a fight, and now I have done so, I don't want any more," recounted one survivor. "I think of all the awful sights … of all the dead and dying lying all about in contorted shapes.… That sight, combined with the cries of the wounded during the night, I shall never forget."[11] Some simply could not believe they had survived: John Matheson wrote home to

Medicine Hat, Alberta, "With the exception of being hit by a rifle bullet on the cheek and a piece of shrapnel in the side, I am still for it.... I have bullet holes in my hat, equipment and clothes, but evidently I am slated to do some more evil in this world yet."[12] Many of the hard men who had withstood the horror of war wept openly when roll call was sounded off after the battle, the voices of sergeants and lieutenants cracking as name after name was called out and met only with silence. In less than a week, the first major Canadian battle claimed half of the infantrymen who had trained together for more than six months.

During those four days of relentless fighting, the infantry battalions had held on, as Lieutenant Colonel George Tuxford recounted, with "nothing more than a handful of disorganized men, sticking it out, having practically no orders, out of touch, and not knowing anything about the situation, nor knowing what to do or where to go, and ready to attach themselves to any definite authority that turned up."[13] When the Second Battle of Ypres degenerated into hundreds of miniature battles, the Canadians kept fighting long past the endurance point in ad-hoc combat groups that were sometimes a few dozen men and sometimes only a few mates watching each other's back.

Despite some awkward failures to properly situate the artillery to support the infantry, the gunners had provided devastating defensive fire on April 23 and 24, often shattering enemy counterattacks. The eighteen guns of the 2nd Canadian Field Artillery Brigade had fired some 12,000 rounds on the second and third day of battle, monumental figures by the standards of 1915.[14] The drivers, horses, and mules that hauled ammunition forward throughout the battle had also played an essential, if forgotten, role in ensuring that the Canadians were not overrun for lack of ammunition.

Although most of the Canadian units had performed beyond all expectation, mistakes had been made. Both Currie and Turner were fortunate not to have been part of a British division, as Turner's miscalculation in pulling back his troops and Currie's unorthodox action of leaving his troops and going to British headquarters himself would likely have resulted in their dismissal. Indeed, Alderson did consider removing Turner from command but felt that his political connections were too strong. Yet Alderson, too, had shown little brilliance. While communication to his divisional headquarters was cut repeatedly, and he sent forward officers to determine what was happening, the desperate situation surely demanded that he move parts or all of his divisional command forward to lessen the distance from front to rear. J.S. "Buster" Brown, a staff officer during the war, and often remembered for planning a possible invasion of the United States in the 1920s, wrote: "I firmly believe that ... we should not conceal any defects—for we had every right to have defects at that time."[15] Instead of finding scapegoats, however, Alderson turned his attention to the heavy losses of men and officers, and focused on rebuilding the combat effectiveness of units with reinforcements from England.

ALTHOUGH FAILURES HAD OCCURRED during the battle, these should in no way overshadow the resilient Canadian defence against nearly overwhelming odds. The inexperienced Canadian troops, who had only recently apprenticed with the British, had shown their mettle in the cauldron of fire and gas. And while the Germans had never planned to push on to the Channel ports, they might have been able to envelop the 50,000 Entente troops in the salient if the Canadians had not held firm. Such a result would have been a disaster of monumental proportions, and the War Office did not exaggerate its praise when it announced: "The Canadians had many casualties but their gallantry and determination undoubtedly saved the situation."[16] Further, more than a few Germans spoke grudgingly of the "tenacious determination" of the Dominion troops.[17] Undeniably, the division's first battle had been a bloody one, but the Canadians had earned a name for themselves as unyielding soldiers.

The Second Ypres survivors carried the honour of their outstanding performance in the battle like a badge. The level of Canadian casualties had been shocking, at more than 6,000 almost evenly divided among the three infantry brigades, and a few hundred more from the artillery and the units along the lines of communication. In the front lines, the Canadians lost almost fifty percent of their infantry strength.

Poison gas had shocked, frightened, and angered the Entente forces, but conventional weapons—small-arms fire, high explosives, and shrapnel—killed in far greater numbers. The 15th Battalion was devastated, losing some 675 men, effectively destroying it; the 2nd and 7th lost 541 and 580 men respectively; five other battalions suffered more than 400 casualties; and no battalion suffered fewer than 250 casualties. Three Canadian battalion commanders had been killed while leading from the front, and a fourth, Lieutenant Colonel John Currie of the 15th Battalion, was sent home. The remaining eight survivors would rise through the ranks, and every officer who became divisional commander in the coming four years had fought through the Second Battle of Ypres. In fact, so too had most of the brigadiers. At lower levels, many junior officers and NCOs who had survived the fighting would rise to command battalions. Over the next three and a half years of battle, Second Ypres veterans would go on to fill most of the senior command positions in the Canadian Corps.

While much of the recognition and glory in the battle went to the commanding officers (as well as some derision to Turner and Currie), the credit for the Canadians' victory (or perhaps more accurately their absence of defeat) must go to the infantry. Time and time again it had been the infantry in the front lines fighting it out against overwhelming odds, often pressured from two or three sides, and dealing with a host of problems, from poor command to lack of food and water, from chlorine gas to jammed Ross rifles. It had been the infantry—those men who many Imperials felt did not have the discipline or the military skills to yet survive on the battlefield— who had shown unshakable resilience in keeping the enemy from cutting off the salient and dealing a crushing blow to the Entente war effort.

Success at Ypres had not been a result of commanders' actions but of those of the soldiers in the firing line. After the first day, it had fallen to the junior officers— majors, captains, and lieutenants—to direct the shifting, confusing defence that often had to be improvised on the spot. Command further devolved to senior non-commissioned officers, and both NCOs and officers depended on resolute bands of privates holding out against impossible odds. The Canadians learned very early in their war service that control could not be exerted through the lieutenant colonels or brigadiers, and that junior officers would need to be empowered to command from the front, as they were the only ones who could direct a battle when all communication was cut from front to rear. This was a hard lesson to accept in the hierarchical context of the army, but a necessary one if formations were to remain effective on the Western Front after heavy casualties.

THE BRITISH AND FRENCH continued to fight in the salient on and off until May 25. The British lost almost 60,000 men, and the Germans admitted to 34,873 casualties, although likely another 8,000 or so lightly wounded German soldiers were not counted.[18] This was one of the few points during the war when defenders lost more men than attackers, although this unusual loss rate could no doubt be attributed to the unleashing of half a dozen additional gas attacks and the overwhelming German artillery fire. Rudimentary respirators and concentrated defensive artillery fire ensured that the British forces blunted these chemical attacks, but they paid a harsh price. While this chemical "frightfulness" did not live up to the claims by some hysterics during the dark days after April 22 that gas would be a "war-winning" weapon, gas would be used increasingly by all armies in the coming years of the war, reaching a saturation point in the last eighteen months of combat, during which every battlefield on the Western Front was blanketed in chemicals and soldiers were forced to fight through the only continuous gas environment in the history of warfare.[19]

In the northern salient, the casualty rates had spiked from the first minutes of the battle, then throughout the day, and then day after day. First the French and Algerians, then the Canadians, then the British were brought in on bloodied stretchers, in the arms of comrades, or dragging themselves back on shattered limbs. The stretcher-bearers and orderlies tried to care for the wounded and apply rough bandages, but hundreds of wounded, bloodied men needed emergency battlefield surgery. Arms red in blood, John McCrae, the medical officer of the 1st Brigade, Canadian Field Artillery, recounted it as "seventeen days of Hades."[20] In a brief respite from the cries of pain and grisly work among shattered bones and lacerated flesh, and moved by the death of his friend Alexis Harmer, McCrae sat outside his dugout and scratched a fifteen-line poem in almost as many minutes: "In Flanders fields the poppies blow / Between the crosses, row on row ..." And so was penned the most memorable poem of the war. It spoke to the tragedy and loss of war, but more importantly it was a clarion call for steely resolve. "Take up the quarrel with the foe / To you from failing hands we throw / The torch; be yours to hold it high. / If ye break faith with us who die / We shall not sleep, though poppies grow / In Flanders fields."

THE CANADIAN DIVISION had suffered a terrible blow, and the shock of war was even more difficult to fathom for those at home, who took great pride in the stalwart defence and were then blindsided by row upon row of the names of the dead and wounded. Despite the overwhelming enemy guns, troops, and use of chemical weapons, the Canadians had fought on, refusing to be broken. And they would continue to fight. As McCrae demanded, they would not break faith with those who were killed in the Ypres salient.

THE SALIENT: APRIL 22 TO MAY 4, 1915

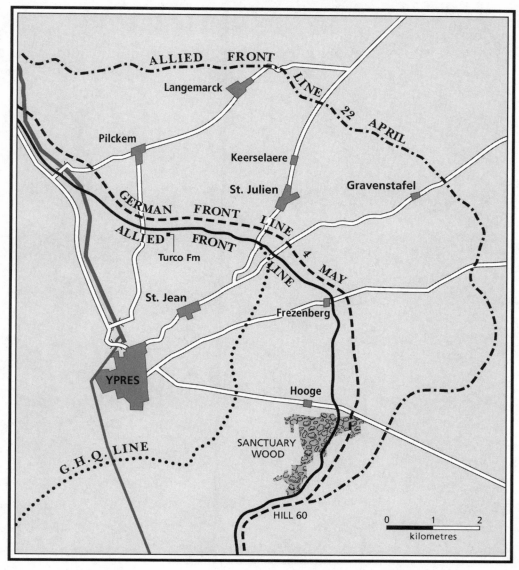

ALLIED FRONT LINE 22 APRIL

Langemarck

Pilckem

Keerselaere

St. Julien

Gravenstafel

GERMAN FRONT LINE

ALLIED FRONT LINE

Turco Fm

4 MAY

St. Jean

Frezenberg

YPRES

Hooge

G.H.Q. LINE

SANCTUARY WOOD

HILL 60

0   1   2
kilometres

CHAPTER 13

INTO THE MAELSTROM

Festubert, May 1915

"Hard fighting and a damned lot of it," was Sir John Colborne's explanation for his rise through the ranks in Lord Wellington's army in the previous century's great war between the European Powers.[1] With his superiors killed off or maimed, or promoted to fill the ranks of others above them, Colborne had shown his competence and had also risen through the ranks. A hundred years later, a similar situation had developed in the First Contingent, which had now lost a third of its force and a little less than half of its infantry. New leaders rose to replace the fallen, knowing there would be a "damned lot" of hard fighting in the near future.

After the devastating trial by fire at Ypres, the survivors marched south, some of them wearing uniforms cut to rags by bullets and shrapnel, while most were missing key parts of their kit that had been abandoned on the battlefield. Many were suffering from shell shock or the effects of gas poisoning. Men fell out of formation during the march to lie down by the side of the road. A few were even reported to have succumbed to their gas wounds after the arduous and, some complained, callous, march. The telegrams of congratulations that flowed into the Canadian Division headquarters from throughout the army and Empire were of little consolation to men who had seen their best friends torn apart during a week of gut-wrenching fighting.

By the beginning of May, however, the men of the Canadian Division began to recover "from the strain and fatigue of the last two weeks" through participation in sports, light drill, and inspections.[2] New clothing was issued, along with early generations of respirators to protect against poison gas. The first of these—cotton pads that were fastened around the mouth and nose after being wetted—had been sent from England by patriotic women who formed sewing groups to meet the army's desperate pleas for protection. But citizens at home also demanded revenge, and soon the British were organizing their own offensive chemical warfare companies. In the meantime, the newspapers and propagandists took every opportunity to remind the public of the Hunnish barbarity.

Reinforcements were also called up and rushed across the Channel to be integrated into the mangled Canadian forces. Four battalions had lost their commanding officers, and hundreds of experienced and trusted officers and NCOs had been killed or wounded. Thousands arrived from England, and many of the units that had considered themselves homogeneous to a certain region of Canada soon found men from across the Dominion in their ranks. To fill the gaps at the higher echelon, a number of sergeants and corporals who had proven their mettle during the Ypres battle were commissioned as officers, while new lieutenants and captains coming from England attempted to find their place among these bloodied veterans.[3] Jack Pinson, a raw recruit for the 7th Battalion, remembered, "We were all goggle-eyed looking at these old-timers who had been there about two months before us."[4] But with another British offensive looming, these new men would soon have a chance to prove themselves, or die trying, at Festubert on the La Bassée front.

THE BATTLE OF FESTUBERT was fought by the British First Army against the German Sixth Army from May 15 to 27, 1915, as part of French commander-in-chief Joseph Joffre's Artois Offensive, which started on May 9 while the British Second Army was still battling in the Ypres salient. On that day, the French launched a twenty-one-division offensive against Vimy Ridge and the high ground around Notre Dame de Lorette. They almost captured the enemy strongpoint on Vimy Ridge, overlooking the French lines—before being hurled back into the mud by German counterattacks. Despite these setbacks, Joffre continued to stoically throw his troops against formidable positions, even though each time they were chewed up by the enemy's guns. Total French casualties numbered around 100,000, a sacrifice that made no appreciable gains around Notre Dame de Lorette and Vimy Ridge, while the Germans lost about three-quarters of that number in trying to deny their enemy the ground.

To support the French, the British First Army also attacked the enemy strong-point around Aubers Ridge. However, like the French offensive, it failed, and eight divisions suffered almost 12,000 casualties.[5] This and previous offensives along the Western Front had demonstrated that German defences were sound, as they forti-fied their positions and held the trenches strongly. The French and British armies lacked sufficient artillery shells to shatter the enemy positions, but they were unwilling to sit in their muddy ditches waiting for the Royal Navy blockade to slowly strangle Germany. This naval strategy might eventually force a cessation of hostilities (assuming the German submarine counteroffensive did not defeat the surface ships), but no one could be certain that the Germans would be forced to turn over all of their newly captured territory. Not only were the occupiers holding Belgian and French civilians against their will—and often brutalizing them—but France had lost fifty-five percent of its coal resources, seventy percent of its steel production facilities, and eighty percent of its iron ore and iron production indus-try.[6] With the French continuing to dictate the strategic priorities of the Entente, and demanding the return of their country, the British and French forces would keep strong pressure on the Western Front and dig the enemy forces out of their occupied positions at the point of a bayonet. However, as Canadian infantryman H.R. Alley noted grimly, "All through 1915 you were on a shoe string and a pretty frayed shoe string at that."[7] The Entente never had enough high explosive shells to blast their way through the strong German defences, let alone the communication tools to coordinate attacks over wide fronts.

The British portion of the offensive was waged against Aubers Ridge, which ran 1.5 kilometres northeastward behind the German front line, about 35 kilometres south of the Ypres salient. This operation was also launched to relieve pressure on the Ypres front by drawing away enemy reinforcements and guns. As in the Ypres salient, which was overlooked by Passchendaele Ridge to the east, Aubers Ridge offered enemy forward artillery observers an advantage over the infantry spread out below them. They called in fire orders, observing the fall of rounds and correcting them to target forming-up areas, trenches, and essential roads. But the British were not defenceless. In grouping their forces for an attack, they had a significant advantage in their number of troops and guns. Aware that a hurried assault would only leave their infantry hanging on the barbed wire, First Army Commander General Douglas Haig planned for a slow, methodical destruction of the German lines, which were so heavily fortified as to include concrete bunkers housing machine guns.

Haig, a dour Scotsman who had risen to command one of Britain's two armies, and who within the year would take over the entire BEF, had never been known for his intelligence. He had barely made it through staff college—often relying on friends for answers—but he did understand warfare, and was far more competent than his legion of critics have assessed over the years. More than a simple-minded cavalryman, Haig actively studied the problems of modern warfare and even wrote a prewar tactical manual, no mean feat for a man whom many considered illiterate. Haig's deep spirituality gave him a sense of certainty that helped him to deal with the stress of command, even if he and his troops might have been better off had he suffered more pangs of doubt. However, he had learned the practical lessons of the 1914 fighting, during which attacking troops that had been shattered by dug-in defenders required the support of larger, more devastating artillery bombardments.

Like all senior officers, Haig was stymied by the unprecedented stalemate on the Western Front, where enemy forces held all the advantages: ground of their choosing, barbed wire that was difficult to cut and that therefore channelled attackers into kill grounds to be mowed down by machine-gunners who barely had to aim, and defenders who could rest relatively safely behind sandbag walls while their attackers were forced to run and stumble forward over shell-cratered fields.

In the past, the armies would have tried to manoeuvre around strongpoints like Aubers Ridge, but at this point, the British and Canadian forces had nowhere else to go on the Western Front. The entire war had become an enormous siege, except that the enemy could not be starved out of their position, as their rear area was largely untouchable, allowing the free movement of men, munitions, and food to the garrison troops in the German forward trench system. Every attack was a frontal attack. Aware that both the French and Germans had often been annihilated in such plunge-ahead offensives in 1914 and early 1915, Haig believed that artillery would help to even the odds. The guns would smash the enemy defences and allow the infantry to cross the killing ground before punching through to the other side. Through this hacked-open gap, the cavalry would push through, wreaking havoc on the enemy's lines of communication and logistical areas, and eventually collapsing the entire front. The siege lines would be broken and the British would harass the broken enemy armies back into Germany, if they did not surrender first.

Haig and his commanders were right in relying on the artillery, but they did not yet have enough guns or shells, or gunners with sufficient tactical skills to hit small targets from several kilometres away. Guns firing in an indirect role—from behind cover—were very hard to hit, as they could not be seen and the interaction between gunners and reconnaissance planes was in its infancy. The German situation was no better, one doctrinal order noting, "It is of no use firing with field guns against artillery in position behind cover: this is merely a waste of ammunition."[8] Only the heavier guns could hit these targets, and they were in short supply. Furthermore, both sides suffered from technical limitations: the fuses that detonated the shells were fragile pieces of machinery and were difficult to mass-produce. Throughout 1915, the fuses were often not sensitive enough to detonate a shell on its contact with barbed wire, and so the shells did not explode until they were in the ground, thereby reducing their effectiveness. Shellfire was one of the components essential to achieving tactical victory, but it was far from perfected.

Heavy British howitzers and field guns blasted the German front with more than 100,000 shells during the sixty-hour bombardment before zero hour when the troops would attack.[9] This was an almost unbelievable weight of fire, and Haig and his officers could perhaps be excused for thinking that now, finally, a breakthrough might be achieved. The attack, to the east of the village of Festubert, was launched at night on May 15 by two British and Indian divisions, followed by a third the next morning.

Haig's forces advanced on an 800-metre front. Not only was the strength of the artillery barrage unprecedented but the British attacked at night for an added surprise. Unfortunately, the inherent confusion of moving thousands of men through cratered, uneven terrain in darkness nearly negated the element of surprise, and the Germans were soon alerted to the advancing troops. But the British had some success and captured the enemy front lines, even beating back counterattacks. In response, the Germans retreated to a new, prepared line, 2,700 metres to the east. It was a wise decision and proved that the Germans were willing to trade useless land for time and space.

The British high command saw the German retreat as a sign that the enemy's armies were disintegrating. The British were infused with a belief in the sanctity of ground and an unwillingness to ever give up an inch to the enemy. Any retreat on the part of their enemy was viewed through that lens. They therefore pressed the attack, Haig calling on General Alderson's Canadian Division to be ready to exploit success.

ELEMENTS OF THE 2ND and 3rd Canadian Infantry Brigades had been moved into the reserve lines on the night of May 15, but they had not been engaged in the fighting. From May 15 to 17, the artillery thundered, but the Canadian infantry were left with tightened stomachs as they waited for the order to enter into battle. Amidst the confusion and the crumbling British attack, the second phase was delayed time and time again. The soldiers suffered under the stress of the unknown.

By May 17, a steady drizzle had turned into rain, and the battlefield, already chewed up by artillery fire, was reduced to a quagmire. This was ideal ground for the defending German forces. As at Ypres, the water table was high and much of the natural drainage had been destroyed by artillery fire. The ground was now a morass of mud, with the water-filled craters, ditches, and streams that crisscrossed the broken expanse making parts of the battlefield nearly impassable. Years of farming in the area had also taken down most of the trees and created a relatively flat ground that allowed defenders broad and uninterrupted fields of fire.

Word that an attack would go ahead finally came on the night of May 17. But orders from corps headquarters were late, and the British and Canadian preliminary bombardment was working over the German lines even as Brigadier Richard Turner briefed his battalion commanders on the impending operation. His words were not inspiring. Most of the tactical intelligence was "little more than guesses; the only course ... to go ahead and make the best of the situation."[10] As at Ypres, however, this would be a battle in which the brigadier would have little control, and any hope of driving home the attack would rest instead with the battalion commanders and even individual company and platoon officers.

Four companies from the 14th and 16th Battalions were to attack in broad daylight on May 18 as part of a larger British offensive. The plan had an air of unreality, as it had been set by staff officers and commanders in the rear who had not surveyed the battlefield. The Canadians were to capture a series of trenches, culminating in the Orchard, a key enemy strongpoint. The operation involved the close coordination of several battalions and companies that were to support one another, or guard open flanks, but no mechanism was in place to allow for communication between British and Canadian units. Worse was yet to come.

The maps provided to the troops were completely inaccurate, off by several hundred metres, and, unbelievably, printed geographically backwards and upside down (with south at the top, east on the left). Some officers resorted to trying to read them as reflected in a mirror and all found them nearly impossible to memorize.[11] The numbers printed on the maps, denoting enemy positions such as M6, meant nothing to anyone, and no distinction was made among a hedge, ditch, or track. Heavy artillery bombardments had also obliterated many of the landmarks, further rendering the maps useless.

As well as these "cartographic monstrosities," as Captain A.F. Duguid, an artillery staff officer with the Canadians, described them, the infantry was not trusted with additional information that might have been useful to them in preparing for battle. Lieutenant Alexander Macphail accused senior officers of hoarding information, stating that the men "were sedulously prevented from knowing anything that was going on."[12] This secrecy was no doubt a misguided attempt by senior officers to control the battle and compartmentalize the fighting units, but it showed a shocking lack of trust in subordinate officers who would, as Ypres proved, end up making most of the command decisions at the front—often under shellfire and cut off from the rear. Without proper information, the battle amounted to soldiers blindly stumbling forward in a frontal assault against dug-in German defenders in broad daylight.

As the minutes ticked down towards the 5 P.M. zero hour, the four companies of front-line troops tensed as their artillery built to a final crescendo. The 18-pounders fired at a low trajectory to clear the wire, and the passing of shells just above the heads of the troops was nerve-rattling. Alerted by the British barrage, which was heavier than normal, the observant Germans guessed that an attack was in store, and not only rushed reinforcements forward but called down heavier artillery fire of their own. Soon, there seemed to be more German shells falling than British ones.

Officers of the 14th Battalion recognized the futility of the operation but had little recourse. They ordered the troops to thin out to five paces between men, and to advance in four skirmish lines of about 200 metres in depth.[13] As per the accepted attack doctrine of the time, the artillery fire was to stop at 5 P.M., just when the infantry was to go over the top. The shelling stopped because most gunners felt that they could not guarantee the safety of their own troops while firing over their heads. All hoped that the enemy's defences were shattered. This was the doctrine of fire preceding movement, as opposed to combining fire and movement that would be introduced a year later.

As the Canadian attackers prepared to leave their trenches at zero hour, they found the barrage still pounding the enemy lines after the 5 P.M. set time for them to go over the top. Confused, the Canadian attackers could not leave their trenches to advance into their own barrage, and were forced to wait for it to stop. This mix-up was due to faulty communication from front to rear, and among the various arms, primarily the infantry and the artillery. Unfortunately, to the north, British troops of the Guards Brigade went over when they were ordered, and many German defenders on the Canadian front fired into their exposed flank of the unfortunate Guards—who also had uncut wire and undestroyed machine guns on their own enemy front to worry about as they moved forward. Worse, the Guards' action brought the Germans out of their trenches. The desultory artillery fire from the Canadian and British gunners did almost nothing to suppress the enemy fire, and when the barrage petered off about twenty-five minutes later, the Canadians realized that if they moved forward, they would be mounting a frontal assault against enemy forces positions that were clearly still manned in strength. Canadian officers were left with a terrible choice: order an advance into likely slaughter, or stay in the relative safety of the trenches but leave the British to the north abandoned and—not knowing if the Guards had succeeded or failed—vulnerable to a counterattack from the enemy forces on the Canadian front. One cannot imagine the terrible tension building among officers who stared uncomprehendingly at each other, weighing such options.

The Canadians would go. In those final seconds as the last shells were fired, the battlefield took on a strange silence, broken by the whistles of the officers urging their men over the top. As the first waves of the 14th and 16th Battalions emerged from their trenches and spilled out into No Man's Land, they were immediately met by German rifle and machine-gun fire. With metal tearing through their ranks, the advance companies fanned out and moved forward, but in the confusion and while traversing over broken ground, the waves began to drift into one another, causing an intermingling of forces.[14] These were not parade-ground conditions and the advance was not pretty; the bunching up of troops—a common occurrence among men under fire who instinctively group together for protection—made them easier targets.

Despite the terrible enemy fire, the Canadians drove forward, overrunning a series of German trenches about 400 metres from their start line. Private Romeo Heule of the 14th Battalion recounted, "A bayonet charge is a street fight magnified and made ten thousand times more fierce."[15] While the Canadians cleared a few trenches with bayonet and bullet at close range, this outer crust was only held lightly, most of the defenders having already pulled back to secondary, strongly fortified defences.

Having crashed through this first line, the Canadians were beset by confusion. Officers found it hard to get the rank and file to move out of their new trenches and forward again into the lethal killing ground that needed to be crossed before the Canadians could close with the main body of German defenders. Commanding B Company of the 14th Battalion, Major Allan Shaw—a former insurance broker who had put in a decade and a half of militia service and had fought in the South African War—rallied his troops even though he had been shot in the head. He was killed by a second bullet while reconnoitring the front in an attempt to push through a soft spot in the enemy line. No such openings were to be found.

With their ranks decimated and officers wounded, few men knew where to go for their secondary objectives. Follow-on forces and the two battalion commanders even further back had little evidence of how the battle was unfolding. The first runner to arrive, however, was not encouraging. Weaving his way to the rear, exhausted and caked in mud, he stammered out a message: "The Canadians are all blown to hell; there is terrible murder up there."[16] This news did not help much since the situation was beyond dire, but if the message lacked detail, its sentiment was very clear.

Under heavy artillery fire and a driving rain, the exhausted, soaked, and cold infantry sought safety by shovelling deeper into the dissolving trenches, heaving liquid mud over the parapet. Of the enemy's fire, C.J. Johnson of the 14th Battalion remarked, "They had the range right down to a science." The Germans shelled the front all day and into the night, only stopping at around 2 A.M.[17] The historian of the German 57th Infantry Regiment, the unit that defended against the attack, noted that the Canadians "encountered such an effective barrage that the attack collapsed after a few minutes."[18] The Canadian and British artillery did little to respond to this overwhelming bombardment, or to the nearly uninterrupted fire from Maxim machine guns and Mauser rifles, as they were too far back and few forward observers were in place to guide artillery fire. Without adequate forward observers or a robust communication system, and with the small divisional staff overwhelmed after having taken control of the artillery batteries from three other divisions, the artillery guns in the rear could not correct the fall of their shells, or even respond to the ever-changing situation at the front. Canadian flesh was pitted against German steel.

Front-line units were situated in a nightmare landscape of charred tree stumps and pulpy ground. But it was the torn and bloody corpses that gave the field its horrific quality. Men had been mowed down in straight lines by machine guns; others were hanging on the barbed wire like bizarre scarecrows. Slain men littered the battlefield—new Canadian corpses and older, decaying British and German ones. The smell of rotting flesh and fresh blood was overpowering. Detached body parts littered the area: a shredded torso in a shell hole, a bloody stump of a leg still wearing puttee and boot. The Canadians captured half a kilometre of French field and, in the military vernacular of the time, "straightened out the line" to ensure that the Germans were not able to drive a wedge into the British positions, but they did so at a terrible cost.

After the punishing shellfire stopped, Brigadier Turner ordered reserve troops to support the 14th and 16th, which were now overextended and vulnerable. But the infantry moving into the nightmare landscape well understood their limited chances on the battlefield. Private Charles Pearce of the kilted 13th Battalion wrote a final letter to his "dear mother." He had enlisted with his best friend, Dick, in Belleville against his mom's wishes. In the letter he handed to Dick should he be killed, he penned, "while I hope to live to come back home I pray more that God will give me strength to fight the good fight.... I hope that it will be comforting to you to know that I feel that happen what may I have achieved one great good in giving my life for others."[19] Pearce survived the battle uninjured despite continual harrowing journeys back and forth carrying wounded soldiers to the advanced medical dressing stations. His friend Dick was not so lucky: he was shot in the mouth, the bullet ricocheting up and out through his right eye, shattering his facial bones. His war was over after less than a month at the front, although he did survive. While Dick eventually returned home, Pearce never did: he was shot down to his death in an aircraft over the Somme after transferring to the Royal Flying Corps to escape the slaughter on the ground.

The Germans were content to let the Canadians wallow in the mud under their heavy shellfire, aware that several hundred metres of No Man's Land still separated their forces. The overextended Canadians suffered as supplies were mired in the rear, with all ground in between raked with fire. Most of the exhausted soldiers were now out of water and food. The brackish, fetid water that pooled in shell craters was strained through handkerchiefs and gagged down for momentary relief of thirst. One infantryman wrote of his section's desperation: "I crawled back on the first night and got some water from a shell hole to make tea. We boiled it and enjoyed our hot drink. Next morning I went back to the same shell hole and was about to fill my tin when I saw the dead face of a German soldier looking up at me through the water."[20] Under such conditions, most Canadians decided to go thirsty.

AS DAY BROKE on May 19, the new Canadian trenches were in full view of German snipers and gunners. With shrapnel air-bursts raining jagged metal and whirling ball-bearings down on their soft-capped heads, the infantry became one with the earth, hugging trench walls and trying to keep out of sight. But most of the trenches had been built in haste, in the dark, and without much planning, and this haphazard construction allowed some of the German snipers to worm their way into deadly positions on the flanks. They fired into the Canadian lines, many of which did not run parallel to the enemy front. Men died all day long. The occasional brave or frustrated Canadian infantryman fired off a few snap shots from his Ross rifle, but as at Ypres, the flawed weapon continued to malfunction and jam. Soldiers risked their lives to crawl around, rooting through British corpses in the hope of securing a Lee-Enfield.

With new troops coming to the front, the Germans realized that the failed British offensive was being prolonged, so they further reinforced the sector. The veteran 2nd Guards Reserve Division was one of the new units sent up to the German front, and their line remained strongly held. In fact, it was the Canadians who were more vulnerable after their attack. The shellfire fell all day, and the Dominion infantry-men caught in these new, weak positions could do almost nothing to respond to their tormentors. Trooper T.L. Golden of Lord Strathcona's Horse, a unit then in reserve, wrote of the shelling: "You hear it coming as a dull moan, then it gradually develops into a weird whistle, then a shriek and the earth rocks under you; you are covered with mud and earth and you are glad you are alive. Simultaneously with the bursting of a shell comes the cries and the moans of the wounded. When you are exposed to this for quite a while it gets rather nerve-racking."[21] Such phlegmatic understatements helped these trench warriors deal with the nearly unbearable strain of battle, which would only get worse.

THE BATTLE OF FESTUBERT: MAY 15 TO 21, 1915

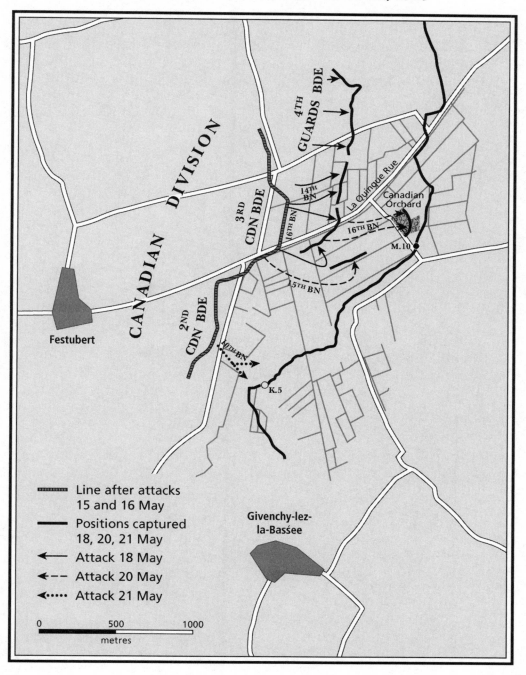

4TH GUARDS BDE

CANADIAN DIVISION

3RD CDN BDE

14TH BN

16TH BN

La Quinque Rue

Canadian Orchard

16TH BN

M.10

15TH BN

2ND CDN BDE

10TH BN

K.5

Festubert

Givenchy-lez-la-Basśee

Line after attacks 15 and 16 May

Positions captured 18, 20, 21 May

Attack 18 May

Attack 20 May

Attack 21 May

0   500   1000

metres

CHAPTER 14

"THIS IS NOT WAR, IT IS SIMPLY MURDER"

The Attack on Canadian Orchard and K.5

Hundreds of Canadian corpses and wounded men lay uncleared on the battlefield, the survivors digging in under life- and limb-shattering fire. In the rear, First Army headquarters ordered another attack for May 20. It was set for 7:45 P.M., just as the sky would slip into dusk, but again without the cover of darkness. Brigadier Richard Turner and Lieutenant Colonel R.G. Leckie of the 16th Battalion could scarcely believe their orders. It had already been proven that sending forward troops against prepared defences in the light of day was akin to suicide. Turner wrote to Alderson's headquarters to ask for a later start time, suggesting a night attack at 10:15 P.M. When he received no reply, the desperate brigadier even went to divisional head-quarters to see Alderson in person. The general refused to meet him, but Turner confronted senior staff officer Lieutenant Colonel G.C. Gordon-Hall, stating that he had crawled forward through the muck and surveyed the ground, and that his battalion commanders had told him the attack could not succeed as currently planned. Uncut barbed wire had been discovered by an infantry patrol, and Turner had been informed by front-line officers that not only had patrols been prevented from crossing some of the waterlogged ditches, but one man had drowned.

Turner was nonetheless ordered to proceed. The Canadian divisional staff indeed seemed to deserve their reputation as callous incompetents out of touch with troops at the front, a distinction that had been intensifying since the beginning of the war, but it should be noted that they were under pressure from their British superiors. The corps and army headquarters were even further removed from the reality of the front, and General Haig was pushed equally hard by his French allies to renew the attack. The objections of a number of battalion commanding officers and their brigadier were not going to register with an army commander, but the Canadian divisional headquarters, and specifically Alderson, should have made a stronger case in the men's defence—at least arguing for an adjusted attack time. But as commander of a fresh division at the front, Alderson lacked the willpower to force the issue. The general had in fact tentatively broached the subject of a delay in order to give his artillery adequate time to break the German defences, but in response he had received a personal visit from an impatient Haig, who had questioned his judgment and ability to carry out an offensive operation. Alderson had folded before the veiled threat. The attack would not be called off. Turner returned to his men with the bad news, but not before he thundered to the divisional headquarters staff that the operation was little more than murder.[1]

Expectations that artillery would destroy or suppress German fire had already proven to be misplaced during the attack two days earlier, and to order a 700-metre assault against a frontal position using exhausted soldiers was nothing short of criminal. But almost a year of military training had prepared soldiers to accept orders without question. The infantry at the sharp end might have thought their assault was part of a larger offensive, or a feint—a greater goal that might justify their sacrifice. Sadly, this was not the case, but the Canadians remained unaware of the reality of the situation and obeyed their orders. Besides, fatigue had numbed some of the men into indifference to their fate. "Before the attack yesterday I was dead tired; I didn't know how I could make it," wrote one infantryman of the 16th Battalion. "But when the fight started and they opened up on us I didn't care one damn. They could do what they like with me. I went on indifferent to my surroundings, and I was thinking quite clearly, too."[2]

The 16th Battalion, and the fresher 15th—which was brought into the line from reserve—moved into the front trenches. But the Canadian artillery barrage leading up to the start time was weak and episodic. Even the infantry waiting to go over the top could sense its ineffectiveness. As the attack time neared, the bombardment reached a brief fury and then stopped. At 7:45 P.M., the officers' whistles could be heard across the battlefield. The Canadians climbed out of their trenches, advancing in waves, with 2 or 3 metres between men.

In accordance with the doctrine of the time, the barrage had stopped before the initiation of the attack, which meant that almost no supporting barrage of shells or small-arms fire was being used to keep the Germans down in their own fortified front lines. Two Canadian Colt machine guns had been added to supplement the artillery fire, but the first position was almost immediately sniped by Germans who well understood the guns' effectiveness, and the second was obliterated by a high explosive artillery shell. Little additional firepower was mobilized to assist the infantry.

Going over the top was a terrifying event, but discipline took over and soldiers went forward. Many described the surreal quality of bullets whizzing past them, shells exploding, and men falling all around them. Still, they advanced, crawling, walking, and stepping over barbed wire, moving around smoking craters, barely looking down at the red-stained heaps of rags and jutting bone that had once been men. Acrid smoke caught in the throat; eyes were dry as soldiers forgot to blink. Time alternately stood still and sped fast in an experience both unsettling and dream-like. In looking back on the mad minutes in No Man's Land, or the hours in a shattered enemy's trench, the Highlanders of the 15th and 16th Battalions might only be able to reconstruct a few images: a red poppy in a sea of mud; a friend torn open and crying out for help; the rustle of the wind on the back of a sweaty neck. In some ways, being out of the trenches, unencumbered by the terrible stress of waiting, was easier for the men—even though this position was far more dangerous.

The Canadians displayed iron discipline in the face of small-arms fire that fell, as one attacker noted in his diary, "like sleet."[3] The German Maxim machine gun— which was similar, if slightly inferior, to the British Vickers machine gun—swept the battlefield with some 500 rounds a minute. It had a heavy sledge mount that resembled a stretcher, and more than a few Entente soldiers were tricked into not firing at machine-gunners moving into position, as they appeared to be medical orderlies. Dug in, and advantaged by a commanding view of the ground, the German gunners laid down a devastating arc of fire, and advancing Canadian infantrymen were hit repeatedly as they fell to the ground.

THAT ANYONE COULD SURVIVE such a hurricane of fire seemed unbelievable, but still the Canadians advanced on the enemy, finding gaps in the barbed wire, firing from their five-round clip, and then alternately running and crawling forward. But the gaps in the advancing waves became wider and wider. Captain Frank Morison of the 16th Battalion's C Company reported that he and his men ran into the "grave obstacle" of a creek eight feet wide and four feet deep.[4] A hedge lined the other side, with only two small openings through which to pass, both of which were covered by machine guns. The Jocks—as Highlanders liked to call themselves—pushed through single file but took terrible casualties. Those who made it to the other side soon built up a weight of fire that eventually knocked out the enemy guns, but the cost in casualties was high. Amidst the horror of men being torn apart, infantrymen could glimpse a few startled rabbits hopping along in these old farmers' fields, a strange pastoral sight in a war of industrialized fury.

"When we made the attack the bullets were so thick that I thought that it was sure death for me," wrote Private Herbert Durand, a former railway brakesman from New Liskeard, Ontario. "The three fellows who went ahead of me were killed as soon as they got over, and I had to crawl over them, and wherever I looked someone was falling."[5] In Durand's platoon, twenty-two of the thirty-three men were killed or wounded, and the survivors went to ground as their officers were all killed. But other platoons pushed forward. Crossing water-filled ditches and trenches, the Canadians drove through the outer German lines, bayoneting and shooting the enemy. Sergeant Jock Thompson, one of the favourite non-commissioned officers in the 15th, single-handedly charged a machine gun that was raking his men. He nearly succeeded but was shot down only metres from the position. Another group of men crept forward during Thompson's charge and were able to knock out the gun. The Canadians made a slow advance, but often only as a result of terrible sacrifices.

Private Thomas Hannah, who had enlisted in the 15th Battalion at the age of forty-one in the first months of the war, wrote home to a friend, "This is not war, it is simply murder." During the daylight attack, "It was hell let loose, shrapnel, machine guns and rifles all at us at once, but we went through it at an awful cost, and I believe I am the luckiest man in the world to-day, for after we got to the trench there were eighteen of us between traverses when a shell got us and sixteen of us went down. I have often read of the battlefield, but this beats everything. What I have seen would turn men's hair white."[6]

By the end of the night, the survivors of the 16th Battalion had captured the Orchard, which had been enclosed in thick hedges and ditches and strengthened with barbed wire. The 15th Battalion had been stopped short of their assigned trenches, two German concentrations labelled L.11 and L.12 on their maps, but they had also overrun a number of difficult positions. The Highlanders' occupation of the Orchard was the farthest point reached by British forces in the Battle of Festubert, and the location was therefore renamed "Canadian Orchard" in their honour. But the battle had cost the four companies an estimated 250 casualties, and in a testament to the futile nature of the operation, even this farthest point was soon pulled back to straighten out the line to avoid enfilade fire (shooting from the flank).[7] In his report to Alderson, Turner noted "a feeling in the brigade that unnecessary heavy casualties were incurred ... on account of the hour at which the attack was ordered."[8] This was the hard truth, but it won Turner few friends at division headquarters.

With his 2nd Brigade located on the right flank of Turner's 3rd, Brigadier Arthur Currie was ordered to coordinate an attack of his brigade in conjunction with Turner's, even though the original plan had not called for an operation by Currie's brigade until the next day. Working on a shortened timetable hurt the ability of Currie's men to reconnoitre the ground—identify potential strongpoints or plot courses through the wire. And such reconnoitring was based on the assumption that they could even find their objectives.

The 2nd Brigade had been ordered to capture K.5, a junction of new and old German trenches not distinguished on any map and not even visible to the Canadian officers who crawled through the mud and barbed wire in the dark. Frustrated and confused by orders that could not be carried out, Currie roared to several of his officers that the "son of a bitch who wrote this order never saw a trench."[9]

Currie was no less fed up with the British and Canadian artillery, whose failure to knock out the enemy's big guns had left the troops in the front line weakly supported. No stranger to a good profanity-laden outburst, Currie frothed, "The damned artillery don't fire on each other but on the infantry on either side."[10] He was correct for the most part, and captured German artillery doctrinal orders observed that targeting an enemy's front line was far more profitable than hunting in the rear for hidden guns.[11] The gunners on both sides lacked ammunition and expertise, but at Festubert the Canadian gunners had also been situated too far to the rear by Alderson's divisional staff. They were nearly blind since most of the forward observers were not close enough to the front, and those few who were there to correct the fall of shells often could not send reliable coordinates back along the unreliable telephone wires.

Along the front, the enemy's barbed wire seemed almost untouched. Although thousands of shells had been fired, most were ineffective, becoming buried in the ground and exploding beneath the wire because the fuses were not sensitive enough to detonate the shells on contact. Wire had simply been tossed around, creating enormous tumbleweeds of sharp metal. Uncut barbed wire would remain a grave problem until more high explosive shells were produced in 1916, followed by more sensitive fuses early in the next year.

On the night of May 19, infantry intelligence patrols had informed Currie that not only were the enemy trenches seemingly untouched by shellfire, but most of the barbed wire remained. Currie attempted to have the attack delayed until more guns could be brought up to provide a suitable bombardment.[12] Inexperienced and unsure of how to press his demand, Currie received a flat rejection from divisional headquarters, as had Turner. A dejected and frustrated Currie selected two companies of the 10th Battalion and a small party of grenadiers from the 5th Battalion to go forward. This was far too small a force to achieve any success against a fortress like K.5, and one suspects that Currie, aware of the hopeless situation, was not willing to commit more men to the futile expedition.

As a location, K.5 meant nothing to the soldiers at the front: it could neither be spotted by forward observers nor be found on the inaccurate maps. K.5, with parapets that were 3 to 6 metres thick in places, was almost untouched in the preparatory bombardment. Worse, Currie's two infantry companies of Calgarians were crowded in battered forward trenches, where the parapet and sandbags were knocked about, allowing snipers to take out victim after victim. Even inexperienced troops could smell blood in the air.

In the hours before the assault, two heavy 9.2-inch howitzers that were to have bombarded K.5 were redirected away from the target for fear that such a bombardment might alert the Germans to the objective of the attack. Such concern was unwarranted, however, as the Germans were already well aware of the impending operation. Situated on Aubers Ridge, the enemy was able to look down into the Canadian and British lines and see exactly where they were forming up.

At 7:45 p.m., the 10th Battalion was forced to attack "in full view of the enemy" and with no protective barrage.[13] With the high command completely unaware of the battlefield conditions, and the soldiers at the sharp end not even sure as to the direction in which they were to attack, the officers at the front found to their horror that the only way forward was through a narrow communication trench. Only one man could fit down and through it at a time, although the bullets continued to whiz over the heads of all troops. After several dozen infanteers had emerged from the same spot, the Germans began to train their fire on the exit. The Fighting Tenth advanced into a death trap in which even a handful of enemy riflemen could have taken apart the two companies.[14]

With only a limited number of men making it beyond the exit of the communication trench, the forward company advanced the line a pitiful 100 metres. But most of the officers had been gunned down within minutes, and the last surviving company commander called off the suicidal attack. Interestingly, the grenadiers of the 5th Battalion appear to have taken matters into their own hands: no record indicates that they left the relative safety of the trench for the slaughter ground beyond. The insignificant 100-metre advance achieved in this operation was a result of the ferocity of enemy fire but also of the Calgarians' decision to go to ground and stay there, no doubt exercising their own judgment in the hopeless battle. In his official report, Currie refused to mince words: the attack was "a complete failure."[15]

AFTER THE CANADIAN OPERATION was stopped dead by enemy fire, General Alderson and senior staff officer Lieutenant Colonel G.C. Gordon-Hall were forced to present themselves to Haig. The general sat at a small table at his headquarters "while we stood in front of him like a pack of school boys," recounted Gordon-Hall. The normally unemotional Haig "raged at the failure of the attacks on the hostile position." Alderson tried to explain the difficulties, but Haig simply "stormed and declared the enemy must be driven from his position." Yet he offered no proposals as to how this was to be done, although he was liberal in pouring "scorn on the efforts of the Canadians," who he felt had given up too easily in taking K.5. Gordon-Hall intervened, arguing that additional attacks would only result in "further useless slaughter," pointing out that inaccurate artillery fire and timid gunners (both British and Canadian) located safely in the rear had abandoned the front-line troops to their fate.[16] Haig ignored him and ordered the Canadians to mount another attack. Gordon-Hall's protest went unknown to battalion commanders such as Turner and Currie, but it certainly left him marked in Haig's eyes, and the staff officer never advanced beyond his rank of lieutenant colonel.

At the front, K.5 was being further reinforced by elite German troops. In addition, to the north of the position, near Canadian Orchard, a fortified house at M.10 remained unhit by shellfire, and the Canadians suspected enemy troops there would pour enfilading fire into any advance. But the Canadians had too few artillery and machine guns to destroy the position or suppress fire coming from it. With this grim prospect, Currie's troops prepared for a third assault.

On May 21, the attack was to begin at daybreak, but the artillery had been unable to coordinate their action with the infantry. The operation was therefore postponed until 8:30 that evening, but once again the sky was still light enough for German machine-gunners to work their devilry. Supported by a weak and sporadic barrage, the infantry was left to its fate.

Two companies of the unlucky 10th were called on again, supported by the 1st Brigade's grenade company, a specialist unit that brought together men from the brigade's four battalions to conduct the dangerous work of tossing hand grenades. Bravery got the Fighting Tenth out of the trenches, but before they set off across No Man's Land, their officers felt it necessary to line them up, as per existing doctrine. They carried out this process in the face of sweeping enemy fire, which, according to E.J. Ashton, the ranking officer leading the attack, "almost annihilated the [two] platoons on the left and caused heavy casualties to those filing to the right."[17]

The troops exhibited iron discipline as they stood and waited for their companions to emerge from the trenches, even as bullets were tearing into their ranks. This type of discipline would not have been out of place at the Battle of Waterloo in 1815. But the weapons of war had become considerably more deadly over the intervening hundred years, and the fact that any of the 10th survived in the open was something of a miracle. When enough men had lined up, they advanced. Moving in leaps and bounds, they pushed forward, but they lost comrades at every step. Still they drove on, going to ground to lay down fire and then moving forward again. But the battlefield afforded few places to hide from the growing weight of enemy fire. While the force on the left was largely annihilated, that on the right cleared 400 metres of trench in fierce hand-to-hand fighting. However, the strongpoint of K.5 refused to fall.

With the Germans temporarily retreating, the surviving Canadians set to constructing sandbag walls, reversing the trench firesteps (tearing them up and rebuilding them on the side of the trench that now faced the enemy), caring for the wounded, and consolidating their ammunition. They waited for the storm. And soon it came. Throughout May 22, the 10th beat back uncoordinated counterattacks along the enemy's communication trenches. Having failed to break the Canadian blocks in the trenches, the Germans came at them over land; but they found this approach no more successful. Three times the Germans launched major attacks and three times they were cut down by massed Ross and Lee-Enfield rifle fire, disproving the widely held belief that the former was useful only as a club. Private Sydney Cox recalled with some delight: "We really murdered them for a while."[18]

The Canadians had a toehold into the German lines, but this gain caused little more than a ripple through the enemy's position. The Germans still had the strategic high ground, and both sides were unwilling to end the battle. A lot of murder was still left for both sides to carry out at Festubert.

CHAPTER 15

"MAINTAINED BY SCIENCE TO BE KILLED BY SHELLS"

Battlefield Medicine

"The Germans rained shells on us…. I was so worked up, I couldn't eat my rations," wrote Private Alfred Andrews, describing the bombardment of May 22. He continued:

> Rankin and I volunteered to go out around a trench to get a wounded man. We got him out and Scotty Cairns came with us. He was suffering from shell shock. I had to put the boots to him to get him to do any work. Our instructions were to bring back ammunition. As we came down the road we saw 6 men lying dead alongside of ammunition they were carrying.

The Germans shelled their return route heavily and, as Andrews remembered,

> a shell burst on Rankin's legs, wounding men on each side of me. I put a tourniquet on the legs which were horribly mangled and with the help of a fellow who was there carried him to the dressing station. I first had to go and get a stretcher. I was so tired I could hardly hold the stretcher and seeing an ambulance man I asked him to help. He refused and said he'd carried all the men he was going to. If I had had my rifle I'd have shot him. I was so mad. Rankin died in the dressing station.[1]

Medical units were overwhelmed as the waves of wounded washed over them. With only sixteen dedicated stretcher-bearers and one medical officer per battalion, long lines of casualties stretched around the makeshift hospitals. Men lay in their own blood and feces, their pitiful groans and glassy-eyed stares revealing that many would not survive the transportation back to a field ambulance further behind the lines. At the front, stretcher-bearers raced across the pitted battlefield and under the rain of shells. They were drawn to the fallen: turning over bodies, looking for pulses, and then trying to breathe life back into the near-dead. Sometimes, a companion of a wounded soldier would plant the man's rifle in the ground next to him to draw the attention of the "body-snatchers," as the stretcher-bearers were informally called. Moving from rifle to rifle—from one informal cross to another—the stretcher-bearers dispensed bandages and iodine. First-aid dressings were ripped from the inside of a wounded man's tunic, where they were sewn inside the front. Occasionally, morphine tablets were issued to ease the pain. When the morphine ran out, the experienced stretcher-bearer reached for his canteen filled with rum. Offering a sip and a word of encouragement, he then moved on to the next victim.

The wounded had two options. With far too few stretcher-bearers to carry the legions of broken and bleeding men, they could wait for someone to help them to the rear medical stations—either a captured prisoner of war on his way to the rear or another wounded ally—or they could try to make it there on their own. Even through the haze of agony, the wounded knew that the longer they waited in a shell crater the greater the chance that the hole would become their grave. Men who had no right to be standing, let alone moving—men with shattered legs or gaping holes in chests—stumbled or dragged themselves to the rear. Shock resulting from loss of blood could strike at any time, and trembling limbs were pushed onward in the search for care.

During the first two days of the Festubert battle, No. 3 Field Ambulance of the Canadian Army Medical Corps provided medical care to 996 Canadians and 111 British troops.[2] Surgeons and orderlies rushed through the bloodied mess, assessing men, sorting the mutilated and maimed into groups: men who needed immediate attention before they bled out, men who could wait, and lost causes— usually anyone with a devastating head wound or an abdominal contusion. In the

MEDICAL ARRANGEMENTS IN THE FIELD.

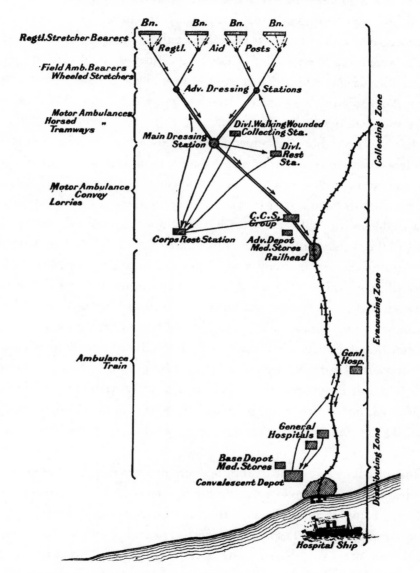

The progression of wounded soldiers from front to rear was long and arduous. The difference between life and death was often determined by the speed at which the wounded were cleared from the battlefield to receive medical care from the doctors in the rear areas.

latter cases, without antibiotics doctors had little hope of staving off a life-ending infection. Private Herbert Burrell recounted his shock when, after leading a badly wounded Canadian who had been shot through the lung across the battlefield to stretcher-bearers, they refused to take him, telling Burrell that they had "other cases who were more likely to live."[3] The medical teams could turn to such nearly dead men after dealing with the mad rush of wounded who had a greater chance of surviving. They might hope to save a few, but in a war of long odds, these seriously wounded men had drawn the worst hand.

"In the dressing station the surgeons work ceaselessly," testified Private George Bell. "A few deft strokes of a knife and a shattered leg is amputated and the stump quickly bandaged."[4] Despite countless stories of surgeons working miracles, too often these doctors were forced to wield the saw and scalpel in the same way that Civil War doctors a half-century earlier had done to lop off shattered limbs. Attesting to the savage nature of the industrialized war, the Canadian Army Medical Corps grew from a prewar strength of 20 officers, 5 nursing sisters, and 102 other ranks to 1,528 officers, 1,901 nurses, and 15,624 other ranks, a 150-fold expansion.[5] These doctors, surgeons, and nurses had a steep learning curve: the wounds were grim, requiring the use of new surgical and healing techniques.

The impact of bullets on Canadian flesh produced shocking wounds. Men advancing on the battlefield were bowled over by the force. Many recounted that they felt as if a sledgehammer had hit them. The entry wound from a bullet could be quite small, but as the projectile passed through a human body it tore or even liquefied flesh. A bullet's exit wound was a horrendous hole, sometimes as large as a fist.

Internal bleeding and tissue disruption were unavoidable, but bullets at the end of their trajectory, and therefore moving more slowly, could do even more damage. Instead of passing straight through the body, they often deformed on impact, tumbling through the soft flesh, leaving irregular wound patterns. Some bullets also broke up on contact with bone, creating a multiple-headed projectile. These were the most ghastly of wounds, as flesh, bone, and muscle were torn, shattered, and even reduced to a pulp of pink mist. Chest and abdominal wounds were usually fatal, as was anything that severed femoral arteries. A surprising number of head wounds did not result in death, and instances occurred of men arriving at wound stations with exposed brain matter or with empty eye sockets.

The most pressing concern of the doctors was the likelihood of infection. Since the fighting was taking place on farmers' soil that had been enriched for centuries by animal and human manure, the vast majority of all wounds became infected.[6] The whirling metal of a bullet or a piece of shrapnel dragged soil-stained, filthy outer clothing through skin likely covered in septic spots due to louse infestation, and into the wound. Even trivial cuts could be infected unless they received quick attention, and each one needed to be viewed as a potential death sentence.

The infection suffered most widely was gas gangrene, which bore no relationship to chemical warfare. The process of the disease began when bullets or shrapnel drove gas bacillus microbes from the soil deep into a wound. In the absence of oxygen, the microbes quickly multiplied in the hothouse environment of crushed bone, tangled blood vessels, and shredded flesh. The infection created a septic swill that soon bubbled up like gas, sometimes within as little as twenty-four hours. Wounds became distended and elephantine, fast turning a greenish colour. The smell was enough to make experienced medical men vomit. Gas gangrene was a lethal and agonizing fate, as wounded men were killed from within.

Yet, since the infection was anaerobic, it could be eradicated by exposing it to oxygen. But accomplishing this required the use of advanced surgical techniques. As thousands died in agony, doctors were forced to turn to more radical methods. Amputation, which had long been a war hospital treatment for wounded men whose doctors had only a few minutes to care for them, became common practice. Major G.S. Strathy of the Canadian Army Medical Corps recorded in his diary in the midpoint of the war: "Gas gangrene and shock are taking a terrible toll, although there is much less than a year ago, owing to efficient wide-open drainage. Amputations have to be very frequent."[7]

After some grisly experimentation, a technique was developed to cut away flesh from around entry and exit wounds and then punch a hole through the limb or body to allow oxygen to enter and kill the infection. Drainage holes the size of clenched fists were not uncommon, and although these holes often controlled gas gangrene, they created other challenges, such as how to dress, drain, and redress

*The rough handling of patients undergoing battlefield surgery left tough men grimacing
in pain, but the cleaning of wounds was essential to reduce the chance of infection.*

these intentionally induced wounds. Gordon Glassco of the PPCLI, a former
Hamilton electrical engineer with a long career in the Canadian militia, described
the debridement technique (as it came to be known) used to clean his wound: "Each
morning they pulled a piece of sterile cord through my wound from front to back,
and after remaining there overnight it was pulled out and another sterile cord was
substituted. This was to prevent any internal infection from developing." The
tough-as-nails infantryman noted rather laconically, "This hurt like hell."[8]

The introduction of new medical techniques—such as how to set wounds, deal
with lung gases, and locate buried steel in flesh through X-rays; when to keep a man
immobilized and when to send him to the rear to reach a hospital more quickly; and
how to get life-giving blood into men who wore most of it on their clothes—
resulted in an astonishing ninety-three percent survival rate of all wounded soldiers
who reached a doctor.[9] Once in the medical system, wounded soldiers received a

high quality of care, although many of the 138,000 Canadians wounded on the battlefield would nonetheless hobble through life on one leg or breathe through damaged lungs. However, despite the impressive medical innovations made during the war, more than a few men might have echoed the sentiments of Sergeant F.W. Bagnall, who noted cynically, "We were maintained by science to be killed by shells."[10] Bagnall would survive the war but was forever maimed by three wounds, including an amputated arm and a poorly reconstructed jaw.

The speed with which wounded soldiers moved from front to rear was the primary factor in saving their lives. From the battlefield, they generally passed first through their regimental aid post (RAP), manned by the battalion's medical officer and his orderlies. But each battalion had only one RAP (although later in the war those battalions not on the front line sent forward their medical officers to offer assistance). Many men therefore bypassed the RAP and moved on to one of the three field ambulances (medical stations) in each division.

Under tents, and sometimes more permanent structures, the wounded were again assessed, triaged, and bound up or sent further to the rear. The field ambulances had trucks to evacuate the men and relieve them from walking, although the agony of a continuously jostled stomach wound or a temporarily set broken femur as trucks lurched from shell craters to potholes along beaten roads was a torment. Luckily, most did not remember the trip, having passed out from the pain. Drivers braved artillery fire and poor roads, and one official report for the Canadian No. 10 Field Ambulance noted that its truck drivers "careened around the dangerous corners and dashed madly down the straight-a-way, weaving through the traffic, slacking, shooting ahead, taking advantage of every opening, in order to save time and make more trips for the wounded."[11]

The trucks' destination was the Casualty Clearing Stations (CCS), a few kilometres behind the lines. The CCS was the first major site where surgery was performed, although doctors closer to the front could and did intervene surgically to save men where necessary. In response to the static warfare of the Western Front, the CCS became large centres that could accommodate hundreds. These facilities were the closest the 2,500 Canadian nurses who served in the war got to the front.[12]

Nurses were almost always unmarried and, in the Canadian Army Medical Corps, had the rank of an officer, which was higher than the status of their British counterparts. Most came from middle-class families and had previous nursing experience. Like the doctors and surgeons they assisted, they endured the hardship of massed medical care and the dreadfully long hours. "The wounds caused by the bursting shrapnel are most severe," wrote Nurse Sophie Hoerner. "It rips, tears, lacerates and penetrates the tissues in a horrible manner. The doctor tries to repair and make good the best he can, but our best is often of little avail. One man completely blind, another with a knee joint blown open. I am witnessing terrible suffering. A weary road these men have trod. Some of them go right to pieces. Their nerve has gone and they cry like babies. Others just stare and say nothing, but have such a vacant look."[13]

These patients with such empty looks had what later generations of American soldiers would call the "thousand-yard stare." They had seen the horror of war and it had broken them—most men temporarily, a few permanently. Combat veteran George Ormsby described one friend who was suffering from the strain of battle: "I was down to the hospital yesterday and saw Percy Graves—poor chap he seems to have had a dreadful shock. He is out of his head at times and is quite sensible at others but he attributes his pain to some disease, says he has been in the hospital three weeks and has not been in any battle, when as a matter of fact I know that a week ago he was out in billets and was in the best of health as I was talking to him then." A corporal told Ormsby that Graves, his friend from back home in Lumby, British Columbia, had been found unconscious in a trench after a savage German attack. "I feel so sorry for poor Percy, he was crying when I saw him. He is a fine soldier—he will be alright after a few months rest."[14]

Percy Graves was suffering from shell shock, a mental breakdown caused by the unending strain of combat. The war at the front could drive men mad. The constant crash of high explosives, the never-ending fear of death, and hours and then days of sleep deprivation, as well as the brutality of what they witnessed and were forced to do to other men, pushed many soldiers over the edge of sanity. Mental breakdowns had been witnessed almost from the first day of the war, and the military was unsure as to how to handle the problem. Heroic soldiers were succumbing to fear, paranoia, bouts of uncontrollable crying, paralysis of limbs, mutism, nightmares, and other typical hysterical reactions. The only explanation that fit the army's view of its masculine warriors was that the physical shock to soldiers' bodies caused by the explosion of shells near them had unbalanced or compressed some men's brains. This interpretation of the problem as the result of a brain hemorrhage saw shell shock as a physical ailment, as devastatingly apparent as a bullet through the hand or a piece of shrapnel through the gut.

But then soldiers who had never been within range of a high explosive shell began to collapse mentally. Breakdowns also occurred when men left the high-stress area of the front and were finally able to relax in the rear. Soon, medical practitioners realized that shell shock was in fact a symptom of battle stress. A soldier who develops shell shock, observed Medical Officer Captain R.J. Manion, "trembles violently, his heart may be disorderly in rhythm, he has a terrified air, the slightest noise makes him jump and even occasionally run at top speed to a supposed place of safety. He is the personification of terror, at times crying out or weeping like a child."[15]

Time at the front wore down the mind. "What few are left of the first contingent have been through so many bombardments, and have seen so much slaughter, and bloodshed, that they dread the thought of the trenches," wrote Roy Macfie. "Fellows that feared nothing when they came out here, are so nervous now that they can't stand anything[.] The sound of shell's [sic] will almost set some of them crazy."[16] Rest was needed—away from the front—and often soldiers were able to recharge their batteries as they were rotated through the line. But the war was a constant drain on one's courage, and over time all men began to wear down.

The military could not deny the existence of shell shock, although it would later try to downplay the implications of the term by refusing to allow doctors to label patients' condition as such; instead, doctors were to use the term "N.Y.D.," standing for "Not Yet Diagnosed," which the men cynically transformed into "Not Yet Dead." Since sufferers of shell shock carried no physical marks of violence, medical officers were unsure about what to do with them. While many medical officers, who were often prewar civilian doctors, understood the psychological trauma inflicted on these men, the army needed every soldier at the front. Medical officers were torn between, on the one hand, adhering to their Hippocratic oath to care for their patients above all other demands and, on the other, meeting the military's needs by returning trembling, shaken men to the line. With soldiers pushed to the edge of both endurance and sanity, many would do anything to escape from the horrors of the front. Medical officers had the distasteful task of ferreting out the truly psychologically damaged from the clever fakers. Malingering indeed happened, but the reality of shell shock could not be denied, and by war's end an estimated 9,000 cases had been recorded in the Canadian forces alone, and countless more cases likely existed of men who were wrongly diagnosed or were killed before they sought or required medical attention.[17]

The best remedy for men on the verge of a breakdown was rest, a bath, and a meal at a location a few kilometres behind the lines, and then a return to their units at the front.[18] But this was hard to do during the war since the men could not be spared and often the facilities were unavailable. Sending men back to England for longer-term care was required for the more severely wounded—those who were unable to sleep without having nightmares or to walk without trembling legs giving out, or those who babbled insanely or stared mutely into space. In England, these men were placed in special hospitals, where specialists treated them, often employing Freudian techniques of discussing deep-seated fears and anxieties, combined with a program of relaxing activities, baths, and rest. Officers and enlisted men received similar treatments, although a myth arose that the rank and file were treated far more harshly.[19]

Although therapy and rest were important, some doctors believed in more aggressive methods. In cases where the "will" seemed to have "lost control of the brain," patients were coerced into regaining control of their bodies and minds.[20] Major W.J. Adie of the Royal Army Medical Corps took on the "treatment" of about a dozen patients a day, specializing in men who had lost the ability to speak. His method was to lash them to an operating table and put a constrictive gas mask on them, after which the doctor left for a while and let the patients suffer in near-suffocation. He returned some time later and, in a soothing voice, promised to remove the mask when they said, "Take it away." For more stubborn cases, he injected ether through the mask while he "pricked the skin over the larynx rather vigorously with a pin."[21] Other experts employed electric shock therapy, which involved the brutal electrocution of tongues, eyelids, and even genitals in order to elicit a response and bring shell-shocked men out of their catatonic state. This method had a higher success rate than did psychotherapy, with greater numbers of men returning to the front after being "cured," but more than a few doctors wondered at the inhumanity of such techniques, as well as the high rate of post-treatment relapse.

At the front, the private demons that each soldier struggled with remained his own, although they were sometimes shared with a close friend or occasionally captured on paper as men tried to exorcise their malignant fears. Basil Craig wrote to his mother shortly before his death:

> I have got quite used now to the sight of wounded men and some of them pretty badly at that. It made me feel a bit queer at first, but have got used to it now. This is not a cheerful line so I will not dwell on it.... I am sorry if I appear a bit blue in this letter, but, Mother, I know you will understand just how I feel. A person gets no sympathy in the army. I have had a nightmare the last two nights and woke up trembling all over. I had dreamed I was in a fight and was nearly bayoneted when I woke up. I don't know what caused such dreams. I hope I don't have one tonight.[22]

These nightmares were the stuff of every trench soldier's combat experience, and often the medical corps could do little to assist them. Only individual courage, endurance, a reward system, and an efficient medical apparatus could keep a fighting force from degenerating into a mob of madmen.

CHAPTER 16

"THE GATES OF HELL OPENED"

Festubert, May 22–24, 1915

"This life is sure hell. I don't know the minute I may get shot. Sometimes the bullets are so thick that it is just like a big rain storm, and while I am writing this the shrapnel is exploding over our heads every minute, and pieces of steel and iron are falling all around us," wrote Private Herbert Durand.[1] Reinforcements could not be moved forward to relieve the exposed troops. Ahead, behind, to the left, to the right, the shells fell in a steady stream. Every man hugged the trench walls as the scrotum-tightening, bowel-loosening explosions crashed all around them.

The survivors of the assault on May 21—the 10th Battalion, now reinforced by the 5th and 7th Battalions—were wasting away under the all-day artillery onslaught. Ammunition was fired off. Water ran out as terrified men gulped their last reserves. Wounded men cried out in agony, and the stench of the dead overpowered the living. Some men grimly held on while others began to break down, whimpering at first, then sobbing quietly. "Not all men behave in the same manner under fire," Private George Bell wrote later, looking back from his position as a veteran of the entire war. "Our battalion, like all others, had those who liked to be considered hard boiled. They were the ones picking fights back of the lines and telling how tough they were. But often these men, toughest back of the line, were weakest when they came to the crucial moment of making an advance, and often the most mild mannered of men made the best soldiers."[2] Under the bombardment, it took an iron will to hold on to one's sanity. Some 200 cases of shell shock were reported during and immediately after the Festubert battle.[3]

With the Canadians outgunned, several Colt machine guns had been brought forward and placed in secondary positions to consolidate the ground. These provided important fire support, and the machine-gun teams fired off belt after belt, the barrels glowing red hot. But the new guns also became the targets of the Germans, who recognized their important role, and snipers soon began to make the exposed gunners pay for their bravery. "It was simply the gates of hell opened and everything let loose at once," remarked Jock Palmer, who earned a Distinguished Conduct Medal for recklessly exposing himself by resting his machine gun on the parapet and fighting off a series of German counterattacks throughout the day.[4] Palmer's bravery kept the enemy at bay in his sector, even though the fact that he avoided being shot in the upper body or head at some point during the battle was perhaps a minor miracle. While the infantry fought for their lives, the artillery again

On the battlefield, even a depth of half a metre made the difference between life and death.

failed to suppress enemy artillery fire. With counter battery fire in its infancy, gunners found it difficult to target enemy guns that were several kilometres away and hidden by folds in the ground or by camouflage. And so these unsuppressed guns relentlessly pounded the exposed Canadian infantry.[5]

Haig visited Alderson's headquarters to communicate once again his displeasure at the lack of success in the colonial advance. A renewed offensive was ordered, and again the Canadians were to attack K.5, with British units supporting on both flanks. How to rectify the failures of artillery and supporting fire, and how to deal with both the lack of surprise of their attack and the recent German reinforcement of the area, were problems left to a bewildered Alderson to solve.

The 10th Battalion having lost 18 officers and 250 men from other ranks—mostly from the two companies of less than 400 that were part of the advance—two additional companies of the 5th Battalion and a small group of bombers were ordered to take K.5. The commanding officer of the 5th Battalion noted stoically that the miniature German fortresses, of which K.5 was the strongest, were nothing short of "unbreakable."[6] Massive artillery bombardments would be needed to smash the strongpoints, but the pitifully few field guns and howitzers afforded to the operation were insufficient.

As the soldiers of the 5th Battalion passed by Brigadier Currie's command headquarters on their way towards the front, Private E.G. McFeat saw the large brigadier kindly patting men on the shoulder and saying in a sad voice, "Now, boys, don't forget, I am relying on you." McFeat was touched by the brigadier's compassion, but wrote that the "citizen soldiers" who filled the ranks "knew only too well the tremendous peril which awaited them."[7] Backed by almost no artillery support, the infantry could rely only on themselves and their own ingenuity to survive the next twenty-four hours. Ross rifles and bayonets were no match for the weapons of the dug-in German defenders, but the Canadians had also been busy building their own miniature artillery in the form of hand grenades.

Canadian trench entrepreneurs had followed the British lead in the black art of bombing. The hand bomb had been out of service for the British infantryman for more than a century, but the new obstacles presented by trench warfare demanded a return to old weapons. Specialists in the infantry, along with engineers, constructed bombs in the trenches and behind the lines by stuffing jam tins with nails, bolts, shredded gun cotton, explosives, detonators, and handmade fuses. These weapons were known by many names, but perhaps most affectionately as "Tommy Tickler's Artillery," because they were made from jam tins often bearing that name.[8]

Enough crackpot weapons were designed in the trenches—from supposedly bulletproof shields to various forms of slings and catapults—for officers to turn a skeptical eye to these handmade bombs lit by match, pipe, or cigarette. But they soon proved their worth, especially in clearing enemy trenches. Nonetheless, they were notoriously unreliable weapons. The fuses burned quickly and they were, initially, almost as dangerous to the thrower as to the targeted victim. Corporal W.S. Lighthall of the Royal Canadian Dragoons remembered eyeing the bombs with trepidation, considering them "very dangerous weapons in untutored hands."[9] Men with such untrained hands soon lost them, along with most of their upper body. And even among experts, the weapons could be deadly. Lieutenant G.B. Glassco of the PPCLI rejoined his unit after being wounded and was appointed bombing officer; he was more than a little shocked later to hear from a friend that the average life expectancy of bombing officers up to that point in his battalion was sixteen days.[10]

Despite the dangers of the job, the bombardiers often attracted good men looking for a fight. Private W.H. Wray noted in a letter that he loved to build his own bombs, crawl into No Man's Land, and toss them into the German lines. The best part was watching the way the "German shit flies."[11] As grenades became an essential trench weapon, the grenadiers, who had been pulled out of their infantry companies to create a specialist force at brigade headquarters, were embedded individually back into their companies by 1916. That same year, most infantrymen went into battle with a handful of grenades as a secondary weapon. By the next year, the grenadiers were considered so important that one-fourth of the men in each platoon were designated bombers.

The grenades had many variations, but they could be placed in one of three categories: percussion, ignition, and mechanical. Percussion grenades were made active by removing a safety pin. They exploded on impact and were dangerous to the thrower, as a backward knock against a trench wall during the throw could set off the grenade. Sometimes, these grenades had streamers to guide them in flight and ensure they landed nose down. Using an ignition grenade involved lighting a fuse, in the same way as a Molotov cocktail; but lighting each grenade took time, and they were unreliable in muddy and wet trench conditions. Very quickly, almost all grenades became mechanical grenades, which had spring-loaded mechanisms that ignited a fuse and detonated several seconds later.

The best British grenade was the No. 5 Mills egg-shaped bomb. Introduced in March 1915, but not available in sufficient numbers until later that summer, the Mills continued to be manufactured in tremendous numbers before reaching a high-water mark of 800,000 per week in July 1916.[12] Its metal exterior had serrated edges that allowed the grenade to be in one hand while the other pulled the safety pin. As the Mills left the hand, the lever flew off, setting off the striker, which commenced a five-second fuse leading to detonation. An exploding grenade could shower an area with dozens of whirling metal bits of fragmentation, although more often the grenade exploded in larger, uneven pieces that were fewer in number but more deadly if stopped by flesh. Any grenade that landed within 3 metres of an opponent would likely fill him with some metal.[13] "They are very simple in working, but terrific in effect," wrote one Canadian infantryman. "The explosion is awful, as the metal casing covering the bomb splits into over twenty pieces which fly in all directions."[14] The No. 5 Mills was an effective and deadly anti-personnel weapon.

The bombs were carried in special bomber pouches around the midsection, and sometimes—if attackers were trying to hold a trench and expected to go through bombs in great numbers—in green canvas buckets. Experienced bombers had their own methods of quick delivery: they would bend the safety pins to allow for a rapid pullout to effect continuous delivery. Unfortunately, they sometimes forgot to straighten the pins after a battle, making the explosion of grenades in trenches a not uncommon occurrence. But they were robust weapons and could withstand a surprising amount of jostling and rough handling.

The grenade was essential in clearing the narrow, winding enemy trenches. Experienced bombers and bayonet men trained together: Emsley Yeo, a twenty-two-year-old schoolteacher and amateur rugby player from Victoria, British Columbia, described breaking into the enemy lines: "The bombing party consists of a number of men armed with hand bombs who are immediately preceded by others with fixed bayonets. Bombs are hurled over the heads of the latter people at the enemy, the demoralized survivors of which are summarily dealt with by the bayonet men."[15] Trench after trench was cleared, and frequent battles took place between bombers from the two sides—with bombers throwing their own grenades, catching enemy grenades in turn, and then tossing them back before they exploded—a deranged game of "hot potato."

Experts could catapult a grenade 30 to 35 metres, throwing them not like a baseball but more like a cricket ball, with a straight arm. Towards the end of 1915, the grenade was modified to be fired from a rifle to achieve a greater distance. This revolutionary development armed the infantry with access to controlled firepower, in effect placing a dozen small mortars in the hands of a platoon. But no rifle grenades were to be had at Festubert, and so the infantry relied on arm power to project their bombs.

ON MAY 24, the Canadians were again ordered to capture K.5. Scouts and officers patrolled the front on the night of May 23 and came away with grim findings. The ground remained a glutinous mess. Ditches criss-crossed the battlefield and an advancing formation would be forced to climb in and out of holes and depressions, which would likely break its coherency. Despite these warnings, however, the attack was not called off. Battalion commanders were pressured by brigadiers, who were pressured by divisional headquarters, which in turn had pressure from corps and army commands. The attack would go forward. But again, the battalion commanders, with the tacit approval of Brigadier Currie, committed only limited resources to this seemingly forlorn operation.

Two companies of about 400 men from the 5th Battalion would lead the assault. Officers hoped to inspire the grim-faced rank and file by urging them on with battle cries of *Lusitania!,* in recognition of the recent sinking of an unarmed civilian ship by a German U-boat. But the soldiers needed more than battle cries. So badly was the ground cut up that the infantry carried footbridges to lay across the swamp. One infantryman testified, "It was a difficult thing to know exactly the position of the enemy."[16] The attackers went in nearly blind, and the artillery was completely sightless, doing very little damage to German defences or defenders.

The infantry took matters into its own hands. With no hope of suppressing the enemy fire, Lieutenant Colonel Tuxford of the 5th Battalion ordered a radical night assault. The two companies of this battalion's infantry were in the front lines sixty minutes before zero hour, which was set for 2:45 A.M. "Here we waited in silence for the word," wrote Harold Baldwin, whose war was about to end when a bullet would nearly sever his ankle, requiring an amputation of his foot. "The steady hammer, hammer of the light guns, the monotonous base muttering of the heavies, the shrill, hysterical crackle of machine gun and rifle and the shrieking and cracking of bursting shells seemed to sing hell's requiem to us poor mortals waiting. My God! That waiting. At such a time man's trivial thoughts sink into utter oblivion and the naked soul shows bare."[17]

As minutes ticked down, the artillery barrage stopped, and the officers shouted "over the top." The men of the 5th charged forward and surprised the defenders, who neither expected an attack nor had the willpower to defend against this desperate push. The Westerners bombed their way through the enemy trenches, and ferocity carried the day. By 4:45 A.M., Currie received information from runners that the 5th now occupied portions of the enemy's trenches, but the battalion was desperate for reinforcements, having lost more than half of its force.[18]

Enduring a hurricane of enemy fire and several counterattacks, the 5th Battalion held on until three companies of the 7th Battalion and one squadron of Lord Strathcona's Horse were rushed forward to consolidate the front. K.5 had not fallen in the attack, but the Canadian advance had made it untenable for the Germans. As a result, the infantry was able to enfilade the powerful redoubt with rifle and machine-gun fire, forcing the Germans to abandon it. The K.5 strongpoint was thus swallowed by No Man's Land, a fitting testament to the futility of the battle.

Haig now ordered a series of further assaults into the German lines to see if the enemy's core was rotten. Unfortunately, it was not. The Canadians' probing attacks were shot down by enemy fire. Even the Canadian Cavalry Brigade was thrown into the line, but the commanders were wise enough to realize that horses would last only minutes in the killing zone. The cavalry went in unmounted to join their infantry cousins in experiencing the terrible battlefield of mud, corpses, and unrelenting fire.

THE BATTLE OF FESTUBERT proved that the infantry needed assistance in crossing No Man's Land. Artillery support was essential to destroy barbed wire and drive the defenders into their protective dugouts. Without such support, further attacks would lead only to slaughter. To date, this frightening truth had not stopped the high command from continuing to order assaults, but on May 25 the British commander-in-chief, Sir John French, came to the conclusion that no further fighting would dislodge the enemy. The Battle of Festubert thus ground to an inglorious end.

At the shocking cost of 2,605 casualties, the Canadians had inched their way 600 metres forward on a 1.5-kilometre front.[19] More than four men had been sacrificed for every captured metre of muddy ground. This casualty rate was just less than half that suffered by the entire Canadian Division at Ypres, but came with none of the glory. The Canadian and British troops deserved better.

The battle, as characterized by Brigadier Richard Turner, was a "pure bloody mess."[20] Confusion and incompetence reigned at and behind the front. Although both Currie and Turner had objected strongly to the operation, they had been overruled by higher levels of command. The British and Canadian artillery had proved ineffective, firing short and inaccurately throughout the battle, and being wholly outclassed by the enemy. The ordering of these operations in the face of unsuppressed enemy machine-gun fire, with riflemen firing over open sights and through uncut barbed wire, was reprehensible—and had resulted in nothing less than butchery.[21]

The Canadian and British attack doctrine would not improve much over the next three weeks, and on June 15 a small attack by the 1st Brigade against Givenchy, just south of the Festubert battlefield, was another futile affair that resulted in several hundred additional casualties. But innovations had been attempted, including the welding of protective armour to the field guns to allow them to be brought forward (thus enabling the firing of shells more accurately into enemy lines) and the detonation of explosives under the German position through a mining operation. The latter proved devastating to both sides, as the force of the uncontrolled blast collapsed trenches and killed at least fifty Canadians, as well as a higher, although unknown, number of Germans. But the Canadian infantry were shot to pieces again as the artillery were plagued by a shortage of shells and by faulty fuses, and were therefore unable to do any significant damage to the German defences and barbed wire. As at Ypres and Festubert, communication was continually severed, leaving troops isolated and vulnerable in the enemy lines once they had sacrificed so much to cross the killing ground. Initially successful Canadian break-in attacks were decapitated and then driven out by fierce counterattacks. The key to battlefield victory in the coming year would be the efficient training and marrying of artillery and infantry into a coherent mailed fist that smashed enemy strongpoints, allowing the infantry a fighting chance at crossing the killing ground, and then helping them hold captured ground against enemy counterattacks.

Since late April, the Canadian Division had suffered more than 8,500 casualties in two battles in which its involvement had spanned about ten days. Most infantry battalions had lost between two-thirds and three-quarters of their men. For the thousands of Canadians who had enlisted in the heady days of August 1914, impelled by adventure, glory, or patriotism, the Western Front proved little more than a charnel house. In a war not short on terror, brutality, or horror, the Battle of Festubert marked the most callous sacrifice of Canadian lives.

CHAPTER 17

LIVING IN A SEWER

Life in the Trenches, 1915–1916

The trenches were areas of safety, and to go above ground was to invite eternal ownership of a white cross. Zigzagging across the continent like angry scars, the trenches of the Western Front cut their way through 700 kilometres of countryside, from the border of Switzerland to the Belgian coast on the North Sea. For soldiers caught within this terrible blasted zone, the terrain seemed like a different planet: a cratered, eviscerated land of mud, wasted vegetation, and unburied bodies. Gregory Clark, who entered the war as a shy man and left as a hardened soldier who would make his career as a journalist and one of Canada's great storytellers, described the Western Front as follows:

> You entered this strange mysterious unearthly land of stealth waving and weaving across Belgium and down through France, over hill and valley and plain and river, never changing, day and night, week after month, year after year, this ribbon of stealth in which no man moved or spoke loudly. And in that stealth, millions of men—British, French, German, Americans, every nationality lived years of their lives.[1]

Along most parts of the front, less than 30 kilometres away in either direction the green fields of France or Belgium teemed with life. This contrast only added to the surreal quality of the wasteland into which the troops were fed.

Trenches were not invented in 1914. For over a century, campaigns and wars had usually featured some sort of trench system, if only a simple, shallow ditch to provide some protection for the infantry. The American Civil War, the South African War, and the Russo-Japanese War had all demonstrated the importance of digging in. However, the opening stages of the Great War had proven that weapons technology had made another leap forward from previous wars, with more soldiers equipped with quick-firing rifles and supported by deadlier field guns firing high explosives and shrapnel shells. In this industrial war, trenches were more important, and more permanent, than ever.

The German defenders dominated the battlefield with firepower. Improvements in rifles, gunpowder, and ammunition extended the killing power of magazine-fed, bolt-action rifles to beyond 500 metres. Machine guns firing 400 to 500 bullets per minute were spread throughout a sector, arranged so that they fired directly and obliquely to the front and in overlapping arcs, making any assault costly, no matter how the attacking infantry approached. In addition, artillery gunners in the rear had plotted out the avenues of advance across No Man's Land, and could almost fire shrapnel and high explosives blindly, knowing that they would likely hit something in the open. In 1915, the firepower afforded to the defenders was nearly impossible to suppress, and therefore impossible to defeat.

The Germans also usually had the best ground since they had captured most of Belgium and much of France early in the war. Their occupation of this land afforded them an enormous advantage. Their strongpoints were usually positioned on the forward slope of a ridge or hill, to force attackers to advance uphill. But just as importantly, these positions provided the defenders with a view into the enemy's lines and their forming-up attacking area, which were raked with small-arms, mortar, and artillery fire. In response, however, the attackers' artillery pulverized these exposed positions on the forward slope, forcing the defenders' trenches backwards onto the reverse slope of a hill. This meant that the defenders' main line was now situated on the other side of the hill, so that its fields of fire against the attackers were limited, but the trenches were harder to hit with artillery. A small defending garrison left as a screen on the forward slope could still exact a terrible toll with massed machine-gun and rifle fire. They usually inflicted enough punishment on the advancing attackers that they would not have the strength of numbers or

DIAGRAMMATIC SKETCH OF PORTION OF A FRONT LINE, WITH SUPERVISION TRENCH, LIVING DUG-OUTS AND, SHELL TRENCHES.

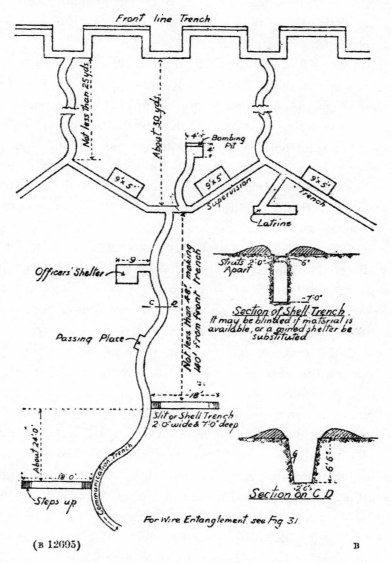

(B 12695)　　　　　　　　　　　　　　　　　　　　B

Note the front-line system, identifiable by its zigzag design,
as well as the straighter communication trenches running to the rear.

willpower to overrun the principal line of defence on the reverse slope, which had remained largely untouched by shellfire. As well, because of the difficulty of carrying out effective reconnaissance, attacks usually went in blind against positions that, in the first three years of the war, were protected by coils of barbed wire that usually had not been cut by artillery fire.

With the power of the defensive stopping most offensive operations in their tracks, the trench system of the Western Front soon resembled a permanent siege. Dirty ditches in the ground soon became homes in which sandbags and timber were used to shore up the oozing walls, and at times corrugated tin was used to protect against the weather. Underfoot, wood or bundles of sticks were laid to provide some sort of dry footing. More permanent trenches had regulation-issued lumber boards and even rudimentary pumping systems to remove water. But as Captain R.S. Robinson wrote of his first winter in the trenches, "One cannot keep dry feet, and one is cold, always cold in the trenches."[2]

The trenches were dug down to a depth of as much as six feet, but were left shallower if the ground was very wet. Sandbags were then piled in front of the trench to create an additional two or three feet of protection. Stone and brick were avoided, as they easily splintered under shellfire, becoming deadly secondary weapons in and of themselves. Along some parts of the front where the water table was close to the surface, trenches were more shallow and additional sandbags had to be stacked up to form breastworks. However, these higher sandbag walls were obvious to most observers, were attractive targets for enemy gunfire, and were easily knocked down by shells.

The wall in front of the trench was called the "parapet," and a similar sandbag protective wall called the "parados" ("dos" being the French word for "back") was placed behind the trench to protect against friendly fire from secondary lines, and to ensure that defenders' bodies were not outlined against the sky should they rise above the parapet. The sandbags—burlap or jute sacks usually a half a metre in length, filled with earth, and pulled shut with cords—were stacked on top of each other and in layered rows. Afterwards, the stack was usually packed down with shovels to create a denser barrier against the penetrating power of ordnance that flew over the battlefield by the millions. Yet the weather and the constant pounding of high explosives often caused the bags to shift, lose their density, or simply rot away, so the parapets were continually being rebuilt. Snipers periodically fired through these dissolving defences in the hopes of finding soft spots. Experienced men with any sort of height learned to walk bent over like ancients.

Along the trench parapet, wood and tin could also be used as revetment to shore up crumbling walls. Special steel loopholes were built into the sandbag wall to allow snipers to fire out through them with greater safety. These camouflaged holes also provided sentries with a little more protection when they observed the enemy. After a few men were shot in the face, however, soldiers learned to open the loopholes

This sentry is likely looking through a hole in the parapet or a periscope. Still, he is standing dangerously high up during daylight hours.

only when placing a dark bag or blanket behind and over their head, as any light from behind the observer would be seen through the loophole, drawing attention to the spot in the parapet. But these "look-sees" were always dangerous: one sloppy mistake could reveal the position, and the next unfortunate soldier to open the loop would meet his fate courtesy of a patient sniper's bullet.

Despite the constant evolution in methods of protection for the men in the trenches, the sandbag remained the most essential life-saving tool. These sacks were probably the single most common sight in the soldier's world, and everywhere he went, everywhere he looked, everywhere he sat, he was either on a sandbag or staring at one. Soldiers wrapped them around their feet to add another layer of warmth in the winter and used them to store food or personal belongings. Many men covered their helmets with sandbags to reduce the glint and glare a sniper could focus on. And in the worst case, sandbags could double as a coffin for a dismembered man hit directly by a shell. As Private Will Bird of the 42nd Battalion wrote, "A 'flying pig' [mortar] had exploded as it left the gun and three men had been shredded to fragments. We were to pick up legs and bits of flesh from underfoot, place all of them in bags and bury them." For Private Bird, only recently arrived at the front by way of Nova Scotia, this was a "harsh breaking-in."[3] Afterward, he was ordered to stand sentry in the same red-tainted spot in the trench, and spent two hours looking anywhere but down at the bloody mess on which he stood.

With most soldiers spending their days staring up at the sky or the sandbag parapet, the phrase "going over the bags" or "over the top" took on a chilling meaning. Such an attack meant that an infantryman was leaving the dirty sanctuary of his trench. The saying "over the top" had initially been followed with "and best of luck." But with one slaughter following another, it seemed advisable to drop the "best of luck," as few men could say this phrase without grimacing. A mixture of adrenaline, fear, discipline, and belief in their leaders carried the infantry forward, but a soldier could never be sure about what would greet him over the bags: would it be a smouldering, ruined trench, shattered by accurate gunfire, or an unscathed machine-gun team releasing arcs of bullets? One is reminded of the ancient explorers' maps whose large blank areas of undiscovered land were denoted only by "Here there be monsters."

BEYOND THE TRENCH PARAPET, barbed wire wove along the front as a buffer. Coiled metal strands, usually adorned with barbed wire or razor blades, protected the trench system and forced attackers to either clear it or pass through gaps that were intentionally left as they were always a part of the defending machine-guns' traverse of fire. Barbed wire was originally designed in the 1870s to corral livestock in the American West. But like many civilian implements, it was easily adapted for the purposes of war, and had been used in South Africa by the British army to limit the mobility of guerrilla Boers, as well as during the trench warfare phase of the Russo-Japanese War. During the Great War, the barbed wire was laid in irregular patterns so as not to provide an obvious outline of the trench for enemy gunners. However, since many soldiers had poor trench discipline and tended to toss their empty bully beef cans and other refuse over the parapet, a thick line of garbage often provided a clear outline of the trenches to any aerial observer.

The primary role of the wire was to slow an attack. Early in the war, it proved a devastating obstacle that kept defenders from being overwhelmed by the sheer numbers of attacking troops advancing in waves. Infantry caught in the deadly maze of barbed wire had little hope of escape or survival. Only artillery could clear these jagged defences, but in the first two and a half years of the war, gunners had neither the required weight of shells, nor fuses sensitive enough to detonate the shells when they made contact with the wire. Often shellfire only blew the obstacles over the battlefield, creating tangled mountains of jagged wire that added to the apocalyptic landscape.

Unsupported by the guns, the infantry were often reduced to cutting barbed wire by hand with special cutters. This method took time—and the cutting often had to be done at night on patrol or, even worse, when troops were on the offensive and caught in a crossfire. Too often, attackers were corralled like livestock and slaughtered by bullets and shrapnel.

THE UNDERGROUND TRENCH CITIES on either side of No Man's Land teemed with life. The front-line trench with its built-up parapet and parados was just the start of the spidery web of fortifications that consisted of many kilometres of criss-crossing support and communication trenches.[4] Estimations suggest that a single square kilometre of trenches contained 1,500 kilometres of barbed wire, 6 million sandbags, 150,000 cubic metres of tin, and 33,500 square metres of corrugated iron.[5] By 1916, for every kilometre across the front, the British system had almost 50 kilometres of trenches running back in lines parallel or at right angles to it. Two years later, in 1918, 10 million spades were issued to the British army.[6] This was as much a digging war as it was a shooting war.

The front-line trenches were ideally some six feet deep, and surmounted by another half to full metre of parapet. The building of firing steps was therefore necessary, to enable sentries to survey the battlefield and, in the case of an attack, to allow soldiers to get above their parapet and fire at the enemy. Although the sentries stood waist-high above the trench parapet at night, when they were largely hidden in the darkness, periscopes went up along the line during the day. Early periscopes were mirrors mounted on sticks, but more complex constructions evolved as the war progressed. The use of later periscopes involved a sentry looking through the bottom of a box into a mirror that contained an image reflected from another mirror above. The mechanism was simple but effective. However, after snipers began to knock these periscopes out for target practice, they were wrapped in sandbags and old rags. The eagle-eyed snipers were not usually tricked, though, and periscopes remained favourite targets. A sentry would receive quite a shock—not to mention a black eye—when the top of the periscope was destroyed by a bullet while he was looking through it.

The same trench wall on which the periscope was mounted—the forward wall—was pitted with depressions that had been carved by soldiers. Called "funk holes," the soldiers rested within them—one man per hole. Curled in the fetal position, a soldier could usually shelter half his body from the rain. The men using the holes suffered the constant kicking or trampling of their jutting legs, as well as the threat of the holes' collapse from rain and the steady pounding of artillery. Yet all such stresses could be absorbed by stoic soldiers in the hope of gaining a few hours of sleep. Alfred Andrews described the funk hole as a means of escaping—however slightly—from the madness and death that surrounded him in the trenches; he lay in the hole and "shivered with fright."[7]

As the living jutted from the walls, so too did the dead. While carving out a funk hole or filling a sandbag, it was not uncommon for a shovel to uncover a maggoty

Often it was difficult to distinguish the living from the dead, as soldiers found a few hours of sleep by carving out funk holes in trench walls.

arm or broken femur. Even in the dark, the rush of putrid air alerted a man to his unwelcome discovery. David McLean described the horror to his sweetheart at home in a gasping, run-on sentence that captured his reaction to his bewildering experience: "I will never forget the last time I went into the trenches there was a skull sticking out of the side of the trench and a couple of nights after I was moving some sand bags in the front trench and there was some poor fellow lying underneath with all his kit on but you have to get used to such things."[8] The dead were rarely buried in the walls of the trenches after 1915, but corpses remained from the first eighteen months of the war. The slow advance into No

Man's Land also meant that the dead, whether buried or not, were incorporated into the front lines unintentionally.

"The acrid smell of stale urine got up my nose when I first arrived but I'm used to it now," wrote Sergeant John MacGregor from Powell River, British Columbia. He was also soon "used to the sickly sweet stench of rotting bodies that gags the throats of newcomers."[9] The smell of the trenches was something that none of the *frontsoldaten*—on either side of No Man's Land—ever forgot. During the winter months, soldiers wore their wet wool clothes for weeks at a time. "We seldom wash. No water to spare," remarked Herbert Burrell, a former cashier from Winnipeg who enlisted at the age of forty-five.[10] Corporal John Harold Becker echoed Burrell: "Filth was part of the soldier's existence and one could not expect to be any more than half clean at any one time."[11] With the soldiers huddled together for warmth, the smell of a fetid dugout could be unbearable. During the summer, the men sweated freely in their heavy uniforms, again without changes of clothes or frequent baths. Hugh Urquhart of the 16th Battalion wrote that in the summer the trenches could be stifling, as "currents of fresh air never penetrated into them, and in their depths the men sweltered in a lifeless atmosphere."[12] And in addition to these seasonal, human smells, all year long the reek of the wet earth burned and tainted by explosives and cordite was unmistakable. Life in the trenches afforded precious few good aromas, but bacon in the morning was one to be cherished, and strong cigarettes were useful in temporarily masking the most unpleasant odours.

Civilians along the English coast could never imagine the smell at the front, but they were often close enough to hear the rumble of a large artillery bombardment on a quiet day. The low murmur of artillery heard from Britain's coast was, however, an ear-shattering, gut-wrenching shock in the trenches. The powerful shells tore up the ground and the men hiding in it. The infantry soon learned from painful experience that trenches had to be dug in zigzag formation to prevent artillery shell blasts or shrapnel from being funnelled down a straight path to kill and maim those in the trench. Furthermore, the trenches were made as narrow as possible in order to limit the blast radius of overhead explosions, and were therefore only wide enough for one or two men to stand in. This limited width was necessary to contain shell blasts, but it created terrible difficulties during big offensives when the wounded from No Man's Land pulled themselves back to their lines and flung themselves into the trenches. With nowhere to go, the wounded were often trodden on and trampled underneath the fighting soldiers, despite their screams of agony.

The trenches were broken up by solid walls of earth, called fire bays, every 30 or 40 metres, to provide another cushion against direct blasts. This division also aided in defence, as the separated sections of trench were set at turned angles to one

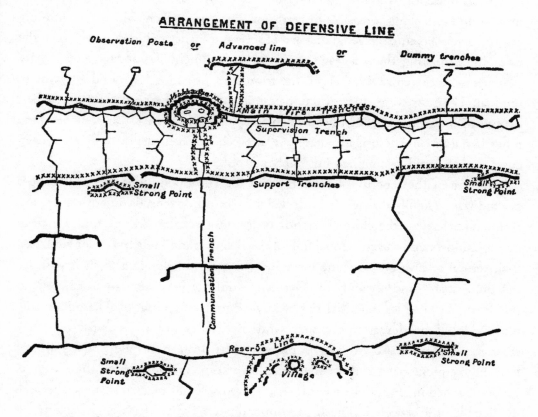

Note the three lines of defence: front line, secondary line, and reserve positions. The x's represent barbed wire; the dummy trench was an uninhabited trench designed to draw enemy fire. The strongpoints in the rear were protective dugouts from which counterattacking forces could launch assaults and drive the attackers back to their lines.

another, creating an irregular zigzag design that protected defenders against raiders slipping into their lines, setting up machine guns, and firing all along a trench. Moreover, if a section of the trench was captured, it could be temporarily sealed off, forcing the attacker to capture one fire bay after the next—a slow and costly process that also allowed time for the defenders to gather together a counterattacking force.

BY 1915, it was clear that a front-line trench could often be pierced by an infantry advance behind a heavy artillery bombardment, but two or more trenches of defenders spread in depth would likely blunt an enemy assault, certainly slowing it down until counterattacking forces could be thrown into the breach. Moreover, thinning out the defenders into a layered defence of several trenches reduced crowding in the front lines, making them a less target-rich environment. Secondary and tertiary trenches were therefore dug behind the front line, usually a few hundred yards to the rear. The four companies of one battalion defended these reinforced trenches: two companies in the front line, two in reserve. Behind these rear trenches were other battalions in the brigade that were also echeloned in depth to create a deep cushion that could be smashed but rarely pierced.

The idea of the sanctity of ground—and the corresponding belief that to lose ground was to signify defeat—were drilled into the officers' heads on both sides, and counterattacks were therefore constantly ordered to recapture lost ground. One can perhaps understand the emotional link of the Belgians and French to their land, and their refusal to give up even one more inch of ground belonging to their nations, but the British—and certainly the Germans—did not have such an attachment to this land. Yet all sides practised fierce, unyielding counterattacks. These lightning attacks could be devastatingly successful in driving out the enemy, but they consistently ground away the troops on both sides. Instead of following a policy of limiting counterattacks to those that were likely to be in one's favour, these assaults were unleashed in almost every battle—and often several times, so that they became predictable and expected. The high commands on both sides were also narrow-mindedly concerned with straightening out the line, which meant attacking enemy positions that jutted into one's own trench system. This tended to result in fruitless assaults to ensure that the maps looked better to those at division headquarters.

Although this straightening helped the artillery to coordinate fire along a wide front, allowing the enemy a salient that jutted into one's lines was usually a wise move since this peninsula would be surrounded in part on three sides and easier to bombard with enfilade fire. However, both sides remained gripped by the sanctity of ground, and only in the last two years of the war did they become more willing to trade land and space for time and a better defensive position.

WHILE THE FORWARD and secondary trenches ran parallel to the enemy trenches on the other side of No Man's Land, the communication trenches linked the various levels of defence. These were the arteries feeding the essential front-line muscle. As Private George Kempling, a thirty-one-year-old machinist from Toronto, wrote, "The inside of the walls are stiffened up by long heavy stakes, 4 ft. long to which is nailed mesh wire, or strips of corrugated iron, solid cross-stick sidewalks are built, leaving a deep drain underneath for the water to flow away for nearly the whole country is low and the earth always very damp."[13] Along the path these trenches provided to the rear, cross-planks were laid to keep the mud from swallowing men alive. Overhead, telephone wires ran along the upper part of the trench walls, but they were too easily cut in this position, and so were later buried in the earth, up to 2 metres deep.

Like the front trenches, these communication routes were dug in a zigzag formation, but with fewer turns since they were traversed by hundreds of men each day. Everything needed by the front-line infantrymen had to come via the communication trenches, which started in the rear and led to the front. Both sides were aware of this set-up, and therefore the communication trenches were regularly swept by enemy artillery fire. Branching off from these trenches were dugouts for company and battalion headquarters, bays to allow for the grouping of troops in the event of a rapid counterattack, and a rough dugout manned by the battalion's medical officer and stretcher-bearers.

Day and night, reinforcements and men carrying water or ammunition moved forward like blood through arteries; along the same network, but coming from the opposite direction, the walking wounded banged from one trench wall to the other. Taking up more space were the stretchers, with their four-man carrying parties. This constant movement occurred in tandem with high explosives crashing above the trench walls, shrapnel raining down, and a steady stream of bullets whirling over-head. Soldiers faced a hard decision when high explosives caved in the communica-tion trenches or rain reduced the pathway to thigh-high gluey mud: either dig their way through or go overland. After a few weeks at the front, exhausted soldiers usually chose the latter option, weighing the odds against being hit by stray fire. "One of the most difficult things to do is not to take fool chances, as the impulse to cross the open rather than walk a mile through a muddy communication trench is irresistible," wrote Armine Norris, who had enlisted as a twenty-one-year-old student from the University of Toronto.[14] Despite the danger posed by snipers and shells, however, the infantry continued to take shortcuts overland, impelled by exhaustion, bravado, and an unhealthy sense of fatalism.

Moving within the high walls of the communication trenches, the soldiers were effectively blind. "These marches into the trenches by night are something never to be forgotten. You go stumbling along in the dark, single file, just like 'follow the leader' and 'obstacle race' combined," wrote Ernest Taylor—the youngest of eleven siblings—to his older sister in his hometown of Vermilion, Alberta, six months before his death.[15] Soldiers were constantly becoming lost in the winding, doglegged, and confusing turns of new trenches. "All the trenches look alike," complained a new man, "after you have plodded along for a time twisting and turning aimlessly with nothing ever before and beside you but mud walls and mud-coloured uniforms of silent men."[16] And since troops moved from the rear to the front lines at night to avoid enemy fire, men could be lost beneath the ground for hours—slithering along the greasy duckboards, stumbling into new shell holes, and stepping over the rubble of torn-up duckboards. Not only was this confusion an annoying part of the trench soldiers' existence, but it could result in unnecessary deaths as men were caught in more vulnerable communication trenches during the daily shelling that typically occurred around dawn. Soldiers could be endangered if an exhausted and confused scout could not get troops to their start line in time for a battle or in time to relieve troops under cover of darkness.

Crudely drawn trench maps helped, as did the signs that marked the dark passages with names alternating from the cryptic and mundane to the sentimental and the silly. Wretched Way, Hellfire Corner, Winnipeg Row, and an assortment of other "street" names helped to designate areas and throughways for the mole-like soldiers. New trenches were named by the units that dug them, and it was not uncommon for a battalion of men from a particular city to name the trenches they dug after landmarks and streets in their hometown. The long reach of home-front memories accounted in part for such labels, and familiar names were also simply easier to remember. Trenches coordinated by the Royal Engineers often had more formal naming structures, with all the new trenches and saps in a particular sector receiving names beginning with the same letter of the alphabet. Throughout the trench system were more informal warnings in danger spots, especially in corners that might suffer from enfilade fire: "Keep down your bloody bean."

Side passages jutted out along the communication trench: cul de sacs, storage areas, and places to step out of the path of foul-mouthed sergeants leading working parties carrying wood or corrugated iron. Latrines were also built in designated spots close to the front after consultation with the medical officer and engineers. They were deep holes in the ground with planks of wood placed over them for some modicum of comfort. A sanitary corporal, often nicknamed "shit wallah," had the unpleasant job of ensuring that the latrines were not filled beyond capacity. He also advised the battalion's second-in-command as to when new ones needed to be constructed. This was, as one might expect, an unpopular job and often reserved for men undergoing punishment.

The stirring up of flies by the constant tramp of men to and from the latrines drew snipers to that area of the trench, making the continual replacement of sand-bags necessary to ensure that snipers did not fire through the ever-rotting bags in search of targets. Fortunately, instructions to squat were perhaps more readily heeded here than anywhere else. And certainly, given the danger and stench, many did not linger at the latrine—although it was a good place to pick up the latest rumour racing up and down the line. Soldiers were not issued toilet paper, and so newspapers and magazines were jealously guarded by the men, even the illiterate ones. Soldiers in search of "bumf," a short form for "bum-fodder," were not above relieving their mates of their "toilet paper" if they happened to leave it in plain sight, or even if it was securely hidden away in a pack.

When a latrine was filled to capacity, chloride of lime was spread over it and then it was usually imploded with a small explosive charge. However, enemy shell-fire would sometimes hit the fetid waste and spray it around the area in a geyser of excrement. These events proved that latrines should be built along secondary passageways further away from front-line trenches; more practical military reasons for such relocation included the control of disease in the trenches.

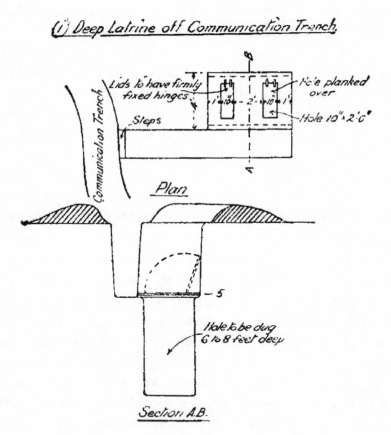

With a male adult unloading an average of 2.4 pounds of feces and urine per day, the latrine became an important structure in the trench.

Dugouts were not initially welcomed by the high command, some British and French generals being unwilling to embrace any sort of comfort for their troops, who might then lose the impetus to drive the enemy from the battlefield. Nonetheless, dugouts became a necessity to protect against weather and increasingly devastating barrages. As trenches solidified, deeper dugouts—similar to underground cellars—were built to offer better protection for soldiers. More dugouts per section of trench were constructed by the end of 1915, when it appeared that soldiers would be forced to endure another winter before open warfare could possibly return to the front. Most of the front-line infantry slowly abandoned their funk holes for dugouts, trading fresh air for the protection of a cave. Inevitably, though, a few men with ragged nerves, and who had been buried alive once too often, would refuse to enter a deep dugout even during the heaviest of bombardments. If their commanding officers did not take pity on them and send them to the rear, these men's life expectancy at the front could be measured in weeks.

Dugouts were situated along the communication trench or in the forward and secondary lines. When constructed in these latter positions, they were always built into the front trench wall to ensure that a chance shell could not be fired straight down the dugout entrance. A heavy blanket was hung in front of the dugout's wooden stairwell to reduce the visibility of the light emanating from within. This covering was replaced in 1917 with a double-layered chemically impregnated blanket that offered good protection against the gas fumes that pooled in the trenches. Officers and men did not bunk together, and the privileges of rank went to the commissioned men, whose dugouts were usually cleaner and often had the luxuries of beds, desks, telephones, and even gramophones.

The Royal Engineers stipulated the exact size of the dugouts, but these specifications were rarely adhered to in the fury of digging. Most often, however, the dugouts were at least 6 metres deep and accessed via a series of descending steps. The smell of a dugout could alert a man to its location even if he could not find it in the dark. These accommodations were rarely ventilated, and the assault on the olfactory senses caused by twenty or thirty unwashed men was overpowering. Within this dank cocoon, soldiers slept on the floor, which was sometimes covered in sandbags.

TYPICAL DUG-OUT.

Scale 1 in. = 12 ft.

Section A.B.

Sandbags

Corrugated Iron Sheeting

Picket driven down as holdfast for uprights at side of steps

Gas Blanket

9" Burster of broken brick, stone, etc.

6'0"

5'3"

4'6"

20'0" This will vary with the soil and whether or no there is a bursting course over the dug-out.

Bomb Pit

Section C.D.
(Method of using Pit Props & Corrugated Iron)

1'6" 1'6" 2'6"

6'0"

Bomb Pit

Section C.D.
Alternative Method using 12" Planks

Note the dugout's recommended depth of twenty feet and its single entrance and exit; these features rendered the soldiers' underground shelter a death trap if the enemy secured the trenches above.

In the wintertime, a central fire in a dugout left men sooty black, and the constant consumption of strong tobacco caused the walls to drip with nicotine.

In the dead of winter, friends huddled together for warmth, and men usually developed sleeping partners. "We wake up, shivering and wet," remarked Lieutenant Stanley Rutledge, an officer with better living conditions than the average Tommy.[17] In the summer, the heat was oppressive and kit was strewn about in the dark (although experienced men always kept their gas mask within reach), presenting an obstacle for new men arriving from sentry duty or a battle patrol. But such hindrances did not stop tired men from kicking their way forward to a spot on the ground. Having a hand or ankle stepped on by heavy hobnailed boots was usually greeted by little more than a good string of profanities that would be lost within the cacophony of snores, coughs, and cries from men wracked with tortured dreams. Privacy was a thing of the past, as with many civilian concepts.

The dugouts were impervious to all but the heaviest of shells, and they were reinforced with sandbags and wooden beams. Despite their sturdiness, however, to reside in one during a barrage was terrifying. Dirt and dust left the air hazy as it silted down and billowed in with every shellfire shock wave. The essential candles that soldiers read and wrote by were snuffed out time and time again by the blast concussions. In worst cases, dugouts were caved in and the survivors— enduring a race against depleting oxygen—prayed for release from their coffin by topside mates. But any soldier who had spent more than a few months at the front had likely been buried alive at least once, and the terror of that experience compelled all men to join in to dig out their trapped companions in a frenzy of activity. Buried soldiers could suffer additional wounds as a result of their saviours' clumsy spadework, but this was preferable to suffocation.

A dugout was little more than a hole in the ground and an automatic death trap should a trench be captured since there was usually no way up. Nonetheless, it provided a welcome psychological and physical relief from the trials of the trenches. A good dugout was indeed something to be marvelled at and jealously guarded. The soldiers found that despite the horrors of their subterranean world of trenches, it was necessary to make the best of it. More than a few soldiers happily hummed along to the popular trench song "My Little Wet Home in the Trench."

CHAPTER 18

MANY A DAMNED COLD MORNING

The Banality of Trench Routine

At daybreak we were told to "stand to our arms." I almost danced with excitement at the anticipation of the attack. And so we stood with bayonets fixed until what some Johnny called "the cold, grey dawn" grew into broad daylight. I was really disappointed that no attack came off. I enquired and found that "stand to" every morning and dusk were a part of the daily routine of trench life. The grey light is very favourable to attacks. Since then I have seen many "cold, grey dawns," some of them merely cold, and some of them damned cold.[1]

Twenty-year-old Private John Baston of the 16th Battalion recounted disappointedly in the above letter his first experience in the line and being "initiated into the mysteries" of the trenches. New men expected constant battles and bayonet charges when they arrived at the front. Instead, they more often found many a damned cold morning. Baston would soon learn to embrace the static nature of the front, but he would not be disappointed by going through the war without seeing an attack: over the next three years, he would be shot in the head and the leg in battle, but he would survive the war.

STAND-TO AT A HALF HOUR before dawn, which brought all the soldiers, half asleep and shivering, into the front lines to wait with rifles and bayonets at the ready for an attack was just one of the strange rituals of trench warfare. The general perception was that enemy forces would come over at dawn, the best time to launch an operation since success would mean that any counterattacking force would have to retake the position during daylight. However, since all sides expected an attack, and called out the full garrison to the firing line, dawn action was rare, as few commanders were callous enough to order a suicidal attack against an alerted garrison. However, such considerations did not stop the artillery from laying down a "morning hate" in the hope of catching the infantry bunched together and outside their protective dugouts. While a few days of these surprise bombardments quickly brought artillery retaliation from the other side's guns, as always the "poor bloody infantry" were the ones caught in the middle.

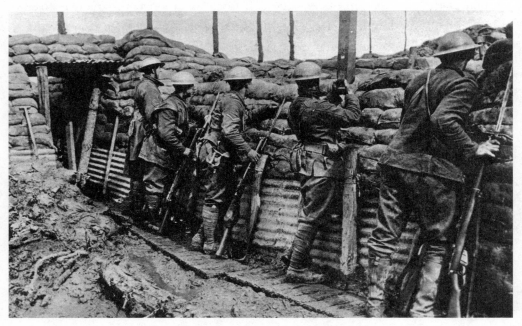

A front-line Canadian garrison standing-to in the cold, grey dawn.

But this stand-to ritual was important as it allowed non-commissioned officers and subalterns (a British term for junior officers) to see all their men, thus reinforcing the officers' presence in the trenches. New orders were given at stand-to, and after waiting for the attack that rarely came, the order to "stand down" was barked out and the day began in earnest. "After we stand-down there are rifles to clean, trenches to be cleaned, a wash to be had—if you can find a shell hole with some water in it—then breakfast," wrote young Sergeant Samuel Honey, a former teacher on a Six Nations reserve. Honey stood only five foot five, but his steel-grey eyes and gentle manner had made him a favourite among his men. He would be commissioned later in the war, and awarded the prestigious Victoria Cross for bravery on the battlefield.[2]

The men cleaned no more than half the rifles in a section at a time, for fear of being caught defenceless by a surprise enemy raid. Rust and dirt—both on and in the barrel—were the key concerns in the cleaning process. Barrels were wiped down with oil and cloth, and a special weighted rag was pulled through the barrel. After a few incidents of rifles discharging in the faces of inspecting officers, strict orders were given to ensure that no cartridge was in the chamber before the firearm was extended for examination. Still, an inordinate number of deaths and maimings were caused by accidentally discharged rifles, with exhausted and fidgety soldiers all too often making fatal mistakes of judgment.

This long-arm inspection was far more pleasant than the "short-arm" one, which sometimes followed it and left everyone involved thoroughly embarrassed. Officers accompanied the medical officer, who examined the men's genitals for telltale signs of concealed venereal disease. Controlling the spread of sexual infections was important, but the indignity of this exam was often reserved for areas to the rear of the trenches, where the men had less chance of being killed with their pants around their ankles.

The genital inspection was done sporadically, but the "sick parade" occurred every day. Those men claiming they were too sick to work lined up to be inspected by the medical officer or his senior medical orderly. This was a difficult job, as the medical officer was torn between the twin roles of physician and detective. For weary, dejected soldiers, being declared sick was a ticket out of the trenches—one that many tried to punch by feigning all manner of illnesses.[3] New medical officers were sometimes fooled by men who claimed to be deaf from explosions or who had deliberately infected weeping boils by rubbing cordite into wounds; but more experienced medical officers had their own tricks for ferreting out the malingerers. Deaf men were asked questions in low voices, and then shouted at in the hopes that they lurched at the sound of a voice, while those who claimed paralysis of limbs were pricked with pins at an unsuspecting moment. More often, however, the medical officers simply prescribed the infamous "pill No. 9"—a mild laxative— for everything ranging from hacking coughs and splitting headaches to skin infections and bleeding gums. Such laxative pills did little for the soldiers' ailments and ultimately deterred sick men from parading themselves before the medical officer. "One nearly had to be on death's door," complained an exasperated Canadian, before a front-line soldier would be sent to the rear.[4] The tension between caring for the men and responding to the high command's orders to keep the soldiers in the line was a trial for doctors who had taken the Hippocratic oath.

The inspection of feet remained a key priority for the medical officer, and this procedure was carried out with almost neurotic insistence. The medical and regimental officers crouched over the men's feet, pushing and prodding them, examining digits for signs of fungus and rot. However, during the first two winters of the war, before thigh-high rubber boots were issued in sufficient numbers, the ailment was hard to avoid. With soldiers standing in mud and icy slush for hours, even days, they often went too long without taking off their wet socks and boots. This immersion in water was like staying in a bathtub for too long: the flesh on the foot began to pucker. Blood was constricted to the extremities, and days in these conditions led to inflamed feet that soon became grossly swollen and discoloured. Blisters formed, and first the toes, then the entire foot became numb from nerve damage. Infantryman Will Bird from Nova Scotia remembered seeing one man hobbling along on "huge blobs of misshapen flesh."[5] After this stage, gangrene usually set in, leading to toes eventually rotting off. Before that, however, the pain felt in between periods of numbness alerted the afflicted. Hard men who did not complain about their plight in life were sometimes known to ignore the agony; soldiers fed up with the troglodytic existence endured the torture through gritted teeth, realizing that they might be sent to a rear hospital if they let the foot rot long enough. They were often "crimed" for this transgression, receiving hard labour after they recovered, but at least their suffering afforded them a temporary escape from the trenches. By war's end, 4,987 cases of trench foot were recorded in the Canadian forces.[6] While only two men died from the affliction, there were many cases of soldiers who had their glutinous, rotting toes and feet amputated.

Trench foot was particularly worrisome to officers, as it was seen by the high command as an indication of weak morale in a unit. Battalion officers were threatened with reprisals by their seniors should their men fall victim to trench foot, and to prevent this perceived threat to discipline and combat effectiveness the battalion officers passed on mass punishment to their men, usually by refusing to grant leave. Officers were to ensure that socks were changed every day and that smelly whale oil was slathered on the feet. Complaints of the noxious smell of greased, unwashed

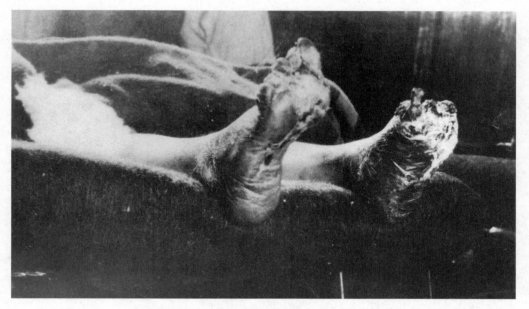

Standing in water for too long resulted in a loss of circulation and, eventually, gangrene. This is an advanced case of trench foot, which will require amputation of several toes and perhaps the left foot.

feet were ignored in the name of discipline, although some men begged for less malodorous solutions such as talcum powder from loved ones at home. These foot inspections remained serious business, and when an obvious imbalance between the numbers of trench foot victims in the 1st and 2nd Canadian Divisions appeared in the winter of 1915–1916, Major General Richard Turner, commander of the 2nd Division since September 1915, was accused of running a loose formation, the charge further damaging his already battered reputation.[7]

Applying smelly oil was an ugly task, but the job was made more palatable by the fact that afterwards the men were usually issued a rum ration. A couple of months before he was killed at Vimy Ridge, Private Ronald Mackinnon noted that he had to cut his letter to his father short because he heard "the joyful cry, 'rum up.'"[8] Men raced up dugouts and down trenches to greet the rum jar–carrying sergeant like a long-lost brother. Infantryman Ralph Bell of the 1st Battalion wrote, "When the days shorten, and the rain never ceases; when the sky is ever grey, the nights chill, and trenches thigh deep in mud and water; when the front is altogether a beastly place, in fact, we have one consolation. It comes in gallon jars, marked simply 'S.R.D.'"[9] This S.R.D. was potent, dark rum, and although few soldiers knew what the letters stood for (Supply Reserve Depot), they had great delight in spoofing the name with interpretations such as "Soon Runs Dry," "Seldom Reaches Destination," "Sergeants Rarely Deliver," and "Soldiers' Real Delight."

Rum was an institutionalized and regimented part of the ritual of enduring the trials of trench warfare. At the discretion of their officers, sergeants doled out two ounces of over-proof Jamaican rum to each man. The coveted liquid was to be drunk in the presence of an NCO or officer to prevent hoarding, and any extra rum was to be poured out. In reality, however, not a lot of rum went into the dirt, with friends of the NCOs and old hands generally benefiting from "leftovers."

As the allocation of rum was left to the prerogative of commanding officers and medical officers, an important agent was placed in their hands.[10] If a commanding officer was a teetotaller, then the men got lime juice and pea soup instead of rum. One of the Canadian Corps' most attack-oriented commanders, or a "fire-eater" in the parlance of the time, was Victor Odlum, who commanded the 7th Battalion and later the 11th Brigade. Because of his missionary background, he refused to issue rum to his troops. Odlum was nicknamed "Old Lime Juice" and, in the words of E.L.M. Burns—a signaller in the 4th Division and a general in the Second World War— Odlum's temperance stance "got minus zero in the front-line opinion polls."[11] Mutinous feelings became so strong that Odlum's superior officer was forced to overrule the usually popular brigadier and instigate the issuing of rum to his men in February 1917. In an organization where soldiers had little if any power, the withholding of rum was an important enough matter for them to raise their collective voices.

"If we hadn't had our rum, we would have lost the war," testified more than a few

HOPE SPRINGS ETERNAL IN THE HUMAN BREAST

This cartoon, published in a soldiers' trench newspaper, speaks to the importance of rum.

soldiers.[12] The troops expected to receive the rum ration, and many considered it to be owed to them for their hard life in the ditches. Perhaps some even saw it as their reward for surviving another day at the front. When rum was issued, men were content. If it was withheld, the result could be a plunge in morale. R.J. Manion, a wartime medical officer and a future parliamentarian and leader of the national Conservative Party, believed that the rum ration was often the only "cheery thing" for the soldiers who eked out an existence in the trenches. Without it, soldiers could turn mutinous or "swing the lead" (malinger), which was their form of protest against a perceived injustice.[13] Front-line soldier Ralph Bell echoed Manion when he wrote that men would work in the rain or stand in mud for hours on end if they knew they would receive a shot of rum in the end: "Deny it to them, and more than half will parade sick in the morning."[14]

Rum was an essential coping mechanism for the trench soldiers. The liquid courage protected men from physically and psychologically crumbling under the rigours of trench warfare. The drink also acted as a sedative, and its potency could knock men out for hours, notwithstanding the cold or heat, the lice or rats, and the constant pounding of the big guns. Claude Williams, who had left his studies at the University of Toronto to enlist, scrawled a letter to his mother stating that rum could be "regarded more as a medicine than a beverage. It is ... absolutely invaluable to put men to sleep when they are wet and cold."[15] But the taste required some getting used to. When J.I. Chambers of the 7th Battalion had his first gulp of rum, he remembered that it felt as if he had "swallowed a red-hot poker."[16]

The issuing of rum to soldiers also helped to reinforce the hierarchical nature of the armies, which was so integral to their success. In the unparalleled slaughter of the Great War, discipline and hierarchy were essential: a few led, and many followed. Soldiers rarely questioned orders openly—even seemingly callous ones. Punishment and discipline were the main deterrents for potential troublemakers, but the issuing of rum also played a role in bolstering the hierarchy of command. Men who were under punishment were excluded, but those who were in the good books lined up, and the more senior-ranking men moved down the line doling out the precious liquid. This was a ritual of war and akin in many soldiers' eyes to that of a religious offering. "A good snort of rum was issued to us this morning by the Priests of the God Rum—i.e., the Sergeant," wrote Private Herbert Burrell.[17] Each soldier waited patiently for his share, all the while aware that the higher-ranking soldier who divided up the portions gave a little more or less depending on his whim. Thus, just as rum was meaningful to the individual soldiers, it was also essential to the officers in helping to enforce their role in the trenches.

AFTER INSPECTION and the dispensing of belly-warming rum, NCOs ordered men to take up sentry duty or begin their work fatigues. Parts of the trench were destroyed by shellfire nearly every night and had to be repaired; sandbags were in continuous stages of rot from the rain and mud, necessitating that new sections of the parapet be rebuilt every day; and fresh latrines had to be dug. Captain David Corrigall, a thirty-two-year-old architect from Toronto who had served more than eight years in the militia before the war, recounted one trying period in November 1915 when the rain had so badly dissolved the trenches that most of the battalion had to work "for forty-eight hours at a stretch without sleep" to ensure that their protective walls did not crumble around them. The men shovelled and stacked sandbags at a frenzied pace, aware that German snipers were smacking their lips in anticipation of the walls coming down. Corrigall's 20th Battalion survived those terrifying two days, but the experience was ingrained in the minds of most survivors.[18]

Life in the trenches for the rank and file consisted of vast periods of manual labour, drudgery, and boredom. Companies were responsible for rebuilding their own sections of the trenches and keeping them intact. While soldiers worked steadily all day, many of them were free from chores for at least a few hours. One of the tasks to be attended to after military duties were completed was the maintenance of personal hygiene. Front-line soldiers were usually allowed to shave every second day. But with a shortage of clean water (cold tea was often a substitute), shaving was always a nick-ridden affair of patience and profanity.

Following a shave and a visit to the latrine, soldiers could search for food. "We live mostly on bully beef and hardtack," recounted Lieutenant Louis Keene. "The first is corned beef and the second is a kind of dog biscuit. We always wondered why they were so particular about a man's teeth in the army. Now I know. It's on account of these biscuits. The chief ingredient is, I think, cement, and they taste that way too.... We have fried, baked, mashed, boiled, toasted, roasted, poached, hashed, devilled them alone and together with bully beef, and we have still to find a way of making them into interesting food."[19] Sergeant Ernest Black recounted that some of the hardtack was edible, but that eating a common variety, Number 4, was "like gnawing a very old bone."[20] Bully beef was eaten for breakfast, lunch, and dinner, but the meat was so full of fat and gristle that only the foolhardy ate it in the dark. All soldiers developed their favourite types of bully, but stretcher-bearer Frederick

Noyes recounted that the William Davies brand from Canada was universally regarded as the worst. "It proved to be practically uneatable—a sort of jellified blob of gristle, fat, and skin. We had fairly strong stomachs, but simply could not swallow it."[21] In a testament to the soldiers' ingenuity, the bully beef cans were often used to pave dugout entrances.

Experienced soldiers learned to light small braziers—watching the smoke anxiously to ensure it was not heavy enough to give away a position—to heat water or soften up the biscuits. And a good quartermaster in charge of supplies made sure that front-line troops had bacon and bread for breakfast, although the movement of food from the rear to the front was a dangerous affair at all times. Canadian soldiers subsisted largely on these basic foods while stationed in the front lines, but although the cuisine was bland and monotonous, it provided a high calorific content so that no one starved.

In this war of inactivity, food became an important focus for the soldiers. Rumour had it that since the company cooks were allowed to ride on the baggage wagon, they were usually men with poor feet or hammer toes, but most fighting infantrymen sniffed that the cooks also obviously had something wrong with their olfactory senses. The establishment of cooking schools was met with quizzical eyes by most of the rank and file, and rarely did cooks return having learned more than a few mundane dishes. But soldiers were occasionally surprised by an excellent stew, although it paid not to look too closely at what had been included in it from the scrap heap. Eighteen-year-old Private James Johnston, who spent the war driving shell-transporting mules, recounted how he and his mates always complimented their company cook on his greasy fried potatoes until one day they examined the cooking grease and found it "alive with maggots." Johnston's horrified mates made sure "that fellow did not do more cooking."[22] Good cooks were hard to find, and when a company got one, they rarely allowed him into the front line for fear that he would be killed. No matter what innate skill a cook might possess, however, with access to only rudimentary kitchen supplies and heavy, starchy foods, few could be called culinary maestros. For the most part, men masticated methodically—and often with little pleasure.

But food remained a focal point for the bored and hungry. George McLean of the 4th Battalion informed his sister that while the food was not very appetizing, "It is amazing how conditions change taste … I have had my 'teeth water' over biscuits and water in a way that often they didn't for the most delicious meals in civil life."[23] The infantry, it would appear, could get used to most things. Soldiers did have access to some more palatable types of food, however. Jam remained a treat during the war, but the front-line soldiers always seemed to be stuck with plum and apple, with the mythical strawberry gobbled up long before it made its way to the sharp end. The infantry blamed the service corps, whom they rightly saw as having cushy jobs and abusing their position on the lines of communication. The questionable contents of their staple foods were reflected in one of the litanies of the trenches: "From plum jam and bully beef, good Lord deliver us."[24]

More damaging for health, soldiers rarely had an opportunity to eat green vegetables, and the men often suffered from skin problems due to shortages of vitamins C and D. This lack of nutrition, combined with the greasy food and dearth of clean water, left tens of thousands of young Canadian lads covered in pimples. No one starved in the front lines, but finding and eating food became an obsession. As one trench veteran grumbled, "The system appeared to have the purpose of keeping us like bulldogs before a fight—with enough to live on but hungry all the time."[25]

Gift packages from the home front were therefore prized for the alternatives to bland rations they offered. A study of soldiers' letters reveals constant pleas for food and treats. Fresh food sent from home was often mouldy when it arrived, but men were hungry enough to scrape away a fuzzy green exterior. They certainly ate worse in the trenches. Sergeant Samuel Honey wrote to his parents thanking them for their care package, which was "acceptable and appreciated, if not all by myself, at least by my 'mates' for of course everything is shared up."[26] The unwritten law in the trenches was to divide the care packages with one's close friends, but the recipient got first choice of treat. These life lines from the home front were essential to augment the "deadly monotonous" food, but also to reinforce in soldiers the feeling that their loved ones had not, in the words of Lieutenant J.E. Ryerson, "forgotten us."[27]

SOLDIERS DID THEIR BEST to avoid their NCO throughout the day. The rebuilding of the trenches was never-ending, and any shell damage occurring in the night had to be repaired the next day. Shovel and pickaxe work was never fun, but it was done in the trenches, and so the soldiers remained relatively safe. Those not selected for work fatigue or standing sentry spent their time cleaning their kit, writing letters, reading newspapers, or catching a few hours of sleep. "The greatest difficulty that we had to contend with was monotony—just utter bloody boredom," recounted H.R. Alley of the 3rd Battalion. "It just went on and on and on and on."[28] The always acerbic Herbert Burrell of the 1st Canadian Mounted Rifles (CMR) vented in his diary, "One wishes for something to read or do. You are liable to go bughouse lying hour after hour on your back gazing at the chalk roof of your funk hole which is only two inches from your nose. I found a diversion in taking a match and scratching little channels to try and persuade the water to trickle into the trench instead of my blanket."[29]

While the boredom was trying, in the summertime life in the front-line trenches was not terrible. The water- and mud-filled ditches dried out and soldiers could take the opportunity to laze around in the sun. During the summer (or even as soldiers fought the more difficult weather

This strange field-service postcard was nicknamed a "whiz-bang" after the fast German shells that often arrived with little warning. It was forbidden to write anything on the cards. Instead, soldiers struck off the pre-written lines that did not apply to them. They were, in short, a quick note from the front to let loved ones know that a soldier was still alive.

conditions through the winter months), artillery bombardments and sniper bullets were not non-stop, day and night. The strange silence of the front was broken by birdsong, although soldiers had to restrain the urge to pop their head up and look around for the warblers. Even in the calm, snipers were always looking for careless men.

For those who could see the battlefield through trench periscopes, it had a strange empty quality. Tens of thousands of men garrisoned the front, yet all were below ground. Lieutenant Allen Oliver, a forward observer for the artillery, wrote to his father, the powerful Liberal member of Parliament Frank Oliver: "This is certainly a funny war. Not that I am a very good judge of wars, this being my first experience. The only evidence which we have of the enemy is a line of trench which can be seen either through a periscope or by poking the head up and immediately withdrawing it, and the fact that at times the air (and sometimes other things) is rent with bullets and shells."[30] Another trench warrior, Coningsby Dawson, noted that the experience of the *frontsoldaten* consisted of "muddy roads leading up through a desolated country to holes in the ground, in which he spends most of his time watching other holes in the ground, which people tell him are the Hun front-line."[31]

WHETHER STANDING SENTRY, ducking for cover, or snoring through a nap, most soldiers did so with a cigarette in the mouth. Almost everyone smoked in the trenches, and this habit provided a significant relief from the stress of war. The cigarettes were supplied by the army, patriotic groups, and loved ones at home. The army ration arrived several times a week, but they were cheap and smoked only when all others had turned to ash.

Woodbines were the most popular brand of "gaspers," but dozens of varieties of cigarettes from all countries made their way to soldiers: Ruby Queen, Red Hussar, 'Arf a Mo, and Gold Flake were all burned down with a relish.[32] Cigarettes helped to calm the nerves and whittle away the time in the trenches. For soldiers faced with the stench of blasted earth, lingering poisonous gases, decomposing bodies, and the rankness of unwashed bodies, cigarette smoke also masked the scent of the trenches. "I have not up to this time succumbed to the tender influences of the lovely lady nicotine," wrote Gunner Frank Ferguson in his diary, but "it is easy to see she is a great friend of most of the lads."[33]

But one could only smoke so many cigarettes. Within the muddy enclosures, much-loved trench pets were one of the few distractions. As in regular life, a wee dog or a cat could offer hours of amusement. "We have adopted an old Belgian mother cat with her family of three kittens in the dugout," wrote Louis Keene. "I like cats, and they will help to keep the rats down. Although some of the rats are nearly the size of cats."[34] Lieutenant Clifford Wells was particularly proud of his little terrier, which caught and killed forty-three rats in only a few minutes after a nest was uncovered. This was a new record, he announced proudly in a letter home, although given the exploding rat population, he suspected the record would soon be broken again.[35] The army allowed the men to keep such pets but could also be cruel, as was the case in September 1915 when an order went out to destroy all dogs owing to a rabies scare. As one commanding officer sighed to his wife, "This will come hard on some of the men."[36]

While dogs and cats were loved, the rats remained a constant and disgusting feature of the trenches. Sleek or scruffy, they lived among the sandbags, underfoot beneath the duckboards, and especially in No Man's Land, where they fed and fattened off the corpses that littered the grim landscape. Sergeant Alexander McClintock remembered the sickening sight of "ravenous swarms burrowing into the shallow graves of the dead."[37] They were everywhere and seemingly unstoppable. Some soldiers took delight in hunting them—skewering them on bayonets or shooting them. However, enough soldiers were wounded by wild shots from overexcited rat-hunters for orders to be issued to desist from discharging one's rifle at rodents. In the end, though, most men found that the solid army boot was their most effective weapon.

For Canadians who had come from clean middle-class homes, living with the rats was bewildering and degrading. "The last time we were out a rat bit me on the head," complained Private Enos Grant. "I came over here to fight the Germans not to fight rats."[38] The squeaking, pudgy rodents with their beady-eyed stare haunted many men. Clothes were gnawed through, especially if food was kept in a pocket or knapsack. "It is very annoying to be suddenly wakened out of sleep by a big rat running across your face," wrote Lawrence Rogers to his wife.[39] Soldiers learned to sleep with their mouths closed.

Despite these disgusting trench companions, most men could not be bothered to expend too much energy on the rats. Poisoned bait was useless in controlling numbers, as a mating pair of rats could produce 880 offspring in a single year. Gas attacks killed the rats by the tens of thousands, but enough blinded and burned rodents always survived to repopulate the horde. Private Romeo Heule, an American barber who had enlisted in Montreal with the Canadian forces, wrote that the rats "still slide on their fat bellies through my dreams."[40]

But worse than the rats were the lice that indiscriminately infested everyone in the trenches. Whether sleeping, reading, or working, all soldiers experienced this constant aggravation in their lives. These "cooties" or "greybacks" were prevalent in crowded, unsanitary living conditions and not uncommon to the men who had lived in slums before the war. But these hidden tormentors, and the numbers in which they infested men, proved one of the greatest shocks for the majority of front-line soldiers. The trenches were a breeding ground, and a single female louse laid between 50 and 300 eggs at a time. Even a few soldiers crawling with critters could infect an entire battalion.

The lice hid in the folds and pleats of clothing, emerging only to feed. Clinging to flesh with claw-like legs, the insects parasitically sucked blood from their victims. They gave off a particularly sour smell, which only added to the generally unpleasant aroma of the trenches. The telltale signs of red rashes on the body proved a man was infected. Even removing one's clothes did not help to kill the lice, as they could survive up to a week without feasting on a host. For soldiers in wintertime, often covered in many layers of clothing like the homeless people that they were, the itching caused by the loathsome bites was infuriating and nearly impossible to alleviate. "The misery from these pests here is some-thing awful," wrote Herbert Burrell in his diary. "My body is covered with sores from scratching so much."[41] Unable to find escape even in their sleep, many men woke up with bloody marks all over their bodies. Scratching also drove infected louse feces into the lesions that then became infected, as the feces were also a carrier of disease.

These men are having a "chat" as they pick lice from their clothing.
Their smiles as they hunt their tormentors might remind us that
soldiers learned to live in the most squalid of conditions.

"We fought them with a variety of soaps, violent washes, such fumigations as we could discover in the French mines or swimming-baths, and our own bare hands," recounted T.W.L. MacDermot of the 7th Siege Battery. "As far as I know they were never conquered."[42] But the impossibility of defeating the tiny vampires did not stop most men from ferreting them out in a process called "reading the shirt" or having a "chat." Others knew the practice as searching for "seam squirrels." Stripped to the waist, men studied the seams of their shirts for the lice. During the summer months, soldiers engaged in the sport almost every day. Candles could be run along the shirt to draw out embedded lice. When the opponent was found, it was squashed between thumb and forefinger with a satisfying pop. While they did this, the men would sit around and talk, complain, gossip, or bet on how many lice they could kill. These happy discussions were known as "chatting," and thus the word seeped into the English language, even if we now "chat" without the accompanying execution of body lice. In the always perverse world of the trenches, where gallows humour reigned supreme, money commonly rode on who could find the largest, most grotesque looking beast, or the greatest number in a period of time.

Trench sickness was common among the soldiers throughout much of the war. This flu-like scourge was a mystery to both the afflicted and their doctors. Severe cases could knock a soldier out for a week to three months. Soldiers were stricken with fever, chills, fatigue, and pain in their shins, which resulted in the alternative name of "shin-bone fever."[43] The fever was officially labelled PUO—"pyrexia of unknown origins"—and most men came down with it at least once in the war. The origin of the fever was not discovered until 1918 when lice were revealed as the cause and transmitter of the infection. Even then, however, no effective preventative was available other than frequent baths and changes of clothes, which were never common for men at the front.

In addition to trench foot and trench sickness, men suffered from the equally distasteful trench mouth. This disease was particularly distressing for the soldiers, as they would have to face loved ones at some point (when on leave) with a mouth full of bacteria known as "acute necrotizing ulcerative gingivitis." The disease caused bleeding lesions and foul breath, and advanced cases required that all teeth be pulled from the rotting, grey gums. Trench mouth was brought on by poor oral hygiene, lack of fresh fruit, heavy smoking, and ongoing stress, all of which were abundantly prevalent among front-line troops. Trench mouth was also highly infectious, and so the sharing of cups and especially respirators resulted in its transmission, as was the case in the summer and fall of 1916 when not enough cups were available to go around. Trench mouth was never an epidemic, although more than 10,000 Canadian cases were recorded, but it was a symptom of the squalor in which the soldiers were forced to live.[44]

Disease remained a problem for all soldiers, but the fact that death from disease was not more prevalent was a remarkable testament to the medical corps' skill. During the winter months, almost every infantryman was plagued by hacking coughs and runny noses, but the fatality rate of disease was proportionally low in comparison with previous wars. Constant wetness, few breaks from the cold, and months of compounded exhaustion made soldiers good candidates for sickness. Typhus, pneumonia, scabies, and diphtheria—with its fatigue and nearly uncontrollable diarrhea—remained a drain on manpower throughout the war. However, the greatest killer would be influenza, which struck heavily in the last year of battle. In the course of the war, some 4,000 men died of disease, but the number could have been far worse in the fetid trenches.[45]

THE INFANTRY held their front against possible attacks within these crypt-like dwellings. They rarely saw the enemy—only his plague of shells, poison gas, and bullets—while bugs, slugs, rats, and lice provided other types of trials. In the summer, the *frontsoldaten* sweated and scratched; in the winter, they shivered and hacked. Yet the trench was their temporary home. It was dirty and debilitating, but it was an area of safety. Boredom and banality were often the soldiers' greatest scourge, but the stasis was frequently interrupted by the crash of shells, reminding men that within this bizarre, subterranean world, someone was trying to end their lives nearly every minute of the day.

CHAPTER 19

"EVERY DAY WE LOST A FEW MEN"

Death in the Trenches

Life in the trenches could be bearable, and even relatively calm, despite the occasional crack of a sniper's bullet or a burst of staccato fire from a machine gun. But calm never lasted for long on the Western Front. "War is a season of intense discomfort punctuated by periods of agonizing fear," wrote Lieutenant J.E. Ryerson, only a few months before he was killed in battle.[1]

The crash of a high explosive shell was both a physically and psychologically jarring force. Daydreaming or napping soldiers were pulled back abruptly to their nightmarish world in which someone was trying to kill them. Death was ever-present—and not only during the "big pushes." Soldiers did their best to downplay its angry sting, nonchalantly assigning nicknames to shells and mortars, and even referring to men killed as having "gone west." But the steady creep of death was not to be avoided. "Every day our defences were leveled," noted Private Harold Peat. "Every night we would crawl out, long hours spent flat on our stomachs, covered to the neck in mud and blood, and endeavor to repair the damage. Every night we lost a few men, every day we lost a few men, and still we held our ground."[2]

The spectre of death loomed over the Western Front, and even new men could feel its oppressive presence. Captain R.J. Manion described the apparent safety of the trenches, where you could be "dreaming of your loved ones at home, when a bullet thuds into the trench wall a few feet from your head, insolently splattering mud in your face. Then you know you are alive only by the grace of God and the poor aim of the Germans."[3] Lieutenant C.B.F. Jones wrote in a letter home, "I have seen chaps that have been all through the heavy fighting … get picked off by a fragment of shell on the quietest of days."[4] Death came in every form in the trenches, and no one could defend against fate when, as the saying went, "your number was up."

"THERE'S TOO MUCH fucking artillery in this bloody war," lamented British infantryman turned novelist Frederic Manning.[5] The image of the deadly machine gun, firing in scythe-like arcs as it mowed down troops, remains paramount in the

The gunners' war.

popular memory of the Great War. But the artillery was the true killer. Gunners set fuse timers on the shell nose to achieve an explosion at the desired height over the target. Ramming home the shell in the breech, the lanyard was pulled and the shell twisted at high speed from the barrel of the gun, propelled by cordite. Depending on whether a field gun or howitzer was used, shells were fired to a distance of 5 or 6 kilometres, arriving at their targets at just under the speed of sound. The crash of high explosives and whirling shrapnel proved early in the war that artillery would decide the fate of empires, as heavy firepower caused an estimated sixty percent of all deaths and injuries in the war's first three years. This percentage dropped in the last two years, and significantly so for Canadians in 1918, when Canadian artillery

The gunners' victims.

This rare photograph captures a shell landing in a nearby trench bay.

gained ascendancy over the enemy guns, forcing the Germans to rely on machine-gun defences and poison gas. But artillery always remained the great killer.

For those caught in the open, shellfire wreaked havoc. High explosive shells exploded like dynamite, killing with the force of the blast, which could collapse lungs, burst eyes from sockets, or kill a man without leaving a mark. Heavy siege shells, such as the 118-pound 8-inch shell, could break eardrums from a distance of 9 metres or more.[6] Dead bodies lacking any wounds or marks left survivors perplexed, and few autopsies were performed to determine whether it was burst intestines or an exploded heart that had rendered a friend a corpse in those split seconds after an explosion. Private Harold Baldwin described the bizarre case of one battalion mate who was killed by a high explosive blast that left his body elongated. "When alive and well he was a man of six feet two, and when we examined him after his death, he easily measured seven feet."[7] Somehow, the terrible blast had shattered the bones and stretched flesh.

But more often the high explosives ripped men apart. Colonel R.P. Cambell of the No. 6 Canadian Field Ambulance noted matter-of-factly in his diary on April 30, 1916: "5th Bde at Walled Garden was shelled today and 10 men in one dugout killed and in pieces—we could not match trunks and legs."[8] Cambell, too, would later be killed by shellfire on the Somme. Arms and legs were blown off by high explosives, with body parts often being carried away by material blown up from the blast. Cases were recorded of men being injured by body parts, as skulls and femurs were turned into projectiles. More often, however, a direct hit from a shell reduced a victim to pieces. The grisly task of picking up the chunks of blackened flesh and jagged bone was necessary for sanitary reasons, but carrying a comrade out in a blood-soaked sandbag was a hard task indeed.

Crouching in a trench under a high explosive bombardment was one of the most terrifying ordeals of the war. When the shells began to fall, soldiers dove for the closest dugout. Usually only a few seconds passed before the full barrage dropped from on high. When the shells hit, the atmosphere was supercharged with pressure waves. Private E.C.M. Knott had a shell explode near him, blowing off most of his clothes, burying him alive, and rendering him unconscious for five days. He was dug out and survived. So, too, did his mate, who had been buried beside him, although his jaw was smashed and all the teeth were ripped from his mouth from the same explosion.[9] The blast and sound of the explosions quickly numbed the mind, and soldiers caught in a bombardment were continually tossed left and right in the trenches, many suffering minor concussions. Dazed and deafened after a bombardment, Lieutenant D.E. Macintyre, at that time the intelligence officer for the 28th Battalion, wrote privately: "To give you some faint idea of the force of the explosion, we found one of our men who had been blown over 100 yards away and the buttons on his coat were pressed flat as though with a hammer."[10]

The dull moan of the shells transformed into a shrieking whistle, and finally into a cacophony of stomach-turning blasts that were an all-out assault on all the senses. "The difference in the sound of our own & Fritzies shells & Machine guns, is very easily picked up," wrote Private Gordon MacKay, who enlisted in Saskatoon at the age of twenty-two, and whose war service lasted only a few months before shrapnel crippled him for life by shattering his right knee and ankle.[11] The infantry could do little under the storm of steel. Explosions rocked the trenches, sending geysers of mud, sandbags, and bodies skyward. Depending on the intensity of the barrage, in between the blasts the wounded could be heard crying out in pain. During drumfire bombardments—when the shelling became one long sonic and physical assault, and no respite could be found—even veterans could crack under the unending pressure.

Staggering under the blasts that felt like body-blow punches, W.R. Lindsay of the 22nd Battalion later recounted, "There are no words for it; it's far beyond imagination."[12] The helpless waiting and agonizing anxiety was too much for some men: many were driven mad as they waited for the shell with their name on it. Lieutenant William Gray recounted watching one underage soldier, a mere lad of sixteen or seventeen, come unstrung during a heavy drumfire bombardment: "He laughed rather hysterically and babbled incoherently. Suddenly he jumped up, climbed into the open, his sole thought to get away, but there, a scant hundred yards, we saw him fall."[13] Others steeled their courage by waiting for revenge. Private Donald Fraser noted, "To get up over the parapet and rush to certain death at the hands of machine gunners or riflemen [was] a welcome mental relief as opposed to remaining stoically in a trench with an avalanche of shells smashing and burying everything."[14] The desire to escape was nearly overpowering, but soldiers realized that their trench was the safest place at the front.

While high explosive bombardments were used to destroy trenches and dugouts—and of course to kill—shrapnel shells were largely an anti-personnel agent. Invented in the early nineteenth century, the hard shot cannon ball had been hollowed out and filled with metal projectiles. Improvements over the century had resulted in a deadly weapon by the time of the Great War. The shrapnel shell was fired primarily by the smaller-calibre guns, especially 18-pounders and 4.5-inch howitzers, with gunners setting the fuse of the shrapnel shell to explode at an optimum height of 5 to 6 metres. As the shell was hurtling downwards from its trajectory, the fuse set off a small charge of black powder at the bottom of the base plate, which detonated and pushed the base plate up, ejecting some 375 metal shrapnel balls that had been packed in trinitrotoluene (TNT). If the fuse was set correctly—and this was very difficult to do—the 375 metal balls exploded downwards in a shotgun-like blast. "When a shrapnel shell bursts the bullets sweep forward and obliquely to the ground, having a forward range of three hundred yards and a lateral zone of fifty yards," described Private Harold Baldwin. "A shell may burst right over your head without injuring anyone, but the men three hundred yards or so to your rear are hit."[15]

The explosive charge hurled the shrapnell shell's solid nosecap, while high explosive shells also shattered the shell casing, which created jagged, whirling shell splinters. The irregular wounds from these shell splinters were deadly and tended to tumble through the body, leaving jagged exit wounds. One medical officer described the effects of shellfire: "Legs, feet, hands missing; bleeding stumps controlled by rough field tourniquets; large portions of the abdominal walls shot away; faces horribly mutilated; bones shattered to pieces; holes that you could put your clenched fist into, filled with dirt, mud, bits of equipment and clothing, until it all becomes a hideous nightmare."[16] During the war, doctors noted that a wounded man was three times as likely to die from a shell wound to the chest than from a bullet wound to the same region.[17]

Shellfire was the great killer of men in the trenches, but mortar fire also contributed to the butcher's bill. The Germans had more eagerly adopted the mortar than the British, and it was a particularly effective weapon in trench warfare, as high explosive plunging shells could be projected into the Entente lines to target suspected strongpoints or areas of resistance. For the Canadians, the "flying pigs," "moaning minnies," or "rum jars," as they nicknamed the various German mortar shells, were terrifying weapons. The shells, which could weigh several hundred pounds, were projected into the air, lobbing in a high arc and leaving a trail of sparks. They were spotted easily because of their slow flight and high trajectory. Soldiers played a terrifying game of trying to gauge where the mortar would fall and then running in the opposite direction down the trench. "You can see them coming and if you can dodge them why so much the better … it is no pleasure to make their acquaintance," wrote Melburn Sprague to his parents in Belleville, Ontario, while he was recovering with broken legs and gas poisoning after being unable to dodge his fate.[18] Running down trenches away from mortars became a sport of sorts for some men, although many would probably have agreed with Private W.C. Millar of Port Arthur, who wrote that this was no joking matter, as the mortar bombs were "filled with very high explosives, and the concussion is the destruction power which makes them, next to gas, the most dreaded agent of Death in this war."[19]

MORTARS COULD ALSO FIRE gas shells, but this was not the preferred method of gas delivery, as a sufficient rate of shellfire could not be built up to create a dense chemical cloud. In 1915, poison gas was released through large metal canisters. Special gas units, who were despised by their own men for what they did and the retaliation they brought, attached rubber hoses to large metal canisters filled with liquid gas that had recently been buried in the front lines.[20] These "gas merchants" waited for the proper wind conditions and then turned on the hoses that released the liquid death, which became gaseous when it cooled in the air. The gas cloud seeped out from the lines, pushing forward lethal green and yellow tendrils that licked along the battlefield, filling the crevices and trenches in which the soldiers took cover. The cold vapour of chlorine and later phosgene—eight times as deadly and harder to detect because of its translucent colour—could claim victims on both sides of the battlefield, as wind conditions could blow the cloud back into friendly lines.

Poison gas remained a terror weapon. Civilians-turned-soldiers had a hard enough time adapting to the lethality of the conventional battlefield weapons; nobody had experience in the deadly and bewildering scientific advancement of chemical warfare. The unleashing of gas at Ypres in April 1915 resulted in a panic in the British high command. The Germans might have discovered a war-winning weapon. Although the army responded quickly with a series of respirators—initially cloth pads, later chemically treated bags that fit over the head, and finally the effective small box respirator—the fear of gas was never controlled.

The arena of the gas war was populated by only the quick and the dead. Each battalion sent gas specialists to schools to learn the intricacies of poison gas, how to gauge wind conditions, and how to devise drills to ensure that soldiers got their masks on in less than ten seconds. But the respirator never reduced the fear of chemicals ravaging lungs or eyes. Wearing a respirator also hampered a soldier's ability to fight: seeing through the goggle-eyed panels that fogged up was difficult, and the sense of isolation was terrifying. Panicky breaths taken in through the small box respirator's chemically filtered canister barely provided sufficient oxygen to survive on, let alone enough to carry out battlefield duties such as advancing under fire or loading and firing artillery guns. "Gassing weakens the morale of troops," observed Medical Officer R.J. Manion. "Men do not fear to stand up and face an enemy whom they have a chance of overcoming, but they do hate dying like so many rats in a trap, when death is due to a gas against which they cannot contend."[21]

With the introduction of the chemical shell in 1916, gas could be delivered more accurately into the enemy lines, and attackers no longer needed to fear blowback from the changing direction of wind. Crash chemical bombardments—which entailed the rapid firing of high concentrations of gas shells—were intended to catch the enemy unaware before they had a chance to raise the alarm and don respirators. The mixing and interplay of gases became a science in itself, with the Germans preferring to use vomit-inducing gases first, thereby forcing their targets to choose between puking uncontrollably into their gas masks and removing them to fall victim to follow-on lethal gases. Trained soldiers learned to endure their own vomit.

The constant gas alarms also harassed soldiers who were wakened night after night by nervous sentries mistaking fog for death clouds. While gas never became the war-winning weapon some thought it would be—as no weapon system did on its own—it was increasingly used in a combined arms role. By 1918, fully one-quarter of all shells fired on the battlefield contained poison gas.[22] By war's end, gas had killed some 100,000 men and wounded more than a million in all armies. Almost 12,000 cases of gas poisoning among Canadian forces were recorded, although the number was surely higher since chemical casualties were not always accurately counted. Gassed men who were also hit by shrapnel or bullets—and more susceptible to them in their vulnerable state—were often recorded as slain by conventional weapons rather than by chemical agents. While the lethality rate of poison gas was a mere three percent, its use, opined Lieutenant Armine Norris, "was murder, not war." Most soldiers would have agreed with him.[23]

Gas was one more horror that ate away at the morale and fighting efficiency of soldiers in this prolonged siege warfare. Shells pounded them from above, and the very air they breathed was poisoned with chemicals. But the Canadians were to find that they could not even rely on the ground beneath their feet. Special mining units on both sides pushed underground shafts and tunnels towards the enemy lines in the hope of burrowing beneath them, setting an explosive charge, and destroying the enemy trenches from below. Dark and claustrophobic, work in the tunnels required special men with iron nerves, most of whom had been miners before the war. They well understood the danger of fragile galleries and mines, made even less stable by the constant pounding of high explosives. Cave-ins were not uncommon. In fact, to defend against and disrupt enemy miners, both sides regularly set traps and attempted to blow charges to collapse the enemy's tunnels, thus crushing or entombing enemy miners alive. "You hear sounds and try to locate them," recounted one tunneller. In this war of cautious action and frayed nerves, "every noise in the gallery seems like a cannon going off."[24] The three Canadian tunnelling companies raised during the war were involved in these deadly affairs. Mining never changed the fighting in the trenches, but soldiers caught above these underground shafts, desperately listening for the telltale sounds of pickaxes or shovels, had one more terror to confront.

Reports of mines being dug beneath the front lines left officers with two options: to pull out of the trench, which would basically hand the position over to the enemy, or to stick it out and hope that a mine did not go off before one's own tunnelling units disrupted the enemy's position by blowing a countermine. Either way, as Lieutenant Colonel Agar Adamson informed his wife, "It is not conducive to sleep."[25] J.S. Williams noted in one cavalier letter home:

> These German sausage-eaters managed to sap a mine under part of our trench and blew about twenty-five yards of it up and about thirty men in it. Some of the bodies of the men were found about twenty-five yards away from the place that was blown up. Immediately [after] they blew it up they hurled all the shells possible into us and their machine-guns simply hammered our parapet. It was a dark inferno…. My batman had his head blown off.[26]

These underground attacks were infrequent, but the mounting pressure of waiting could destroy the mind. Ralph Lewis described one fellow officer who was so terrified of mine blasts after being blown up and buried once that he went about his tour in the trenches "wearing armored body plates, and every time he heard a rat scratch he thought it was a mine."[27]

However, despite their terror of enemy miners, the men were capable of impressive acts of sympathy for their tormentors. The 14th Battalion's chronicler recounted the unit's taking over of a battered part of the line in the Vimy section of the front in late November 1916. As the men settled in, they heard tapping noises beneath them, which they discovered were SOS signals from German miners who had been buried alive under tons of mud and debris. Putting aside their hatred of the enemy, relief parties attempted to dig the entombed Germans out. For two days the Canadians dug, but the tapping gradually grew fainter and finally died out before the rescue could be completed.[28] Miners were despised, but few wished a slow suffocating death in pitch darkness on even their own worst enemy.

FACED WITH THESE HORRORS in addition to the conventional weaponry, soldiers could do little to respond. Impotent with rifle in hand, new men had to be restrained from standing on the firestep and firing off a few rounds. Those who refused to heed the urgings of experienced mates to avoid such pointless ventures often paid for it with a bullet in the face. Some men countered the enemy's tactics by rigging rifles to periscopes so they could fire from the safety of a trench. With the periscope and rifle barrel jutting through the parapet, a soldier could study the enemy lines from within the trench. Then, by depressing a secondary trigger linked to the rifle's trigger by aligning rods, he could fire without exposing his head or body to enemy fire. This method was later extended for use with light machine guns, and sometimes as many as half a dozen rifles were set on a brace and fired at once when a patient infantryman saw a target to his liking. Little evidence indicates that these fixed firing platforms had much effect, but their use relieved some of the soldiers' frustration.

While respites from the trenches could be had, and as much boredom as brutality was suffered, the swiftness of the carnage wreaked on the men left them reeling. The experience was akin to being involved in a car accident every day: someone around you was always being killed. "It is the not knowing what is coming next that gets you," testified one Canadian trench soldier.[29] Shoulders ached from the tension of anticipation; backs were knotted in stress; headaches came and went with blinding speed; lines of fatigue were etched in the faces of young men. Many soldiers wrote home that everyone looked like they had aged a decade over the last few months. Hair turned white, eyes were sunken, hands began to shake.

Amidst this destruction, soldiers had to find ways to cope. "You can't dodge your fate; it searches you out," wrote Coningsby Dawson.[30] The unpredictable had to be made predictable. Soldiers reassured themselves that they would "get it" when their number was up, and only then. "Of course there are dangers," testified George McLean, "but one learns to feel the same towards them that he does at home to the danger of being struck by lightning or run down by a crazy chauffeur. You learn to take what precautions you can, you know there is some chance of being hit, and you gradually get into the way of forgetting about it and going on with your work in a sensible way."[31] This nonchalance indeed helped men cope with the vagaries of fate, even if McLean likely laid it out too neatly for his worried sister.

Magic talismans were carried and rubbed by almost every soldier at the front. "I have sufficient faith in your goodness and prayers that I believe if I carry your photo with me I shall not meet with any serious injuries," wrote Corporal Harry Hillyer to his wife. Sadly, his belief did not succeed in warding off death.[32] "I was intimately aware of the presence of a sardonic, malign Fate, whose eyes were ever on the watch for tricks to play," wrote Lieutenant Gregory Clark. "And I felt that the less I counted on living, the more was I likely to live." Despite this fatalistic attitude, however, Clark, like many soldiers, had his talismans to ward off death: "I carried lucky stones, coins, and little brass match cases full of little souvenirs of Helen [his wife]—bits of cloth, faded flowers, coins; and the nails out of a horseshoe I picked up one noisy night on the Coulette road."[33] These coping mechanisms—from the psychological to the magical—helped men to deal with the unpredictable, and, in their own minds, even the odds.

In the wet miserable days that stretched from December 1, 1915, to March 31, 1916—when the two divisions of the Canadian Corps were involved in no battles and were only holding the line and carrying out the occasional trench raid—2,606 men were recorded as killed, wounded, or missing.[34] The high command's clinical term for these effects was "wastage." This steady rate of loss was hard on all units, which found their leaders and rank and file to be ever changing. Lessons had to be continually taught and retaught as men moved to new positions or were knocked out. After having two of his officers killed by enemy fire in as many days, Lieutenant Colonel John Creelman lamented in his diary, "The changes in this life are appalling. We are always changing. Nothing is ever finished. Just as soon as officers are trained for their particular jobs, changes come about and we have to begin all over again."[35] As the war progressed and losses deepened, the senior command was forced to confront its old prejudices. The knowledge and skills necessary for a battalion or battery to succeed in battle could not be hoarded among the leaders; they had to be disseminated throughout the lower ranks of the units. Senior NCOs and even privates had to be trained in effect to fight the war at several levels above their rank, in order to take over the job of their superiors should they be wounded or killed in battle. This was a hard lesson to swallow in 1915, when the levels of hierarchy in the army were starkly laid out, but it was slowly embraced over the coming years.

While staff officers studied the casualty lists and worked out monthly wastage rates—such as ten percent of each infantry or machine-gun unit, only three to five percent of the artillery, and less than three percent of railway and medical troops— these cold figures meant far more to the soldiers.[36] These figures were made up of their friends and family members, who were being chewed up in the Western Front's steady grind.

With the infantry taking most of the punishment and a disproportionate part of the losses, some *frontsoldaten* found it difficult at times to remember who the enemy was. The opposing artillery killed and maimed, but it was one's own high command that kept the soldiers in the line or sent them off in desperate attacks. Across from the freezing or sweating front-line troops were other miserable sods—men sharing similar deprivation and terror in their trenches. While both sides still had their trained killers—the snipers—often an infantryman could go months without ever firing a shot in anger against the opposing troops. This did not mean that a fraternity of brothers existed across the divide of No Man's Land, but the demonization of the enemy by the home-front propagandists and editors often sat uneasily with the troops.

The language of the troops often reflected this strange relationship: as opposed to the barbaric "Hun," the moniker that was spat with venom at home, the enemy was

"Jerry" or "Fritz" to the rank and file, and more often "the Boche" (French slang for "the rascal") to officers. Soldiers found it harder to think of massacring the enemy when they realized that he too had a family. Throughout the war, the opposing front lines were sometimes close enough for the men to shout across to enemy troops on the other side of No Man's Land. Usually such communication took the form of taunts and insults, and sometimes snide comments from soldiers that a trench they had occupied, deep in mud and in terrible condition, was undesirable and not worthy of any further fighting. In the Ypres salient in the summer of 1916, J.K. Patterson of the 26th Battalion recounted, "A dog appeared in our lines one morning with a message on its collar, saying, 'We have sunk four of your battle cruisers [at Jutland].'"[37] The New Brunswickers tried to send the animal back with a reply message—no doubt with some colourful comments on the nature of the enemy troops' mothers—but the poor beast got confused and kept returning to the Canadian lines. The back-and-forth ribbing and taunting could escalate into revenge patrolling and raiding, but a curious lack of animosity towards the enemy tended to prevail.

Often it did not make sense to the men to shoot at an enemy who did not want to shoot back. This "live and let live" policy developed from the perspective of the infantry, who saw little value in exposing themselves to greater danger in the hope of killing their opposite, who was just as badly off. The truces that were made could be small—for instance, between individual sentries—or larger—along several hundred metres of front, spanning two or more battalions. Occasionally, German troops put up signs suggesting a truce—such as one posted opposite the 4th CMR in early April 1916, which read: "Go easy. We are Saxons."[38] "Hello Canadians, I have nothing against you, but for God's sake keep your head down, for I shoot straight," was the written greeting of one hidden German sniper to a new group of 3rd Division men entering the Ypres salient in April 1916.[39] The Canadian front-line troops sometimes responded with the popular song written by fellow countryman Lieutenant Gitz Rice, "Keep Your Head Down, Fritzie Boy."

The Canadians had a reputation for ferocity, and so not many cases of these truces are recorded, but sometimes they occurred when lines were close together or after a terrible slaughter, with both sides agreeing to a temporary respite to collect the dead. One story of a necessary truce was recounted by Private Victor Wheeler: The trenches were in extremely poor condition from the mud and rain, making digging into the ground to create a latrine impossible. After a few days of soldiers defecating in the trenches, something had to be done. "A gentlemen's agreement, mutually entered into by silent consent, permitted each other's men to get up on top of the trench whenever it was necessary to relieve their bowels. No shots would be fired during this necessary personal hygiene chore. Either Fritz or [Tommy] was quite safe to expose himself and his bare bottom on top of the trench."[40] Within hours or a few days, however, the front usually returned to its lethal nature, as it did on Wheeler's sector when an officer passed along the forward trench, looked through the periscope, and saw to his great surprise a German naked bottom staring back at him. He grabbed a rifle and shot the indecent fellow.

A truce could also be halted by a battalion's burning hatred of the enemy after a fierce bombardment or a successful trench raid. And despite being a party to a truce, the man who lost a friend to a sniper might be inclined to "take no prisoners" the next time he encountered a German soldier. The war could return quickly, but elsewhere the calm of peace would be felt, as these temporary peaceful cycles broke out all along the front, with men managing their urge for personal and collective violence. The unwritten rules and regulations of the Western Front took time to decipher; they were always changing, and often only understood by those at the sharp end.

EVERY NEW INVENTION of war could take more lives, and in greater numbers. Most *frontsoldaten* wondered what fresh new horror they would soon encounter in the enemy's bid to break the deadlock. Fear of the unknown often manifested itself in outlandish rumours of super weapons, including poison gas that made eyes fall out of heads, or death rays.[41] But such fantastic rumours might be forgiven in men who faced machine guns firing 500 rounds per minute, 9-metre-long metal tanks, gas lethal to lungs and skin, and even liquid fire dispensed by flamethrowers. New weapons would continue to be introduced, and old ones were employed in a deadlier manner, within a refashioned doctrine, and with evolving tactics to make them more efficient on the battlefield.

With soldiers living amidst sites of mass murder, often with the corpses of slain comrades and enemies jutting from the very walls of their homes, death was a constant companion in the front lines. While the trenches were an area of safety, one's fate was inescapable, or so believed many soldiers. "It's all arranged for you, if there's a bit of shell or a bullet with your name on it you'll get it, so you've nothing to worry about," wrote Louis Keene, a graphic artist turned machine-gunner. "You are a soldier—then be one. This is the philosophy of the trenches."[42] Keene survived at the front longer than most of his mates, but eventually a high explosive shell landed near him and left his hand a mangled mess. He lived through the incident, however, and rehabilitated his hand. He must have felt he got off lucky, as the other man in the casualty clearing station with him was a corporal who suffered fifty-six wounds, including having both hands blown off—his arms ending in charred flesh, hanging tendons, and two white, broken arm bones jutting out from a frayed and bloodied uniform. Fate caught most soldiers on the Western Front, but not everyone's fate was the same.

CHAPTER 20

INTO THE ABYSS

No Man's Land

Writing to his wife about the stalemate of trench warfare, Sergeant George Ormsby declared that he would "rather risk a battle and accomplish something" than suffer more of "this inaction [which] is hard to endure."[1] The enormous battles of the Great War—Ypres, the Somme, and Passchendaele—act as grim signposts in charting the evolution of fighting, but they were infrequent affairs. Even when the battles raged for weeks or months on end, the experience of individuals in battle might last only a few days, as men could not stand much longer in the grinding warfare. The Canadian part in the Second Battle of Ypres lasted four days for most units; the men who formed the few battalions involved at the Battle of Festubert in May 1915 spent only two or three days in the line; and future battles would be no different. In the gaps between these titanic struggles, the front returned to its seeming inactivity, the quietness broken only by the sounds of men working and sporadic machine-gun fire and shelling.

FROM FEBRUARY 1915—the date of the Canadian Division's arrival in France—to the early months of 1918, little changed geographically on the Western Front. The static trench system shifted gradually only after fierce fighting, as one side ate into No Man's Land, forcing the other back a few kilometres at most. The Western Front had solidified into two strong defensive lines, hundreds of kilometres long and often several kilometres deep, separated by the blasted ruins of No Man's Land.

The name "No Man's Land" originated in the Middle Ages, and was a designated slaughter ground to the rear of a castle where the bodies of slain criminals were left to rot as a warning to others. The name transferred well to the Great War. This land of corpses and craters was a menacing ribbon of ravaged landscape that ran as long as the Western Front. No Man's Land could be as narrow as 100 metres (and even narrower in a few bizarre areas of the front) or stretch to over 1 kilometre wide in parts, but most often it was 300 to 400 metres wide. The dimensions continually shifted as both sides pushed their lines outward from their trenches, eating into the shell-cratered, rat-infested, corpse-ridden ruins. But closing the gap too tightly between the opposing lines made little sense since the trench soldiers would suffer from constant raids, mortar fire, and even grenades if the two sides had no buffer zone.

In parts of the front where the trenches were close enough for both sides to engage in constant harassment, the front-line troops who knew the futility of bombing each other to death in relentless battles often established informal truces. These could last for a few hours or a few days, but often the rotation of troops or inspection by a senior officer returned the front to war conditions. Yet No Man's Land was still considered a prize. Trench patrols and trench raids were continually weaving their way through the blackened tree stumps and slimy craters in this territory in order to exert control over the uncontrollable. Despite this activity, however, No Man's Land remained a haunted, unconquerable place. It formed the central motif of the Western Front: a shattered landscape continuously fought over but which neither side could ever hold. As one army advanced, the other fell back, creating another empty space, and always No Man's Land glowered back at the combatants forced to defend the front lines.

Tens of thousands of soldiers manned the underground trench fortresses, and while the battlefield was empty during the day, below ground soldiers were always rebuilding the crumbling trenches, pushing additional saps into No Man's Land, preparing new jumping-off points for future attacks, and extending communication trenches in the rear. And at night, the once empty battlefield above ground swarmed with activity. The most common nighttime activity for the infantry was work patrols, which were carried out beyond the parapet, in No Man's Land, or anywhere along the defensive grid extending back to the rear. Units holding the secondary line or reserves were also called on to provide work parties. Sergeant Samuel Honey noted in one letter to his parents: "Believe me, a working party on a pitch black, foggy, rainy night, when you are sometimes up to your knees in water and mud with no light to show the way except the intermittent flash of guns and flare of star shells is certainly some party."[2] Sentries were alerted to the outgoing parties to prevent nervous men from firing on their own troops, and scouts cleared paths through the tangle of barbed wire.

Men going on work parties or patrol studied the weather and light conditions before setting out. Rain, cold, or sleet was not enough to cancel an operation, but leaving the trenches during a full moon was considered akin to suicide. The presence of fresh snow was equally dangerous, as patrollers were revealed against it as targets for sentries and snipers. Even when special white suits were issued for such circumstances, the troops' tracks in the snow usually provided a map of their movements for the enemy, who could then set up an ambush. Most often, the parties went out only under the protective cover of complete darkness: the soldiers—usually 40 to 50 men, but sometimes as many as 200—stumbled forward, shovels and sandbags in hand.

The soldier-labourers were to carve out a new trench that an engineer had mapped out with tape, or to unroll the seemingly endless coils of barbed wire. Digging a new trench was no easy task as men went to work on uneven ground, trying to cut through not only the ruptured earth but also buried barbed wire, canvas, armaments, and anything else that was found in the churned-up soil. "Sappers digging a new trench cut away limbs of the buried as if they were roots of trees," remarked one veteran.[3] The smell of rotting flesh wafting through the darkness alerted a man instantly to what was on the other end of his pick or shovel.

Aware that blindly searching machine guns could open fire at any time, the members of the working party did not need the encouragement of the NCOs who urged them onward in whispers. Most dug like fiends, recounted Private W.H. Wray, only days before his death, because "the quicker they get a hole made the safer [they] are."[4] Like prisoners in a chain gang, each man was allotted about a metre of ground, and told to dig down to at least 1.5 metres. In spots that were raked with fire, soldiers learned to dig in a prone position, with face and body as close to the earth as possible. No matter how onerous their fatigue, the infantry always kept their rifles within reach.

The laying of barbed wire required the men to carry large wire rolls as well as steel stakes. Early in the war, the soldiers pounded wooden and metal stakes into the earth, but even if the mallets and stakes were covered in sandbags, this hammering often sent clanking noises drifting over the front, invariably drawing fire. A safer method adopted later in the war involved screwing threaded metal stakes into the ground. The clank of steel on steel was thereby minimized, but no method could dampen all of the noise resulting from such work.

OTHER FRONT-LINE FATIGUES involved the disagreeable task of looking for the dead in No Man's Land. Most men felt a strong obligation to bury their fellow soldiers' corpses—especially those of battalion comrades. Even if the slain were too close to enemy lines, or were suspected of being used as a trap to draw more men to their own deaths in an enemy ambush, identifying those listed as missing was considered essential for the sake of families at home. Yet this was a grim task, as corpses that had lain out in the open would be in various forms of decomposition after being subject to the effects of weather and hungry rats for days or weeks. Flesh the consistency of cottage cheese gave off a smell that could direct the gravediggers, who spent much of their time skulking through the darkness following their noses. Twenty-eight-year-old Private Deward Barnes, a former machine factory worker from Toronto, recounted in his diary: "On burial detail all night, burying dead on our front-line trenches we had lost. Buried ten half-rotten; smell was awful—pulled one poor fellow's leg off."[5] They tended to put two or three men in each shallow grave of half a metre to a metre deep, first making sure, however, to remove the identity disk and personal effects from each body. Each soldier was issued two identity disks that contained rank, name, regimental number, unit, and religious affiliation, the latter to indicate the type of last rites or burial required. The disks differed in size and colour, but most were either round or hexagonal, red or green. When a corpse was buried, one of the disks was taken, the other left with the body. The collected disks were passed to the battalion's second-in-command to record the losses, and then sent to chaplains, who often wrote letters to families.

But painful last letters were not penned only by chaplains: friends did their best to convey their feelings to a man's family about a chum who had become a member of their family in the trenches. The educated and the illiterate struggled to find the right words: the fallen were always cheerful and well liked; their deaths were always instant and painless; their sacrifice was always for the greater good of the army and Empire. Few spoke of the men who were sniped through the head as they carried wood into the lines or blown to atoms by high explosive shells as they dug latrines. Writing these letters was no easy task, but the bonds of camaraderie demanded the effort. Some officers, such as Major J.R. Ralston—who was loved by his men and would rise to become minister of national defence in the Second World War—wrote a letter to the family of every man killed under his command. He could often be seen working late into the night, his staff asleep around him, his body curled over a rough table trying to find a phrase or a cheery anecdote that might ease the suffering of a grieving family he would likely never meet.

For those back home, the death of a family member was a terrible blow, but to receive a note that a loved one was missing kept a faint hope alive. Too many families were left in desperation, but some held forlorn hope that a son or father listed as "missing" might somehow be a prisoner or, in a story line that became a favourite of novelists after the war, had somehow escaped death on the battlefield and made it to the rear, but was shell-shocked into amnesia.[6] With time, they believed fervently, their missing loved one would regain his memory and be reunited with his family. Most often, though, the missing had simply been killed, were lying alone and unburied, and would eventually be swallowed into the earth.

The Commonwealth War Graves Commission—the wartime and postwar organization that cares to this day for the dead of the Commonwealth—notes that forty-nine percent of its 1,146,982 Great War soldiers have no known graves. With regard specifically to Canada, the 11,285 names on the Vimy Memorial and the nearly 7,000 names on the Menin Gate account for roughly 18,000 Canadians killed with no known graves. As grim as these figures are, Canada's number of graveless dead from the Great War is far less than the average for other armies since the Canadian force was in an attacking formation for much of the war, making its dead easier to locate as waves of successive troops moved over them to establish new trenches in the enemy's lines. Many other forces had to abandon their dead on the battlefield as they attacked and then retreated.

For much of the war, these front-line and No Man's Land fatigues fell to the infantry, who were to fight during the day and work at night. This type of work was frequent and constant: the 49th Battalion, for instance, was involved in seventy-eight working parties, twenty-four carrying parties (which transported supplies—anything from sandbags to duckboards), and one wiring party over the month of November 1915.[7] "It had been my understanding that an infantryman did nothing but fight and that trench digging, road building and work of that nature was performed by members of the Engineers or Labour Battalions," muttered John Lynch, a nineteen-year-old American serving with the PPCLI. "I was due to learn that the infantry not only fight the wars but also do all the work connected with a war, particularly the dangerous and disagreeable work."[8] The infantry grumbled and groaned through the backbreaking work, for, as another commentator noted, it was "hard and dangerous without compensating glory or excitement."[9] Digging trenches had the uncomfortable similarity to digging a grave. However, such thoughts could be banished from men's minds by the post-job reward of a healthy shot of rum and maybe a greasy bacon sandwich to take the edge off their fatigue and anger.[10]

AS THE INFANTRY STRUGGLED with the pick-and-shovel work, sentries kept watch, rifles at the ready. Work parties from the opposing sides rarely ran into each other since they remained close to their front lines, but roving battle patrols seeking intelligence on the enemy were known to venture far and wide across No Man's Land. The Canadian battle patrols were renowned for their aggressiveness, as most battalions took it as a point of pride that they would rule this blasted territory, driving the enemy into his trenches behind his protective band of barbed wire. Indeed, as infantryman Arthur Chute claimed, with patrollers looking for a fight, "the name of No Man's Land had been changed to the 'Dominion of Canada.'"[11]

But control of No Man's Land was more than just a question of pride. Battle patrols were an important tool for gathering intelligence on the static front. "The best security against attack is active patrolling and constant observation of the enemy's line, so that he cannot undertake any new work without steps being taken to prevent an advance," intoned one standing order.[12] Almost from the start of the war, the Canadians followed the British lead and aggressively patrolled their front lines, slinking over the bags in the dead of night, advancing close to the enemy lines, under their wire, to lie in shell holes and listen to enemy activity. Bomber Ernest Taylor described one such action: "We spent our nights lying prone on the wet ground seven yards from the Huns. The idea was to take them by surprise if they came out to throw [grenades], but principally to discover what they were up to. They were always at work, we could hear their footsteps on the wooden bath mats and hear them talking and coughing. A good deal of hammering and sawing went on and there was a continuous sound like pumping. I think they must have been mining under us."[13]

Every battalion had a few men who all but lived in No Man's Land. Private Lance Cattermole of the 21st Battalion spoke reverently of the multiply decorated Captain Albert Miller, who "never missed a night, walking and crawling over No Man's Land reconnoitering, always bringing back a snippet of the German wire to show he had been there."[14] Active intelligence was needed to gauge the enemy's intentions, to ensure that their own barbed wire was intact, or to prepare for a raid on the enemy. A new machine-gun nest might be spotted and the information conveyed back to the battalion's intelligence section, which might order an artillery bombardment to fall on the area or a stealth raid to be carried out against it.

All along the front, these patrols—or "stunts," as they were often called—acted as important eyes and ears for the battalion, brigade, and divisional commanders in the rear. Intelligence officer Lieutenant D.E. Macintyre noted in his diary that part of his job was to know every path and dead alley in "Never Never Land," his name for No Man's Land.[15] Each battalion had a small team of scouts who went out almost every night, and usually the intelligence officer went with them. The officer's reports were sent up the chain of command, and became essential reading for rear-situated commanders, who were not much better informed than the Duke of Wellington had been a century earlier. Indeed, these commanders would well have understood Wellington's observation: "I have spent all my life trying to guess what lay on the other side of the hill."[16]

While patrolling could lead to murderous mayhem in the dark, the ghosts lurking in No Man's Land were not always there for a fight. Some men hopped the bags, skulking into the blasted landscape to fulfill their nearly insatiable desire for souvenirs. All the soldiers of the various armies collected trophies on the battlefield, but the Canadians had a reputation for being among the most voracious collectors. Afflicted by a "souvenir-hunting craze ... we gathered and hoarded everything," recounted Herbert McBride.[17] As proof of this penchant, an article in *The Twentieth Gazette,* a trench newspaper printed by the 20th Battalion, read only half jokingly, "A Hun prisoner who had been captured at the Somme, in the course of conversation, remarked: 'English fight for what he think is right. German fight for what he think is right. Canadian—he fight for souvenirs.'"[18] Many a soldier went on patrol to locate valuable material in No Man's Land that could later be sent home as material evidence that the man in question was close enough to the front to see action; or he might sell his booty for hard cash to bomb-proof soldiers in the rear who wanted the same evidence. Even robbery of the dead for such mementoes occurred, but such violations were not openly accepted or practised.

The battle patrollers were well known and generally admired within a battalion, but most regular infantrymen shunned the job. Lieutenant James Pedley described his shuddering reaction to No Man's Land: "This earth was soaked with gas and chemicals and rich in metal from exploded shells and rotting flesh. As one advanced, one put a hand always in front to feel the way along. Once my hand came into contact with the end of a bone. It was dry and clean. I felt along this bone and followed it into a boot."[19] Most men were not anxious to enter into the terrifying darkness of No Man's Land, with its real and imagined horrors. Too often they knew of comrades who had been hit by stray fire, got lost, stumbled into the enemy trenches by mistake, or simply never returned, ambushed by the enemy, swallowed in the darkness.

Another reason to fear going forth on patrol was that a surprising number of soldiers were shot by their own battalion's sentries. Despite warnings that their own men had gone out, tired and scared sentries often forgot that their countrymen were prowling in the darkness. Shocked out of the numbness of inactivity by a glimpse of movement or the clink of metal on debris, twitchy sentries fired in haste, or paused for a few seconds, calling out through tentative, shaky voices passwords that the patrollers, also fatigued, could not remember. Private Victor Wheeler of the

50th Battalion recounted the experience of his first patrol. Stuck out in No Man's Land, with flares lighting the battlefield and every sound seemingly alluding to an ambush, "We were wholly unnerved from the strain." As the patrol made its way back to the front lines after a few hours, their group was separated in the darkness and while passing over the broken ground. An anxious officer who was watching the patrollers from the Canadian trench saw the bunched shadows of the group come in through the wire, but also a lone figure seemingly stalking them from the rear. In a split-second decision, he tossed a Mills grenade at the unlucky, lagging Canadian, who was severely wounded by the whirling metal. "In the nervous confusion that followed, our Patrol Officer, not giving the 'enemy' a chance to identify himself as Comrade K.C., fatally bayoneted him as he tried to crawl away. C'est la guerre!"[20] Confusion and friction—as well as fratricidal battles—were a part of war, but they were exacerbated at night, when men engaged in dangerous operations with their nerves frayed. Many of the sentries in the trenches, who were fighting their own private fears, had a "shoot first, ask questions later" policy.

THE ROLE OF THE SENTRY was difficult at the best of times. Sergeants often selected privates to work in pairs, with one watching over the parapet while the other rested below in safety. Two-hour shifts were found to be the limit for soldiers who were already suffering from the fatigue and stress of their regular infantry tasks. Stories of entire sections found with their throats cut after their sentry had fallen asleep passed along the trenches. These stories, mostly apocryphal, belonged to the constant mill of rumours that circulated along the front, but the army threatened the most severe penalty—death by firing squad—for sentries who fell asleep at their post. While most men did not need such threats to do their job, and understood their crucial role in protecting their mates from enemy raiders, the exhaustion of standing sentry could be overwhelming. Even the pairing of soldiers did not always help. Desperately tired men learned to rest their chins on their rifle's bayonet, fresh blood and pain bringing them back to consciousness when they nodded off to sleep.

Soldiers on sentry duty stood at waist height above the sandbags. As half-dozing soldiers leaned on the sandbag parapet, the rats would run along the bags, over their hands and up their bodies if they did not shake them off quickly enough. Equally startling, the periodic sweep of enemy machine-gun fire could drop them down like prairie dogs, with bad luck sometimes dictating that they were shot at the beginning of an arc before they could be warned by the sound or sight of the bullets sparking off the barbed wire. But even the fear of machine-gun fire was dulled by fatigue, and often soldiers could not be bothered to flinch.

For the soldier standing sentry, staring into the yawning darkness of No Man's Land was like staring into the abyss. But at frequent intervals throughout the night, flares were shot above the trenches to illuminate the battlefield. A ghostly white light settled over the full destruction of No Man's Land in a radius of some 3 or 4 kilometres. With the flares kept in the air by parachutes, they often burned for two or three minutes. During this time, sentries were warned not to move, despite the uncomfortable nakedness of standing above the trench, vulnerable to all fire. "I found it tested one's nerve to the limit," wrote Private E.W. Russell.[21] As alarming as it must have been to have one's upper body exposed, any movement under the flare's cold light could draw the attention of a sniper who would train his rifle on the area and fire the next time a flare went up. The sentries had little protection in these situations. Armoured breastplates were issued in limited numbers, or men could purchase their own private Dayfield or Chemico body armour, but most soldiers had witnessed the killing power of high-velocity small-arms rounds, and believed that thin steel plates could do little to deflect it. With most infantrymen refusing to wear the chest armour (which although thin was nonetheless heavy), perhaps an unnamed Canadian staff officer was correct in opining, "I do not believe that any system of shields or helmets or any form of portable amour will provide a remedy."[22]

At all times, sentry duty was terrifying and bewildering. Private Lew Perry of the 8th Battalion remarked that a sentry, wrapped in several blankets and ground sheets, and trying to avoid thinking about the lice biting him in places he couldn't scratch, just looked out "across that dismal, desolate strip of domain that men feared and watched and hated."[23] The blowing wind heightened anxiety by producing strange sounds in the night. "A little imagination on a dark night is a very dangerous thing," remarked one Canadian trench soldier after his first experience as a sentry.[24] However, sentries soon developed a feel for the front: they listened for the extraordinary rather than spooking themselves by the ordinary sounds that played tricks on tired men. The periodic firing of rifles and machine guns or the rhythmic firing of flares indicated that the enemy was keeping an active defence in the opposing trenches, and likely did not have troops in No Man's Land. However, as Private Donald Fraser—a native of Calgary who had enlisted at the age of thirty-two and kept a detailed diary throughout the war— noted, "It is when his lights are not going up often or his shooting nil or high, you should be suspicious and on the alert."[25] Eyes straining, ears attuned to every rustle, nerves taut, sentries left their shifts absolutely exhausted. Indeed, Private Deward Barnes expressed the feelings of many men when he wrote, "I dreaded those long nights."[26]

An even more terrifying night activity was the garrisoning of a listening post. Located at the front end of saps dug forward into No Man's Land, usually some 20 to 40 metres beyond the safety of the front-line trench, listening posts were an advance warning station that would give the alarm of a major enemy night assault. The danger faced by the men in these positions could not be sugar-coated: isolated and vulnerable, the listening posts were the primary targets of enemy trench raiders. At each post, a few men with faces blackened tried to stay absolutely still, listening for enemy troops with their "ears, nose and eyes all at one time," observed one trench veteran."[27] Private Victor Wheeler testified to the nerve-racking quality of the job: "For the next twenty-four hours we would lie coiled, watching, waiting, listening. Our heart thumped furiously for we were less than a 5-seconds-Mills-bomb-throw away from Heine's front line."[28] Every sound, every whistle of wind, could be an enemy raiding party stalking the post.

Sometimes the best method of survival for those manning the post was to stay silent as enemy raiders skulked in the darkness around them. The listening-post men usually had a string winding back to their trenches, where a stronger garrison waited, ready to rush forward after receiving the silent alarm via the pulled string. The anxious pulling of the lifeline by the occupants of the listening post signalled an impending attack, or the fact that enemy raiders were moving too close to the concealed position. Too often, however, when the garrison soldiers moved up to the listening post through a narrow communication link, they found only signs of a struggle and a few dead bodies.

FEW SOLDIERS ever came to grips with the swiftness of death at the front. While the trenches were dirty and claustrophobic, they remained an area of relative safety. But the fighting on the Western Front required not only that soldiers live in a strange, nocturnal world of activity but that they periodically leave their dirt homes to enter this world's unchartered realms. No Man's Land was always out there, just beyond the littoral of the front lines. As the infantry peered and guarded against the monsters that might come out of the darkness, the abyss was always beckoning, always staring back.

CHAPTER 21

SNIPERS

Silent Killers

Lieutenant William Gray of the 52nd Battalion wrote to his mother in anguish over the fact that enemy snipers had killed a number of his men in one particularly costly tour in the front lines: "All hit by these devils of Huns—hit by snipers who use explosive bullets—a bullet that tears a hole as large as a tomato can, and if it strikes anything hard bursts into three pieces, each the size of a quarter, that maims and wounds—a bullet that if it hits the head tears off the top."[1]

Enemy raiders were a periodic dangerous threat, but enemy snipers were always lurking in No Man's Land. Day or night, they offered no rest to the infantry. At the start of the war, the British Expeditionary Force had included no specialist snipers, but soldiers with good shooting skills were encouraged to hunt the enemy. These elite gunmen slowly evolved into a more permanent group of dedicated snipers. In the army training schools established by the British in 1915, and the Canadian one set up the next year, two-week courses taught snipers how to stalk their prey and stay alive on the battlefield. While snipers never achieved the same level of killing as massed machine-gun or artillery fire, they lowered morale, restricted movement, and passed a death sentence over those foolish enough to show their heads above the trenches. These sharpshooters also reminded the infantry that the war was not just about impersonal killing—as carried out by artillery shells—and that the enemy was actively seeking men's individual deaths.

Snipers were specialists and did not partake in regular trench chores. Their job was solely to kill. Working alone or in teams, these marksmen established firing positions from the trenches, usually through metal loops built into the trench parapet. Others set themselves up in posts to the rear of their own front line, which provided greater safety but were less likely to offer good targets. More aggressive snipers wormed their way into the destruction of No Man's Land, constructing nests in shell craters, ruined farm houses, or any other cover, from which they waited for careless or inexperienced men to show themselves.

Experienced snipers always ensured that they had at least one escape route to the rear: an abandoned sunken road, a broken communication trench, or a low rock wall. More important to their survival, however, was the art of camouflage. These hunters donned black balaclavas, or special sniper camouflage clothing— such as the Boiler Sniper's Suit, consisting of linen bulky overalls with a removable hood—or simply a sandbag over the head with eye holes cut in it, all of which helped them to blend into the earth. Their lives depended on becoming invisible.

The marksman sighted his rifle on firing points, picking out targets such as a shattered tree stump or a body half immersed in a crater, usually a few hundred metres away, before firing a few ranging shots. More experienced snipers avoided this

" THE BOILER" SNIPER'S SUIT.
(Made of Painted Linen.)
USED ALSO BY SCOUTS

Snipers donned suits like these to camouflage themselves amidst the destruction of No Man's Land. Then they waited for their prey.

ranging, as it could give away their position. Weather was factored into a gunman's aim, as rain or even a breeze could push a bullet's trajectory.[2] To make it harder for the enemy to pinpoint their position, most snipers preferred to shoot at the front from an angle, firing across the battlefield rather than straight at the enemy's front line. The second man in the sniper team, the observer, employed a scope or binoculars to study the enemy trenches for any sign of movement. And then they waited. Silent. Motionless. The damp ground seeping into their clothes, the lice feeding off their blood, tobacco cravings countered by the slow, methodical chewing of tobacco or gum.

It took hard men to kill so intentionally and methodically. The majority of infantrymen rarely fired their rifles, spending most of their days behind cover and most of their nights working. But snipers were a different breed. While each Canadian sniper was unique, most often the marksman's weapon of choice was the Ross rifle. The Ross had failed as a robust weapon for the infantry, but it was considered an accurate rifle in the hands of experts firing off only a round or two at a time. Telescopic prismatic sights were added to the rifle to ensure that anything that moved within a 500-metre radius, and likely further, could be put in a grave in a few seconds.

In response to the threat snipers posed, the men exercised caution. As former schoolteacher Samuel Honey remarked in a letter to his parents, "I considered discretion the better part of valour and kept my head very low the whole time."[3] And experienced infantryman John Sudbury wrote home of the bent-over shuffle: "I now wish I wasn't so tall for my back is nearly broken bending about so much where parapets are low and can't be built higher."[4] Most experienced soldiers were smart enough not to "pop up" during the day, but occasionally new or careless men allowed their heads to rise above the parapet. Moreover, exhausted and suffering under the strain of the trenches, the infantry often took stupid chances. Considering the danger snipers presented, the fact that soldiers inured with a false sense of bravado or fatalism made it a habit to jump out of their trenches at night and walk overland to the rear rather than endure the crowded and narrow communication trenches is hard to believe. "Many of our casualties have been the result of not obeying orders. We are all prone to take chances," testified Armine Norris, who would survive three years of trench warfare before he was killed less than two months before the Armistice.[5]

Such unsafe behaviour made the snipers' task easier, but these stalkers posed a deadly threat at all times. Textbook-perfect sandbag walls that had been flattened down by shovels to appease officers intent upon neatness were a sniper's dream, since a head showing above the parapet, even for a second, was easily distinguishable above the straight, flat surface of the stacked sandbags. Private Will Bird of the 42nd Battalion recounted the experience of a new man who was intrigued by the nearness of the German lines and the accuracy of snipers. When one unseen sniper shot away a periscope that Bird put up, the new man popped his head above the parapet for a quick look, curious as to whether he could spot the sniper. Bird described his fate: "'Don't!' I yelled and grabbed his coat. He stretched up in spite of my protest. The bullet entered his forehead and went out the back, breaking the strap of his helmet and carrying it to the rear of the post. I lowered the body to the trench floor and covered the face with a clean sandbag."[6] This man had forgotten the first warning to every soldier who entered the trench system: "Fear God and keep your head down."[7]

Snipers found their mark other ways, too, and did not always need a target above the sandbag parapet. Observers studied the parapet, looking for unrepaired holes knocked in it by artillery fire. Unsuspecting soldiers marching by such gaps could be taken by surprise if they were new to the sector. If the parapet contained no breaks, snipers sometimes simply drilled a shot through the sandbags. A high-velocity bullet fired from only a few hundred metres away could penetrate through half a metre of stacked sandbags or a full metre of earth.[8] The sandbag defences of older trenches were usually weaker, having lost their density over time. A careless group of men, perhaps talking loudly, revealing themselves with shovels jutting up on shoulders, or simply stirring up the thousands of flies that settled over the front in the summer, provided an excellent target for snipers who could gauge their movement behind the sandbags. The superstition about sharing a match among three people was born of soldiers' hard experience with snipers. "I have been reaching over to light up when a match is going," wrote Lieutenant Stanley Rutledge, "only to have it blown out in my face—'sorry, old man, have another match, two of us lit up already from this one.'"[9] Such behaviour was a response to snipers' three-part process of noticing the match strike and the lighting of the first cigarette, aiming at the faint glow of the second lit cigarette, and firing through the sandbags at the glow of the third lighting. Three seconds of faint light was one second too many on the cruel Western Front, or so the infantry believed, and these men were, after all, the snipers' targets.

All soldiers knew they could expect little mercy at the front, and almost none from snipers. Lance Corporal Herbert McBride of the 21st Battalion—one of the 15,000 Americans who eventually served with the Canadians in France and Belgium—was one such expert sniper.[10] During the month of December 1915, his shooting alone accounted for the deaths of at least a dozen enemy soldiers. He killed those above the trench and far behind the lines, who thought they were safe; he killed those who tried to drag wounded comrades into the trench; he killed men who showed themselves for only a few seconds; he killed an entire machine-gun crew who, having had their camouflaged nest destroyed by a shell, were stumbling around the front in full view, stunned and defenceless. "We got them when and where we could get them and we damned their souls to hell."[11]

After successfully targeting their mark, sniper teams were wise to go to ground or slink to the rear, as enemy observers and snipers looked for any telltale sign of their tormentor, hoping for an opportunity to erase the threat. Deadly silent duels were carried out in No Man's Land as sniper teams hunted their opposites. Each battalion usually had eight snipers, but some units doubled or tripled that number, thereby ensuring that No Man's Land could host several teams on any given day.

Complex triangulation of fire could be worked out to roughly locate the enemy snipers, after which a crash artillery bombardment was called down on that part of the front in the hope of a saturation kill. Elaborate ruses were prepared to force snipers to show themselves: by the summer of 1916, "dummy heads" made of papier mâché were used to draw enemy fire. With the head mounted at the end of a pole, soldiers took turns walking back and forth in the trenches to simulate human movement. A more advanced model allowed for a lit cigarette to be put in the dummy's mouth, and smoked through a tube attached inside the head. The red glow from the cigarette intake usually attracted the concealed sniper's attention.[12] When a bullet

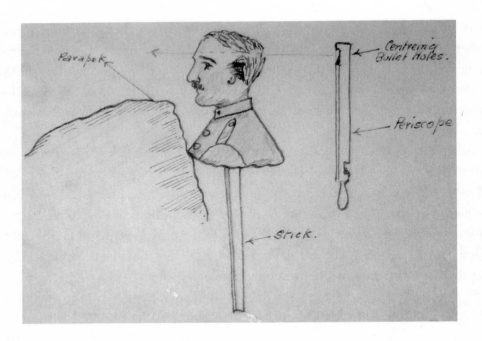

Soldiers fashioned papier mâché heads and deliberately placed them above a trench in the hope of drawing out a sniper. The dummies were walked back and forth, and advanced versions could be "smoked" through a special tube to provide the even more enticing target of a red cigarette ember.

passed through the head, the now shattered papier mâché skull was brought down and examined for entrance and exit wounds, in order to determine the angle of the bullet's trajectory. Often, this crude method showed the direction from which a sniper had fired, thus providing a focus for retaliatory fire. Just as importantly, if the use of the dummy succeeded in drawing a sniper out to take a shot, a counter-sniping team could seize the opportunity to execute him.

The Germans responded in kind. Lance Corporal Alwyn Bramley-Moore of the PPCLI recounted to his son that one of his friends was almost counter-sniped by a German team when he shot at a dummy head, gave away his position, and was fired at from several directions.[13] Lance Corporal J.A. McLean of the 25th Battalion was not so lucky: on September 25, 1915, after sniping two Germans, he was killed by another sniper, whose bullet tore off the top of his head.[14] He lived for two hours before death took him.

Aware of the danger of revealing their position by firing, patient sharpshooters waited for the mark. Snipers, according to Captain W.W. Murray, "lived in a murderous world of their own, developing feuds with unseen enemy snipers, contriving ways and means of getting the Boches to betray themselves so that their end might thus be hastened."[15] One of the most famed snipers of the war, Lance Corporal Henry Norwest—a Métis with the 50th Battalion who scored 115 confirmed kills before he was counter-sniped in the last months of the conflict—was legendary for his patience: "On one occasion he waited two days for two enemy snipers who had heard his rifle, as he accounted for another of their friends, knowing they were suspicious of his post. At last he caught them off guard and one went down followed by the other in fifteen minutes."[16] Other Natives, too, developed a reputation as efficient killers. Two members of the 8th Battalion—Patrick Riel, a relative of Louis Riel, and Philip McDonald, an Iroquois from Ontario—had more than a hundred confirmed kills before they were killed only days apart in January 1916.[17] Francis Pegahmagabow from Ontario's Parry Island Band was another utterly fearless sniper and scout who accounted for dozens of German deaths.[18] Although most snipers were white, these high-profile Natives helped to shape the reputation of the Canadians as natural hunters and soldiers.

Not only did the opposing snipers hunt each other, but so too did the infantry search for the despised murderers of their comrades. Bounties were not uncommon for confirmed kills of snipers.[19] Perhaps the infantrymen felt such anger and hatred because the sniper hunted other men, actively seeking out their deaths, choosing his victims. The artillery gunner fired from several kilometres away and rarely saw what he was hitting; the machine-gunner swept the front in arcs of fire; but the sniper was a conscious killer. The infantry took to meting out revenge on these shadowy assassins with relish. Battle patrols searching the front went looking for enemy snipers in a deadly game of cat and mouse; when found, little mercy was extended to the skilled killers. An unwritten rule dictated that snipers would be executed on the spot. Snipers were trained killers, but their prey did not consist solely of helpless victims.

CHAPTER 22

WINNING CONTROL OF NO MAN'S LAND

Canadian Raiding, 1915

"We have been lying low for so long that the idea was to show that we still had a good kick with us, and could put it up to them any time we wanted," wrote Lieutenant Victor Tupper.[1] Tupper noted with satisfaction that although the Canadians spent much of their time in a standoff against their German opposites, they would periodically impose their will on the enemy. He was referring to the deadly art of trench raiding.

Soldiers spent their tour in the front lines enduring assaults by death-dealing weapons, which resulted in a steady hemorrhage of casualties. Striking back at their tormentors helped soldiers to cope, and this desire for action underpinned the aggressive policy of trench raids. Some units within the BEF, including the four Canadian divisions, developed a fierce reputation as elite troops. Yet while "fire-eating" colonels and everyone up the chain of command viewed raiding as a perfect tool for inculcating the attacking spirit in soldiers, many of the men were often less thrilled about engaging in these night stalkings. Raiding provided important battle-field experience, but the casualties could be high when plans went wrong. In such cases, the losses comprised the most effective and bravest of a battalion's soldiers.

Raids could be orchestrated at any level. Major generals or brigadiers might call for a raid to test enemy defences or secure intelligence. At the battalion level, the same reasons resonated with commanding officers, but they also felt a pressing need to provide an active defence where their men patrolled No Man's Land aggressively and threatened the enemy at every opportunity.

The first raids were carried out by Imperial troops, but although the Canadians did not pioneer raiding, they elevated it into a grim art. When the Australians moved from the failed Gallipoli campaign to the Western Front in early 1916, they deliberately sought out the Canadians to train them in raiding, as their fellow Dominion troops were regarded by friend and foe as one of the most aggressive forces fighting on the Western Front.[2] The Canadians' reputation as elite raiders originated in a raid against La Petite Douve farm, in Belgium.

On the night of November 16–17, 1915, raiding parties from the 5th and 7th Battalions attacked enemy positions around the Belgian farm. The German defenders were complacently dug in behind the Douve River, which after weeks of rain had swollen to double its size and, at 3 metres deep and 9 metres wide, was considered impassable. By patrolling through No Man's Land, however, the Canadians found a way to flank the river, and planned a unique "butcher and bolt" operation rather than a customary "bite and hold" attack to capture a few hundred additional metres of Belgian territory.

In the days leading up to the operation, Canadian gunners had been firing all along the German front to clear enemy barbed wire. Although the artillery gunners and the infantry had not worked well together in many of the Canadians' previous engagements, here they had more time to plan and coordinate the attack. Captain Huntley MacPherson noted in his diary that officers of the 3rd Battery, Canadian Field Artillery, were so pleased with their shooting on this occasion that they claimed "there is not enough wire left on their front to hang washing on."[3] The gunners were required to clear a path for the raiders, but to also lay down a punishing fire on the enemy lines to protect the retreating parties as they made their way back across No Man's Land at the end of the operation.

Prepared with detailed plans worked out over the better part of two weeks, 10 officers and 170 men slunk into the night. Travelling light, with their kit and all forms of identification left behind in sandbags marked with their names, the raiders were divided into parties of wire-cutters, "shovel men," bombers equipped with grenades, rifle attack groups, and reserve rifle units who would support success or provide fire in case the attacking parties needed to retreat while engaged with the enemy.[4] The primary group of raiders carried conventional weapons such as rifles, as well as ladders and mats to lay across the barbed wire. Previous battle patrols had mapped out pathways across the flooded ground, but a tangle of barbed wire remained (regardless of what the gunners in the rear thought), and so additional men equipped with wire cutters led the groups, snipping to clear areas where the shells had failed to provide adequate paths.

Despite their intense preparation, however, elements of the 5th Battalion, attacking from the south to the north, ran into hidden barbed wire in a water-filled 3-metre-wide moat. The men's struggle to cross the obstacle alerted the enemy, and a firefight occurred. The 5th suffered no casualties, but the raiders were forced to retreat. Three hundred metres to the west, the 7th continued to slink forward in a driving rainstorm, moving in a northeasterly direction towards the fortified German lines. Careless German sentries, blinded by the rain, were not watching for an attack. They were surprised and killed by a force led by Captain J.L. Thomas. The Canadian raiders, their faces covered by black masks, slipped quietly into the enemy trench.

Then all hell broke loose. Canadian grenadiers spread out down the trenches, throwing their bombs into the next bays and hugging the trench walls to protect against shrapnel flying back at them. Riflemen supported the grenadiers, shooting and bayoneting the confused defenders emerging from their dugouts. In the course of a few mad minutes, an estimated thirty Germans were killed or wounded. The attackers left the trenches after twenty minutes, herding twelve scared prisoners before them, and carrying a new type of rubber gas respirator that was immediately sent to the battalion's intelligence section. About twenty minutes later, German counterattacking forces charged into their forward trenches aiming to push the attackers out, assuming they would still be there holding the prized ground. The trench was empty. On cue, however, the Canadian guns opened fire, catching and killing many of the trapped attackers who milled about in their trenches or had begun to follow the Canadians into No Man's Land. The only Canadian casualties suffered were the shooting and killing of one man when a comrade stumbled over wire in the dark and discharged his rifle accidentally, and the wounding of a second man by stray enemy fire.[5] Few raids in the Great War were carried off with such unqualified success.

The Petite Douve raid attracted the attention of senior officers, all the way up to the First Army Commander, General Douglas Haig, who approved of the aggressive tactics and called it a model raid. The 7th Battalion's commanding officer, Victor Odlum, was singled out for praise, and Brigadier Louis Lipsett told Major General Arthur Currie, "the 7th has gone up to the top of the class in the Brigade."[6] Private Lew Perry of the 8th Battalion noted that his commanding officer, after hearing about the raid carried out by those "salmon skinners and timber busters from B.C.," demanded volunteers to match that success.[7] The 7th's exploits were acknowledged in other brigades, too, with Lieutenant Victor Tupper of the 16th Battalion writing proudly to his people that the raid was the "slickest little job I've heard of so far.... We are doing a somewhat similar stunt, the first dirty night."[8] And so began a competition among the Canadian battalions to pull off bigger and more damaging "stunts" to prove their worth and earn bragging rights.

Such stunts did not always work, however. The 10th Battalion launched a raid on the night of February 4, 1916, against an enemy strongpoint just south of Petite Douve, with the aim of killing Germans and capturing the prize of a machine gun. The raiding party trained for weeks, preparing to assault the enemy in a complicated operation that involved cutting through extensive wire and sending two raiding parties into the enemy trenches protected by a covering party, all of which was coordinated by a signals post in No Man's Land to transmit information back to command headquarters. The night was dark and quiet, and the rain that had come down all day let up by 10 P.M. At this point the attackers, numbering some seventy men, had been in No Man's Land for three hours cutting wire. Another five and a half hours got them through the enemy's thick outer defences, and then the raiders moved forward, single file, through a narrow gap. They crawled to within bomb-throwing distance of the enemy trenches, but bad luck revealed an enemy working party there. The raiders waited quietly, hoping they would move off. But a small German protective patrol stumbled on the Canadians, now isolated in a vulnerable position. Around 4:30 A.M., according to the official report, "hand-to-hand combat took place in which rifles, bayonets, revolvers, knobkerries [clubs], bombs and even fists were freely used."[9] The alarm went off, and the working party jumped into the German trench. The Canadians tossed eight bombs into the enemy's packed ranks and retreated under a hail of fire without the prized machine gun—but not before snatching some prisoners. However, in the chaotic retreat, the wire constrained the Canadians, and they made the difficult decision to execute at least eight of the prisoners because getting them back to the lines would be too difficult. From 5 A.M. onward, the raiders slithered back into their own lines, carrying some seventeen wounded mates and having lost four who had been killed in the fighting. German Mauser bullets cut through the air, but eight 18-pounders from the 1st and 4th Canadian Field Artillery batteries put a stop to their harassing fire. The officer leading the raid estimated optimistically that at least forty or fifty Germans had been killed or wounded in the operation. Some of the 10th Battalion men—and most of the ranks of the gloating 7th Battalion—were not so sure. Corporal Alfred Andrews, who had been promoted from the rank of private after gaining months of experience and having many of his seniors killed and wounded, observed that his 10th Battalion company believed the raid "was a useless waste of life and that it was put on for the glorification of the C.O. and to show we could do as much as the 7th. We were joshed over this for weeks. Every time we went in [to the front lines], the 7th would say, 'Are you taking a machine gun this trip?'"[10] Instances of such taunting reveal how raids built reputations, and that the Canadian battalions could indeed be riven by petty jealousy.

CANADIAN BATTALIONS were increasingly encouraged to be "offensive," which became a running joke among the men. "Are you offensive enough, mate?" "Ah, you sure smell offensive." Dark humour helped the soldiers cope, but raids were no laughing matter. For some men, the worst part of raiding was the anticipation of meeting the enemy in battle, an enemy who most often was never seen. For others, it was the anxiety of leaving the safety of the trench. "A trip to No Man's Land is an excursion which you never forget," testified Louis Keene. "It varies in width and horrors. My impression was similar to being on Broadway without any clothes—a naked feeling."[11] Corporal John Harold Becker from St. Thomas, Ontario, lamented the necessity of raids that seemed to bring only death and destruction to his mates: "I know there were some fire-eaters out there who were strong for getting on with the War—I wasn't one of them. I had all the bravery knocked out of me."[12]

Raiders had a reputation as hard men, and were often able to avoid the regular fatigues of the trenches since it was felt that they were paying their dues by engaging in such dangerous missions. Some battalions instigated policies of identifying their elite raiders with a long vertical patch along the left arm. A small corps of patrollers, most of whom were drawn from a battalion's intelligence section, went for nightly walks in No Man's Land, but larger raids involved men drawn from the battalion's infantry companies. Most often they were volunteers, but usually with the promise of a reward of some sort. A ration of rum was an almost obligatory payment, but men who captured a prisoner might also be given ten days of leave, which was considered worth risking anything for, including one's life. At other times, prisoners under punishment could be offered a reduction in their sentence if they agreed to join a raiding party. If greater numbers were needed for a larger raid, or if an officer wanted his men "bloodied" to gain battlecraft experience, unwilling soldiers might be "volunteered" for the job.

Special raiding schools later trained the men to "mystify, surprise, and mislead" the enemy.[13] Experience at the front and doctrine emanating from the training schools taught that maintaining secrecy prior to the raid was crucial, and coordinating a raid with a feint further up the line was important to draw off enemy reserves and gunfire. But the key to success was intricate planning and a thorough knowledge of the raid's detailed timetable down to the minute. All of these skills would later be incorporated into the Canadian attack doctrine for planning larger setpiece battles.

Raiders dressed lightly and in dark colours, and burnt cork was rubbed over the face to lessen the chance of skin showing. Dark balaclavas were issued, which could be pulled down to cover the face and present a shapeless target, unlike a helmet. These head coverings eventually became so popular that they were adopted as official issue in the summer of 1917. Identifying patches and rank insignias were ripped from jerkins. Men with colds or sniffles were left behind.

At the appointed time, with sentries warned, the stalkers crept up the trench ladders, crossed over the parapet, and crouched through their barbed wire and into

No Man's Land. The raiders' greatest ally was stealth. But the garbage-strewn ground, ghostly white flares that illuminated the sky, attentive enemy sentries, and even cracking ice could give away a party of men. Skulking forward cautiously, the raiders threaded their way through the destruction. Foul-smelling craters filled with fouler-smelling bodies of the dead were passed with barely a glance. Barbed wire clutched at arms and legs, snaring and scraping. As raiders moved closer to the enemy lines, scouts looked for gaps in the wire, or took out the wire cutters and, on their backs, silently snipped their way through the entanglements. The rest of the party found safety in craters, scanning for enemy patrols or work parties. More than a few men must have felt like Lieutenant D.E. Macintyre, who had volunteered for a raid: "As we lay there waiting, I wondered why I had ever sponsored this mad enterprise. If I had kept my mouth shut and gone about my regular duties, nobody would have ordered me to do this. The planning and training part of it had been fun, anticipation of danger and possibly glory for some had kept us keyed up, but now we were in the ring and there was no way to back out."[14]

Nearing enemy lines and anticipating battle, the raiders fingered their specialist weapons. The Ross and Lee-Enfield rifles were generally too long for the close-quarter fighting that was expected, although big raids employed riflemen to lay down covering fire. Revolvers and knives were popular, and sharpened entrenching tools were the weapon of choice among some men as they could be swung effectively in the narrow trenches. Some hard men even sported brass knuckles, although perhaps more as a display of toughness than for any operational reason. Handmade clubs could also be effective, and two types were wielded: metal bars or hardened wood bats that could knock a sentry senseless so that he could be taken prisoner, or more lethal varieties, often with nails jutting from them, which were meant to kill quickly and silently. However, too much should not be made of these clubs, as they were infrequently used. Most soldiers were experienced enough to arm themselves with projectile weapons, even rifles, which could still be used to deadly effect in and outside the trenches. Grenades also remained an essential component of a successful raid, proving efficient for clearing dugouts.

After finding a gap in the enemy's defences, or making a new one through barbed wire to avoid an area that might be under observation, the raiders jumped into an empty part of the trench. They crept along until they found a sentry, dispatched him, and then crashed down front-line and communication trenches in an orgy of destruction, tossing grenades in dugouts, and stabbing and shooting as they went. Satchels of more powerful explosives, including ten-pound ammonial explosive charges, were also carried to demolish defensive positions, such as redoubts, machine-gun nests, and deep dugouts.

Private John Campbell described a successful, if vicious, raid: "The attack was a complete surprise to the enemy and after putting the machine-gun out of action with a shot from a revolver, the bombers succeeded in getting into the trench in both places and found it full of Germans who were tumbling out of their dugouts at the first cry of alarm (which was given by the sentry before he got his), without any definite idea of what was happening." Campbell's account of the raiders' actions in the enemy trenches conveys the zeal with which some men carried out their job: "Our men fought like demons and they found the Germans who were in the trenches at that time to be rotten fighters and more than one tried to save himself by throwing up his arms and crying 'Mercy Kamerade.' Others who thought [to] escape ran down the trench and when the boys got to work with their automatics and bombs they squealed like pigs."[15]

Battles fought in the trenches were harsh and deadly. The attackers had the advantage over the surprised enemy, but the confusion inherent in night fighting made it difficult for the attackers to maintain command and control. Strict training for such battles, based on timetable tactics, was essential. Multicoloured flares were usually fired to alert raiders to retreat at a certain scheduled time. Raiding parties typically limited themselves to a few minutes in the trenches, sometimes a little longer if the operation involved several dozen or more men. But the key was to hurt the enemy and get out.

Hitting and running fast was important since the roused defenders, once organized, could quickly overwhelm a raiding party. For the enemy, organizing was difficult, however, and confusion always reigned, for commanders were uncertain whether the attack was full-scale or if only a few enemy raiders were in their trenches. The impact of the chaos cannot be overestimated: explosions erupted all along the lines; cries of pain were mixed with shouts of alarm; flares were fired into the air to call down artillery fire in No Man's Land; and machine-gunners on the flanks swept the front, firing in long arcs to catch the attackers as they scurried back to their lines. As the raiders streamed back to safety, they made a confusing and disorienting scramble that often involved running and dropping from shell crater to shell crater to avoid enemy fire. When the front quieted down, soldiers sometimes found themselves lost, having travelled in a direction perpendicular to the lines. Aware that the coming of dawn would leave them easy victims for snipers, they set off following guess and instinct, hoping that their own sentries were not trigger-happy and that they remembered to expect incoming raiders to arrive in staggered processions.

Raiders, prisoners, and the wounded slid back in under the wire all night long. The prisoners were trundled roughly to battalion headquarters, interrogated by intelligence officers, and sent to the rear. Little is known about interrogation methods, but terrified prisoners, perhaps wounded from the fighting, often passed along whatever they knew.[16] Cigarettes, water, or even rum could be offered to win trust; force was used on the uncooperative.[17] "In civilized war, a prisoner can be compelled to tell only his name, rank and religion," testified decorated combat veteran Alexander McClintock. "But this is not a civilized war, and there are ways of making prisoners talk."[18]

Battalion intelligence officers wanted to know about German tactical issues, from the nature of their defences to the morale of their troops. At this first level of inter-rogation, the prisoners' unit and other elements of the enemy order of battle were identified to help piece together a picture of the enemy front, especially which units were opposite the Canadians. Speed was of the essence, and after this level of inter-rogation was complete, prisoners were quickly shunted to the rear under guard for the next round, by higher-ups. Brigade and divisional intelligence officers wanted to know different things than their counterparts in the battalions, such as information that might assist in better understanding the state of the morale in the enemy forces. Letters or diaries captured in the raid were translated in the hope of gleaning insights into German actions, worries, or preparations; accounts of negative morale were published with satisfaction in intelligence reports that were circulated within the army. But young and terrified front-line soldiers often had only minimal knowledge of the army in which they served, and the interrogation of prisoners would only have produced the most limited of intelligence for the brigade or division intelligence officers.

"THE INFANTRY is the place where you have the satisfaction of killing Germans, and that's what will end the war," wrote Roy Macfie of the 1st Battalion.[19] Without doubt, the large-scale muggings carried out during raids allowed for much killing of the enemy. Raiders engaged in aggressive combat, and it taught them essential battle-craft skills. "Raids were extremely effective," claimed Robert Christopherson of the 5th Battalion. "They did more to unnerve the enemy than the battles."[20] Spirits were raised after an operation had gone as planned and all knew that the enemy had been pushed back on his heels. "They say the men in our trenches lined the parapet during the scrap and rooted and cheered us as though it were a hockey match. When they saw us come out they sent up such a cheer that it could be heard away back a mile," recounted Lieutenant D.E. Macintyre after one successful raid.[21]

"I hope that the Canadians are not in trenches opposite you," wrote one shaken German infantryman. "On the darkest night they jump suddenly into our trenches, causing great consternation and before cries of help can be answered disappear again into the darkness."[22] The Canadians developed a reputation for fierceness as a result of these successful nocturnal snatch-and-grab operations. Lieutenant General Edwin Alderson, who by September 1915 had become Canadian Corps commander, did not always like his troops' disdain for spit-and-polish discipline, but he reconciled himself to the unconventional Dominion actions: "I've concluded that men who display initiative and resourcefulness of that kind are just the kind of men we'll need to beat back the Hun."[23] The Canadians' reputation for skilled raiding helped to strengthen their image as elite troops, although they did not stand alone, as the Australians and many British and Scottish units were similarly respected for their raiding prowess.

Raiding also fit into Haig's policy of attrition. In between the big battles, the enemy would be harassed and killed—ground down until he snapped. But the soldiers were not always happy to comply with taking on dangerous raiding missions—sometimes even going so far as to call secret truces with the soldiers in the opposing trenches—and the necessary rate of attrition threatened to dwindle away in some of the quiet sectors where the infantry were not willing to "waste" themselves against the enemy. In those parts of the front loomed the hard reality— at least in the minds of the generals—of the phrase "live and let live."

Raids ordered by higher echelons could be avoided by performing "ritualized raiding," which entailed groups going out into No Man's Land, finding a safe hiding spot, and waiting for several hours. Raiders usually had to bring back a few strands of enemy wire to prove they had gone close to the enemy lines, but this difficulty could be overcome by keeping extra German wire on hand from earlier raids or patrols. Engaging in too much of this feigned warfare was not possible, though, since brigadiers or other staff officers who were expecting to have prisoners to interrogate could order new raids until a prisoner or useful intelligence was delivered.

AN AGGRESSIVE RAIDING POLICY carried many advantages for the Canadians, but the policy was never without its costs in casualties and a wearing down of morale. The nature of the effects of raiding—whether more positive or negative— was difficult to judge, as the dead were counted hastily and enemy casualties could never be accurately tallied, especially when raiding German troops who were caught in deep dugouts. The practice of aggressive patrolling and raiding helped to deliver victory by continually honing the blade of essential battlecraft skills among fighting formations; but overuse also dulled this blade, as the best men of the unit were invariably killed or wounded during these aggressive actions. As well, the constant raiding carried out in the winter of 1916–1917, in response to pressure from senior officers, ruined any chance of maintaining secrecy and the element of surprise. While the Canadians took pride in owning No Man's Land, the Germans could be sure that an attack was coming almost every night, at least somewhere along the line, a certainty that kept them tense and alert but also ready to unleash fire on raiders.

More raids also meant less time to prepare. Without strict timetables and the coordination of various arms such as the artillery, machine-gunners, engineers, and the infantry, a raid might simply degenerate into a mad battle in the dark. Both attackers and defenders would be the victims. Even when operations were tightly controlled, they were unpredictable. An alert enemy sentry could rouse the trench garrison; the gaps in the wire could have been found by an enemy patrol and an ambush established; a cough or the rustle of movement could bring down a hurricane of fire. Trench raiding could therefore be detrimental to fighting efficiency insofar as it killed off a battalion's best men and left the rest wondering when their turn would come.[24]

IN 1915 and the early parts of 1916, the majority of raiding orders originated from battalion commanders or from brigade headquarters. By the summer of 1916, however, raiding became more systemic within the Canadian "way of war," with divisional and corps commands ordering active patrolling and raiding along the front on nearly every tour. Raiding provided an arena for acquiring key battlecraft skills: men learned especially the importance of developing tightly coordinated operations and carrying out intricate pre-raid planning. They also came to appreciate the need for decentralized tactics, which required that soldiers fight independently instead of being corralled into long lines marching methodically into the mouth of the guns. In addition to providing this essential training for the British and Canadian troops, raids and their outcomes were intricately wrapped up in reputations, both of commanders and units. Every successful raid therefore had a triumphant ring, accompanied by a downplaying of evidence that the best and most aggressive men of the battalion were those who took the brunt of the casualties. Perhaps the final word on the subject should belong to trench warrior Edmund Blunden: "The word 'raid' may be defined as the one in the whole vocabulary of the war which most instantly caused a sinking feeling in the stomach of ordinary mortals."[25]

CHAPTER 23

CREATING THE CORPS

September 1915–March 1916

"The war keeps up its everlasting grind and everyone plods unrelentingly on," wrote discouraged front-line officer Lieutenant F.G. Newton to friends at home.[1] Soldiers at the front understood well that the Germans were far from cracking. With politicians and kings refusing to negotiate, the only way to end the war was to hack a hole in the German lines to get to the open country beyond, but that would mean a series of frontal assaults against barbed wire, trenches, and hardened defences protected by machine guns, artillery, and a seemingly never-ending flow of reinforcements.

The summer of 1915 had provided a respite for the Canadians to recover from the shock of the Second Battle of Ypres and the Battle of Festubert. During this period, soldiers spent more time fighting lice and loneliness than Germans, but still the ever-present spectre of snipers and shells took its daily toll on the men in the trenches. Lives continued to be lost in disconsolate dribs and drabs: a man dismembered by a shell in one part of the trench, another shot through the arm somewhere in the next bay, or a raid gone bad, leaving a handful of corpses in No Man's Land. Companions were slowly claimed, one after another.

The troops were also suffering from a reinforcement problem, as most of the men in England were being trained for a second division, and so were not yet ready to be sent forward. In August, a strength report for the Canadian Division's infantry battalions in Europe noted that their number of men ranged from a high of 1,025 in the 16th Battalion to a shocking low of 426 in the 1st Battalion, with most of the battalions fielding around 800 men.[2] Not until the end of the year did infantry battalions return to full strength.

In September 1915, a new Canadian division arrived in France. The 2nd Division had been raised in Canada almost immediately after the First Contingent's armada had sailed. The thousands of men who had been turned down in disappointment in August 1914 responded to the new call to arms. Units were raised from across the country, although the West provided a disproportionate number of enlistees. The new 4th Infantry Brigade comprised four battalions raised in Ontario: the 18th (London), 19th (Toronto), 20th (Toronto), and 21st (Kingston). The division's middle brigade, the 5th, included a mixture of forces drawn from Quebec and the Maritimes: the 22nd Battalion, raised in Quebec, would be the only French-Canadian battalion in the entire corps, while the 24th was formed largely around the English-speaking Victoria Rifles of Canada, a militia regiment from Montreal. The 25th and 26th Battalions were raised from recruiting stations at Halifax, Nova Scotia, and Saint John, New Brunswick, but men from across the two provinces were among the enlistees. The 6th Brigade was raised in the West and consisted of the 27th (Winnipeg), 28th (Winnipeg), 29th (Vancouver), and 31st (Calgary) Battalions.

While the new division's battalions were linked to major cities and sometimes even to militia units, most often they also drew from surrounding cities and communities. Several additional battalions went overseas with the 2nd Division but were broken up for reinforcements. Engineers, medical and service corps, machine-gun units, and the division's artillery accompanied the infantry, all to varying degrees lacking proper equipment, especially the gunners who were dismayed to find they had few, if any, guns with which to train. Almost all of the units had caretaker commanders, who would be replaced in England by more experienced officers pulled back from the Western Front.

Within the corps, Alderson, the Canadian Corps commander, and Turner, the new commander of the 2nd Division, continued their uneasy relationship. Turner felt the British general had twice failed to adequately support him and his troops in battle, while Alderson had little faith in Turner. But Alderson had been unable to remove Turner since his political backers, especially Sam Hughes, had "been too strong."[3] Staff officer J. Sutherland Brown later noted that Alderson, while a kindly, old professional, "did not have the strength of character to contest a politician of the type of Colonel Sam Hughes nor impress upon the British Authorities the necessity for supporting him."[4] The apolitical Alderson's objection to Turner was overturned (he did not press the matter beyond writing adverse reports), and the Victoria Cross–winning Turner was given command of the new division even though his senior officer had little faith in him. The rancorous relationship between the two men would further degenerate within the next half year.

The 2nd Division joined the 1st in the field by mid-September to create the Canadian Corps. General Alderson assumed command of the corps, and a number of officers were transferred from his old 1st Division to form the senior corps command staff. This "general staff" was the nerve centre of the force. It took Alderson's orders and implemented them within the corps, but it was a small organization numbering only about twenty-five men.[5] This cadre was responsible for all military operations, plans, training, movements, communications, supply, and anything that had to do with the fighting machine. Simply feeding and watering a formation of 37,800 men and several thousand additional horses was an enormous task, and when the corps' strength rose to more than 80,000 men by the end of 1916, the combined force would take its place as one of Canada's largest "cities." The general staff oversaw the running of this city— one that was experiencing severe trauma and had a "murder rate" of shattering proportions.

Britain's War Office sent some of its best staff officers to the Canadian Corps to assist in the maturing process. Brigadier General C.H. (Tim) Harrington was appointed brigadier general, general staff (BGGS), the highest-ranking staff officer in the corps. The BGGS organized the general staff, and he had a number of subordinate staff officers: a general staff officer (GSO) 1, who was responsible for operations; several GSO2s, including two devoted to intelligence and one devoted to training; and three or four more officers at the GSO3 level, who assisted in carrying out delegated tasks that changed depending on whether the corps was in the line, in reserve, or in preparation for active operations.

The training branch of the general staff incorporated into the men's training lessons gleaned from soldiers' experiences at the sharp end. Reports of all battles, raids, and engagements were circulated up the chain of command, as were daily war diary entries about events occurring during combat and while holding the line. Important lessons were drawn together from the Canadians' experiences and compared with similar reports circulating through the entire BEF to fashion new doctrinal lessons that resulted in a continuous learning process. Instruction in subjects such as new methods of cutting barbed wire or how to use phosphorus grenades to clear out enemy dugouts soon benefited Canadian officers.

Specialists, including the general officer commanding, royal artillery (GOCRA), chief engineer, corps machine-gun officer, and corps chemical advisor, assisted the corps commander in ensuring that his orders—as well as training and operations— were carried out. Some of these specialists also controlled firepower assets. Brigadier Harry Burstall was appointed to the position of GOCRA, and oversaw and refined the gunners' art while coordinating the artillery in the two divisions as well as an increasing number of heavy artillery and mortar brigades that were attached to the corps. Later in the war, corps training schools were set up to codify the lessons of battle and disseminate them throughout the force. Specialized schools taught an evolving curriculum and doctrine relating to trench warfare, sniping, signals, chemical warfare, machine guns, engineering, artillery, and a few additional arms.

A part of the general staff, and also reporting to the BGGS, was the administrative staff, in which a deputy adjutant and quartermaster general administered all matters relating to running and replenishing the corps. The administrative staff comprised two distinct sections: Q branch, directed by the quartermaster general, and A branch, headed by the adjutant general. Q branch dealt with supply, transport, and even duller, if essential, functions such as bathing, transfer of documents, and veterinary services. This mundane part of war required experts to run it efficiently, for without supplies and ammunition the fighting units would have ground to a halt. The A branch administered issues relating to military law, discipline, postings, prisoners of war, and burials.[6]

These three branches, the general staff, and the Q and A branches of the administrative staff functioned as the nervous system of the corps, and all information passed through these channels, thus keeping the fighting and logistical arms linked to the corps commander. The functions of these branches were duplicated at lower levels of command—at the division, brigade, battalion, and even company level—to establish a hierarchy of command and knowledge.

The Canadians were lucky to have excellent British staff officers in their general staff throughout the war, and when Brigadier Harrington was promoted to become General Herbert Plumer's senior staff officer for the British Second Army in the summer of 1916, he was replaced in the Canadian Corps by a string of brilliant professional soldiers—including Percy Radcliffe and G.J. Farmar. While some of the more strident nationalists, such as Sam Hughes, demanded that the Imperials clear out of the corps' general staff and hand the reins over to the Canadians, officers at the front realized that few Canadians would be able to successfully take over as general staff officers. Arthur Currie, himself a strong proponent of a national forma-tion, wrote that it was not "a question of whether a man is a Canadian or otherwise, it is one of the best man for the job."[7] These "bloody red tabs," as the soldiers often dismissively called the general staff officers after distinctive markings on their uniforms, were essential in inculcating greater professionalism in the high command, and in running the enormous movable city known as the Canadian Corps.

While corps headquarters sorted itself out, with new staff officers learning to work together and with subordinate formations, the forty-year-old Currie was promoted to major general as commander of the 1st Division in September 1915. Alderson had viewed him as his best brigadier, considering him "dogged, depend-able, thorough and increasingly knowledgeable," and he felt it fitting that Currie receive the corps' veteran division.[8] Turner was given the 2nd, and Mercer would soon be appointed commander of the 3rd Division, which was then being raised. All of the senior officers—Alderson, Currie, and Turner—had had their reputa-tions marred by the Ypres and Festubert battles, but had acquired much-needed experience during the summer of 1915.

THE CANADIANS were maturing and gaining experience in the hard environment of the Western Front and were increasingly making a name for themselves as dependable troops in the line. Often perceived as brawlers, voyageurs, trappers, and prizefighters, the Dominion troops had supposedly been shaped by the ravages of the Canadian winter. These conquerors of the frozen north seemed to have innate fighting qualities. The First Contingent had reinforced this wild image through its drunken ramblings and punch-ups, which, although involving only a minority of men, were well publicized across Britain. Stories featuring Canadians had them refusing to salute officers and, when they did, often calling them by their Christian names. While some of the standard army discipline took time for the Canadian civilian-soldiers to accept, their reputed disdain for discipline was quickly reforming in 1915. Divisional commanders Currie and Turner were strict in enforcing discipline, and by the end of the year the Canadians had tightened up behaviour in every unit.

The Canadians also had a darker stain on their reputation. After the Second Battle of Ypres, rumours circulated that the Canadians did not take prisoners, choosing instead to execute captured enemy soldiers on the battlefield. Although more than 43,000 Germans were eventually taken prisoner by the Canadian Corps alone—almost eighteen times the number of Canadians who fell into enemy hands—the perception of colonial savagery remained strong. Canadian soldiers clearly killed prisoners in the heat of close-quarters battle, usually during the time of uncertainty between combat and capitulation, but such actions were by no means unique to the Canadians, and similar allegations clung to the Australians, as well as to some Scottish, Indian, and British units.[9] The practice was, however, particularly associated with the Canadians. British infantryman and poet Robert Graves echoed the accusation voiced by many Tommies when he described the Canadians as having "the worst reputation for acts of violence against prisoners." But Graves also noted,

> The Canadians' motive was said to be revenge for a Canadian found crucified with bayonets through his hands and feet in a German trench.... How far this reputation for atrocities was deserved, and how far it could be ascribed to the overseas habit of bragging and leg-pulling, we could not decide. At all events, most overseas men, and some British troops, made atrocities against prisoners a boast, not a confession.[10]

The Canadians' reputation for ferocity was indeed based on both fact and fiction. Yet although many Entente and German troops still saw the Canadians as wild voyageurs or "red Indians," the vast majority of Canadian troops were workers— either skilled, unskilled, or clerical; far more were students than ranchers; and far more were drawn from the urban workforce than hunters from the wild.[11] The Canadians likely performed no more executions than any other troops on the battlefield, whether Entente or Central, but they tended to be more vocal about those executions they did commit, partly because they had experienced the shock of one of their own men supposedly being crucified on the battlefield, and likely also because this image suited their emerging reputation as elite fighting troops.

THE 2ND DIVISION came into the line near Ploegsteert Wood in the Ypres sector late in the fall of 1915. Opposite them, the Germans held a trench system only a few hundred metres away, based around the strongpoint of Messines. Like the units of the 1st Division half a year earlier, men of the 2nd Division were apprenticed to combat veterans, but this time the apprenticeships were to other Canadians instead of to British comrades. Friendly and not-so-friendly barbs were traded back and forth about the rowdy reputation of the First Contingent in England, or about the tardy arrival of the 2nd Division to the front. A chippy Lieutenant Colonel John Creelman of the First Contingent noted of the 2nd Division men: "The airs which they are putting on are very amusing. They never fail to point out that they were carefully selected. In fact, hand picked, inferring [sic], of course, that we are not.... [They are] a good looking crowd ... but with much too big an idea of their superiority over the old First Division."[12] Notwithstanding the rivalry, however, 1st Division soldiers felt an obligation to teach the new men how to survive at the front, and 2nd Division soldiers who wanted to live listened to them. In fact, the veteran 1st Division also had British units posted to it for instruction, just as they had benefited from experienced British divisions a little more than six months earlier. Informal lessons were also passed on from man to man, and one of the veterans of the Second Battle of Ypres advised, "Kill and keep up the reputation so hardily won at Langemarck, St. Julien, Ypres, Festubert, and Givenchy. The First Contingent has set the pace, let the young men that are coming up now keep it up or beat it, always remembering that they are fighting for humanity, justice, and right."[13]

As the new Canadians learned the ropes in the trenches and in training sessions at the rear headquarters, the British were preparing for a renewed offensive. The 95 French divisions, 38 British divisions (including the two Canadian), and 6 Belgian divisions faced off against 117 German divisions on the Western Front.[14] The BEF forces under the command of General Sir John French were still very much the junior partner to the French on the Western Front in terms of size, and the British commander was therefore often forced to fight in support of French-conceived and -led operations.

In September 1915, as part of a larger French offensive in the Champagne, Artois, and Vimy Ridge sectors, the British attacked Loos, a mining town surrounded by slag heaps that had been fortified by the enemy. This strongpoint would not fall easily, and many weaker spots could be found along the Western Front. But the French forces needed a diversionary attack here to draw off enemy reserves, and so the British prepared to launch this offensive. Lord Kitchener admitted that coalition warfare required that "We had to make war as we must, and not as we should like to."[15]

The 2nd Division was lucky to avoid an immediate trial-by-fire engagement like the Second Battle of Ypres, but the division was involved in the British diversionary attack during the September 25, 1915, Battle of Loos. At Loos the British released their first chlorine gas attack of the war. "We gassed them this morning, and I hope they are dying in thousands, for I'll never forget what they did to us at Ypres," wrote William Hay, a Canadian serving in a British artillery regiment.[16] Indeed, the British did their best to exact a chemical revenge for what they had suffered at Ypres, but the fickle nature of gas revealed itself when large parts of the cloud blew back over their lines when the winds changed. More than 2,000 Tommies were gassed. Yet other parts of the gas cloud blew through the German lines, and small advances were made throughout several days of battle. General French pushed the battle on and off for another six weeks, but with only minimal gains and more than 60,000 British casualties. The French armies to the south involved in the primary offensive had failed on a larger scale, losing some 200,000 men, but the battle on the British front cost

General John French his job. He was replaced as commander-in-chief of the BEF by General Douglas Haig—who had long waited in the wings as an ambitious army commander and had made a habit of undermining his commander-in-chief. Now, the largest army ever fielded by Britain in its history was his.

The Canadians played an insignificant part in the battle at Loos. They had been ordered to lay down an intense fire on the enemy troops across from them at 4:56 A.M., and to further harass them by burning straw and pitch and 100 pounds of red phosphorus, augmented by 500 smoke candles, to simulate a gas attack. The enemy front was lit up with artillery fire, and through the smoke only "flashes were visible."[17] But the diversion kept the Germans occupied, as they called down artillery fire in response to an expected attack. The operation cost the Canadians 100 or so casualties, but many felt they had helped, and the corps had been ready to push through as an exploitation force should the German lines have been broken. This had not happened, though, and so the front-line soldiers turned their attention again to their ever-present enemy, the constantly worsening winter conditions.

Winter on the Western Front was harsh—even for the frontiersmen. For the vast majority of shopkeepers, students, and clerks who formed the Canadian Corps, however, it was a nightmare. Under the weight of fire and the eroding effects of water, the trench walls collapsed. Most of the day and night was spent shovelling the slop back into sandbags and rebuilding the parapet, with this backbreaking labour often being conducted in knee-deep sludge and slush. Major Arthur McNally of the 7th Battalion, who would be wounded three times during the war, wrote exasperatedly in his diary in early November: "Still more rain." The trenches were a "perfect slough of mud and water. Subsidiary line dissolving and flowing away.... Two or three feet of water from one end of the trench to the other."[18] Private George Ormsby communicated to his wife on November 11, 1915, that he had to wade through trench after trench of mud that was two and a half feet deep. After completing several tours in the front lines, he wrote in early January 1916 that he had not had a "dry foot for nearly three months. The mud was something like the snow in Canada, up to our knees and sometimes our waist."[19] A shortage of rubber boots kept the soldiers miserable and wet, but the number of cases of trench foot was remarkably low, as NCOs and officers enforced precautionary measures.

The 14th Battalion spent sixteen days in the firing line during November, in four tours. By the second week, sheets of rain caused floods in the trenches. On November 9, the front-line trenches had to be temporarily evacuated for fear of soldiers drowning.[20] Some men swam to the rear. In such conditions, the infantrymen worked day and night filling sandbags to hold back the elements. With their homes washing away, troops holding ground with low water tables often had to build up rather than down. These higher sandbag defences were more easily scattered by artillery fire, thereby leaving gaps in the trench wall where snipers could shoot unsuspecting victims.

Within this swill of slush, the Canadians battled with the rats for dry ground. Wrapping themselves in layers of clothes, groundsheets, sandbags, and anything else that might help, the *frontsoldaten* began to take on the appearance of puffy, homeless people. Soldiers hacked their greatcoats to above the knee to lighten twenty or thirty pounds of mud that clung to their lower bodies, willing to draw the ire of officers who might charge them for destruction of army property.[21] Under these layers of clothes, parasitic invaders thrived, and up and down the line, rasping coughs and wild sneezing rang forth from every bay and dugout.

WHILE THE WEATHER remained the most persistent foe of most men in the trenches during the winter of 1915, the enemy continued to kill Canadians. Snipers and artillery shells ran up the death total every day along the front. The Canadian gunners, too, had begun to receive more ammunition from mid-1915. But gun teams considered it a good day if they could fire half a dozen shells. This was a far cry from the massive barrages that would accompany offensives during the next year.

The infantry also received new weapons. The Ross rifle had been mired in controversy since its inception at the turn of the century, and its poor performance during the battle of Second Ypres had resulted in Canadians being killed as they stood defenceless. Although not every Ross jammed, the robust Lee-Enfield suffered much less from the uneven quality often seen in small-arms ammunition that was produced by the millions. The Ross had failed the test of battle. Many commanding officers complained bitterly, with the 31st Battalion reporting in one practice shoot that its riflemen had suffered no fewer than 138 jams after 10 to 25 rounds of rapid fire.[22]

But the Ross was more than a rifle. It was Canada's national arm, and many soldiers and politicians had reputations that marched in lockstep with the weapon. One of its strongest supporters was Minister Sam Hughes, who viciously attacked all who attempted to question its value, engaging in what W.A. Griesbach, an infantry brigadier, called a form of "military terrorism." "Many Generals and Colonels spoke their disapproval of the Ross in whispers, but in official communications temporized and wrangled—said that the rifle might be improved or altered, that perhaps it had not had a fair trial, or that the ammunition was perhaps unsuitable—anything indeed but the truth they knew."[23] Hughes's friends and supporters in the CEF, including his son and Richard Turner, refused to condemn the weapon, while others such as Arthur Currie and Malcolm Mercer were against it. General Alderson eventually sent out a survey to the corps' brigadiers and battalion commanders, forcing them to commit their recommendations to paper. They split evenly down the middle, revealing the partisan lines in the CEF and, likely, that the Ross did not perform poorly for all formations. However, a second survey that went out to junior officers—the men who interacted most closely with the rank and file, and heard their grousing—came back overwhelmingly against the Ross.[24]

Though the politicized Canadian Corps was split, Alderson cared not a whit about these nationalist sensibilities and urged the War Office to have the Ross replaced with the Lee-Enfield. Hughes reacted with characteristic anger, deriding Alderson in a letter he sent to all commanding officers in the Canadian Corps, belittling the general's judgment and, in no uncertain terms, telling him that his opinion was not wanted. It was a shocking and callous move, even from a man who had made a career out of shocking and callous outbursts. But Alderson stood his ground against this political meddling.

Responding to the controversy, Lieutenant Armine Norris summed up the non-political reality of the situation: "There are Canadians who prefer the Lee-Enfield and there are Imperials who like the Ross, but the man who doesn't love his rifle will never fight as well."[25] In mid-1916, too many Canadians had lost faith in their rifle. Infanteers in units such as the PPCLI, which were equipped with the Lee-Enfield, found they were ill-advised ever to put down their rifles, as other Canadian soldiers made it routine policy to walk through their trenches and billets looking to see if they could rearm themselves.[26] The Ross had to be changed. While Alderson was no doubt angered and embarrassed by Hughes's reprimand, he had learned some political skills and he continued to work through the British high command to have the rifle replaced. The Ross was slowly pulled from the field, and divisions were rearmed with the Lee-Enfield throughout 1916.

IN ADDITION to the adoption of the Lee-Enfield, other tactical reforms were made in the Canadian Corps, mirroring those made in the larger BEF. By mid-1915, infantry battalions had begun to pull specialists out of their companies. The fighting units clearly needed more than just rifle and bayonet men, but less clear was where the grenadiers and machine-gunners could best be deployed to augment combat effectiveness. First snipers and grenadiers were removed from the infantry companies, then machine-gunners and other specialists, including certain signallers and anti-gas experts. By grouping these specialists outside the infantry companies, and sometimes even outside the battalion at the brigade level, senior officers and the high command thought they could be more easily deployed. In the case of a major operation, for example, machine-gunners could be grouped together from the four companies, or four battalions, to create high concentrations of firepower. But company commanders complained that pulling out the specialists resulted in infantry companies, platoons, and sections being denuded of much-needed firepower. Often a forty-five- to fifty-man platoon was reduced to twenty to twenty-five men, when wounded soldiers, those on leave, and the removed specialists were accounted for. As well, since elite troops were often drawn off to bomber and machine-gun units, riflemen tended to be left with the sense that they were considered the lowest of the low. The brunt of the fighting was still falling to these infantry units, but now they were missing their key men and essential firepower. After much experimentation, it was decided by the high command in early 1917 to return most of the specialists to the infantry company and platoon commanders. Although it would take more than a year for this reversal to take place, it was an important step toward re-embedding the essential flexible firepower in the hands of the infantry who were forced to carry out the difficult missions.

The British Vickers machine gun could fire 500 bullets per minute. It was a deadly defensive weapon and could lay down indirect fire to harass enemy troops.

The main heavy Canadian machine gun remained the Colt. Before the decision was made to group heavy machine guns into specialist units, the Colt added essential firepower to any battalion, and all four teams of gunners in a battalion could be massed to create a wall of fire. But like the Ross rifle, the Colt had a tendency to jam after repeated use. It was replaced in the summer of 1916 with the Vickers, a far more reliable, water-cooled heavy machine gun. The Vickers could fire some 500 rounds per minute, which were fed from fabric belts, and could spray the beaten ground in a flat, sweeping trajectory some 500 metres wide and up to 2,200 metres deep. This hail of fire could also be deployed in a more vertical position in an indirect fire role, causing the bullets to come down behind the enemy lines. This indirect barrage was thought to saturate trenches and sunken roads more effectively than flat, horizontal fire that might be blocked by parapets or other structures.

The Vickers, like the Colt, was a complex machine that required five men to work it as a team. It was also very heavy and hard to drag forward in an assault: the gun weighed 28.5 pounds, plus another 10 pounds when the water jacket was full; the tripod weighed 48 pounds, and each box containing 250 rounds added another 21 pounds. British private George Coppard described the choreographed drill of moving a Vickers machine gun into the line:

> Number One dashed five yards with the tripod, released the ratchet held front legs so they swung forward, both pointing outwards, and secured them rigidly by tightening the ratchet handles. Sitting down, he removed two metal pins from the head of the tripod, whereupon Number Two placed the gun in position on the tripod. Number One whipped in the pins and then the gun was ready for loading. Number Three dashed forward with an ammunition box containing a canvas belt, pocketed to hold 250 rounds. Number Two inserted the brass tag-end of the belt into the feed block on the right side of the gun. Number One grabbed the tag-end and jerked it through, at the same time pulling back the crank handle twice, which completed the loading operation.[27]

With these steps completed, the Number One gunner then flipped up the sights, lifted the safety, and was ready to depress the double thumb trigger to send out an arc of destruction. The gunners fired in short bursts, sweeping the ground in front of them, knowing their range, but usually producing fire to take down advancing bodies of men, not individual soldiers. Because of the bursts, the fire was not like a continuous scythe, and the spray of bullets contained gaps. This was a weapon of mass destruction and not sniping; yet tightly packed men—even those advancing with several metres between them—were hard to miss.

If the Number One was hit, the Number Two took over, with Number Three in turn taking his spot. The two most inexperienced men, the Four and Five, usually ran ammunition back and forth, or water, which was needed to cool down the guns. The water jacket could boil the 7.5 litres of water after only a few minutes of nearly continuous fire, and the escaping steam could give away the gun's position. Asbestos gloves were needed to remove the barrel and replace it with a second one, and the water was burned off at about 1.5 litres every thousand rounds. As well, sustained fire raised the chance of barrel blockages, and gunners were continually dealing with jammed ammunition. These jammings were no doubt a terrifying prospect as gunners frantically scrambled, now for the most part defenceless, to clear the blockage, while the enemy continued his steady advance in trying to close the distance. Despite these interruptions, a Vickers could be expected to fire roughly 10,000 rounds per hour, saturating what became known as the "beaten zone." A Vickers machine gun, wielding the potential firepower of some forty or fifty riflemen, was an essential tool on the battlefield, and all the more devastating when two or more were set up to sweep the same part of the front in interlocking fields of fire. Worth noting, however, is that wiping out a Vickers machine-gun nest was far easier than eradicating a platoon of rifle-wielding infantrymen, who themselves could deliver a devastating rate of fire. Nonetheless, it comes as no surprise that the rank and file viewed the removal of these guns from the battalion as an act of lunacy.

To replace this loss of firepower at the sharp end, a light machine gun was issued to the infantry platoons. The American-designed Lewis machine gun became an essential assault weapon for the infantry platoon, and was even installed on many types of aircraft. A forty-seven-round drum was situated on top of an oversized barrel, and the infantry version of the Lewis could fire off all rounds in a few seconds and be reloaded by experts just as quickly, assuming the next pan was already filled. While it was air-cooled, and therefore had a greater propensity to jam after sustained firing, this automatic rifle was a key infantry weapon from the summer of 1915 until the end of the war. Although it could be carried and fired by one man, it was heavy at thirty-five pounds, and a team of ammunition carriers was needed. Without them, the rifle was just a hunk of useless metal. The Lewis gun provided enormous firepower for the infantry platoon, and was essential in augmenting the attack against and the holding of captured positions. While the Lewis never matched the robust Vickers in firepower, it could be more easily brought forward in the attack, to exactly where the infantry needed it the most. By the end of 1915, one Lewis gun was issued to each of the sixteen platoons in a battalion, although this number would

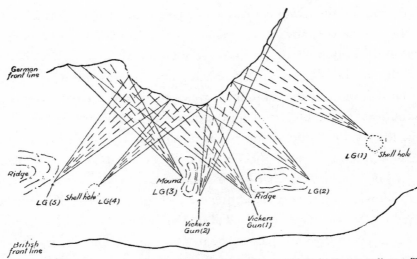

EXAMPLE of arrangement of Lewis (5) and Vickers (2) Guns to cover attack on German salient. The Vickers sweep the whole length of the parapet in their zones. The Lewis guns are allotted sections which they must watch for M.G. emplacements. These are always likely to be found in the sides of a salient.

This doctrinal diagram from a Canadian training manual illustrates the use of machine-gunners to sweep enemy strongpoints to support the infantry in penetrating enemy positions.

be doubled by the last year of the war. The Lewis gunners were one of the keys to victory in the years to come, and as a sign of its usefulness, the Lewis was one of the few weapons that the Germans sought to capture and use against the Allies.

Grenades and rifle grenades rounded out the infantry's roster of primary weapons. These were always popular among the men, and essential for clearing trenches. The rifle remained the primary weapon throughout the war, but in 1916 senior officers complained that the infantry relied too heavily on grenades. They worried that rifle skills were being lost as soldiers instead turned to frantically tossing grenades ahead of them. One British colonel in the summer of 1916 lamented that his infantry-men's shooting skills had deteriorated to the extent that they could no longer hit enemy soldiers fully visible at the range of 200 metres, a full 100 metres short of the longbow range at the Battle of Crécy in the fourteenth century.[28] An emphasis on training ensured that by the second half of 1917 the rifle would emerge again as the key infantry weapon, although grenades always remained important, even if they were used up quickly.

By mid-1915, the rifle grenade was tentatively introduced on the Western Front, and thereafter became increasingly important. Special grenades attached to a long metal rod that could be inserted in a rifle barrel allowed the grenade to be projected up to 80 metres. Although the new weapon was inaccurate in the hands of amateurs, trained men became adept at dropping essential miniature artillery fire into enemy strongpoints. Later, a cup discharger containing the Mills bomb was placed at the end of the rifle, extending the grenade's range to an astonishing 200 metres.

The bayonet was the final weapon in the infanteer's arsenal. Attaching a seventeen-inch bayonet to the end of the Lee-Enfield turned the rifle into a spear. The psychological sense of security men felt when advancing behind a sharpened blade may have been more important than the soldiers even realized themselves. But many historians—and a good number of soldiers—derided the functionality of the bayonet, claiming it was used for little more than opening bully beef cans or jabbing into a sandbag in order to hang one's gas mask. Confusing casualty figures that reveal an extremely low number of bayonet wounds recorded at hospitals are frequently trotted out as evidence that no one used the bayonet.[29] And another wartime report on 698 cases of eye wounds found that only one wound was caused by a bayonet.[30] Such figures are unreliable, however, since they do not account for those men killed by the bayonet who never emerged from No Man's Land or their trench systems to be treated in the rear.

The bayonet was attached for every battle, proving that it had some worth to the men who chose to use it. And almost every single operational report describes trenches being cleared by soldiers employing bombs and bayonets. Some of the reporting about bayonet use in the official records was couched in the language of "cold steel"—which was no doubt metaphorical, and used to connote hard fighting—but too many references to successful bayonet use are made in after-battle reports and in the accounts of medal citation winners to discount the effectiveness of this weapon in battle. Infantrymen were also not trained to aim for the eyes, as a stab to the head was more likely to slide off the skull than to penetrate it. The centre of the body was the primary target, especially the stomach. The fact that men who received such wounds did not make it back to the rear-echelon doctors to be included in their casualty figures is not surprising, as centre-body wounds were frequently lethal. The psychological threat of the bayonet was devastating, too, and enemy troops often gave up when the onrushing, bayonet-wielding enemy got within stabbing range. The bayonet remained a fearsome weapon up until the last day of the war, and both its functional and psychological roles are evident in the fact that it was used—and continues to be used—in every major war fought by Canadian forces in their history.

THE TINKERING with infantry platoons' organization and the implementation of additional firepower taking place in the Canadian Corps was part of the learning process that was occurring in all armies. While this evolution was carried on at the sharp end, evidence of senior commanders' and politicians' learning was harder to find. Although many of the above lessons were orchestrated by—or at least supported by—the high command, the failure of command and control, and the difficulty of influencing the battle after soldiers went into combat, continued to leave senior officers largely impotent. Failure to coordinate the various battle arms—primarily the infantry and the artillery but increasingly the machine-gun formations as well—also revealed that staff officers, commanders, and the soldiers forced to implement the attack doctrine within the British and Canadian assault formations still had much to refine before offensive forces could compete with the inherent advantages of those on the defensive.

By early 1916, the war was not going well for the Entente. The Germans had won significant victories on the Eastern Front while holding off the clumsy French and British attacks in the west. While the Royal Navy continued to tighten the noose with its naval blockade, few assumed that it alone could deliver victory. After considerable infighting within the British cabinet, the politicians had also demanded a new theatre of operations. In the early months of 1915, Britain had taken command of an ambitious naval campaign to push through the Dardanelles to capture Constantinople. The Entente had been at war with Turkey since late 1914 over the country's general support of Germany, and specifically because Turkey was allowing German ships to pass through its territorial waters to attack Russian warships along the Black Sea coast. The first phase of this naval operation against Turkey in

February 1915 was a disaster, with the British losing several prized warships to mines and bad luck. They pulled back at the moment when the Turks had almost nothing left to throw at the Royal Navy, but such are the ways of war for generals and admirals lacking the benefits of clairvoyance or historical hindsight. Instead, the British launched a massive amphibious campaign against the Gallipoli peninsula to capture key forts by land. The campaign degenerated into another version of the Western Front, albeit one plagued by a driving sun, millions of flies, and battles over rocky terrain. This was the trial by fire for the Australians and New Zealanders, but the bulk of the fighting and dying was carried out by the British Tommy. By January 1916, the British enacted a masterful retreat, removing an entire army without the Turks realizing what was happening. But retreats—no matter how impressive—do not win wars, and the British forces, including the Australians and New Zealanders, suffered 205,000 casualties in that fateful campaign. British "sideshows," such as this one in Turkey and those in Salonika and Italy, could not help the Entente forces in defeating the German troops on the Western Front, and succeeded only in sapping hundreds of thousands of troops and precious resources.

In February 1916, the Germans shifted their attention back to the Western Front after propping up the Austrians and inflicting heavy losses on the Russians. Attacking the French at Verdun, they launched the operation behind a hurricane bombardment and quickly captured precious French ground and forts. But the offensive was intended to do more than just overrun more of France. The German chief of staff, General Erich von Falkenhayn, believed that by capturing a series of important forts around Verdun, which had both military and symbolic value, he would force the French to attack him at a disadvantage. The Germans planned for such an attack and situated their artillery and machine guns to bleed the French armies white. The Germans accomplished this goal, but the French held on and soon responded in kind with their own artillery. For the soldiers at the front, the world was reduced to a few metres of muddy shell craters and unending shellfire. The battle dragged on for most of the year, and regiments literally evaporated like water in a scalding frying pan as they were thrown into the holocaust. Within a battlefield covering just 10 square kilometres, some 700,000 men became casualties in the longest single battle of the war.

WITH THE BATTLE OF VERDUN, the war took on a new level of savagery. The balance sheet of suffering and death went deeper and deeper into the red, with everyone losing. The Western Front offensives of 1915 had ended in failure because the attackers had been ill supported by their artillery, which did not have enough heavy siege guns or shells to clear enemy defences. But the situation had begun to change by early 1916, as the full weight of nations was thrown behind the war effort. All of the belligerents manufactured millions of shells and thousands of guns. The battles of 1916 were a harbinger of the industrial warfare that would shape the last three years of the war. Within the maelstrom of steel and fire, lives were lost in astonishingly high totals. But still the armies fought on.

CHAPTER 24

THE MURDER HOLE

Battle of St. Eloi, April 1916

After the terrible bloodletting during the Battle of Festubert in May 1915, the Canadians passed almost a full year on the Western Front without engaging in a major offensive operation. But 1916 would bring a year of mayhem and battle. In the early part of the year, the Canadians were holding the southern part of the Ypres front, near the village of St. Eloi, about 5 kilometres south of Ypres. As a result of earlier advances by the Germans, the trenches within the sector ran almost from east to west, rather than from north to south, as was usual on the Western Front. Like the northern part of the salient, this southern sector had been hotly contested, with the Germans in command of a slight rise called "the Mound" and able to direct accurate artillery fire over the battlefield. To even the odds, General Sir Herbert Plumer's British Second Army had spent months burrowing under the ground preparing for a new assault.

Underneath the Western Front, sappers on both sides dug elaborate systems of mines, excavating beneath enemy positions to place explosives and destroy strong-points. The German practice had been to work at a depth of 3 to 9 metres, pushing their subterranean labyrinths forward. British counter-sappers attempted to locate these enemy shafts and collapse them with timed explosives. By 1916, the Entente miners had honed their skills, and with more modern equipment, they were able to dig 15 to 25 metres beneath the ground.[1] Using these combat miners, Plumer planned to capture the small German salient that jutted into British lines near St. Eloi.

Here, beneath the Mound, a clay bank under which some thirty-three mines and thirty-one smaller explosive packages had already been exploded in an area of less than 4 hectares, British miners laid thousands of pounds of explosives.

On March 27, the British opened up with their heavy guns and blew up a series of new mines. Although unencoded chatter about the operation over radio waves had alerted the Germans to a possible attack and allowed them to thin out their lines, two companies of a German Jäger Battalion were consumed in the geyser of fire and earth when the mines were detonated at 4:15 A.M. The enormous multiple-mine explosions—which were heard in Folkestone, England—were so powerful that they caved in trenches along the battlefield.[2] Once the blasted ground came back down, the aftermath of the explosions revealed seven yawning craters and dozens of smaller ones pockmarking the Mound. These new craters, the largest numbered 1 to 7 from left to right, could easily swallow several houses each in their cavernous depths, and the largest crater was some 55 metres across and 20 metres deep.

Into the morass of mud and remains rushed the British and German troops. It was kill or be killed in a week of savage fighting as both sides struggled to occupy the tactically important craters. Torrential rain turned the battlefield into a quagmire. Officers lost control of their units as men disappeared in the mud and shell craters; wounded soldiers drowned in the muck, their cries heard over the battlefield. Soon, none of the maps matched up to the now battle-ravaged terrain, and soldiers found themselves wandering into the enemy lines.

The intensity of the struggle required that the 2nd Canadian Division hastily prepare for an unplanned relief of the now exhausted 3rd British Division, several days in advance of the set time. It would be the 2nd Division's premier engagement on the Western Front. Due to the emergency nature of the relief operation, front-line officers were unable to reconnoitre the enemy trenches adequately, and the staff officers in the rear were forced to hurry preparations and plans.[3] However, Major General Richard Turner investigated the front by crawling through the porridge-like mud and was nearly killed by shellfire. Turner was shaken by what he found, and was under no illusion that holding the forward position would be easy: "There is absolutely no front line, every vestige being blown away."[4] Covered in mud, the experienced general protested at Alderson's corps headquarters against his troops being sent into the salient. What was the use of holding the craters? he asked. And how would they be held? Despite Turner's moral bravery in questioning the operation, he was overruled and ordered to consolidate the position. Too much work had evidently gone into rendering the terrain a wasteland to allow it to be engulfed by No Man's Land.

On April 4, the 6th Canadian Brigade, commanded by Brigadier General H.D.B. Ketchen, a former officer in the Royal North West Mounted Police and a member of the Permanent Force since 1901, took over from the 76th British Brigade to the south of the newly captured craters, moving into shallow trenches that ran along the lips of the craters and that were riven with serious gaps. The Canadians were ill-prepared and untrained for what awaited them. Private Donald Fraser of the 31st Battalion wrote in his diary that the outgoing British troops could furnish them with no information, offering only the blank stares of men who had been pushed beyond endurance. As the naive Canadians passed by the mud-spattered British, one Canadian shouted jovially, "Cheer up! Don't be downhearted!," a customary greeting among troops on the Western Front. "You'll be downhearted, when you see what's up there," whispered a Tommy. "I have lost my best chums."[5]

Rushed and unplanned reliefs were never easy, but this one was terrible. Faced with seven enormous craters, as well as dozens of smaller depressions, the Canadians found it hard even to locate their own lines, let alone the enemy front. Forward Canadian units had been led into what passed for the forward trench (just beyond the craters) by exhausted British scouts who had no idea where they were going and wanted only to get out with their skin intact.

Wading into the 600-metre-wide salient, the infantry of the 27th and 31st Battalions squeezed into the constricted battlefield, finding only shallow ditches and no continuous linking trench. Sergeant A.H. Bell described the Canadian line as being "on a forward slope, in full view of the enemy."[6] Because of the narrowness of the salient, the Germans were able to fire their guns into the Canadian lines from three sides. This was a miniature Ypres salient, but in far worse condition. The mud was choked with dead and dying men, as the British had been too exhausted to remove them. Soon, the bodies of Canadians would be added to the grim swill. The message to the Canadians was very clear: keep your head down. Hedgehogging above the trenches for any amount of time attracted sniper fire or a few whiz-bangs. Even if one could take a leisurely look, not much remained for the eye to see, as the battlefield had been both aerially and subterraneously eviscerated.

In this open grave, the Canadians hunkered down and attempted to devise some sort of defensive position. But how? Little barbed wire was left, and only a few machine guns had not already been knocked out. Soldiers dug into the ground but soon found themselves sinking deeper and deeper into the oozing muck. They might as well have been consolidating water. Sandbags filled with the runny slop were thrown up on parapets that soon collapsed, oozing back onto the soldiers seeking shelter beneath them. The sheer exhaustion of just moving around in thigh-deep mud left soldiers depleted and wasted. Even worse, the Germans knew of the weak defences and used their artillery to good effect from their superior position that looked into the Canadian lines. One exhausted defender remarked wearily that the enemy employed his artillery guns as a sniper would: "If they see even one or two men exposing themselves they send over a shell."[7] By noon on April 4, every second man in one of the 27th Battalion's forward companies had been hit by shrapnel or sniper bullets.[8]

But more deaths and maimings would have been sustained if not for the newly issued Brodie steel helmets. Although men found the helmets strange-looking— deriding them in letters as inverted soup bowls and even using them to cook food over a fire—they stopped complaining about "tin hats" (which weighed more than a pound) after they began to save lives. While a helmet usually could not stop a high-velocity bullet, it did protect the head against smaller, irregular shell splinters and shrapnel balls that might hit the helmet's top or steel rim and be deflected off. Ringing ears or a concussion were far preferable to whirling steel passing through the skull. Medical authorities confirmed what soldiers already knew: that head injuries and brain wounds were reduced dramatically after the introduction of the helmet.[9]

The Brodie became an essential part of the soldier's uniform, even though a few British generals at first refused to let their men wear them for fear it would make them go soft. But all were soon convinced of the helmets' necessity. The German bucket helmet protected the back of the neck better and had a superior design, but it could not be adopted for Entente forces since soldiers were trained to distinguish enemy troops in the chaos of fighting by the shape of their helmet. Even as the men were better protected, the helmeted soldier began to look more industrial, a development not lost on some men who already felt like replaceable cogs within the war machine.

The Canadians soon found that St. Eloi was a battle of industrial might and medieval fury. Frank Maheux, an Ottawa Valley lumberjack who wrote to his wife in run-on sentences that may remind us that the average education level of soldiers was grade 6, recalled the horrific conditions: "We were walking on dead soldiers and the worse was they was [in] about three feet of mud and water. I saw poor fellows trying to bandage their wounds, bombs, heavy shells falling all over them.... it is the worst sight that a man ever wants to see."[10] Commanders rushed forward rum and hot food, but as one 27th Battalion infantryman attested: "We had a drink of rum, but nobody wanted anything to eat. These dead bodies lying around there took your appetite right away."[11] Private Donald Fraser recorded with revulsion that his crater was filled with at least thirty corpses. He and his companions clung to the top of the crater walls, scrambling in the mud to keep from sliding back into the corpse-filled muck. Throughout the day, shells landed among the bodies, dismembering them and plastering the survivors with rotting flesh. Vomit was soon added to the unimaginable swill at the bottom of the crater.

Recognizing that clusters of soldiers made easy targets, Lieutenant Colonel I.R. Snider of the 27th Battalion ordered a thinning out of his lines after crawling through the mud and observing the murderous shellfire. He knew that such an order weakened his defensive positions, but it at least gave his men a chance at survival. No continuous front existed, with platoons and sections cut off from their company headquarters since the multiple craters and shallow trenches required a patchwork defence. Communication had broken down almost immediately after the Canadians had entered the fray. Runners went out from company headquarters and were shot down or riddled by raking shrapnel fire. "There was no communication in the daytime," remembered William Pinkham of the 27th Battalion, a twenty-four-year-old who had been born in South Africa before immigrating to Canada.[12] Equally trying for soldiers was the realization that red cigarette embers drew fire; they were ordered to avoid all smoking. Most followed orders, but some of the hard cases tried their luck: life was not much worth living without one's "coffin nails."

Under such conditions, a German assault was not long in coming. On April 6, Bell's Bulldogs, as the 31st Battalion nicknamed themselves after their admired colonel, were blasted by the German artillery for seventeen continuous hours as the forward troops remained defiantly entrenched in and around Craters 6 and 7 on the far right. The shelling was, as one soldier recounted, "painfully accurate."[13] The battalion's war diarist noted, "Hundreds of shells must be bursting per minute. We must expect heavy losses."[14] Private Donald Fraser, one of the few survivors, wrote that "it was a miracle that anyone emerged alive."[15]

Casualties began to flow back to the medical officer, who recorded "cases of shattered nerves ... [due to] some men being buried by shells" and "a number ... coming in with chilled, sodden feet.... [from] standing in water and mud for 48 hrs."[16] "It was impossible to remove the wounded for twelve hours," wrote Andrew Macphail, a respected academic and doctor turned medical officer. "Some were hysterical, and some maniacal, bound to their stretchers.... the wounded officers were gaunt with pain, loss of sleep, and the general horror."[17] Among the psychiatric casualties also came a steady stream of mangled and dead.

Those soldiers mired in the mud at the front were blue with cold, but they continued to face the enemy. Major Patrick Daly of the 31st Battalion recorded that his platoon of 35 men was cut off from the rest of their company during the bombardment and attacked by a raiding party of 150 Germans. His "platoon opened up with rapid rifle fire under heavy bombardment, and accounted for about 25 dead at close range."[18] Mud-slathered soldiers, with only a few rivulets of sweat marking their filthy faces, cheered as the enemy survivors were driven into the muck. Lost from sight, the Germans waded back to their trenches under cover of darkness. The 31st may have been demoralized and battered, but it refused to break.

In the dark hours of April 6, the 29th Battalion relieved the badly mauled 27th Battalion.[19] One report noted that the 27th Battalion's officers "had not slept for over 100 hours."[20] In three days of fighting—or more accurately, in three days of being pulverized by artillery—the 27th had suffered 40 killed and 189 wounded.[21]

However, since only one narrow communication trench was in place for both the exhausted and injured defenders of the 27th and the fresh troops of the 29th to traverse, the relief took much too long to carry out. The Germans, aware that inexperienced or careless troops were coming into the line, attacked behind a violent artillery barrage of shells and Minenwerfer mortar explosions.

Using infiltration tactics learned at the Battle of Verdun (concurrently raging to the south), the Germans launched four attack companies, pushing from the south to the north towards the craters. Isolated Canadian positions were destroyed, or soon found themselves overrun, now caught behind enemy lines.[22] The Germans were unhindered by Canadian gunners, who were firing inaccurately, with most of their shells landing behind the enemy attacking troops that had quickly moved forward to get inside the safe area of the barrage (which was closest to the Canadian lines) to escape the shell slaughter.[23] While the newly arrived 29th Battalion caught some of the Germans with small-arms fire, the attackers swept through the Canadian positions. Hand-to-hand fighting among desperate men struggling for their lives went on for several hours. Little mercy was afforded by either side, and there was almost no place to hold prisoners. By the end of the battle, the Canadians were pushed out of the craters or annihilated.

Reacting to the doctrine of refusing to give up any ground—which the British and Canadian high command repeated like a mantra—Turner ordered the position recaptured, although he must have realized this was a nearly hopeless task. Several Canadian counterattacks were smashed as the infantrymen floundered in the mud and the battlefield was swept with German shrapnel and small-arms fire. Despite the appalling conditions, further counterattacks on the night of April 6 by Canadian bombers using grenades rather than mud-clogged rifles seemed to have more success.

Lacking a bird's-eye view of the battlefield, however, the Canadian raiders mistakenly occupied a number of small craters to the north of the intended larger craters that had been their original objective. None had seen their objectives before the attack, and instead of seven craters they found at least seventeen large ones and dozens of smaller ones. As Sergeant A.H. Bell wrote after the war: "At this time we did not realize that this part of the front was pelted with a mass of craters of varying sizes (but all of them very large to us) and therefore firmly believed that we had made Nos. 4 and 5 secure."[24] From the infantrymen's position, one large crater looked like another, especially without maps. When news of the supposed success filtered back to headquarters, commanders were relieved that the infantry had seemingly reoccupied some of the lost craters, thereby mitigating the blow of losing the line.

But the information coming from the front remained unclear. With most of the forward communication trenches blocked, collapsed, or raked with fire, the 2nd Division's staff was forced to rely on aerial photographs, but the weather was so poor that the flights were grounded or failed to deliver clear images. At least one spotter plane did go up on April 8, sending back photographs of the battle-field to create trench maps.[25] Poor-quality images and shoddy staff work at both division and corps headquarters failed to identify the German defenders in the large craters. As well as those photographs, though, several German prisoners stated that their forces—and not Canadians—held the craters.[26] To add to that confusion, however, Turner and his staff officers continued to receive conflicting reports from front-line soldiers that the Canadians were in the craters.

Those at the front may have had no idea as to where they were situated on a map, but they quickly realized the futility of trying to hold useless terrain. One company commander was correct in assessing the ground and suggested that the infantry pull back from the untenable salient: "To even attempt to hold [the salient] if we are successful in winning it, in the first place, would be rather like committing useless murder."[27] But with the British and Canadian commands both believing in the "sanctity of ground"—instead of the importance of trading ground for time or space or simply a more secure line of trenches—they could not see beyond this flawed concept and see fit to order a withdrawal from the untenable position. This meant, sadly, that the Canadian infantry were effectively abandoned because no one in the rear really knew where they were and the artillery could not adequately support them with fire.

Both commands saw clearly, however, that several of the craters were still in German hands. During the night of April 9–10, Brigadier General Robert Rennie of the 4th Infantry Brigade ordered the recapture of Crater 3. Despite the muddy conditions compelling one lieutenant to assert, "No one could crawl along this ground without getting his arms into such a state that they would be useless to him," at daybreak brigade headquarters received a report that a raiding party of fifty men from the 18th Battalion were holding the crater.[28] Unfortunately, the report was again inaccurate, as the weather, darkness, and inexperience of the troops had left them confused. The Canadians were not in Crater 3, but rather in smaller craters to

The horrendous conditions at St. Eloi had to be imagined by artists. This fanciful rendition depicts the Canadian infantry somehow attacking a German trench while wearing what appear to be saucepans on their heads.

the northeast of the German fortified position. The raiding parties had little idea of where they were going, and without proper maps or guidance from the rear, could only attack craters which were in front of them while moving over the blasted landscape at night.

Battles are difficult enough to reconstruct with the aid of documents, operational orders, histories, and maps. For soldiers who had nothing to go on but the word of a sergeant or a quick view over a muddy parapet, it was nearly impossible to have any idea of where they were headed or what part they played in the larger scope of battle. "Local, limited and incoherent," was how infantryman Edmund Blunden described the perspective from the sharp end.[29] For Turner to have relied on these men for information was to have failed to grasp the complete bewilderment prevailing on the front at St. Eloi. The 2nd Division's command staff in the rear peered at their clean maps and could not understand why their orders were not being carried out. Surely this was a case of the blind leading the blind.

Several German attacks the following night were beaten back by the Canadian infantrymen in the front-line trenches and smaller craters that dotted the battlefield. These soldiers were now relying almost exclusively on rifle fire and grenades, as their own artillery had few available shells and were still supporting the wrong infantry positions. The Canadians who were supposedly holding the centre craters wondered from where the Germans were launching these raids. A probing assault on April 12 against forward companies of the 18th and 19th Battalions was supported by heavy "machine gun fire from the enemy trench in rear of the craters."[30] In fact, the fire was coming from Craters 4 and 5, which the Canadians thought they were occupying, but which the Germans had now firmly consolidated.

During the night of April 14, the 24th Battalion prevented a German bombing party from retaking Craters 6 and 7—which remained in Canadian hands—in a ferocious forty-minute battle.[31] While the Canadians were being furiously shelled, the Germans were launching raids free from return fire because the divisional artillery thought the enemy line was the Canadian one. In contrast, any movement among the Canadians drew German artillery fire, and the 24th Battalion was effectively cut off from its commanders in the rear. Brigadier David Watson feared that the 24th had been annihilated, and runners were unable to penetrate the German artillery "box barrages," which effectively put down a screen of artillery fire between front and rear. Surviving officers of the 24th Battalion were eventually able to send a homing pigeon back to the rear, informing Watson's 5th Brigade headquarters that the battalion still held the front but had suffered heavy casualties.[32]

On that same night, a roaming patrol, slithering through the mud of No Man's Land, weaving in between the rotting bodies, heard the faint cries of a

Mass graves were not uncommon during high-intensity battles. Weeks, months, even years later, the bodies were often dug up and reinterred in individual graves.

wounded soldier. They investigated and stumbled across Private S.H. Warn of the 29th Battalion. He had been lying out in No Man's Land for nine days, with wounds to his arms, thigh, and head, and his feet having nearly rotted off from being submerged in freezing mud and slush.[33] He had survived by scavenging food and water from the corpses around him. Left for dead by his unit in the confusion of fighting, he had lived among the corpses but had refused to join them. The distance across No Man's Land was only a few hundred metres, but for men peppered with steel, this blasted zone might as well have been the size of the Atlantic. Warn was carried out and survived the war.

That Private Warn lay so long in No Man's Land was just one more testament to the degree of confusion on the battlefield. Without maps or aerial photographs, the infantry did not know where they were, did not know where they were supposed to be, and worst of all, did not know where they were in relation to the enemy. Not until April 16 did aerial photographs reveal that the Germans were indeed in the largest of the craters that gouged the battlefield. Realizing the futility of recapturing the now strongly fortified craters that the Germans had incorporated into their front-line system, General Alderson withdrew the Canadians from the muddy morass and went about trying to find a scapegoat. There were many to choose from, including the general himself.

The St. Eloi Craters: April 10, 1916

St. Eloi

—— Actual Canadian Line

• • • Supposed Position
of Canadian Line

– – – Actual German Line

–·–·– Supposed Position
of German Line

Water

0   50   100   150   200
metres

CHAPTER 25

DEFEAT AND SCAPEGOATS

April 1916

The question of who was to blame, or who would be forced to fall on their sword, spawned countless rumours throughout the Canadian Corps after the St. Eloi debacle. On April 26, press baron Sir Max Aitken (later Lord Beaverbrook), who had the unprecedented job of investigating, reporting on, and creating favourable publicity for the Canadian Corps, cabled Sam Hughes that the British viewed St. Eloi as a serious breakdown within the Canadian command.[1] Second Army Commander Sir Herbert Plumer had been reprimanded by Sir Douglas Haig, commander-in-chief of the BEF, for the failed operation, and Plumer in turn ordered Canadian Corps commander General Alderson to take "severe disciplinary measures." Plumer wanted Major General Richard Turner and Brigadier H.D.B. Ketchen removed from command for their apparent incompetence.[2]

Although Alderson could have used this justification to remove Turner, with whom he had had problems since Ypres in early 1915, the corps commander sympathized with the 2nd Division's difficult predicament and first asked Turner to sacrifice Ketchen of the 6th Brigade, hoping to save the general's job. However, the impeccably brave and angry Turner refused to serve up Ketchen. While his stand was honourable, it nonetheless surprised almost everyone, given Turner's precarious position. In a stormy confrontation with Alderson, Turner refused to lay the blame on Ketchen, who had done his best in the battle, and had even mucked through the slop—nearly being killed by shellfire—to get to his men and see the true conditions at the front. An angry Turner went one step further and accused Alderson of once again inadequately supporting him in battle by not heeding his request to pull his forces back to a safer position.[3]

Fed up with Turner, the normally reserved Alderson—described by one Canadian as a "kind gentle little man"—went to Plumer demanding that both Ketchen and Turner be removed from command.[4] Alderson dredged up a report he had penned the previous year, where he had questioned Turner's suitability as a divisional commander, citing a lack of "necessary qualification" other than being "physically brave to a fault."[5] Plumer, who was also looking for a scapegoat, found Alderson's assessment acceptable. But they had not cleared it with the Canadian government, which was always prickly about how its forces were handled by the British.

At the behest of Sam Hughes, who had appointed Sir Max Aitken to his role as Canada's military representative at the front, as well as bestowing upon him a host of other duties that allowed him to travel freely among various military headquarters, Aitken took it upon himself to save Turner.[6] The thirty-six-year-old diminutive newspaper magnate, with his enormous grin and twinkling eyes, was a charmer in business and among female company. But he had steel in him, and had made his millions through wily deals, tough negotiations, and ruthless business practices. In his accumulation of enormous wealth, he had made many enemies, and some accused him of having fled Canada rather than facing down official inquiries into his business dealings. Arriving in England in 1910, he was shortly thereafter knighted and elected as a British member of Parliament. Despite receiving these accolades in Britain, however, Aitken was a fierce Canadian nationalist all his life. He had a wicked sense of humour and liked to tweak the upper British establishment by always talking in an exaggerated Canadian accent. After first considering whether he should cut bait on Turner, whose division had indeed performed badly, Aitken used his considerable influence to arrange a personal meeting with General Haig on April 23 to clear the air. Face to face with Haig, Aitken warned the British general that the Canadian government would not stand to see their war hero denigrated and scapegoated for the battlefield loss.

The fifty-five-year-old veteran of the British army, Sir Douglas Haig, had won more than a few political battles to get to his senior position. While he knew almost nothing of the Canadian Corps, he realized that they were different from most of the forces under his command. He could have made a stand against this political interference, but he came to the conclusion that only one route of action was viable, noting privately that the importance of avoiding a "serious feud between the Canadians and the British is greater than the retention of a couple of incompetent commanders."[7] Turner and Ketchen kept their jobs, but Alderson was sacrificed. It appears that Sir Max, the kingmaker of British politics who would play a key part in disposing of British prime minister Raymond Asquith later that year, first honed his blade on British generals.

To be sure, Alderson had not exhibited a firm hand in controlling the Canadians at either Ypres or St. Eloi, but his greatest failing in the eyes of Sam Hughes (and therefore Aitken's) was his condemnation of the Canadian-built Ross rifle. Alderson had done the right thing in following the wishes of his troops by demanding that the British War Office replace the Ross rifle with the Lee-Enfield, but he ultimately paid the price for it in the partisan and political Canadian military organization.[8] The disposal of Alderson enraged Plumer and left Haig shaking his head at the mysterious ways of these colonials.[9]

Alderson was parachuted into an important job as inspector general in England, in the hope of clearing up the worsening quagmire within the Canadian training system. But he was given few powers and no one listened to him, as he was now little more than a cast-off, and several competing generals in England—all vying for control of the enormous training system—were not willing to back down even for the sake of increased effectiveness. After six frustrating months, the War Office allowed him to exit the position with what little dignity he had left. There is no doubt that Alderson's career had suffered from his association with the Canadians, and he was never given another command in the field. Many of the Canadians felt sorry for Alderson, who had clearly been done in at the political crossroads by Hughes and Aitken, but he was little remembered by Canadians within a few months, even though a mountain overlooking the Waterton Lakes in Alberta bears his name.

While Turner refused to give up his brigadier, he did remove four of his battalion commanders: E.S. Wigle of the 18th Battalion, J.A. MacLaren of the 19th Battalion,

J.L. McAvity of the 26th Battalion, and I.R. Snider of the 27th Battalion. Snider's case was particularly sad. In early 1916, much of the battalion's fighting efficiency still relied heavily on the commanding officer. He not only organized training, but often led his troops into battle. The fifty-two-year-old Irvine Snider, a veteran of the North-West Rebellion of 1885 and the South African War, had not slept for six straight days and nights during the battle, as he desperately did everything he could to relieve the strain on his beloved boys caught at the St. Eloi salient. Having lost so many men weighed heavily on him, and according to his medical file, when he finally returned to his billet and saw his bed, he went "to pieces and broke down and cried." Snider was removed from command having been diagnosed as suffering from exhaustion and shell shock. By war's end, of the 179 men who commanded an infantry battalion for more than one month, fully one-third would be killed, maimed, or rendered incapable of command due to illness or exhaustion.[10] The "Old Man" of the battalion, as the commanding officer was almost universally known—even though by the end of the war seven battalion commanding officers would be twenty-five to twenty-nine years of age—was often in the thick of the fighting with his men, and these commanders wasted away at similar rates of attrition.

At least one more battalion commander was on the chopping block, but J.A. Gunn of the 24th Battalion kept his position through a backroom deal with his brigadier, David Watson. During the later desperate stages of the battle, after it had been found that the Germans controlled the craters, Watson had insulted and abused Gunn in front of his staff for his refusal to carry out Watson's orders for further attacks. Gunn had refused to send his men back into the mud. Later, he offered his resignation, but asked to be paraded before Watson's senior commander to plead his case, as was his right under military traditions. The shocked brigadier pleaded obsequiously with Gunn not to resign, realizing rightly that having one of his officers go before his superiors for such a purpose would reflect poorly on him and might jeopardize his nomination for command of the 2nd Division should Turner be fired, as many officers expected at the time.[11] Gunn accepted Watson's apology, but later regretted this decision, feeling he had "made a very grave mistake in not pushing the matter through, as Watson later, through bad judgment and looking for kudos, cost the lives of many Canadians."[12] Watson would eventually rise to command the 4th Division, and would reveal himself to be one of the weakest, if longest serving, Canadian divisional commanders of the war.

While real failures had occurred at St. Eloi, men who had tried their best in the most deplorable of situations had also found themselves scapegoated. With the Canadians having cleaned out some officers, the British also threw some senior staff officers to the wolves, including Plumer's major general, general staff, and a corps commander.[13] Plumer could also have been "degummed"—the French slang for fired, which was adopted by the British and Dominion troops—for his role in the entire operation, but replacing staff officers was much easier than replacing army commanders, and was certainly less of an admission of failure.

Although Turner survived, his reputation was damaged permanently. The high command knew of his difficulties at Ypres, and definitely held him accountable at St. Eloi. He was rightly seen as being protected for political reasons. It may not be fair to blame Turner for the bewildering situation at St. Eloi, but someone had to be held accountable. Having visited the front and sent junior officers to ascertain the situation, Turner did not sit idly like some château general as his soldiers wallowed in the mud. As at Festubert, Turner tried to convince the British to allow him to pull back his formation out of the quagmire, but he was not supported by his superior, Alderson. Turner and his staff were plagued by inaccurate intelligence throughout the battle, but the division's inexperience also worked against it. Furthermore, throughout the Battle of St. Eloi Turner failed to fully comprehend the utter confusion and chaos in which his front-line troops were mired. To allow the blind to lead the blind could only result in failure, and that failure must be laid at the feet of the commanding officer. For surely the role of the command staff was to find out what was happening to its division, especially if it was being torn up by German attacks. Turner's failure in two battles ensured that he would never rise to command the corps.

THE BATTLE OF ST. ELOI certainly proved that a limited objective could be attained by using surprise and a hurricane bombardment to paralyze the enemy. But the question remained: how was that objective then to be held? Troops that were bottlenecked into a small area because of the limited width of the attack were soon susceptible to murderous enemy artillery fire massed on shallow defences that could be bombarded on three sides. The failure at St. Eloi may have strengthened General Haig's belief that attacking on a small front made the achieved ground impossible to hold. But as he was to find out on the Somme in a few months' time, attacking on a wider front would not lead to success either.

Although the outcome of the St. Eloi battle had almost no impact on the overall war effort, the failure to recapture the craters was an embarrassment to Alderson and his Dominion troops, damaging the Canadians' reputation. Far worse, many of the infantry had been abandoned in the mud, unsupported by artillery fire. All of the ensuing political intrigue and attempts to master the lessons of the battle meant very little for the soldiers of the 2nd Canadian Division. They had been thoroughly beaten and they knew it: more than 1,300 casualties had been incurred in losing British-captured ground. The defeat could not be easily sloughed off.[14] Yet, as described by Captain Maurice Pope, who fought at St. Eloi and was later a general in the Second World War, more than a few Canadians felt that the 2nd Division had been "asked to do the impossible.... We were handed over a strange area and the newly won ground was in simply hellish shape and the consolidation supposed to have been done by the Imperials was a [bad] job."[15] While more blame should have fallen to the British high command—both Plumer and Haig—for not having had the courage to pull back from the morass and let the Germans keep the bog, one well-connected Canadian in England noted that post-battle allegations of "slackness" in the Dominion forces rendered the unfortunate Canadians ready scapegoats.[16] Putting aside the rumours, the men of the 2nd Division, ragged, verminous, and exhausted, were relieved to simply depart from a battlefield that Private Donald Fraser called nothing more than a "murder hole."[17]

CHAPTER 26

"IT WAS A DAY
OF OBLITERATION"

The Battle of Mount Sorrel, June 2, 1916

As the 2nd Division regrouped and reintegrated new men into their mauled battalions, the Canadian Corps also found itself with a new corps commander. Alderson's loss was mourned by few Canadians. Most had respected the old Imperial general, but the grumbles and disquiet after Second Ypres, Festubert, and St. Eloi had revealed that perhaps he did not have a firm enough hand with his subordinates. John Creelman, who disliked almost everyone above him in rank, noted uncharitably: "Gen. Alderson leaves next Monday and will be replaced by Gen. Byng, who is said to be a very good soldier. I do not think he will be the type of person the retiring gentleman has shown himself to be. If a man has no self-respect he cannot expect to be respected by others."[1]

Alderson exerted a gentle command style with his Canadians, which some men responded to but others took to be weakness. Although the general had rarely revealed brilliance on the battlefield, it was the political challenge of serving two masters that had eventually left him crucified. The Ottawa politicians demanded that he keep them informed when decisions by British command impinged on Canadian autonomy, and they also expected the right to influence appointments; on the other side of the issue, the British War Office was aghast that one of their officers was breaking the chain of command and reporting directly to Canada. Alderson sometimes successfully played the two sides off against each other, but more often he was mauled at every turn.

Even if Alderson had proven to be a general of the second rank, the Dominion force had been supported by several excellent British general staff officers during the first two years of the war. Moreover, while Sam Hughes would have liked to have seen a Canadian command the corps, preferably himself, no Canadian was yet suitable, and certainly no one on par with Alderson. Although there was some dickering by Hughes to get a few of his favourites installed in command after Alderson was fired, General Sir Douglas Haig turned to an experienced and respected British cavalry general, Sir Julian Byng.

Lieutenant General Sir Julian Byng commanded the Canadian Corps from May 1916 to June 1917. He was the single most important figure in transforming the Canadian Corps into a battle-hardened formation.

Known as "Bungo" to his friends— who included Haig and King George V—Byng came from an aristocratic family and had a grandfather who had been a field marshal. He was known for his enviable record during the South African War as a thrusting cavalry officer, and in the current war, had received much praise for organizing the bloodless strategic retreat at the end of the Gallipoli campaign. His service on the Western Front as a corps commander had marked him for an army command. Receiving the Canadian Corps was therefore not a step up for him. Nor was the position initially welcomed. "Why am I sent to the Canadians?" wrote Byng. "I don't know a Canadian. Why this stunt?"[2] But Haig realized that the Dominion troops, who had proven their valour at Second Ypres, but had also been shaky at St. Eloi, needed a firm and experienced commander to guide them to maturity.

While Hughes viewed Byng as some blue-blooded, patrician general, the new corps commander was far from it. His manner and dress were casual, and he was easygoing and fatherly to the men in the ranks. Byng was the opposite of everything that the aloof British generals seemed to represent, and he won over the hearts of the Canadians. "This is a soldier!—large, strong, lithe, with worn boots and frayed puttees. He carries his hands in his pockets, and returns a salute by lifting his hand as far as the pocket will allow," wrote the hard to please Andrew Macphail.[3] In fact, the Canadians soon began to call themselves the "Byng boys," after a famous show playing in London, but also no doubt as a show of affection for their general. "He was literally adored by the men," wrote Lieutenant Colonel Andrew McNaughton, himself a man of enormous charisma who would rise to army commander in the next world war.[4]

But Byng could be a hard man. Although casual in dress and habits—Haig once derided the food at Byng's headquarters as not being fit for a pig—Byng was no slacker, and certainly no pushover. He saw his job as instilling discipline and fighting inefficiency in the supposedly wild Dominion troops. The Canadians engaged in strong rivalries—not only among divisions but also among brigades and even battalions. One of Byng's goals was to take this regimental pride and forge it into pride for the Canadian Corps as a whole. He was also intent on stiffening discipline in the Canadian Corps, a process he embarked upon slowly as he realized that part of the Canadians' reputation and sense of identity was wrapped up in the notion that they were wild colonials from the outer reaches of the Empire.

With his corps consisting of three divisions now, Byng set about instigating new training and reform. He knew only his senior staff officer, the very competent Tim Harrington, and had never even met his three divisional commanders, or any of the more junior officers. But he soon got to know them, and they him. Byng had always been an unorthodox thinker, as evidenced by his attempts before the war to reform the cavalry into a mounted infantry force. Taking a similar attitude towards his new role, he harnessed the Canadians' initiative and fostered in them a stronger sense of identity based on rugged discipline and professionalism. "I give him credit for the welding of the Corps together and giving it that first Corps spirit," wrote one Canadian soldier.[5] Byng also went a long way towards cutting the corps' political ties with England and weakening Hughes's hold over the Canadian forces. He increasingly blocked the "suggestions" of appointments from Hughes and other politicians, noting in one letter to Second Army headquarters that he would prevent this "pandering to political patronage."[6] Accomplishing this goal would take time in the highly politicized Canadian Corps, but Byng was a soldier through and through, and he had no problem with jeopardizing his career as corps commander with the Canadians, partly because he knew that he would be received back eagerly as an Imperial corps commander.

Byng arrived in late May 1916 at his new corps headquarters in the Ypres salient. But before he had a chance to meet most of his officers and men, or to instigate any reforms, the Germans unsettled everything by unleashing a ferocious bombardment against the untried 3rd Division, then holding the most easterly point of the Ypres salient.

THE 3RD DIVISION was dug in to the Ypres salient along a frontage of 2,225 metres, anchored in a semicircular trench that ran from Hooge to Sanctuary Wood and then continued down through Hill 62/Tor Top, Hill 61, and Mount Sorrel (the hills designated by their height in metres above sea level). A gradual spur, known as Observation Ridge, cut across the front, projecting from west to east. Its capture would imperil the entire British front as it ran through the lines and would allow the enemy to fire into the rear of trenches further to the north, forcing the evacuation of the salient. The Canadian-held wooded hills and spurs were the last remaining high points in British hands within the salient, offering important views over the enemy lines. The Germans wanted them.

Holding key tactical features in the Ypres salient mattered not a whit to Canadians in the front lines. Most grumbled about their return to the hecatombs of the Ypres salient, where shell and bullet had plagued them among the blasted landscape of unburied corpses and rats. Sergeant F.W. Bagnall, a long-serving veteran of the 14th Battalion who still wore the First Contingent blue epaulettes, remembered Ypres as little more than a "death trap ... the grave of so many good men."[7]

Although the 3rd Division had been on the Western Front since the beginning of the year, they had not yet participated in a significant operation. Supporting them in the line was the veteran 1st Division, while the 2nd Division was still situated to the south, near St. Eloi.

The 3rd Division had been established on December 24, 1915, and comprised three brigades of far different character. The division was commanded by Major General Malcolm Mercer, a veteran of the Second Battle of Ypres. Brigadier A.C. Macdonell, who had earned the name "Batty Mac" for his fearless fighting, commanded the 7th Brigade. The "Fighting Seventh" was home to the Royal Canadian Regiment (RCR), derided as the "Shino Boys," as they were a Permanent Force regiment and, other Canadians believed, spent much of their time grooming (including shining their buttons), saluting, and marching. The 42nd and 49th Battalions, the former a Highland unit raised in Montreal and the latter consisting of men from Edmonton, soon developed close ties and the men tended to pal around together.[8] The brigade's last battalion was Princess Patricia's Canadian Light Infantry (PPCLI); it was the first Canadian infantry unit to fight in Europe and had already earned a proud reputation for its service with the 27th British Division. "We didn't have much to do with the PPs, as we were a bit in awe of all the gong [medal] ribbons a lot of them wore from South Africa," remembered Private Roy Henley of the 42nd Battalion.[9] Most of the South African War veterans had been killed or wounded by early 1916, but the PPCLI kept their reputation as elite troops, even though the battalion was now reinforced with the same Canadian recruits as the other thirty-five front-line infantry battalions within the corps.

The 8th Brigade consisted of four mounted rifle units, now permanently unmounted to become "gravel crushers," as one of them noted mournfully.[10] The 1st, 2nd, 4th, and 5th CMRs, which formed the brigade, had often faced inter-service friction with the infantry. Brigadier General Victor Williams had a full job in integrating them into the division. He was the only brigadier to date who lacked combat experience, having up to this point been an adjutant general responsible for, among other things, running the Valcartier camp in 1914.

The 9th Brigade, commanded by Brigadier General F.W. Hill, consisted of the 43rd, 52nd, 58th, and 60th Battalions. The 43rd (the Cameron Highlanders of

Canada) had been raised in Winnipeg; the 52nd had been mobilized in Port Arthur, Ontario; and the 58th had its recruiting headquarters at Niagara-on-the-Lake, but drew from Central Ontario. The brigade's final unit, the 60th, was the corps' second still-serving French-Canadian battalion, after the 22nd Battalion. One other had existed—the 41st—but it had been broken up after major discipline problems that included murders and a series of crime sprees in England. But the 60th would also eventually be broken up after the Battle of Vimy Ridge and replaced with the 116th Battalion when the number of Quebec recruits dried up and the battalion could no longer keep its "French" character.

The 3rd Division comprised a far higher number of Canadian-born soldiers than the first two divisions, and it began to reflect the changing nature of the Canadian Corps, with British and Scottish accents slowly being replaced by the flatter, Canadian dialect. Though the Canadian units were still deeply British at the core, the subsequent waves of Canadians who had answered the increasingly desperate calls for men ensured that, by war's end, fifty-one percent of the CEF would be Canadian-born. However, the implied meaning behind these percentage break-downs (that half the Canadian force were in fact British) is perhaps a present-day construct, since at the time of the Great War all Canadians were British citizens— lacking distinct passports until after the Second World War. Furthermore, many of the British-born had lived in Canada for decades before the war and tended to see themselves as Canadians. Almost immediately these British-born Canadians, who initially outnumbered all others, were incorporated into the Canadian Division (and later the Canadian Corps) as "Canadians," revealing a gradual process of defining a new sense of identity among the Dominion troops. But even here, the Canadian Corps was a proud member of the BEF, and while there was occasional friction with British forces, these incidents were generally derived from the increasing desire among the officers and men to redefine themselves as Canadians first, proud Imperialists second. This forging of a Canadian identity would increase in impor-tance, and intensity, during the last two years of the war.

IN THE SALIENT, the 3rd Division had divided its front into two separate sections held by the 7th and 8th Brigades, each with two battalions in the forward lines, a third in support, and the fourth in reserve. These front-line units held the forward trenches and patrolled the narrow No Man's Land that separated the Canadian and German lines. Numerous skirmishes took place as raiders stalked one another. To the south, the 8th Brigade was situated on the high points of Mount Sorrel, which gave the men a commanding view of the enemy lines. To the north, the 7th Brigade held trenches that ran along the eastern edge of Sanctuary Wood. Unfortunately, the Ypres salient, including the Canadian sector, was weak in supportive artillery since much of the heavy firepower had been moved south to support the soon-to-be-unleashed joint Entente offensive on the Somme.

The Germans hoped to make the salient less tenable for their enemy and to draw reserves away from the obvious marshalling of British forces on the Somme. Two German assault divisions of 13 Corps from Württemberg had been training intensely for the attack over several weeks. The Württemberg corps took pride in its separate identity within the Imperial German Army, much as the Canadians did in relation to the Imperials. Continuous German activity along the front, including new communication and assembly trenches, had been observed by both airplanes and Canadian forward defences.[11]

Despite this buildup of enemy fortifications and firepower, the inexperienced Canadians took a curiously passive role in their own defence. The front-line soldiers were cold and wet from unseasonably rainy weather, and many of the trenches were clogged with mud. An ongoing shortage of labour units meant that much of the work of maintaining the trenches fell to the exhausted infantry, and many commanders were hesitant to call on the men to not only fight and train but also work. Barbed wire and machine-gun nests were in place, of course, but reports from forward officers recorded that the front was only thinly held, with the forest terrain working against effective defences-in-depth, which was the more common and effective system of holding ground at this point in the war.

Despite these warnings, the division's commanders and staff officers inexplicably failed to order the artillery to prepare fire zones in front of the Canadian lines to break up expected attacks. Nor did the Canadians keep counterattacking forces close to the front to drive the enemy back should they successfully attack and capture parts of the line. However, these issues were in the process of being addressed in the early morning hours of June 2. To assist in the preparation of a stronger defence and to form a better appreciation of the dangers, divisional and brigade commanding officers Mercer and Williams were reconnoitring the front. They had invited General Byng to join them, but he had cancelled at the last moment. Nonetheless, a brigadier and major general touring the front lines might be seen as giving the lie to the oft-recurring image of generals and other commanding officers resting comfortably far from the front.

Mercer and his staff arrived in the forward trenches only minutes before the Germans opened up with a hurricane of fire. At 8:30 A.M., shellfire exploded over the Canadian lines and the weight of artillery left the defenders stunned and deaf at best, blasted from the earth at the very worst. The Germans had learned from their ongoing grim experience at Verdun. The tornado of enemy fire concentrated on less than a 1,000-metre portion of the front. The Canadian gunners tried to retaliate but were completely overwhelmed and ineffectual. This was one of the most staggering bombardments of the war to date, and it continued to rupture the Canadian trench system for nearly four and a half hours. "The ground just shook like jelly," recounted Lawrence Rogers, a thirty-eight-year-old sergeant. Rogers, who would later be awarded the Military Medal for carrying wounded men out while under fire during the battle, wrote to his wife, "I was horribly afraid and there was not a man in the whole outfit who was not."[12]

Trenches caved in; communication lines were obliterated; defenders were buried alive or dismembered. "It seemed," penned another non-commissioned officer in a letter afterwards, "as though that part of the line had been transformed into an active volcano, so continuous were the flashes of bursting shells."[13] The divisional command was decapitated when shelling killed Major General Mercer and wounded Brigadier Williams, who was later captured, becoming the highest-ranking Canadian prisoner of the war. Very few of the front-line garrison survived to tell their tale: they simply disappeared in a cloud of dust and fire. Maple Copse, Armagh Wood, and Sanctuary Wood were cleared: the trees were uprooted and, even worse for the men garrisoned near them, transformed into deadly slivers and stakes that whirled across the battlefield. Soon, charred, jagged stumps added to the apocalyptic landscape.

Not having dug enough deep dugouts due to the wet ground, whole Canadian sections were wiped out under the weight of fire. "All sorts of shells were coming over," recounted R.C. Bradford of the PPCLI. "Some great big ones would come with a roar like the CPR and land with a crash like thunder that would almost lift us off our feet. The air was thick with bits of shrapnel, shell-case, and nose caps."[14] At 1 P.M. the barrage let up, but the men were afforded no respite. Four mines were detonated below the Canadian lines, further collapsing trenches and projecting into the air reddish-brown bursts of mud and human remains. The German assault parties finally advanced after the detonation. The few survivors who had their senses and rifles still at hand laid down a desultory fire into the onrushing ranks of grey. The enemy were cut down but continued to push through by sheer numbers, some units aided by flame-throwers.

Even if the men hadn't faced a ferocious bombardment and the blowing of four large mines, as well as the periodic explosions of Canadian ammunition piles that rocked the earth, six Württemberg assault battalions, with five in close support and six more in reserve, were thrown against four battalions of Canadian defenders.[15] The results were predictable. Ill supported by artillery that were firing blindly because of shattered communication lines or slain forward observers, the surviving garrison of Canadian soldiers put up a brief resistance but were quickly forced into retreat, or were killed or captured. Private Courtney Tower, a twenty-seven-year-old farmer who enlisted from Robbin, Manitoba, wrote in his diary, "It is nothing more or less than God's good providence that I am here and able to write up what happened yesterday."[16] Too many of his friends were not, and Tower was indeed lucky to be alive, as he had been shot in the face. Of the 692 officers and men in the 1st CMR, only 135 made it to the rear. The 4th CMR, also holding the front, suffered an eighty-nine percent casualty rate. "It was a day of obliteration," one of them would later write.[17]

Yet the attacking Germans were subject to high casualties themselves. Two 18-pounder field guns from the 5th Battery fired over open sights at the advancing enemy, holding on to the bitter end. "It is fitting to stress that here too the Canadians did not surrender," wrote one German regimental historian chronicling the battle, "but at their guns defended themselves with revolvers to the last man."[18]

The entire gun crews were killed, but they made the Germans pay for advancing through a hail of shrapnel.[19] Sergeant John Caw of the 5th Battalion, whose unit was on the southern flank of the attack, and who would later be shot in the arm, described the German vulnerability to enfilade fire: "We had him where we wanted him; halfway up a slope, no cover, and digging himself in, in full view in broad daylight, range about six hundred yards."[20] The 5th Battalion did not stop the attack, but they made it a costly one.

Harris Turner of the PPCLI was situated in Warrington Avenue, a support trench in the northern sector. After this position was pounded by German artillery and mortar fire, only about 30 or 40 of the half-company's garrison of 125 men were left standing. "The landscape in front of us had been torn to pieces," wrote the five-foot-nine, blue-eyed twenty-eight-year-old from Saskatoon. Trying to find a description that made sense to his kinfolk at home, Turner wrote that the battlefield "looked like a dirty old farm might look after it had been made the subject of an intensive search for buried treasure by mobs of crazy excavators."[21] And according to the account of a stretcher-bearer, "Trees were uprooted or snapped off like matchwood. Great chunks of earth and fragments of dugouts were thrown high in the air." Communication trenches were "clogged with dead—singly and in agonised heaps—buried under portions of parapet, until only bloody limbs were exposed … the wounded lay quivering at the bottom of the trench or crawled desperately along, dragging their mutilated bodies to some place of shelter."[22] Smoke and dust obscured the front, and the ground shook from the blast of the high explosives.

Over this wasteland, surviving PPCLI infantrymen could see groups of grey-clad figures advancing through the haze. They shot at them, but were unsure if their targets were dropping from being hit or were simply taking cover. On the right, a German flame-thrower opened up with a stream of liquid fire. Being burned alive was a terrifying prospect, and almost every soldier turned his rifle on him. The flame-thrower went down peppered with bullets within seconds, but the battle continued. Harris Turner's mate was killed beside him, with a bullet through the head. Turner barely had time to look down and see the life draining from his comrade's eyes before returning to the fight for his own life. The last thing he saw was a German soldier, whom he watched collapse from the bullet Turner had put in him. Then everything went black, as a shell exploded on the parapet. Although the last thing he ever saw was the Germans advancing on his position, the permanently blinded Turner survived both the war and a prisoner of war camp. When he returned to Saskatoon, he would later serve as an MPP, a publisher of the agricultural newspaper known today as the *Western Producer,* and director of publications for the Canadian National Institute of the Blind.

Most of the Canadians caught within the path of the German juggernaut were in a similarly hopeless position on the battlefield. The experience of Captain Alan Crossman of the 1st CMR was not unique: "The fire became steadily heavier and ... I found that part of the line I was in was untenable and moved the men from it to a more sheltered trench close by." High explosive bombardments left the steadily dwindling survivors shaken and stunned. The barrage fell like a drumbeat, and the sound of individual shells could no longer be heard. "Men were being hit on all sides," continued Crossman, "a thing absolutely unavoidable owing to the fact that we had no dugouts. We were waiting anxiously for our artillery to reply but of course as we afterwards found out that was quite impossible as it wasn't there." By mid-afternoon, Crossman's position was cut off by shellfire and his small detachment soon realized that German troops had slipped behind their lines. "Smith and myself, with two men, were attacked on all sides by Germans with bombs and were eventually driven along to the dressing station which then was full of wounded. Here, rather than have all the wounded killed, I gave the order to surrender."[23]

With the Germans having successfully overrun the Canadian trenches on a front of about 1,000 metres and having captured the heights of Mount Sorrel, Hill 61, Hill 62, as well as the eastern portion of Observation Ridge by early afternoon, this was a second bitter pill for the Canadians to swallow after the St. Eloi debacle. The result was equally troubling for Byng, who had been in command for less than a week.

The only good news was that the Canadian flanks were holding against the onslaught. The veteran PPCLI refused to allow the Germans to expand their precarious position, notwithstanding the loss of their beloved commanding officer, Lieutenant Colonel H.C. Buller, who was killed while rallying the troops. The second-in-command, Hamilton Gault, was also knocked out with a severe leg wound that later required amputation. But men took their place in the line as leaders. Despite having its right forward company virtually annihilated in the bombardment and suffering through the nearly twenty-four hours of continuous fighting that followed, the PPCLI refused to break, eventually funnelling the enemy into a narrow salient that left them dangerously exposed. "The resistance of the officer and some men who remained to the last in a portion of an almost obliterated trench was magnificent," wrote an admiring German officer.[24]

The PPCLI lost more than 400 men in their desperate stand. "Hardly a man survived to tell the story of this defence," noted Lieutenant Ralph Hodder-Williams. "In the Battalion papers there is little beyond an eloquent list of killed and missing."[25] This moving statement could well have stood for any of the front-line battalions that absorbed the terrible German assault at Mount Sorrel.

THE BATTLE OF MOUNT SORREL: JUNE 2, 1916

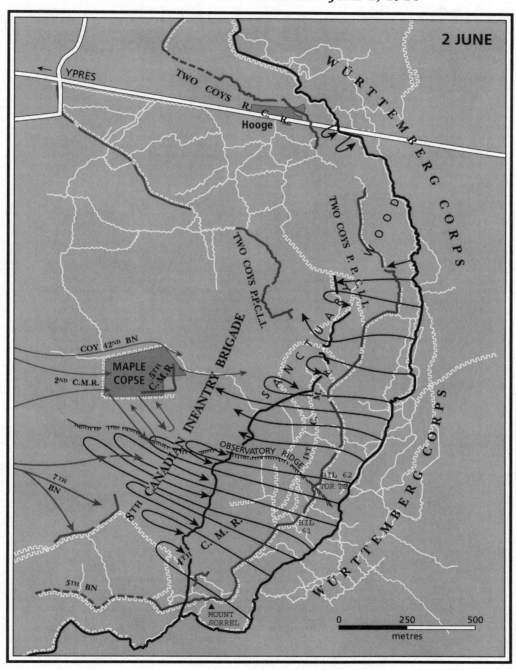

2 JUNE

YPRES

WÜRTTEMBERG CORPS

TWO COYS R.C.R.

Hooge

TWO COYS P.P.C.L.I.

SANCTUARY WOOD

TWO COYS P.P.C.L.I.

COY 42ND BN

MAPLE COPSE

5TH C.M.R.

2ND C.M.R.

CANADIAN INFANTRY BRIGADE

1ST C.M.R.

OBSERVATORY RIDGE

HILL 62

TOR TOP

HILL 61

8TH

7TH BN

C.M.R.

4TH C.M.R.

5TH BN

MOUNT SORREL

WÜRTTEMBERG CORPS

0   250   500

metres

CHAPTER 27

"LIKE POURING METAL INTO A BLAST FURNACE"

Counterattack, June 3–4, 1916

With the Canadian Corps reeling from the loss of Mount Sorrel and the surrounding high ground, a shocked Sir Julian Byng assessed the disaster and demanded that all ground be recaptured. Sometime after 5:00 P.M., he ordered an immediate counterattack, and by 5:42 P.M., he was receiving reports that counterattacking units were forming up.[1] However, since communication to the front had effectively been cut, Byng's headquarters had little idea as to where the Germans were or which portions of the front their own troops still held.[2] But Byng felt tremendous pressure to prove the mettle of his new corps. Some Canadians in the rear recounted how British units "were cheerfully rude concerning the ability of the Canadians to hold the salient."[3] Rumours even circulated that the Canadian Corps would be moved to a quiet sector where they could do less damage to the Entente cause.

Putting aside questions of pride, an immediate counterattack was necessary to ensure that the Germans did not launch a second attack to push out from their newly won trenches, thereby breaking into the Ypres salient and possibly cutting off British forces further to the north. But the Dominion troops were ill prepared to respond to the catastrophe. Just as the Canadian artillery had not been properly sited on the front lines, so too were no counterattack reserves stationed close to the front. Further delays resulted from the confusion left by the death of Mercer and the capture of the wounded Williams. After several hours of confusing orders and counter-orders, it fell to the 7th, 10th, 14th, 15th, 49th, and 60th Battalions to spearhead the charge to retake the lost ground, with another four battalions in support. This would be the largest Canadian concentrated attack to date in the war.

The Germans were in an untenable position: they had followed their near-perfect bombardment into the Canadian lines but were now exposed and susceptible to enfilading fire and counterattack. However, as a result of the Canadian staff's inability to supply guides to the front, as well as broken communications that left units unable to coordinate their attack, and inadequate covering fire in the form of artillery counter-battery work that could not effectively harass the enemy guns, the counterattack took several hours to develop, was delayed several times, and gave the Germans precious time to fortify.

All through the night of June 2–3, spearhead battalions marched to the front over roads choked both with traffic and with the movement of wounded to the rear. Command and control by senior officers cut off in the rear was nearly impossible, and the zero hour attack at 2 A.M. was repeatedly delayed. The 7th Brigade was nominally in charge of organizing the operation, but Brigadier Macdonell could not get close enough to the front, so coordination of the assault devolved to the commanding officer of the 49th Battalion, the very competent William Griesbach. A veteran of the South African War, and known as Edmonton's "boy mayor" for having taken office before the age of thirty, Griesbach was an experienced and able officer who would eventually rise to command a brigade. It was said that before the war he had consumed military history, reading between three and five hours per day on the subject.[4] To him fell the task of organizing several battalions in the dark and without adequate communication, and then of somehow finding a way to coordinate their attack after marching several kilometres and assaulting over a wide front.

As the Canadians advanced to the front in piecemeal fashion, the Germans laid down a withering artillery and gas-shell barrage, causing further casualties, confusion, and delays. To combat the gas, the hated PH helmets were pulled over the heads of the marching infantry. This protective move further delayed the marching forces, as any activity while wearing the PH helmet left soldiers wheezing and weak from lack of oxygen.[5] These gas hoods—composed of a double layer of light blue-grey flannel with two glass eyepieces—had a rubber piece that was gripped tightly in the mouth, which tended to result in drool and saliva dripping down a wearer's chin and chest. The hoods were treated with a chemical solution (giving the helmet its name) that helped to dilute the effects of chlorine and phosgene gas, but the solution also burned the soldiers' eyes, as well as the skin when it mixed with sweat. Over the bodies and body parts of their former comrades, the Canadians, still in their short-pants summer kit, stepped forward wearing their chemically impregnated gas hoods.

The Germans had dug in furiously throughout June 2 and into the early hours of June 3, setting up barbed wire, and even building eight communication trenches back to the rear to move supplies and men within the relative protection of the trench system. But an active defence of shells and gas remained their key to keeping the Canadians at bay. One Colt machine-gunner, Sergeant F.W. Bagnall, recounted that his formation moved alternately over open ground and shattered communication

These two infantrymen are wearing the bulky PH helmet. When forced to wear gas helmets, soldiers complained that they could barely breathe, let alone fight.

trenches when they could, entering the latter to avoid artillery fire, but also finding these potential shelters largely blocked by cave-ins, corpses, and the wounded. "I never thought a battalion had as many men as were left lying here.... It was a sickening mess."[6]

Stumbling forward nearly blinded by their PH helmets, the Canadians would pay for the ill-planned counterattack. The start time was delayed, as preparations were not complete—with some units not even in the jumping-off trenches when they were supposed to be, due to the delay from gas and a "heavy hostile barrage."[7] Lieutenant William Gray led his men forward through this artillery fire, noting oddly that it was "one of the prettiest sights I've ever witnessed. The average pyrotechnic display pales considerably in comparison. This arc of light was continuous for some few minutes, mingled with the lurid yellow red of shrapnel. The colour of shrapnel bursting at night is hard to liken; it resembles more than anything a deep tiger lily which bloomed for an infinitesimal space, then melted into black oblivion."[8] An artillery barrage could indeed be as beautiful as it was deadly. As the attackers advanced over open ground to their start lines, past the desolation of shattered trees and horses splayed open on the side of the road, they could hear the guns booming in the near distance. Any chance of surprise was ruined by the weak Canadian barrage that did little to destroy or suppress the enemy. The Germans would now be alert for the coming attack.

During the advance, the Canadians also had to deal with the terrifying experience of friendly fire. While the gunners tried to support the attack, they had little idea as to where the Canadian or German lines were after the lines had shifted on June 2. Shells were therefore continually falling short onto the Canadian troops. This added to the men's confusion and terror, especially since veterans could easily pick out the sound of the Canadian shells that were supposed to be hurtling towards the enemy, and instead were crashing amongst them. Attempts to call off these short barrages usually failed, as runners "sent with messages seldom ever lived to deliver them," noted Major Agar Adamson of the PPCLI.

THE GUNNERS FIRED blindly for an hour and then stopped abruptly when they heard they were killing Canadian troops. But this cessation of artillery fire left the soldiers at the front largely defenceless. As the gunners had few forward observers in place to pass along information to the rear, the infantry was ordered to fire off a series of flares when they reached their objectives, in order to indicate when the bombardment should be recommenced. But most of these flares either malfunctioned or were obscured in the enemy barrage, and so many of the anxious and confused gunners searching the sky failed to open up their bombardment at the required time to support the men at the sharp end. Communication was lacking not only from front to rear but also laterally, as the attacking battalions missed the signals from other striking formations. But by this time these counterattacking formations were close enough to the German front lines that they were already taking heavy casualties from enemy fire.

The infantry attack had begun to come apart before a single Canadian on the battlefield ever saw a German. Between 7:00 and 8:30 A.M., the assault battalions went forward from their start lines in uncoordinated charges, in broad daylight, advancing uphill over unknown broken ground, and with no supporting artillery barrage. Furthest to the south, the 7th and 10th Battalions were ordered to retake Mount Sorrel, while the 14th and 15th went forward in the centre against Hill 62, supported by the 16th and 13th Battalions in reserve. To the north, the 49th and 60th Battalions, with the 52nd in support, were to attack to the north of Hill 62, against Sanctuary Wood, and meet up with Canadian units still holding the original front lines near the ruined village of Hooge. The advancing three arms' lack of coordination allowed the Germans to concentrate their fire on active sectors of the front before moving to meet subsequent attacks further down the line.

The 49th Battalion had been left to attack alone, as the 52nd Battalion had been shot to pieces before it even made it to the front. Private W.C. Millar of the 52nd recounted the inspiring leadership of his commanding officer, Lieutenant Colonel A.W. Hay, who raced back and forth encouraging the men forward, even with the shells blasting holes through the ranks. And forward they went, stepping "over the writhing wounded and dying men.... Every face was drawn with agony and horror."[9] The advance into enemy fire held no romanticism for the terrified soldiers, and the battalion took crippling losses of several hundred men before Hay, too, was killed by the incessant fire. With their colonel knocked out, the crippled 52nd lost heart, and soon dug in, never even making it to the start line. This was a case of the rank and file, with their officers' support, making an on-the-spot decision not to go forward into certain death.

The 60th Battalion—who were to attack alongside the 49th—also hesitated in this inferno. Private A.Y. Jackson, who had enlisted in his early thirties and would return from his war experience with a new eye for painting Canada as a member of the Group of Seven, described the strain of advancing into the firestorm with the 60th. The lead infantry formations were forced to march over corpses and through smoking craters, with eyes watering from the gas. For Jackson, the worst sight was that of an adolescent Canadian, his young face staring up at the sky with surprised eyes and the rest of his body torn apart, with legs ripped from the torso and arms ending in bloody stumps. Jackson never forgot that face, which he made sure to step over, even as he was forced to march through the young boy's entrails.[10] In the face of such slaughter, the commanding officer of the 60th Battalion, Lieutenant Colonel Frederick Gascoigne, refused to order his men to advance further, later writing that "words failed" to describe the situation but that his men were "hammered to pieces."[11] While his order resulted in the abandonment of the men at the front holding onto the flanks, as well as of the 49th Battalion that was still intent on attacking, it likely saved his men's lives, although many of them were cut down—including Jackson, who was wounded by shrapnel in the shoulder, back, and neck.

Griesbach stuck to his orders to recapture the lost ground, even after he failed to rally the 60th Battalion to move forward. The PPCLI on the flank could not hold out much longer, and not to attack would leave them to bear the brunt of further probing assaults from the Germans aiming to extend their dangerously exposed position. As well, the complete breakdown in communication made it unclear whether the operations in the centre or further to the south had succeeded or failed, but the heavy fire heard from that direction indicated that the Canadians from the 7th, 10th, 14th, and 15th Battalions had indeed gone forward, or were preparing to do so. "Billy's Own," as the men of the 49th sometimes referred to themselves, went over the top around 7 A.M., in broad daylight, against an alert front, and with no artillery barrage. "It was just like pouring metal into a blast furnace," remembered Stanley Bowe of the 2nd CMR, a former farmer from Red Deer, Alberta, whose unit was supporting the main attack from the flank.[12] The 49th was ripped apart by gunfire, losing 16 officers and 345 men in under half an hour.[13] One of the experienced Forty-Niners' sergeant's last words were, "Well, mates, it looks like bloody suicide, but it's orders."[14] He was right on both accounts.

In the centre, the Royal Montrealers (14th Battalion) charged at 8:17 A.M., followed by the Highlanders of the 15th Battalion about twenty minutes later. The 15th's war diary described the assault as a "Perfect HELL of Artillery and Machine gun fire."[15] Victor Gordon Tupper, an intelligence officer whose 16th Battalion was laying down supporting fire for the assaulting 14th and 15th, described this part of the battle: "The thing was impossible. They were mown down by machine-gun and shrapnel, but succeeded in establishing a trench about 300 yards from the enemy's new position."[16] Sergeant George Ormsby of the 15th Battalion was more optimistic, although no less certain about the fate of his companions as he charged forward as part of a Colt machine-gun crew:

> Such bravery it would be hard to imagine and unless seen cannot be realized. I saw our boys go over the crest of the hill running for all they were worth and as they poured along in an irresistible charge they were mown down in hundreds. But they actually chased Fritz right back into the trenches and followed him in but of course none of them came back as they were outnumbered 50 to 1.... I don't think that any of the boys ever figured on coming out of that fight and personally I gave myself up as a goner.[17]

To the south, the 7th and 10th Battalions had done no better. The attacking forces stumbled over the cratered ground and "were subjected to heavy machine-gun fire from both flanks."[18] This unsuppressed fire, which was almost impossible to locate as the Canadians were on lower ground and could not observe the camouflaged German positions, soon compelled the last few surviving officers to call off the attack and have their men dig in before everyone was destroyed in a crossfire of shot and shell.

THE CANADIANS had shown their inexperience in their preparation of a disorganized and delayed counterattack that had given the enemy too much time to dig in and then allowed them to focus on separate piecemeal assaults. Discipline and grit had carried the Canadians forward, but they should never have been asked to attack without proper artillery support or, at the very least, a chance to coordinate their counter-thrusts. In the absence of a supportive bombardment, the infantry had been left on their own, forced to knock out enemy machine guns with rifles, bayonets, and bombs, and unable to suppress any long-range fire from the flanks or rear.

Moving among the new and old corpses, German and Canadian forward infantry companies traded small-arms fire throughout the rest of the day, all the while enduring sporadic artillery barrages. Trenches like China Wall—named because it was constructed on hard ground that could not be dug into, and so was almost entirely built up from sandbags—were a horror show, filled with dead, dying, and dismembered troops. In parts of the trench, the blood was ankle deep. George Adkins, the youngest of three brothers who enlisted from Westlock, Alberta, recounted the terror of those on the receiving end of the German bombardment of high explosives and shrapnel: "Two or three times they nearly landed one in our trench. The force of the explosion threw us down and I couldn't hear nothing but ringing in my ears. I was hit on the head about four times but my steel helmet saved me. Then I had a bullet go right through a mess tin strapped on my back."[19] George survived the battle, and the war, but his older brothers, Bill and Martin, were killed within a month of each other. The high command, feeling that his family had suffered too much, pulled George from the front lines and gave him a "bombproof" job in the rear.

"Here for the first time the hell of the war came to me," recounted Lieutenant William Gray, who was wounded by shellfire later on June 3.

The trench, or what was left of it, was congested with dead and dying. Men crawled along, over dead bodies distorted beyond only the ken of one who has been there. We lifted wounded men a little to one side while from each turn of the trench came the heart-rending, throaty sob of the dying. Ghastly!, well I don't suppose there's a word been coined in English to describe it. Meanwhile, shrapnel rained on its horrible hail, high explosives lifted sandbag and bodies househigh. Everywhere men lay half buried, gasping. Some, reason fled, climbed out only to be struck down a few yards away.[20]

The less effusive Major Cy Peck of the 16th Battalion, a future Victoria Cross winner and member of Parliament, jotted his thoughts tersely into his diary: "No Sleep. Shelling all day. Steady evacuation of the wounded."[21] And another officer, Lieutenant Victor Tupper, wrote home, "You can't imagine what a modern barrage is like. Hell is not strong enough."[22]

The Canadian attack on June 3 ended in failure, with most of the multiple assault forces stopped cold by the German counter-barrage even before they reached the enemy trenches. The Canadians limped back to their reserve lines, and Byng prepared for another attack. But cooler heads prevailed and a second counteroffensive was delayed until further preparations could be made.

On June 4, 1916, army commander Herbert Plumer wrote to Haig's chief of staff, Lieutenant General L.E. Kiggell, that the Canadian counterattack had not succeeded but that Byng would soon go back in with stronger artillery support. "The Canadians have lost pretty heavily," Plumer reported, "but it was a severe ordeal and they have fought well."[23] Indeed they had, but the losses had been staggering. The 3rd Division was all but shattered, with an estimated 3,750 casualties spread among the fighting battalions alone.[24]

Each of the dead lost in this battle left behind grieving comrades and loved ones at home. Private Walter Wray of the 13th Battalion, a popular soldier because of his musical skills with flute and drum, was one of the slain. As a specialist bomber, he had been moving forward into the line to support the counterattack when a high explosive shell exploded over his position, killing him instantly. The thirty-six-year-old Wray's death left his three children orphans, as his wife, Minnie, had died the previous year while he was in uniform.[25] The real cost of battle was not always represented in casualty statistics.

THE BATTLE OF MOUNT SORREL: JUNE 3, 1916

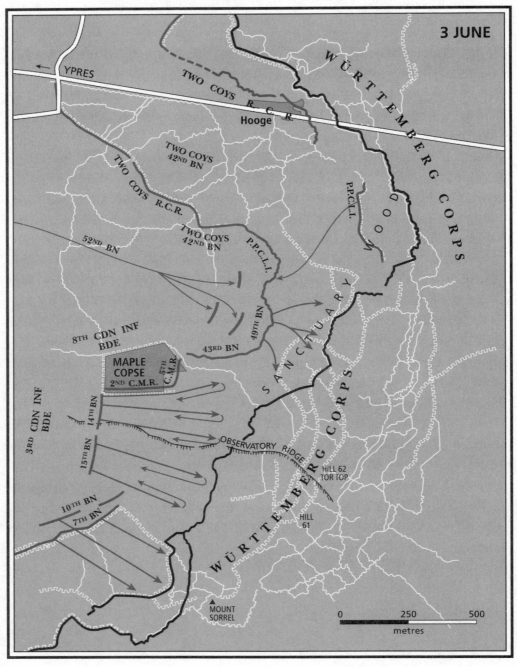

3 JUNE

YPRES

TWO COYS R.C.R.

Hooge

WÜRTTEMBERG CORPS

TWO COYS 42ND BN

TWO COYS R.C.R.

52ND BN

TWO COYS 42ND BN

P.P.C.L.I.

P.P.C.L.I.

SANCTUARY WOOD

49TH BN

43RD BN

8TH CDN INF BDE

MAPLE COPSE

2ND C.M.R.

5TH C.M.R.

3RD CDN INF BDE

14TH BN

15TH BN

OBSERVATORY RIDGE

WÜRTTEMBERG CORPS

HILL 62 TOR TOP

HILL 61

10TH BN

7TH BN

WÜRTTEMBERG CORPS

MOUNT SORREL

0   250   500

metres

CHAPTER 28

BITING BACK

June 6–13, 1916

Conditions at the Mount Sorrel front following the failed Canadian counterattack continued to be harrowing. "During the day, a man could get no sleep or peace for the shelling, and at night every man was required for patrol and working parties," complained Sergeant J.A. Caw. "Gas alarms were the thing of the days, and, believe me, it is not pleasant business to 'stand to' with gas helmets on for a matter of two hours or so, every minute expecting the Boches to come over. They gave us all kinds of tear gas, and at the end of a week my eyes began to feel as if they were stuck on the end of poles like crabs' eyes. I was as deaf as a post and as dirty as a tramp. Water was very scarce, that is, good water; even the tea tastes of dead men."[1] Every man at the front had countless narrow chances and close calls with death.

Although the Canadians' debacle on June 2 had not been redeemed by their sloppy piecemeal attack the next day, they had stopped the German drive with their bloodied bodies. The two sides had dug in, trading small-arms fire from June 3 to 6, with the steady fall of rain, high explosives, shrapnel, and gas adding to the misery. Little was achieved other than the slow creep of casualties.

June 6 meant very little to the Canadian Corps writ large, but for the 28th Battalion, situated around the shattered village of Hooge, the day brought another disaster far too common in the war. In mid-afternoon, the Germans exploded four mines under the battalion's front-line positions, and almost two entire companies—some 300 of the 650 men in the 28th—were wounded, buried alive, or taken prisoner. "The ground rocked for a great distance. I was hanging on the side of the trench, and the sensation was for all the world like being in a rowboat in a gale," wrote Lance Corporal Stanley Rutledge. The Germans unleashed a heavy shellfire and mortar bombardment to coincide with the mine explosions, and then rushed forward. Despite the enemy attack having "practically wiped out" the two forward companies, the 28th recovered, with B Company making a resolute stand at Menin Road Culvert to limit the extent of the German advance.[2]

B Company was supported by Canadians firing on the flanks, too—primarily the 31st Battalion. Private Donald Fraser of the 31st described the troops' ravaged yet determined state after the German attack:

> notwithstanding the difficulties we were in, encumbered with the dead and wounded; the firing step smashed in many places; in mud and wet; rifles half clogged; and though dazed and crazed we pull ourselves together, line the serviceable parts of the parapet and blaze into the advancing enemy, who recoil in confusion.[3]

The Canadians held their position. Still, as Stanley Rutledge noted, the two companies of the 28th that fell victim to enemy mines "might as well have been swallowed up by a great mediaeval dragon, so completely did they become lost to us."[4] Rutledge, a law student before the war, would also be lost to his family when he was killed in an aircraft accident after being transferred to the Royal Flying Corps.

While the Germans made limited gains and captured what was left of the ruined village of Hooge, Byng's headquarters refrained from ordering a knee-jerk response. Instead, the Canadians waited and prepared for a decisive counterattack all along the line. But the units at the front found it hard not to strike back, especially when German placards taunted the Canadians about the fate of Lord Kitchener, the British war hero and minister of war who had drowned on June 5 when his ship, the HMS *Hampshire,* sank en route to northern Russia. "Terrible news of Kitchener's death in the French papers today," wrote Gunner H.W. MacPherson. "One can hardly realize it yet."[5] The loss was felt deeply in Britain and Canada, and, one suspects, far more among Canadian troops than if Sam Hughes had gone down with a ship (although martyrdom might have helped

Hughes's fast-sinking reputation). In the coming months, rumours and hopes circulated that somehow Kitchener had survived, and would return to lead the Empire to victory. He did not, and his death was probably beneficial to the British war effort since he made for a better poster image than an actual war minister. But the Germans' taunts about Kitchener's death were one more reason for the Canadians to arrange for some payback.

High winds and driving rain delayed the counterattack for several days, until June 13, but the Canadians used the extra time to thoroughly bombard the German lines. They were assisted by the Royal Flying Corps, which had driven many of the German planes from the skies over Ypres. From June 3 to 7, the corps' official artillery report noted that the enemy "trenches could not be accurately located," but aerial photographs were finally taken on June 7 and 8.[6] Gunners used the photos to target strongpoints and forming-up areas, and their use marked the beginning of the interaction between artillery and aircraft, a relationship that would help to hone the gunners' ability to target and destroy.

A heavy siege gun laying down crushing high explosive fire on the enemy lines.

Realizing the importance of the lost Canadian position, General Haig wanted it recaptured. Although he did not wish to divert troops from his soon-to-be-launched Somme offensive, he advocated the release of important artillery batteries to support the Canadian assault. The Canadian counterattack would go in behind a devastating barrage from 218 guns, nearly half of them heavy howitzers. The senior corps artillery officer, Brigadier Harry Burstall, coordinated and controlled one of the greatest concentrations of guns to be directed on a limited objective up to this point in the war. Almost every Canadian gun was put into action, and this firepower was augmented by British, Indian, and South African batteries.

From June 9 to 12, four heavy bombardments were laid on the opposing trenches, each one severe enough to throw the enemy into full alert and compel them to rush troops forward. Four times the Germans were dragged to attention by their officers to prepare to respond to an attack, and each time they lost men to shellfire and waited for an attack that did not materialize. The Entente artillery fired over 45,000 18-pounder shells and over 30,000 howitzer shells, which pounded the enemy trenches and rear areas into mush.[7] Casualties "mounted in horrifying numbers," wrote one German contemporary historian."[8] In a reversal of the June 2 battle, the Württemberg corps was subjected to a heavy concentration of fire, as well as gas attacks on the flanks and diversionary raids by elements of the 20th British Division.

The real assault was to be mounted at 1:30 A.M. on June 13, and Major General Arthur Currie's veteran 1st Division was directed to retake the lost frontage between Hill 60 and Sanctuary Wood. The failure of June 3 was partially attributed to the artillery's forward observation officers (FOOs) not having been close enough to the front to correct the fall of shells—both those going short into the Canadian lines and those going long past the German positions. During the counterattack on June 13, the FOOs would be working closely with the infantry, often being stationed in the same headquarters, as greater coordination was needed between the two arms in battle.

To maximize the level of surprise, the innovative Currie planned to launch a night attack. Having endured a ten-hour bombardment of their lines on the 12th, the German troops were weary and battered, and many had collapsed in exhaustion from the unending stress. Moreover, after weathering the fifth day of heavy gunfire, few of the Württemberg officers expected a night attack, as neither side felt confident enough to launch complicated assaults in the darkness. Currie understood well that the operation would be difficult, especially given the cratered state of the ground, but he needed a victory and felt a night operation would give his troops the advantage of surprise, since this edge had obviously been lost in the long artillery buildup.

WAITING IN THE TRENCHES before the attack, every soldier realized that these could be his last moments. Time was spent praying, thinking of loved ones, or nervously waiting for the NCO with the rum jug. "I have seen pictures in the movies and in pictorial papers of the boys going 'over the top' with smiling, cheery faces," wrote Private W.C. Millar, who would survive the battle only to have his war ended by a bullet in the thigh a few weeks later. "Personally, I have grave doubts as to where these pictures were taken....We all knew only too well that, before we reached the enemy positions, thousands of machine gun bullets would be facing us, as well as shell-fire, bombs, minnenwerfers, rife-grenades, and the final bayonet thrust when we reached our goal."[9]

The Canadian barrage continued all day on June 12 and into the early hours of June 13, up until thirty seconds before the attack at zero hour: 1:30 A.M. An amazed Archie MacKinnon of the 58th Battalion noted, "Nobody can imagine what kind of night it was on June 12. When you see 5 acres of bush going up in the air there is something doing."[10] From 12:45 A.M. to 1:30 A.M., the barrage became heavier and was "thickened up" by machine-gun fire from Brigadier Raymond Brutinel's now dismounted Motor Machine Gun Brigade, which fired tens of thousands of bullets. Behind these curtains of fire, the enemy was alerted to a change in the bombardment's intensity, but few of the defenders were in shape to pull together a coherent defence. The Germans had been unable to excavate many deep dugouts, so they were vulnerable to the devastating drumfire. A German lieutenant in the 127th Infantry Regiment called the bombardment a "catastrophe." "The trenches are quite destroyed or levelled, one shell hole joins the next. And besides this fearful devastation, the dreadful spectacle of the many dead, and the number of missing, depresses everyone."[11] Major W.H. Hewgill, a company commander with the 31st Battalion, which was providing flanking fire, recounted in his diary that German prisoners spoke of their "trenches filled with the dead."[12]

At 1:30 A.M., the barrage lifted off the enemy lines and landed several hundred yards in the rear in order to block enemy counterattacking troops seeking to move forward.[13] Four primary attacking battalions—from right to left, the 3rd, 16th, 13th, and 58th—plus several battalions in reserve, went over the top in a rainstorm, advancing uphill, through deep mud, and over broken ground. Unfortunately, the high command had not yet processed the lessons of the previous year regarding the necessity of keeping the barrage on the enemy lines while the infantry left their trenches. There was now no barrage in between the German front line and outposts to keep the enemy in their trenches, leaving the attacking Canadian infantry with little protection. Shellfire would fall on the enemy's secondary lines to confuse the defenders and keep counterattacking forces away from the Canadian objectives, but this meant little to the infantry who were going in unprotected against the enemy's front-line troops. It would be a race between the attackers and the defenders: the stunned Germans, ears bleeding from the bombardment and dazed from the seemingly unending concussions, were lurching to their guns just as the panting Canadians tried to close the gap. Stray artillery shells, SOS flares, and tracer bullets lit the front in a pyrotechnic light show that would have been beautiful if men were not being torn apart by slashing steel at the same time.

Some battalions, such as the 3rd, ordered a bayonets-only policy to control the chaos inherent in night fighting, as the chances of comrades shooting each other were greatly increased in the darkness.[14] Bayonets at the ready, the infantry advanced slightly hunched over, a posture that was a natural reaction for men walking into the mouth of hell. Most kept their eyes slightly averted, as it did nobody any good to taunt death. But such precautionary measures did not mean that the infantry were cowed. Lieutenant H.R. Alley of the 3rd Battalion recorded that the infantry advanced in small groups of ten to twelve, picking their way through the holes in the barbed wire, trudging along the shattered landscape, finding their way only by the light of the artillery explosions and the enemy's small-arms fire. "We were on top of them before they knew it and the rain was at our backs and it was in their faces. There was some pretty bloody bayoneting," recounted Alley.[15]

While many of the German front-line defences were overcome easily, fierce hand-to-hand fighting took place on the left flank, as well as when the Canadians charged the second line at 1:50 A.M. The first two waves of the 16th Battalion encountered Halifax Trench, which was strongly held by a machine-gun team and groups of riflemen. The attackers swarmed forward in the dark. Although sectional rushes were held up by enemy fire, troops infiltrated past these strongpoints in the night, dealing with them from the flanks. "The trench was soon taken and any of the enemy who resisted were bayoneted," wrote one officer.[16]

Despite the successful push, this was no parade-ground advance. The battlefield was a shambles, all landmarks had been obliterated, and soldiers stumbled around in the dark, falling into shell holes. Control of these forces by a major or a lieutenant colonel was impossible, and so these officers relied on their junior officers, the lieutenants, as well as non-commissioned officers, to lead the infantry towards, and then through, the targets. More than a few cases of Canadians killing Canadians occurred in the confused fighting, especially given the use of grenades with their uncontrollable spray of shrapnel. But such accidents did not unduly hinder the operation, and soon the Germans were surrendering in droves. One official report noted that the enemy trenches were in a "shocking condition," with the dead and dismembered mixed with the wounded. Prisoners reported being buried alive, freed from their dirt graves, and buried again by the seemingly never-ending fall of shells.[17] Only the survivors could tell the tale of how many times they were rescued from this grim fate.

This determined Canadian push, ably supported by the artillery, successfully recaptured most of the ground lost two weeks earlier by 2:30 A.M. Grey-faced soldiers tensed in anticipation of the enemy's counterattack. Bombers prepared their grenades by straightening the pins for quick access; Lewis gun teams double-checked their ammunition pans; riflemen wiped the mud from their weapons. Officers moved back and forth across the new, ragged Canadian front line, bringing the scattered attackers together and coordinating the defence. One such officer was thirty-five-year-old Major D.H. Mason of the 3rd Battalion, a former chemical engineer from Toronto with a dozen years of prewar militia experience. Despite being wounded in the head, shoulder, and foot, Mason tried to organize a coherent defence in the dark. But he was also forced to kick many of his men awake, as the incredible stress and rush of adrenaline that coursed through the infantry during an attack quickly fled the body after battle, leaving men utterly exhausted and spent, notwithstanding their fear and terror of an expected enemy attack.[18]

The attack did not come, but soon the entire Canadian front was jolted awake. Instead of a counterattack in the dark, the Germans responded with a massive barrage that had been previously sighted on the lost trenches in case of a reversal. The Canadians paid for their victory with a merciless pounding of their entire front and rear. Telephone lines were cut, but pigeons "proved most valuable" in getting essential information from the soldiers enduring the bombardment to their commanders in the rear.[19]

The casualties from shell and steel began to mount. Private Frank Walker, a twenty-two-year-old stretcher-bearer and gifted poet, noted grimly in his diary: "The wounded are falling faster than we can pick them up…. The dead and wounded lie everywhere: in trenches, in shell pits, and along the sodden roads. Two thousand wounded have passed through our hands since the attack. Hundreds more are dying of exposure a mile away, and we cannot reach them. The wounded who are already here must lie outside the Dressing Station, in the open, under rain, until their turn comes."[20] Many of the victims succumbed to their wounds before a doctor could care for them.

Amidst this carnage, the enemy counterattacked several times over the next two days, but accurate Canadian artillery and small-arms fire broke up the assaults. One forward observer noted that "the whole face of the hill [was] one brown bog," and the Württembergers therefore could not close with the Canadians quickly. Artillery supporting the Canadian infantry remained ready for SOS calls: when the signal flares went up in the front lines, a sheet of artillery fire hammered down on prearranged parts of the front—the exact areas where the Germans crossed before storming the newly consolidated Canadian front lines.[21] Having honed some of these tactics in the complicated trench raids over the previous six months, the gunners were now expected not only to support the infantry's assault but also to protect newly captured trenches by smashing enemy counterattacks with prearranged shellfire. The gunners were increasingly becoming an integral part of the defence. Through the next few nights and days, both sides inched their way forward until they had a No Man's Land of only about 150 metres between them.

TWO WEEKS OF FIGHTING at Mount Sorrel had resulted in almost no change in the ground held by both sides. But the battle had cost the Canadians more than 8,700 casualties, with the Germans suffering about two-thirds that number.[22] "It is strange how a person becomes hardened to seeing comrades blown to pieces and living in the midst of blood and death," wrote Canadian infantryman Elmer Bowness after surviving these weeks of fighting. "I have seen sights in the blood-stained trenches of Flanders that I will never forget. If the people at home could see the real horrors of the battle-field they would be worried to death."[23] Thousands of telegrams reporting deaths were sent out to loved ones at home. Parents' dreams of seeing their children again were shattered after reading the first line: "Deeply regret to inform you…." Many would be left with only their memories and a sepia photograph; others who were more well off, such as the multi-millionaire Molson family, could take more elaborate steps in memorializing their lost kin. After hearing that their son Percy had fallen in battle, the Molsons ensured that his name would live on by renaming the McGill University football stadium in his honour. But whether wealthy or poor, no one back home escaped the shock delivered by the telegrams.

A PPCLI infantryman who survived the counterattack at Mount Sorrel, while so many of his mates fell, remarked, "Those three days stand out in my memory and the rest of the War was [an] anti-climax."[24] Others shared the feeling of Lieutenant Frank Mathers of the 43rd Battalion: although Mount Sorrel had been a harsh introduction to battle, now the survivors were "real soldiers, with a name to uphold."[25] Whatever the case, the 3rd Division, much like the two divisions that had preceded it, had undergone a difficult introduction to the Western Front.

The "June Show," as the battle was known informally, had been costly and had proved that continued diligence at the front was necessary. Although overshadowed by the ongoing bloodletting at Verdun, the Russian Brusilov offensive on the Eastern Front, and the preparation for the Somme offensive, the retaking of the lost ground at Mount Sorrel on June 13 was an important victory for the Canadians, and it helped to restore the men's confidence after their poor performance at St. Eloi.

G.

personal

Dear Mrs. Ring,-

Will you kindly accept my sincere sympathy and condolence in the decease of that worthy citizen and heroic soldier, your son, Private Alexander Ring.

While one cannot too deeply mourn the loss of such a brave comrade, there is a consolation in knowing that he did his duty fearlessly and well, and gave his life for the cause of Liberty and the upbuilding of the Empire.

Again extending to you my heartfelt sympathy.

Faithfully,

Sam Hughes

Major General,
Minister of Militia and Defence,
for Canada.

Mrs. William Ring,
Waba,
Ont.

*Thousands of Canadian families were forever devastated
by these telegrams bearing news of the death of loved ones.*

In stark contrast to the hurried counterattack on June 3, the setpiece battle by the 1st Division on June 13 was methodically planned and organized. Although the 1st Division troops faced the same problems as the 3rd Division had—of approaching the enemy trenches and finding suitable assembly areas while under fire, and dealing with inadequate supplies of hand grenades and stretcher-bearers, as well as failed communications—the staff officers and men at the front had begun to understand the limitations of war-fighting and the need for detailed planning.

Mount Sorrel also raised the curtain on a new level of ferocity and intensity in the war. The German bombardment had been an unprecedented experience for the Canadians, with almost entire battalions shattered by shellfire. In turn, Byng, his staff, and his men recognized that in taking back the ground they had similarly relied on their own artillery to pave the way to success. This reliance on heavy guns did not take away from the Canadian infantry's accomplishments, but it did reveal that improved cooperation of the infantry with the artillery was an essential component of any successful operation. The trauma of early June forced a renewed concentration on the importance of firepower within the Canadian Corps. A limited operation, based on a "bite and hold" principle—which involved planning not only the attack but also how to hold the captured position—would become the hallmark of Canadian operations over the next two and a half years. Still, the Canadians were far from being considered elite troops, and General Haig had written in his diary, after the German attack on June 2: "This seems bad and goes to prove that men with strange equipment and rugged countenances and beards are not all determined fighters."[26]

ONE OF THE MANY SIDEBARS of the Mount Sorrel battle was the friction and acrimonious relations that developed between the 1st and 3rd Divisions. The Canadians and their Dominion counterparts, the Australians, always had an uneasy relationship with their British comrades in arms. However, after Mount Sorrel, a rift formed among their own, as the veterans of the 1st Division made "sneering remarks" towards members of the 3rd Division's 8th Brigade, which had borne the brunt of the attack on June 2.[27] Clearly, tensions existed not only between the Canadians and other national armies but also within the supposedly homogeneous corps.

While much goodwill and friendship was shared among Canadians, competition and rivalries also marked the working relations within brigades and between them in the divisions. But what had started as a healthy rivalry had increasingly become damaging to combat effectiveness and cohesion. In fact, when Byng had taken over the corps, he had commented on the competitiveness and pride among units, which was sometimes detrimental to their cooperation. He hoped that more cross-pollination between the divisions, especially at training schools, would help to lessen regimental and divisional chauvinism and strengthen the entire corps' identity. He was ultimately proved right. Under Byng's guidance, the Canadian Corps became a more unified and cohesive force, and was set on its way to becoming an elite formation.

Byng also looked to sever ties with interfering Canadian politicians. It was true that the amateurism of the Canadians at the sharp end would result only in deaths, but the amateurism that was revealed in England and Canada—evident in countless ways, from the confusing training structure in England to Sam Hughes's proclivity for demanding that his friends be rewarded with command appointments—also had to be reformed. Byng, tired and worried about his Canadian Corps, increasingly had no reason or compunction to listen to Hughes and his cabal. And since Byng had not initially wanted the job of commanding the Canadians (although he would turn down two opportunities to leave before he was forced by Haig to take command of an army), he was willing to risk a falling out with the bullying Hughes.

This lack of respect or concern for Hughes's authority on Byng's part was demonstrated when, after Mercer's death at Mount Sorrel, Byng's headquarters received an urgent telegram reading, "Give Garnet 3rd Division, Sam."[28] Brigadier General G.J. Farmar, one of Byng's experienced and professional staff officers, tried to make sense of the message, assuming it was code for something, as it had arrived in the middle of the heated Mount Sorrel battle. It wasn't, and Byng knew this, but he ignored the request by Sam Hughes to make his son divisional commander. Command of the 3rd Division went instead to Louis Lipsett, a British officer who had been in Canada before the war and who carried a strong reputation among the British as well as with his own Canadian troops. (Hughes objected to the appointment, of course, but he and his son were later appeased when Garnet was given the 5th Division, although the division was fated to be broken up for reinforcements before it ever saw battle.)

From Byng's point of view, the Canadians were "too good to be led by politicians and dollar magnates, and if the credit of the Corps is to be augmented, the men must be led by leaders."[29] Byng avoided a no-holds-barred brawl with Hughes—the type of dirty fighting that the minister had excelled at during twenty-five years of political survival in the rough-and-tumble House of Commons—but he started the process of freeing the Canadian soldiers from the yoke of political interference. The war, Byng insisted, could not be run like an election.

With Lipsett at the helm, the 3rd Canadian Division began the arduous task of integrating new recruits into its mangled battalions. To the south, Haig was putting the finishing touches on his planned summer offensive on the Somme. Known as the "Big Push," this operation was expected to finally break through the German lines. It was not to be.

THE BATTLE OF MOUNT SORREL: JUNE 13, 1916

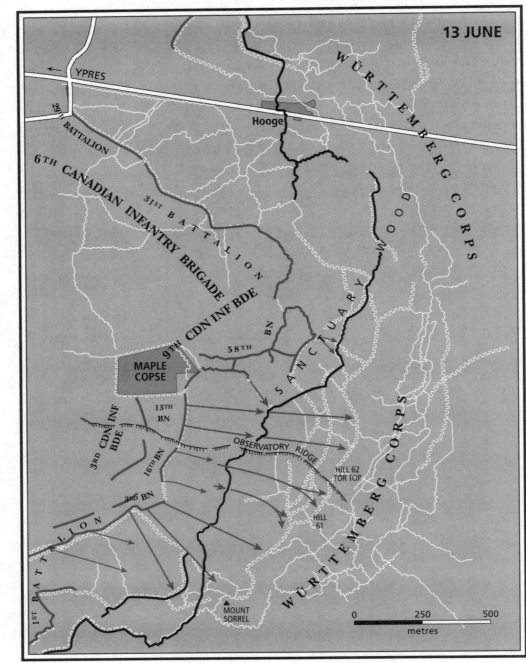

13 JUNE

YPRES

Hooge

WÜRTTEMBERG CORPS

29TH BATTALION

6TH CANADIAN INFANTRY BRIGADE

31ST BATTALION

9TH CDN INF BDE

58TH

BN

MAPLE COPSE

SANCTUARY WOOD

13TH BN

3RD CDN INF BDE

OBSERVATORY RIDGE

16TH BN

3RD BN

HILL 62 TOR TOP

HILL 61

WÜRTTEMBERG CORPS

1ST BATTALION

MOUNT SORREL

0   250   500

metres

CHAPTER 29

"REDEEMED FROM THE GRAVE"

Escape from the Front

"When I first joined, the 'tour' was six days in each position—front line, then to support 200 to 400 yards back, then to reserve, 800 to 1000 yards back, then to rest billets, a half ruined village four or five miles in rear," wrote Lieutenant Gregory Clark. "The six days in the front were naturally the worst, strict holding, patrolling, wiring, repairing and under shellfire, machine gun, rifle-grenade, and trench mortar. While in support and reserve, we did regular working parties, digging trenches, repairing, wiring, carrying ammunition, wire, and materials of all kinds. Thus while we lived in comparative comfort, at nights we were up in the dirty work."[1] Shells easily reached the second and third lines, and only when a unit was in brigade reserve, some 6 or 7 kilometres in the rear, was it truly safe.

The unceasing stress at the front and the constant possibility—increasing to likelihood for long-service veterans—that the men who manned the firing line would fall victim to shot or shell necessitated a rotation through the front lines. While the most common image of the Great War infantryman is that of him "going over the top" or sitting in abject misery in a muddy trench, the high command well understood the terrible pressure on its troops, and created a system to ensure they had a break from the front. Battalion headquarters tried to help the men by keeping the rotation time in the front lines as short as possible. The numbers in forward trenches were thinned out to allow a greater part of the force to rest in drier rear billets. The reward of periodic escape helped soldiers get through their tour. The 16th Battalion's experience typifies a unit's rotation. This unit spent 1,240 days of the war in France, putting in roughly 41 months of service. Of this time, thirty-four percent was spent in the front line or support, thirty-five percent in brigade or divisional billeting areas, and thirty-one percent in corps reserve far to the rear.[2] Although most of a soldier's combat experience was not in the front or secondary lines, the constant cycle ensured that the trenches dominated the soldiers' lives even when they were not in them.

Trench reliefs were carried out at night to ensure maximum protection of the men under the cover of darkness. Staff officers at brigade and divisional headquarters worked out the schedules of rotation, and then battalion headquarters—usually the second-in-command—implemented them. New men went in by companies, but

Life in the trenches involved long bouts of work and boredom interspersed with never-ending stress and brief moments of terror.

these were often further broken down to platoons of roughly thirty-five to forty men to keep the numbers manageable, since all would be travelling along narrow communication trenches. Captain Bruce Bairnsfather, the famous originator of the "Old Bill" cartoons, remarked candidly, "taking over trenches was one of the most remarkably dangerous feats of the war."[3]

Scouts led the parties through the pitch-black subterranean city. A long line of heavily burdened infantrymen grunted, swore, and stumbled in the dark over broken duckboards, catching their rifles on the low-lying wires, running face-first into the man in front, and continually listening for whispered harsh warnings to avoid this muddy hole or that rubble obstacle. The march was exhausting and annoying work, and made all the worse as the men moved closer to the increasing danger of the front lines. Throughout this ordeal, guides and officers commonly got lost, and a chorus of cursing could be heard when orders were passed down the line for the exasperated rank and file to turn the "snake" around, march back 100 metres to the last "T" junction, and wait. Anxiety built among men as the first haze of dawn pierced the gloom on the horizon and they realized that they would soon be vulnerable targets for the ritualistic "morning hate" fired by the enemy gunners.

Most reliefs were carried out without these problems, however. Men were ordered to be quiet and to avoid feeding their raging nicotine addictions. Some followed these orders, realizing the potential consequences of a long line of burning embers snaking into the lines; other units, though, had notoriously bad discipline. Seemingly petty regulations like these grated on soldiers, but adhering to them mattered. The faint glow of several dozen cigarettes or loud talking would indicate that new and possibly unprepared troops were coming into the line. Alert enemy troops could launch a lightning raid at the moment when two battalions were involved in a trench handover, likely catching both units scattered and disorganized. The front-line soldiers were at their most vulnerable when in the midst of a rotation.

As incoming officers met the outgoing, exhausted ones, they shook hands and passed along intelligence. Enemy strongpoints were identified on crude trench maps; trench stores such as grenades and shovels were counted and signed for; and information about the condition of the barbed wire was passed on, creating immediate fatigue work for the rankers.[4] Sometimes the handover was sloppy, as the outgoing officers and men, plagued with the trials of a bad tour and grey with exhaustion, only wanted out of the lines. But regardless of the parties involved, as one anxious officer noted, "It is always a difficult job placing your men when you take over in the dark."[5]

"I HAVE COME through some fearfully stiff fighting, and sometimes I pinch myself to make sure I am still alive," wrote Lieutenant J.M. Walton after rotating from the front lines. "I have seen some sights which I shan't forget in a hurry."[6] With the stress of firing-line service etched on their faces and resting stiffly on hunched shoulders, the outgoing battalion trudged along the communication trenches to the rear. The battalion was usually missing a few men if it had got off lucky, or more if it had been subject to raids or heavier than normal artillery fire. Although the infantry were exhausted, the troops were relieved to be leaving death behind; for the British poet and warrior, Siegfried Sassoon, quitting the line was akin to being "redeemed from the grave."[7] In darkness, the tired warriors kept moving until they arrived at their billets, usually a ruined village several kilometres behind the lines.

Company commanders reported to battalion headquarters, situated in one of the village's best houses. The battalion headquarters remained a strange beast—at times sharing the danger with the front-line infantry companies, but also often considered as something distinct, as the commanding officer, a lieutenant colonel, was forced to command from the rear, even if it was only from a slightly larger dugout a few hundred metres behind the firing line. The battalion staff included the medical officer and his sixteen (later thirty-two) stretcher-bearers, many of whom also doubled as members of the battalion's band. The regimental sergeant major, who was the senior NCO and struck terror in the rank and file—and in a good many officers, all of whom heeded his experience and authority—also remained at battalion HQ, unless he was on the rampage. Specialist officers for the scouts, machine-gunners, and bombers, as well as the second-in-command, who carried out many of the administrative and disciplinary issues for the commanding officer, usually bunked together in the same dugout or house. Additional rank and file specialists, such as armourers who repaired rifles and Lewis guns; signallers (sixteen per battalion); transport men responsible for wagons, pack horses, and water carts; runners (nine per battalion); the quartermaster, who kept the men fed and supplied; company cooks; and the all-important boot-repairers, essential for an army that travelled on its feet, all stayed at battalion headquarters and rarely went into the front lines.[8] Although usually viewed by the infantry with a good deal of suspicion—and even more envy—the battalion staff continued to do its best in providing for the men, and were their link-up to the brigade's high command.

While the commanders were getting settled at battalion headquarters, lieutenants ensured that their men were given adequate billets. Certainly some junior officers would look out for themselves first, but more often they tried to ensure that the men were cared for as best they could be within the limited circumstances. As one soldier observed, horses were "treated better than men because they're harder to replace."[9] In fact, the men were often treated the same as horses and other livestock, with whom they shared their billets in a barn, as French and Belgian civilians continued to inhabit houses near the front throughout the war. Despite some soldiers' anger about being treated like livestock, it was nonetheless better than the trenches and good officers ensured that a company cook would have a hot meal ready for the men.

Officers and NCOs with any sense allowed the exhausted infanteers to sleep in the next day. Most awoke to the smell of cooks frying up sizzling bacon and brewing strong tea. After shaving away days of stubble, chipping the mud from their kit, and making minor repairs to their clothing, soldiers were marked off by platoons and marched to local bathing facilities, if they were available. These facilities were crude even by the standards of the day. In true military fashion, men lined up and waited outside a brewery or hastily built structure that could accommodate huge vats of water and hundreds of filthy men per day.

Louse-infested shirts and underwear were tossed in a pile, where they were steam disinfected in hopes of killing the hidden tormentors. Huddled in naked masses, the men moved into the showers in groups, generally receiving a minute or two of water, a break to apply soap, and then a few minutes more to rinse. The experience was glorious in the summer, but wintertime left bathers hopping on gradually developing blocks of ice as frigid water washed over them. Nonetheless, in the words of one trench veteran, after a shower, the men might feel "almost human again."[10]

Lieutenant William Gray, who as an officer would never have bathed with the men, remarked that a shower was nothing short of an "indescribable pleasure. You will understand that after, say, twelve days of filth and slush, of fecundence and slime, when your clothes are coated with a sticky veneer, which percolates through in spots, and that before meals you use a knife to scrape the ooze from between your fingers, a bath is somewhat of a glorified affair."[11] The steamed clothes were handed out to the wet men as they passed through the rear of the shower house. Much grumbling took place as no attempt was made to measure the man to the clothes, leaving the soldiers to trade and sort their kit out among themselves. The relief the men enjoyed was temporary: within a few hours they were lousy again from billets that were crawling with lice.

BACK AT THE BILLETS, the men lined up to receive their pay: paybooks were handed over to the battalion paymaster and were returned filled out and accompanied by a wad of French francs. Married men assigned most of their pay to dependants, but the unmarried soldiers who made up eighty percent of the ranks were temporarily flush. Most rushed off to spend their money in the villages that dotted the rear areas.

Estaminets in every town and village served steak, eggs, and chips to the men, all of which were washed down with watery beer and "vin blanc." These small restaurants and taverns catered to the soldiers, who spent their pay with wild abandon. Once soldiers got over the sometimes shocking sanitary standards of these makeshift restaurants, which could simply be the living room of a house, they were all too happy to consume what was offered. As Samuel Honey informed his parents, however, the Canadians' well-deserved reputation for high pay often resulted in their paying prices that approached "highway robbery."[12]

Most of the eating and drinking establishments were maintained by old men and women, but some were run by younger women whose husbands had gone off to war or who had been widowed. Mixing with women tended to awaken repressed sexual appetites in the soldiers, who had pushed these thoughts aside in the struggle for survival in the trenches. Now, a buxom or petite maid with even a hint of beauty could drive young men to fits of passion, although most of the women became well experienced in fending off amorous advances.

The time spent in the rear, and especially in the *estaminets,* was some of the soldiers' happiest in the entire war. The men munched on their greasy food, drank, and sang. If the mood struck, songs such as "Mademoiselle from Armentières" and "I Don't Want to Join the Army" could be sung either clean or dirty, depending on the company or the amount of alcohol imbibed. Private Courtney Tower of the 44th Battalion recounted in his diary that most of the soldiers carried on their masculine culture from the trenches even in the presence of the serving ladies; his companions were "great drinkers and swearers, but really the best fellows in the world…. [They] tell their smutty yarns and drink just as if there were no women around."[13]

Of course, soldiers and drink did not always mix well. Men with money tended to cause "trouble and indiscipline," remarked William Kerr, who was wounded three times, was awarded the Military Medal, and rose from private to lieutenant colonel in the 5th Battalion.[14] Lieutenant Colonel Agar Adamson, the stern PPCLI commander and South African War veteran who was much admired by his soldiers—even though he was the subject of jokes about his affectation of wearing a monocle—bewailed the number of his men that got drunk in rear areas, but wrote to his wife that "You cannot prevent the French people selling them rotten spirits."[15] Drunkenness remained a problem in the CEF, as it was throughout the BEF, and accounted for more courts martial than all other offences combined.[16] Although the high command fretted over alcohol-related indiscipline and crime, the problem was long-standing and therefore somewhat understood. So too did the army understand the soldiers' undeniable need for sex, even if it was considered a yet more sordid and morally damaging vice.

When soldiers found food and alcohol behind the lines, they often then went in search of women. While sexual enjoyments were far less common than the other temporary pleasures, desperate soldiers would go to great lengths to pursue them. If a unit spent any time in the rear, the officers and rank and file were often billeted with French families. Inevitable coupling occurred among desperate young people looking to wring some joy out of a tension-filled life.

If they had no luck among the local population, soldiers looking for sex often had liberty to walk to local villages, as long as the military police had not cordoned them off. There is ample evidence from the men that many of them bought and bargained for sexual services; others benefited from their status as the nations' liberators, rewarded by women who—with local French and Belgian men away at the front—were often caught in a "demographic No Man's Land."[17] An estimated 50,000 homeless and hopeless displaced persons turned to prostitution to survive.[18] Private Victor Wheeler mulled over the possibilities when one young woman propositioned him, wondering "whether her motive was to earn a few francs for desperately needed food; or for pure personal pleasure to relieve loneliness and the rigours of war; or was an invitation extended out of a sense of appreciation for what we *soldats Canadiens* were doing to help liberate their beloved country."[19] He never found out, turning her down shyly.

Visiting bigger city brothels was a more common way for Canadians to meet their sexual needs. Trips to Paris or other large French cities provided ample opportunity for soldiers on leave to meet women. Single men, and even some married ones, free from the shackles of the trenches and with money in their pockets, found red-light districts. Brothels in such districts were regulated by army medical officers, who inspected the prostitutes and jailed those who had sexually transmissible diseases. Later in the war, the YMCA struggled with the issue of soldiers' sexual urges: the Christian organization strongly encouraged men to observe abstinence, but once it was clear that this message was largely being ignored, the YMCA made the painful decision to offer free prophylactics to Canadians who were taking their leave in areas offering significant temptation.[20] "He who hopes to wage war without wine and women is living in a fool's paradise, for there are no half-measures in war, try how one will," wrote F.P. Crozier, an experienced Imperial soldier.[21] Most Canadians would have agreed with him.

W.R. Morison, an inveterate diarist in the Canadian Field Artillery, who throughout the war penned more than 2,000 pages in 19 notebooks, described the crude content of conversations among his mates: a fellow soldier bragged about "detailed incidents of his experiences with Paris whores. He can talk of nothing else since he got back…. As this is the most delicate of conversations I won't record further."[22] Of course, rarely did the men's stories reflect their true experiences. One British Tommy recounted his shocked reaction to the women in the brothels: "As for the resident ladies, the least said of them, poor things, the better. They were old and worn and hideous, with death's heads instead of faces."[23] Some officers, fearful of the moral degeneracy that these brothels would engender in their men, petitioned to have them closed. But the army refused to take such action, acknowledging the right of soldiers to negotiate some of their own comforts. Furthermore, since separate blue-light districts existed for the use of officers, clearly not all commissioned men were against the idea of paying for sex. With brothels left open for business and prostitutes meeting demands closer to the front, venereal disease remained a problem throughout the war, and no amount of threats, control, or punishment curbed development of sexually transmitted disease, which would rise to epidemic proportions.

Yet not all of the soldiers' affairs were tawdry, pay-for-sex relationships. Canadians fell in love with French and Belgian women, who, lonely or having experienced their own wartime traumas, could also return the sentiment. Those soldiers with some knowledge of the local language had a better chance of cementing a relationship, but many unilingual men tried their best nonetheless. Thomas Dinesen, a Dane serving with the Canadians—and an eventual recipient of the Victoria Cross—recounted how he walked several miles to a local French village in the hope of meeting a "sweet, pretty and kind-hearted French girl." Dinesen also noted disdainfully that the feeling among many men was that "with the girls you may use any trick, however mean and shabby—the only thing is to get what you want from them and then beat it."[24] Competition for female attention was fierce, especially when a battalion of 800 descended on a village all at once. Men memorized key French phrases, purchased gifts, or simply stared starstruck at the women. However, despite soldiers' fervent efforts to win the local women's favour, of the estimated 350,000 Canadians who served in Europe, only a few hundred marriages resulted, although several thousand unions between Canadian soldiers and British women took place in Britain. Although this low marriage rate in Europe is attributable in part to soldiers' failed attempts to woo the objects of their affection, no doubt some unions were blocked by commanding officers who had the right to approve or disapprove of any marriage application, as well as the constant rotation of troops who rarely stayed in the same rear village twice.[25]

The tone of interaction between civilian and soldier was generally positive, but the relationship was not without its fault lines. Even though the BEF did not have an official policy of "living off the land," as had armies of the past by taking what they wanted and needed from farmers and merchants, the soldiers still experienced friction with the local civilians. The tension between the two groups revolved around the soldiers' image as both liberators and occupiers. Some civilians greeted the Canadians with open arms, sharing their food and homes; others grew tired of these men who destroyed their fields with hobnailed boots, drank their water, and urinated wherever they wanted. The soldiers' propensity to augment their meagre supplies by hook or by crook—in opposition to the official policy—also meant that often civilians suffered the loss of eggs, milk, and even farm animals. But local residents received some compensation beyond the return of their country someday: French and Belgian civilians were paid a billeting fee of five centimes for each enlisted man and one franc per officer.[26] A private bunking in a hayloft above a herd of cows likely did not consider the accommodations worth the fee, although the price was the equivalent of only a little more than a Canadian penny.

In addition to day-to-day tensions between the soldiers and their local hosts, more serious crimes were committed—of assault, theft, rape, and murder. Such incidents were usually perpetrated by drunken soldiers. One of the most egregious cases involved Driver T.H. Bryans, who was convicted of raping a sixty-six-year-old woman near Malvinière Moulton. Bryans had a good prior conduct sheet, but he was given a long sentence and was still in a prison after the Canadians left France in 1919.[27] However, while brutal cases such as this did occur, the archival records do not contain an exorbitant number. In fact, one is struck by the limited incidence of serious crimes in a corps whose population ranged at various times from 80,000 to 100,000 men, most of whom were suffering from terrible stress, were deprived of the calming influences of loved ones, and were armed. Although Canadians were caught and punished for these crimes, it is also true that the military and civilian police apparently turned a blind eye to some of the offences, especially to crimes committed against women selling their bodies.[28]

Although news of most of the Canadians' serious transgressions was prevented from reaching the home front through the stringent censorship of not only soldiers' letters but also journalistic accounts, stray rumours and sordid stories inevitably seeped back to Canada through letters or injured soldiers who returned home. Mothers, wives, and social activist groups worried about the welfare of their boys, and especially about their ability to withstand the evils of drink and women. More than a few soldiers had such worries, too. Arthur Chute, a junior artillery officer, remarked that with few other types of entertainment available in the towns, soldiers often found "nothing to welcome them but the cafes and the harpies," and in the absence of the "steadying influences ...[of] loved ones and friends and home," soldiers would inevitably be tempted to act out in undesirable ways.[29] Legitimate amusements were clearly needed.

CHAPTER 30

"THE BLIGHTER—
HE-SWINGS-LIKE-A-GATE"

Rest and Recuperation

To keep soldiers from embarking upon the "downward path," as the YMCA called it, the army and unofficial organizations invested considerable time and resources into developing leisure activities for soldiers. Although some officers at first had reservations about unsoldierly pursuits such as games, sports, theatre, and other cultural manifestations, they soon acknowledged the importance of these events for the army of civilian-soldiers.

For those who did partake of blowout evenings in the local villages, returning to billets with only a few francs to their names, solace could be found in the YMCA and the Salvation Army. These organizations established huts to care for the men's health and spiritual well-being, and most sold sweets and gave away free coffee and tea. Many of the products available at these huts were Canadian, stirring up prewar memories for the men as they consumed their favourite food, tobacco, and chewing gum. "We would have been utterly lost without it," recounted one trench soldier, "although we grumbled at the terrifically high prices we had to pay."[1] The YMCA and the Salvation Army were places for the soldiers to have a hot drink, "swap stories or just talk & jolly one another," remembered Corporal J.C. Stothers, a twenty-eight-year-old teacher from Toronto.[2]

These spiritual shops were also a place to write letters home. Soldiers could be seen at the rough wooden tables with a faraway look in their eyes. The YMCA or Salvation Army sometimes even had staff on hand to pen a quick letter for one of the thousands of illiterate CEF soldiers. "The good old Sally Ann," wrote Private William New of the 3rd Division Supply Column, and his sentiment likely summed up the feelings of most Canadians.[3]

Back at billets, soldiers relaxed, smoking their cigarettes sprawled on the ground. Frank Ferguson, a prewar chauffeur driver from Nova Scotia, remembered one gunner who spent many hours of his time in reserve tending to the graves of the fallen behind the lines, pulling weeds, straightening crosses, and saying prayers. "Someone asked him why he spent so much time looking after a stranger's grave," remembered Ferguson. The gunner replied, "Well, I might be in his place someday."[4] Sadly, Ferguson buried the gunner on the Somme.

FOR THOSE MEN with too much money in their pockets, a few old hands could always be counted on to whip out a Crown and Anchor board game with the intention of fleecing their mates. The rambling patter that accompanied the game was part of the fun—enticing, harassing, pleading, and cajoling onlookers to dance with lady luck:

> Plunk your money down thick and heavy; the more you put down the more you pick up. You must speculate if you expect to accumulate. The last fellow came here in a wheel-barrow and rode off in an auto. Come on me lucky lads. Break me and you break the Bank of Monte Carlo.[5]

Relaxing with Crown and Anchor was illegal in the army, but the tradition of playing the game subversively had long been handed down. The game board was divided into six sections: spades, diamonds, clubs, hearts, crown, and anchor, and these six symbols were displayed on the six sides of each of the game's three dice. The gamers placed their money on one of the board's symbols. If that image came up on all three dice, the gambler won three times his stake, if on two dice, he won double, and a single meant that he kept the original amount bet. All other combinations of dice meant the bet was lost. The odds were always in favour of the "house," the man who owned the board, and he usually walked away with most of the francs. Poker and bingo (known as "housey-housey") were also played, although the latter was usually regarded as a sissy's game.

NCOs and officers were on the lookout for games of Crown and Anchor, and often knew who ran the outfits. Yet since many of the NCOs also partook in the gambling, they were not always adamant about breaking it up, unless the purpose of doing so was to give a partner an opportunity to set up as the new "house." Canon Frederick Scott, among others, made it his mission to stamp out gambling; he was still loved by the men—although perhaps just tolerated by some of the gamblers—even if he had the annoying tendency of breaking up their games by riding his horse through the group of players. Gambling was a regular pastime for the men, second only to smoking. "The odds at Crown and Anchor were, we knew, against us," remembered Sergeant Ernest Black, "but we loved the action and we were used to unfair odds."[6]

Those who worried about suffering spiritual degradation as a result of their gambling and drinking—and, among the most puritanical, smoking—could usually find some solace with the padre. The army's padres—in conjunction with the YMCA and the Salvation Army—tried to reach the men spiritually. But a very fine line always existed between preaching to and comforting the men, with the former approach tending to drive many of them away.[7] Herbert Burrell of the 1st CMR recounted his experience with what he called a "padre's *estaminet*": "A captain and a major make and serve the coffee. One of them in answer to my enquiry said he was a Presbyterian, his friend was an Anglican, and the Anglican chiming in said, 'yes, but the coffee is undenominational.' This drink was a godsend."[8]

Soldiers were ordered to attend the religious parades usually held on Sundays, and most did so willingly. Of those occasions, Major Arthur McNally remarked incredulously, "It is hard to realize that it is Sunday and the fighting goes on just the same."[9] Religion was important to most Canadian soldiers: 30.9 percent listed themselves as Anglicans, 22.9 percent were Catholic, 21 percent were Presbyterian, and 13.6 percent were Methodist; the remaining 11.6 percent were divided among various other denominations and atheism.[10] Many men were deeply spiritual, even though most found ways to accommodate the idea of taking lives within their belief system. Other lowly activities could be similarly reconciled, as attested by A.L. Barry, who would rise from a batman to a brigadier in the course of his long military career. Barry remembered seeing a twisting line of soldiers giving their confessions to a padre. "About 50 yards away a poker game was in progress. Occasionally a soldier would fall in, hat in hand, at the end of the line for confession, move on to say his penance and then rejoin the poker game."[11] As the war ushered in changes in many areas of the soldiers' lives, the spiritual aspect, too, was reshaped to fit the men's new reality.

AFTER DRINKING A COFFEE, reading a newspaper, or talking to a padre, the soldiers might go for a walk through the farmers' fields. Good soil produced bountiful crops, and while those near the front were left to rot in the fields, 5 to 10 kilometres behind the lines, thriving farms could be found. Walking gave men a chance to clear their heads and even straighten out their bodies, as most had grown accustomed to moving in a perpetually crouched-over position in the trenches. While they took a stroll, they could look around and see as far as the rolling hills or horizon allowed, as no eight-foot-high, sandbagged trench wall was continuously staring them in the face. "It is warm and the air balmy with the odors of the first fruits of spring," wrote Herbert Burrell in his diary after one such walk. "The trees are brilliant in their fresh green and the earth teems with a thousand spring plants and flowers. The birds sing the happiest of songs, and it is

The war was not all about mud, rats, and misery. This lucky Canadian has found some wild blueberries.

the Sabbath, and yet, desecrating all this beauty, we hear the thumping roar of the big guns, the throbbing of aeroplane engines overhead."[12]

Many of the farms dotting the pastoral surroundings were still populated, as thousands of civilians in the war zone had refused to be chased from their farms. "The land is being tilled—the peasants are about in their pantaloons and huge shoes," wrote Stanley Rutledge. "One can quite easily forget there is such a thing as war."[13] Many Canadian farmers marvelled at how the Belgians harnessed their dogs and used them to labour the land, and they scratched their head in wonderment at running across Canadian-made Massey-Harris farm equipment in France.[14] Those men with a hankering for their old farms sometimes jumped in and offered a hand to grateful farmers who could barely imagine why those colonials were fighting their war, let alone why they were also helping to till their land. For a few sweaty hours, men lost themselves in the welcome work of creating rather than destroying. Taking their lead from the farmers, some units established large gardens behind the lines. This required some investment of time and effort, and some guarantee that a unit would not be moved immediately, but by the summer of 1918, large and profitable gardens were used to feed the Canadian troops.[15]

The bucolic scenes of farmers setting up produce stalls along roads, or the cows that watched the long lines of men and materiel move towards the front, were common images of war, much more so than were sights of fighting German soldiers. These gentle scenes were also a reminder of that which was left behind. Corporal Harry Hillyer, who had enlisted at the age of thirty-eight, wrote achingly to his wife and newborn son after staying with a Belgian family: "[I] became homesick and I have not got over the feeling yet although I've been out with a working party today and have seen a little of the sterner side of life."[16] Hillyer would never be reunited with his family, as he would be killed while leading a raid on enemy lines.

The more adventurous men wanted to record what they saw not only in print, but visually as well. Those shutterbugs, or "Kodak-toters" as Frederick Noyes called them, took the time (and risk) to capture an image of the green fields at the rear, or the blasted lines they had just left.[17] Snapping pictures like tourists allowed the men to inject a temporary sense of normalcy into their lives. However, such photography was illegal. The army ordered in March 1915 that no cameras were to be carried into the front or rear lines for fear of captured film providing the enemy with battlefield information. This order was as ignored as the appeals to the men to refrain from keeping diaries; however, the prosecution of photographers was carried out with much zeal, while diarists were left alone. Although those who took photos were simply trying to find a means to understand, order, and capture the experiences of their strange world, headquarters missives continued to circulate throughout the war demanding that the prohibition of amateur photography be enforced. It clearly was not, although snapping pictures in the trenches was never easy. "Among some of the minor military transgressions I committed was carrying a small camera in my pack," confessed Private George Bell. "Probably every man in my platoon knew that I had a camera, but none gave me away. The boys were anxious to have their pictures taken to be sent home, particularly pictures which showed life in the trenches. My sister mailed films to me from England and I sent them back by soldiers to London, where they were developed and printed and the prints mailed to my sister who, in turn, mailed them to me, a roundabout method which worked quite successfully."[18] At least one of Bell's officers knew of the pictures, but he did nothing to enforce the military rule. Determined men such as Bell refused to be cowed, and they left a valuable, if illegal, photographic legacy.

WHILE INDIVIDUALS CHOSE various ways to regain their old form—whether gambling, seeing friends, engaging in hobbies such as photography, or simply having a desperately needed rest—sports were an almost universally shared pastime. "The moment our men get out of the trenches they begin to play baseball, football, cricket," wrote Lieutenant Coningsby Dawson.[19] The Canadian troops were mad for sports, as were most men in the BEF, and the games were encouraged by the army to relieve stress, build fitness, and keep soldiers out of trouble.

The most popular game was baseball. The Canadian baseball matches within or between battalions, and then against other armies' teams, especially the Americans' once they joined the war, attracted enormous crowds.[20] One lieutenant colonel recounted the jovial atmosphere at a game: "The supporters of different teams ... shouted such witticisms and jeering remarks at the players—irrespective of rank— as bewildered the British officers.... It was bad enough to hear a private tell a non-commissioned officer who was pitching that he had 'a glass eye', but it seemed to them as if discipline had completely broken down when a crowd of all ranks kept yelling in chorus at the batting of a Brigadier-General, 'He swings like a gate, the blighter—he-swings-like-a-gate.'"[21] Other officers played the men in sporting events, and this undoubtedly helped to break down some of the hierarchical barriers between leaders and the led.

Sports also had an important role in fostering reputations and rivalries between units. The men played hard for bragging rights, and officers seem to have invested even more in the games, believing that they offered insight into the morale, even ferocity, of their formations. Staff officers and commanders were attracted to these sporting matches, and this exposure to scrutiny by higher-ups meant that a lot was riding on the games' outcome. Professional players were recruited in the ranks, and divisional championships might feature teams consisting solely of peacetime sports pros. Winning teams were recorded in regimental histories and the 1918 Dominion Day games in France attracted crowds numbering in the tens of thousands.

CONCERTS AND THEATRICAL REVUES were also established behind the lines for the men's pleasure and relaxation, although these events did not elicit the rabid spirit seen at sporting events. These vaudeville and music hall–inspired shows started off as informal routines staged by the jokers in a company or battalion. Drawn from the ranks, these soldier-performers understood the war in a way that civilian entertainers never could. As the shows grew in popularity, they expanded in scope and size. Often mimicking prewar humour and exploiting common cultural references from films and music hall shows, the performers used songs, skits, and monologues to explore the soldiers' experience.

Some songs from this period, such as "Keep the Home Fires Burning" and "Tipperary," remain forever tied to the Great War. They were sung throughout the entire British Empire, and they buoyed spirits. The soldiers also sang these uplifting songs in formal performances and in singalongs with friends (although "Tipperary" soon fell out of favour with the men in uniform as it was too closely associated with civilians), and to further distinguish themselves the soldiers also updated prewar songs and hymns to better reflect their wartime lives. New, raunchy words or an anti-authoritarian rant might be inserted into a popular song; the tune remained the same, but the words spoke to the reality of the men's experiences, thus contributing to the development of an exclusive soldiers' culture. One of the popular sentimental songs of the period, "My Little Grey Home in the West," was revised into several versions by the Canadians, one of which was known as "My Little Wet Home in the Trench":

> I've a little wet home in the trench
> Where the rainstorms continually drench
> There's a dead cow close by,
> With her hoofs towards the sky
> And she gives off a beautiful stench.
> Underneath, in the place of a floor
> There's a mass of wet mud and some straw
> And the "Jack Johnsons" tear
> Thro' the rain sodden air
> O'er my little wet home in the trench.
>
> There are snipers who keep on the go
> So you must keep your napper down low
> And their star shells at night
> Make a deuce of a light
> Which causes the language to flow.
> Then bully and biscuits we chew
> For 'tis days since we tasted a stew
> But with shells dropping there
> There's no place to compare
> With my little wet home in the trench.[22]

The soldiers' songs were owned by no one, and they were continually updated, their words blurring and shifting with the changes of the war.

Formal entertainment units, such as the Dumbells or the PPCLI Comedy Company, achieved army-wide acclaim, and the performers in these units became full-time actors, many parlaying their wartime popularity into successful postwar careers. As J.A. Bain recounted, "The boys crowd into the tents glad to get a chance to hear some songs and jokes and have their minds distracted from the stiff work that has been going on up the line lately."[23] "They made us laugh, uplifted our spirits and helped lighten the leaden weight of our recent losses," remembered Victor Wheeler.[24]

Among the most popular parts of the act was the troupe's alluring "women." No show was complete without its drag performer, and cross-dressing remained highly appealing in a world that was largely devoid of women. "The girls were excellent; one of the officers fell in love with one of them, and had to be told it wasn't a real one," snickered a soldier to his family. This was likely an apocryphal story, but the ranks enjoyed poking fun at their officers whenever they had a chance.[25] The cross-dressing performances also provided a sense of escape from the harsh, masculine world of soldiering. Some historians, in considering the appeal of such performances, have projected twenty-first-century values backwards by ascribing homosexual urges to the soldiers.[26] However, the appeal of drag queens in wartime revues was in fact more akin to the prewar popularity of cross-dressing in the music hall shows, and isolated army garrison units also had a long tradition of similar drag performances. The power of illusion wielded by talented soldier-performers can also not be overlooked.

These shows at the rear were important for maintaining morale. They also played a part in reducing the rigidity of the army hierarchy. Officers sat in the same darkened theatre or tent as the enlisted men, with all having an opportunity to enjoy the show. Rank ceased to matter for a while, as the gaze of all was directed towards the performers. These concerts and revues were acknowledged by officers and men as an important respite from the fighting, and as essential to keeping up morale. Officers even allowed for anti-authoritarian jokes and pokes in the shows. Major Agar Adamson of the PPCLI chortled along with his men as one of his battalion's entertainers did an impression of the major's stringent manner and personal affectations: "His efforts at mimicking me highly amused both men and officers and I really had a rather bad time, though in a most friendly way."[27]

In addition to doing impressions, entertainers fired off silly jokes and presented satirical sketches, with most shows playing on the absurdity of life in the trenches or in the army in general. Much of the darker humour was exclusively intended for front-line troops.[28] Civilians did not understand it and they were not meant to. Jokes about the dead, about being killed, and about getting back at the officers were simply another form of grousing. An uninitiated observer might have thought the British and Canadian Tommies were on the verge of mutiny. Yet the songs and skits, like the ever-circulating rumours and the trench newspapers that poked fun at authority, were all part of the soldiers' culture, which revelled in the blackness of their situation. It is said that German intelligence was highly excited one night upon hearing singing coming from a British trench: "I want to go home, I want to go home / I don't want to go in the trenches no more, where coalboxes and whiz-bangs they whistle and roar / Take me over the sea, where the Alleyman can't get at me / Oh my! I don't want to die, I want to go home." The German report came to the conclusion that the British morale was at its breaking point and the troops were on the verge of a mutiny.[29] They were not, of course, and the soldiers simply liked to dream in song about a future without war. While raucous singalongs and profanity-laden sketches were most common at the evening revues, a wistful song about Canada or the girl left behind often brought the crowd to tears.

Films were also popular among the troops, although in the early years of fighting, they were less common at the front. As the war went on, however, the YMCA responded to the demand for this form of entertainment by establishing theatres behind the lines, often in old barns. In a letter written from the front before his death on the Somme, Lieutenant J.E. Ryerson described such cinematic amusements: "We made it a holiday and I went to a Movie Show, where there was a band which played some good music. It may seem strange but the Movie Show is within three or four miles of the front line trench, and is crowded every afternoon and evening. It is a great boon to Tommy and only costs him five cents."[30] Charlie Chaplin was a favourite among almost all soldiers of the BEF, and his humour crossed national boundaries.[31] The antics of the little tramp who tweaked and beat the upper classes appealed to the soldiers, who enjoyed any shot at authority. Sergeant Ernest Black believed that Chaplin had a "great dignity" despite his shoddy clothes; Black and his mates took inspiration from him in their struggle to survive the indignity of army life and sudden death.[32]

REST, SPORTS, AND ENTERTAINMENT at the rear helped to humanize the war experience and rejuvenate men who had lived in squalor and experienced the unimaginable. For the men, these times in reserve were precious breaks from the trials of the trenches. But life behind the lines did not consist only of sports and entertainment. After the officers judged that the men had had some time to recoup mentally and physically, new work fatigues and training were carried out. "They don't let one rest much, and in some ways it is more tiresome having to do silly old drill that you have done dozens of times than to listen to the booming of guns," wrote Alwyn Bramley-Moore, a former provincial member of Parliament from Alberta.[33] The infantry's work fatigues in the rear area were largely centred on improving the logistical line—either roads or railways—although much of this work was alleviated in 1918 as larger labour battalions were established to relieve the infantry, who could then focus on training.

The rotational cycle continued throughout the war: from service in the front line to the secondary trenches to reserve, and finally billets, and then back to the front. The circle was rarely broken, and soldiers knew that no escape was to be had unless it was by being given a bombproof job or being carried out on a stretcher. While temporary respites from the front were necessary to maintain the men's physical strength and psychological endurance, the trenches always loomed in the back of the soldier's mind. Within a few days or a week at best, he would be marching up the line, back into the killing ditches of the Western Front.

CHAPTER 31

THE "BIG PUSH"

The Somme, July 1–September 1, 1916

The Entente needed a victory after nearly two years of defeats and crippling casualties. The second year of the war had illustrated the bankruptcy of existing tactics, as battle after battle squandered lives in shocking numbers. The failures in preparation, fire support, and communications had often pitted the infantry alone against uncut barbed wire and dug-in machine-gunners. But the sharp end was not the only place where tactics had ground to a halt. The entire Entente war effort was showing signs of strain: Serbia was overwhelmed, its army sent reeling, the country overrun and occupied; the Italians, who entered the war as an ally of the Entente in May 1915, had fruitlessly attacked the Austrians in frontal assaults that had been repulsed, with resulting heavy losses; and the Russians had seen several offensives crushed as their lumbering armies were often beaten because of ammunition shortages, uncoordinated operations, and incompetent commanders. Even when the British high command and politicians directed their focus away from the Western Front in attempts to reduce the strength of Germany's allies—the Gallipoli landings in the Dardanelles, for example—those efforts failed, as costly stalemates on those fronts sucked men and materiel into them just as greedily as did the European front.

DESPITE ITS LONG LIST of defeats and setbacks, the British high command was trying to understand the reason for its failures, and then learn the important lessons in preparation for a new onslaught. After the munitions scandals of 1915, which revealed that the BEF was in danger of losing the war because of a lack of shells, the British arms industry had been invigorated under the leadership of David Lloyd George, who would soon become Britain's prime minister and war leader. Equally important, new armies had been raised. From all backgrounds, classes, and regions, the British male population responded to the call to arms. The men joined up together—in groups of pals or entire city blocks. From farmers and miners to clerks and aristocrats' sons: more than five million signed on by the end of the war.[1]

In a December 1915 conference at Chantilly, France, politicians and generals from the Entente nations reached a consensus to coordinate attacks on the Central Powers throughout the next year. But coalitions were easily divided, riven with national prejudices and hindered by divergent economic, political, and military goals. Political and military leaders fought against the fear that such cooperative action might result in commanders of some nations surrendering their strategic initiative to other Allied forces, perhaps putting them in the position of being forced to attack when they were not ready. It is reported that General Ferdinand Foch, who would become France's greatest military commander during the war, scoffed, "I lost some of my respect for Napoleon when I learned what it was to fight a coalition war."[2] While coalitions might create larger forces, the necessity of taking the positions of all parties into account often made such associations unwieldy, and they were always vulnerable to fissures under sustained pressure. One of the most important goals of the French and British military and civilian commanders was to ensure that the military coalition remained unbroken, even in the aftermath of catastrophic battles.

In early February 1916, General Douglas Haig again confirmed his support for French commander General Joffre's proposal of a joint attack on the Somme. He offered twenty-five divisions to take part, sometime in late summer, in what would be the largest British offensive to that point in the nation's history.[3] While Haig believed in the need to mount a synchronized offensive, and to reclaim the occupied parts of France that were now being strip-mined to support the enemy's war machine, he well recognized the difficulty of coordinating two massive army groups that had different cultures, doctrines, and sometimes even objectives. Haig was willing to support the French, but he needed at least six months to integrate his new forces into the line. More heavy howitzers were also required to break up the German defensive system that was now a "fortified zone ... constructed in depth," with individual trenches, strongpoints, and machine-gun nests affording mutual flanking support.[4]

However, the Germans upset the Entente plan for a joint assault by launching their Verdun offensive on February 21, 1916. The battle raged for nine months and bled both the French and Germans white in attritional warfare that would eventually leave 700,000 dead and maimed. As the terrible fighting went on, the French high command was slowly forced to pull back forces planned for the joint Somme offensive to stem the bloodletting at Verdun. The Somme offensive, which initially consisted of almost double the number of French divisions in comparison with the British, therefore increasingly became a British battle, with less and less French support in the south. As well, the French pleaded with the British to move up the launch date, even though preparations were not complete. At one meeting between the allies in May—meetings that were usually held in French, in acknowledgment of the leader of the alliance—Joffre exploded that if the British waited until August 15 to attack, as Haig believed necessary to properly harbour his resources, "The French Army would cease to exist."[5] Joffre pleaded, cajoled, and cried for a second front to reduce the pressure at Verdun, and Haig eventually agreed to assist with a rushed offensive, aware that the war would be lost if his principal ally folded.

Even though the British were forced to shoulder a greater load and had less time to prepare for the largest army operation in the history of British warfare, the goal of the Somme offensive remained largely the same as in smaller battles: to grind away at the enemy and break through the stalemated trench situation to the green fields beyond. The Somme region, relatively flat and devoid of ridges and built-up towns, was also the point where the British and French armies joined hands. To attack anywhere else along the line would require the disruptive moving of corps and armies of several hundred thousand men, and so those logistical constraints were avoided by attacking where the allies were already situated. This approach did not, however, help much in surprising the Germans.

The assault's utter lack of strategic surprise hardly mattered, though, as the Germans had long anticipated an attack here, and had for months been heavily fortifying towns and villages that checkered the Somme region. Within this defensive grid, the methodical defenders had prepared strong fixed defences based on deep dugouts, reinforced trenches, and the best fields of fire. What could be seen above ground—comprising raised fortifications and barbed wire—was supported by a deep underground labyrinth of defences. Unlike siege warfare of old, the fortifications were built not up but down. These underground fortresses would be hard to crack, but few other spots existed on the Western Front where the British and French could attack side by side.

AS THE HEMORRHAGE of the French forces continued at Verdun, the BEF took over the Somme operation. Kitchener's armies—divisions raised from volunteers—had arrived on the Western Front, but Haig and his generals believed those forces were unready for battle. With not enough time available to put the new men through a complete training regimen, the only solution was to subject them to a rigid doctrine. The infantry tactics were simplistic: lines of men—nearly standing shoulder to shoulder—would advance en masse to occupy the smoking remains of the enemy trenches after massive artillery bombardments first destroyed all resistance. "The artillery conquers, the infantry occupy," was a common, if glib, phrase during the war.

With such an unswerving faith in metal, the high command believed the infantry would only have to get to their targets in order to take control of what remained. The challenge was thought to lie not in overcoming enemy defenders, but in getting one's force into the shattered trenches as soon as possible. Officers feared that unless they monitored their newly arrived soldiers closely, ensuring that they advanced across No Man's Land in long lines, they would drop to the ground at first fire, find cover, and never get up again. In contrast, the French, who had learned in the cauldron of Verdun that lines of advancing men were apt to be cut apart by machine-gun fire, moved forward in small groups, supporting each other with fire, and then advancing again. One could accuse the British generals of butchery for enforcing such unimaginative tactics, but with insufficient time to prepare their forces for battle, they believed they had solved the riddle of the trenches by employing a weight of artillery fire that would simply wipe out the enemy front line, making it necessary only to advance in unison, a formation that could not be guaranteed if isolated platoons of men were firing and moving at their own speed.

Although the infantry tactics had now been established, the overall strategy for the Somme operation remained opaque. The two primary architects of the British part in the battle had contradictory visions. General Haig, commander-in-chief of the entire BEF, which now consisted of five armies each with its own army commander, wanted a breakthrough battle, and he pushed his army commanders to plan for grandiose operations that would allow for a breaking of the enemy line, followed by an immediate breakout into the German rear areas to restore mobility to the battlefield. He did not want a halting, limited operation, in which each phase of the battle required the infantry to wait for the artillery bombardment before advancing. Army commander General Henry Rawlinson, who was tasked with planning the operation, also wanted an end to the stalemate, but he could not see how his forces would break through the strong German lines without engaging in a series of setpiece, limited battles. The enemy defences were simply too strong, and the infantry's assault had already been tied to the massive artillery barrages, which, because of the range of the guns that were already situated far behind the lines, could only reach a few kilometres into the enemy lines. Haig's method of breaking through would require the limited number of British guns to be spread too thinly since many of the batteries would have to be ready for the exploitation phase and therefore not firing. This reduction in firepower would jeopardize the break-in phase of the battle. But each time Rawlinson and his staff presented their limited operation to Haig, the field marshal demanded something more ambitious that would allow him to send his cavalry through the "gap" to hunt the Hun in open fields. Or this is at least what Rawlinson thought was said, since he often misunderstood his superior's directives. Haig tended to grunt his way through most conversations, at best offering a few disjointed words, and after a meeting with him, officers could leave with diametrically opposed ideas but all believing they were following the field marshal's directives. As the planning unfolded, Haig continued to push for a breakthrough and Rawlinson continued to plan for his limited setpiece battle.

But both men were in agreement over the need for a devastating artillery bombardment to kick off the campaign, regardless of how it proceeded from there. After much analysis, the British believed their 1915 battles had come apart because the attacking forces had advanced on too narrow a front and without sufficient artillery support.[6] In contrast, at the Somme, the British would launch a hurricane bombardment of unprecedented fury, weight, and length, over an enormous front of 24,500 metres, and to a depth of several kilometres. The week-long artillery attack promised to crush the enemy as he cowered in his trenches: 1,732,873 shells would crash down on the German lines, making the bombardment the largest to that point in the history of warfare.[7] "We have the preponderance in artillery and in everything else, in fact, and we give them twenty shells to one," wrote one Canadian artillery officer. "How they live through our terrific bombardments is a wonder to me."[8]

Yet if the war proved one thing, it was that the infantry on both sides were resilient. Deep dugouts allowed many soldiers to survive a heavy shelling, even if the occupants were nearly driven mad by the concussion of fire. Further, a secondary German line of defence, some 3 kilometres behind the front line, was largely out of range of many of the field artillery guns, making the task of cutting the barbed wire there even more difficult. Another problem for the British was their reliance on shrapnel shells: although deadly against soldiers' bodies, these shells were not effective in cutting wire, and were almost entirely useless against troops submerged in deep dugouts. High explosives were needed, and these were in insufficient supply. Even worse, a high proportion of the British high explosive shells, both light and heavier calibres, were duds that failed to explode. The Entente munitions factories had begun to produce millions of high explosive shells per month, but many still remained crude and unfit for battle. Finally, the British gunners—who were just beginning to work with Royal Flying Corps planes and embrace scientific principles—had little proficiency in hitting hidden targets such as the dugouts and the enemy batteries in the rear, and many of the shells simply tore up the empty farmers' fields.

Despite these setbacks, the Entente guns rained down hell through the sheer enormity of their shellfire. The German defenders suffered terribly under the bombardment. Stephen Westman, a medical officer with the Germans, who, interestingly, served with the British in the Second World War, wrote of the shelling around Beaumont Hamel:

> For seven days and seven nights the ground shook under the constant impact of light and heavy shells, and in between the bombardments gas alarms were sounded, and we could hardly breathe. Our dugouts crumbled, tumbled on top of us, and our positions were razed to the ground. Again and again we had to dig ourselves and our comrades out of masses of blackened earth and splintered wooden beams. Often we found bodies crushed to pulp, or bunks full of suffocated soldiers. The 'drum-fire' never ceased. No food or water reached us. Down below, men became hysterical and their comrades had to knock them out, so as to prevent them from running away and exposing themselves to the deadly shell splinters. Even the rats panicked and sought refuge in our flimsy shelters; they ran up the walls, and we had to kill them with our spades.[9]

The Germans lost several thousand men who were buried alive, dismembered, or driven mad from the pounding shellfire. But enough of the defending garrison survived. With gritted teeth and tightened belts, many whispered that they would soon get their chance to strike back against their tormentors.

The Germans had used the previous two years to fortify the area, and they had prepared a vast underground city. The trench systems were visible to the aerial observers, but the deep dugouts remained hidden from the cameras. In their underground shelters, the Germans cowered under the sonic barrage of shells that pounded the earth and reverberated through the chalk. Many of the dugouts were 9 to 12 metres deep, and therefore largely impenetrable to all but the heaviest of British shells. Above ground, the German barbed wire had been thrown around the battlefield, but few clear paths could be found through the tangles of shredded steel. Much worse for the attacking infantry forces, hundreds of machine-gun positions in concrete dugouts remained unscathed. The front-line system was manned by some 32 German battalions, but about 65 battalions remained in reserve. Should the 158 attacking British battalions punch through the front lines, they would encounter even stiffer fighting to the rear.

AT BRITISH GENERAL HEADQUARTERS, while Haig was planning for the break-through attack, Rawlinson was trying to assess the barrage's damage to the enemy trench system. Aerial photographs indicated little activity in their lines or behind it. The continuous barrage made the front look like an endless series of factory chimneys spewing out white smoke. Yet no white flags of surrender were waved, and no signs of a general retreat were made. Did this mean that the defenders were dead, or were they simply holed up in the dugouts and waiting for the infantry to come out in the open, at which point they would exact their revenge? Whatever the case, both sides knew that an offensive was imminent, as all surprise was eliminated by the obvious hive of activity behind the British lines.

Closer to the front, British brigadiers and battalion commanders sent scouts and patrols forward to inspect the damage. Without access to the full array of intelligence that was fed to G.H.Q. or the army headquarters, their vision at the front was far more limited. But they did not like what they were seeing. Intelligence patrols reported that the preparatory barrage had not cut the barbed wire. While munitions industries had pumped out shells by the millions, the perfection of fuses remained problematic. British fuses were still not yet sensitive enough and therefore tended not to go off until a shell buried itself in the ground, leaving much of the wire unscathed. The intelligence patrols travelled over ground pitted by hundreds of thousands of shells, but still the barbed wire lay deep. The infantry tried to take care of the problem themselves by blowing holes in the wire with Bangalore torpedoes—steel pipes up to 6 metres long, filled with explosives—but even as they did this, hurried reports were compiled by battalion officers at the front for their superiors in the rear, noting that no attack could possibly succeed.

In the extremely hierarchical structure of the British high command, generals and staff officers did not encourage criticism or dissenting remarks. Even though General Rawlinson, commander of the Fourth Army, was a forward-thinking senior officer, he came from a generation that brooked little creative input from his juniors; one shocking order from him before the Somme battle warned, "All criticism by subordinates ... of orders received from superior authority will, in the end, recoil on the heads of the critics."[10] Rawlinson was not alone in holding this rigid view; for instance, it was not uncommon for officers who reported on the failure of shelling to clear wire to be removed, as they were derided as insufficiently aggressive or as too fixated on determining the state of enemy defences rather than instilling aggressive qualities in their men.[11] But even the high command could not ignore the series of reports up and down the line indicating that the artillery had failed in its task, and the offensive was delayed two more days to clear the wire. So much faith had been funnelled into the "Big Push" that it would have taken a strong man, very secure in his position, to call off the battle, especially given the desperate situation at Verdun. Haig was not such a man, and none of his army or corps commanders pressed the issue. And so the British Tommies prepared for battle.

THE BOMBARDMENT, accompanied by a series of mines that were blown under the German positions, continued until 7:30 A.M. on July 1. In its last hour, the barrage escalated to a hurricane of some 3,500 shells fired per minute, becoming what the Germans called *Trommelfeuer* (drumfire).[12] But when the bombardment reached its crescendo, it stopped as synchronized watches struck 7:30. Silence fell.

Whistles blew, and thousands of Tommies followed their officers out of their trenches into the dusty, shell-cratered battlefield, slowly walking towards the enemy lines that had been annihilated—or so they were told. A jovial attitude prevailed among some of the troops, as this, they believed, was finally the beginning of the end. After the battle, newspapers widely reported that a few plucky officers and men kicked soccer balls, urging the troops forward. One suspects, however, that men went forward with a grim determination, and that the supposed laddish activities of boys "out for a stroll" were few and far between. The rank and file were more likely focused on the crippling weight on their backs, as they were laden like pack mules, carrying more than sixty pounds of equipment each. Panting and sweating from the exertion and anxiety, the infantry wanted only to dump their packs in the supposedly still-smoking enemy trenches, and then light up a Woodbine.

Then the German MG-08s opened up, each gun firing up to 500 bullets a minute. The unsuspecting infantry, stumbling forward, were mowed down, as gunners swept their weapons in situated arcs, first from right to left, and then from front to rear.[13] Not all Tommies were advancing in straight lines, with some instead rushing forward in smaller groups to present fewer targets, advancing in short bounds, shooting and moving, before going to ground and then advancing again.[14] No matter what was tried, however, the enemy machine-gunners laid down a terrible fire, slaughtering soldiers en masse. Then, German artillery in the rear, much of which had remained silent in order not to be identified before the battle, opened up with a plunging counter-barrage of shrapnel that further tore apart the advancing infantry, killing and wounding thousands even before they reached their start lines.

Although no Canadian infantry units were involved in the attack on July 1, two CEF batteries of heavy artillery supported the assault. But Canadians did participate in the battle: those forgotten men serving in British units. One of them, Lieutenant F.A. Day, had been commissioned early in the war with the Middlesex Regiment, which served in the 29th British Division. That division had fought with distinction in the Gallipoli campaign, and one of the other twelve battalions in the division was the 1st Newfoundland Regiment, which was to be wiped out on the first day of the Somme. Of his experience at the Somme, Day remembered, "The first of July was a beautiful summer day, and I do not think that any person who is living today who went over the parapet that day will ever forget it. A slight breeze was blowing towards the German line, and everything seemed dead in front of us; the grass had lost its colour from the gas we had sent over during the seven days' bombardment. Our line could be traced as far as the eye could see by the difference in the colour— green on our side…. I shall not dwell on the attack; it was too awful for words…. The Germans simply annihilated us with machine-guns."[15] Day was one of the few survivors from his regiment, and he eagerly accepted a transfer to the Canadians, who were desperate for his experience and made him a brigade musketry officer. While the Canadian infantry battalions were lucky to escape involvement in the slaughter on July 1, their time would come.

By the end of the day, of the estimated 120,000 Tommies who had attacked, more than 19,000 had been killed and another 38,000 wounded.[16] "As far as you could see there were all these bodies lying out there…. Some were without legs, some were legs without bodies, arms without bodies. A terrible sight. They'd been churned up by shells even after they were killed," recounted one British corporal.[17]

THE FIRST DAY of the Somme offensive has gone down as one of the greatest disasters in military history, partly because so much was expected of the operation. Generations of commentators have derided the uninspired infantry tactics without acknowledging the rushed nature of the operation, which necessitated, at least in the minds of the British high command, tight control over the advance. Even when a number of British fighting units took matters into their own hands and attacked using more flexible tactics, or pushed forward into No Man's Land before the barrage ended in order to get a jump on the enemy, they too achieved little success. But despite the carnage at the sharp end, Haig did not call off the battle, as he was well aware that the first day of the Somme was the 132nd day of the campaign at Verdun. There, the French were being bled white in their position of dogged defence, as summed up in their rallying cry, *"Ils ne passeront pas"* ("They shall not pass"). Although the July 1 battle at the Somme is etched into the collective memory of the war, it is worth remembering that the campaign on this front continued for another 141 days. Hope and enthusiasm for a breakthrough were eventually replaced by a grim determination to see it through to the bitter end; even Sir Douglas Haig began to describe the operation as a "wearing-out battle," although he hoped that when the Germans broke, his forces would exploit the situation.[18]

The British armies continued to be thrown against the German positions in a series of battering-ram onslaughts. In the two weeks following the July 1 disaster, the British attacked along the line, often in piecemeal battles, to capture key tactical positions that would provide more favourable areas from which to launch future operations. After two weeks of bloody skirmishes, Rawlinson launched an audacious and successful night attack on July 14, but it achieved only limited gains. For the following two months—until the next push, on September 15—the BEF chipped away at the German lines, and both sides concentrated their artillery on smaller areas of the front, wasting precious resources. The July 14 to September 14 phase seemed to have little strategic direction, with the fighting being done for the sake of straightening out lines or simply wearing down the enemy. The "Big Push" was increasingly being called the "Big Fuck-up" by soldiers.

The battles of Pozières, Longueval, Delville Wood, and Guillemont—all fought during these two months—left thousands of dead, and for little gain. These nondescript villages and woods had been objectives since the first day of the offensive, and they all held out under the strongest bombardments. Capturing these strongpoints entailed hand-to-hand fighting as the bloody tide of battle swept back and forth through the ruined villages and blackened shards of once-full forests. Convergent fields of fire and mutually supporting strongpoints, along with ample counterattacking reinforcements, made victory in the morning easily reversible by the afternoon, and, if anyone was left alive, another attack and counterattack was possible that same night. The seesaw nature of the fighting chewed up battalions in a relentless grind. In two months, only 8 square kilometres were captured—at a cost of another 100,000 British casualties.[19] These figures recalled the worst losses of the first day of July, but soon even these shocking numbers of casualties were washed away in a sea of blood. More troops were needed, and soon almost all the British divisions were being funnelled into the battle. Few would escape the slaughter. The British and Dominion soldiers steeled themselves for the unimaginable when they heard they were heading to the Somme.

CHAPTER 32

"YOU PEOPLE AT HOME CAN'T REALIZE HOW BLOODY THIS WAR REALLY IS"

Preparing for Battle

"It may be taken for granted that in attacking the front system of the enemy's trenches the first three lines will be wiped out; the fourth may reach the enemy's second line; the fifth may take it."[1] Such doctrinal predictions, which were revealed in training manuals and shared with officers and men, were less than inspiring for those at the sharp end. Faced with these odds, the Canadian infantry and their commanders at headquarters strove to devise new tactics, in the hope of reducing the blood sacrifice required to achieve victory on the Western Front. Although the Canadians had missed the first part of the Somme campaign, they were preparing furiously for the moment when they would be ordered to that front.

A British Expeditionary Force and Canadian Corps attack doctrine stipulated the importance of wave attacks in overrunning enemy strongpoints through the sheer force of numbers. Most infantry attacks involved two companies, with their platoons echeloned in a number of waves and these waves in turn broken down to the section level. The platoon and company commanders tried to keep the waves

THE PLATOON

Taking an average strength of 36 O.R. and H.Q. at 4 O.R.

(Showing 2 Platoons in 2 Waves, with the right the outer flank.)

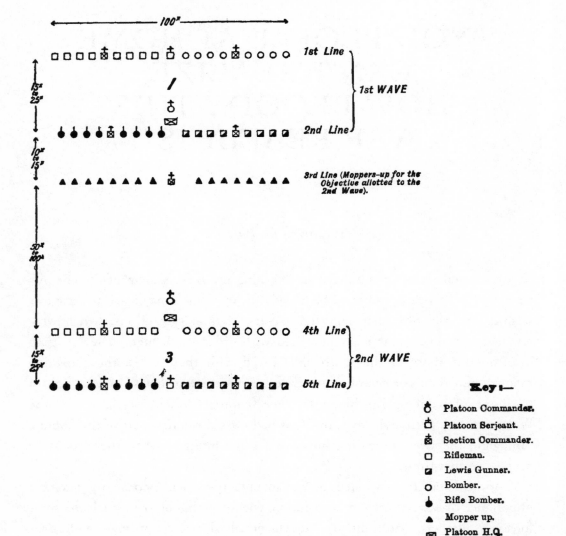

*Note the platoon and company formations advancing in echeloned
waves of Lewis gunners, riflemen, bombers, and "mopping up" units.*

50 metres apart, and sometimes further, with the main push coming from the first wave of riflemen moving forward behind an artillery bombardment.

Lessons learned from 1915 battles indicated the necessity of dispersing troops on the battlefield; but without corresponding firepower or tactics, such thinning out left attacking forces too weak. The Canadians were struggling with the proper weighting and ratio of men on the battlefield, and variations to the attack doctrine were made throughout the corps. Some infantry battalions had begun to experiment with having soldiers move forward in looser formations in the hope of achieving greater dispersal on the battlefield, and the "waves" thus did not always take the form of long lines of men advancing in lockstep. Brigadier Archibald Macdonell, the fiery commander of the 7th Brigade, joked that if they kept thinning out their forces, "the order of battle of the future will be eight men and a boy in column."[2] Operational and training reports from the period show some attacks going in behind three or four waves, with Lewis machine-gunners up in the first wave or second, and grenadiers holding back or kept on the flanks. But the attack doctrine lacked uniformity within the corps, which was in fact beneficial since it had been acknowledged that applying cookie-cutter tactics to varying enemy formations, time requirements, and terrain would likely result in failure. Despite these useful variations in tactics, however, the British and Canadian doctrine continued to tie the infantry's advance to the artillery's barrage, as only the latter could destroy the enemy defences. This often meant that the infantry lacked the ability to manoeuvre on the battlefield and was lashed to strict artillery timetables that allowed for almost no deviation from pre-planned orders, notwithstanding what was happening at the sharp end.

But still the infantry experimented with finding ways to solve the deadlock of trench warfare. Private George Kempling of the 26th Battalion—a former machinist from Toronto whose amputated index finger served as a mark of his trade—offered important insight into this new training in late August and early September: "We practiced open order work, going ahead in short spurts and flopping quickly in the mud, then getting up quickly, running a few yards and dropping again behind any cover you could get. This is all practice for the open fighting we are to have down on the Somme."[3] This increasingly decentralized infantry advance, which was less reliant on commanders to keep the soldiers in rigid lines, drew not only on updated tactics described in manuals such as SS 109, which had been issued across the British army in May 1916, but also on the prewar tactics of the British regular army and even the Canadian militia, which had practised advancing in fire and movement tactics, with sections bounding forward, going to ground, and laying down fire to allow other sections to advance, as they slowly closed the distance with the enemy. Some of this prewar initiative had been lost in the fighting in 1915 and early 1916, when the high command tried to protect the infantry by tying them closely to the artillery. This doctrine had, however, been unsuccessful, as the artillery proved it could not offer enough suppressing or destructive fire to smother the enemy's defences or guns, and so the infantry were often left abandoned and without the tools to fight their way forward.

But these revised tactics were more than a return to prewar manoeuvres of fire and movement, as they included a new degree of decentralization and empowerment of junior officers and NCOs to deal with the ever-changing situation on the battlefield. Kempling jotted in his diary that his battalion prepared for "the new kind of fighting on the Somme":

> [V]ery important, we practiced open fighting with the responsible men falling out (killed or wounded) and the next in command automatically taking charge. This took place simultaneously in several positions both in major and minor positions. We practiced in company formation—two platoons in line, with fixed bayonets, with bombers on both flanks and a couple of Lewis gun crews in front a little. The third platoon supported and carried picks, shovels, and sandbags. The 4th platoon was in reserve. Every man in the company is made conversant with the immediate plan of battle and the battalion and brigade headquarters.[4]

Kempling's statement that "every man in the company is made conversant with the immediate plan" reveals an important breakthrough in the devolution of command. Surprisingly, historians have generally associated this training in decentralized tactics solely with the winter of 1916–1917, more than half a year later—and after the slaughter of the Somme had revealed a necessary change in tactics. But the Canadian Corps was already applying the principles of decentralization before the troops arrived on the Somme, as the high command was aware that the infantry needed more flexible tactics. Such tactics included the greater application of firepower by Lewis gunners and grenadiers, which in turn freed units at the sharp end to practise greater decentralization, as massed riflemen were no longer needed to win the fire-fight. If Lewis gunners could lay down a steady stream of fire, the other components of the section or platoon could advance on the enemy in leaps and bounds, firing as they moved, but taking cover when necessary. The infantry was further empowered by the instruction that, should their officers be knocked out, they were to continue on to their objectives. The brutal fighting that would follow on the Somme revealed that leaders would indeed fall within the firestorm, and that the success of the operation would depend on the NCOs and privates, who would have to drive the push home. The high command underscored its new-found faith in decentralization in its revised doctrine: "All subordinates must be prepared to act on their own initiative. The one unforgivable sin when in difficulties is to do nothing and wait for orders."[5]

OVER THE SUMMER of 1916, the mistrusted and frequently malfunctioning Ross rifle was finally discarded by the few Canadian units still using it. Now, all soldiers were equipped with the robust Lee-Enfield. No more bayonets rattling off when the rifle was discharged; no more backsights that were easily broken; and most important, significantly less jammed ammunition. However, though the evidence of the Ross's failure was monumental, some infantrymen continued to swear by it even as it was removed.[6] Others testified that it really didn't matter what rifle the infantry carried, as they rarely had a chance to fire their long arm. For example, in four months of service, which included the Battle of Festubert, Private Charles Pearce discharged his weapon only four times: "once at a bird, once at an aeroplane, once at a fish, and once at a German," whom Pearce thought he hit.[7] On the empty battlefield, with soldiers stuck in deep holes in the ground, regular infantrymen had few opportunities to practise their marksmanship. Pearce became so fed up with the trenches that he transferred to the Royal Flying Corps, only to be shot down over the Somme.

Also during the summer, and into the fall, the Canadians were issued identification flashes, known as "battle patches." Each of the divisions had a distinguishing colour: red for the 1st, blue (initially black) for the 2nd, grey for the 3rd, and green for the 4th, the last of which had not yet joined the Canadian Corps. Worn on the upper sleeve, the badges displayed additional symbols—squares, circles, and triangles—distinguishing every unit in the corps. The patches became an enormous source of pride for the soldiers. The men of the 1st Division eventually referred to their division as the "old red patch," and these battle patches became akin to the traditional regimental colours that fighting units had carried into battle for generations. The divisional patches and colours also soon made their way to a prominent position on the soldiers' steel Brodie helmets, further allowing troops to recognize one another and reinforcing units' esprit de corps.

As the corps had suffered almost 9,000 casualties at Mount Sorrel, the surviving core of Canadian veterans was again augmented by new recruits, who were promptly taught the lore of the battalions, the unwritten rules, and how to even the odds during the first terrifying weeks at the front. These new men would need all the help they could get. The addition of an entrenching battalion for each of the divisions also meant less work for the infantry. Upon hearing of this development, more than a few men must have scoffed at such a seemingly wild rumour, but it proved to be true. As the poor bloody infantry were celebrating their good fortune, Haig ordered General Byng and his Canadians to the Somme battlefield.

Canadian forces relieved the 1st Australian Corps at Pozières at the beginning of September. Moving the Canadian Corps from Ypres in Belgium to the Somme battlefield had been an enormous challenge and had tested the resources and skills of the staff officers, to whom had fallen the task of working out marching timetables, arranging food, and tending to all the other necessities of moving the equivalent of a large Canadian town across a distance of 140 kilometres. The accomplishment of this task was a sign of the growing professionalism among the staff of the Canadian Corps.

When the Canadians arrived, they were integrated into General Sir Hubert Gough's Reserve Army, later renamed the Fifth Army. At age forty-five, Gough was the youngest army commander in France. He came from an illustrious British military family, where, incredibly, his uncle, father, and brother had all been awarded the

Victoria Cross. As a thrusting cavalry commander, he made a meteoric rise from brigadier in 1914 to general by 1916. His aggressive attitude appealed to Haig, who felt that many of his army commanders were too plodding and slow. But Gough's men often paid for his haphazard approach to planning at the Somme, as he tended to look beyond his initial objectives—objectives that had already proven to be extremely difficult to achieve. Infantrymen grumbled that talking about a break-through was pointless when they could not walk 10 metres without encountering massed machine-gun fire.

Haig wanted Byng and his men to acclimatize themselves to the Somme battlefield by arriving almost two weeks before the September 15 offensive, as the

Tens of thousands of Entente soldiers marched through Albert on the Somme, under the watchful eye of the Leaning Virgin. According to legend, the war would end when she fell. Hopeful soldiers prayed for the Virgin's descent and their salvation.

fighting here was far more intense than anything they had seen, even in the terrible Ypres salient. Thousands of Entente troops were under canvas on what was called the Brickfields, northwest of Albert, creating an awe-inspiring sea of tents. The Somme district and battlefield was divided into three zones—those of fighting, assembly, and rest—with three corresponding headquarters located at Albert, Rubempre, and Canaples. Soldiers rarely spoke of the latter two areas, but Albert stood out in their minds as a sepulchre. Along with hundreds of thousands of British troops, the Canadians passed through the bombed-out husk of Albert, and saw, high atop the ruined cathedral, a golden statue of the Virgin Mary over-looking a wasteland of destruction. She had been knocked askew, and lay below the horizontal line, but engineers had bolted her down. The broken virgin seemed to be offering her blessing or weeping for the soldiers as they marched into damnation. Superstitious soldiers attached symbolic significance to the image, infusing it with their hopes for deliverance: "The Legend is that when the statue falls the war will be over. If I was sure of this the Virgin would certainly come down tonight," wrote Major W.H. Hewgill of the 31st Battalion in his private diary.[8] More than a few soldiers echoed Hewgill's silent prayer, but the Virgin Mary refused to fall. And so the Canadians moved into the line, beneath her outstretched arms.

THE VAST EXPANSES of land on the Somme front would remind many of the Western Canadian boys of the wide, flat prairies. There was no extensive intercon-nected system of communications; no large industrial base that had to be captured in order to strangle German industry; in fact, no major cities. The strategic objec-tive was to break through the enemy lines. Later, when that had failed, the goal was to punish the enemy and break his will. One of the longest and largest battles of all time was fought over blasted farmers' fields and tiny villages.

On September 3, before the Australians left the dirty region where the Canadians would fight, the "Diggers," as the Australians were known, launched one final attack against Mouquet Farm, a fortified defensive system that was situated on the main German line. Its capture would compromise the Germans' position at Thiepval, a strongpoint that acted as a hinge connecting several enemy trench systems. Known as "Mucky Farm" to the men, the position had been held for months and was built on an underground city of concrete bunkers and cellars.

This final Australian attack failed, as artillery had been unable to destroy the dug-in defenders, and when the Australians attacked over open ground, they were shot to pieces. The 13th Canadian Battalion reinforced the shattered Australian units, and in the battle's bloody aftermath, Lieutenant Harry McCleave of the 13th Battalion noted in his diary that both he and his German opposites had sent men out under a Red Cross flag as part of an informal ceasefire to collect the dead and wounded. The 13th's stretcher-bearers brought in one stoic Australian who had lain in No Man's Land for four days, and whose fortitude compelled McCleave to comment, "[I] have changed my opinion of the Australians. Individually, the men are splendid and if given a job to do they carry it out."[9] McCleave clearly did not blame the Aussies for failing to capture Mouquet Farm, and too many soldiers had already given their lives in attempts to conquer this position for anyone to think it would fall easily. McCleave would also do his job in the coming fight, eventually dying from gunshot wounds to the right arm and thigh in the failed Canadian attempt to capture Regina Trench on October 8, 1916.

As their relief of the Australians continued throughout early September, the Canadians found little sanctuary in their trenches, as the chalk in the ground often showed as white streaks against the mud, making the trenches highly visible to the enemy. The artillery pounded the positions, and experienced German snipers—who had studied the landscape and knew the weak parts of the defences—took their toll. First Division commander Arthur Currie noted privately in his diary: "absolutely continuous shelling night and day. Our casualties very severe and trenches very bad."[10] This was a hard introduction to the Somme for the bloodied Canadians. Two companies of the 13th were nearly annihilated by hammering shellfire as the men crouched in their trenches. In the first seven days of September, the Canadian Corps lost 769 men although the troops almost never strayed from their forward trenches.[11]

Death came every hour—nearly every minute. George Magann, an artillery forward observer from Toronto and a future Canadian diplomat, recounted in his diary: "I had the rather unsettling experience of having a man pass me in the trenches and be shot a moment later.... It sounded so close (the rifle discharge) that

I thought it must have been the accidental discharge of a rifle in the trenches. The man had had the top of his head blown off…. the trenches were in a frightful condition and snipers were always lurking to fire through gaps."[12] With the intense shelling rarely slowing, let alone stopping, the infantry dug deep, encountering rotting bodies and other sickening sights. Regiments that had passed through the area could be identified by corpses' rotting uniforms and tarnished cap badges.

Even a few hours in the front lines convinced soldiers they were in for a new type and intensity of warfare. "My heart went down to my boots for a while, but I got it back again. I guess it was too wet for it to stay there," joked Private John McNab of the 38th Battalion after his first time in the line.[13] In a quick letter to his father, Private Ronald Main, a former surveyor from Amhurst, Nova Scotia, conveyed the indescribable quality of life in the front lines: "I am writing this in an old trench (not so very old either) and only wish I could tell you where I am and what I see just around here, but am a poor hand at describing anything on paper, so will not attempt it, all I can say is that I have seen more in the last few days than I ever saw in my life before or expected to and then I haven't seen anything compared with some of the boys who have been out here months."[14] There was no means of escape and nowhere to run. The infantry could only go deeper into the earth to hide from the terrible fire.

But the Canadians were not content simply to sit back and be used as cannon fodder. To prepare for the offensive that they knew was coming, commanders launched a series of minor operations in order to push out the Canadian lines and gain favourable jumping off positions. The 2nd Battalion was ordered to attack in the early hours of September 9. The infantry in this three-company assault were equipped with two Mills grenades each and 170 rounds of small-arms ammunition; select troops were also issued with stores of grenades, sandbags, and Very lights (flares) to alert headquarters of progress. The barrage opened up at 4:45 A.M., and the infantry, with bayonets fixed, followed behind it three minutes later in evenly spaced waves.

The barrage was strong, but shells were firing short—into the advancing Canadians. Captain W.W. Murray noted that the Germans refused to be cowed, and instead of diving into their dugouts, they rose above the trench to fire at the onrushing attackers. "Men dropped into shellholes, seeking to exchange shots with the Germans, while at the same time working their way forward on their stomachs."[15] As the 2nd Battalion closed the gap, officers rose up, exposing themselves to fire, and led a bayonet charge. The Canadians lost about fifteen percent of their strength in the attack, but destroyed the defenders from the German 212th Reserve Regiment, bayoneting them to death or shooting them as they retreated overland and down communication trenches.

But the real challenge would be in holding the newly captured ground. A second wave of troops, 50 metres behind, with shovels fastened across their backs, immediately began to consolidate the trench, reversing the firesteps and digging new communication trenches back to the original lines. Annoyed at having lost the trenches, the Germans laid down a heavy machine-gun barrage to isolate the attackers from reinforcing troops coming from the rear, and then launched several counterattacks. The German doctrine was *"Halten, was zu halten ist,"* meaning "Hold on to whatever can be held."[16] Following this policy, quick counterattacks were arranged to throw back the weakened and likely confused enemy forces, who always lost troops in the advance and who would be working hard to strengthen the shattered trenches they had occupied. Such lightning counterattacks often worked, although they could be costly, as troops were roused from their dugouts and thrown into battle with almost no opportunity to reconnoitre the ground or fully apprehend the situation.

Several counterattacks were beaten off in a frenzy of fighting by the 2nd Battalion, but they kept coming. After more than twelve hours of fighting, the Canadians were hemorrhaging badly. And front-line morale plummeted later in the day when the troops were bombed by their own artillery. Most of the errant guns were quickly called off, but desperate officers searched all day for a lone 18-pounder firing somewhere in the rear, dutifully dropping shells short into the Canadian lines. From the other side, the Germans continued to probe the steadily weakened forward defences. Cut off from the rear, Canadian officers grimly sent runners back through the shellfire, aware that this was likely a suicide mission, but knowing also that the front could only be held with the aid of more Lewis-gun ammunition and Mills bombs, of which only a handful of the 1,000 they had started with remained by the end of the day.

Although the Canadians were pressed in on all sides, individual acts of staggering bravery kept the Germans at bay. With many of the 2nd Battalion's officers knocked out, it fell to men such as Corporal Leo Clarke to exert authority. All day long, "Nobby" Clarke, as the good-looking and popular corporal was known, manned a tenuous block in the trench. As trenches ran for miles, it was essential to carve out a manageable position at a point along their length and then build a block or barrier from sandbags, wood, wire, or any other available materials. But the Germans pressed against these positions, with the fighting degenerating into hand-to-hand combat after grenades, rifles, and bayonets had taken their toll in the narrow trenches. At one point, with his companions all wounded or killed, Clarke alone held off a group of twenty-two Germans, emptying his revolver into their ranks twice, then grabbing captured enemy rifles and firing those until he was out of ammunition. One German officer lunged at him, spearing him through the leg below the knee with a bayonet, but still Clarke fought on, wrestling with and eventually impaling the man with his own bayonet. All but one of the enemy was killed, and the one survivor was taken prisoner. Clarke was awarded the Victoria Cross for his desperate defence against overwhelming odds.

Clarke had lived in Winnipeg on Pine Street, and, incredibly, two other Victoria Cross winners—Sergeant Major Frederick Hall and Lieutenant Robert Shankland—had lived on the same street. Three recipients of the Victoria Cross coming from one street is no doubt a situation unique throughout the entire British Empire, and it was fitting then that the residents of Winnipeg later renamed the street Valour Road. Clarke would never see the rededication ceremony, however, or even know that he had been awarded the Empire's highest award for bravery, as he was killed five weeks after his valiant stand in further Somme fighting. A shell did to Leo Clarke what nearly two dozen Germans could not. He was buried alive, entombed under dirt and sandbags. His brother, Charlie, who was with Leo at the time, desperately dug for him in the debris, and found him under the crushing weight of the earth and sandbags. He was paralyzed from a broken back, and died a week later on October 19.

Back on September 9, the 2nd Battalion's bombers, riflemen, and Lewis gunners were increasingly being wiped out by enemy attacks. Water and ammunition remained in critically short supply and the wounded suffered terribly, many bleeding to death for want of stretcher-bearers, who had all been pressed into the desperate defence. But the battalion held on, throwing back the Germans.

The survivors were relieved on September 10, having lost 48 killed and 147 wounded in clearing a trench front of some 500 metres across and 200 metres deep. This amounted to almost a man killed or wounded for every metre of advance.[17] "You people at home can't realize how bloody this war really is. There are some awful sights," wrote William Curtis, a veteran of the First Contingent and a machine-gunner. But he remained optimistic nonetheless, vowing: "Our turn will come soon. I'd like to see the Kaiser do a bit of suffering."[18] The Canadians would indeed have their turn in the coming months, but Curtis, like more than 6,000 of his mates, would be killed in the fierce fighting that was to follow on the Somme.

CHAPTER 33

"LOOKING FORWARD TO A CRACK AT FRITZ"

The Canadians on the Somme, September 1916

Robert Clements of the 25th Battalion, a former employee of the Bank of Montreal in Yarmouth, Nova Scotia, had a harsh introduction to the Somme. He was sent forward as part of a large working party to dig a 2-metre-deep line in which telephone wires would be laid from the front to the rear. As the weary infantrymen moved forward, picks and shovels resting on shoulders, a German barrage began to fall around them. Almost no cover could be found, except for an old, unused communication trench about 100 metres away, known as "Dead Man's Trench." The trench was full of the rotting bodies of Germans who had been caught in the middle of a relief rotation by a British artillery barrage, and so bad was the mess of three-week-old decomposing and maggoty men that no one had the stomach to clean it up. "It was either pile into Dead Man's Trench among the rotten bodies or stay above ground and get killed," remembered Clements. The combat veterans made the hard call, and ran like hell for the trench. Diving in to the mush of former human beings was an indescribable experience for Clements, and he noted that although his comrades "were all tough experienced men who had been through all kinds of dirty combat conditions, within minutes every man had lost his last three meals."[1] After the target-rich area was cleared, the German fire moved off to harass other parts of the front. The slime-covered infantry stumbled to the rear in a daze, expecting some sort of bath to be arranged for them, but their officers sent them back 9 kilometres to the front a few hours later to finish the job. The men worked all night digging the telephone line, sweating in their rotten, flesh-sodden uniforms. Rest eluded everyone on the Somme, and all men would be pushed to the limits of endurance. As Clements put it, "There were not any decorations or medals in the ration bags in recognition of that kind of activity. Just another weary and dirty job completed and then forgotten, with scarcely a word of thanks or encouragement from on high."[2]

SEVERAL DAYS of trench raiding and bombing followed the fighting for trenches around Mouquet Farm on September 9, after which the Canadians made final preparations for their part in the Battle of Flers-Courcelette on September 15. This second major Somme offensive (the first being the July 1 debacle) would be fought over an 11-kilometre expanse and would involve three British armies. After two and a half months on the Somme, and with few gains to show for over 100,000 deaths, Sir Douglas Haig hoped that this offensive would break the stalemate, crush the now weary German defenders, and allow his exploitation force, the cavalry, to charge through the gap and fan out to wreak havoc in the enemy's rear.

In captured letters and diaries, the British found evidence that German morale might be broken. For example, one unnamed German wrote: "We are here on the Somme in such an artillery fire as I have never experienced—indeed no-one has in the whole war. Cover there is none, we live in a hell-hole and defend ourselves to the last man.... It's frightful; such murder here."[3] But were letters like this representative of the entire German army, and did such feelings of fear and desperation translate into a loss of combat effectiveness? When the chief of the imperial general staff, General Sir William Robertson, was asked by a senior British politician if the Germans were close to breaking, Robertson replied truthfully that he did not know the extent of the enemy's losses but felt they "were losing as many and more than we were."[4] Such vague calculations were not likely to win the battle, or the war.

The only solution to the stalemate seemed to be to attack again. Perhaps, it was hoped, one more push would knock in the German front door, and the rotten walls would collapse with it. With no other way to force Germany's hand, and with sideshow expeditions to other fronts having ended in absolute failure or in stale-mates that consumed men and resources, the main battle front had to be against the German armies in the west. The naval blockade around Germany was tightening its noose, but no one expected capitulation for several years. And in the meantime, the French were still losing thousands of men a day at Verdun, and the Russians were pleading for a renewed offensive to draw off the terrible mauling they were receiving in the east. In this coalition war, General Haig felt compelled to order another round of attacks.

The British forces would drive forward with eleven divisions on an 11,000-metre front between the villages of Flers and Courcelette. The Canadians, as part of Sir Hubert Gough's Reserve Army, would advance with two divisions to capture Courcelette and the surrounding region, north of the important Albert–Bapaume road. Formerly innocuous farming villages and woods were now deadly patches of ground that had to be won metre by bloody metre. The names of ridges, trenches, and rubble that had once been villages were bandied about as if their capture was as important as taking Berlin or Munich. Given the amount of chatter surrounding Courcelette's importance, more than a few Canadians would be surprised to find the place no bigger than a small Canadian hamlet. Thousands fell in the fighting over this now ruined farmland—soil that for years after the battle would harvest only iron and corpses.

This second major offensive was planned on the assumption that the German defenders had been ground down to a point where one more major setpiece battle would break them. Having lost some 320,000 men by early September, the German combat divisions were indeed worn out. Their infantry were outnumbered 2 to 1 and their artillery outgunned by a ratio of 1.5 to 1.[5] But the Germans continued to have the advantage of being on the defence, with their deep and multi-layered forti-fications providing essential protection from the drumfire bombardments.

For the Entente forces, the last two months of fighting had revealed that limited objectives could usually be captured, but massive bombardments alerted the enemy to where exactly the attack would occur. In previous costly battles, German rein-forcements had been rushed to back up forward units, and making any headway beyond minor bites into the opposite lines had proved nearly impossible. The

Entente needed to find new ways to sharpen their attack doctrine, or their forth-coming offensive would likely be destroyed in a storm of enemy fire and fierce counterattacks.

Deep trenches, barbed wire, and machine guns had to be knocked out or masked to allow attackers an opportunity to get to their objectives. But German defences were linked and interlocking. When one trench fell, it did not automatically make the others untenable. Most often, the attacking troops found that capturing a position not only failed to destabilize the enemy line but that the occupiers in fact became more vulnerable because the newly won position jutted into the enemy line, and counterattacks frequently decapitated the weakened lead forces. Added to this very real problem, the British, always looking to prepare for the big breakthrough, were obsessive about straightening the line—like neurotic housecleaners. While this straightening in fact made sense from one perspective, since straight trenches made it easier to coordinate artillery barrages, for the soldiers engaged in these isolated but still costly attacks on enemy positions jutting into their lines, the result seemed nothing more than useless slaughter. Thousands of soldiers were lost in these minor engagements that seemed to epitomize fighting for the sake of fighting.

But Haig and his generals were not simply callous butchers, rubbing their blood-stained hands with glee as they planned pointless attacks from their safe château miles behind the fighting, even if this is how popular memory tends to construct these men. The generals were desperate to find some way to support the men at the front, and much faith was put into a new tactic and a new weapon: the creeping barrage and the tank.

THE CREEPING BARRAGE was born out of both the failure of artillery to fully support the infantry in previous battles and the impossibility of having shellfire destroy all enemy strongpoints before the infantry went over the top. Artillery support was essential to an infantry attack, but the gunners had to have an over-whelming concentration of fire to match the inherent power of the defensive. To assist the infantry at the sharp end, the gunners had to not only saturate the objective but also target positions on the flanks that could lay in enfilading fire. They were further tasked with stopping the enemy from rushing up reinforcements, and preventing the enemy guns from laying down a counter-barrage, which required carrying out heavy shelling behind the primary objective, in an interdiction role. In turn, the artillery fire alerted the enemy to the direction and location from which the attack was coming, and their artillery could fire almost blindly into that part of No Man's Land through which any attacking force would have to advance. Interdiction fire was also part of the defensive fire plan, as it would cause additional casualties to reinforcing units and to those groups tasked with rushing supplies forward to support the spearhead. Despite heavier and longer barrages that chewed up the enemy lines in advance of Entente offensives, some defenders always survived, including troops at the front, isolated and hidden machine-gunners between the first and second trench lines, and gunners in the rear. Attackers were always met with fire.

The creeping barrage was therefore based on suppressing, not destroying, the enemy. Previous barrages, such as those at Mount Sorrel three months earlier, had not only smothered the front but had also dropped down on specific enemy objectives before lifting to new targets further to the rear. But these "lifts" were several hundred metres apart and were often targeted far in front of the infantry in order to reduce friendly fire incidents. No matter how effective this lifting barrage, however, once the shells moved off the target, the German defenders were able to rise from their dugouts and shoot the attackers caught in the fire zone. Therefore, the creeping barrage used tighter lifts, leaving longer intervals between them. This allowed the infantry to catch up to their barrage, "hugging" it all the way to the objective, thus reducing the time the enemy had to emerge from his dugout.

High explosive and shrapnel shells in the creeping barrage rained down on the enemy front. Like a steel rake dragging through No Man's Land, the barrage first tore through the enemy outposts, then through the front lines, and finally into the rear areas. Major General Arthur Currie, who was increasingly becoming Byng's most trusted general, studied artillery barrages in past operations and recommended that the "infantry should be taught to follow the artillery barrage as closely as a horse will follow a nosebag filled with corn." Currie acknowledged that hugging the wall of fire would inevitably result in casualties from what has come to be known as "friendly fire," but in the harsh world of the Western Front, he declared, "it is far better to lose a few of our men from our own Artillery fire than to sacrifice hundreds by hostile machine gun fire."[6] This revolutionary use of artillery was based on the bloody lessons learned by the British in the Somme cauldron of the previous two and a half months, and the method had been shared freely with the Canadians, who willingly embraced these new tactics to augment their attack doctrine.

Variations of the creeping barrage had been in play since the start of the Somme campaign, but often the barrage lifts moved too quickly or were not dense enough to allow the infantry to stay with the barrage. After practice barrages indicated that the worn artillery guns—which were forced to fire far more shells than the barrels were ever designed to withstand—often sent shells long or short, senior artillery and infantry officers considered it extremely unsafe for the infantry to get closer than 50 metres from the ragged barrage line. While the Canadians would later hug the barrage within this dangerous range, the real trouble remained in staying with the barrage for 20 to 30 minutes, across 500 to 700 metres of shell-cratered ground, and with the enemy firing small-arms and shells to disrupt the advance. With 75 to 100 metres between the troops and the barrage, when it moved off to the next lift some 100 metres away the infantry scrambled desperately to close the gap. Weighted down with a helmet, full kit, rifle, 200 rounds of ammunition, additional grenades, sandbags, shovels, water bottles, and a host of other necessary kit and tools that could add up to at least sixty pounds, the infantry often could not run what amounted to the length of a football field before the dazed enemy troops emerged from their dugouts. Amidst the still-smoking ruins of the battlefield, enemy fire began to thicken and take lives, and all knew they were in a race for survival. If the defenders won, they raced up from their deep dugouts or cleaned off their mud-splattered machine guns from within their shell-crater defences to mow down the waves of infantry left vulnerable in the open; if the attackers won, they penetrated the trenches, bombing the defenders as they rushed up their deep dugout stairs, or killed isolated and stunned defenders who were situated in the shallow shell-crater defences. Both sides consisted of sweating, straining men: the Germans with ears ringing and noses bleeding from the brutal shell concussions, and fearful that the barrage might return; the Canadians panting heavily, exhausted from flopping into shell holes and running during the breaks in the fire. Soldiers risked all, racing towards death in hopes of escaping death.

The new creeping barrage tactics offered the infantry a better chance of survival on the battlefield, but Haig also unleashed a new weapon. The devastating enemy machine guns that were destroying countless attacking troops had to be defeated, suppressed, or distracted. The British, urged on by Winston Churchill—then First Lord of the Admiralty—sought a bulletproof machine that could overrun enemy defences, especially hard-to-cut barbed wire, and then grind out the machine guns. Trials for these new land cruisers—which were code-named "tanks"—proved successful, although they were pitifully slow (moving at less than the speed of a walking person) and mechanically unstable.

The 28-tonne Mark I tank was a lumbering monster at almost 4 metres wide, 2 metres tall, and 8 metres long, with a 2-metre tail for stabilization and steering. "Male" versions were equipped with two 6-pounder guns and four Hotchkiss machine guns, while "female" versions carried only machine guns: five Vickers and one Hotchkiss. If enough ammunition was available, each tank could spew out more than a thousand bullets per minute. But their primary role was to push through the enemy defences by crushing barbed wire, trenches, and shell holes.

Haig was urged to hold off using the new weapons in order to allow time for the massing of tank forces, but he felt these machines needed a battlefield test. In a war in which the shell was king, he could not imagine investing enormous resources into a massive fleet of tanks only to find they did not work on the battlefield. (Such was in fact the concern of the Germans, too, who avoided putting a tank on the Western Front until the last year of the war.) Furthermore, Haig, his army, and the British people were desperate for a victory. Although the field marshal would later be condemned for introducing the tanks in penny packets, and thus squandering the element of surprise a mass tank attack would have had, one cannot fault him for throwing the new weapon immediately into battle at a time when it was desperately needed. It is difficult to argue that Haig should have held on to the tanks for another nine months to a year while his troops were massacred as they ran up against uncut barbed wire.

Haig's embrace of the tank, and of gas warfare earlier in the war, revealed that he was no closed-minded, ossified cavalryman. He was desperate to find an advantage for his infantry in battle, and was eager to try new methods, but the problem remained of hammering out a tactical doctrine that would efficiently place the tank within the comprehensive attack system of the British forces. The fact that this doctrine took some time to develop—and then perfect—and that this process could only be carried out within the trial-by-fire battlefield conditions of the Western Front, surely should not be used to further bludgeon Haig's already maligned reputation. This time of integration and experimentation was necessary, and the process could not have been accomplished more quickly. While he was not the brightest or most articulate general, Haig was no technophobe, and he was always searching for new weapons that would help his armies break the stalemate.

Forty-nine tanks would be committed to the battle, and the Canadians would have seven to support their main thrust. Most of the other British divisions ordered the tanks to lead the assault, but this required that 90-metre-wide lanes be left clear in the creeping barrage to keep the tanks from being knocked out by friendly shells. Unfortunately, this arrangement allowed German defenders to gravitate forward to these areas of safety and lay down crippling defensive fire.[7] On the Canadian front, Byng placed his tanks in secondary waves, and so was able to avoid this slaughter. At the sharp end, the tanks proved a surprise to the infantry, who had received no warning about this secret weapon (although many were informed through the rumour mill), and were provided no time to train with them. But the surprise would be far worse for the Germans.

WHILE THE USE OF TANKS might turn the tide of battle, allowing the attackers to overcome the inherent power of dug-in defenders, the artillery would continue to be tasked with crushing enemy defences. Already the Somme had turned into a gunners' battle. The Canadian and British gunners kept up a steady fire on the enemy trenches and rear areas in the days before the battle, raining down hundreds of thousands of high explosive and shrapnel shells. The air swirled with chalk dust, reminding many Canadians of snow from back home, and the saturation bombing blew miles of ground to mush. "Imagine an area of tranquil rolling countryside a bit larger than the city of Red Deer, dotted with small villages, farms and orchards," remarked one Canadian. "First, blast this panorama with 30 million artillery shells, each leaving a hole the size of a swimming pool. Next, flood the area with rain for days and days to transform the surface into grey, sticky slime. Finally, throw in nearly a million men from two great armies and have them slaughter each other for four months with bayonet, machine-gun and bomb."[8] Within this wasteland, the German defenders may have lost every poor sentry unlucky enough to draw guard duty, and the remaining garrison were left shell-shocked, bleeding from the ears, deafened, and vomiting due to the ceaseless concussions, but enough survived and waited for the barrage to move over them. The heavy bombardments erased all possibility of surprise: all knew that an attack was coming.

The Canadians planned to advance on a two-division front of about 2,000 metres. Brigadier Burstall's artillery wielded an incredible 234 field pieces and 64 heavy howitzers, the highest concentration of guns for a Canadian battle up to that point in the war; many of the guns, including most of the howitzers, were supplied by the British.[9] On the left, the 3rd Division was to capture the strongpoints of Mouquet Farm and Fabeck Graben trench, which would provide a powerful flank to support the main attack by the 2nd Division against the area surrounding the ruined village of Courcelette to the east. The 2nd Division infantrymen would have to fight through a series of trenches named "Sugar" and "Candy," and then capture the Sugar Factory, a fortified warehouse located about 900 metres from the Canadians' start line. To the north was the village of Courcelette, which would only be attacked if the operation went well and fresh troops could be sent through the captured lines.

The first waves of infantry moved into their jumping-off positions on the night of September 14. Despite the carnage around them, many Canadians were keen to avenge the carving-up they had suffered in the battles at Mount Sorrel and St. Eloi. "The time is now very close and I feel we are going to get a little of our own back," wrote Major Agar Adamson of the PPCLI.[10] Machine-gunner Frank Mathers was also "looking forward to a crack at Fritz," especially since his closest friend had been killed only a few months earlier when a piece of shrapnel passed through his back and lodged in his heart. The loss was still fresh: "This is just one more score to pay out."[11]

Yet every man knew that these could be his last days. Some prayed and made sure their wills were filled out in their paybooks; others talked loudly with bravado; most whispered to themselves that no bullet had their name on it. Hart Leech, a junior subaltern of the 1st CMR, who was a well-known vocalist and pianist in Winnipeg before the war, wrote in a last letter to his mother, "All the gang are writing post mortem letters and kind of half ashamed of themselves for doing it. As one of our officers said: 'If I mail it and come through the show, I'll be a joke. If I tear it up and get killed I'll be sorry I didn't send it.'" After softening the potential blow with this self-effacing humour, Leech starkly noted, "I am 'going over the parapet,' and the chances of a 'sub' getting back alive are about nix."[12] Perhaps Leech had second thoughts about scaring his mother, and never sent the letter, keeping it in his paybook. But his precaution had been warranted and he was killed the next day. Leech's family eventually received the letter, but only twelve years after his death. A British officer, Edgar King, had taken over the Canadian front after the battle, and in burying the dead, he had searched Leech's body for effects that could identify him. King had stuffed Leech's letter in his valise, but he had been wounded the next day, and his equipment had been sent to his home. Twelve years later, in 1928, King opened the valise, found the letter, and forwarded it to Leech's parents in Winnipeg. For many families, the war never ended.

SEVEN BATTALIONS of attacking troops lay waiting in the front lines, where they watched a fine mist greet the dawn on what would be a lovely autumn day. Behind them were follow-on forces and reinforcements. Shallow jumping-off trenches had been dug the night before to allow the infantry to push into No Man's Land and further close the gap with the enemy. In places, these ditches were 150 metres forward of the front lines, which meant that on the 3rd Division's front, the two lead attacking battalions, the 1st and 5th CMRs, would have to cross only 250 metres before crashing through the enemy front lines. On the 2nd Division's front, the five attacking battalions had about 850 metres to go. The minutes ticked down to zero hour—6:20 A.M.—with nervous energy passing along the line from man to man. Extra ammunition was fingered as it hung around the body in cotton bandoliers. Dry-mouthed soldiers took the offered shot of rum to calm their nerves and get the blood lust up. "After drinking the stuff," recounted one soldier, "I would have killed me own mother."[13] Waiting in their shallow jumping-off trenches, the infantry struggled with their private fears and the realization that soon they would leave behind even this limited protection for the terrors of the open ground.

Behind the front lines, Canadian guns were standing almost wheel to wheel in Sausage Valley, a low depression to the south of Pozières, which kept them out of sight of enemy ground observers. While in less danger than the infantry at the sharp end, the gunners were strafed by enemy fire day and night. But they grimly continued at their posts, firing shell after shell in support of the forthcoming assault. Gunner Sergeant Reginald Grant kept his resolve by declaring, "I had the firm conviction that death would come when it would come and not till then, and I went about my work absolutely careless of any possible hurt."[14] Many others, whether in artillery or infantry units, survived the ordeal of waiting with a similar sense of fatalism. They had no choice: the only way out of the army was feet first or a foot under.

With an ear-shattering crash, the German lines were enveloped in fire and whirling steel at 6:20 A.M.—about the time that the defenders would have been

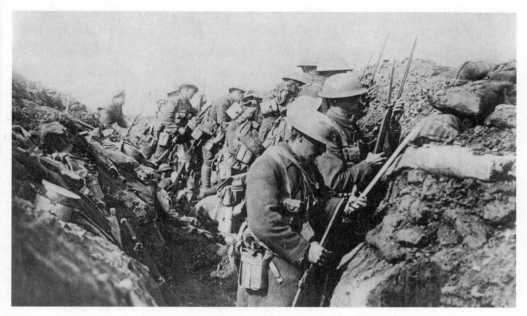

Canadian troops attaching bayonets to go over the top.

preparing their breakfast. The field artillery hammered the enemy's forward and communication trenches, while the heavier 6-inch howitzers "walked up and down the enemy's front" with 118-pound high explosive shells.[15] "Terrific bombardment from all kinds of guns," wrote Sergeant John Davis in his diary. "One continuous stream and din that could be felt."[16] The infantry went over the top behind the moving "wall of death," which jumped forward 90 metres every three minutes, and a further heavy barrage was targeted some 300 to 500 metres beyond, creating a thick wave of fire.[17]

A failure of Major General Louis Lipsett's 3rd Division to capture Mouquet Farm and Fabeck Graben trench would be acceptable, but the troops were above all to ensure that the left flank was secure and that the Germans did not cut off any advances made by the 2nd Division. The 3rd Division's 1st and 5th CMRs pushed into the enemy lines as part of the first wave, but suffered heavy casualties from friendly artillery fire and especially from defenders in trenches further to the north, around Zollern Redoubt, who poured machine-gun and small-arms fire into their massed ranks. One German infantryman described the Canadians' tactics: "The enemy went over to the attack, by advancing waves of troops, divided into section-sized groups and interspersed with machine guns. These waves were supported by compact columns.... They suffered in the process, but their numerical superiority made the cost acceptable."[18] This enemy account implies that the Canadians were moving in tight waves, with their Lewis gunners in support, which was indeed true for the first phase of the battle, but the Canadian attack soon lost its cohesion as the troops went to ground and then bounded forward in small groups, with men seeking protection where they could find it, in shell craters or other depressions in the land. They moved forward not as automatons but as infantrymen aware that they had to somehow cross the killing zone to survive another day on earth.

While the German heavy MG-08s could fire 500 bullets per minute in wide arcs, they could not fire continuously without burning out their barrels in a matter of minutes; nor did they have enough ammunition to keep up sustained fire indefinitely. Experienced German gunners fired off short bursts at a time, but their Canadian attackers listened for the breaks in fire within the cacophony of explosions before rushing for the next shell hole. Not all of them made it, and more than one

German machine-gun fired at them, but the Canadians inched forward. When they got close enough, the CMRs crashed the line, bayoneting Germans and destroying dugouts. "Fritz is fairly cowed by the bayonet," wrote Norman Lowther of the 5th CMR. "He simply can't face it."[19]

One revealing Canadian report noted that a conservative estimate of enemy casualties in this attack was some 900. The 1st CMR bayoneted 50 to 60 of these men and made it as far as the outskirts of Mouquet Farm, while the 4th CMR (in a follow-up role) and 5th CMR killed 150 and 250 respectively by bayoneting.[20] The rest of the enemy troops were shot down by gunfire or shredded with grenades. This official report is revealing, since historians have often claimed that in this industrial war the bayonet was next to useless. While the term "bayoneting" in such reports might encompass other forms of harsh hand-to-hand combat, these figures clearly indicate the value of the seventeen-inch blade in battle.

IT WAS KILL OR BE KILLED in the frenzy of battle, and retreating enemy soldiers were shot in the back by the conquering 1st and 5th CMRs as they scrambled to escape the trenches. Support units such as the 2nd and 4th CMRs, which had been reconstituted from their virtual annihilation at Mount Sorrel three months earlier, were then ordered to capture key portions of Fabeck Graben (only a few hundred metres to the north) later in the day. The purpose of this mission was to deny the Germans access to their underground counterattack routes, which were driven throughout the chalk in the region to allow troops to move about unhindered by sniper fire.

The barrage directed against Fabeck Graben lifted at 6:00 P.M., and the first wave went forward in a "slow run." German small-arms fire caused a few casualties as wire held up the attack, but most of the attackers surged forward. Sergeant R.L. Layton of the 4th CMR, who would later rise to the rank of captain and be awarded the Distinguished Conduct Medal for his inspired leadership, recorded that his men overran the enemy positions, "killing all the Germans who showed any stubborn resistance, and taking prisoner any who gave themselves up."[21] But this forward trench had only been held lightly. The follow-on wave of 4th CMR, pushing deeper into the enemy lines, ran into machine-gun and shrapnel fire from the now alerted

German second-line defenders. But more positions were captured and blocks were established in trenches after several grenadiers had raced down blind alleys, blasting and bombing the Germans as they went from dugout to dugout, from trench to trench.

Although the break-in was successful, the enemy responded with a heavy bombardment that cut all communication back to the Canadians' original lines. The weakened attackers were isolated, with counterattacking German forces massing towards them and a wall of high explosives trapping them as it cordoned off the rear. Battalion headquarters, Layton bitterly recounted, "left us alone. They did not seem to realize our considerable losses, our uneasiness for our wounded, and our position against a possible counterattack. Our rations were low, the water supply was almost nil, ammunition was not forthcoming and BHQ sat tight in a deep dugout five hundred yards away and would have left us to our fate." With the 4th CMR in disarray, the surviving company officer, Major William Coleman, reacted to the situation by establishing forward posts, redistributing ammunition, and caring for the wounded. An exhausted and dispirited Sergeant Layton later remarked of Coleman, "I discovered what a soldier he was in a military sense and what a man he was in a human sense."[22]

This junior leadership—delivered at the front without instructions from battalion, brigade, or divisional command—carried the day.[23] Coleman would survive the war, twice earning the Military Cross for bravery. After the battle, though, he wrote to his wife: "I am so tired I can hardly see. For forty-eight hours I had about two hours of dozes, snatched at odd times, and only had time to eat two or three slices of bread and jam and a few dates and part of a can of pork and beans." As he had trudged from the line, he had "wept purely from exhaustion." Some hot tea and breakfast helped to warm Coleman's body, and a waiting letter from his daughter, Francis, along with a crudely cut-out paper doll, helped to warm his heart.[24]

THE CANADIANS on the left flank thus captured their positions and drew fire to their own lines, which helped to relieve the pressure on the main axis of the attack against Courcelette. Fabeck Graben had fallen to the attackers, but the fortress of Mouquet Farm, now reduced to shattered bricks and wood, was still in German hands. The mounted rifles suffered heavily for stirring up the hornet's nest: in the 1st CMR, 70 were killed, 179 wounded, and 11 missing, while the 5th CMR had 55 killed, 150 wounded, and 20 missing. Attesting to the savage nature of the warfare, after the battle some twenty members of the 5th CMR were diagnosed with shattered nerves. They were led from the front, some having lost the ability to speak, and others having developed hysterical conditions.[25] The Somme fighting destroyed both bodies and minds.

CHAPTER 34

BLOODY VICTORY

Courcelette, September 15, 1916

The Somme battlefield was a wasteland of ruined farmers' fields; scummy, water-filled shell holes; and acres of unburied corpses. Soldiers might be excused for thinking that not a single metre of the war zone had escaped being chewed up by artillery fire, and they were probably right. The mixture of blackened flesh and broken bones with thousands of tonnes of metal and shattered structures created a nightmare landscape. The British had been fighting here for three months, trading more than 250,000 men for less than 8 kilometres of German trench system. It is no wonder that more than a few soldiers joked that it was still "Berlin or Bust"—but likely not before the 1940s.

With the 3rd Division protecting the left flank, the main attack on September 15 was by the 2nd Division, northward towards Courcelette. "What villages there were are as flat as ploughed fields, and most certainly the country is one of desolation," wrote Lieutenant A.B. Morkill, who enlisted at age thirty-three, was awarded the Military Cross, and survived the war despite being shot three separate times and receiving a shrapnel wound in the leg. "Not a tree, but occasionally the stump of one to accentuate the barrenness, and at night when it is lit up by the flames and the flashes of the guns, it leaves the impression of a very modern hell."[1]

General Richard Turner ordered five battalions forward in the initial assault, and fresh units would subsequently pass through them to exploit success. As in the operation on the 3rd Division's front, Turner's 2nd Division, too, was set to go over the

On the Somme, the battlefield—and everything on it—was pulverized. Strongpoints such as this, the former village of Courcelette, were blasted with tens of thousands of high explosive shells.

top at 6:20 A.M. But the Germans launched a pre-emptive barrage, followed by an attack in the middle of the night. In Turner's words, it nearly "upset the applecart and it was only the men's determination and high spirits that saved the situation."[2] The Canadians repulsed the attack, and then waited a few more hours for their own artillery to open up and signal the advance.

Shellfire erupted as hundreds of synchronized officers' watches reached zero hour, and the barrage moved ahead 90 metres every three minutes. Turner's infantry stormed forward from their shallow jumping-off trenches, advancing in evenly spaced waves of men, with a light breeze at their backs and a storm of steel in front of them. The barrage started about 50 metres from the enemy front line, and then moved through it. That was close enough to keep the Germans in their dugouts, but it moved over the front line too quickly. Defenders swarmed from their dugouts after the creeping barrage lifted off their position, and while the barrage had bought precious time for the Canadians to cross the fire zone, they had not reached the enemy front line before they were being fired upon. The five first-wave battalions, from left to right the 28th, 27th, 21st, 20th, and 18th, were stranded in the open, but they were within 100 metres of the enemy trench system.

Caught in No Man's Land, the Canadians were reduced to inching forward on their bellies. The bodies of the slain, men who had for months been companions and friends, were frequently used for cover in the barren No Man's Land, and set up as makeshift, fleshy sandbags on the lips of the shallow craters where the infantry took refuge from the scythe-like sweep of bullets and shrapnel. The situation was grim. But in the words of Lance Corporal Ralph Lewis, a prewar second mate on a Newfoundland steamboat, the 2nd Division men had "a lot of old scores to pay off."[3] And so forward they pushed.

In the terror of battle, soldiers often need to be led through the firestorm, and one man can turn the tide of defeat towards victory. The slaughter that raged around the Canadians at Courcelette dulled the mind. They knew that they had to get across the killing zone, and they knew that they were being shot down in the open or as they crouched in shell holes, but many were transfixed. The terror of moving forward into the face of the guns created paralysis, even when taking such action was safer in the long term than staying in an indefensible shell hole. But this was the point at which discipline took over. The annoying saluting and marching were a part of instilling obedience among the troops, but the continuous drill also encouraged self-control by freeing the mind from its torpor in times of terrible stress and allowing it to govern the body's actions. The advance in the face of this terrible fire started with one man, maybe an officer, maybe a senior NCO, maybe a private, who moved forward into the storm. That simple advance broke the hypnotism of fire, and the infantry scrambled out of their craters and from behind the bodies of the slain to close the distance. While battles are won by all of the various parts of the army working together in unison, success often comes down to the man at the sharp end who must force himself to push forward into the mouth of hell.

On the 21st Battalion's front, in the middle of the advance, the Central Ontario battalion attacked with two companies, each in four waves comprising its four forty-man platoons, and with a fifth wave in support. Each man had a bright yellow, triangular pennant on his back so that spotter aircraft flying over the battlefield in contact patrols could monitor the troops' forward movement. Machine-gunner Armine Norris recounted the advance of his own battalion, the 20th, and that of the 21st, on their left: both battalions' wave attacks soon degenerated into a "mob of men just like the crowds that swarm onto Varsity Stadium after a football game."[4] But the men were still going forward, even after most of the company commanders were knocked out by small-arms fire early in the attack. Sergeant Frank Maheux felt compelled to write to his wife about the battle even though he was never comfortable putting pen to paper.

> The worse fighting here since the war started, we took all kinds of prisoners but God we lost heavy all my comrades killed or wounded, we are only a few left but all the same we gain what we were after.... I went thru all the fights the same as if I was making logs. I bayoneted some killed lots of Huns. I was caught in one place with a chum of mine he was killed beside me when I saw he was killed I saw red.... The Germans when they saw they were beaten they put up their hands but dear wife it was too late.[5]

Although the Canadians made good progress, their casualties mounted in staggering numbers. The survivors were in no mood to offer mercy. "Some of the enemy offered to surrender," wrote the commanding officer, Lieutenant Colonel Elmer Jones, "but in most cases these men were bayoneted by our advancing troops."[6]

The lack of clemency shown by these battalions was not an aberration. According to nineteen-year-old Private Lance Cattermole, the infantry had been instructed to "take no prisoners until our objective had been gained." In the past, a perception had taken hold among the infantry—likely based on apocryphal stories or a few real examples that circulated up the line like wildfire—that German prisoners being taken to the rear had killed their escorts, grabbed weapons that lay abandoned on the battlefield, and shot at Canadians in the front lines. Cattermole attested that the grim "no prisoners" order was reluctantly carried out in his battalion, and recounted coming upon a trench where the enemy dead lay in heaps, steam rising as their hot blood and urine soaked the ground. A steady line of terrified captured Germans was still emerging from a dugout, seemingly oblivious to the slaughter that awaited them as Canadians herded them around the corner and put a bullet in them. One German tried to escape the slaughter by jumping out of the trench, "dodging in and out amongst us to avoid being shot, crying out 'Nein! Nein!' He pulled out from his breast pocket a handful of photographs and tried to show them to us in an effort to gain our sympathy…. As the bullets smacked into him he fell to the ground motionless, the pathetic little photographs fluttering down to the earth around him."[7] This was indeed brutal fighting, in which the attackers were machine-gunned, sniped, and bombed as they advanced on the enemy, and the survivors refused mercy to surrendering men who had been trying to kill them only minutes before.

But the battle for Courcelette went on for several hours, and after the blood frenzy had been satiated, hundreds of prisoners were captured. Cattermole later observed small groups of wounded prisoners making their way to the rear, and two Canadians "who could not have been more tender in their ministrations" to one sad prisoner who had been shot in the head, leaving "one eye bouncing about on a cord below his chin and the other socket empty."[8] Another officer in the PPCLI noted that when one of his subordinates captured and took prisoner thirty-five men in a dugout, "they were so scared, he had not the heart to shoot them."[9] Mercy did exist in the trenches, but it was often handed out sparingly, depending on the soldiers, the informal rules of surrender, and whether the desire for revenge had run its course.[10]

All along the front, sections of infantrymen pushed forward, moving from crater to crater. "I cannot understand how anyone could have crossed that inferno alive," wrote Private Donald Fraser. "As I pressed forward with eyes strained, to the extent of being half closed, I expected and almost felt being shot in the stomach. All around our men were falling, their rifles loosening from their grasp. The wounded, writhing in their agonies, struggled and toppled into shell holes … I expected my turn every moment."[11] Fraser survived, though many did not. Yet even as men were mowed down by small-arms fire, new men pushed through and over them, driving into the enemy lines. When these forward trenches were overrun, the force spread out along the communication trenches, moving at top speed to kill or incapacitate the enemy, thereby allowing more Canadians to slip into the trenches. The fighting was confused and desperate, with the infantry confined in the narrow, muddy trenches, racing forward, tossing grenades in dugouts, driving on to the next bay. Surprised Germans were bayoneted or shot without sympathy, while other Canadian troops blundered into ambushes as they rounded corners, running face-first into a hail of bullets. As the first waves pushed forward, secondary lines of mopping-up units, known as "rat hunters," followed them, throwing bombs down dugouts to make sure no Germans popped up in the rear.

The 2nd Division bit deep into the German lines, but the Sugar Factory would not fall to the 20th and 21st Battalions. German defenders from the 45th Reserve Division refused to surrender, and at least one machine-gunner had reportedly chained himself to his gun, indicating that he would fight to the death (or so it may have seemed to the soldiers from a distance; more often the heavy machine guns were chained down to make them harder for the attackers to turn them around against the defenders in retreat). With these two battalions pinned down in the open and taking casualties, even as other Canadian units surged forward, from behind them out of the smoke came the sound of grinding metal. An 8-metre-long metal tank emerged from the smoke and dust, wobbling like a "queer monster of iron, which dipped into trenches and huge craters and crawled crazily up the other side."[12] A few brave men were near it, hugging its metal walls, their job being to dash out and move wounded men from the beast's path.[13] The unfortunate staff

In order to crush barbed wire and enemy defences, the British developed the tank.
Unleashed for the first time in the history of warfare on September 15, 1916,
the new weapon had only a limited impact on the battlefield.

officer who was forced to pick the men to carry out this task considered it akin to suicide since the tanks were liable to draw fire from all corners of the battlefield. Machine-gunner Armine Norris saw those "heroes" go into battle and thought it was "positively ... [the] bravest thing I've heard of in my life."[14]

The Mark I tanks were very different from those that rolled across Europe a generation later, in the Second World War. They were slow, mechanically unreliable, and easily knocked out by artillery fire. Training soldiers to operate inside the metal coffins was difficult; preventing them from being rendered unconscious by the petrol exhaust that flowed into the stifling, confined space that heated up to 40 degrees Celsius or higher was even more difficult. Many tank attacks failed because the vehicles' operators were too sick to continue on to their objectives. Providing absolutely deplorable visibility, tanks often crossed the battlefield with a seemingly drunken stagger, making it difficult for the infantry to move anywhere near them since the massive weapons had a tendency to get lost or turned around, fire on their own troops, and crush everything in their path.

Fortunio Matania, The Capture of the Sugar Refinery

Despite their unreliability, the tanks still inspired shock and terror in the hearts of the enemy. Infantrymen could especially appreciate the futile ping of enemy bullets on invulnerable metal. While a few tanks helped to clear out the German positions, they were most important as a terror weapon. The tanks "rambled along like great monsters with their guns firing in all directions," recounted Arthur Goodmurphy of the 28th Battalion.[15] Many Germans surrendered as the metal monsters lurched towards them—but not all. As one tank advanced towards the Sugar Factory, it drew fire, allowing the previously pinned-down infantry from the 20th and 21st Battalions to push forward. The same tank was especially effective later, in running along the German trench, grinding out positions with its enormous tracks and "doing good execution."[16]

The tanks were a fitting technological rebuttal to the German unleashing of poison gas a year earlier. But like the chemical agents that were increasingly polluting the Western Front, tanks did not provide the key to the breakthrough. Of the six tanks that went forward on September 15 (the seventh remained in reserve), all were out of action by the end of the day, having broken down mechanically, bellied down in the mud, or been destroyed by shellfire.[17] Still, the tanks played a role in shocking the Germans, as evidenced by one bewildered German prisoner who blurted, "What in hell was the meaning of waging war in such fashion?"[18]

Having made deep advances into the enemy trenches and captured key strong-points including the Sugar Factory, all positions to the south of Courcelette were in Canadian hands by 8:00 A.M. But the exhausted soldiers could not hope to rest. The consolidation phase began and the infantry traded rifles for entrenching tools. Caved-in trenches were expanded; new communication lines were dug to the rear; and sandbags were filled to provide some protection in trenches that were now facing the wrong direction. And all the while the Canadians waited for the attack they knew would come.

BEHIND THIS FURY of activity in the front lines, Canadian stretcher-bearers moved through the heaps of wounded and dead, bandaging gaping holes, providing water for parched lips, and offering final words for those beyond saving. The infantry were

A shell goes off too close for comfort for wounded soldiers at an advanced dressing station.

instructed not to stop for the wounded during the battle, but many invariably knelt to a bleeding pal and planted the fallen man's rifle into the ground so that stretcher-bearers could later find him. But the constant fall of shells could atomize the vulnerable wounded, while those shells falling further away bounced the men along the cratered ground until they were dropped into a hole, ditch, or trench, leaving them stranded and alone with their agonizing injuries. When the firing briefly subsided around noon, the wounded began to surface from their hiding places like worms, wriggling and dragging themselves back to the safety of their own lines. The effect was as if the earth was disgorging its dead.

Stretcher-bearer parties of four ferried the worst of the wounded to the battalion medical officer, some 300 to 700 metres behind the forward lines. The mud created such a quagmire, however, that often these stretcher-bearers had their boots sucked off their feet. The recently invented wheeled stretcher was absolutely useless here, as it was on most shattered battlefields. Amidst the destruction, a team of four bearers often took several hours to make it to the rear. German prisoners were also enlisted in the cause; they stripped off their greatcoats or took those worn by the dead to create makeshift stretchers. "I caught two Fritzies and made them take me out," recounted Private John McNab, who had been wounded in the leg. He had spent the morning watching his gravely injured companions in his shell hole slowly succumb to their wounds, and had witnessed one friend having most of his head blown away while he was trying to apply a bandage to McNab's leg.[19] While the shells fell, German prisoners could be seen looking for wounded Canadians to carry to the rear. They were eager to save the men they had previously been trying to kill as this assistance endeared them to their captors and made it harder for the Canadians to justify their execution on the battlefield.

The bundles of spreading crimson were dropped in a triage area, and the medical officer, or his orderlies, attempted to bind the wounds, apply a quick shot of rum, or perform emergency surgery on those who were in danger of slipping into shock. From the forward trenches, the wounded were rushed to casualty clearing stations, usually a few kilometres behind the line. Again, the wounds were examined, and triage performed. Dying men took on a grey pallor as blood flowed from their bodies. Veterans of the front could take it all in with one glance. Those who were not in danger were sent back to rear hospitals, those who could be saved with emergency care were operated on, and those too badly wounded were left to die.

Sometimes survival depended on blind luck. While taking a break from assisting surgeons in the charnel house that passed for an operating room, medical orderly R.A. Morgan stumbled across his badly wounded brother, Jack, bleeding to death from the shrapnel lodged in his side. He had been triaged into a group of men left to die. R.A. Morgan pulled him out of the triage area and bound him up, thus saving his life.[20] Most men had no guardian angels looking out for them, however, and it is not surprising that many of the cemeteries that dot the Western Front today had their origins in clearing stations and hospitals.

But such grim revelations are not meant to imply that the medical services were callous or incompetent. Quite the opposite was true: the vast majority—more than 90 percent—of the men who arrived at the dressing stations were saved by the expert medical care of surgeons and doctors. The real problem lay in getting the soldiers from front to rear quickly enough, and many died before they ever saw a doctor. But even for those who did make it to the rear, the medical system was strained to the breaking point at Courcelette, and staff officers had planned insufficiently for the rush of casualties. Wounded men often lay waiting for twelve to eighteen hours before they were tended to by a medical officer. Although thousands were saved, the medical corps still had a stiff learning curve to master.

WHILE RESILIENT STRETCHER-BEARERS and doctors cared for the wounded, the battle raged on at the front. With the Canadians occupying most of their objectives by early morning, the Germans responded by laying down an offensive of heavy artillery fire to punish the successful Dominion troops and soften their defences. A few desultory counterattacks were also launched, only to be beaten back by small-arms fire. But the battle was not over for the Canadians. Forward observers and alert officers noted confusion in the enemy lines: small groups of defenders were retreating and the Germans were offering little return fire. At 11 A.M., General Byng ordered a new push north into Courcelette, in the hope of exploiting the successful advance of the morning. The attack would go in at 6 P.M.

For this second phase, elements of the 7th and 8th Brigades—the PPCLI, the 42nd and 49th Battalions, and the 4th CMR—supported the attack on the left, pushing out from the trenches captured by the 1st and 5th CMRs earlier in the day. But the main effort would be undertaken by the 2nd Division's 22nd and 25th Battalions, which would charge straight into Courcelette. Brigadier Archibald Macdonell, known as "Long Archie" to distinguish him from his cousin, A.C. Macdonell, did not receive the order to attack until 1 P.M. Although he and 2nd Division commander Turner had prepared for a possible exploitation phase in the battle, the orders left them little time before zero hour. Macdonell hurried forward from his 5th Brigade headquarters to meet with his four battalion commanders. They, in turn, scrambled to find their company commanders and senior NCOs, most only finishing their briefings at around 4 P.M. With every minute counting, the first-wave troops of the 22nd and 25th Battalions were rallied and rushed forward to get to the start line before the barrage opened up less than two hours later. That they succeeded—and under the fall of searching enemy shellfire—was a sign of the growing Canadian professionalism.

With little time to prepare, the forward units had almost no chance to reconnoitre the ground. They might soon be marching into massed machine-gun fire, and would have little idea of where to concentrate their forces until the enemy opened up with their guns. Obviously, this did not bode well for the attack. But it was the brigade's failure to transport morale-raising rum to the front lines that most worried Captain Joseph Chabelle, commander of D Company of the 22nd Battalion. The men had only a few minutes to compose themselves, and the liquid courage was sorely missed. Chabelle, married and a father of two, scribbled a letter to his family, handing it to an officer who was being held back in the battle in case the unit was annihilated. He departed, filled with emotion, and asked his friend to tell his wife "my last thoughts were for her and the children."[21]

The attack was launched at 6 P.M., in broad daylight, and with no jumping-off trenches to reduce the distance to the enemy. The troops would have to advance over 2 kilometres of open ground: first behind their own lines, then through the devastated battlefield around the Sugar Factory, and finally on to Courcelette. The operation was a recipe for slaughter. Army commander General Hubert Gough would later comment that the audacious assault was "without parallel in the present campaign."[22]

Hugging the artillery barrage, which had been thickened up by machine-gun fire, the lead elements of the 22nd and 25th Battalions, with the "Fighting 26th" 150 metres to the rear, pushed forward with determination. They were laden down with the necessary trench supplies to hold the position, although experienced soldiers soon discarded what they felt they did not need. But no one dropped ammunition or grenades, which would mean the difference between success and failure if they ever got to Courcelette.

Officers clutched maps and used the sun, over their left shoulder, to help guide themselves through the dust and shellfire, which were even denser since the enemy counter-barrage was keeping pace and devastating the advance troops. A little past the halfway point, the Canadians marched through the battlefield around the Sugar Factory, which the 20th and 21st Battalions had captured earlier in the day. The ground looked like an abattoir, with the Canadians literally stepping over red soil, long loops of intestines, and other shredded body parts of men who had been killed and then dismembered by shellfire. The sight was not an encouraging one for troops who were soon to face the Germans in their fortified positions, and still with some 800 metres of open ground in front of them. "The Light Brigade at Balaclava at least had horses for reasonably fast movement. The unfortunates at Courcelette had to traverse that frightful field of slaughter yard by yard on foot," wrote Robert Clements.[23] But the Canadians had the advantage of their creeping barrage, which crashed down ahead of the lead troops: "one mass of flame and smoke" raked over the battlefield.[24]

By this point in the war, experienced Canadian commanders estimated that about twenty minutes after zero hour in a battle, the battalion commander lost his influence over the men engaged in combat.[25] One of the solutions to this problem was for the "old man" to lead his units into battle, an approach that was used during the assault on Courcelette. In the mad march across the open ground, Lieutenant Colonel Edward Hilliam of the 25th Battalion was in the front waves, rallying the troops with a cigar in his mouth and a hand hanging at his side, bloody from shrapnel. The 22nd Battalion's commander, Lieutenant Colonel Thomas Tremblay, was also leading from the front, striding up and down the line, shouting out encouragement, refusing to duck as the shells crashed around them. Three times Tremblay was buried by dirt and debris thrown on him by exploding shells, and each time his men dug him out and he continued to urge them onwards, even as more shells burst around him. Future Canadian governor general Georges Vanier, then an officer in the 22nd Battalion, felt that "as long as I followed him no harm would come to me."[26] Inspiring leadership and iron will would be needed in equal parts if the attack was to succeed.

The Nova Scotians and Quebeckers of the 25th and 22nd Battalions pierced the enemy's forward defensive crust bayonets first, but left behind a path of their own killed and wounded men. "It was the longest and bloodiest half mile" ever faced by troops, according to one survivor.[27] The remaining members of the battalions moved straight into town, overrunning what was left of the advance German positions held by elements of I Battalion, 211th Reserve Regiment, in the overgrown fields and low stone walls that formed part of the southern trenches. (The Canadians had fought the 211th before in the Ypres salient, although few men would have recognized any foes from a year and a half earlier.) One official report noted that the lead units engaged in "smart bayonet fighting" and crashed through the town before many of the dug-in German defenders had come out of their reinforced cellars.[28]

But the sanitized term "smart bayonet fighting" fails to capture the brutality inherent in hand-to-hand fighting. Captain Joseph Chabelle described the action of using his Lee-Enfield with bayonet attached, which was in total just over 1.5 metres long:

> The fight at first was fierce, a hand-to-hand, no-weapons-barred combat: bayonets, rifle-butts, shovels, feet, teeth all came into play....Blood spurted out of punctured breasts; brains spilled from skulls shattered by rifle-butts. Bayonet fighting is a bitter struggle to the end, with no mercy shown.... Oh! the sensation of driving the blade into flesh, between the ribs, despite the opponent's grasping efforts to deflect it. You struggle savagely, panting furiously, lips contorted in a grimace, teeth gnashing, until you feel the enemy relax his grip and topple like a log. To remove the bayonet, you have to pull it out with both

hands; if it is caught in the bone, you must brace your foot on the still heaving body, and tug with all your might.[29]

Against an onslaught of such savage intensity, the Germans fought for about ten minutes and then began to flee or surrender.

Splitting up into small groups, the lead waves—or what was left of them—pushed through the village. Platoons leap-frogged each other four times to reach the northern edge of the village in minutes and set up a defensive perimeter. Two hundred metres behind the now dispersed lead units, the 26th Battalion—consisting mostly of New Brunswickers—killed the remaining confused defenders "at the point of the bayonet and bomb," as one junior officer grimly attested.[30] But not all positions fell easily to the 26th; Corporal Arthur Fleming led twenty-two men against an enemy strongpoint, where they fought back and forth to first clear a position and then hold it against several counterattacks. By the end of the battle, some thirty-five Germans had been captured, several dozen more had been killed, and only Fleming and one other man remained unwounded.[31] Fleming alone accounted for almost two dozen enemy deaths, and was awarded the Military Medal for his ferocity. These small-scale battles continued for two days since pockets of German defenders refused to surrender as they expected to be relieved by their own forces' counterattacks.

With the village of Courcelette burning around them and black smoke obscuring the front, the survivors of the 22nd and 25th, as well as the supporting 26th Battalion, waited for the storm to hit. It did not take long to come. Furious about losing such an important hinge of their defensive line, the German high command unleashed seventeen counterattacks. All of them were beaten back by the Canadians, who often fought in isolated pockets, supported by Lewis gunners firing in wide arcs to cover the gaps in the line.[32] No other Canadian brigade ever defended against such a sustained fury of attacks during the war.

In this battle for survival, the defence involved every single man, including batmen and signallers. Acts of astonishing stoicism and bravery were performed by officers and men alike. Lieutenant Denis Stairs of the 25th Battalion, for example, continued to organize the defence of the all-important machine guns even though he had been shot in the arm and his hand had been reduced to a bloody stump.[33] Captain Chabelle wrote that although the troops were "outnumbered ten to one, we had the advantage of position…. Mercilessly we gunned them down at almost point blank range."[34] Chabelle would survive the battle and be awarded the Military Cross for his bravery and distinguished leadership, but he would later be buried alive twice within a four-day period at the end of April 1917. The second time broke his will and when he emerged from his crypt, he was shaking and crying uncontrollably.[35] He was diagnosed with shell shock and never returned to a combat command.

Grenades were essential in holding off the enemy, but trench mortars were nearly useless since they consumed their ammunition too quickly. The Lee-Enfield, Mark III remained the infantryman's main arm, and with its muzzle velocity of 740 metres per second, accurate fire chewed up the enemy forces coming over open ground. The German 210th and 211th Reserve Regiments lost nearly seventy percent of their strength in these brutal battles.[36]

But each enemy attack killed and wounded more Canadians, and the bombardment left the extended troops increasingly vulnerable and cut off. The men could find no way back over the fireswept ground, but aircraft contact patrols flying dangerously low to observe the battlefield soon informed 5th Brigade and 2nd Division headquarters of the forward extent of the Canadian advance, which was indicated by flares and the signal patches on infantry uniforms. Headquarters was therefore able to order much-needed artillery fire in support of the hard-pressed Canadians. As well, the last reserve battalion of the 5th Brigade, the 24th, along with several machine-gun crews, were moved forward during lulls in the enemy counter-barrage, further consolidating the positions. During four days of desperate fighting, the Canadians refused to relinquish the village, even though the German artillery was accurately bombarding their lines. "It was like a bad dream … shells falling by the thousands, blowing up everything, fighting with grenades, bayonet charges, battles, corpses everywhere and the constant writhing of the wounded. Man's mental and physical endurance is incredible," wrote Lieutenant Colonel Thomas Tremblay. "If hell is as horrible as what I saw there, I wouldn't wish it on my worst enemy."[37]

The 5th Brigade captured more than a thousand Germans, killed probably that many again (and reported that a multitude more had been cut down by their own artillery fire as they moved through the Canadian lines), and lost 1,267 casualties among the four attacking battalions and support units.[38] Seeking an explanation for his survival against such odds, bombardier William Rowat of the 22nd Battalion wrote: "The hand of God has guided and protected me through every seeming death trap."[39] All of the front-line infantry had had countless brushes with death. Men had been killed beside them while they survived unscathed. They had bullet and shrapnel holes through their uniforms. Survival seemed attributable only to chronic good luck or some higher power. Lieutenant Coningsby Dawson endured the psychological strain of battle by repeating the mantra, "You can't dodge your fate; it searches you out."[40] Such beliefs helped men to cope with the imponderables of fate and combat.

THE CANADIAN CAPTURE of Courcelette had been a stunning success. Major General Richard Turner certainly deserved praise for the 2nd Division's exploits, and the positive outcome went some way to restoring the general's damaged reputation. Few such decisive victories—even small ones—had been achieved during the Somme fighting. To the left of the Canadians' front, the 2nd British Corps had advanced some 400 metres closer to the fortress of Thiepval, with its vast underground concrete cellars, but the Germans made the British pay for every step. On the Canadians' right, the British had carried out the main thrust of the attack, finally capturing Flers and Martinpuich; but key villages, including Morval and Gueudecourt, had held out. There would be no breakthrough. The tank had achieved some tactical success in supporting the infantry, but it had done little to sway the battle. The relentless British attacks had ground out more German defenders, but the war of attrition was killing thousands daily, on both sides. In the following days, the Canadians enlarged their gains, capturing spurs or small trench systems that overlooked their lines. But the battle soon ground to a halt. The first major operation of the Canadian Corps had cost 7,230 casualties.[41] It had been a bloody engagement, but unlike so many on the Somme, the Canadians could point to their success.

Such victories were important for morale, but they did little to leaven the survivors' grief for their fallen mates. New troops were rotated into the line, allowing the now-shattered battalions to trudge to the rear. There, sympathetic officers divided the regular allotment of 1,000 rum rations per battalion among the pitifully few survivors. The infantry were weak with exhaustion, and when they were finally allowed to rest, they slept where they fell, in mud or even under sporadic fire. Private W.H. Gilday of the 31st Battalion, a twenty-five-year-old farmer from Rosebud Creek, Alberta, whose unit had helped to consolidate the newly won positions, confided to his sister after the battle: "You know how anxious I was to get into the front line. Well, now I am just as anxious to be far away. I am afraid my nerves won't stand many battles."[42] But the Somme operations were far from over, and the Canadian Corps would hammer away at the enemy trenches to the north of Courcelette. They would have few breaks, and no escape from this foul battlefield with its "acres of sacrificial corpses."[43] The Canadians' tour on the Somme would

become, in the words of Canon Frederick Scott, who would lose his son in the forthcoming fighting, "a time of iron resolve."[44]

THE NEWS of the Canadian victory at Courcelette was greeted with pride on the home front, but many braced themselves for the death telegrams, which arrived first in a trickle and then in a gut-wrenching flood. In Portage la Prairie, Manitoba, David and Isabella Peden, the parents of five brothers serving overseas, received two separate wires towards the end of the month. The first noted that Private J. Peden of the 28th

After a battle, bone-weary survivors usually collapsed into sleep, with nightmares deadened by rum and exhaustion.

Battalion had been killed in action; the second noted that Private J. Peden of the 28th Battalion had been wounded in action. No Christian names had been given, and they had two sons, James and John, serving with the 28th. Perhaps, they prayed, the first wire had been sent by mistake, and only one was wounded. They agonized for weeks in trying to sort out the administrative mess, and it was only a month later that they learned that their youngest son James had been killed, and that his older brother John had been wounded in the head and was recovering. A year later, David and Isabella were rocked again: their eldest boy David was killed while fighting at Passchendaele.[45] For many Canadian families, victories such as the one at Courcelette were marked only by unimaginable grief.

The Battle of Courcelette: September 15, 1916

RESERVE DIVISION

Courcelette

26TH BN
22TH BN
25TH BN
5TH CDN INF BDE

Candy Trench
SUGAR FACTORY

P.P.C.L.I.
7TH CDN INF BDE

Sugar Trench

18TH BN
20TH BN
21ST BN
4TH CDN INF BDE

49ND BN
42ND BN

27TH BN
6TH CDN INF BDE
2ND CDN DIV

15TH

Fabeck Graben
4TH C.M.R.
5TH C.M.R.

28TH BN

15TH (S) DIVISION

Grandcourt Road

Regina Trench
Hessian Trench
Zollern Trench
Stuff Redoubt
Zollern Redoubt

MOU QUET FARM
1ST C.M.R.

8TH CDN INF BDE
3RD CDN DIV

0   .5   1
kilometres

CHAPTER 35

"WE WERE MET WITH DEADLY FIRE"

The Battle of Thiepval Ridge, September 26, 1916

"The battlefield of the Somme is some awful looking place. Those towns you hear of are simply torn to pieces.... You have a hard time to find a brick that is not in two pieces.... Dead men and broken shells and shell holes, barbed wire, wagons, guns, horses, are strewn around. The stink would turn a skunk sick. In some places it is beyond a man's imagination and can't be believed until it is seen by your own eyes. They speak of a place called Hell. If they can beat this they have to show me."[1] So wrote James Kirk of Summerside, Prince Edward Island, who, like all of his companions in the Canadian Corps, felt he was a long way from home.

THE CANADIAN CORPS had delivered victory at Courcelette through the sheer determination of the infantry at the sharp end. German intelligence assessments had been right to rate the 1st and 2nd Canadian Divisions as among the top eight divisions in the entire BEF.[2] Other than the break-in by Canadian troops, which dislodged the enemy lines, the larger British offensive had achieved minor results at best.

But Haig stubbornly believed that the Germans must be steadily attacked and worn down. The Entente forces could not let up. At the front, new units were rotated into the line, recommencing the chewing up of men as each battalion took its turn in the forward trench, was wasted away, and returned to the secondary lines and rear in a cycle of four- to six-day periods. John Davis of the No. 9 Field Ambulance noted in his diary, "The fields past Pozières on the way to C[ourcelette] are literally ploughed by the artillery fire. Hardly a sq. yd. of ground can be seen without its shell hole; indeed we have to walk on shell cases and duds all the way. Many kilties lay as they fell in the charge, several others cast up turned faces in the communication trench."[3] Major General Richard Turner noted laconically in his diary that "many dead lie about. The cleaning of a battlefield is a big problem."[4] Rotting, maggot-ridden corpses mocked new men who entered this nightmare. The "odor from the dead bodies is something fierce," lamented a nauseated Gunner Cecil Climo.[5]

Amidst this open graveyard, the infantry dug deeper to find some protection. The Somme's white chalk trenches lay like great bleached bones in the moon's light. Private Willard Melvin of the PPCLI wrote to his family at home: "The two chief elements of trench life here are working with a shovel and taking turns on guard watching that 'Fritz' does not come creeping over looking for mischief."[6] The infantry carried out night patrols and the occasional raid, but much of their time was spent in building trenches. All the while, the wet, white chalk clung to soldiers, leaving most of them looking like they had been dunked in flour with a coat of slime over it.

"It is nerve shattering to be under shell fire," wrote William Curtis, a long-service veteran who was killed on the Somme. "No matter how strong a man's nerves are they are affected. I have seen many a poor fellow break under strain."[7] Studies of soldiers' morale and breakdown in the Second World War noted that men burned out after 200 to 240 days of combat. Those in the First Contingent had now been fighting for over a year and a half, although most of the Canadian battalions serving on the Somme consisted of recruits or formations who had come later.[8] Still, some of the longer-serving soldiers—those who had replaced the Ypres casualties before Festubert, or even those who came afterwards—had been in front-line rotation for over a year. "A man can face death for an hour, with a laugh; for a day, with quiet self-control; but when again, again and again he comes within a hair's breadth of disaster and escapes, and when he just has to *sit* and *wait* for whatever luck brings, every fibre in his being cries for an end—*any* end—to the strain," wrote Armine Norris in a letter to his family.[9]

While they waited for such relief, the Canadians continued to face off against the German trenches. To the left were Mouquet Farm and Zollern Redoubt, which were on the crest-line of a ridge that dominated the Canadian lines; to the right, to the outer ridges of the Courcelette, lay Kenora Trench, and beyond that Regina Trench. The Canadians had cheerfully named these latter German fortifications after familiar spots back home, but they would soon be viewed as dark, foreboding places, and would become the graves of thousands.

In between the German and Canadian trenches lay hundreds of unburied corpses, the only men who occupied No Man's Land. The bodies and their dismembered pieces were covered with a quivering black fur of bluebottle flies, several inches deep. The buzz of flies was everywhere, and the filthy insects entered the nose, ears, and mouth of the soldiers crouched in their trenches. Food was covered in seconds. The coming rain and cold of late September killed off many of these tormentors, but the wet weather brought new trials.

THE CANADIANS and Germans pushed at each other along the line, in night raids and even full-scale operations, such as the

Harold Mowat, Trench Fight

3rd Division's three-battalion attack at dawn on September 20. With the infantry willing to fight and recapture every last bit of ground in relentless counterattacks, hundreds of lives were traded for a few hundred metres of shattered earth.[10] Trenches were lost and recaptured, but the guns on both sides, firing from several kilometres away and largely unassailable, dropped shell after shell into this constricted battlefield where forces had little room to manoeuvre. Defended trenches could be lost and still the attacker could be pounded remorselessly. A dispirited Lieutenant Maurice Pope wrote home to his kin, "We are indeed cannon fodder."[11]

As a result of the heavy casualties, infantry battalions instigated the "left out of battle" (LOB) rule, whereby fifteen to twenty percent of the officers, NCOs, and men were kept in reserve to form a nucleus in the event of a unit being "knocked to pieces."[12] Although keeping men back weakened the attackers at the sharp end, it ensured the possibility of resurrection for a battalion after the firestorm of battle. As long as a core group of men survived, the battalion could be rebuilt, traditions passed on to new men, and the essential lessons of trench survival inculcated in new recruits. As well, the steady injection of men into the battalion maintained the fighting unit as a coherent battle group—the effect being much like giving a continuous blood transfusion to a dying patient. New men, while scared, were not jaded, and therefore the battalion had an internal ability to renew itself and ensure an esprit de corps that mitigated the attrition of morale by the ravages of trench warfare.

This type of rebuilding occurred throughout the war, with most infantry battalions losing 400 to 500 percent of their initial strength.[13] The 16th Battalion had some 5,491 men and officers pass through it, and suffered the loss of 4,846 who were killed, wounded, and taken prisoner—a shocking 79 percent casualty rate even if men who were wounded (and removed to hospital) more than once are accounted for.[14] The 2nd Battalion, another First Contingent unit, had 5,126 officers and men pass through its ranks from September 1914 to April 1919. Of them, 1,279 were killed in action or died of wounds, totalling to a death rate of 25 percent.[15] Long-service veterans would have had virtually no chance of surviving the war unscathed if they were not given a bombproof position in the rear.

With battalions steadily losing men, it might be assumed that morale would always be low as the survivors agonized over the steady loss of their mates. Soldiers did have such reactions, but they got over the pain or simply became inured to it. Some made new friends, while others found they could not get close to anyone as men were wounded or killed each time they invested the time to get to know them. Yet these old hands also soon became the leaders, mentoring new men or rising to fill the gaping holes above them—privates becoming corporals, corporals becoming sergeants, and some sergeants being commissioned as officers. Drawing from the ranks was far preferable to receiving officers from the pool of untested men in England. The battlefield commanding officers knew of the privates and NCOs who had performed with distinction at the front, and even if their education level was low or they did not come from a middle-class background, they were fighters forged in battle. Soldiers with combat and trench experience were needed. The Canadian Corps was learning to survive in the cauldron of fire.

ON SEPTEMBER 26, as part of a four-division British and Canadian attack on a 6,000-metre front, the Canadians were to drive the Germans from their positions along Thiepval Ridge, which was about 1,000 metres northwest of Courcelette, running parallel to the new Canadian lines. By capturing the ridge, they would have a commanding view and jumping-off point for future battles in the Ancre region beyond. But there was little deception as to where the attack would fall, as Germans expected future operations against this portion of the front. All the while, the guns on both sides battered the infantry holding the existing lines. Byng had a frontage of 3,000 metres, and he ordered two divisions to participate in the offensive, which would involve crashing through three separate trench systems: Zollern Graben, Hessian Trench, and Regina Trench, which had a secondary trench—Kenora—branching off it.

On the left, Currie's 1st Division would attack Zollern Graben, Hessian, and the western end of the Regina trench system. While parts of Zollern were in Canadian hands, this long trench criss-crossed the battlefield and was still partly held by the enemy. On the right, Turner's 2nd Division had a far more limited attack: they were to push north into a series of minor German trenches, providing a protective screen for the 1st Division, which was given the primary objective.

For three days, the Canadian artillery pounded the enemy lines, softening up positions, killing defenders, and clearing the barbed wire. Lieutenant Allen Oliver, a forward observer for the 26th Battery, recounted to his family in a letter that he was dirty and verminous, but that "the general idea seems to be to get revenge on the enemy for the five months pounding which he gave us in the [Ypres] salient."[16] In late September, the Canadians were indeed looking for revenge; however, the Germans, too, felt they had more than a little payback coming their way. Both sides would fight to the bitter end.

The assaulting forces were brought into the line to survey the battlefield and wait for zero hour, which was set at 12:35 P.M. Two waves of infantry from eleven battalions of the 2nd, 3rd, and 6th Brigades lay ready in their shallow jumping-off trenches. In the first wave were the 8th and 5th on the far left, the 15th and 14th in the centre, and the 31st, 29th, and 28th on the right, pushing out north of Courcelette.

But the preparation for the assault was difficult to obscure because the confined front did not allow for feints up the line or, in fact, any sort of manoeuvre. The attack would be little more than a desperate plunge forward, and when the bombardment opened, the enemy was not surprised at all. Their counter-barrage came down almost immediately, catching the Canadians in the open ground. "You see two walls of flame in front of you, one where your own barrage is playing, and the one where the enemy guns are firing, and you see two more walls of flame behind you, one where the enemy barrage is playing, and one where your own guns are firing," wrote one Canadian infantryman. "And amid it all you are deafened by titanic explosions which have merged into one thunderous sound, while acrid fumes choke and blind you."[17] Attacking northeast through Courcelette, the 29th Battalion quickly overran the enemy trenches, but on the left, the 31st ran into strong opposition. The operation had been problematic from the start, when the assault companies had been unable to fit into their jumping-off trenches, which were too narrow, as well as overcrowded since the 13th Battalion further to their left were mistakenly occupying 200 metres of the 31st's trenches. The artillery barrage, which placed an intense shrapnel barrage 100 metres short of the enemy front lines, and then, one minute later, crashed down on the German front-line trench for seven minutes before jumping 150 metres beyond, had been effective in suppressing enemy fire from the front-line trench but not from rear positions that had remained largely untouched. Added to the cacophony of sight and sound was the steady barking of small-arms fire. Lieutenant Hector Kennedy, the only officer of the 31st Battalion who was not knocked out, reported that "we were met by a deadly fire of machine-guns and I lost nearly all of my men in the first 75 yards."[18] While the 29th were clearing the German trenches opposite them, the 31st was caught in shell holes in front of their objective, where they spent the entire day suffering under terrible fire. After the punishing day, the 31st attacked again at 10:50 P.M., supported by the 27th Battalion, and pushed to their objectives, shooting, bombing, and bayoneting the survivors in the smoking ruins.

"One of the easiest tasks in this war is to capture a trench, but to hold on to it is something totally different," wrote Lieutenant J.S. Williams.[19] The 31st had proven that, in fact, capturing a trench on the Somme was no easy task, but Williams was correct in assessing that holding a trench was even harder. In crossing No Man's Land, the attacking Entente infantry always lost significant parts of their force to enemy fire, and then used up much of their ammunition, grenades, and manpower in clearing the trenches. At this stage, if success was achieved, the German rapid counterattacks were very hard for the attackers to defeat in such a weakened state, even if Entente supporting artillery laid down heavy fire on the secondary lines. The battle of Thiepval Ridge proved to be no exception to this typical pattern. Seesaw battles raged below the earth, in narrow trenches where men fell and were ground into the mud in the frenzy of fighting. But these German tactics became increasingly costly as Entente artillery prepared for them, and as the attacking infantry set up ambushes and prepared fields of fire as part of the holding phase.

The Entente forces' difficulty in holding trenches was a direct result of logistics problems. The British had revamped their logistical system by bringing in civilian professionals, who better understood how to modernize and ensure the efficient transportation of millions of tons of war supplies by ship and rail; as a result, the supply from munitions factories in Canada and Britain was now efficiently crossing the English Channel to enormous depots on the coast.[20] From there, the military provisions travelled along rail lines to army depots. Corps arranged for the distribution of the essential goods—everything from shells to mail, from timber to food—and all of these moved steadily towards the fighting men at the front. Divisional logistical units brought them closer, stockpiling them to create reserves. Ultimately, trucks, light rail vehicles, mules, and horses hauled the supplies nightly to within a few kilometres of the line, where the heavy ammunition was distributed among gun batteries and the other materiel was pushed towards the front lines. The final journey into the line was humped in by the pack mules of the army: the infantry. This system operated fairly efficiently by the time of the Somme battles, and rarely were the armies starved for supplies.

However, the devil of logistics was not in getting the supplies to the front but in getting those essential stockpiles—food, water, rum, grenades, barbed wire, sand-

By the time of the Somme battles, gunners were firing hundreds of thousands of shells before, during, and after attacks. These shell casings reveal the importance of not only the shells, but also of the logistical system needed to transport this weight of metal to the front.

bags, and everything else—across the 200 metres of No Man's Land during a battle. Like campers on some mad adventure into the unknown, the infantry had to carry all supplies on their backs. The weight of their normally heavy equipment was increased further by crushing supplies, which could include bombs, 5 to 7 sandbags, 170 rounds of small-arms ammunition, extra water bottles, and sometimes wooden ladders, flares, petrol tins filled with water, and medical supplies. Infantrymen might be forced to trudge into battle with over 60 pounds of kit each—no small feat for men who weighed between 120 and 140 pounds on average.[21] Even if webbing— or special tumpline carrying tools—helped to distribute the weight, this ratio of load to body weight was much greater than that which mules or horses were expected to bear.

Although it seemed cruel and unusually stupid to load up the men with such crushing loads, all of these war supplies were used up quickly in the desperate battles of survival that raged back and forth in the blasted trenches. Husbanding grenades or ammunition was nearly impossible when fighting for one's life. Exhausted men suffered from burning thirst and needed to be resupplied. But the enemy, aware that the attacking troops (now turned defenders) were isolated in their forward trenches, laid down a curtain of interdiction fire over No Man's Land. This forced the attackers to make the hard choice of either sending reinforcements and supplies forward in near suicidal rushes or abandoning their own troops. The armies of all nations could get their supplies across hundreds, even thousands, of kilometres, but the challenge of the final two hundred metres often reduced the warfighting on the Western Front to a stalemate.

ON SEPTEMBER 26, the battle raged back and forth. The 28th Battalion was to attack on the far-right flank, to the east of Courcelette, and was given the only two functioning tanks in the Canadian Corps since they had an open flank on the right. But the first tank broke down before the start line, and the second exploded when a German shell hit its ammunition, burning alive the operators inside. The commanding officer decided that any attack would only result in useless casualties, and the forward companies therefore did not leave the trenches, although a small group of bombers were sent to raid the opposite lines. The raiders succeeded in capturing a number of prisoners, but they saw clearly that this was only an outpost, and that the Germans had pulled back their main force sometime during the previous night.

To the west of the 2nd Division's attack, the 1st Division had a longer front and more battalions committed to battle. On the divisional right, the 14th and 15th Battalions attacked Hessian Trench and the equally strong Regina Trench behind it, with this latter position being largely hidden as it lay just over the crest of a spur on Thiepval Ridge. To get a sense of this operation, it is profitable to follow young James Owen, who was in the trenches before his sixteenth birthday, and who fought alongside his two seventeen-year-old brothers, Cecil and Iorwerth, in the 15th Battalion.

The first waves went over the top at 12:35 P.M., and soon the sunny day was shattered by screaming men and ear-shattering explosions. Private James Owen advanced towards the enemy, his companions cut down all around him by shrapnel and small-arms fire. The ground was bouncing under his feet as the artillery barrage rocked the landscape. After a few minutes, Owen and another man, who was charging ahead of him, were leading the attack, with everyone else having either gone to ground or been sent to it by the whirling metal. His companion "was engaged in a most grisly bit of action," recounted Owen. "A German had come out of his trench to meet him with the bayonet ... [but] had chickened out and tried to surrender. Our boy would have none of it. He lunged at the German again and again, who each time lowered his arms and stopped the point of the bayonet with his bare hands. He was screaming for mercy. Oh God, it was brutal!"

Owen pushed past the grim spectacle, and encountered two more Germans trying to surrender, both of whom were shouting "Kamerad, Kamerad!" As he slowed to consider his options with the prisoners, another Canadian, who had caught up to Owen and perhaps was unsure as to what was happening, fired at the Germans but missed them, the bullets slamming into the trenches near their heads. The would-be prisoners scattered, and Owen jumped into the enemy trench, where he later killed several Germans while they were sniping at onrushing Canadians. German resistance was broken in one section of trench and, in Owen's words, "the remaining Germans were then allowed to surrender. It was indicated to them that they should go to our rear. They left us hurriedly…. No guard or escort was sent with them even though the ground was strewn with weapons. They were not a threat anyway. All they wanted was out."

Owen and his few surviving mates tried to consolidate their position in the enemy trench, now filled with dead and dying Germans. They had no time to attend to these unfortunates, as a German counterattack was soon expected. They turned to working furiously on making the captured trenches defensible. Their first job was to reverse the trench firesteps, but they did not have enough shovels and picks, and were left staring up at the tall sandbagged walls. As the small party of Canadians was confronting this dilemma, a shell landed at the end of the trench, killing a soldier at Owen's side and wounding him in the thigh.

The impact of the shell knocked Owen off his feet, but adrenaline pushed thoughts of rest from his mind. After picking himself up, Owen joined the steadily thinning ranks of the Canadians, who continued to drive their wedge into the German lines, heading off down communication and side trenches to consolidate their weak position. Bleeding profusely, but stumbling forward on adrenaline, fear, and discipline, Owen encountered another German and killed him immediately with a rifle shot to the head. As Owen recounted years later, "I should have given him a chance to surrender and I've felt sorry about it ever since. However, we had always been told to shoot first and talk afterwards, and life was extremely cheap that day."

James Owen was close to collapse when a lieutenant found him. The officer had captured two prisoners and, no longer needing them, ordered them to the rear. One prisoner scurried off, but the second began to argue with the officer—possibly, Owen thought, because he wanted "an escort to assure their safety when next they met other Canadians." The lieutenant ordered the prisoner to the rear again. When he did not move, the officer shot him through the head with his revolver. At this point, Cecil, James's brother, ran into him. They embraced, and Cecil bound his brother's wounds, happy that he was alive. The officer, realizing that two brothers were in the front lines, and noting that the position was soon to be attacked and likely overrun, ordered young James to the rear. James gruffly tried to plead that he was all right, but the officer—who had already proven he was not to be trifled with—was having none of it. James limped back, but not before waving goodbye to his brother, whom he never expected to see again. Cecil survived the German counterattack, but James's other brother, Iorwerth, was shot in the stomach and died of his wounds in agony three days later. At roll call the next day, James was one of only two men from the twelve-man section who had made it back.[22]

Despite the chaos of James Owen's personal battle, both the 14th and 15th Battalions captured their objectives within a few hours. On the right, the 14th consolidated parts of Kenora Trench against counterattacks, while on the left, the Kilties of the 15th Battalion were pushed out of Kenora Trench junction in a series of battles, but dug in to a series of large shell holes to the south of the trench. The casualties ran deep for the Canadians as the forces were sheared away in attack and counterattack. By 6 P.M., for instance, the 15th had been forced to bring up every available infantryman to their vulnerable position.[23] Most of this new Canadian line was held after almost forty continuous hours of battle, and the German defenders in the area—the 26th Regiment—lost nearly every single man in the forward trenches.[24]

Further to the left, the 8th and 5th Battalions, along with elements of the 10th, attacked the highest part of Thiepval Ridge. The 8th and the 5th advanced some 600 men strong each, and a supporting company of 150 men went forward from the 10th Battalion. Firepower was essential: the 8th Battalion had ten machine guns and the 5th had sixteen to suppress enemy strongpoints and mask tougher positions with fire. But the artillery barrage failed to destroy the enemy defences, and the creeping barrage was too thin to smother the enemy fire: the first wall of fire landed 50 metres in front of the objective and then lifted at zero hour over the objective, in effect leaving the trenches largely unharmed when the infantry crossed No Man's Land.[25] The first two infantry waves were to race to their final objectives and capture them before the enemy realized the extent of the attack. Three more waves would consolidate the captured positions or try to punch deep into the German trenches if the initial attack bogged down.

But even one enemy machine-gun team could hold up an attack. Unfortunately, the attacking components of the 2nd Brigade ran into a number of them, both on their own front and firing from the British sector to the left. The Germans had learned to situate their machine guns behind the first and second lines, as these trenches were often the primary targets of the artillery bombardment. Camouflaged and situated between these lines—German doctrine stated that "the best sites are in the open, or concealed under hedges"—they were far harder to identify, and could still lay down sweeping fire when targets presented themselves.[26]

The lead infantry units of the 2nd Brigade attacked in waves, many of them tucking their chins low to the chest, bending over as if in a heavy rainstorm. The need to avert one's eyes from the terror of advancing in the open can perhaps only be understood by those who were there, facing a nearly solid wall of whirling steel. Whatever few actual protections the trenches offered against high explosive shells, at least these shelters gave the men a psychological sense of safety from the rigours of the modern battlefield. Discipline kept soldiers moving in the chaos of battle, but as they followed a creeping wall of metal and explosives while also suffering under additional dropshorts (friendly fire) and the German counter-barrage, the infantry were under no illusions about their mortality. Soldiers strayed to the left and right, some dove into the first shell hole they could find, and others charged off into their own barrage, blown apart by the shells. Officers and NCOs attempted to lead the men forward and keep them spaced in formation, while always fighting their own fears.

The forward wave of the 5th Battalion crashed the German outposts, but as the war diarist noted phlegmatically, the lead forces were "thinned down considerably" by the time they reached Hessian Trench. "During the advance quite a lot of sniping took place, and needless to say, no mercy was shown to the Huns who kept that up until cornered, and then threw up their hands."[27] The deep dugouts that had offered the enemy protection from artillery fire were now "death traps," in the words of one soldier.[28] The Canadians tossed grenades or phosphorus bombs down the dark entrances; these terrifying bombs spewed toxic smoke and chemical incendiaries that could burn flesh down to the bone. But more and more men were lost in the fighting; the deeper they went into the enemy lines, the more eagerly the "mincing machine," as one infantryman described it, began to swallow them.[29] Hessian Trench, which ran along the entire Canadian front, and was therefore attacked in places by several Canadian battalions, was finally captured and held, but at a terrible cost. On the 5th Battalion's portion of the front, 16 officers were killed or wounded, and of the ranks, 52 were killed, 291 wounded, and 122 missing. After the latter figure was adjusted for men found in hospitals and mixed up with other units, those included in it were usually killed rather than prisoners, their bodies shredded beyond recognition or blown to unidentifiable scraps of flesh.[30]

The 8th Battalion—or the "Little Black Devils," as they called themselves—had overrun Zollern Graben (situated about halfway between the Canadian lines and Hessian Trench further to the north), even though they had sustained crippling casualties from machine-gunners firing from untouched positions further to the west in Zollern Redoubt. Furthermore, the enemy artillerymen had sighted their guns on the now lost trench and then bombarded it with painfully accurate fire. Lieutenant Clifford Wells, who had left graduate school to enlist in 1915, described to his brother how it felt to be trapped in a trench under shellfire: "Everything seemed unreal. I could not make myself feel that the shells bursting around us were really intended to harm us, and it was a shock to see a shell which burst in the German lines and hurled two bodies 75 feet or more into the air."[31] But the lieutenant well understood the severity of the operation, and had included a letter for his mother in case he should not survive the battle. Wells did survive his "baptism of fire" but was later killed in the fighting near Vimy Ridge.

With junior officers, NCOs, and the privates driving forward, objectives were captured as enemy strongpoints fell to bomb and bayonet attacks. Almost three hours after the assault, C and D Companies of the 8th Battalion on the right had pushed on and captured parts of Hessian Trench, but they had been reduced to three officers and eighty men from the ranks.[32] Hundreds of prisoners were captured, but the Canadian losses had been too heavy to allow for many escorts. The Germans were disarmed and sent to the rear, but it was later found that a few picked up stray weapons and harassed follow-on troops or fired at the Canadians from behind. After that, T.G. Caunt of the 8th Battalion grimly noted, "there weren't any more prisoners taken."[33]

The Little Black Devils pushed on, but the strong objectives to the north, which because of their fortified nature would normally be assaulted by an entire company, now had to be captured by what amounted to a reinforced platoon. The deaths of officers, machine-gunners, and bombers always left units unbalanced, and the organization of the new ad hoc battle group required a quick sorting out by the highest-ranking man, who was often a lieutenant or a long-serving sergeant. Aware that their pathetically weak force could not possibly capture anything, let alone hold it, the 8th Battalion dug in.

Counterattacks came, but not from the front, being instead directed from the left flank, where elements of the 11th British Division had been unable to capture their part of Hessian Trench. The Germans tried to decapitate the weakened Canadian force, which had placed its neck on the block by jutting deep into the enemy lines. A period of ominous silence from that portion of the front ensued. Eighth battalion runners darted to the rear, passing through the enemy's

A battalion could go in 700 strong and come out with
half that strength (or less) two or three days later.

barrage, and were able to inform the brigade headquarters of the dangerous situation, which rushed up a small force from the 10th Battalion. The injection of the 10th Battalion troops defeated the German attack and held the front, but two days after the battle the 8th Battalion's war diarist reported starkly that the battalion had lost 13 officers and 446 other ranks, a staggering casualty figure for a battalion that was about 600 rifles strong.[34]

With only parts of the enemy line captured, and with a gap between the British and Canadian corps, General Gough ordered a series of attacks the next day. But the Germans had coolly appraised their broken lines and pulled back their troops to the fortified Regina Trench in the middle of the night. Enemy outposts were systematically destroyed by Canadian raiders over the coming days, but probing attacks against Regina Trench revealed that it was strongly held, and protected by deep rows of barbed wire. It could only be captured behind a full set-piece battle with extensive artillery support.

THE BATTLE OF THIEPVAL RIDGE, which officially ran for three days on the Canadian front, had been a study in nearly unimaginable brutality. Attacks raged back and forth over the same shell-torn ground, with the infantry savagely fighting for every square metre of territory. Lewis machine gun and Lee-Enfield rifle fire had proven essential in holding off counterattacks, while grenades had been the weapon of choice in clearing the winding and shattered trench systems. The fragmentation Mills grenade was deadlier than the German explosive stick grenade, but the German weapon could be thrown further by as much as 3.5 metres.[35] But despite this weapon's greater range, the Canadians preferred their own grenade, which could wreak havoc on enemy troops stuffed in a trench, bay, or dugout. Yet a finite number of grenades were available, and they were often used up quickly by men in the heat of battle, desperate to clear enemy strongpoints or hold off counterattacking forces. When they were gone, much of the defence crumbled with them.

After the battle, which could be called a partial victory at best, the shattered assault battalions were rotated out of the line and new units were marched into the open graveyard. "The Somme is a dreadful place," wrote Sergeant George Ormsby to his wife. "The man that gets a decent wound there is lucky as I certainly consider myself."[36] Ormsby took shrapnel through his shoulder and back during the September 26 battle, and his war, like many, ended on the Somme. He had served since May 1915, and in his fifteen months of battle he had watched most of his friends and mates be killed or wounded. He would have over a year of painful recovery before he saw his family again.

THE NIGHTMARE LANDSCAPE and the ferocity of battle pushed men to the limits of endurance. The Canadians had sustained more than 10,000 casualties on the Somme in September, and the German army lost a total of 135,000 men across the entire Somme front during that one month, a casualty rate that nearly destroyed its fighting efficiency. German crown prince Ruprecht could not believe the intensity of fighting, remarking on the "persistence with which the attacks are continued," and declaring, "This simply cannot last."[37] In this war of attrition, both sides were now fighting for survival.

THE BATTLE OF THIEPVAL RIDGE: SEPTEMBER 26, 1916

CHAPTER 36

"WE POUND, POUND, POUND"

Regina Trench, October 1, 1916

"Our advance is slow, methodical, irresistible—We pound, pound, pound, blasting our way. Land, houses, men and beasts are destroyed. There was never a plague like it."[1] Such was Talbot Papineau's view of the Somme fighting. This captain had been born into a famous Quebec family, whose grandfather was Louis-Joseph Papineau, the leader of the Patriote rebels in 1837. After fighting for more than a year at the front, Papineau's political backers at home, who envisioned him as a future politician, used their influence to pull him out of the fighting and transfer him to a bombproof job in the rear. Papineau accepted the move, but he had earned the respect of his men in the PPCLI, and he agonized over leaving them. Sheltering in the bombproof post would surely save his life, but could he live with himself? "More friends are gone. By what strange law am I still here?" Papineau wondered.[2] Unable to shake his belief that he had abandoned his men, Papineau returned to the front, where he was killed a year later while leading his troops in battle.

AS PART OF A BRITISH OFFENSIVE planned for mid-October, the Canadians were ordered to capture Regina Trench in what would be known as the Battle of the Ancre Heights. The powerful Regina trench system ran the entire length of the Canadian front—more than 3,000 metres—and it had withstood all previous assaults. Built over the crest of a spur on Thiepval Ridge, the trench was difficult for the British and Canadian artillery to hit, as the shells usually fell behind or crashed in front of the line.

Although he had little time to prepare for an assault, General Byng accurately appraised the strength of the position, which was protected by barbed wire, and ordered a severe bombardment all along the front to shatter the fortress. But as in so many of the Somme operations the conditions allowed little room for an innovative plan: positions could not be flanked since no flanks existed, and even the time of the attack was rigid, as dozens of units in many formations were ordered to attack concurrently. Nor could the position be ignored or masked with fire (to allow the infantry to slip around it as the enemy was driven into the ground to take cover), as Regina dominated the British lines. Therefore, even when the failure of shellfire to destroy the defences was revealed, Byng was left with little choice but to inform his two divisional commanders, Turner and Lipsett, that the attack "must take place."[3] Both divisional commanders had objected that their men would have no chance against such strong positions, but the British army commander, Hubert Gough, had overridden Byng, demanding that the attack take place so that other troops could advance. This was generalship by guess and by God. There was no room for manoeuvring on the ground or, apparently, in the headquarters behind the lines.

The 2nd Division was in for more grinding warfare, although its soldiers had been fought out in battles since September 15. Byng's decision to keep Turner's men in the line was unwise, and the corps commander was clearly frustrated by the division's slow advance. In his diary, an exhausted and dispirited Turner lamented the inability of the Canadian artillery to cut the barbed wire, and even worse, their periodic shelling of his own lines. Of his infantry, he enthused, "From my heart I thank God at being privileged to serve with such gallant men. No recompense on earth can adequately reward them for their sacrifices in so many cases, 'loyal until death,'" adding angrily, "We have to attack again!"[4]

The main assault would be delivered by the 2nd Division's 4th and 5th Brigades attacking north from beyond the Canadian strongpoint at Courcelette, and supported on the left flank by the 4th and 5th CMRs from the 3rd Division's 8th Brigade. After several days of patrolling and studying the ground, scouting officers reported that the barbed wire had barely been touched by the artillery barrage, and that few paths could be found through the jagged brambles. Front-line officers waited for guidance from headquarters as to how to proceed, and more than a few of them must have remembered the line from Tennyson's poem "The Charge of the Light Brigade"—"Theirs but to do and die"—when they heard that the infantry assault would nonetheless go ahead as initially planned.[5]

In the meantime, Robert Clements of the 25th Battalion was in the front lines monitoring the work of the heavy artillery in trying to cut the barbed wire. The gunners were not having much success when the shells suddenly began to work their way back towards the Canadian lines. Clements and his mates looked on with horror as the six-inch shells began to land in front of, and then in their trenches down the line. "It was bad enough to face everything that the enemy could throw, but getting killed by [our] own shells was just too much," wrote Clements. Luckily, the 25th had experienced officers—recent combat-veteran NCOs who were promoted from the ranks—and these men had no qualms about abandoning the trench and getting their men to the rear. Their quick action saved the lives of many, and Clements was grateful not to be another fatality statistic, especially one who had been "killed by accident."[6] The Canadians would have ample opportunity to be killed by deliberate action in the days to come.

THE NIGHT BEFORE the battle, the trench stormers waited in a steady drizzle, battling their nerves and counting down to zero hour: 3:15 P.M. on October 1. The time for battle had been set by Gough, as army commander, and units within the British Fourth Army were also coordinating their offensive to ensure that the forces attacked in unison.[7] There is no indication as to why a mid-afternoon zero hour was decided upon, and the timing seemed to offer all the advantages to the enemy. Also, unbeknownst to Canadian intelligence officers, a fresh marine division had been moved into the line opposite them, and its companies were almost up to full strength, unlike many German divisions at this point that were severely weakened and had not yet received reinforcements.[8] These marines were prepared to fight to the bitter end, and one prisoner later revealed that it was "generally believed" that the Canadians killed prisoners, so the enemy troops were unlikely to surrender.[9]

Even though many of the German field guns and howitzers had long burned themselves out through massive overuse, the marines were now situated on the axis of advance through which the Canadians would have to pass. And they were waiting with machine guns, mortars, and Mauser rifles.

On the left, two companies from each of the 4th and 5th CMRs were to break into Regina Trench, capture a portion of it, and hold it to ensure that the main attack on the right was not harassed by flanking counterattacks. But the artillery barrage, although heavy, had done little damage to Regina Trench or its defenders since most of the shells had landed behind the first trench, leaving the original line unscathed. When the barrage opened up in the broad daylight and the officers ordered their men over the top at 3:15 P.M., the telltale sound of machine-gun fire was heard above the din on what was otherwise a lovely fall day. The creeping barrage had failed to destroy or suppress the enemy positions, and some Germans had moved out of their trenches to occupy shell craters in advance of the trenches.[10] Normally, the rest of the defenders would have taken refuge in their dugouts by this point. German doctrine indicated that during a creeping barrage, it was the role of an unlucky sentry, standing at the top of the dugout stairs, to race outside when the barrage seemed to move off their position and survey the battlefield for advancing troops. Most of the garrison was to stay below, for as one captured German report noted, "It is wrong for all the occupants of the dug-out to hurry to the parapet immediately after the enemy's fire has ceased: the enemy frequently only makes a pause in his firing and then, suddenly re-opening fire, inflicts casualties on the garrison."[11] In the case of this attack, however, Canadian survivors noted that although the ineffective and erratic barrage was supposedly playing on the enemy lines, in reality shells were falling short or going long, and the Germans were so unhindered that they were seen standing above the trench firing at the Canadians as they advanced.[12]

The Canadians found themselves facing a frontal assault against one of the most fortified positions on the Western Front. That anyone survived above the ground in such a firestorm was amazing. But it was not easy to hit a man while he was moving. Machine guns fired along fixed lines in wide arcs that created a beaten path, but they could not fire continuously. They laid down bursts, and in between these flashes, or during the changing of ammunition belts, or after the arc of fire passed the men's positions, the infantry moved forward. These gaps in fire allowed advancing soldiers to survive on the open battlefield within a hail of gunfire.

But the CMRs were far from safe. Within minutes, the lead units were cut to pieces, as several machine guns swept the ground and riflemen engaged in rapid fire. Dozens of Canadian corpses could be seen hanging on the wire. Almost the entire D company of the 4th CMR, attacking on the right, was wiped out before they even crossed the killing ground; A Company made it to the trench, passing their slain companions, and then stormed it. They held Regina Trench for a few hours, but were annihilated to a man by relentless enemy counterattacks coming from the secondary German lines.

The 5th CMR fared little better, suffering terrible casualties in simply attempting to reach the enemy trench. When the survivors arrived, most of the Germans had fled, although the men of the 5th took some pleasure in shooting many in the back as they scrambled over the ground since their communication trenches were caved in from the shellfire. It was clear, though, that a strong counterattacking force would soon be on them since both flanks were "in the air"; the 4th CMR on the left and 24th Battalion on the right had been unable to keep up as they had, for the most part, been shot down in No Man's Land. The few surviving officers of the 5th quickly recognized that they were in a very vulnerable position.

The battalion's receipt of much-needed reinforcements, grenades, and ammunition was delayed, as all communication to the rear was cut off by artillery fire. Signaller Sergeant R.B. Givson recounted in a letter that there were "forty-three breaks [in the telephone wire] in that small 300 yards, and when anybody went out to fix same, it was the last we expected to see of him.... Linemen work practically sixteen hours a day and are under the most intense shell-fire during that period. But telephone communication has got to be kept up, for on it rests the success and cooperation of the whole front." Givson survived, but noted, "the majority of my chums were not quite so lucky."[13] Because of these communication difficulties, commanders in the rear were effectively blind to the ever-changing situation at the front.

The 5th CMR was locked in vicious combat throughout the rest of the day. An effective supporting barrage that rained down high explosives and sweeping shrapnel fire had been set up to fall to the north of the newly won trenches to keep the Germans from massing their forces; but because the flanks were not protected, the Germans eventually attacked along communication and secondary trenches. Although the CMRs were able to hold on longer because reinforcements were eventually fed forward, their casualties were staggering. Lieutenant George Pearkes, who had the most combat experience of the battalion's surviving officers, led four platoons from the 5th CMR and the reinforcing 1st CMR in a bombing raid at 10:30 P.M. in the hope of linking up with the 24th Battalion on the right. This vanguard force pushed 500 metres into enemy lines using innovative tactics: the bombers rushed through the trenches, while supporting bayonet men crawled along outside of the trenches in the dark, dropping on the enemy when the bombers ran into severe problems. Throughout the night and the next day, Pearkes's steadily dwindling battle group fought and retreated, fighting over the same wrecked trenches for more than ten hours.[14] But the 24th could not push forward to link up with the CMR battle group, and so Pearkes was forced to retreat in the face of steady enemy pressure. By 5 A.M. on October 2, the Canadians were eventually pushed out of Regina Trench and back into Hessian, having lost 962 men.[15]

TO THE RIGHT of the CMRs, the 5th Brigade, as part of the main assault, would attack on a 1,000-metre front, and was tasked with overrunning two formidable defensive systems: Kenora Trench and Regina Trench. Brigadier Archibald Macdonell of the 5th Brigade realized that his depleted force, which had lost heavily in the fighting for and around Courcelette, would need at least three battalions to achieve their objectives since most of them were down to at most half strength. From left to right, the 24th, 25th, and 22nd Battalions would storm the enemy positions. Yet all along the front, the artillery had failed to cut the barbed wire. And so, sharing the fate of the 8th Brigade's CMR battalions, Macdonell's men were channelled into killing grounds. During the preliminary barrage, the heavy artillery consistently fired short, and, despite the frantic work of liaison officers, this continued on for half a day. Equally disheartening was the fact that when the creeping barrage opened up, it fell behind the forward assault troops and then raked through them, killing and maiming dozens of Canadians before righting itself.[16] As a result, a staggering 130 casualties were attributed to friendly fire.

But even without this added horror, the attack would likely not have achieved its objective of capturing two trench systems. The battalions simply did not have enough men, with the 25th, for example, mustering only 200 among all ranks and 12 machine guns.[17] More than half of the Maritimers in the 25th fell during the battle, but the weakened unit still succeeded in capturing Kenora Trench, which had been levelled by weeks of artillery fire. The battalion's remaining soldiers established Lewis guns as their main line of defence, one of which was manned by Lance Corporal Ralph Lewis, a former Newfoundland steamboat second mate who was awarded the Military Medal for his performance in the battle. With the Canadians holding the newly won position, the Germans pounded Kenora all day, and the lance corporal was twice nearly killed by artillery fire. Lewis recounted that the second time a shell burst over his position, "It got one of the men who was just behind me, tore off his leg and a big chunk went into his back, missed me, and the concussion took the chap that was in front of me and landed him about 5 yards away dead."[18] The path of shrapnel and explosives was impossible to predict, and it is no wonder that so many men became fatalists.

In the centre, the 25th Battalion had been ordered to attack and capture Regina Trench "at all costs." But this order was simply impossible to follow. By the end of the day, the crossfire of enemy machine guns and artillery fire had reduced the 25th to a skeleton of itself, and almost every man who could carry a rifle, including those from the transport and quartermaster stores, was sent to hold the front. The 25th held Kenora, but at one point the battalion's frontage was held by only one officer and two other ranks.

On the left, the 24th Battalion pushed past Kenora and into Regina Trench, but they were unable to close the gap with the CMRs on the left flank. The Victoria Rifles, as the 24th Battalion still called themselves, in allegiance to their prewar militia designation, held parts of Regina, but were soon under unending attacks and "owing to the lack of men, they were annihilated."[19] On the right, the 22nd Battalion was ordered to advance over 700 metres on a 370-metre front, only to be cut up by friendly fire, enemy machine guns, and an accurate

German SOS counter-barrage that caught the second and third waves in the open. A mere few dozen men were left to push into Regina Trench, and they were crushed in a wave of attacks. One officer recounted sadly that the 22nd Battalion "ceased to exist as a unit."[20]

The 5th Brigade had been given neither the support nor the men to capture Regina Trench, and while its pre-battle trench strength of 1,717 had been pathetic enough, the brigade of four battalions—which at a full strength had been about 4,000 men—had now been reduced to 773.[21] As Sergeant Percy Willmot, a long-serving Cape Bretoner in the 5th Brigade, noted in a letter home to his cousin, "I am fast becoming a hardened and calloused old Soldier. The loss of dear friends is a matter of every day occurrence and awakens little deep feeling."[22]

On the far right of the assault, the 18th and 20th Battalions of the 4th Brigade suffered under unceasing machine-gun fire, but their creeping shrapnel barrage was far more effective here than along the rest of the Canadian front, and it successfully kept the Germans in their dugouts. The two battalions pushed 500 metres into the enemy front, but the 20th also had the misfortune of being assigned a part of the front that contained no enemy trenches. When they reached their objectives, they were to dig new trenches, in the open and under fire. This was the type of order that read like a suicide note and was completely unbefitting the brigade or divisional officer who penned it. But the infantry did their duty, diving into still-smoking shell craters and linking these up through desperate digging.[23]

During a miserable night of desultory rain and shellfire, the 18th and 20th Battalions, reinforced by elements from the 4th Brigade's two other battalions in reserve, beat back a German counterattack, leaving the Canadians in control of the front. But they had not captured Regina, succeeding only in helping to straighten out the line to protect the flanks of British units on their right. William Wright of the 19th Battalion, a prewar teacher who would be killed at the Battle of Hill 70 almost a year later, and whose unit helped to consolidate the gains on the 4th Brigade's front, wrote that the infantry fought hard, but that "the shelling was fearful." After several days enduring this terrible strain, he and his comrades "looked like wild beasts."[24]

THE OPERATION against Regina Trench had failed because the artillery had been unable to accurately destroy the trench or the barbed wire protecting it. Shellfire could tear barbed wire apart, but it also threw it around the battlefield like enormous metal tumbleweeds, creating new obstacles. "My heart breaks … when I think of the brave young men that I have seen hanging on the wire," recounted J. Keiler McKay of the Canadian Field Artillery.[25] Often the gunners had neither the proper shells nor the skills to hit the enemy line situated on the reverse slope of the ridge from their positions several kilometres in the rear. As well, many gun barrels had been worn down from overuse. An 18-pounder was supposed to have its barrel changed after firing 20,000 rounds, since the intense heat of prolonged fire often melted it slightly, rendering it increasingly inaccurate; many Canadian guns had fired double or triple that number of shells, and now the guns were firing long and short. Furthermore, faulty ammunition that was covered in mud tended to travel in irregular paths or, occasionally, explode in the gun barrel. As infrequent as the latter type of event was, it only had to happen once to a gunner to put an end to his war. As a result of such problems, enemy defences were often left undestroyed, and the garrisons were not forced into their deep dugouts before the Canadian infantry went over the top. Equally debilitating to the attacking infantry was the Canadian artillery's focus on the enemy front, to the detriment of also focusing counterbattery fire against the opposite gunners. But the Canadians did not have enough heavy guns to reach the enemy batteries far to the rear, and had not yet developed a reliable means of locating, targeting, and destroying them. This was unfortunate for the infantry, as entire enemy trenches and their garrisons might be wiped off the face of the earth, but every German shell fired into the path through which the assault groups had to pass would continue to take a terrible toll.

The gunners' unreliability was, however, not the only reason for the failure at Regina Trench. The normally solid General Byng can be faulted for pushing the Canadians, and particularly the 2nd Division, to capture the position, even though the infantry battalions were played out. No excuses can be made for the high command that ordered attacks to capture strongpoints along Regina Trench even though the forward units were indicating the near impossibility of the task. These rushed and callous operations indicated that although the corps had learned from

The Battle of the Ancre Heights: Regina Trench, October 1, 1916

The Battle of the Ancre Heights: Regina Trench, October 1, 1916

Courcelette

20TH BATTALION

18TH BATTALION

4TH CANADIAN INFANTRY BRIGADE

Dyke Road

Pys Road

3RD MARINE INF REGT

1ST MARINE INFANTRY REGT

E. Miraumont Road

Courcelette Trench

W. Miraumont Road

Regina Trench

Kenora Trench

22ND BATTALION

25TH BATTALION

24TH BATTALION

5TH CANADIAN INFANTRY BRIGADE

Desire Support Trench

5TH C.M.R.

ELEMENTS 2ND C.M.R.

ELEMENTS 1ST C.M.R.

CQY 4TH C.M.R.

Hessian Trench

4TH C.M.R.

2ND MARINE INF REGT

8TH CANADIAN INFANTRY BRIGADE

0 250 500 metres

the setpiece battles of June 13 and September 15, a further refinement of tactics and the overall approach to battle had to be worked out. In particular, the artillery and infantry needed to be welded into a combined arm, and high command needed to accept that it was necessary to delay operations until success was possible. A lack of flexibility on the latter score was a hallmark of the British fighting on the Somme and had led to tens of thousands of deaths.

General Haig's assessment of the Canadian operation on the 1st was ungenerous to say the least: "I think the case was that in the hope of saving lives they attacked in too weak numbers....They [the Canadians] have been very extravagant in expending ammunition! This points rather to nervousness and low morale."[26] Such things were perhaps easier to say several kilometres behind the line, where the general did not have to personally witness the 5,509 casualties suffered by the Canadians from late September to early October.[27]

CHAPTER 37

NO REST, NO RETREAT

Regina Trench, October 8, 1916

"Mud under me, water around me and hell above me," grumbled Gunner Reginald Grant.[1] The weather turned foul in early October, with drenching rains reducing the shattered landscape to a quagmire of sticky, deep mud. The smell of sodden wool clothing and equipment pervaded the infantry, and some found the odour more trying than the stench of rotting corpses. As shells pummelled the battlefield, trenches began to dissolve in the rain. Front-line troops battled the enemy and the weather, and soldiers engaged in a constant struggle to shore up defences in the sea of mud. Lieutenant Colonel Andrew McNaughton, who had been wounded at Ypres but who had returned to his unit and was applying his scientific mind to improving gunnery skills, remembered walking through spongy trenches and finding the resilient ground a relief from the quagmire of mud until he realized that he was tramping "through the bodies of our own men."[2] The mud sucked greedily: boots were pulled from feet; artillery guns slowly sank out of sight; stockpiles of shells disappeared into the muck; the dead returned to the earth.

The Canadian and German artillery continued to rake the battlefield, adding new names to the already sickening list of killed and wounded. "When they struck, the ground looked like Resurrection Day with the dead elbowing their way into daylight and forcing back the earth from their eyes," wrote Lieutenant Coningsby Dawson of the shellfire. "There were actually many dead just beneath the surface and, as the ground was ploughed up, the smell of corruption became distinctly unpleasant."[3]

Yet the fighting stopped for nothing. At night, all along the front, battle patrols were crawling through the mud and over bodies of their countrymen, gauging enemy defences and especially whether or not barbed wire had been cut. The artillery continued their program of blasting the enemy wire in front of Regina Trench, but intelligence reports indicated that neither the wire nor the strongpoints in and around the objective were sufficiently cleared or demolished. Thousands of additional shells were fired.

General Haig wrote to King George V on October 5 regarding the recent fighting: "I venture to think that the results are highly satisfactory, and I believe the Army in France feels the same as I do in this matter. The troops see that they are slowly but surely destroying the German Armies in their front, and that their Enemy is much less capable of defence than he was even a few weeks ago."[4] Haig also believed that his divisions were becoming more and more effective. While survivors of these brutal battles were indeed hammering out new skills to ensure they drew another day's breath, few front-line troops could see beyond the mud and misery of their trench, and fewer would have concluded that the German army was "surely" being destroyed.

"O JESUS, MAKE IT STOP!" This pleading conclusion to British war poet Siegfried Sassoon's poem "Attack" would have resonated throughout the trenches. But the war at the front never stopped: there was no escape from the shells; no rest from the constant pressure of sentry duty while the enemy patrolled No Man's Land; no place to run from the tendrils of poison gas that worked into the trenches or polluted the shell holes; no respite from the enormous rats that fed on the rotting corpses; no way to avoid the hollow eyes of the living and the dead. And no stopping the orders to attack.

"It was straight slugging," wrote Major Dan Ormond, in an attempt to categorize the Somme fighting.[5] Eight battalions from the 1st and 3rd Divisions were ordered to assault Regina Trench at 4:50 A.M. on October 8. Gough's army was pushing forward despite the terrible losses on October 1, and the general needed the Canadians to capture Regina Trench to allow for further operations in that region.[6] Byng was urged on. Unfortunately, the Canadian high command had had little time to make many changes to the attack doctrine, and except for the new assault being carried out under cover of darkness, this "push" would have few differences from the one attempted a week earlier.

The operation on October 1 had failed largely because the artillery had been unable to sever the wire and suppress enemy fire. Intelligence reports compiled from aerial photographs and ground patrols indicated that while the enemy trench was "considerably damaged in parts by our Artillery, it [was] still very strong."[7] The German positions also continued to dominate the Canadian lines, a geographical advantage that allowed the enemy to look down into the zone of preparation.

General Currie of the 1st Division made a special visit to the Canadian Corps headquarters to implore the artillery to fire everything they had in support of his troops. A young Major Alan Brooke, an Imperial officer attached to the corps, and who would later rise to chief of the Imperial general staff in the Second World War, remembered Currie telling him, "Brooke, I want you to realize how much depends on the guns: my boys haven't got the kick in them which they had; I look to the guns to put them into Regina Trench."[8] Alan Brooke was deeply moved by Currie's plea and his desire to save his men's lives; he promised to do his best.

The corps threw thousands of tonnes of metal into the battle, including twenty-four Vickers machine guns to thicken up the barrage with small-arms fire, but many of the Regina positions still remained in the dead ground behind the reverse slope and were not easily hit. Scouting parties were sent out to locate the strength of the wire, but since most of the experienced men had been killed or wounded in previous operations, much of the intelligence was insufficient, often being too optimistic.[9] But even inexperienced men could look down at the ankle-deep mud and wonder how they would discharge their rifles in battle after they and their weapons had become slathered and clogged. Above them, however, the ever-present wall of shells helped to assuage some nerves, as the overwhelming supportive shellfire smashed the enemy lines day and night. The Canadian artillery did its best in laying down a heavy barrage on the enemy's reverse slope position, but without an accurate method of locating and silencing enemy artillery guns further to the rear, any attacking troops leaving the relative safety of their own trenches would have to contend with shrapnel in the open.

On the far right, the 1st Division's 3rd and 4th Battalions followed their creeping barrage into No Man's Land, passing through the brambles of barbed wire and into the enemy position. They had crossed the kill zone, but now they found themselves in a series of fortified trenches known as the Quadrilateral. It was a maze, and although the Canadians pushed out their gains, most units stumbled forward blindly. Bombing parties caused considerable damage to the enemy, but men and grenades were used up quickly. Even after robbing the dead of their extra bombs, and then turning to the German stick grenades as a last resort, constant pressure from German counterattacks split the Canadian defences, eventually driving the men of the 1st Brigade out and back to their start lines at around 6 P.M. The 3rd Battalion suffered 339 casualties, for a loss rate of sixty-eight percent; the 4th Battalion suffered 359 casualties, leaving sixty percent of their force wounded or killed (since they attacked with 100 more men).[10] This was the most successful of the operations on October 8.

To the left of the 3rd and 4th Battalions, the 3rd Brigade's 13th and 16th Battalions had been ordered forward. Their first waves of men ran into uncut barbed wire and were "practically wiped out by machine-gun fire," and the follow-on platoons bunched into the killing ground as the leading waves were driven into craters seeking cover from the fire.[11] Most of the Highlanders were planning their fighting retreat back to their own trenches when the sound of bagpipe music wafted over the battlefield above the cacophony of explosions. Piper James Richardson, a baby-faced twenty-year-old with the 16th Battalion, strode up and down the line, with bullets flying around him but miraculously missing him. The Highlanders pulled themselves together, and 100 of them rushed the enemy lines, using their bayonets to clear the wire aside before fighting their way into Regina Trench. Later in the day, Jimmy, as he was known to his friends, put down his bagpipes to carry out a wounded soldier. Although he returned to the safety of his trench, Richardson refused to leave his pipes behind, and so he went back across the fire-swept battlefield to retrieve them. He was never seen again, but was awarded the Victoria Cross for his inspirational piping earlier in the day.

Most of Jimmy's mates at Regina Trench disappeared too. The successful defence of a newly captured trench boiled down to knowing what to hold. Commanders at the rear did not have the benefit of a bird's eye view, and concerned reports were emanating from the forward troops by 7:35 A.M. that the "ground was very exposed." The situation was no better in the captured parts of Regina Trench, where officers were finding it exceedingly difficult to gauge the location of their troops or the enemy. Small groups of scouts were sent forward down the German communication trenches, warily rounding each traverse, until they ran into the enemy doing the same thing. It was left mainly to junior officers in the enemy trenches—such as Lieutenant Edward Hall of the 16th Battalion who wrote that after two and a half hours into the battle that he was the only commissioned man still on his feet—to direct and coordinate the few attackers who were consolidating what was left of the portion of Regina Trench they had captured. What should they hold? What should they reinforce with their pitifully small garrison? From which direction would the enemy attack? Soon, each time an attacking party was sent forward down a communication trench, its members were swallowed by enemy forces, and none returned to tell what the Germans were preparing. A Lewis gun post was set up on the far left, as this position offered a good field of fire, but the Germans, after taking casualties when they tried to go over ground, attacked along the trenches, and from several directions. About seventy-five survivors were slowly pushed back, and, by the end of the day, most of the Highlanders had been wiped out or forced to retreat to their original jumping-off trenches.[12]

On the left flank, the four attacking battalions of the 3rd Division met with similar hurdles of uncut barbed wire—coils 1 to 1.5 metres high. In other places, the Germans had screwed additional wire on top of the coils, to create barriers almost 3 metres high. "They shelled the hell out of us going in," recounted M.J. Cunningham of the 43rd Battalion. He felt sorry for a group of new recruits—just "kids ... scared stiff" and crowding together like "sheep."[13] A few older veterans tried to help them, but when the whistles went to go over the top, survival would depend on more than just experience. The attackers fought their way forward with grenades and rifle fire, but most could not pierce the barbed wire and then the fortified trench defences further on.

Only the Royal Canadian Regiment (RCR) of the 7th Brigade achieved much penetration into Regina Trench. The men of this battalion had crawled behind their creeping barrage, which had slowly and methodically torn up the ground and the

German forward positions. The men of the RCR won the "race to the parapet," entering the enemy trench and killing many defenders as they were running up their dugout stairs. Mopping-up units destroyed dugouts and accumulated prisoners, but as they were organizing the sending back of these prisoners, the Germans launched a series of fierce counterattacks. Officers such as Captain William Sapte and Lieutenant Frederick Dickson—two prewar professional soldiers who had served in the South African War—organized a resolute bombing defence, and both men continued fighting even though peppered with shrapnel from grenades. Dickson was eventually knocked out when a grenade exploded in his face, shredding his flesh with the force of the blast. He pulled himself to the rear. Sapte was last seen racing down a trench, tossing bombs and bleeding from a head wound. He disappeared into history, fighting to the death.

Weakened and spread out in foreign trenches, the men of the RCR succumbed to a third counterattack and were forced to engage in a fighting retreat, with Lewis gunners and riflemen sacrificing themselves to buy time for a new forward trench to be dug in a series of shell craters 100 metres from Regina. When the Shino Boys were relieved the next day, only 140 marched into billets.[14]

THE TWO ATTACKS on Regina Trench had been repulsed with crippling casualties: the second attack, on October 8, had cost some 1,364 men, and another 1,324 had been killed or wounded by shells and snipers while preparing for the operation and while holding the front in the days after the attack.[15] There could be no denying the strength of the German position, but the Canadian infantrymen had been ill-supported by their artillery, which had been unable to properly target the enemy defences. Not one to mince words, Lieutenant Colonel W.A. Griesbach noted in one report, "Our field artillery is, in my opinion, quite useless for wire cutting and the destruction of the enemy's works."[16] Indeed it was, and heavier shells were needed. So too was a more sensitive fuse that could detonate shells on contact with barbed wire. Artillery skills were evolving, but the Somme proved that much room remained for improvement.

Communication had remained a problem throughout the battle. Even laddered telephone wires—two or more lines usually buried 0.5 to 1.5 metres deep—were almost consistently cut by shellfire. Signallers used flags or other lights to contact the rear, but they often attracted the unwanted attention of snipers looking for these actions in battle. And even when such attempts at signalling were unhindered by sniper fire or high explosives, gas, smoke, and dust stirred up by the pounding shells usually created an impenetrable blanket over the front. After two years of the greatest industrial war ever witnessed by human beings, runners therefore remained the only reliable method of communication, no different than at Marathon twenty-four centuries earlier.[17] But estimates suggested that a message would take four and a half hours to reach battalion headquarters from a forward company position on the Somme.[18] And when the messages finally arrived, they were usually out of date and often more damaging because of their unreliability. For instance, an order that was four hours old and asked for an artillery bombardment on a certain trench to silence a machine gun might result in the guns bombarding a Canadian position that had been captured in the intervening time. Commanders generally had little idea of what was happening when troops were pushing into No Man's Land and enemy trenches. This meant that lead units often fought their battles alone, cut off, and against a surging enemy defence that gained in strength as the hours wore on. Brigade, division, and corps headquarters did not know where to direct their reinforcements to support success, and without accurate intelligence they did not know where to direct their artillery to break up counterattacks. They were thus reduced to the worst sort of generalship: the planning of operations and ordering of attacks to recapture lost ground in the absence of sufficient intelligence. The normally supportive and stoic Agar Adamson of the PPCLI, who saw his own battalion and the other three that made up the 7th Brigade nearly annihilated during the October 8 attack against Regina Trench, observed ruefully: "They gave us a job that was almost impossible to carry out."[19] The infantry needed and deserved better.

The infantry, too, underwent its own gut-wrenching analysis after the Regina Trench battles, including a consideration of what had succeeded and what had failed. Fighting on the Somme was hammer-and-tongs warfare of the worst kind, lacking all elements of finesse and offering no chance to find a flank and no opportunity to surprise the enemy. Moreover, many of the orders for attack had allowed the infantry almost no time to prepare for battle. A lesson garnered from soldiers' experience with trench raiding was that every operation needed to be practised and planned down to the smallest detail. Infantrymen who did not know what they were doing or where they were going were not likely to succeed in the hail of gunfire and smoke that deluged the battlefield. This and other important lessons would be implemented in postbattle training to assist the men at the sharp end. Every battalion was ordered to strike a court of inquiry that would produce detailed reports on the successes and failures of the Regina Trench battles. The Canadians would learn from their blood sacrifice.

But some lessons were already known. Too often the infantry had been forced to fight their way forward when their barrage had broken down or in the face of stiff opposition, but often they did not have the firepower to do so. Nor did the junior officers know their objectives, as much of the information was hoarded at higher levels. This would have to change if lives were to be saved in battle. Improvements to the infantry platoon and to infantry–artillery cooperation would be the key to victory, and later, combined-arms fighting included tanks, chemical weapons, mortars, and airpower. The need for thorough planning, accurate intelligence, and an ongoing process of refinement to solve the logistical problem of supporting overextended forces was understood. But although such lessons had been learned, they had not yet been mastered.

AFTER SEVERAL MONTHS of slogging through the chalk and mud, and only inching their way forward, the Canadian Corps was pulled out of the line. The fighting on the Somme had cost the 65,000-strong three-division Canadian Corps nearly 20,000 casualties. The survivors were scarecrow-thin, sunken-eyed men who looked as if they had just recovered from a life-threatening illness. The situation was scarcely better for the German defenders. One letter captured with a soldier in the 17th Bavarian Infantry Regiment confessed: "You can no longer call it war, it is mere murder. All my previous experiences in this war, the slaughter at Ypres and the battle in the gravel pit at Hulluch, are purest child's play compared with this massacre, and this is much too mild a description."[20] The Somme was a bloodbath for Canadians and Germans alike, and it would continue for one more fruitless and savage month.

The Battle of the Ancre Heights: Regina Trench, October 8, 1916

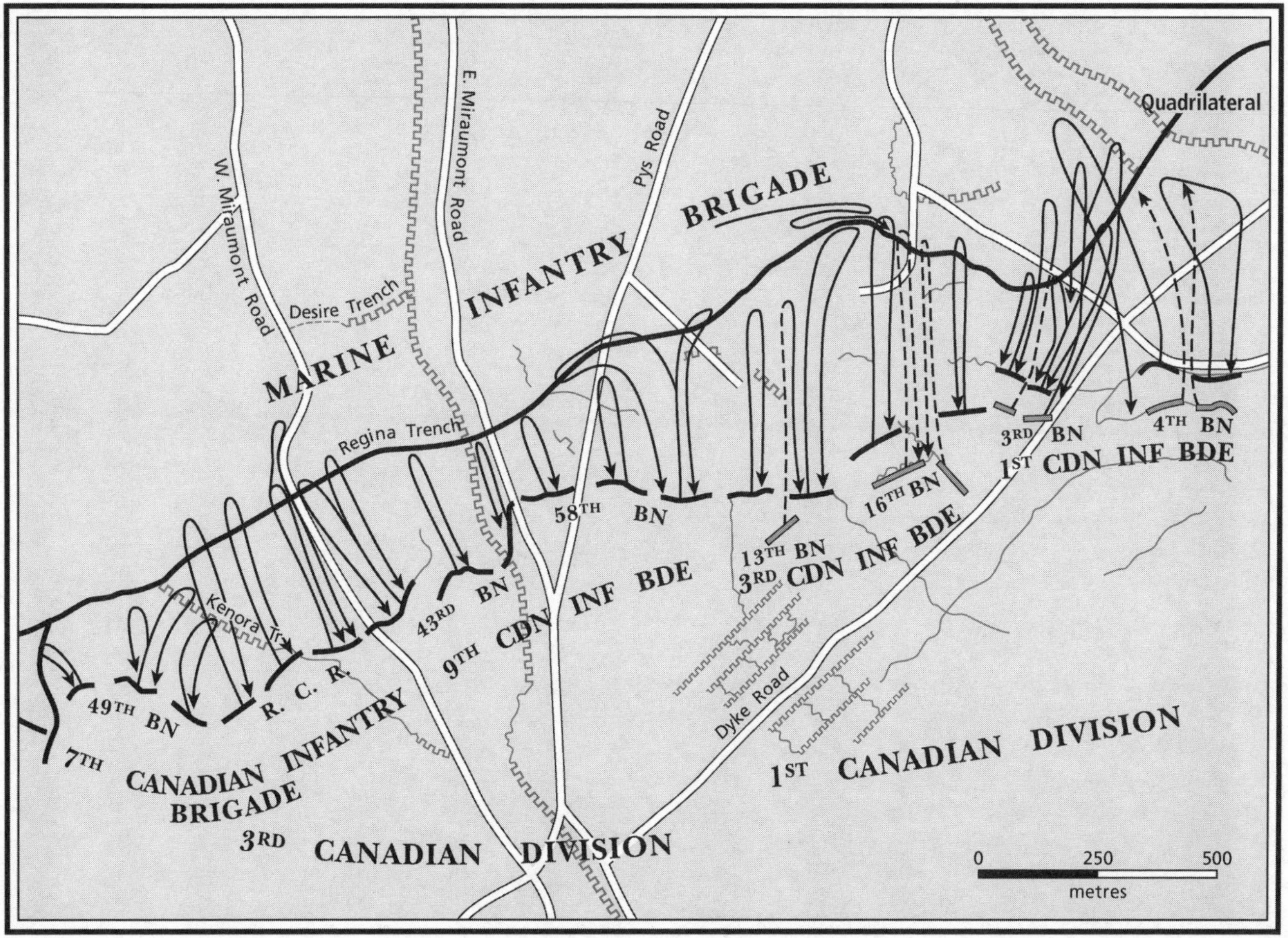

Quadrilateral

4TH BN

1ST CDN INF BDE

3RD BN

16TH BN

1ST CANADIAN DIVISION

2ND INF BDE

13TH BN

3RD CDN INF BDE

BRIGADE

Dyke Road

Pys Road

INFANTRY

58TH BN

2ND CDN INF BDE

E. Miraumont Road

MARINE

43RD BN

9TH CDN INF BDE

Regina Trench

Desire Trench

W. Miraumont Road

Kenora Trench

R. C. R.

3RD CANADIAN DIVISION

49TH BN

7TH CANADIAN INFANTRY BRIGADE

500

250

metres

0

CHAPTER 38

"EXPERIENCES TOO HORRIBLE TO RELATE"

The 4th Division on the Somme

"One cannot praise or perhaps sympathize with the rank and file of the infantry too much," wrote Maurice Pope, a junior officer from Rivière-du-Loup, Quebec, and son of Sir Joseph Pope, a prominent Canadian civil servant.[1] To the infantry fell the worst tasks, in the worst conditions, during which they invariably paid the highest price. For much of the first two years of the war, these Canadians had kept up an indomitable spirit, but the Somme had been too much. It had broken many men, in body and in spirit. Attritional warfare had worn down the attackers as much as, if not more than, the defenders.

Although the infantry battalions of the Canadian Corps' first three divisions were limping into reserve, Canadian fighting on the Somme was not over. Regina Trench still had to fall, and the raw, untried 4th Canadian Division would be called on to deliver victory. The new division would be assisted by the Canadian Corps' field artillery, which had orders to fire a nearly unlimited number of shells to ensure that Regina's defences were pounded beyond recognition. The 4th Canadian Division was commanded by Major General David Watson, a prewar newspaper editor from Quebec City, renowned hockey player, and veteran who had served at the Second Battle of Ypres as a battalion commander. Watson's rise through the ranks was due to his own skill, but also to the efforts of good staff officers and a close friendship with Sir Sam Hughes. Minister Hughes and his cronies had cleared a path for Watson, removing possible competitors for the divisional command. The forty-six-year-old Watson, whose lined face and bushy moustache made him appear older, got his coveted divisional command and then promptly turned his back on the minister by refusing to appoint Hughes's friends to command positions.

It did not take much to make Sam Hughes froth at the mouth, but this betrayal by Watson had Hughes demanding retribution against what he perceived as ungrateful officers who owed him. He did not get his revenge against Watson, but Hughes was increasingly angry about having been blocked by Byng from interfering in the operations of the Canadian Corps, and he would look to even the score someday. But it would be some time before that happened, and Hughes was only a month away from being fired as minister. He would remain in the House of Commons, however, anger radiating out from him as he plotted retribution against the government, and against some of the officers in the CEF who he felt had betrayed him.

Watson's 4th Division consisted of the 10th, 11th, and 12th Brigades, as well as the regular allotment of artillery, engineering, medical, and supporting units. The 10th Brigade was commanded by Brigadier General William St. Pierre Hughes, Sir Sam's brother. His appointment as brigadier was Watson's price for getting the division, although Watson removed Hughes in January 1917 on the basis of a perceived lack of command ability during the Somme battles, and after his brother had been fired as minister. The brigade consisted of four Western battalions: the 44th from Manitoba; the 46th from Saskatchewan, which gave itself the disquieting name of the "Suicide Battalion"; the 47th Battalion from British Columbia; and the 50th Battalion from Alberta, with its core raised from Calgary.

Brigadier General Victor Odlum commanded the 11th Brigade. Odlum had earned his reputation as a fire-breather who had held his shattered 7th Battalion together at Second Ypres, and who had later made his name as a pioneer of raiding in the Canadian Corps. Although as a former journalist he might have been expected to be reserved or bookish, Odlum was in fact well suited for war, studying every aspect of battle, continually training his men, and ensuring a high level of aggression. His four battalions were the 54th from British Columbia, the 75th from Toronto and

Mississauga, the 87th Grenadier Guards from Montreal, and the 102nd from Northern British Columbia, who went by the nickname "The Buck Twos."

The 4th Division's final brigade was commanded by J.H. MacBrien, a professional prewar soldier who had served in South Africa, and one of the corps' few men with staff training and experience. He was the 3rd Division's first quartermaster general, before receiving the 12th Brigade. Unlike most of the brigadiers and battalion officers, he had risen through the general staff, but he was twice wounded in the war, awarded the Distinguished Service Order and Bar (the bar indicating that he received the award twice), and would leapfrog dozens of men with higher ranks to become Canada's postwar chief of the general staff. His battalions were the 38th from Ottawa, the 72nd Seaforth Highlanders from Vancouver, the 78th Winnipeg Grenadiers, and the 85th Nova Scotia Highlanders.

The 4th Division had been allotted a quiet sector in Belgium, where they were to learn about the Western Front. A few months of trench duty, with periodic trench raids and patrols to provide battlecraft skills, had provided some experience for the new men, but the Somme was unlike anything anyone could possibly imagine. However, Watson's men benefited from arriving at the end of the Somme battles and being taught the accumulated lessons learned from the last three months of bitter fighting. Line tactics were out, although soldiers were still to attack in waves of men. Now they were in looser formations, and the infantry were instructed to flow around strongpoints, pushing on to their objectives, and allowing secondary mopping-up units to snuff out the resistance that had been enveloped. These were important lessons, and constituted a genesis for changing the doctrine. But just because the new doctrine was understood, and even codified in documents, did not mean that it had been transmitted to the infantry or accepted by the soldiers or their officers. The training cycle of the last two years, in which the infantry were rigidly controlled, was not easily broken. Furthermore, the problem on the Somme was not in attacking around strongpoints but in finding somewhere along the front that was not a strongpoint.

AS THE TROOPS MOVED into the devastated Somme region in mid-October, rain and cold weather further accentuated the bleakness of their situation. "The road is all shot full of holes, and there is everything lying down there you can think of, dead Germans, and I noticed one or two of our fellows, and rifles and equipment, dead horses, broken wagons, all kinds of dud shells and all kinds that are not duds," recounted Private John McNab in his personal diary. "When a horse is shot down carrying rations and ammunition it is just thrown to one side or in a hole, and the road cleared to let the rest go on."[2] Shaken by this horrific flotsam of battle, Lieutenant A.K. Harvie wrote: "On the way down I began to realize that our first experience in Belgium was almost child's play in comparison with what we were going into."[3]

Holding the same trenches that the three other Canadian divisions had captured, and surrounded by the makeshift cemeteries and graves of their dead countrymen, the 4th Division, as part of the 2nd British Corps, was ordered to capture Regina Trench. This deep system of fortified trenches had provided protection for the German defenders and had allowed them to repulse the series of Canadian attacks throughout September and October. The gunners of those battles had remained behind to assist the 4th Division and they now had orders to fire an unlimited number of shells, curtailing the barrage only when "each section of trench [was] completely obliterated."[4] This weight of shellfire steadily reduced the defences, and the Canadian artillery cleared the German wire faster than it could be put up. Eventually, it became too costly for the Germans to keep sending men out night after night to rebuild the wire. "We have to watch carefully that the English are not shooting; if they see us they open fire directly with a machine gun, and then by day as well as by night they give us heavy [shell] fire," wrote a German pioneer in the 258th Company. "The blackguards sometimes send over gas shells too."[5] Another German soldier testified to being under sustained shellfire: "We hover more or less in danger of death, and have no longer any chance of getting out.... May it all just come to an end; how, I don't care."[6]

The Germans responded with their own shelling, and though it was not as heavy, it left forces at the front bloodied. Private Percy Hewitt was one of the hundreds of Canadians who were killed by shellfire in between the big battles. Hewitt was a cyclist who passed information from front to rear; he was obliterated on October 14 when a shell killed him and a comrade as they read their Bibles in a shell crater.

His mother was another victim of the Somme, as she died shortly after receiving a telegram that her son was never coming home.[7]

The 10th and 11th Canadian Infantry Brigades assaulted portions of Regina Trench on October 21, the plan of attack ordering components of the 50th, 87th, and 102nd Battalions into battle on a small, 550-metre section of trench. The order was printed, perhaps appropriately enough, on the back of "last will and testament" forms.[8] Although the shells rained down heavily on the enemy lines, the attacking infantry were understandably nervous as they stood in their trenches waiting to go over the top. Sergeant Alexander McClintock, a blue-eyed, five-foot-ten, Kentucky-born American serving with the 87th Battalion, discussed frankly the agonizing minutes before battle: "Some of our men sat stupid and inert. Others kept talking constantly about the most inconsequential matters. One man undertook to tell a funny story. No one listened to it, and the laugh at the end was emaciated and ghastly. The inaction was driving us all into a state of funk. I could actually feel my nerve oozing out my finger tips, and, if we had had to wait fifteen minutes longer, I shouldn't have been able to climb out of the trench."[9]

McClintock did not have long to wait in his condition near the breaking point, as the three battalions rushed forth at 12:05 P.M., behind a lifting wall of shells that was later described by some survivors as a "perfect barrage."[10] In the centre, the 87th Battalion attacked in four waves, with the men spread three to four paces apart. The mud was so deep in places that infantry sank to their hips. But they struggled forward, desperation overcoming exhaustion, knowing that every minute spent in No Man's Land courted a meeting with the enemy's counter-barrage, which was expected to fall as soon as ninety seconds after their own barrage had opened up. The four waves moved forward very tightly, and then spread out as they crashed into the enemy trenches. The Germans mounted little resistance, and Regina Trench was nearly flattened by the enormous weight of shellfire directed against it, with only mangled German corpses and dazed survivors mixed amongst the rubble.

With the battalions having captured their objective a mere fifteen minutes after zero hour, mopping-up parties now bombed the surviving defenders who had taken shelter in their dugouts. The fighting and consolidation were done, as one officer testified, "under incessant shell-fire," but the expected German counterattacks were

THE BATTLE OF THE ANCRE HEIGHTS: REGINA TRENCH, OCTOBER 21, 1916

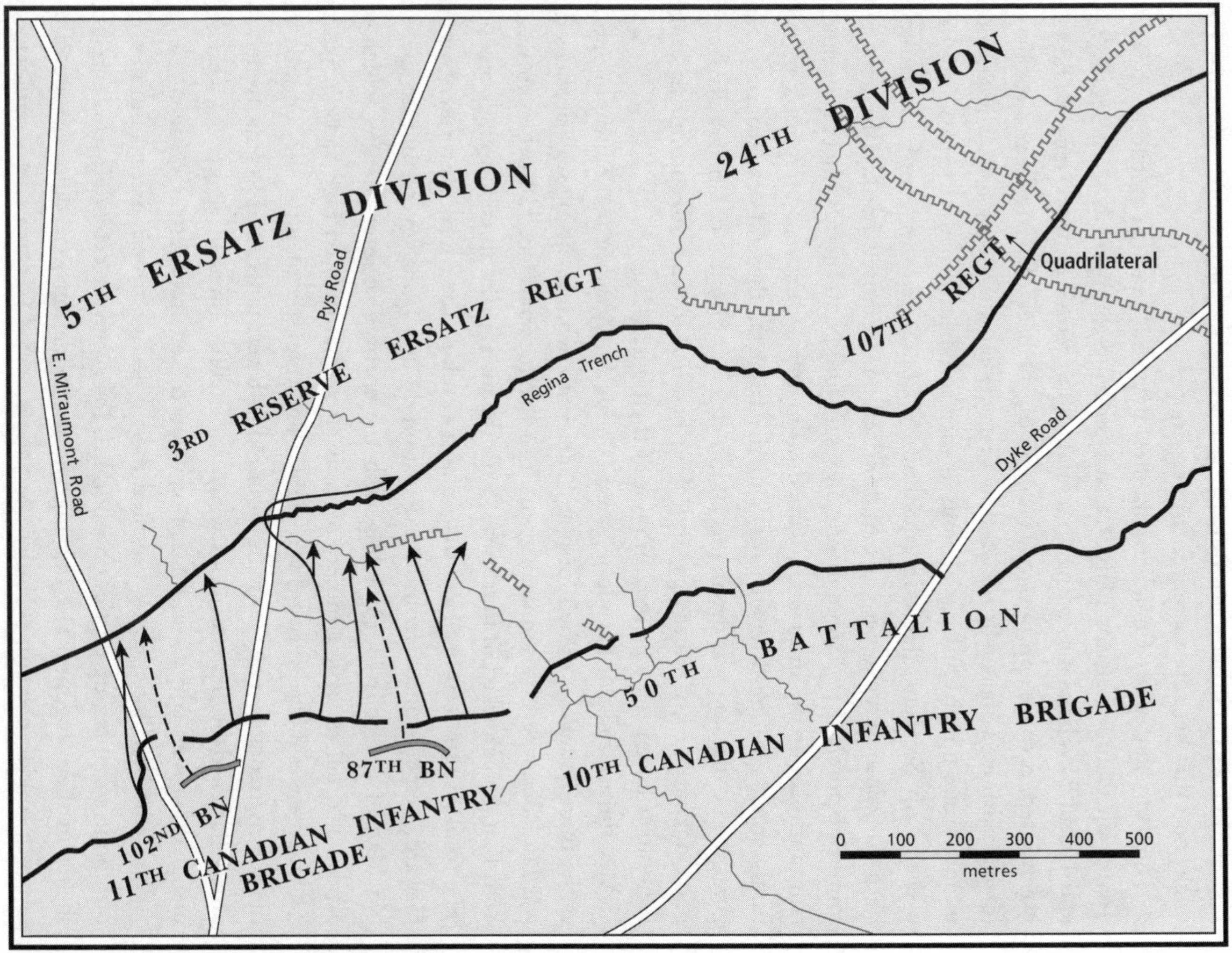

24TH DIVISION

5TH ERSATZ DIVISION

3RD RESERVE ERSATZ REGT

107TH REGT

Quadrilateral

Regina Trench

Dyke Road

Pys Road

E. Miraumont Road

50TH BATTALION

10TH CANADIAN INFANTRY BRIGADE

87TH BN

11TH CANADIAN INFANTRY BRIGADE

102ND BN

metres

0   100   200   300   400   500

beaten back in savage battles that raged over the front.[11] Sergeant McClintock recounted after the death struggle that he could not shake a particularly incongruous thought: "I had lost the address of a girl in London along with some papers which I had thrown away, just before we started over, and which I should certainly never be able to find again."[12] The mind works in strange ways during times of terrible stress.

The Canadian attackers, now turned defenders, held the trench. Their defence was assisted by indirect machine-gun fire, which provided an interceding barrage of 500,000 bullets on the enemy's known communication trenches and support lines.[13] This indirect fire was shot over the heads of the infantry, much like an artillery barrage, and was intended to force German troops to stay below ground. While the forward troops were understandably nervous about this tactic since they could easily be in the line of fire, it soon became a regular feature of future battles. This robust defence kept many of the Germans away from the new Canadian lines, but much hard fighting was carried out in those subterranean crypts. Captain John Preston, a South African War veteran with five children, could only write in his diary that the battle had brought "experiences too horrible to relate."[14]

After the success of the limited three-battalion assault, a second offensive was ordered only three days later against another portion of Regina Trench. The target was the same fortified part of the line where German defenders had repulsed the 1st Division's attack on October 8. The 10th Brigade had no better luck than Currie's veteran division, however, and was caught in a crossfire of machine-gun fire and counter-barrage explosions from artillery that had not been knocked out by the Canadian guns supporting the attack. The survivors crept back to their trenches under cover of darkness. Torrential rainstorms postponed further attacks, and another assault could not be contemplated until a cold spell solidified the ground on November 8. The waiting was insufferable, and, as Private Victor Wheeler observed, "Fighting men who may never have prayed in peacetime prayed on the Somme."[15]

A three-battalion attack was launched under a full moon at midnight on November 10. At that point, the trench had been pounded by thousands of tonnes of high explosives over several months, so in portions it was nothing more than a dip in the ground. While this once formidable position was no longer the obstacle

THE BATTLE OF THE ANCRE HEIGHTS: REGINA TRENCH, NOVEMBER 11, 1916 that it once was, there were still German defenders holding the ground, including numerous machine-gunners. The attackers in the three battalions—the 46th, 47th, and 102nd—assisted themselves by leaving their trenches and infiltrating into forward saps or into the mud of No Man's Land before zero hour to be closer to their objectives, thereby getting a jump on crossing the fire-swept battlefield. The barrage opened up at midnight and the first wave of assault companies moved forward eight minutes later, hugging their creeping barrage into the enemy lines, which they cleared through hand-to-hand fighting. "Parties of the enemy put up a strong resistance but were mopped up and many others who retired hurriedly ... when the barrage moved forward were killed by rifle fire and by the barrage."[16] German general Erich Ludendorff later recounted in his memoirs that the loss of the trench system was a "particularly heavy blow, for we considered such an event no longer possible, particularly in the sectors where our troops still held good positions."[17] However, the Germans were able to fall back to another strong position in the hope of waiting out the end of the campaign season. After bearing the brunt of tens of thousands of high explosive shells, Regina Trench was not just captured in the end—it was erased.

AS PART OF THE LAST British offensive on the Somme, the 4th Division was next ordered to storm Desire Trench, which lay three-quarters of a kilometre north of their position in Regina Trench. Both sides were completely spent by this point. "The mud—and rain—has been our most disagreeable enemy," wrote Sergeant Cecil French. "Mud, mud, mud, ankle deep, knee deep, hip deep, mud. Mud to walk in, to sit in, sleep in; mud on our clothes, on our equipment, on our rations— mud everywhere. I never knew that mud could make itself so abominably beyond the power of words to describe."[18] The wet chalk covered soldiers in a slime, which glistened in the moonlight. Muddy, frozen boots were held on by frozen puttees, pants and jackets were soaked and waterlogged, packs oozed slime down the back: a soldier's kit could weigh in excess of 100 pounds, making every step feel like the tail end of a marathon.[19]

Freezing rain and sleet pelted the front for days, and soldiers were so cold that they could not hold their rifles. "No man cared how serious a wound was," recounted a sniper from the 46th Battalion, "just as long as he got a Blighty."[20] "Blighty" was a term used by the soldiers, denoting a "soft" wound that would take a soldier out of the line for a few months and back to England, which was known as "Blighty" in soldiers' slang. Although receiving a soft wound still meant taking a bullet through the hand or shrapnel through the shoulder, temporary, if agonizing, pain was easier to face than the likely fate of worse maiming, insanity, or death if the men stayed in the trenches.

The cold was even more dangerous for aggressive soldiers who were called on or volunteered to engage in active patrolling and searching for weak points in the enemy lines. The raiders were often given away in No Man's Land by the cracking of ice as they tried to traverse thousands of pits of frozen water. In and outside of them, corpses lay as macabre statues, splayed out or curled up in the fetal position. Sergeant Cecil French, who before the war was studying to be a missionary in India and was now a machine-gunner, wrote of the dead: "once seen one does not forget."[21] He would join the ranks of the slain in the last months of the war.

Still the fighting continued. The Germans harassed the Canadian lines with shrapnel and poison gas bombardments. "Most batteries losing heavily. The whole place certainly is not healthy," wrote Brookes Gossage, a gunner with the 13th Battery.[22] The Canadian and British artillery responded in kind. Forward observers crawled into the muck with the infantry in the hope of coordinating the hammering guns. One of the forward observers, Lieutenant Allen Oliver, who had been awarded the Military Cross for his bravery only weeks before, was killed while straining to observe the fall of the shells in the snow and rain. Forsaking his safer position, he went forward and was shot through the body and bled to death on the battlefield. One can only imagine what this top graduate of McGill University, star athlete, and son of a famous politician might have achieved had he lived.

When the weather broke a little, components of seven Canadian battalions from the 10th and 11th Brigades attacked on November 18. Going over the top in four waves, the infantry once again followed their creeping barrage as it rolled over No Man's Land and through the German trenches. Some fierce fighting, combined with low German morale, resulted in the capture of Desire Trench. But the success was not achieved without terrible sacrifices, repeated among hundreds of small

THE BATTLE OF THE ANCRE HEIGHTS: DESIRE TRENCH, NOVEMBER 18, 1916

battle groups. One example must suffice: Sergeant Alexander McClintock of the 87th Battalion was ordered by his commanding officer to take out a machine-gun nest in what both of them knew was a suicide mission. McClintock selected thirteen bombers and twelve bayonet men to storm the position. They charged forward, bombing and sniping as they closed the distance, and when McClintock finally killed the last German, he and another man were the only two who had survived. McClintock was later wounded, suffering twenty-two shrapnel wounds to his legs.[23] Although he was listed as dangerously ill for several weeks, he survived, was awarded the Distinguished Conduct Medal, and returned to his home in the United States to recover. There, he penned a best-selling memoir and was commissioned in the United States army as a hero. But the pain of his wounds and debilitating insomnia drove McClintock to commit suicide even before the

The Canadian Corps suffered some 24,000 casualties on the Somme.
About one in four of those was fatal.

war had ended. Unable to find solace in sleep, and tormented by what the Western Front had done to him, Alexander McClintock was a casualty of the war, no different from the comrades and enemy soldiers he had buried on the Somme.

Although the 4th Division had captured Desire, as in all battles on the Somme, holding it was another challenge altogether. But the 4th Division was learning, and an innovative smokescreen allowed the desperate defenders to consolidate their trenches without being picked off by German snipers.[24] Nevertheless, the battalions of the 10th Brigade on the right were forced back to their start lines by unsuppressed artillery and machine-gun fire. On their left, the battalions of the 11th Brigade had more success, holding 700 metres of ruined trenches.[25]

"There will be quite a few homes that will be sad after this," wrote Private Stephen Dalton of the 38th Battalion. His friend, Nelson Lachance, was killed in the advance, and Dalton remained distressed for many days as he was unable to find his comrade's body and give him a proper burial.[26] Thousands of other men who were killed during the final November push would also have no known graves, as their bodies were dismembered beyond recognition by shellfire. In a month of fighting, the 4th Division contributed 4,311 more casualties to the almost 20,000 suffered by the other three Canadian divisions since early September.[27] Heavy rain on November 19 reduced the battlefield to a quagmire, and Haig decided to call off any further attacks. The Battle of the Somme was over.

CHAPTER 39

THE BLUDBATH

Assessing the Somme

The Somme yielded no winners. The British had advanced 9.5 kilometres over four months and had lost 432,000 men, with every metre captured to close the gap with the enemy costing dozens of lives. Most of the objectives that were to have been overrun on the first day remained in German hands after months of grinding warfare. The French fared no better, and although they fought on a smaller front, they still contributed 204,000 men to the shocking Entente casualty list.[1] Those on the other side of No Man's Land had it no easier, with the Germans losing an estimated 500,000 men, although this figure is more ambiguous since the Germans did not count men who were considered lightly wounded. A vigorous postwar debate would take place regarding the exact number of killed and wounded on the Somme, with historians, politicians, and body-bag accountants employing all manner of figures in the hope of either embarrassing or supporting the British high command. That the Entente casualties were higher should not be too surprising, however, since it was their infantry who were forced to attack, time and time again. While being on the defensive offered significant advantages, the high German casualty rates reveal that they too were unable to escape the terrible slaughter of shellfire and close-quarter combat; and since the German army had fewer divisions on the Somme, its fighting formations therefore took a higher ratio of casualties, which was ultimately more damaging to morale. The Somme was a touchstone of horror no matter how the butcher's bill was compiled, and its bottom line became the standard against which every other battle was measured.

Regardless of the contested figure of dead and wounded on the Somme, most historians—and many veterans—have condemned General Haig for achieving little other than the grinding away of his armies in fruitless assaults. Haig's policy of attrition indeed looked bloody-minded, but one wonders what the strategic alternatives were to bleeding the enemy white in order to break the stalemate and restore mobility to the Western Front. Sideshow campaigns were proving less costly—but not by much—and all of them quickly degenerated into stalemate as well. The troops had nowhere to go but through the Germans on the Western Front, which both the Entente and German forces agreed was the decisive theatre of war. While Haig's plodding attacks are easy to condemn if they are compared with the great manoeuvre operations of the German blitzkrieging armies of the Second World War or the Israeli 1967 lightning campaign, most wars in history have included some sort of attritional campaign, which reduced the combat efficiency of enemy troops through death and maiming and ground down morale.[2] That the Germans refused to fold in the face of hundreds of thousands of dead is perhaps not a reason to bludgeon Haig; but of course looking beyond the thousands upon thousands of white crosses is not easy. The Somme offensive did, however, accomplish the goal of relieving the French at Verdun and showed, perhaps in a bloody-minded way, that the British were in for the long haul. The greatest navy in the world now had an army to match it.

If Haig should be saved from the gallows, he cannot, however, emerge from any analysis of the Somme undiminished. His greatest failure was his seeming inability to reassess the battle as it unfolded. His "Big Push" had been reduced to push, push, push. Thus, at first, his emphasis was on more guns and shells. Then, it was on the introduction of the tank, which had proven unequal to the task of passing over the cratered battlefield under fire. Finally, it was simply on throwing everything he had—men, guns, and munitions—into the battle with the hope that this onslaught would somehow overwhelm the enemy. It almost did, considering the number of German casualties, but Haig persisted in a battle that cost too much for the small returns it yielded, although it should be noted that the French were continually pushing the British to greater exertions. And overly optimistic intelligence assessments about the German breaking point led the high command further astray. The German army appeared always on the verge of crumbling, or so thought senior intelligence offers who could not imagine how the enemy endured the shellfire and casualties. However, when the weather turned in October, Haig should have ended the campaign. The general's eternally hoped-for breakthrough was no longer possible in the mud of autumn, for should his infantry have ever hacked that envisioned hole in the enemy line, his mired guns would never have made it through the gap to follow the cavalry before the Germans rushed to close it. Even though the Somme was accepted as a battle of attrition, it seemed clear that his own forces were close to the breaking point, and certainly hemorrhaging casualties at a shocking rate. But Haig refused to call off the battle, feeding everything he had into its maw in the hope that the Germans would crack. His belief in providence guiding his hand helped him deal with the terrible losses, but acting on such blind faith was, without a doubt, a disservice to his troops. Estimates indicate that a serviceman of British birth or speech was killed or wounded every forty-five seconds throughout the bloody year of 1916.[3]

Yet the Germans did not escape the Somme *Schlacht*—their word for the catastrophe, signifying both battle and slaughter—without their own terrible scars. The massed Entente artillery fire and tenacious infantry, added to the Germans' own rigid defensive doctrine of holding their ground and then constantly counterattacking to regain lost portions, resulted in a steady stream of wounded and dead. The Germans' slavish devotion to the tactic of immediate counterattack was generally successful, but it also wore down their forces as the British and Canadians learned to prepare for this expected phase of the operation. Also damaging to morale was the refusal of the German high command to rotate their troops out of the high-intensity fighting until they were nearly torn apart. The constant exposure to battle and bombardment broke the spirit of the survivors. "The Somme was the muddy grave of the German field army," remarked Captain von Hentig of the Guards Reserve Division.[4] Another German who fought there lamented, "The tragedy of the Somme battle was that the best soldiers, the stoutest-hearted men were lost; their numbers were replaceable, their spiritual worth never could be."[5] In the battles of Verdun and the Somme, the Germans lost a total of around 850,000 men. The Entente forces lost even more, but they were better able to replace the materiel and men.

After the stalemates of the Somme and Verdun, General Falkenhayn was removed as German commander-in-chief and replaced by an old war hero, Paul von Hindenburg, and his able second-in-command, Erich Ludendorff. The new high command realized that the German forces could not continue to take such devastating casualties, as even if they won the war, the country would be ruined for a generation. Victory was needed, and somehow the emerging Entente superiority in armaments had to be curtailed. "We must save the men from a second Somme battle" was the German high command's rationale for supporting the risky U-boat campaign.[6] In early 1917, unrestricted submarine warfare was reinstated to sever the Entente's lifeline that stretched across the Atlantic. (The use of submarines had been curtailed in September 1915 for fear of dragging the United States into the war through the sinking of its merchant ships.) This tactic did not succeed in blocking the essential flow of war materiel—although sailors and civilians paid with their lives—but, as feared, it did bring the United States into the war once its ships were targeted and sunk.

The German army also learned important lessons from the Somme that led to changes in strategy and tactics. In the battle's aftermath, the Germans developed a defence-in-depth system. By spreading out in a patchwork, checkerboard, elastic defence that relied on machine guns and counterattacking troops, the defenders created a flexible grid offering their *frontsoldaten* a better chance of surviving the devastating artillery bombardments that now preceded all operations. The German defensive battle zone could now stretch back several kilometres, with defenders willing to trade ground for space. The attacking Entente troops would pay for every step.

The Canadians and British, in turn, learned the essential skills of planning and preparing for major offensives. Fanciful flights of planning that called for break-throughs were shelved in the face of methodical bite-and-hold operations. The tighter coordination of the artillery and infantry, and, in the coming year, tanks, chemical weapons, mobile machine guns, trench mortar teams, and airpower, were required to help the infantry fight through the enemy defences-in-depth. The emerging success of the creeping barrage proved an important step in securing an offensive advantage over the inherent power of the defensive, but it also stifled infantry tactics that were continually evolving under the increasingly decentralized command structure. It was initially believed that in order to harness the creeping barrage, officers needed to tightly control their attacking men, binding them to the established timed lifts of the barrage. But by the end of the Somme, the horrendous casualties suffered by junior officers—a fifty-four percent casualty rate during the war—meant that success could occur only if the infantry were trained to fight their way forward.[7] They would have to use the creeping barrage, but also find a way to manoeuvre within it when the barrage invariably failed to destroy, or even suppress, enemy strongpoints. Flexible tactics, empowered soldiers, and increased firepower would create a robust warfighting tactical doctrine that would allow the infantry to overcome the German defensive grid.

"Whatever you do, you lose a lot of men," lamented French general Charles Mangin.[8] Indeed, he was right, but experienced staff and soldiers lost fewer men in battle than inexperienced ones did. The British and Canadian senior officers learned their hard lessons on the Somme and were becoming adept at planning, even though they have been, for the most part, derided as bumblers and butchers in postwar histories and the collective memory. The logistical chain had worked well in bringing supplies thousands of kilometres to the front, but the final push through No Man's Land on the Somme had resulted in the failure of countless operations. The irony of the Western Front fighting was that success always put a greater strain on the supply lines, and any deep penetration made attackers more vulnerable as they left behind their heavy guns, supplies, and medical system. The planning and support of armies still had a long way to go before break-ins at the sharp end could be converted into the much-hoped-for breakthrough of the enemy's trench system.

For the Canadians, the Somme was a slaughter. The corps suffered 24,029 casualties out of a total strength of roughly 85,000. Of those terrible losses, the infantry, including machine-gun units, made up over 90 percent.[9] It had been the "poor bloody infantry" who bore the full weight of battle, and they had paid for the sometimes clumsy and haphazard planning, the weak artillery support, and the higher command's failure to fully take into account the consolidation phase that marked the battles from late September to mid-November. Flesh was pitted against steel in shelling that was so heavy that parts of the Somme were subjected to more than

1,000 shells per square metre.[10] Perhaps we should not be shocked by the crippling casualties but instead wonder why they were not higher.

The Battle of the Somme marked a transformation among the Canadians.[11] Like steel tempered in fire, the Canadian Corps emerged with the tools and harsh experience to become one of the most effective fighting forces on the Western Front. Even first-class commanders such as Byng and Currie had been only mediocre on the Somme, with Turner's victory at Courcelette standing out as the one shining moment for the corps. But if the Somme forced most commanders to engage in plunge-ahead warfare at its most uninspired level—with little room to manoeuvre, and almost no chance to break out of the straitjacket of timetable warfare set by commanders in the rear trying to coordinate several different corps or armies—it was the lessons absorbed that would distinguish the Canadians and their commanders. During the months of recuperation and training in the aftermath of the Somme, Byng and his senior officers focused on improving artillery and infantry coordination. Limited bite-and-hold operations, such as that carried out on June 13 at Mount Sorrel or at Courcelette on the Somme, seemed to provide a way forward. The Canadians, self-contained in their corps structure but still benefiting from the lessons disseminated throughout the larger BEF, were able to work on perfecting their setpiece battle. These limited engagements would become more effective in the months that followed, when the corps commander was able to delay operations to find an advantage for the attacking troops rather than fighting according to rigid timetables.

The four-month-long Battle of the Somme cannot be pigeonholed as a clear-cut victory or defeat. One can marshal evidence suggesting that it was nothing but a bloodbath of incredible proportions—for example, the diary entry written by a Canadian captain who experienced the holocaust: "we simply can not win."[12] However, other records show that some soldiers were proud of how their armies slowly but inexorably steamrolled forward, learning the art of war and driving the Hun back with crippling losses. It is not surprising that no consensus has been achieved regarding what was gained and lost in a series of battles that involved millions of men, ranged over hundreds of square kilometres, and lasted for more than a third of a year. During the Great War, and especially on the Somme, victory was often difficult to distinguish from defeat.

CHAPTER 40

THE RECKONING

The "Brooding Soldier," his head bowed and hands resting on a reversed rifle, stands at the Keerselaere crossroads, one kilometre north of the village of St. Julien at a spot renamed Vancouver Corner. The statue is an enduring memorial of the Canadian sacrifice during the Second Battle of Ypres. Regina sculptor Frederick Clemesha's design took second place in a Canadian postwar competition to create a memorial to the fallen, with Walter Allward's striking design at Vimy coming first. The Brooding Soldier's single shaft of flagstone granite rises from a garden of flowers and trees, with the soldier's head and upper torso seeming to grow from, and be one with, the granite. Gazing down from this great height, the infantryman keeps watch over the fallen. The soldier is sombre, not celebratory, but while his head is bowed, he is not broken.

The first half of the Great War had not gone well for the Entente, and many of the soldiers—and the armies they formed—had been bent, some even broken, but most were enduring the terrible conflict like men made of granite, demanding to see the fighting through to the end. The quiet defiance of the Brooding Soldier was not unlike that of the Canadian soldier, even after the slaughter at Ypres, St. Eloi, Mount Sorrel, and the Somme.

By the end of 1916, who was winning the war? The obvious answer that the *frontsoldaten* would have given to the politicians was that no one was winning. Victory remained elusive for both sides, as the armies remained deadlocked in the thickening trench systems that seemed to resist all attempts to break through to the open ground beyond. Moreover, in almost every battle in which the Entente forces

The "Brooding Soldier," erected in 1923, marks the Canadian sacrifice during the Second Battle of Ypres in April 1915, where more than 2,000 Canadians were killed in less than a week of battle.

had strived for such a breakthrough, they had been turned back, had left objectives uncaptured, and had witnessed their own soldiers hanging on the barbed wire by the tens of thousands. Despite these horrendous losses, however, no revolution had erupted in the ranks or at home. Too much blood had been spilt thus far in the name of victory for the Entente forces to give up, or even seriously seek a compromised peace.

At the front, the soldiers in the fighting armies had found ways to cope with the unfettered and unending slaughter. The survivors were improving, and emerging lessons were being codified and institutionalized. The British bulldogs, with their tough Dominion troops, did not acknowledge that they should perhaps have given up a long time ago. They persisted and kept pressing the attack, driving the German troops through the sausage machine. While the victories were never bloodless, the Entente formations were getting better.

Nowhere was this more evident than in the Canadian Corps, now 85,000-men strong. Its four divisions had been through murderous trials by fire. At Ypres, 6,000 casualties had been sustained in a week of battle; at Festubert, another 2,500 had been killed and wounded; at St. Eloi, some 1,300 had been added to the wastage; at Mount Sorrel, the mounting casualty list had been augmented by almost 9,000 more; and the brutal fighting on the Somme had contributed 24,000 to the butcher's bill. The time in between battles had also resulted in death and maiming among the trench soldiers, and most of this burden fell on the infantry. In total, from February 1915 to the end of 1916, the Canadians suffered almost 61,000 casualties, of which about 15,000 resulted in death.[1] British infantryman Guy Chapman summed up this mass carnage: "Between this war and the last, we did not die: we ended. Neatly, in the shelter of a room, in the warmth of a bed. Now, we die. It is the wet death, the muddy death, death dripping with blood, death by drowning, death by sucking under, death in the slaughter house."[2]

AT THE SHARP END of battle, the Canadians had used these losses to hammer home in the survivors and new recruits the hard lessons of warfighting. They had embarked upon the blood curve of learning with no lesson book to show them how to effectively fight in this new kind of warfare: only costly experience could provide a way forward. Many of the Canadian defeats in battle, most notably those suffered during the battles of Festubert and St. Eloi, the first counterattack at Mount Sorrel, and the assaults against Regina Trench on the Somme, had often occurred because of a breakdown of artillery support—the failure of barrages to suppress the enemy and cut his barbed wire—and of planning and communications. With regard to the latter, the front had been cut off from the rear by heavy enemy shellfire, leaving the assault troops abandoned and fending off constant counterattacks; forces were cut to shreds as all ammunition and bombs were steadily used up. Even though the tactics had evolved and new weapons, such as bombs, rifle-grenades, and Lewis guns, had been introduced to the infantry, too often the infantry had been poorly supported by their artillery as a result of inadequate communication channels. When the gunners received more guns and shells on the Somme, one of the key lessons learned was the need for greater integration between the two most powerful offensive arms, the infantry and the artillery, which would be fused together through better communication tools and an emerging doctrine. This combined-arms approach to warfare would become the hallmark of the Canadian way of battle in the final two years of the war.

By the end of the Somme, the Canadians had been cut to the bone. The Canadians and the British realized they could not go on fighting in the same manner. Offensive operations had been too costly. A new attack doctrine with revised tactics and new weapons had to be employed to assist the infantry when it went over the top. While the front rarely moved, a constant hive of activity buzzed below ground and further to the rear. All soldiers and generals were desperate to move along the learning curve as they mastered the difficult art of warfighting. But this evolution was not some ever-steady climb to success. The curve was more akin to stairs that went up and down as lessons were mastered and it was then found that they could not be applied to battlefield conditions that were constantly changing—and so the lessons would have to be revised, reapplied, and so on. This learning curve, or series of steps, rose and fell over the bodies of the slain. There is no doubt that some of the dead were sacrificed in hopeless and cruel battles such as Festubert and St. Eloi, but not all—in fact few—casualties were the result of reckless callousness and waste. Most men died in hard fighting, in which no immediate solutions to the stalemate could be found: there were no flanks to attack around, and ground had to be captured or held—this combination meant brutal combat conditions.

Throughout the first two years of battle, there was tension between the Canadians and Imperials. The Canadians bristled at being treated as amateurs, and an emerging sense of identity and nationalism, paid for dearly through the sacrifice of their troops, drove the Dominion forces to distinguish themselves from the British. This identity was codified during and after the war by veterans and historians, who often justified Canada's terrible losses in the war as part of the Dominion's evolution to nationhood. And the war was certainly a key event in this evolution. Amidst the monstrous loss of life, however, many Canadians also looked for villains to blame; but while the British high commanders remained an identifiable target because they were ultimately responsible for orders to attack, and critics can point to disasters like Festubert and St. Eloi, these British generals more often did their best to assist the Canadians at every turn during the war.

British high command shared information and lessons and sent their best staff officers and one of their best corps commanders, Sir Julian Byng, to help the Canadians mature. Further, at the sharp end, the British often supported the attacking Canadian infantrymen with artillery assistance and logistical support. Many Canadians did not forget this essential Imperial support. The Dominion shock troops that would emerge in the last two years of the war—elite troops that would be thrown against the most formidable positions and still deliver victory—owed a debt to the patient British soldiers who had nurtured them into the efficient and deadly war machine.

"THE WAR HAD BECOME undisguisedly mechanical and inhuman. What in earlier days had been drafts of volunteers were now droves of victims," wrote Siegfried Sassoon in his postwar memoirs about 1916, the year of slaughter.[3] While the Canadian combatants suffered horrendous casualties in the second and third years of the war (1915–1916), they were more than victims, more than cannon fodder. Soldiers did not stumble around in a blind, despondent daze until put out of their misery by a shell or sniper. They developed new weapons and tactics in their deadly environment. These resilient men also grasped onto, and were forced to forge, new coping mechanisms. Endurance was the key to victory on the Western Front, and few Canadians were willing to give up until victory was achieved. In this industrial war, the human factor remained paramount to success on the battlefield.

Behind the Canadians lay two years of wreckage and war, the bodies of friends and countrymen left on the battlefield like bloody flotsam. Ahead lay the fortress at Vimy Ridge in France, one of the most strongly defended German positions on the Western Front. The French and British had attacked it three times and had failed to either capture or hold it; these operations had cost the Entente forces more than 150,000 casualties. The shock troops from Canada would be called on to snatch the position away from the dug-in Germans in half a year's time. An army was staring up at the gallows. With a death sentence on their collective heads, they had a strong incentive to learn not only how to survive on the battlefield but also how to drive the Germans from their strongpoints.

CANADIAN INFANTRYMAN Private J.P. Baston wrote of his mates: "Our khaki is dirty and stained, and our packs are heavy; but our rifles are clean and well-oiled as we plod along the road to our 'spell in.' Our faces are red, as the rain drips down from our bonnets and runs down our cheeks or drops from our noses. We don't look like a bunch of 'bleedin' 'eroes,' but we are not at all downhearted."[4] The Canadian combat soldiers may not have always looked like heroes, but their ability to survive and endure on the battlefield would eventually enable them to drive the enemy before them and recapture all that *geography* that was so important to the combat soldier, his commanders, and the politicians and kings who kept them in the field. But there would be no easy victories. Captain H.E. Taylor, looking back on his six weeks on the Somme, noted, "One cannot describe the situation clearly—it is all a nightmare."[5] And this nightmare would continue to torment tens of millions of soldiers and civilians for another two years, cost millions of lives, and forever change world *history*.

Notes on Sources

Citations for sources are located within the endnotes linked to the text. Volume II will contain a full bibliography, but this brief account provides an outline of available sources relating to the Canadian Corps and its operations. Readers should keep in mind that an enormous international literature exists on all facets of the subject, and a number of Canadian studies explore the impact of the war on the home front.

Owen Cooke's bibliography, *The Canadian Military Experience, 1867–1995*, provides a comprehensive list of books on the subject, and a bibliographic essay, "From Colony to Nation," also compiled by Cooke, is available on the Library and Archives Canada (LAC) website. Tim Cook's *Clio's Warriors* examines the historiographical trends and historical battles within the canon of war writing.[1]

Histories of the war have been published since the second year of the conflict, and while works by Lord Beaverbrook and other wartime journalists must be treated with caution, they contain unique information and contemporary observations.[2] These "instant" histories were later supplanted by regimental histories and the first official history, written by Colonel A.F. Duguid. While Duguid produced only one of eight projected volumes, the regimental histories remain an important source for readers to understand the inner workings of a battalion, battery, or other unit.[3] About half of the infantry battalions have some form of regimental history (although they are less common among the engineering and artillery units), and these works often contain first-hand testimonials, letters, and keen insight into the soldiers' experience at war. A one-volume essential official history of the Canadian Expeditionary Force was published in 1960 by G.W.L. Nicholson.[4] It has stood the test of time—although it documents the Canadian war experience from the high command to the battalion level, and rarely below that. In recent decades, a number of essential histories have been published in Canada—including those by A.M.J. Hyatt, Daniel Dancocks, Bill Rawling, Desmond Morton, Shane Schreiber, Tim Cook, and, J.L. Granatstein.[5] These works build upon early histories but are distinguished by their extensive use of archival records. The Great War also continues to attract scholarly study from graduate students, and some of the best works have remained unpublished.[6]

At the time of writing, only one Canadian Great War veteran is still living. While we will soon no longer be able to talk to the veterans, we can continue to "listen" to them. From the first years of the war to the present, Canadian soldiers' letters, memoirs, and diaries have been written. While the historian must be wary of men who wrote with an eye on history or to protect or destroy reputations, there are few better sources than the soldiers' own words, cross-referenced with archival records, to shed light on soldiering on the Western Front. Collections of first-hand accounts and oral histories also provide deep insight into the soldiers' experiences. The most important of these is the Canadian Broadcasting Corporation's (CBC's) interviews of some 600 veterans in the early 1960s for a multi-part radio program, *Flanders Fields*. The audio tapes and original interviews, as well as the transcripts of those interviews, are held at LAC, and they are an invaluable resource for any historian.[7] Putting aside the vagaries of memory and the occasional error of fact, these interviews provide searing accounts of men at war. This study has drawn on the interview transcripts and the tens of thousands of pages that formed the raw interviews. Other resources have become more accessible over the last decade as museums, universities, and archives have increasingly digitized their Great War collections, and readers should be aware of The Canadian Letters and Images Project, a valuable resource for writers, scholars, and students of Canadian military history that continues to expand monthly.[8]

While this volume builds upon a long tradition of historical writing, remarkable gaps remain in our understanding of the Great War. Throughout the book, I have returned to archival sources in order to better understand events, especially as they were first recorded—before they were filtered through the perspectives of historians or other writers. This is a history from the bottom up. Battles and engagements were reconstructed from the official archival records, including the daily war diaries, intelligence reports, battlefield maps, postbattle reports of operations, casualty lists, and dozens of other types of sources. Most of these are held at LAC, with the core of the records in Record Group (RG) 9 (Records of the Department of Militia and Defence), RG 24 (Records of the Department of National Defence), and RG 150 (Records of the Overseas Ministry), although Great War records can be found throughout most government collections. These archival sources, numbering in the millions of pages, are the bare bones of history, and they have been used extensively in this book. The maps in this volume have been based on the maps from G.W.L. Nicholson, *Canadian Expeditionary Force, 1914–1919: Official History of the Canadian Army* (Ottawa, 1960).

Of these sources, the daily war diaries—kept at the battalion, brigade, division, and corps level—document decisions taken in the planning and execution of trench warfare or setpiece battles, as well as revealing the consequences of such actions. LAC has recently digitized these rich records, and they are now available to all Canadians. In this history, I cite not only the digitized sources but also the original paper copies, as the time frame for my research stretches back to the years before the war diaries were digitized. Moreover, tens of thousands of the subject files in RG 9 related to every aspect of the soldiers' experience remain available only in textual (undigitized) form, and these too must be examined to gain a full appreciation of the complexity of soldiers' experiences in battle. Additionally, valuable research files from the Department of National Defence's Army Historical Section contain statistical information and aggregate data.

Equally important are the private papers of Canadian soldiers, from the highest-ranking general to the lowest members of the rank and file. All contain valuable insight into the war, and serve to round out the official records that rarely document the human condition: fear and anxiety, grim humour and belief systems, and how soldiers dealt with the daily reality of the trenches are revealed in these private collections. Several hundred private collections were consulted at LAC, the Canadian War Museum (CWM), and in archives across this country and overseas. The contents of these collections range from a few letters to detailed memoirs, diaries, and even official or semi-official reports. Each collection furthers our understanding of the war and its effects upon ordinary Canadians dealing with extraordinary circumstances. While hundreds, perhaps thousands, of these collections exist in archives, museums, and other historical repositories across the country—and increasingly on the internet—thousands more lie abandoned in attics and basements, slowly succumbing to climate and time. They are all valuable and should be archived for future generations.

Finally, less conventional sources, such as photographs, maps, war art, postcards, ephemera, poetry, trench cartoons, material history artifacts, and walks taken on the battlegrounds in Europe have provided additional perspectives on factors that shaped the combat efficiency of the Canadian Corps in the Great War.

ENDNOTES

INTRODUCTION: AT THE SHARP END (PP. 1–8)

1. Hugh Kay, *The History of the Forty-Third Battery, C.F.A.* (self-published, 1916) 5.

2. David Stevenson, *Cataclysm: The First World War as Political Tragedy* (Basic Books, 2004) xvii.

3. Significant debate occurs among historians over whether the war should be seen as a break with the past or as an event of continuity. Cultural historians frequently portray the war as an event of continuity rather than a break from the past, with the arguments of Jay Winter having superseded that of the now dated, although still useful, Paul Fussell, although one must still come to grips with Modris Ekstein's "birth of the modern." With regard to grand politics and war, the Great War remains the catalyst that changed the modern world in fundamental ways. See Jay Winter, *Sites of Memory, Sites of Mourning: The Great War in European Cultural History* (Cambridge: Cambridge University Press, 1995); Paul Fussell, *The Great War and Modern Memory* (New York: Oxford University Press, 1975); Modris Ekstein, *The Rites of Spring: The Great War and the Birth of the Modern Age* (Toronto: Lester & Orpen Dennys, 1994). For political and military breaks with the past, the scholarship is legion: for starters, see Ian Beckett, *The Great War, 1914–1918* (New York: Longman, 2001); Margaret Macmillan, *Paris 1919: Six Months That Changed the World* (New York: Random House, 2002).

4. Omar Bartov, *In Our Midst: The Holocaust, Industrial Killing, and Representation* (Oxford University Press, 1996).

5. Robin Prior, *Churchill's "World Crisis" as History* (London: Croom Helm, 1983) 221.

6. John H. Becker, *Silhouettes of War: The Memoir of John Harold Becker, 1915–1919* (Ottawa: CEF Books, 2001) 110.

7. Library and Archives Canada [hereafter LAC], Records of the Department of National Defence [hereafter RG 24], volume [hereafter v.] 1843, 10-47E, Statistics OMFC; G.W.L. Nicholson, *Canadian Expeditionary Force, 1914–1919* (Ottawa: Queen's Printer, 1964) 548.

8. Joseph Chaballe, "Courcelette: The Glorious Battle Fought by the 22nd French-Canadian Regiment," *La Canadienne,* October 1920 [translated copy at Canadian War Museum, Military History Research Centre] 14.

9. Coningsby Dawson, *Khaki Courage* (Toronto: S.B. Gundy, 1917) 164.

CHAPTER 1: EUROPE MARCHES (PP. 9–20)

1. Cited in Ian Passingham, *All the Kaiser's Men: The Life and Death of the German Army on the Western Front, 1914–1918* (Phoenix Mill: Sutton Publishing, 2003) xii.

2. Paul Kennedy, *The Rise of Anglo-German Antagonism, 1860–1914* (London, 1987).

3. Gary Cox, "Of Aphorisms, Lessons and Paradigms: Comparing the British and German Official Histories of the Russo-Japanese War," *Journal of Military History* 56 (1992).

4. Jack Snyder, *The Ideology of the Offensive: Military Decision Making and the Disasters of 1914* (Ithaca: Cornell University Press, 1984); Stephen Van Evera, "The Cult of the Offensive and the Origins of the First World War," *International Security* 9.1 (Summer 1984) 58–107.

5. Samuel Williamson and Russel Van Wyk, *July 1914: Soldiers, Statesmen, and the Coming of the Great War* (New York: St. Martin's Press, 2003) 57.

6. Niall Ferguson, *The Pity of War* (New York: Basic Books, 1999) 91–5.

7. Samuel Williamson, "The Origins of War," Hew Strachan (ed.), *The Oxford Illustrated History of the First World War* (London: Oxford University Press, 1998) 12.

8. David French, *The British Way in Warfare, 1688–2000* (London: Unwin Hyman, 1990).

CHAPTER 2: "THE COUNTRY WENT MAD!" (PP. 21–34)

1. Stephen Leacock cited in G.R. Stevens, *A City Goes to War: History of the Loyal Edmonton Regiment* (Brampton: Charters, 1964) 8–9.

2. Daphne Read (ed.), *The Great War and Canadian Society: An Oral History* (Toronto: New Hogtown Press, 1978) 90.

3. Robert Bothwell, *The Penguin History of Canada* (Toronto: Penguin Canada, 2006) 217.

4. As one popular Newfoundland anti-Confederation song warned: *Men, hurrah for our own native isle, Newfoundland, Not a stranger shall hold one inch of her strand; Her face turns to Britain, her back to the Gulf, Come near at your peril, Canadian Wolf.*

5. Richard Clippingdale, *Laurier: His Life and World* (Toronto: McGraw-Hill Ryerson, 1979) 72–4.

6. Quoted in Henry Borden (ed.), *Robert Laird Borden: His Memoirs,* v. I (Toronto, 1938) 456.

7. Joseph Levitt, *Henri Bourassa on Imperialism and Bi-Culturalism, 1900–1918* (Toronto: Copp Clark Pub. Co., 1970) 162.

8. Stevens, *A City Goes to War,* 17.

9. Harold Peat, *Private Peat: His Own Soldier's Story* (Bobbs-Merrill, 1918) 3.

10. CBC Radio program *Flanders Fields,* radio transcripts [hereafter *Flanders Fields*], G.T. Boyd, program 2/page 13 [hereafter 2/13].

11. *Flanders Fields,* R.L. Christopherson, 2/10.

12. Hugh MacIntyre Urquhart, *The History of the 16th Battalion: (The Canadian Scottish) Canadian Expeditionary Force in the Great War, 1914–1919* (Toronto: MacMillan, 1932) 9.

13. The Canadian Letters and Images Project, http://www.canadianletters.ca [hereafter CLIP], Alfred Andrews papers, diary/memoir, 30 August 1914.

14. See Desmond Morton, *Fight or Pay: Soldiers' Families in the Great War* (Vancouver: UBC Press, 2004).

15. LAC, RG 24, v. 1813, file 4-15L, *The Expansion of the Canadian Militia for the War, 1914–18,* 1; Urquhart, *The History of the 16th Battalion,* 355.

16. C.A. Sharpe, "Enlistment in the Canadian Expeditionary Force: A Regional Analysis," *Journal of Canadian Studies* 18.4 (1983–84). There were another almost 200,000 Canadian men not counted as British subjects who were not technically allowed to serve. Many did.

17. *Flanders Fields,* J.M. MacDonnell, 2/9.

18. On the cadet movement, see Desmond Morton, "The Cadet Movement in the Moment of Canadian Militarism, 1909–1914," *Journal of Canadian Studies* 13.2 (Summer 1978): 56–69; For the influence of prewar literature and military messaging, see Mark Moss, *Manliness and Militarism: Educating Young Boys in Ontario for War* (New York: Oxford University Press, 2001).

19. CLIP, George Broome, letter to mother, 27 June 1915 and 1 July 1915.

20. For "hungerscription," see John Thompson, *The Harvests of War,* 24; for men giving up good jobs, see Ian Miller, *Our Glory and Our Grief: Torontonians and the Great War* (Toronto: University of Toronto Press, 2001).

21. *Flanders Fields,* R.L. Christopherson, 2/15.

22. Colonel A.F. Duguid, *Official History of the Canadian Forces in the Great War, 1914–1919,* General Series, v. I (Ottawa: J.O. Patenaude, Printer to the King, 1938) 59 [volume and page numbers hereafter I/59].

23. Urquhart, *The History of the 16th Battalion,* 10.

24. LAC, Records of the Department of Militia and Defence [hereafter RG 9], v. 3751, Major G.S. Strathy's diary, 10 August 1914.

25. LAC, RG 24, v. 1810, GAQ 2-1, v. 1, Enlistment 1st Canadian Contingent.

26. J.L. Granatstein and J.M. Hitsman, *Broken Promises: A History of Conscription in Canada* (Toronto: Oxford University Press, 1977) 23–4.

27. J.A. Currie, *The Red Watch: With the First Canadian Division in Flanders* (Toronto: McClelland, Goodchild and Stewart, 1916) 38.

28. Harold Baldwin, *Holding the Line* (Toronto: George McLeod Ltd., 1918) 2–3.

29. Deborah Crowly (ed.), *Georges Vanier, Soldier: The Wartime Letters and Diaries, 1915–1919* (Toronto: Dundurn Press, 2000) 19.

30. James. W. St. G. Walker, "Race and Recruitment in World War I: Enlistment of Visible Minorities in the Canadian Expeditionary Force," *Canadian Historical Review,* LXX.1 (1989) 1–26.

31. See Michael L. Hadley and Roger Sarty, *Tin-Pots and Pirate Ships: Canadian Naval Forces and German Sea Raiders 1880–1918* (Montreal: McGill-Queen's University Press, 1991).

32. For biographies of Hughes, see Charles F. Winter, *Lieutenant-General The Hon. Sir Sam Hughes* (Toronto: The Macmillan Company of Canada, 1931); Alan R. Capon, *His Faults Lie Gently: The Incredible Sam Hughes* (Lindsay: Floyd Hall, 1969); and R.G. Haycock, *Sam Hughes: The Public Career of a Controversial Canadian, 1885–1916* (Ottawa: Canadian War Museum, 1986).

33. LAC, RG 24, v. 1810, file GAQ 1-4, Notes re: Mobilization scheme.

34. Hansard, Debates, House of Commons, 2 January 1916.

CHAPTER 3: CONTROLLED CHAOS (PP. 35–54)

1. Canadian War Museum (hereafter CWM), Ralph Gibson Adams papers, 19760345-007, letter to mother, 29 March 1916.

2. Daniel Dancocks, *Gallant Canadians: The Story of the Tenth Canadian Infantry Battalion, 1914–1919* (Calgary: The Calgary Highlanders Regimental Funds Foundation, 1990) 7.

3. RG 24, v. 1824, file GAQ 5-42, *The Growth and Control of the Overseas Military Forces of Canada,* 2–3.

4. G.C. Johnston, *The 2nd Canadian Mounted Rifles* (Vernon: Vernon News, 1932) 18.

5. RG 24, v. 1813, file 4-15L, *The Expansion of the Canadian Militia for the War, 1914–18,* 8.

6. Duguid, *Official History of the Canadian Forces in the Great War, 1914–1919,* I/47.

7. W.W. Murray, *The History of the 2nd Canadian Battalion* (Ottawa: The Historical Committee, 1947) 2.

8. Carman Miller, "The Crucible of War: Canadian and British Troops During the Boer War," Peter Dennis and Jeffrey Grey (eds.), *The Boer War: Army, Nation and Empire* (Canberra: Army History Unit, 2000).

9. Gordon MacKinnon, "Major-General Malcolm Smith Mercer," *Stand To!* 74 (September 2005) 40.

10. Kenneth Radley, *We Lead, Others Follow: First Canadian Division, 1914–1918* (St. Catharines: Vanwell, 2006) 63.

11. Daniel Dancocks, *Welcome to Flanders Fields: The First Canadian Battle of the Great War: Ypres 1915* (Toronto: McClelland and Stewart, 1988) 37.

12. On French Canadians, see Desmond Morton, "French Canada and War: The Military Background to the Conscription Crisis of 1917," J.L. Granatstein and R.D. Cuff (eds.), *War and Society in North America* (Toronto, 1971).

13. John Macfarlane, "The Right Stuff?: Evaluating the Performance of Lieutenant-Colonel F.-L. Lessard in South Africa and His Failure to Receive a Senior Command Position with the CEF in 1914," *Canadian Military History* 8.3 (Summer 1999) 48–59.

14. CWM, 19710147-001, R.E.W. Turner papers, diary/memoir, 10 September 1914.

15. LAC, RG 24, v. 1824, GAQ 5-51, Notes on the contribution of Montreal to the CEF, 5.

16. Urquhart, *The History of the 16th Battalion,* 15.

17. LAC, RG 24, v. 1812, GAQ 4-6, Notes on conversation with Major General G.G. Hughes, 11 January 1934.

18. For more details, see Craig Brown and Desmond Morton, "The Embarrassing Apotheosis of a Great Canadian: Sir Arthur Currie's Personal Crisis in 1917," *Canadian Historical Review* (March 1979).

19. Harold Baldwin, *Holding the Line* (Toronto: George McLeod Ltd., 1918) 118.

20. Ronald Clifton, "What Is an Artillery Brigade?" *Stand To!* 35 (Spring 1991) 34.

21. *Flanders Fields,* 2/22.

22. Scott, *The War as I Saw It,* 17.

23. John Macfie (ed.), *Letters Home* (Meaford: Oliver Graphics, 1990) 4.

24. *Flanders Fields,* 3/3.

25. LAC, RG 24, v. 1811, GAQ 3-9, Disposal of Troops.

26. LAC, RG 9, v. 3751, Diary of Captain P.G. Bell, 15 September 1914.

27. On age, see Desmond Morton, *When Your Number's Up: The Canadian Soldier in the First World War* (Toronto: Random House of Canada, 1993) 279; LAC, RG 24, v. 1844, GAQ 11-8B, Number of ORs Served by Years of Age.

28. R.C. Fetherstonhaugh, *The Royal Montreal Regiment 14th Battalion, CEF* (Montreal: The Gazette, 1927), 10.

29. Macfie, *Letters Home,* 5–6.

30. Duguid, *Official History of the Canadian Forces in the Great War, 1914–1919,* v. I, pt. 2. Chronology, Appendices, and Maps, Appendix 111.

31. J.L. Granatstein, *Canada's Army: Waging War and Keeping the Peace* (Toronto: University of Toronto Press, 2002) 61.

32. CWM, 20020112-004, Harry Coombs papers, diary, 29 August 1914.

33. Macfie, *Letters Home,* 6.

CHAPTER 4: CARNAGE (PP. 55–68)

1. Stevenson, *Cataclysm,* 60.

2. John Schindler, "Disaster on the Drina: The Austro-Hungarian Army in Serbia, 1914," *War in History* 9.2 (2002) 159–95.

3. See Graydon A. Tunstall, *Planning for War Against Russia and Serbia: Austro-Hungarian and German Military Strategies, 1897–1914* (Boulder, 1993).

4. Stevenson, *Cataclysm,* 58.

5. For the Russian army, see Norman Stone, *The Eastern Front, 1914–1917* (London: Hodder & Stoughton Ltd., 1975).

6. Beckett, *The Great War,* 48.

7. Dennis Showalter, *Tannenberg: Clash of Empires* (Hamden, 1991) 143.

8. *The Bryce Report: Report of the Committee on Alleged German Outrages* (London, 1915).

9. See John Horne and Alan Kramer, *German Atrocities 1914: A History of Denial* (London, 2001).

10. Anthony Clayton, *Paths of Glory: The French Army 1914–18* (London: Cassell, 2003 [2005]) 18.

11. David Clarke, *The Angel of Mons: Phantom Stories and Ghostly Guardians* (West Sussex: Wiley, 2004).

12. Major T.J. Mitchell and G.M. Smith, *Medical Services: Casualties and Medical Statistics of the Great War* (The Imperial War Museum, reprint 1997) 40.

13. D.E. Showalter, "Manoeuvre Warfare: The Eastern and Western Fronts, 1914–1915," Hew Strachan (ed.), *The Oxford Illustrated History of the First World War* (Oxford University Press, 1998) 53; Beckett, *The Western Front,* 59.

14. Peter Vansittart, compiler, *Voices from the Great War* (London: Jonathan Cape, 1981) 54.

CHAPTER 5: "DRINKING AND GETTING INTO ALL THE TROUBLE THEY CAN" (PP. 69–82)

1. CLIP, Alfred Andrews papers, diary/memoir, 14–20 October 1914.

2. LAC, MG 30 E300, Victor Odlum papers, v. 15, file: Newspaper Clippings, "Canadians Arrive," *The Western Morning News, Plymouth,* 15 October 1914.

3. CWM, 20020112-004, Harry Coombs papers, diary, 15 October 1914.

4. Urquhart, *The History of the 16th Battalion,* 35.

5. CWM, 58A 1 92.1, Alfred Baggs papers, diary, 19 October 1914.

6. *Flanders Fields,* 3/17.

7. Desmond Morton and J.L. Granatstein, *Marching to Armageddon: Canadians and the Great War 1914–1919* (Toronto: Lester & Orpen Dennys, 1989) 48.

8. LAC, RG 9, v. 3751, Diary of Captain P.G. Bell, 14 January 1915.

9. Dancocks, *Gallant Canadians,* 10.

10. Peat, *Private Peat,* 19.

11. *Flanders Fields,* E. Seaman, 2/7.

12. Macfie, *Letters Home,* 11.

13. Baldwin, *Holding the Line,* 35.

14. Fetherstonhaugh, *The Royal Montreal Regiment,* 10.

15. LAC, RG 24, v. 1813, GAQ 4-15K, W.A. Griesbach, "Lieut-Gen. Sir Edwin Alderson, KCB," *The Khaki Call* XII.1 (February 1928) 1.

16. See E.A.H. Alderson, *With the Mounted Infantry in the Mashonaland Field Force* (London: Methuen, 1898); *Pink and Scarlet, or Hunting as a School for Soldiering* (London: William Heinemann, 1900 [1913]); and *Lessons from 100 Notes Made in Peace and War* (Aldershot: Gale and Porden, 1908).

17. LAC, RG 24, v. 6931, file "canteens," narrative, 1. Quote from Sam H.S. Hughes, "Sir Sam Hughes and the Problem of Imperialism," *Report of Annual Meeting of the Canadian Historian Association* (1950), 30.

18. Ted Byfield (ed.), *Alberta in the 20th Century: The Great War and Its Consequences,* v. IV (Edmonton: United Western Communications, 1994) 21.

19. LAC, MG 30 E565, Frank Benbow Fox papers, transcript of diary, 40.

20. LAC, MG 27 II-B-9, A.E. Kemp papers, v. 118, file 8, despatch note; R.C. Fetherstonhaugh, *The 13th Battalion Royal Highlanders of Canada, 1914–1919* (Montreal: Privately printed by the 13th Battalion, 1925) 22.

21. "Alderson Announces End of Teetotal Rule for Canteens," *Mail and Empire,* 21 October 1914. Clipping found in LAC, MG 27 II-D-7, v. 17, file 1525.

22. R.H. Tupper, *Victor Gordon Tupper: A Brother's Tribute* (Oxford University Press, 1921) 11.

23. LAC, RG 24, v. 6931, file "canteens," Currie to Camp Commandant, West Down South Camp, 28 October 1914.

24. CWM, 20020112-004, Harry Coombs papers, diary, 31 October 1914.

25. LAC, MG 30 E505, William Howard Curtis papers, letter to mother, 6 December 1914.

26. Duguid, *Official History of the Canadian Forces in the Great War, 1914–1919,* I/126.

27. Cited in John Swettenham, *To Seize the Victory: The Canadian Corps in World War I* (Toronto: Ryerson, 1965) 50.

28. Charles Lyon Foster (ed.), *Letters from the Front: Being a Record of the Part Played by Officers of the Bank in the Great War, 1914–1919* (Toronto: Southam Press, 1920–21).

29. Currie, *The Red Watch,* 65.

30. Barbara Wilson, *Ontario and the First World War: A Collection of Documents* (Toronto: Champlain Society for the Govt. of Ontario, 1977) viii.

31. Clive Law, *Khaki: Uniforms of the Canadian Expeditionary Force* (Nepean: UpClose, 1997) 8.

32. LAC, MG30 E8, J.J. Creelman papers, diary, 10 December 1914.

33. Duguid, *Official History of the Canadian Forces in the Great War, 1914–1919,* I/141–2.

34. Jay Cassel, *The Secret Plague: Venereal Disease in Canada, 1838–1939* (Toronto: University of Toronto Press, 1987) 123.

35. Trevor Wilson, *The Myriad Faces of War* (Cambridge: Polity Press, 1986) 152–63.

36. LAC, MG30 E432, Ian Sinclair papers, diary, 25 December 1914.

37. CLIP, Robert Hale, 19 February 1915.

Chapter 6: "An Iron Division for Service in an Iron War" (pp. 83–94)

1. F.W. Bagnall, *Not Mentioned in Despatches* (North Vancouver: North Shore Press, 1933) 20.

2. Alexander McClintock, *Best o' Luck* (Ottawa: CEF Books, 2000) 10.

3. Baldwin, *Holding the Line,* 49, 97–8.

4. A.P. Birchall, *Rapid Training of a Company for War* (London: Gale & Polden, 1915) 140–2.

5. For the best account of training in the 1st Division, see Andrew Iarocci, *1st Canadian Division at War, 1914–15: A Study of Training, Tactics and Leadership* (Ph.D. Dissertation: Wilfrid Laurier University, 2005) chapter 2.

6. John Swettenham, *McNaughton* (Toronto: Ryerson Press, 1968) 37.

7. See Cameron Pulsifer, "Canada's First Armoured Unit: Raymond Brutinel and the Canadian Motor Machine Gun Brigades of the First World War," *Canadian Military History* 10.1 (Winter 2001) 44–57.

8. Jonathan Vance, *High Flight: Aviation and the Canadian Imagination* (Toronto: Penguin, 2002) 41.

9. Ralph Hodder-Williams, *Princess Patricia's Canadian Light Infantry, 1914–1919,* v. I (Edmonton: Executive Committee, Princess Patricia's Canadian Light Infantry, 1968) 7–10.

10. These brigades stayed uniform throughout the war: 1st–3rd Brigades were always part of the 1st Canadian Division; 4th–6th Brigades formed the 2nd Division; 7th–9th formed the 3rd Division; and the 10–12th formed the 4th Division.

11. Peat, *Private Peat,* 51.

12. Arthur Hunt Chute, *The Real Front* (New York: Harper and Brothers, 1918) 16.

Chapter 7: Welcome to the Western Front (pp. 95–108)

1. LAC, MG 30 E113, George Bell papers, "Back to Blighty," memoir, 3–6.

2. LAC, RG 24, v. 1810, GAQ 2-1, v. 1, Short History of the 1st Canadian Division, 16.

3. Baldwin, *Holding the Line,* 72–3.

4. LAC, Digitized Online War Diary [hereafter WD], 1st Battalion, 12 February 1915.

5. Figure in Nicholson, *Canadian Expeditionary Force,* 548.

6. LAC, RG 24, v. 1811, GAQ 3-6, Divisions in France.

7. Dancocks, *Gallant Canadians,* 15.

8. Murray, *The History of the 2nd Canadian Battalion,* 29.

9. Sir Max Aitken, *Canada in Flanders,* v. I (London: Hodder and Stoughton [13th Edition], 1916) 28.

10. Foster, *Letters from the Front,* 9.

11. Fetherstonhaugh, *The Royal Montreal Regiment,* 29.

12. Dancocks, *Welcome to Flanders Fields,* 139.

13. CWM, 19900227-005, Alfred Baggs papers, diary, 18 February 1915.

14. LAC, MG 30 E8, J.J. Creelman papers, diary, 23 March 1915.

15. Stephen Bull, *Trench Warfare* (Havertown: Cassmate, 2003) 7.

16. Duguid, *Official History of the Canadian Forces in the Great War, 1914–1919,* I/207.

17. Foster, *Letters from the Front,* 108.

18. See Chris Madsen, *Another Kind of Justice: Canadian Military Law from Confederation to Somalia* (Vancouver: UBC Press, 1999); Gerard Oram, *Military Executions during World War I* (New York: Palgrave Macmillan, 2003); and Morton, *When Your Number's Up.*

19. LAC, MG 30 E113, George Bell papers, "Back to Blighty," 15–6.

CHAPTER 8: TRIAL BY FIRE (PP. 109–122)

1. Foster, *Letters from the Front,* 128.

2. LAC, Records of the Canadian Broadcasting Corporation [hereafter RG 41], Transcripts from taped interviews for *Flanders Fields,* v. 9, Ian Sinclair, 13th Battalion, tape 1/page 13 [hereafter 1/13].

3. On the state of the trenches in the Canadian sectors, see the reports in WD, 1st Brigade, Canadian Engineers, April 1915; LAC, RG 9, v. 3751, Diary of William M. Hart, 14 April 1915.

4. John Dixon, *Magnificent but Not War: The Second Battle of Ypres 1915* (London: Leo Cooper, 2003) 42.

5. LAC, RG 41, v. 9, 13th Battalion, J. Jeffery, 1/2-3; RG 41, v. 9, 13th Battalion, Ian Sinclair, 1/15; RG 41, v. 8, 10th Battalion, W. Gritchley, 1/1A.

6. LAC, RG 24, v. 1832, GAQ 8-15D, E.W.B. Morrison account.

7. LAC, RG 9, v. 4823, Report of Operations.

8. Duguid, *The Canadian Forces in the Great War, 1914–1919,* Appendix 357, 241.

9. CWM, 19710147-001, R.E.W. Turner papers, diary/memoir, 3 May 1915.

10. Armine Norris, *Mainly for Mother* (Toronto: Ryerson Press, 1919) 84–5.

11. LAC, RG 9, v. 4011, 15/2, Summary of work performed by the Divisional Engineers.

CHAPTER 9: DESPERATE COUNTERATTACK (PP. 123–134)

1. J. Clinton Morrison Jr., *Hell Upon Earth: A Personal Account of Prince Edward Island Soldiers in the Great War, 1914–1918* (self-published, 1995) 56.

2. WD, 10th Battalion, 22 April 1915, 11:44 P.M.

3. LAC, RG 24, v. 1755, DHS 10-10 pt. 2, D.M. Ormond to Duguid, 8 June 1926.

4. Urquhart, *The History of the 16th Battalion,* 58.

5. Morrison, *Hell Upon Earth*, 56.

6. Foster (ed.), *Letters from the Front*, 10. The official war diary for the 10th Battalion also notes frankly, "very few prisoners were taken." WD, 10th Battalion, 22/23 April 1915, 12:01 A.M.

7. WD, 16th Battalion, 22 April 1915.

8. LAC, MG 30 E84, R.G.E. Leckie papers, Leckie's untitled account of the Second Battle of Ypres [ca. May 1915].

9. WD, 2nd Canadian Brigade, Counterattack by the 10th and 16th Battalions.

10. WD, 1st Battalion, Narrative of Operations, 23 to 30 April 1915.

11. LAC, MG 30 E113, George Bell papers, memoir, "Back to Blighty," 25.

12. Andrew Iarocci, "1st Canadian Infantry Brigade in the Second Battle of Ypres: The Case of 1st and 4th Canadian Infantry Battalions, 23 April 1915," *Canadian Military History* 12.4 (Autumn 2003) 13.

13. LAC, RG 24, v. 1755, DHS 10-10 pt. 2, R.G.F. Hayter to Duguid, 15 June 1926.

14. WD, 1st Battalion, Narrative of Operations, 23 to 30 April 1915; WD, 4th Battalion, 23 April 1915.

15. LAC, RG 24, v. 1756, file DHS 10-10-E pt. 1, Duguid memo, n.d. [ca. 17 October 1934].

16. Radley, *We Lead, Others Follow*, 119.

17. Bill Rawling, *Surviving Trench Warfare: Technology and the Canadian Corps, 1914–1918* (Toronto: University of Toronto Press, 1992) 64–5.

18. Dancocks, *Welcome to Flanders*, 188.

CHAPTER 10: ATTACK AND HOLD (PP. 135–144)

1. Duguid, *Official History of the Canadian Forces in the Great War, 1914–1919*, I/238.

2. Imperial War Museum, 91/3/1, R.J. Clarke, Memoir.

3. See LAC, MG 30 E300, Victor Odlum papers, v. 24.

4. Dancocks, *Gallant Canadians*, 35.

5. University of Manitoba Archives, MSS 56, box 21, folder 4, Lt. Hugh Urquhart to C.W. Gordon, 9 May 1915.

6. CWM, 19900227-005, Alfred Baggs papers, Baggs to [wife], 6 May 1915 and diary entries for 22–24 April 1915.

7. Ibid.

8. Foster, *Letters from the Front*, 5.

9. LAC, MG 30 E69, David Watson papers, diary, 23 April 1915.

10. LAC, RG 24, v. 1825, GAQ 5-61, Narrative of Brigadier General Tuxford, 10 March 1916.

11. LAC, MG 30 E321, William Johnson papers, letter to wife, 3 May 1915.

12. Suzanne Kingsmill, *Francis Scrimger: Beyond the Call of Duty* (Toronto: Hannah Institute and Dundurn Press, 1991) 81.

13. J.H. Elliot and Harold Murchison Tovell, *The Effects of Poisonous Gases as Observed in Returning Soldiers*, December 1916, see LAC, RG 9, v. 3618, File 25-13-6; R. Dujarric de La Riviere, "Lecture on the Effects of the Gases Employed by the Germans," *The Canada Lancet*. XLIX. 4 (December 1915) 157–8.

14. Victor Wheeler, *The 50th Battalion in No Man's Land* (Ottawa: CEF Books, 2000) 108.

15. LAC, RG 9, v. 3751, Diary of Captain P.G. Bell, 25 April 1915.

16. Kingsmill, *Francis Scrimger*, 14–17; LAC, RG 9, v. 3751, Diary of F.A.C. Scrimger, 22–25 April 1915.

CHAPTER 11: TO THE LAST MAN (PP. 145–160)

1. Peat, *Private Peat*, 179.

2. See *Private Peat* (USA: 1918), which starred Harold Peat as himself.

3. George Cassar, *Beyond Courage: The Canadians at the Second Battle of Ypres* (Oberon Press, 1985) 115.

4. H.H. Mathews, "An Account of the Second Battle of Ypres, April 1915," *Canadian Defence Quarterly* 1.3 (April 1924) 38.

5. LAC, RG 41, v. 9, 13th Battalion, T.S. Morrissey, 2/3.

6. Morrison, *Hell Upon Earth*, 235–6.

7. LAC, MG 30 E46, Richard Turner papers, v. 1, file 4, Report of No. 3 Coy. 15 BN. 48th Highlanders, 20–24 April 1915—2nd Battle of Ypres.

8. LAC, RG 24, v. 7734, file D.H.S. 3-4, Casualties 15th Battalion, March & April, 1915. For a discussion of gas casualties at the Second Battle of Ypres, see Tim Cook, *No Place to Run: Canadian Corps and Gas Warfare in the First World War* (Vancouver: UBC Press, 1999).

9. WD, 7th Battalion, Report of Events, Ypres, 22–26 April 1915, A Company Report.

10. LAC, RG 24, v. 1811, file 2-1, v. 2, comments on draft of 1st Division history, 26.

11. Fetherstonhaugh, *The Royal Montreal Regiment*, 14.

12. LAC, MG 30 E300, Victor Odlum papers, v. 16, file: Report of Events, No. 1 Company, April 22–26, 1915, 7th Battalion, Report of Narratives, No. 1 Company.

13. CWM, 19750128-004, A.L. Mackay papers, diary, 24 April 1915.

14. On the problem of communication, see Bill Rawling, "Communications in the Canadian Corps, 1915–1918: Wartime Technological Progress Revisited," *Canadian Military History* 3.2 (Autumn 1994) 6–21.

15. LAC, RG 24, v. 1755, DHS 10-10 pt. 2, Duguid to Edmonds, reply to letter 25 January 1926.

16. CWM, 19710147-001, R.E.W. Turner papers, diary/memoir, account of Second Battle of Ypres.

17. LAC, RG 24, v. 1755, DHS 10-10 pt. 2, Gordon-Hall to Duguid, 27 April 1926.

18. Duguid, *Official History of the Canadian Forces in the Great War, 1914–1919*, II/Appendix 580. Ten days after the battle, Turner noted to his wife, "I have not been able to get my head clear." CWM, 19710147-001, R.E.W. Turner papers, diary/memoir, 3 May 1915.

19. Fetherstonhaugh, *The Royal Montreal Regiment*, 50.

20. W.A. Dymond, "Kitcheners Wood," *Stand To!* 34 (April 1992) 14.

21. LAC, RG 24, v. 1822, file GAQ 5-29, OC, 2nd Battalion to OC, 3rd Brigade, 27 April 1915.

22. LAC, RG 24, v. 2680, file HQC 4950 (pt. 2), Appendix: Points Raised by Turner and Hughes on 2nd Battle of Ypres, 19 June 1936.

23. LAC, MG 30 E1, William Alexander Alldritt papers, diary, 24 April 1915.

24. LAC, RG 24, v. 1755, DHS 10-10 pt. 1, G.S. Tuxford to Duguid, 15 April 1926; RG 24, v. 2680, file HQC 4950 (pt. 2), G.S. Tuxford to Duguid, 19 July 1926.

25. WD, 2nd Canadian Brigade, 8th Battalion Narrative of Events.

26. LAC, MG 30 E75, v. 2, Statement of Major E.F. Lynn, MC.

27. For the postwar acrimonious debate over this event between the British and Canadian official historians, see Tim Cook, *Clio's Warriors: Canadian Historians and the Writing of the World Wars* (Vancouver: UBC Press, 2006). For an eyewitness account, see LAC, MG 30 E100, Sir Arthur Currie papers, v. 18, file 58, E.F. Lynn to Currie (n.d., ca. 6 April 1928). For Currie's remark on Snow, see ibid., v. 41, file 186, Comments on 2nd Draft, British Official History, n.d. [ca. 1926].

28. LAC, RG 24, v. 2680, file HQC 4950 (pt. 2), C.H. Mitchell to Duguid, 12 June 1926.

29. LAC, MG 30 E300, Victor Odlum papers, v. 3, file: Colonel A.F. Duguid, Odlum to Duguid, 26 September 1934.

30. A.B. Tucker, *The Battle Glory of Canada* (London: Cassell, 1915) 131.

31. Rawling, *Surviving Trench Warfare*, 35.

32. Dancocks, *Welcome to Flanders Fields*, 162.

CHAPTER 12: A REPUTATION FORGED (PP. 161–170)

1. Duguid, *Official History of the Canadian Forces in the Great War, 1914–1919,* I/359.

2. Rudolf Binding, *A Fatalist at War* (London: George Allen & Unwin Ltd., 1929) 64–65.

3. Stephen Carthy, "A Letter from Ypres," *The Beaver* (December 2005) 35.

4. Morton, *When Your Number's Up,* 44.

5. Morrison, *Hell Upon Earth,* 209.

6. Gerald Sanger, *The Svenhonger Diary* (self-published, 2000) 173.

7. Canadian Field Comforts Commission, *With the First Canadian Contingent* (Toronto: Hodder and Stoughton, 1915) 88.

8. LAC, MG 30 E28, G.D. Scott papers, *3 Years and 8 Months in a German Prison* by Private G.D. Scott.

9. LAC, MG 30 E100, Sir Arthur Currie papers, v. 27, file 7, Currie to Reid, 20 April 1925; and see testimonials in LAC, RG 24, v. 817, HQ 54-21-8-48-1.

10. Paul and Audrey Grescoe, *The Book of War Letters: 100 Years of Canadian Wartime Correspondence* (Toronto: Macfarlane, Walter & Ross, 2003) 112–13.

11. Canadian Field Comforts Commission, *With the First Canadian Contingent,* 88.

12. Foster, *Letters from the Front,* 11.

13. LAC, RG 24, v. 1755, DHS 10-10 pt. 2, G.S. Tuxford to Duguid, 19 July 1926.

14. LAC MG 30 E6, J.J. Creelman papers, v. 3, file 17, Creelman to Burstall, 16 June 1916.

15. LAC, RG 24, v. 2680, file HQC 4950 (pt. 1), J. Sutherland Brown to MacBrien, 25 November 1925.

16. See Sir John French's communication issued by the War Office on 24 April 1915 in LAC, RG 24, v. 1811, GAQ 3-5.

17. LAC, RG 24, v. 1838, GAQ 10-18B, Translation of *DerWeltkrieg, 1914–1918,* 13.

18. Sir James Edmonds, *Military Operations, France and Belgium, 1915, v. I* (London: Macmillan and Co., 1927) 359; Passingham, *All the Kaiser's Men,* 67.

19. See Cook, *No Place to Run.*

20. On McCrae at Second Ypres, see Dianne Graves, *A Crown of Life: The World of John McCrae* (St. Catharines: Vanwell, 1997).

CHAPTER 13: INTO THE MAELSTROM (PP. 171–184)

1. Quote from A.T. Hunter, "The Battle of Festubert," *Canada in the Great World War Vol. III* (Toronto: United Publishers of Canada, 1919) 156.

2. WD, 14th Battalion, 6 May 1915.

3. See this file for correspondence relating to reinforcements: LAC, RG 9, v. 4011, 15/6.

4. *Flanders Fields*, Jack Pinson, 6/2.

5. Sir James Edmonds, *Military Operations, France and Belgium, 1915,* v. II (London: Macmillan and Co., 1928) 39.

6. Beckett, *The Great War,* 47.

7. LAC, RG 41, v. 7, 3rd Battalion, H.R. Alley, 1/11.

8. CWM, Military History Research Centre (MHRC), C.D.S./88, Ia/9700 D, Artillery: General Principles, 12 July 1915.

9. Nicholson, *Canadian Expeditionary Force,* 97.

10. Radley, *We Lead, Others Follow,* 130.

11. LAC, RG 24, v. 20541, file 990.009 (D6), Duguid to Burns, 2 April 1937. On the failure of maps, see Jeffrey S. Murray, "British–Canadian Military Cartography on the Western Front, 1914–1918," *Archivaria* 26 (Summer 1988) 52–65.

12. LAC, RG 24, v. 20541, file 990.009 (D6), Alexander Macphail to Duguid, 23 March 1937.

13. WD, 14th Battalion, Report of operations, May 18–20, 1915.

14. LAC, RG 9, v. 4011, 15/8, Diary of Operations, 3rd Brigade.

15. Romeo Heule, *Horrors of Trench Fighting: With the Canadian Heroes* [n.d., sometime during the war]—digitized at http://www.greatwardifferent.com/Great_War/Canada/Canada_01.htm.

16. Urquhart, *The History of the 16th Battalion,* 77.

17. *Flanders Fields*, C.J. Johnson, 6/4.

18. Nicholson, *Canadian Expeditionary Force,* 99.

19. CWM, 58A 1. 141.2, Charles Pearce papers, Pearce to "my own dear mother," 22 June [sic, May] 1915.

20. Fetherstonhaugh, *The Royal Montreal Regiment,* 57.

21. Foster, *Letters from the Front,* 20.

CHAPTER 14: "THIS IS NOT WAR, IT IS SIMPLY MURDER" (PP. 185–194)

1. LAC, RG 24, v. 1504, HQ 683-1-30-5, Turner to Duguid, 5 February 1937.

2. Urquhart, *History of the 16th Battalion,* 343.

3. Ibid., 79.

4. LAC, MG 30 E68, H. Lamb papers, 1/2, Report of Captain Frank Morison, OC, 3 Company, 16th Battalion, Festubert.

5. CLIP, *The New Liskeard Speaker* Collection, Herbert Durand, letter, 20 June 1915.

6. CLIP, Thomas Hannah, letter, 9 July 1915.

7. Duguid, *Official History of the Canadian Forces in the Great War, 1914–1919,* I/474.

8. CWM, 19710147-001, R.E.W. Turner papers, diary/memoir, 23 May 1915.

9. McGill University Archives (MA), Currie/Urquhart papers, 4027, box 1, file 12, Lt-General Archie Macdonell, n.d. (ca. 1934); LAC, MG 30 E300, Victor Odlum papers, v. 3, file: Colonel A.F. Duguid, Duguid to Odlum, 16 February 1937.

10. MA, Ibid, Lt-General Archie Macdonell, n.d. (ca. 1934).

11. CWM, MHRC C.D.S./89, Ia/445, Barrage Fire in Case of Attack and the Necessary Expenditure of Ammunition.

12. Hugh Urquhart, *Arthur Currie: The Biography of a Great Canadian* (Toronto: J.M. Dent, 1950) 106–7.

13. WD, 1st Division, Narrative of Events, Festubert Action, 2nd Infantry Brigade.

14. LAC, RG 24, v. 1504, HQ 683-1-30-5, Ashton to Duguid, 9 February 1937.

15. LAC, MG 30 E68, H. Lamb papers, 1/2, Narrative of Events, Festubert Action, 2nd Brigade, 1.

16. LAC, RG 24, v. 1504, HQ 683-1-30-5, G.W. Gordon-Hall to Duguid, 20 March 1937; Gary Sheffield and John Bourne, *Douglas Haig: War Diaries and Letters* (London: Weidenfeld & Nicolson, 2005) 126.

17. LAC, RG 24, v. 1504, HQ 683-1-30-5, Ashton to Duguid, 9 February 1937.

18. *Flanders Fields,* Sydney Cox, 6/6.

CHAPTER 15: "MAINTAINED BY SCIENCE TO BE KILLED BY SHELLS" (PP. 195–206)

1. CLIP, Alfred Herbert Andrews, diary, 21–22 May 1916.

2. Sir Andrew Macphail, *The Medical Services* (Ottawa: F.A. Acland, 1925) 37.

3. CWM, 19920187-002, H.H. Burrell papers, diary, 9 April 1917

4. LAC, MG 30 E113, George Bell papers, "Back to Blighty," 92.

5. Macphail, *The Medical Services,* 5–6.

6. Ibid., 265.

7. LAC, RG 9, v. 3751, diary of G.S. Strathy, 17 March 1917.

8. Robert F. Zubkowski, *As Long as Faith and Freedom Last, Stories from the Princess Patricia's Canadian Light Infantry from June 1914 to September 1919* (Calgary: Bunker to Bunker Books, 2003) 203.

9. Morton, *When Your Number's Up,* 181–2; Geoffrey Noon, "The Treatment of Casualties in the Great War," Paddy Griffith (ed.), *British Fighting Methods in the Great War,* 87–112.

10. Ex-Quaker [F.W. Bagnall], *Not Mentioned in Despatches* (North Vancouver, B.C.: North Shore Press Ltd., 1933) 64.

11. CWM, 58C.1.1.1., 10th Canadian Field Ambulance, Second of June Strafe, 2.

12. For nurses, see G.W.L. Nicholson, *Canada's Nursing Sisters* (Toronto: Samuel, Stevens and Hakkert, 1976); and Susan Mann, *Margaret Macdonald: Imperial Daughter* (Montreal: McGill-Queen's University Press, 2005).

13. LAC, MG 30 E290, Sophie Hoerner papers, letter, 4 July 1915.

14. CWM, 20000013-008, George Ormsby papers, 7 June 1916.

15. R.J. Manion, *A Surgeon in Arms* (Toronto: McClelland, Goodchild and Stewart, 1918) 163.

16. Macfie, *Letters Home*, 54–5.

17. Tom Brown, "Shell Shock in the Canadian Expeditionary Force, 1914–1918: Canadian Psychiatry in the Great War," in Charles G. Roland (ed.), *Health, Disease and Medicine: Essays in Canadian History* (Toronto: Clarke Irwin for the Hannah Institute for the History of Medicine, 1984) 309.

18. This was better understood in the Second World War; see Terry Copp and Bill McAndrew, *Battle Stress: Soldiers and Psychiatrists in the Canadian Army, 1939–1945* (Montreal: McGill-Queen's University Press, 1990).

19. Mark Humphries, "The Treatment of Evacuated War Neuroses Casualties in the Canadian Expeditionary Force, 1914–19" (Wilfrid Laurier University: MA Thesis, 2005).

20. Bill Rawling, *Death Their Enemy: Canadian Medical Practitioners and War* (Ottawa: B. Rawling, 2001) 89–93.

21. *Report of the War Office Committee of Enquiry into "Shell-Shock"* (London, 1922) 17–18.

22. Grace Morris Craig, *But This Is Our War* (Toronto: University of Toronto Press, 1981) 51.

CHAPTER 16: "THE GATES OF HELL OPENED" (PP. 207–216)

1. CLIP, *The New Liskeard Speaker* Collection, Herbert Durand, letter, 30 May 1915.

2. LAC, MG 30 E113, "Back to Blighty," by George V. Bell, 44.

3. LAC, RG 24, v. 1844, GAQ 11-11E, Neurasthenia, Shell Shock and Hysteria Admissions.

4. Dancocks, *Gallant Canadians*, 53.

5. WD, 1st Division, Narrative of Events, Festubert Action, 2nd Infantry Brigade, n.d. [ca. 30 May 1915].

6. LAC, RG 9, v. 4011, 15/8, untitled report [5th Battalion attack on 24 May 1915].

7. A.T. Hunter, "The Battle of Festubert," *Canada in the Great World War, Vol. III* (Toronto: United Publishers of Canada, 1919) 169–70.

8. Rawling, *Surviving Trench Warfare*, 24.

9. IWM, 81/9/1, W.S. Lighthall, memoir, 49.

10. Zubkowski, *As Long as Faith and Freedom Last*, 217.

11. CWM, 19990089, W.H. Wray, Wray to father, 19 May 1916.

12. Sir James Edmonds, *Military Operations, France and Belgium, 1915*, v. II (London: Macmillan and Co., 1928) 89.

13. Bull, *Trench Warfare*, 67–8.

14. W.C. Millar, *From Thunder Bay Through Ypres with the Fighting Fifty-Second* (self-published, 1918) 18.

15. Foster, *Letters from the Front*, 22.

16. Ex-Quaker, *Not Mentioned in Despatches*, 52.

17. Baldwin, *Holding the Line*, 262.

18. WD, 1st Division, 5th Battalion, Narrative of Events. 29 May 1915.

19. The casualties occurred from May 18 to midnight on May 24/25. The fighting units of the Canadian Division lost 2,204 officers and men; Seely's Cavalry Brigade lost 198; and divisional troops suffered an additional 203 casualties. See RG 24, v. 1820, file GAQ 5-11, Casualties, Canadian Division, Festubert.

20. RG 24, v. 20541, file 990.009 (D6), Meighen to Duguid, 22 March 1937.

21. CWM, Sir Arthur Currie papers, 58A.1.59.1, Narrative of Operations at Festubert, 2nd Brigade.

CHAPTER 17: LIVING IN A SEWER (PP. 217–236)

1. *Flanders Fields*, Gregory Clark, 6/16

2. CLIP, *The New Liskeard Speaker* Collection, R.S. Robinson, 14 February 1915.

3. Will Bird, *Ghosts Have Warm Hands* (Ottawa: CEF Books, 1997) 9.

4. For the building of trenches, see *Trench Fortifications, 1914–1918: A Reference Manual* (Imperial War Museum, 1998).

5. J.M. Bourne, "A Personal Reflection on the Two World Wars," Peter Liddle, et al. (eds.), *The Great World War 1914–45, Volume I, Lightning Strikes Twice* (HarperCollins, 2000) 19.

6. John Laffin, *The Western Front Illustrated, 1914–1919* (London: Grange, 1997) 27.

7. CLIP, Alfred Andrews, diary, 20 May 1915.

8. CLIP, David McLean, Dear Lettie, 9 December 1916.

9. James MacGregor, *MacGregor V.C.* (Victoria: Victoria Publishing Company, 2002) 51.

10. CWM, 19920187-002, H.H. Burrell papers, diary, 27 December 1916.

11. Becker, *Silhouettes of the Great War*, 69.

12. Urquhart, *The History of the 16th Battalion*, 81.

13. CLIP, George Kempling, diary, 25 July 1916.

14. Norris, *Mainly for Mother*, 28.

15. CLIP, Ernest Taylor, My dearest Nance, 4 December 1915.

16. James H. Pedley, *Only This: A War Retrospect* (Ottawa: The Graphic Publishers, 1927) 68.

17. Lieutenant Stanley Rutledge, *Pen Pictures from the Trenches* (Toronto: William Briggs, 1918) 106.

CHAPTER 18: MANY A DAMNED COLD MORNING (PP. 237–254)

1. Foster, *Letters from the Front*, 123.

2. CWM, 58A 1 112.10, Samuel Honey papers, Sam to parents, 31 August 1916.

3. On malingering, see Joanna Bourke, *Dismembering the Male: Men's Bodies, Britain and the Great War* (London: Reaktion, 1999).

4. Norma Shephard, *Dear Harry: The Firsthand Account of a World War I Infantryman* (Burlington: Brigham Press, 2003) 178.

5. Bird, *Ghosts Have Warm Hands*, 27.

6. Macphail, *The Medical Services*, 270.

7. Dave Campbell, *The Divisional Experience in the C.E.F.: A Social and Operational History of the 2nd Canadian Division, 1915–1918* (Unpublished Ph.D: University of Calgary, 2003) 69–72.

8. LAC, MG 30 E547, Mackinnon family papers, letter, 27 January 1917.

9. Ralph Bell, *Canada in War Paint* (London: J.M. Dent, 1917) 123.

10. LAC, MG 30 E442, Aubrey Wyndham Griffiths papers, Memoirs, 13. Griffiths remarked that the rum was 186 proof strength. LAC, MG 30 E300, Victor Odlum papers, v. 24, file Trench Discipline, Extract of Trench Routine Orders, n.d. [end of 1916]; LAC, MG 27 II-B-9, A.E. Kemp papers, v. 147, file L-4, Memorandum for the Honourable Minister on the Subjects: (a) sale of Liquor on board Transports. (b) Wet Canteens in England and France. 18 June 1918.

11. E.L.M. Burns, *General Mud* (Toronto: Clarke, Irwin & Company, 1970) 14; Pierre Berton, *Vimy* (Toronto: McClelland and Stewart, 1986) 113; LAC, RG 41, v. 16, 54th BN, R.H. Sinclair, 1/9; LAC, RG 41, v. 8, 7th BN, F. Dawson, 2/14.

12. As noted by Pte. G. Brownbridge of the 13th Northumberland Fusiliers in Martin Middlebrook, *The First Day on the Somme* (London: Penguin Books, 1971, 1984) 160. In addition, one medical officer testifying before a 1922 parliamentary committee investigating the nature of shell shock offered his opinion: "Had it not been for the rum ration I do not think we should have won the war." As quoted in Paul Fussell, *The Great War and Modern Memory* (London: Oxford University Press, 1975) 47.

13. R.J. Manion, *A Surgeon in Arms* (New York: D. Appleton and Company, 1918) 107–8.

14. Bell, *Canada in War Paint*, 125. Also see Robert Graves as quoted in Richard Holmes, *Firing Line* (London: Pimlico, 1985) 249; LAC, RG 41, v. 11, 26th Battalion, W.R. Allen, 3/1.

15. LAC, MG 30 E400, Claude Vivian Williams papers, Williams to mother, 28 December 1916.

16. LAC, RG 41, v. 8, 7th Battalion, J.I. Chambers, 1/7.

17. CWM, 19920187-002, H.H. Burrell papers, diary, 6 April 1917.

18. Corrigall, *The Twentieth Battalion*, 43.

19. Louis Keene, *"Crumps," The Plain Story of a Canadian Who Went* (Boston: Houghton, 1917) 109–10.

20. Ernest G. Black, *I Want One Volunteer* (Toronto: Ryerson Press, 1965) 97.

21. Frederick Noyes, *Stretcher-Bearers ... at the Double: History of the Fifth Canadian Field Ambulance Which Served Overseas During the Great War of 1914–1918* (Toronto: Hunter-Rose, 1937) 60.

22. James Robert Johnston, *Riding into War: The Memoir of a Horse Transport Driver, 1916–1919* (Fredericton, N.B.: Goose Lane Editions, 2004) 47.

23. CWM, 58A 1 188.34, George McLean papers, George to sister, 6 October 1917.

24. Armine Norris, *Mainly for Mother* (Toronto: Ryerson Press, 1919) 59.

25. McClintock, *Best o' Luck,* 19.

26. CWM, 58A 1 112.9, Samuel Honey papers, Sam to mother and father, 26 December 1915.

27. D.E. Macintyre, *Canada at Vimy* (Toronto: Peter Martin Associates, 1967), 18; Foster, *Letters from the Front,* 108.

28. *Flanders Fields,* H.R. Alley, 7/29.

29. CWM, 19920187-002, H.H. Burrell papers, diary, 30 May 1917.

30. CWM, 19740046-001, Allen Oliver papers, scrapbook, Oliver to Dodo, 26 February 1916.

31. Coningsby Dawson, *The Glory of the Trenches* (New York: John Lane Company, 1918) 23.

32. Chris McCarthy, "Not All Beer and Skittles? Everyday Life and Leisure on the Western Front," in Geoffrey Jensen and Andrew Wiest (eds.), *War in the Age of Technology: Myriad Faces of Modern Armed Conflict* (New York: New York University Press, 2001) 153.

33. Peter G. Rogers (ed.), *Gunner Ferguson's Diary* (Hantsport: Lancelot Press, 1985) 45.

34. Keene, *"Crumps,"* 143.

35. Clifford Wells, *From Montreal to Vimy Ridge and Beyond: The Correspondence of Lieut. Clifford Almon Wells, B.A. of the 8th Battalion, Canadians, B.E.F., November, 1915–April 1917* (Toronto: McClelland, Goodchild and Stewart, 1917) 194.

36. N.M. Christie (ed.), *Letters of Agar Adamson, 1914 to 1919* (Ottawa: CEF Books, 1997) 76.

37. McClintock, *Best o' Luck,* 23.

38. CLIP, *The New Liskeard Speaker* Collection, Enos Grant, 6 March 1915.

39. CWM, 20040015-005, Lawrence Rogers papers, Lawrence to May, 9 February 1916.

40. Romeo Heule, *Horrors of Trench Fighting: With the Canadian Heroes* [n.d., sometime during the war]—digitized at http://www.greatwardifferent.com/Great_War/Canada/Canada_01.htm.

41. CWM, 19920187-002, H.H. Burrell papers, diary, 22 February 1917.

42. T.W.L. MacDermot, *The Seventh* (Montreal: the Seventh Canadian Siege Battery Association, 1953) 19.

43. Dr. David Payne, "'Trench' Diseases of the Western Front," *Stand To!* 73 (April 2005) 16.

44. Macphail, *The Medical Services,* 271.

45. Morton, *When Your Number's Up,* 138.

CHAPTER 19: "EVERY DAY WE LOST A FEW MEN" (PP. 255–270)

1. Foster, *Letters from the Front,* 108.

2. Byfield, *Alberta in the 20th Century,* 29.

3. Manion, *Surgeon in Arms,* 25.

4. Foster, *Letters from the Front,* 181.

5. Frederic Manning, *The Middle Parts of Fortune* (London: Peter Davies, 1929) 222.

6. Leonard Heaton, *Wound Ballistics* (Washington: Office of the Surgeon General Department of the Army, 1962) 106.

7. Baldwin, *Holding the Line,* 163.

8. LAC, RG 9, v. 3951, Diary of Colonel R.P. Cambell, 30 April 1916.

9. Foster, *Letters from the Front,* 32.

10. LAC, MG 30 E241, D.E Macintyre papers, diary, 8 October 1915.

11. CLIP, Gordon Rae MacKay, Dear Mother, 28 May 1917.

12. LAC, RG 41, v. 11, 22nd Battalion, W.R. Lindsay, 2/2–3.

13. William Gray, *A Sunny Subaltern: Billy's Letters from Flanders* (Toronto: McClelland, Goodchild and Stewart, 1916) 164.

14. Reginald H. Roy, *The Journal of Private Fraser* (Victoria: Sono Nis Press, 1985) 151.

15. Baldwin, *Holding the Line*, 195.

16. J. George Adami, *The War Story of the Canadian Army Medical Corps* (Toronto: Canadian War Records Office, 1918) 118–19.

17. G.D. Sheffield, *Forgotten Victory: The First World War, Myths and Realities* (London: Review, 2002) 111.

18. LAC, MG 30 E523, Sprague family papers, Sprague to Jim and Eva, 9 November 1916.

19. Millar, *From Thunder Bay*, 37.

20. For the British gas units, see Donald Richter, *Chemical Soldiers: British Gas Warfare in World War I* (Lawrence: University Press of Kansas, 1992).

21. Manion, *A Surgeon in Arms,* 79.

22. For gas in 1918, see L.F. Haber, *The Poisonous Cloud: Chemical Warfare in the First World War* (Toronto: Oxford University Press, 1985).

23. For gas death rates, see Cook, *No Place to Run*, 215–18; Norris, *Mainly for Mother*, 18.

24. Craig, *But This Is Our War*, 52.

25. Christie, *Letters of Agar Adamson,* 246.

26. Foster, *Letters from the Front*, 58.

27. Lieutenant R. Lewis, M.M., *Over the Top with the 25th* (Halifax: H.H. Marshall, 1918) 16.

28. Fetherstonhaugh, *The Royal Montreal Regiment*, 132.

29. D.L. Matthews (ed.), *The Oslers During World War One* (Gravenhurst: The Artstract Co., 1999) 71.

30. Coningsby Dawson, *Living Bayonets: A Record of the Last Push* (London: Lane, 1919) 179.

31. CWM, 58A 1 188.34, George McLean papers, George to sister, 12 September 1918.

32. Shephard, *Dear Harry*, 76.

33. LAC, R8258, Gregory Clark papers, file 2-3, undated memoir.

34. WD, Sketches and Locations—Extracts and Flank (handwritten notes from A.F. Duguid), Canadian Casualties, pp. 25–6.

35. LAC, MG 30 E8, J.J. Creelman papers, file 1, diary, 4 December 1915.

36. Report of the Ministry: *Overseas Military Forces of Canada 1918* (London: Printed by Authority of the Minister Overseas Military Forces of Canada, 1918) 59.

37. Foster, *Letters from the Front*, 130.

38. K. Weatherbe, *From the Rideau to the Rhine and Back: The 6th Field Company* (Toronto: Hunter-Rose, 1928) 98.

39. WD, 3rd Cdn Division, Assistant Director of Medical Services, 7 April 1916.

40. Wheeler, *The 50th Battalion in No Man's Land*, 43.

41. LAC, RG 9, v. 3982, 3/7, "Report on the Periodical Outbursts of Reports Announcing Extraordinary Discoveries Made by the Enemy."

42. Keene, *"Crumps,"* 106.

CHAPTER 20: INTO THE ABYSS (PP. 271–282)

1. CWM, 58A 1 153.5, George Ormsby papers, letter to Maggie, 22 June 1916.

2. CWM, 58A 1 112.9, Samuel Honey papers, Samuel to parents, 24 October 1916.

3. Macphail, *The Medical Services,* 56.

4. CWM, 19990089, W.H. Wray papers, Wray to father, 1 June 1916.

5. Bruce Cane (ed.), *It Made You Think of Home: The Haunting Journal of Deward Barnes, CEF 1916–1919* (Toronto: Dundurn Press, 2004) 89–90.

6. For postwar writings on the war, see Jonathan Vance, *Death So Noble: Memory, Meaning, and the First World War* (Vancouver: UBC Press, 1997).

7. G.R. Stevens, *A City Goes to War: History of the Loyal Edmonton Regiment* (Brampton: Charters Pub, 1964) 31.

8. John William Lynch, *Princess Patricia's Canadian Light Infantry, 1917–1919* (New York: Exposition Press, 1976) 45.

9. Fetherstonhaugh, *The Royal Montreal Regiment,* 64.

10. The Adjutant, *The 116th Battalion in France* (Toronto: E.P.S. Allen, 1921) 81; William Ogilvie, *Umty-Iddy-Umty: The Story of a Canadian Signaller in the First World War* (Erin: The Boston Mills Press, 1982) 46–7; Middlebrook, *The First Day on the Somme,* 91.

11. Chute, *The Real Front,* 106.

12. LAC, MG 30 E54, F.R. Phelan papers, folder 3, Trench Standing Orders, November 1915.

13. CLIP, Ernest Taylor, My dearest Nance, 24 March 1916.

14. LAC, MG 31 G29, Lance Cattermole papers, "Attack on the Somme, 15th and 16th September 1916," 5.

15. LAC, MG 30 E241, D.E. Macintyre papers, diary, 3 November 1915.

16. For intelligence in the corps, see D.R. Jenkins, *Winning Trench Warfare: Battlefield Intelligence in the Canadian Corps, 1914–1918* (Unpublished Ph.D.: Carleton University, 1999). Wellington quote cited in A.L. Rodger et al., *Surveillance and Target Acquisition Systems* (Oxford: Brassey's Defence Publishers, 1983) 157.

17. McBride, *A Rifleman Went to War,* 44–5.

18. CWM, *The Twentieth Gazette* 2.3 (December 1916) 23.

19. Pedley, *Only This,* 157–8.

20. Wheeler, *The 50th Battalion in No Man's Land,* 7.

21. LAC, MG 30 E220, E.W. Russell papers, Memoir, *A Private Soldier's View of the Great War, 1914–1918,* 10.

22. J.H. Johnson, *Stalemate!: The Great Trench Warfare Battles of 1915–1917* (London: Arms and Armour, 1995) 117.

23. Lew Perry, *Pickinem-Up-n-Putinem-Down* (self-published, 1932) 64.

24. George B. McKean, *Scouting Thrills: The Memoirs of a Scout Officer in the Great War* (Ottawa: CEF Books, 2003) 12.

25. Roy, *The Journal of Private Fraser,* 42.

26. Cain, *It Made You Think of Home,* 139.

27. CWM, *The Listening Post* 6 (20 October 1915) 1.

28. Wheeler, *The 50th Battalion in No Man's Land,* 206.

CHAPTER 21: SNIPERS (PP. 283–290)

1. Gray, *A Sunny Subaltern*, 128.

2. For snipers' tactics, see Leslie Mepham, *Making Their Mark: Canadian Snipers and the Great War, 1914–1918* (M.A. Thesis: University of Windsor, 1997).

3. CWM, 19950008-014, Samuel Honey papers, Sam to parents, 31 August 1916.

4. CLIP, John Sudbury, 7 May 1916.

5. Norris, *Mainly for Mother*, 212.

6. Bird, *Ghosts Have Warm Hands*, 17.

7. McClintock, *Best o' Luck*, 19.

8. CWM, 58A 1.171.29, T.W. MacDowell papers, Notebook, School of Musketry, 20 June 1916.

9. Rutledge, *Pen Pictures from the Trenches*, 57–8.

10. LAC, RG 24, v. 1874, file 22-21, Some figures regarding American-born serving with the CEF. A total of 35,599 American-born served in the CEF; 15,057 made it to France and 2,138 were fatal casualties.

11. McBride, *A Rifleman Went to War*, 86–7.

12. LAC, MG 30 E2, N.A.D. Armstrong papers, *Notes on the Training of the Battalion Intelligence Section*. n.d. [before 1947], chapter XIX.

13. Ken Tingley (ed.), *The Path of Duty: The Wartime Letters of Alwyn Bramley-Moore, 1914–1916* (Alberta: Historical Society of Alberta, 1998) 75–7.

14. F.B. MacDonald and John J. Gardiner, *The Twenty-Fifth Battalion Canadian Expeditionary Force: Nova Scotia's Famous Regiment in World War One* (Sydney, N.S.: J. Chadwick, 1985) 71.

15. Murray, *The History of the 2nd Canadian Battalion*, 76.

16. WD, 50th Battalion, 28 April 1918.

17. Dancocks, *Welcome to Flanders Fields*, 125.

18. Adrian Hayes, *Pegahmagabow: Legendary Warrior, Forgotten Hero* (Sault Ste. Marie: Fox Meadow Creations, 2003) 8.

19. Currie, *The Red Watch*, 163.

CHAPTER 22: WINNING CONTROL OF NO MAN'S LAND (PP. 291–302)

1. Tupper, *Victor Gordon Tupper: A Brother's Tribute*, 29.

2. For the Australian opinion, see *C.E.W. Bean, The Australian Imperial Force in France 1916*, v. III (St. Lucia, Queensland: University of Queensland Press, 1982) 244.

3. LAC, MG 30 E23, H.M. MacPherson papers, diary, 16 November 1915.

4. WD, 7th Battalion, Operational Order No. 59.

5. WD, 7th Battalion, 17 November 1915; RG 24, v. 6992, Account of the Raid on Petite Douve.

6. LAC, RG 24, v. 1825, file GAQ 5-66, Lipsett to Currie, 20 November 1915.

7. Perry, *Pickinem-Up-n-Putinem Down*, 95–7.

8. Tupper, *Victor Gordon Tupper*, 29.

9. WD, 10th Battalion, Appendix 3, Report of minor operation on the night of February 4th [1916].

10. CLIP, Alfred Andrews papers, diary/memoir, 4 February 1916.

11. Keene, *"Crumps,"* 96–7.

12. Becker, *Silhouettes of the Great War*, 82.

13. LAC, MG 30 E50, Elmer Jones papers, v. 1, file 3, Trench Raids (a lecture to Corps Officers' School), n.d.

14. LAC, MG 30 E241, D.E. Macintyre papers, v. 2, *Men of Valour*, 5.

15. Morrison, *Hell Upon Earth*, 236.

16. For German interrogation and tricks, see CWM, MHRC, S.S. 730, Leakage of Information through Prisoners of War.

17. LAC, MG 30 E2, N.A.D. Armstrong, "Notes on the Training of the Battalion Intelligence Section," n.d. [before 1947], chapter 1.

18. McClintock, *Best o' Luck*, 27.

19. Macfie, *Letters Home*, 39.

20. *Flanders Fields*, R.L. Christopherson, 6/24.

21. LAC, MG 30 E241, D.E. Macintyre papers, v. 1, diary, 31 January 1916.

22. Dancocks, *Sir Arthur Currie*, 64.

23. Murray, *The History of the 2nd Canadian Battalion*, 32.

24. James Brent Wilson, *The Morale and Discipline of the BEF, 1914–1918* (M.A. Thesis: New Brunswick, 1978) 67–117, 310–13.

25. Quote attributed to Edmond Blunden, cited in Rawling, *Surviving Trench Warfare*, 47.

CHAPTER 23: CREATING THE CORPS (PP. 303–322)

1. Foster, *Letters from the Front*, 115.

2. LAC, RG 24, v. 1811, GAQ 3-2, Strength Return for 1st August 1915.

3. Dancocks, *Sir Arthur Currie*, 60.

4. LAC, RG 24, v. 1813, file 4-15L, The Expansion of the Canadian Militia for the War, 1914–18, by J. Sutherland Brown, 16.

5. "The Role and Composition of the Army Corps in the BEF," *Stand To!* 29 (Summer 1990) 19.

6. See David Love, *A Call to Arms: The Organization and Administration of Canada's Military in World War One* (Winnipeg: Bunker to Bunker Books, 1999); and LAC, RG 9, v. 3827, 5, Staff Work in Armies, 13 January 1916.

7. A.M.J. Hyatt, *General Sir Arthur Currie: A Military Bibliography* (Toronto: University of Toronto Press, 1987), 52. Turner agreed with Currie. Stephen Harris, *Canadian Brass: The Making of a Professional Army, 1860–1939* (Toronto: University of Toronto Press, 1988) 118.

8. Radley, *We Lead, Others Follow*, 134.

9. See Tim Cook, "The Politics of Surrender: Canadian Soldiers and the Killing of Prisoners in the Great War," *Journal of Military History* 70(3) (July 2006) 637–65.

10. Robert Graves, *Goodbye to All That* (London: Penguin Modern Classics, 1960, original in 1929) 154.

11. See LAC, RG 24, v. 1883a, file 28, statistics. For the Canadian reputation, see Tim Cook, "Documenting War & Forging Reputations: Sir Max Aitken and the Canadian War Records Office in the First World War," *War in History* 10(3), 2003, 265–95.

12. LAC, MG 30 E8, J.J. Creelman papers, file 1, diary, 13 July 1915.

13. Morrison, *Hell Upon Earth*, 236.

14. Anthony Clayton, *Paths of Glory: The French Army 1914–18* (London: Cassell, 2003 [2005]) 98.

15. David French, "The Strategy of the Entente Powers, 1914–1917," Strachan (ed.), *The Oxford Illustrated History of the First World War*, 59.

16. CWM, 20030142-001, William H. Hay papers, Hendrie to mother, 25 September 1915.

17. LAC, RG 9, v. 3842, 42/1, Report of Operations, September 24 and 25, by 1st Canadian Divisional Artillery; Ibid., Proceedings of Corps Commanders Conference, 18 September 1915.

18. CWM, 19770531-011, Arthur McNally papers, diary, 2 November 1915.

19. CWM, George Ormsby papers, George to May, 11 November 1915 and 11 January 1916.

20. Fetherstonhaugh, *The Royal Montreal Regiment*, 72.

21. This happened to the 116th Battalion; see The Adjutant [E.P.S. Allen], *The 116th Battalion in France* (1921) 18.

22. Karl Weatherbe, *From the Rideau to the Rhine and Back* (Toronto: Hunter-Rose, 1928) 53.

23. LAC, RG 24, v. 1813, GAQ 4-15K, W.A. Griesbach, "Lieut-Gen. Sir Edwin Alderson, KCB," *The Khaki Call* XII.1 (February 1928) 4.

24. On the junior officers, see Griesbach, "Lieut-Gen. Sir Edwin Alderson, KCB," 4.

25. Norris, *Mainly for Mother*, 79.

26. Hodder-Williams, *Princess Patricia's Canadian Light Infantry*, I/94.

27. Bull, *Trench Warfare*, 15.

28. Griffith, *Battle Tactics of the Western Front*, 72.

29. Geoffrey Noon, "The Treatment of Casualties in the Great War," Paddy Griffith (ed.), *British Fighting Methods in the Great War* (Portland: Frank Cass, 1996) 101.

30. T.H. McGuffie, "The Bayonet," *History Today* v. 12 (August 1962), 593.

Chapter 24: The Murder Hole (pp. 323–336)

1. For mine warfare, see Peter Barton et. al, *Beneath Flanders Fields: The Tunnellers' War 1914–18* (Kingston: McGill-Queen's University Press, 2005).

2. Major H.C. Singer, *History of the 31st Canadian Infantry Battalion, C.E.F.* (Unknown publisher, 1938) 75.

3. LAC, RG 9, v. 4688, 42/15, Protest by Brig-Gen. Ketchen, against adverse Report of G.O.C., Cdn. Corps, addressed to 2nd Cdn. Division, 18th April 1916, 1.

4. LAC, RG 24, v. 1501, HQ 683-1-28, J.A. Gunn to Duguid, 3 October 1938. For Turner's protest, see CWM, 1971-0147-001, Sir Richard Turner papers, diary, Narrative of St. Eloi Crater.

5. Roy, *The Journal of Private Fraser*, 113.

6. LAC, RG 9, v. 4937, 429/1, Personal account by A.H. Bell, 2.

7. Foster, *Letters from the Front*, 106.

8. LAC, RG 9, v. 4935, War Diary of the 27th Battalion, Summary of Operations, Appendix II.

9. Middlebrook, *The First Day of the Somme*, 38; Donald Simpson, "Brain Wounds in the First World War: Lessons from the Steel Thunderstorms," *War and Society* 23 (September 2005) 53–7.

10. Desmond Morton, "A Canadian Soldier in the Great War: The Experiences of Frank Maheux," *Canadian Military History* 1(1) & 2, 82.

11. *Flanders Fields*, H. Snape, 7/5.

12. *Flanders Fields*, V.C.H. Pinkham, 7/6.

13. LAC, RG 9, v. 4937, Report of Operations of the 31st Battalion, April 3–9, 1916, Appendix 16.

14. LAC, RG 9, v. 4937, War Diary of the 31st Battalion, April 6, 1916.

15. Roy, *The Journal of Private Fraser*, 117.

16. On the night of April 3, the battalion had a nominal strength of 24 officers and 703 men. When the 31st were relieved on April 8, they had suffered 29 killed, 154 wounded, and four missing. RG 9, v. 4937, War Diary of the 31st Battalion, April 4–7, 1916.

17. Macphail, *The Medical Services*, 61.

18. LAC, RG 9, v. 4937, 429/1, Report of Operations of the 31st Battalion, April 3–9, 1916, Appendix 16; LAC, RG 9, v. 4694, 56/7, The Gallant Stand of Major Daly's Company, 2. It was reported that thirty-six Germans were killed.

19. This was the start of the relief for the 6th Brigade by the 4th Brigade. To relieve an entire brigade could take up to two days, and as a result some battalions from different brigades were in the line together. When the 6th Brigade was finally fully relieved, it had suffered 617 casualties. See RG 9, v. 4688, 42/14, Casualties During Tour in St. Eloi Trenches, 4th–8th, 1916.

20. LAC, RG 9, v. 4935, War Diary of the 27th Battalion, April 6, 1916.

21. Ibid.

22. On the German tactics, see CWM, 1971-0147-001, Sir Richard Turner papers, diary, Narrative of St. Eloi Crater.

23. LAC, RG 9, v. 3859, 85/3, 2.C.D.-G.S. 723, 7 May 1916.

24. LAC, RG 9, v. 4937, 429/1, Personal account written by A.H. Bell, 7.

25. DHH, Duguid Bio file, 3/Colonel A.F. Duguid, pt. 1, Duguid to Lt. Col D.E. MacIntyre, 18 June 1928; also see Campbell, *The 2nd Canadian Division*, chapter 3.

26. LAC, MG 30 E46, Richard Turner papers, 9/2 C.D.-G.S. 592, Summary of Operations April 17, 1916.

27. LAC, RG 9, v. 4098, folder 42, 3/2 C.D.-G.S. 611, Memo from Lieutenant-Colonel E. Hilliam to General Watson, 12 April 1916.

28. Ibid.

29. As cited in Samuel Hynes, *The Soldiers' Tale: Bearing Witness to Modern War* (London: Penguin, Allen Lane, 1997) 12.

30. LAC, RG 9, v. 4098, 42/3, 2 C.D.-G.S. 611, April 12, 1916.

31. R.C. Fetherstonhaugh, *The 24th Battalion, C.E.F., Victoria Rifles of Canada 1914–1919, Regimental History* (Montreal: Gazette Printing Company, 1930) 47.

32. LAC, MG 30 E46, Richard Turner papers, 9/Summary of Operations 15–21, April 1916; Fetherstonhaugh, *The 24th Battalion*, 48.

33. Will Bird, *The Communication Trench* (Ottawa: CEF Books, 2000) 42.

Chapter 25: Defeat and Scapegoats (pp. 337–342)

1. LAC, MG 30 E49, Richard Turner papers, folder 9, Alderson to Turner, 16 April 1916.

2. Nicholson, *Canadian Expeditionary Force*, 145.

3. See DHH, Duguid Bio File, box 2, folder E, file 75—Relations between General Turner and General Alderson, 14 March 1934; RG 24, v. 1739, DHS 3-17 (v. 4), Turner to Duguid, (ca. late 1929).

4. H.F. Wood, *Vimy!* (Toronto: Macmillan of Canada, 1967) 55.

5. WD, Sketches and Locations—Extracts and Flank (handwritten notes from A.F. Duguid, ca. 1938), G.271, II Army (AMS).

6. LAC, MG 27 II G 1, Beaverbrook papers [hereafter BP], series E, reel A-1764, Aitken to Hughes, 20 April 1916; 21 April 1916; and especially 24 April 1916.

7. Robert Blake, *The Private Papers of Douglas Haig, 1914–1919* (London: Eyre and Spottiswoode, 1952) 140. LAC, RG 24, v. 20542, file 990.011 (D1), excerpt from Haig's diary, 21 April 1916.

8. LAC, MG 30 E15, W.A. Griesbach, v. 1, file 1, Sam Hughes to Alderson, 7 March 1916.

9. Aitken informed Hughes of Plumer's anger; see BP, Aitken to Hughes, 4 May 1916.

10. Granatstein, *Canada's Army*, 87; Patrick Brennan, "Good Men for a Hard Job: Infantry Battalion Commanders in the Canadian Expeditionary Force," *Canadian Army Journal* 9.1 (Spring 2006) 9–28.

11. BP, reel A-1764, Aitken to Hughes, 20 April 1916.

12. LAC, RG 24, v. 1501, HQ 683-1-28, J.A. Gunn to Duguid, 3 October 1938.

13. DHH, Duguid Bio file, folder 3, box 2, folder E, file 75—Relations between General Turner and General Alderson, 14 March 1934.

14. German casualties were calculated as 66 killed, 299 wounded, and another 118 missing (most of whom were killed on the battlefield). LAC, RG 24, v. 1892, file 108, Translation of draft German History supplied by Reichsarchiv and forwarded by Gen. Edmonds, ca. 1928.

15. Lieutenant-General Maurice A. Pope, *Letters from the Front, 1914–1919* (Toronto: Pope and Company, 1996) 47.

16. Beckles Willson, *From Quebec to Piccadilly and Other Places, Some Anglo-Canadian Memories* (London: Jonathan Cape, 1929) 221.

17. Roy, *The Journal of Private Fraser*, 109.

Chapter 26: "It Was a Day of Obliteration" (pp. 343–356)

1. LAC, MG 30 E8, J.J. Creelman papers, file 1, diary, 25 May 1916.

2. Jeffrey Williams, *Byng of Vimy* (Toronto: University of Toronto Press, 1983, 1992) 115.

3. Macphail, *The Medical Services*, 57.

4. Wood, *Vimy!*, 56.

5. *Flanders Fields*, C.B. Price, 7/14.

6. LAC, RG 24, v. 1811, file 2-1, v. 2, comments on draft of 1st Division history, 46.

7. Ex-Quaker, *Not Mentioned in Despatches*, 68.

8. On the battalion friendship, see Bird, *Ghosts Have Warm Hands*, 184.

9. Ian McCulloch, "The 'Fighting Seventh': The Evolution and Devolution of Tactical Command and Control in a Canadian Infantry Brigade of the Great War" (M.A. thesis: Royal Military College of Canada, 1997) 66.

10. G.C. Johnston, *The 2nd Canadian Mounted Rifles* (Vernon, 1932) 18.

11. LAC, RG 9, v. 3834, 21/5, Canadian Corps, Summary of Intelligence, 1 June 1916; WD, 3rd Division, Summary of Intelligence, 2 June 1916.

12. CWM, 20040015-005, Lawrence Rogers papers, Lawrence to May, 9 June 1916.

13. Lieutenant-Colonel C. Beresford Topp, *The 42nd Battalion, CEF. Royal Highlanders of Canada in the Great War* (Montreal: Gazette Printing, 1931) 39.

14. Zubkowski, *As Long as Faith and Freedom Last*, 181.

15. William Frederick Stewart, *Attack Doctrine in the Canadian Corps, 1916–1918* (M.A. thesis: University of New Brunswick, 1982) 44.

16. CWM, 58A 1.47.9, Courtney Tower papers, diary, 2 June 1916.

17. For 1st CMR casualties, see Wayne Ralph, *Barker VC* (Doubleday Canada, 1997) 38. For the 4th CMR, see LAC, RG 9, v. 4947, 467 (1), War Diary of the 4th CMR, 2 June 1916; quote in S.G. Bennett, *The 4th Canadian Mounted Rifles 1914–1919* (Toronto, 1926) 19–20.

18. Nicholson, *Canadian Expeditionary Force*, 150.

19. Major-General A.G.L. McNaughton, "The Development of Artillery in the Great War," *Canadian Defence Quarterly* (January 1929) 171.

20. Foster, *Letters from the Front*, 143.

21. LAC, MG 28 I233, v. 26, file 8, narrative by Harris Turner, n.d. I would like to thank Dr. Serge Durflinger for bringing this record to my attention.

22. CWM, 58C 1.1.1., Second of June—Strafe, 10th Canadian Field Ambulance.

23. LAC, MG 30 E36, Alan Crossman papers, Account of capture at Mount Sorrel, n.d.

24. Hodder-Williams, *Princess Patricia's Canadian Light Infantry*, I/114.

25. Ibid., I/123.

CHAPTER 27: "LIKE POURING METAL INTO A BLAST FURNACE" (PP. 357–366)

1. LAC, RG 24, v. 1739, file DHS 3-17 (v. 4), Sir A.C. Macdonell to Duguid, "Mount Sorrel" (ca. August 1929).

2. WD, 3rd Division, Report of Operations, 2 to 8 June 1916.

3. H.R.N. Clyne, M.C., *Vancouver's 29th* (Vancouver: Tobin's Tigers Association, 1964) 13–14.

4. Stevens, *A City Goes to War*, 3.

5. For some of the problems confronting the counterattacking force, see LAC, RG 24, v. 1739, file DHS 3-17 (v. 4), Notes on Mount Sorrel, Brig-Gen G.S. Tuxford, 3rd Brigade, ca. August 1929; LAC, RG 9, v. 4146, 8/8, Report on Operations on Front of 3rd Canadian Division in Ypres Salient from 2nd to 8th June, 1916.

6. Ex-Quaker, *Not Mentioned in Despatches*, 76.

7. LAC, RG 9, v. 3842, 43/1 and 1a, Operational Log, untitled [2nd June 1916], 5:42 P.M.; WD, 3rd Division, Summary of Operations, 2 to 8 June 1916.

8. Gray, *A Sunny Subaltern*, 142.

9. Millar, *From Thunder Bay*, 45, 55.

10. LAC, RG 41, 85th Battalion [misfiled], A.Y. Jackson, 3/3.

11. Ian McCulloch, "The Fighting Seventh," 110; CWM, 20020073-001, F.A.D. Gascoigne, letter to Mabel, 3 June 1916.

12. *Flanders Fields*, J.H. Lee, 7/19.

13. WD, 3rd Division, Summary of Operations, 2 to 8 June 1916.

14. Stevens, *A City Goes to War*, 47.

15. WD, 15th Battalion, 3 June 1916.

16. Tupper, *Victor Gordon Tupper*, 41.

17. CWM, 58A 1 153.5, George Ormsby papers, George to Maggie, 7 June 1916.

18. WD, 2nd Brigade, Appendix A, Report Describing the Operation for Ypres Salient.

19. CLIP, George Adkins, Adkins to "Dear Mother," 5 June 1916.

20. Gray, *A Sunny Subaltern*, 146.

21. LAC, MG 30 E134, Cy Peck papers, diary, 4 June 1916.

22. Tupper, *Victor Gordon Tupper*, 41.

23. LAC, RG 9, v. 3842, 43/1a, Plumer to Kiggell, 4 June 1916.

24. LAC, RG 9, v. 3842, 43/1a, 3rd Canadian Division, Estimated casualties, 10 P.M., 3 June 1918.

25. See documentation in CWM, 19990089, W.H. Wray.

CHAPTER 28: BITING BACK (PP. 367–380)

1. Foster, *Letters from the Front*, 143.

2. Rutledge, *Pen Pictures from the Trenches*, 114–17; WD, 28th Battalion, 6 June 1916.

3. Roy, *The Journal of Private Fraser*, 152.

4. Rutledge, *Pen Pictures from the Trenches*, 114–17; WD, 28th Battalion, 6 June 1916.

5. LAC, MG 30 E23, H.W. MacPherson papers, diary, 7 June 1916.

6. WD, June 1916, Report of Operations of Artillery Canadian Corps, 2 June to 14 June 1916; S.F. Wise, *Canadian Airmen and the First World War: The Official History of the Royal Canadian Air Force* (Toronto: University of Toronto Press, 1980) 364.

7. WD, Canadian Corps Artillery, June 1916, Report of Operations of Artillery Canadian Corps, various appendices.

8. D.J. Goodspeed, "Prelude to the Somme: Mount Sorrel, June, 1916," in Michael Cross and Robert Bothwell (eds.), *Policy by Other Means: Essays in Honour of C.P. Stacey* (Toronto: University of Toronto Press, 1972) 155.

9. Millar, *From Thunder Bay*, 62.

10. LAC, MG 30 E547, Archie MacKinnon papers, 3 September 1916.

11. CWM, 20030011-014, A.J.R. Parkes papers, Ia/18086, "Diary of Lt. … 127th Inf. Regt," 13 June 1916.

12. LAC, MG 30, E16, W.H. Hewgill papers, diary, 13 June 1916.

13. LAC, RG 9, v. 4011, 16/1, Operational Order No. 23; WD, 3rd Battalion, 13 June 1916; WD, 1st Divisional Artillery, 13 June 1916.

14. D.J. Goodspeed, *Battle Royal: A History of the Royal Regiment of Canada, 1862–1962* (Toronto, 1962) 142–5.

15. *Flanders Fields*, H.R. Alley, 7/25.

16. LAC, MG 30 E83, John Edward Leckie papers, v. 1, file: Reports and Routine Orders, Report of Operations, Mount Sorrel, 16th Battalion.

17. RG 9, v. 3842, 43/1a, Untitled [Log of Communications], 13 June 1916, 6:00 A.M.

18. LAC, MG 30 E300, Sir Arthur Currie papers, v. 18, file: Ypres Salient, 2 June to 14 June 1916, Report of Operations, 2nd Brigade, 2 June to 14 June 1916.

19. WD, 3rd Battalion, 13 June 1916.

20. Mary F. Gauder (ed.), *From a Stretcher Handle: The World War I Journal and Poems of Pte. Frank Walker* (Charlottetown: Institute of Island Studies, 2000) 93.

21. WD, Canadian Corps Artillery, June 1916, Report of Operations of Artillery Canadian Corps, 2 June to 14 June 1916.

22. Bill Rawling, "A Resource Not to Be Squandered: The Canadian Corps on the 1918 Battlefield," in Peter Dennis and Jeffrey Grey (eds.), *Defining 1918 Victory* (Canberra: Army Historical Unit, 1999) 71; LAC, RG 9, v. 3842, 43/1a, Report of 1st Canadian Division operations, 2 to 14 June 1916.

23. Morrison, *Hell Upon Earth,* 84.

24. Zubkowski, *As Long as Faith and Freedom Last,* 183.

25. CWM, 58A 1. 34.3, Frank Mathers papers, Frank to Mom, 9 June 1916.

26. Dominick Graham, "Sans Doctrine: British Army Tactics in the First World War," in Tim Travers and Christon Archer (eds.), *Men at War: Politics, Technology and Innovation in the Twentieth Century* (Chicago: Precedent, 1982) 89, endnote 3.

27. Currie sent out a letter to all officers demanding that they stop this type of slander among their men. LAC, RG 24, v. 6993, file XVIII, Currie to 1st Division, 16 July 1916.

28. Desmond Morton, *A Peculiar Kind of Politics: Canada's Overseas Ministry in the First World War* (Toronto: University of Toronto Press, 1982) 74.

29. Williams, *Byng of Vimy,* 118.

CHAPTER 29: "REDEEMED FROM THE GRAVE" (PP. 381–392)

1. LAC, R 8258, Gregory Clark papers, v. 2, file 2-3, Memoir, written in 1919 [n.d.].

2. Urquhart, *The History of the 16th Battalion,* 416.

3. Bruce Bairnsfather, *Carry on Sergeant!* (Indianapolis: The Bobbs-Merrill Company, 1927) 61.

4. For a list of points, see CWM, Sir Arthur Currie papers, 58A 1.60.1, "Canadian Corps Trench Standing Orders," January 1918.

5. Christie, *Letters of Agar Adamson,* 127.

6. Foster, *Letters from the Front,* 172.

7. Cited in Denis Winter, *Death's Men: Soldiers of the Great War* (Middlesex: Penguin, 1979) 141.

8. Ronald Clifton, "What Is a Battalion?" *Stand To!* 30 (Winter 1990) 17–19.

9. Norris, *Mainly for Mother*, 97.

10. CWM, 19650038-014, William Coleman papers, diary, 4 December 1915.

11. William Gray, *More Letters from Billy* (Toronto: McClelland and Stewart, 1917) 40–1.

12. CWM, 58A 1 112.9, Samuel Honey papers, Samuel to parents, 7 January 1917.

13. CWM, 58A 1.47.9, Courtney Tower papers, diary, 27 May 1916.

14. IWM, 86/53/1, William Kerr papers, Memoirs, 69.

15. Christie, *Letters of Agar Adamson*, 91, 182.

16. For crime and punishment in the CEF, see Morton, *When Your Number's Up*.

17. K. Craig Gibson, "Sex and Soldiering in France and Flanders: The British Expeditionary Force along the Western Front, 1914–1919," *The International History Review* XXIII.3 (September 2001) 552.

18. Ibid., 555.

19. Wheeler, *The 50th Battalion in No Man's Land*, 68.

20. Charles W. Bishop, *The Canadian Y.M.C.A. in the Great War* (The National Council of Young Men's Christian Associations of Canada, 1924) 234.

21. Brig.-Gen. F.P. Crozier, *A Brass Hat in No Man's Land* (London: Cape & Smith, 1930) 127.

22. LAC, MG 30 E371, W.R. Morison papers, diary, 2 September 1917.

23. McCarthy, "Not All Beer and Skittles?" 160.

24. Thomas Dinesen, *Merry Hell! A Dane with the Canadians* (London, 1929) 185; and Heather Robertson, *A Terrible Beauty: The Art of Canada at War* (Ottawa: National Museum of Man, 1977) 74.

25. Marriage figure in Morton, *When Your Number's Up*, 240.

26. McCarthy, "Not All Beer and Skittles?" 146.

27. LAC, RG 9, III A 1, v. 93, 10-12-50, pt. 2, Recommendations, Dvr. T.H. Bryans, CFA, 87140.

28. Gibson, "Sex and Soldiering," 565–7.

29. Chute, *The Real Front*, 261, 257.

CHAPTER 30: "THE BLIGHTER—HE-SWINGS-LIKE-A-GATE" (PP. 393–404)

1. Lynch, *Princess Patricia's Canadian Light Infantry*, 84.

2. Grescoe, *The Book of War Letters*, 166.

3. William New, *The Forgotten War* (self-published, 1982) 29.

4. Rogers (ed.), *Gunner Ferguson's Diary*, 44.

5. William Breckenridge, *From Vimy to Mons* (self-published, 1919) 17.

6. Black, *I Want One Volunteer*, 71–2.

7. Duff Crerar, *Padres in No Man's Land: Canadian Chaplains in the Great War* (Montreal: McGill-Queen's Press, 1995).

8. CWM, 19920187-002, H.H. Burrell papers, diary, 19 August 1917.

9. CWM, 19770531-011, Arthur McNally papers, diary, 2 May 1915.

10. Morton, *When Your Number's Up*, 279.

11. A.L. Barry, *Batman to Brigadier* (self-published, 1969) 31.

12. CWM, 19920187-002, H.H. Burrell papers, diary, 20 May 1917.

13. Rutledge, *Pen Pictures from the Trenches*, 105.

14. Ellis (ed.), *Saga of the Cyclists in the Great War, 1914–1918*, 26.

15. S.F. Wise, "The Gardeners of Vimy: Canadian Corps' Farming Operations during the German Offensives of 1918," *Canadian Military History* 8.3 (Summer 1999).

16. Shephard, *Dear Harry*, 201.

17. Noyes, *Stretcher-Bearers at the Double*, 130.

18. LAC, MG 30 E113, George Bell papers, "Back to Blighty," by George V. Bell, 115–16.

19. Dawson, *Living Bayonets*, 129.

20. See Andrew Horrall, "Keep-a-fighting! Play the game!": Baseball and the Canadian Forces during the First World War, *CMH* 10.2 (Spring 2001) 27–40.

21. Urquhart, *The History of the 16th Battalion*, 221.

22. *The Listening Post* 6 (20 October 1915) 3.

23. J. Alexander (Sandy) Bain, *A War Diary: A Canadian Signaller, My Experiences in the Great War* (Moncton: self-published, 1986) 72.

24. Wheeler, *The 50th Battalion in No Man's Land*, 129.

25. Tingley, *The Path of Duty*, 74.

26. For an especially egregious article, see David A. Boxwell, "The Follies of War: Cross-Dressing and Popular Theatre on the British Front Lines, 1914–18," *Modernism/modernity* 9.1 (January 2002) 1–20.

27. Adamson, *The Letters of Agar Adamson*, 268–9.

28. For an analysis of the content of the shows, see John Wilson, "Soldiers of Song: The Dumbells and Other Canadian Concert Parties of the First World War" (M.A. thesis: University of Guelph, 2003).

29. Max Arthur, *When This Bloody War Is Over: Soldiers' Songs of the First World War* (London: Piatkus, 2001) xx.

30. Foster, *Letters from the Front*, 108.

31. See Andrew Horrall, "Charlie Chaplain and the Canadian Expeditionary Force," *Canada and the Great War* (Montreal: McGill-Queen's University Press, 2003) 27–45.

32. Black, *I Want One Volunteer*, 76-7.

33. Tingley, *The Path of Duty*, 109.

CHAPTER 31: THE "BIG PUSH" (PP. 405–416)

1. See Peter Simkins, *Kitchener's Army* (Manchester University Press, 1988).

2. Elizabeth Greenhalgh, *Victory through Coalition: Britain and France during the First World War* (Cambridge: Cambridge University Press, 2005) 6.

3. Trevor Wilson, *The Myriad Faces of War* (Cambridge: Polity Press, 1986) 313.

4. CWM, MHRC, S.S. 544, Experience of the Recent Fighting at Verdun.

5. Sheffield and Bourne, *Douglas Haig*, 188.

6. See Tim Travers, "Learning and Decision-Making on the Western Front, 1915–1916: The British Example," *Canadian Journal of History* XVIII, no. 1 (April 1983).

7. Figure from Martin Gilbert, *The Battle of the Somme: The Heroism and Horror of War* (Toronto: McClelland & Stewart, 2006) 37.

8. Foster, *Letters from the Front*, 172.

9. Stephen Westman, *Surgeon with the Kaiser's Army* (London: Kimber, 1968) 94.

10. See Martin Middlebrook, *The First Day on the Somme* (London: Penguin Books, 1971, 1984) 99.

11. Tim Travers, "The Hidden Army: Structural Problems in the British Officer Corps, 1900-1918," *Journal of Contemporary History* 17 (1982) 523–44.

12. Gilbert, *The Battle of the Somme*, 50.

13. CWM, MHRC, S.S. 450, Regulations for Machine-Gun Officers and Non-Commissioned Officers.

14. Sheffield, *Forgotten Victory*, 163–7.

15. Foster, *Letters from the Front*, 163.

16. See Middlebrook, *The First Day on the Somme* and John Keegan, *The Face of Battle* (London: Pimlico, 1976).

17. Lyn Macdonald, *The Somme* (London: Penguin Books, 1983) 114.

18. Captain Wilfrid Miles, *Military Operations, France and Belgium, 1916: 2nd July 1916 to the End of the Battles of the Somme* (London: Macmillan, 1938) viii.

19. There are dozens and dozens of books devoted solely to the Somme campaign; the best is by Trevor Wilson and Robin Prior, *The Somme* (New Haven & London: Yale University Press, 2005).

CHAPTER 32: "YOU PEOPLE AT HOME CAN'T REALIZE HOW BLOODY THIS WAR REALLY IS" (PP. 417–430)

1. LAC, RG 9, v. 4044, 3/5, Notes on Recent Operations, 29 October 1915.

2. Stevens, *A City Goes to War*, 48.

3. CLIP, George Kempling, diary, 29 August 1916.

4. Ibid., 1 September 1916.

5. Rawling, *Surviving Trench Warfare*, 61.

6. For the story of the Ross, see A.F. Duguid, *A Question of Confidence: The Ross Rifle in the Trenches* (Ottawa: Service Publications, [2000]).

7. CWM, 58A 1 141.2, Charles Pearce papers, Pearce to George, 7 September 1915.

8. LAC, MG 30 E16, W.H. Hewgill papers, diary, 8 September 1916.

9. CWM, 20020189-001, Harry McCleave papers, diary, 5 September 1916.

10. LAC, MG 30 E100, Sir Arthur Currie papers, v. 52, diary, 5 September 1916.

11. RG 9, v. 3843, 44/4, extract from 1st Division's war diary, 6:20 P.M., 9 September 1916.

12. LAC, MG 30 E352, George L. Magann papers, diary, 2 September 1916.

13. LAC, MG 30 E42, John P. McNab papers, memoirs, 3.

14. CWM, 58A 1 44.18, Ronald W. Main papers, Ronald to father, 17 October 1916.

15. Murray, *History of the 2nd Battalion*, 124–5.

16. Timothy T. Lupfer, *The Dynamics of Doctrine: The Change in German Tactical Doctrine During the First World War* (Fort Leavenworth, Kansas: Combat Studies Institute: U.S. Army

Command and General Staff College, 1981) n.p., digitized at http://www-cgsc.army.mil/carl/resources/csi/Lupfer/lupfer.asp.

17. WD, 2nd Battalion, 9–10 September 1916; WD, 1st Infantry Brigade, Appendix J, Report of Operations, 9–10 September 1916.

18. LAC, MG 30 E505, William Howard Curtis papers, undated letter to mother, [ca. mid-September 1916].

CHAPTER 33: "LOOKING FORWARD TO A CRACK AT FRITZ" (PP. 431–446)

1. LAC, MG 30 E156, Robert Clements papers, "Merry Hell," memoir, 197.
2. Ibid.
3. CWM, MHRC, S.S. 515, Extracts No. 2 from German Documents and Correspondence.
4. Gilbert, *The Battle of the Somme*, 160.
5. Christopher Duffy, *Through German Eyes: The British and the Somme* (London: Weidenfeld & Nicolson, 2006) 200.
6. LAC, RG 9, III, v. 3842, 43/8-9, G3-649 [Currie artillery report], 15 August 1916.
7. Prior and Wilson, *The Somme*, 234.
8. Fred Bagley, *A Legacy of Courage: "Calgary's Own" 137th Overseas Battalion, CEF* (Calgary: Plug Street Books, 1993) 19.
9. Ibid.
10. Adamson, *Letters of Agar Adamson*, 219.
11. CWM, 58A 1 34.3, Frank Mathers papers, Mathers to Dad, 6 April 1916.
12. CLIP, Hart Leech, Dear Mother, 13 September 1916.
13. LAC, RG 41, v. 11, Crooks and McCorry, 25th Battalion, 7/13.
14. Reginald Grant, *S.O.S.—Stand To!* (New York: Appleton and Company, 1918) 189.
15. WD, 5th CMR, 14–15 September 1916.
16. IWM, 87/51/1, J.S. Davis, diary, 15 September 1916.
17. Foster, *Letters from the Front*, 152.
18. Duffy, *Through German Eyes*, 216.
19. Morrison, *Hell Upon Earth*, 92.
20. LAC, RG 9, v. 3842, 43/13-14, Summary of Operations, 8th Brigade, 11 to 17 September.
21. CWM, 19650038-014, William E.L. Coleman papers, "The Attack of 15 September 1916," written by Sergeant R.L. Layton, B Company, 4th CMR, 24 September 1916.
22. Ibid.
23. S.G. Bennett, *The 4th Canadian Mounted Rifles* (Toronto: Murray Printing, 1926) 35.
24. CWM, 19650038-014, William E.L. Coleman papers, Coleman to wife, 18 September 1916; 29 September 1916.
25. WD, 1st CMRs, 15 September 1916; WD, 5th CMRs, 15 September 1916.

CHAPTER 34: BLOODY VICTORY (PP. 447–466)

1. Foster, *Letters from the Front*, 147.

2. LAC, RG 24, v. 1739, file DHS 3-17 (v. 5), Comments by Turner on Somme (26 October 1936).

3. Lewis, *Over the Top with the 25th*, 26.

4. Norris, *Mainly for Mother*, 101.

5. LAC, MG 30 E297, v. 1, Frank Maheux papers, letter, 20 September 1916.

6. WD, 21st Battalion, Account by Lt. Colonel Elmer Jones, O.C., 21st Battalion, n.d.

7. LAC, MG 31 G29, Lance Cattermole papers, "Attack on the Somme, 15th and 16th September 1916," 2–5.

8. Ibid., Cattermole, 7.

9. Adamson, *The Letters of Agar Adamson*, 219.

10. For the complicated actions during the surrendering process, see Tim Cook, "The Politics of Surrender," 637–65.

11. Roy, *The Journal of Private Fraser*, 204–5.

12. C.S. Grafton, *The Canadian Emma Gees* (London: Hunter Printing Company, 1938) 49.

13. WD, 20th Battalion, To O.C. Units, 20th Battalion, 14 September 1916.

14. Norris, *Mainly for Mother*, 116.

15. LAC, RG 41, v. 12, Arthur Goodmurphy, 1/7–8.

16. WD, 5th Brigade, Canadian Corps Summary of Intelligence, 16 September 1916.

17. For the tanks, see LAC, RG 9, v. 3843, 45/3, Report on operations of the tanks, 16-9-1916.

18. Reginald Grant, *S.O.S.—Stand To!* (New York: Appleton and Company, 1918) 176.

19. LAC, MG 30 E42, John P. McNab papers, memoirs, 12.

20. LAC, RG 41, v. 15, various men from the 52nd Battalion, 1/14.

21. Lieutenant Colonel Joseph Chabelle, "Courcelette: The Glorious Battle Fought by the 22nd French-Canadian Regiment," *La Canadienne*, October 1920 [original in French, translated copy at CWM] 16.

22. WD, 5th Brigade, G.B. 8, 22 September 1916.

23. LAC, MG 30 E156, Robert Clements papers, "Merry Hell," memoir, 202.

24. Lewis, *Over the Top with the 25th*, 33.

25. Radley, *We Lead, Others Follow*, 154.

26. Maxime Dagenais, "Une Permission! … C'est Bon Pour Une Recrue": Discipline and Illegal Absences in the 5th Canadian Infantry Brigade, 1915–1919 (M.A. thesis: University of Ottawa, 2006) 68.

27. LAC, MG 30 E156, Robert Clements papers, "Merry Hell," memoir, 203.

28. WD, 5th Brigade, Formations adopted by the Battalions of the 5th Canadian Infantry Brigade in the Attack on Courcelette, 24 September 1916.

29. Chabelle, "Courcelette: The Glorious Battle Fought by the 22nd French-Canadian Regiment," 14a.

30. Foster, *Letters from the Front*, 187.

31. S. Douglas MacGown et al., *New Brunswick's "Fighting 26th"* (Neptune Publishing Company, 1994) 121.

32. WD, 5th Brigade, report from 25th Battalion to 5th Brigade, 20 September 1916; WD, 5th Brigade, 5th Brigade Report of Operations for 15–17.9.16, 20 September 1916.

33. WD, 25th Battalion, Report of operations by E. Hilliam, n.d. [ca. 20 September 1916].

34. Chabelle, "Courcelette: The Glorious Battle Fought by the 22nd French-Canadian Regiment," 15a.

35. LAC, RG 150, 1992-93/166, box 1592-55.

36. Passingham, *All the Kaiser's Men,* 123.

37. Serge Bernier, *The Royal 22e Regiment* (Montreal: Art Global, 1999) 47–9.

38. WD, 5th Brigade, 15 September 1916; 5th Brigade Report of Operations for 15–17.9.16, 20 September 1916.

39. Grescoe, *The Book of War Letters,* 129.

40. Coningsby Dawson, *Living Bayonets: A Record of the Last Push* (New York: John Lane Company, 1919) 179.

41. Nicholson, *Canadian Expeditionary Force,* 172.

42. Byfield, *Alberta in the 20th Century,* 73.

43. L. Moore Cosgrave, *Afterthoughts of Armageddon* (Toronto: S.B. Gundy, 1919) 20.

44. Scott, *The Great War as I Saw It,* 94.

45. Murray Peden, "Lest We Forget Those Who Stayed Behind," *The Citizen,* 11 November 2004.

CHAPTER 35: "WE WERE MET WITH DEADLY FIRE" (PP. 467–484)

1. Morrison, *Hell Upon Earth,* 94–5.

2. Duffy, *Through German Eyes,* 51, 65.

3. IWM, 87/51/1, J.S. Davis, diary, 20 September 1916.

4. CWM, 58A 1.9.1, Sir Richard Turner papers, diary, 28 September 1916.

5. Climo, *Let Us Remember,* 220.

6. CWM, 19840484-001, 58A 1 57.5, Willard Melvin papers, Melvin to People, 4 November 1916.

7. LAC, MG 30 E505, W.H. Curtis papers, letter to mother, 2 June 1915.

8. Morton, *When Your Number's Up,* 227.

9. Norris, *Mainly for Mother,* 127.

10. CWM, MHRC, S.S. 485, Army Order Regarding the Execution of Counter-Attacks.

11. Pope, *Letters from the Front, 1914–1919,* 57.

12. Adamson, *Letters of Agar Adamson,* 219.

13. RG 24, v. 1821, file GAQ 5-16, Total and average number of other ranks who passed through the four divisions' infantry battalions.

14. Urquhart, *The History of the 16th Battalion,* 408. For the wounded men, this included 2,577 first wounds, 452 second wounds, 73 third wounds, and 6 fourth wounds.

15. Murray, *The History of the 2nd Canadian Battalion,* 353.

16. CWM, 19740046-001, Allen Oliver papers, Frank to Father, 1 October 1916.

17. McClintock, *Best o' Luck,* 56.

18. WD, 31st Battalion, Report of operations, 25–29 September 1916.

19. Foster, *Letters from the Front,* 105.

20. For the story of British strategic logistics, see Ian Brown, *British Logistics on the Western Front 1914–1919* (Westport: Greenwood, 1998).

21. Rawling, *Surviving Trench Warfare*, 71.

22. CWM, AQN 20030308, Owen Brothers papers.

23. WD, 3rd Brigade, Resume of Events, 26 September 1916.

24. "The Other Side of the Hill: The Capture of Thiepval, 26th of September 1916, Extract from the *Army Quarterly* XXVII.2 (January 1934) 2, in RG 24, v. 1825, GAQ 5-59.

25. WD, 8th Battalion, Operational order, No. 12.

26. LAC, MHRC, S.S. 487, Order of the 6th Bavarian Division Regarding Machine Guns, 3 September 1916.

27. WD, 5th Battalion, 26–28 September 1916.

28. LAC, MG 30 E66, Cruickshank papers, v. 71, Gilfoy to Cruickshank, 4 August 1916.

29. Australian War Memorial, PR 83/232, "Recollections" by Douglas Joycey, 4.

30. WD, 5th Battalion, 26–28 September 1916.

31. O.C.S. Wallace (ed.), *From Montreal to Vimy Ridge and Beyond* (Toronto: McClelland and Stewart, 1917) 210–14.

32. WD, 8th Battalion, Report of operations, 30 September 1916.

33. *Flanders' Fields*, T.G. Caunt, 9/14.

34. WD, 8th Battalion, Report of operations, 30 September 1916.

35. WD, 49th Battalion, Report on operations of the 49th on 8 October 1916.

36. CWM, 58A 1 153.2, George Ormsby papers, George to Maggie, 12 October 1916.

37. Duffy, *Through German Eyes*, 253.

CHAPTER 36: "WE POUND, POUND, POUND" (PP. 485–496)

1. LAC, MG 30 E52, Talbot Papineau papers, v. 4, letter to dear B., 23 September 1916.

2. Ibid., 30 September 1916.

3. LAC, MG 30 E241, D.E. Macintyre papers, diary, 1 October 1916; WD, 4th CMRs, Narrative of events during the action of the 1st October 1916; Captain Wilfrid Miles, *Military Operations, France and Belgium, 1916,* 413.

4. CWM, 58A 1.9.1, Sir Richard Turner papers, diary, 30 September 1916.

5. WD, Canadian Corps, General Staff, 1 October 1916, log, 9:10 A.M.

6. LAC, MG 30 E156, Robert Clements papers, "Merry Hell," memoir, 211.

7. WD, Canadian Corps, General Staff, Appendix I, Reserve Army Operation Order No. 29.

8. WD, Canadian Corps, General Staff, Appendix IV/1-IV/10, No. 374, Examination of prisoner, 3rd Company, 2nd Marine Infantry Regiment.

9. Ibid.

10. WD, Canadian Corps, General Staff, Appendix IV/1-IV/10, Intelligence Report on Regina Trench, 4 October 1916.

11. CWM, MHRC, S.S. 466, Conclusions Drawn from the Study of Raids Carried Out by the British.

12. WD, 4th CMRs, Notes of operation by Lt. Col. H.D.L. Gordon.

13. Foster, *Letters from the Front*, 174–5.

14. WD, 5th CMRs, 1 October 1916; Reginald Roy, *For Most Conspicuous Bravery: A*

Biography of Major-General George R. Pearkes, V.C., Through Two World Wars (Vancouver: UBC Press, 1977) 48–50.

15. WD, 8th Brigade, Report of operations from September 27th to October 3rd.

16. WD, 5th Brigade, 24th Battalion report of operations, covering tour, September 27th to October 2nd, 1916; 5th Brigade, Summary of Operations, B.M.L. 330.

17. WD, 5th Brigade, 25th Battalion report to 5th Brigade, 5 October 1916.

18. Lewis, *Over the Top with the 25th,* 47.

19. WD, 5th Brigade, 24th Battalion report of operations, covering tour, September 27th to October 2nd, 1916.

20. WD, 5th Brigade, Summary of Operations, B.M.L. 330; WD, 22nd Battalion, Report 22-175.

21. WD, 5th Brigade, 25th Battalion report to 5th Brigade, 5 October 1916; WD, 5th Brigade, Summary of Operations, B.M.L. 330.

22. Brian D. Tennyson, "A Cape Bretoner at War: Letters from the Front, 1914–1919," *Canadian Military History* 11.1 (Winter 2002) 44.

23. WD, 20th Battalion, 1 October 1916.

24. LAC, MG 30 E521, William J. Wright papers, letter to Mr. Martin, 13-11-16.

25. *Flanders Fields,* J.K. McKay, 9/16.

26. Sheffield and Bourne, *Douglas Haig,* 236.

27. WD, Canadian Corps, General Staff, Appendix III/1-III/3, Return of Casualties, Canadian Corps, 27 September–4 October 1916.

CHAPTER 37: NO REST, NO RETREAT (PP. 497–506)

1. Grant, *S.O.S.—Stand To!,* 210.

2. Swettenham, *McNaughton,* I/64.

3. Dawson, *The Glory of the Trenches,* 96.

4. Gilbert, *The Battle of the Somme,* 207.

5. Dancocks, *Gallant Canadians,* 95.

6. WD, Canadian Corps, General Staff, Appendix I, Reserve Army S.G. 66/2 and S.G. 66/19.

7. WD, Canadian Corps, General Staff, Appendix IV/1-IV/10, Intelligence Report on Regina Trench, 4 October 1916.

8. Dancocks, *Sir Arthur Currie,* 78.

9. LAC, RG 9, v. 4011, 17/1, 1st Division [Lessons Learned], 25 November 1916.

10. WD, 1st Brigade, Report of the operation carried out by the 1st Brigade, 8th October 1916.

11. WD, 3rd Brigade, 8 October 1916, Message 112.

12. WD, 3rd Brigade, Resume of Events, 8 October 1916.

13. LAC, RG 41, v. 13, M.J. Cunningham, 43rd Battalion, 1/16.

14. WD, Royal Canadian Regiment, Report of operations, 7–9 October 1916.

15. Nicholson, *Gunners of Canada,* I/267; WD, Canadian Corps, General Staff, Appendix III/1-III/3, Canadian Corps, Summary of Operations, 6-13 October 1916. The Corps suffered 2,688 casualties from 4 to 11 October.

16. WD, 49th Battalion, Report of Operations of the 49th on 8 October 1916.

17. Rawling, "Communications in the Canadian Corps," 11.

18. Stewart, "Attack Doctrine," 53.

19. Adamson, *The Letters of Agar Adamson*, 223.

20. Malcolm Brown, *The Imperial War Museum Book of the Somme* (London: Pan Books, 1997) 169.

CHAPTER 38: "EXPERIENCES TOO HORRIBLE TO RELATE" (PP. 507–520)

1. Pope, *Letters from the Front, 1914–1919,* 37.

2. LAC, MG 30 E42, John McNab papers, diary [first part is a narrative] 8.

3. Foster, *Letters from the Front*, 168.

4. Nicholson, *Gunners of Canada*, I/267.

5. CWM, MHRC, S.S.532, Extracts No. 4 from German Documents and Correspondence.

6. Ibid.

7. *Their Name Liveth: A Memoir of the Boys of the Parkdale Collegiate Institute Who Gave Their Lives in the Great War*, 60.

8. James L. McWilliams and R. James Steel, *The Suicide Battalion* (Vanwell Publishing Limited, 1990) 51.

9. McClintock, *Best o' Luck*, 28.

10. Nicholson, *Gunners of Canada*, I/270.

11. Foster, *Letters from the Front,* 168.

12. McClintock, *Best o' Luck,* 57.

13. LAC, MG 30 E537, Ernest William Sansom papers, v. 1, file 2, 4th Canadian Division, History of the 10th, 11th, 12th and 16th M.G. Corps and 4th M.G. Battalion, (n.d., written sometime during World War I).

14. CWM, 20030140-005, J.R. Preston papers, diary, 24 October 1916.

15. Wheeler, *The 50th Battalion in No Man's Land,* 62.

16. WD, 46th Battalion, Report of Operations, 12 November 1916.

17. LAC, MG 30 E50, Elmer Jones papers, v. 1, file 10, Translation of Ludendorff's *My War Memoirs,* n.p.

18. LAC, MG 30 E558, Cecil French papers, v.1, file 1, letter, 8 November 1916.

19. Stevens, *A City Goes to War,* 65.

20. McWilliams and Steel, *The Suicide Battalion,* 55.

21. LAC, MG 30 E558, Cecil French papers, French to McAulay, 10 November 1916.

22. CWM, 58 A1 13.7, Brookes Ferrar Gossage papers, diary, 11 November 1916.

23. McClintock, *Best o' Luck*, 60–3.

24. LAC, MG 30 E153, 38th Battalion Association, "War Record of the 38th Ottawa Battalion—Somme Battles."

25. LAC, RG 24, v. 1820, GAQ 5-8, Employment of 10th Canadian Infantry Brigade, 18 November 1916; LAC, MG 30 E40, v. 1, file 4, Report on the Canadian Divisions on the Somme (n.d., ca. December 1916).

26. Grescoe, *The Book of War Letters*, 128–9.

27. By the end of November, the 4th Division was down to a strength of 12,712. See LAC, RG 24, v. 1874, file 22(8), Monthly Strength returns. 4th Division casualties listed in LAC, RG 24, v. 1844, file 11-11b.

CHAPTER 39: THE BLUDBATH (PP. 521–526)

1. For British casualties and the controversies surrounding them, see Wilson, *The Myriad Faces of War*, 348–50; Sheffield, *Forgotten Victory*, chapter 7; Prior and Wilson, *The Somme*, chapter 27.

2. On attrition, see Brian Bond, *The Pursuit of Military Victory: From Napoleon to Saddam Hussein* (Oxford: Clarendon Press, 1998) and Carter Malkasian, "Toward a Better Understanding of Attrition: The Korean and Vietnam Wars," *The Journal of Military History* 68 (July 2004) 911–42.

3. Philip J. Haythornthwaite, *The World War One Source Book* (London: Arms and Armour, 1996) 55.

4. J.H. Johnson, *Stalemate!: The Great Trench Warfare Battles of 1915–1917* (London: Arms and Armour, 1995) 86.

5. Gilbert, *The Battle of the Somme*, 246.

6. Miles, *Military Operations, France and Belgium, 1916*, xii.

7. Campbell, *2nd Division*, 40; Nicholson, Appendix C.

8. Sheffield, *Forgotten Victory*, xxii.

9. Nicholson, *Canadian Expeditionary Force*, 198; for infantry percentage, the British infantry and machine-gunners suffered ninety-four percent of the losses: see T.J. Mitchell and G.M. Smith, *Medical Services: Casualties and Medical Statistics of the Great War* (London: The Imperial War Museum, reprint 1997) 43; the Australian infantry suffered ninety-two percent of all losses on the Somme: see Ross Mallett, "The Interplay between Technology, Tactics and Organisation in the First AIF" (Masters: Australian Defence Force Academy, 1999) chapter 3.

10. H. Clout, *After the Ruins: Restoring the Countryside of Northern France after the Great War* (Exeter: University of Exeter Press, 1996) 46.

11. For this evolution in the Canadian Corps, see Rawling, *Surviving Trench Warfare*. Paddy Griffith and other historians have also noted this for the BEF as a whole. Paddy Griffith, *Battle Tactics of the Western Front* (Yale University Press, 1994).

12. Jeffrey A. Keshen, *Propaganda and Censorship During Canada's Great War* (University of Alberta Press, 1996) 183.

CHAPTER 40: THE RECKONING (PP. 527–532)

1. Compiled from Rawling, *Surviving Trench Warfare*, Appendix B.

2. Guy Chapman, *Vain Glory* (London: Cassell, 1968) 519.

3. Siegfried Sassoon, *Memoirs of an Infantry Officer* (London: Faber, 1965) 104.

4. Foster, *Letters from the Front*, 123.

5. Ibid., 171.

Notes on Sources (pp. 533–536)

1. Owen A. Cooke, *The Canadian Military Experience, 1867–1995: A Bibliography* (Ottawa: Department of National Defence, 1997); "From Colony to Nation: A Reader's Guide to Canadian Military History": http://www.collectionscanada.ca/military/025002-6000-e.html; Tim Cook, *Clio's Warriors: Canadian Historians and the Writing of the World Wars* (Vancouver: UBC Press, 2006).

2. See, for example, Sir Max Aitken, *Canada in Flanders: The Official Story of the Canadian Expeditionary Force*, v. I. (London: Hodder and Stoughton, 1916); J.F.B. Livesay, *Canada's Hundred Days: With the Canadian Corps from Amiens to Mons, Aug. 8–Nov. 11, 1918* (Toronto: T. Allen, 1919).

3. Colonel A.F. Duguid, *Official History of the Canadian Forces in the Great War, 1914–1919, General Series*, v. I. (Ottawa: J.O. Patenaude, Printer to the King, 1938).

4. G.W.L. Nicholson, *Canadian Expeditionary Force, 1914–1919* (London: Queen's Printer, 1960).

5. For a sampling, see A.M.J. Hyatt, *General Sir Arthur Currie: A Military Biography* (Toronto: University of Toronto Press and Canadian War Museum, 1987); Daniel Dancocks, *Welcome to Flanders Fields: The First Canadian Battle of the Great War: Ypres, 1915* (Toronto: McClelland and Stewart, 1988); Bill Rawling, *Surviving Trench Warfare: Technology and the Canadian Corps* (Toronto: University of Toronto Press, 1992); Desmond Morton, *When Your Number's Up: The Canadian Soldier in the First World War* (Toronto: Random House of Canada, 1993); Shane B. Schreiber, *Shock Army of the British Empire: The Canadian Corps in the Last 100 Days of the Great War* (Wesport: Praeger, 1997); Tim Cook, *No Place To Run: The Canadian Corps and Gas Warfare in the First World War* (Vancouver: UBC Press, 1999); J.L. Granatstein, *Canada's Army: Waging War and Keeping the Peace* (Toronto: University of Toronto Press, 2002).

6. William Stewart, "Attack Doctrine in the Canadian Corps, 1916–1918" (M.A. thesis: University of New Brunswick, 1982); Ian M. McCulloch, "The 'Fighting Seventh': The Evolution and Devolution of Tactical Command and Control in a Canadian Infantry Brigade of the Great War" (M.A. thesis: Royal Military College of Canada, 1997); David Campbell, "The Divisional Experience in the C.E.F.: A Social and Operational History of the 2nd Canadian Division, 1915–1918" (Ph.D. thesis: University of Calgary, 2003); Andrew Iarocci, *1st Canadian Division at War, 1914–15: A Study of Training, Tactics and Leadership* (Ph.D. thesis: Wilfrid Laurier University, 2005).

7. The transcripts are held in the Records of the CBC (RG 41).

8. http://www.canadianletters.ca

ACKNOWLEDGMENTS

I first visited the Western Front while in high school, and was shocked and fascinated by the vast cemeteries and memorials to the fallen. My interest was rekindled at Trent University under the tutelage of Dr. Stuart Robson, who encouraged me to explore the writings of Great War soldiers. Several years later, Professor Terry Copp of Wilfrid Laurier University invited me to lead a battlefield tour of the Western Front. It was a moving experience for me to return to the battlefields, study the terrain, and walk in the soldiers' steps. For the last decade, the Western Front has rarely been far from my imagination, and I continue to attempt to understand how Canadians dealt with this terrible conflict that interrupted and ended so many lives.

This history draws upon old and new scholarship, and I am indebted to veterans, historians, and writers who have come before me. Senior scholars within the field of military history in Canada have always been very generous in their support, with Dr. Desmond Morton, Dr. Jonathan Vance, Dr. Bill Rawling, Dr. Patrick Brennan, Dr. Steve Harris, Dr. J.L. Granatstein, Professor Terry Copp, and others offering advice and constructive criticism over several years of study. I am also grateful to fellow Great War historians from my generation—David Campbell, Wes Gustavson, Mark Humphries, and Andrew Iarocci—for sharing their ideas over the last few years.

At the Canadian War Museum, where it is my privilege to be the First World War historian, I have had tremendous support from colleagues and senior managers. Dr. Dean Oliver, director of research and exhibitions, has been a champion of historical scholarship, and I am a much better historian for having worked with him. My colleagues in the historical section are as gifted a group as I have ever known, and I learn something new from them every day. I would like to highlight the generosity of Dr. Cameron Pulsifer and Dr. Peter MacLeod, who have read almost everything that I've published in the last five years, including this volume. Dr. Bill Rawling of the Department of National Defence's Directorate of History and Heritage was a third reader, and I am deeply grateful for his careful edit and penetrating questions. My colleagues at the CWM in the Collection Management Division have freely shared their knowledge of material history and wartime technology, and the ever cheerful and diligent staff in the museum's Military History Research Centre are always willing to assist researchers.

I'd like to thank my agent, Rick Broadhead, for rounding up interest in the two-volume history and for delivering the goods. At Penguin, Diane Turbide, editorial director, took on the project, and rightly prodded me into explaining things in clear English, especially mysteries such as enfilade fire, flanks, and reverse slopes. Her support and expertise have been invaluable. Tara Tovell also provided a painstaking line and copy edit, which has saved me much embarrassment. The entire team at Penguin has been exceedingly professional and generous, and I'd like to extend my appreciation to Elizabeth McKay, Yvonne Hunter, David Leonard, Tracy Bordian, and Kristin Shensel.

Jennifer Lazuk, one of my brilliant students at Carleton University, also assisted in ferreting out personal information on soldiers from Library and Archives Canada. I am especially grateful for having the opportunity to teach at Carleton and to engage with such stellar minds. The students in my senior seminar on Canada and the First World War have enriched my understanding of the war, and I looked forward to meeting them every Thursday night as their passion, cleverness, and good humour buoyed my spirits.

Five-hundred-page books don't get written overnight, and the long grind of writing a two-volume history during weekends, early mornings, and late nights, in addition to my museum duties, sometimes left me questioning whether the entire effort was worth it. During this process, I have relied heavily on friends and loved ones, and I suspect this volume simply could not have been completed without their support. My parents, accomplished historians and educators, instilled in me a love of history. As a parent myself now, I better understand the sacrifices made by Terry and Sharon on behalf of my brother Graham and me.

But it is my own family of Sarah, Chloe, and Emma who have most intimately borne the burden of this work. To them I owe everything. Sarah, a gifted historian and archivist in her own right, was unwavering in her support and love. Our sweet girls, Emma and Chloe, have brought more joy to us than we thought possible, and they put everything into perspective. I'd give it all up for them tomorrow if they asked, but they never would. This book is dedicated to them.

Index

CREDITS

Permission to reproduce the following copyrighted works is gratefully acknowledged.
Note: Canadian War Museum (CWM); Library and Archives Canada (LAC)

Photographs

Page 25: Author's collection
Page 37: George Metcalf Archival Collection,
    CWM, 19880069-645001
Page 51: CWM, 19770495
Page 53: LAC, C-068841
Page 70: LAC, PA-02278
Page 72: LAC, PA-004981
Page 75: *With the First Canadian Contingent*
    (1915) 30
Page 84: LAC, PA-22705
Page 115: CWM, 19700140-077
Page 117: LAC, PA-8275
Page 124: Sir Max Aitken, *Canada in Flanders*
    (1916)
Page 127: CWM, 19940001-887, #1
Page 146: Sir Max Aitken, *Canada in Flanders*
    (1916)
Page 157: LAC, PA-1370
Page 200: LAC, PA-3231
Page 208: CWM, 19820103-001, p. 66c
Page 221: LAC, PA-568
Page 225: LAC, PA-1326
Page 238: LAC, C-006984
Page 241: LAC, PA-149311
Page 248: CWM, 1972-0232
Page 252: LAC, PA-1400
Page 256: LAC, PA-1884
Page 257: LAC, PA-128
Page 258: LAC, PA-742
Page 315: LAC, PA-635
Page 331: *The War Illustrated,* 13 May 1916
Page 333: CMW, 20030172
Page 344: LAC, PA-1284
Page 359: CWM, 19830277-005
Page 369: LAC, PA-743
Page 376: CWM, 19730208-002
Page 382: Author's collection
Page 396: LAC, PA-3419

Page 423: Author's collection
Page 441: CWM, 19830277-005
Page 448: CWM, 19940001-420
Page 453: Author's collection
Page 454: CWM, 19870268-001
Page 455: LAC, PA-625
Page 464: LAC, PA-2468
Page 469: CWM, 19710261-0434
Page 474: LAC, PA-001349
Page 481: LAC, PA-22705
Page 518: LAC, PA-4352
Page 528: Photograph by Allan Jennings

Illustrations

Page 98: *Notes on Trench Warfare for Infantry
    Officers. December 1916.* Figure 30
Page 102: S.S.122, *Some Notes on Lewis Guns
    and Machine Guns,* Figure 1
Page 197: A.E. Snell, *The CAMC During the
    Last Hundred Days* (1924) 11
Page 219: *Notes on Trench Warfare for Infantry
    Officers, December 1916.* Figure 6
Page 227: *Trench Warfare, 1916*
Page 232: *Notes on Trench Warfare for Infantry
    Officers. December 1916.* Figure 34
Page 234: *Notes on Trench Warfare for Infantry
    Officers. December 1916.* Figure 62
Page 243: *The Forty-Niner* 1.4, 23
Page 284: LAC, MG 30 E2, Major N.A.D.
    Armstrong, *Notes on the Training of the
    Battalion Intelligence Section*
Page 288: LAC, MG 30 E2, Major N.A.D.
    Armstrong, *Notes on the Training of the
    Battalion Intelligence Section*
Page 318: S.S.122, *Some Notes on Lewis Guns
    and Machine Guns,* Figure 1
Page 418: *The Organization of an Infantry
    Battalion, April 1917.* Plates A and B